Published in the United
States by Times Books, a
division of Random House,
Inc., New York.

This work was originally
published in two volumes
in Great Britain in 1995
and 1996 by BBC Books, an
imprint of BBC Worldwide
Limited.

This combined edition was
first published in 1998.

ISBN 0-8129-2843-1

EDITED AND DESIGNED
BY
*B·C·S Publishing Ltd,
Chesterton, Oxfordshire*

PRINTED AND
BOUND IN FRANCE

COLOUR ORIGINATIONS
BY
*Fotographics,
London – Hong Kong*

Set in Bembo and Futura

RANDOM HOUSE
WEBSITE ADDRESS:
www.randomhouse.com

98765432

FIRST U.S. EDITION

People's Century
20th

From the dawn of
the century
to the eve
of the
millennium

Godfrey Hodgson

Series Consultant
J.M. ROBERTS

 TIMES BOOKS

RANDOM HOUSE

Contents

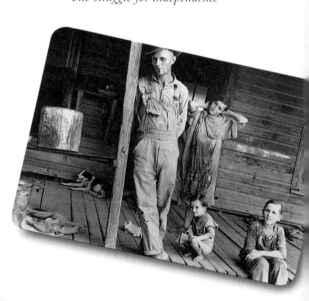

Foreword

by

J.M. ROBERTS

MOST HISTORY IS NOT WRITTEN IN WHAT WE might call a democratic mode. It is not about 'ordinary people' – people like us. This is both understandable and defensible. Individual decisions by remarkable individuals, or those taken by people in power, can make big differences to the lives of the rest of us: the course of the Second World War – and therefore the lives of millions of people – might have been wholly different if Hitler had not decided to go to war formally with the United States. Much time and attention has been given by historians to powerful or distinguished men and women and to the things they did, and rightly so.

But there is a sense, too, in which history cannot but be concerned with the lives of anonymous millions, as well as those of the great shapers of events. Individuals are historically important because of the impact they have had on the lives of huge numbers of their fellow human beings. History is the story of what has been done by and made a difference to human beings. The more of them that have been affected, the more historically important the events, influences and decisions that shape the story are. That is how historical importance is measured; I know of no other way.

Perhaps this has become more obvious during the present century. Not only have there been many more people than before on whom its events have played, sometimes with terrible effect, but we know more about them than about their predecessors in more distant times. More important still, a number of processes have been going forward – some political, some technological, some economic – all of which have tended to give large numbers of people a more active role in events, or at any rate the illusion of one. More and more countries have, for instance, at least formally become democracies, with elected governments. The world has grown richer in this century, too (if it had not done so there would probably be fewer people alive today than there were in 1900). As more people have had access to some wealth, they have come to matter more as consumers; whole industries have grown up to supply what they could be persuaded to buy. With wealth came life: huge numbers of people now live much longer than their great-grandparents' generation. In many parts of the world mass education became available for the first time in this century, with incalculable effects on wants, the way people saw those wants, and their visions of what might be possible. Mass communication (particularly, in the second half of the century, television) led to more shared experience: events that would once have had only a local or at most a regional impact suddenly took on global significance.

When the television series on which this book has been based was devised, it was hoped that it would bring to a large audience a historical emphasis that would show just what was this unique new feature of the twentieth century. Even if the involvement of 'peoples' in history in a new way was already foreshadowed before 1900, its mass character is clearer than ever as the year 2000 approaches. Huge numbers of men and women have been caught up in processes that transform their lives.

As the people's century draws to a close, it is clear that even more change is on the way: a prospect that, depending on where you stand, may seem inspiring, intimidating, exciting, liberating, oppressive or many other things. Many of the changes will turn out to have deep roots in the past. There will be nearly six billion human beings alive in the year 2000. We should not be too confident that we can guess what their future will be, but it will have a lot of history mixed up in it, including unfinished business of our own.

Introduction

YOU WILL HAVE HEARD OF few of the people in this book. It belongs not the the giants – to Lenin or Hitler, Roosevelt or Churchill, Gandhi or Mao Zedong – but to the men and women who fought in their wars, voted in their elections, worked in their factories, and died for their crimes or their mistakes. These are the voices of men and women who experienced the century's great events – as actors, victims or eyewitnesses – or who lived through the slow but almost equally dramatic transformation of everyday life by new machines and new medicines, new media and new ideas.

You might expect to find these people's stories strung like beads on the narrative of the century's great events. Instead, we have given the main thread of the chapters over to what might be called their 'little histories' within the framework of 'big history' in which their experiences took place. Yet there has been a thread running through the century. It began in hope, based on the illusion of new ideologies and the promise of new technologies; but the European political system, which had come to occupy the centre of the world stage, broke down. War led to revolution, and to the collapse of empires; to famine, inflation, the rise first of communist, then of fascist totalitarianism, and a second world war even more deadly than the first.

In the East, the story was of the slow fading of the dream of a socialist utopia. In the West, the second half of the century promised to be a golden age of prosperity; it turned out to be prosperous but unpredictable, violent, full of conflict and change. Where once most of the world's people watched Europe's quarrels as spectators, by the end of the century almost the whole of the human race had marched up out of the auditorium and taken its place on the stage.

In the last third of the century, an age of plenty was replaced by an age of protest. Black people demanded equality with whites; women with men. Young people challenged the autority of their elders, and people of all kinds shouted urgent warnings about what we humans were doing to the environment. As at its beginning, as the century neared its end old political structures abruptly collapsed, and new technologies again offered new hope.

All human beings live at the centre of their own universe, so there are as many true histories of the twentieth century as there are people who have lived through it. We have tried to hint at the sheer variety of their experience rather than to pass judgement on how its events may later come to be seen, let alone to predict what the future may bring.

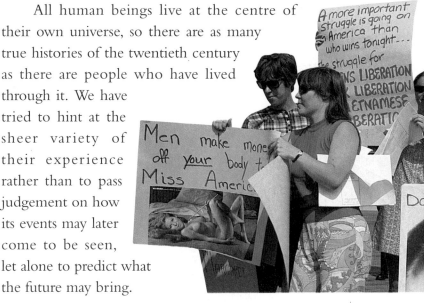

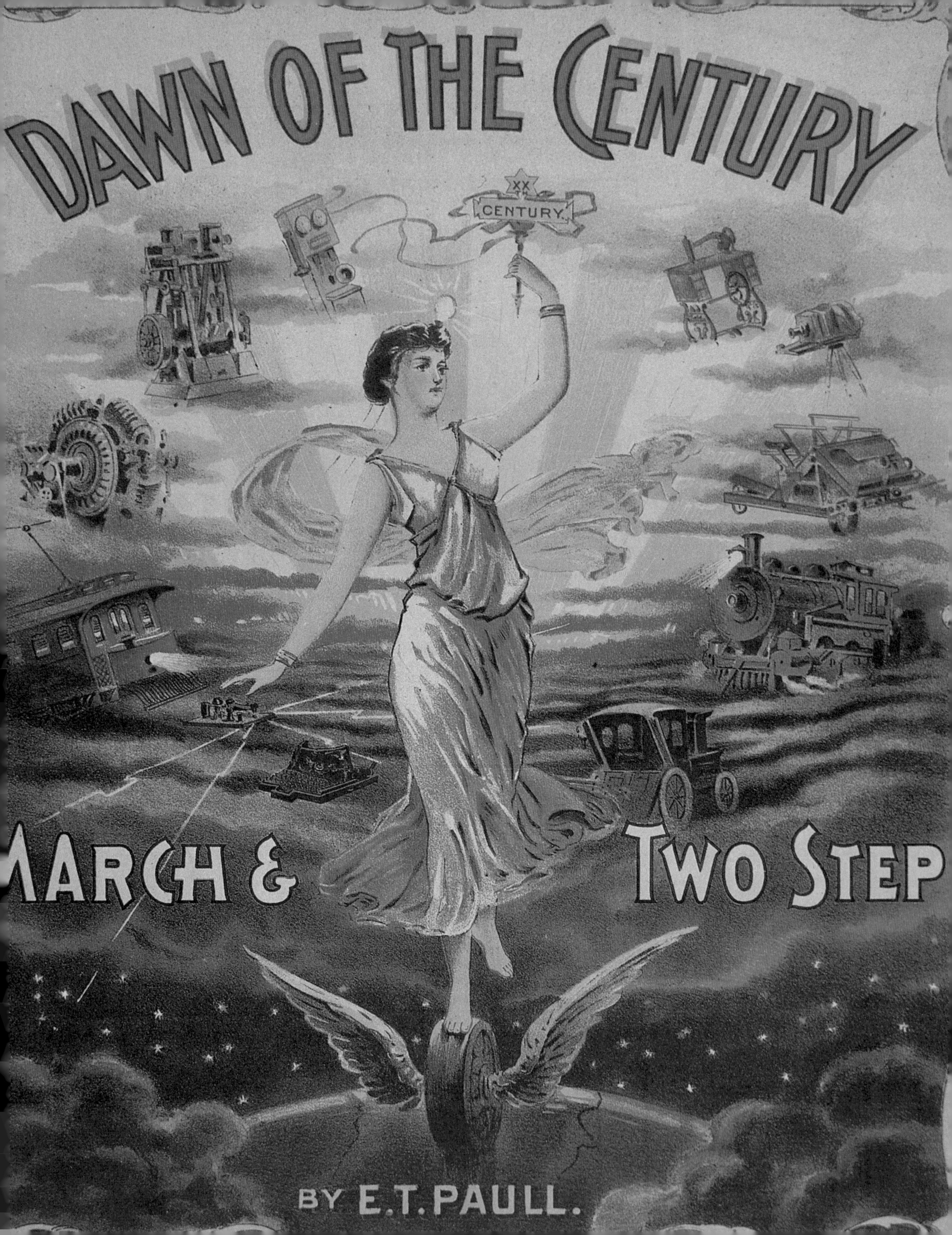
DAWN OF THE CENTURY
XX TH
CENTURY
MARCH & TWO STEP
BY E. T. PAULL.

Age of Hope

THE TURN
OF THE
CENTURY

THE TWENTIETH CENTURY made a dazzling entrance at the Paris Exhibition of 1900. Special trains brought people from all over France and other European countries, to a display designed to show what the new century might hold. Millions of visitors were whisked along moving walkways, carried high above the stands, and plunged into displays from far-flung corners of the globe that heralded a future in which their work and leisure would be transformed.

Raymond Abescat was nine years old when he visited the exhibition. 'It really opened my eyes to everything that was going on around us outside Paris, seeing all those stands – stands of every nationality. I was able to compare what was going on in England, in Germany and so on. It gave me the urge to travel.'

One of the highlights of the exhibition was the Palace of Electricity, with its hall full of lamps, generators and motors, and its grand façade lit up at night. Raymond Abescat remembers, 'At home we used oil lamps and candles – we didn't have electricity....For me the electricity stand, which was about as wide as the Champs de Mars and brightly illuminated by all those lights – that was the most impressive sight of all.'

As the new century dawned in Russia, the young Alexander Briansky joined the celebrations in the port of Odessa, where he lived. 'The streets were illuminated. There were fireworks, drinkers. Nobody stayed at home – crowds of people were on the street....The twentieth century gave everybody some kind of specific hope.'

The hope went beyond a desire for material progress in a world characterized by deep social inequalities. Democracy, literacy and good health were privileges still denied to many. The struggle for emancipation, education and better working conditions accelerated as the century unfolded and people struggled to control and change their lives. In the years to come some of humanity's most cherished hopes and greatest dreams would be fulfilled, but many people would be confronted by horror beyond their worst nightmares.

DAWN OF THE CENTURY *The cover of a song published to herald the new century, decorated with symbols of progress.*

The old order

'The Queen is dead' blazed newspaper headlines all over the world. It was January 1901. Queen Victoria, British monarch, empress of India, ruler of half a billion people and a quarter of the world, had reigned for sixty-four years. At her funeral tens of thousands of mourners watched silently as the gun carriage bearing her coffin passed by. Two emperors, two kings, twenty-four princes and thirteen dukes followed it.

The crowned heads who followed Victoria's coffin between them governed most of the world. The major European powers had established empires far beyond their own borders. Nearly three-quarters of the world's people lived under foreign rule, and not only in Europe but also in Africa, Australia, the Far East, India and North America indigenous peoples had been subjugated.

The century dawned on a society based on privilege and obedience, on simple certainties and prejudices. In Britain only men with some wealth and over a certain age were able to vote, while women in Germany could not go to university. American factory owners could fire their workers simply on suspicion of joining a union. Elaborate social codes determined relations between the sexes and between people of different rank. It was a world built on Victorian notions of hard work and thrift, and it looked as though it would endure for ever. Donald Hodge grew up in a small English village at the turn of the century. He remembers how people were expected to touch their caps to show respect to their social superiors the squire, the vicar and the doctor. He also recalls his childhood conviction that nothing would change. 'It was going to go on. We were the greatest democracy in the world, and we felt a kind of pride in our empire.'

Confidence in the established order was echoed in Japan. Mohei Tamura, who grew up in the town of Maebashi north-west of Tokyo, remembers that at the beginning of the century 'People worshipped the emperor as God'. He believes it was this devotion to the emperor that united the nation. 'I think that was why the Japanese soldiers were so brave. We, the ordinary people, had the same feelings. Everyone remembers the time when the emperor

DRESSED TO KILL *in India. Hunting was one of the familiar sporting activities that Europeans continued to pursue throughout their empires. Hunting clothes were hot and uncomfortable to wear in tropical climates, but Western traditions were rigidly maintained.*

Toys for teaching

JIGSAW PUZZLES *were originally designed as a way for children to learn geography, and they became extremely popular in the early 1900s. Piecing together pictures such as this one, which shows King George V in royal regalia at the centre of imperial activities, taught children about the extent and influence of the British empire.*

A SOLEMN SPECTACLE
(LEFT) *Crowds line the pavements and rooftops to catch a glimpse of Queen Victoria's funeral procession through the London streets. Her death marked the end of an era. Within just two decades, most of the people riding behind her coffin had lost their crowns.*

NATIVE LABOUR (ABOVE)
A group of Malagasy, the people of Madagascar, pause with their French overseer in their construction of a new railway. France had greatly extended its empire by the early 1900s, ruling much of west and central Africa as well as lands in Indochina and South America.

THE NEW JAPAN *Millions of Japanese citizens flooded into the growing industrial towns to find work in the new factories. By 1900 Japan had left feudalism behind, and had launched into a programme of modernization that soon rivalled economic development in the West. Coal, iron and steel production all expanded rapidly, the textile industry flourished, and Japan's decisive victory in the war with China in 1894–95 demonstrated the power of its army and navy. In the West Japan's emergence was viewed with admiration and disquiet.*

died; people from all over the country gathered at the front garden of the Imperial Palace and cried bitterly.'

The rise of Japan, the one country in Asia modernizing itself successfully, was regarded with some suspicion in the West. Mohei Tamura remembers that when Japan invaded China in 1894 the Europeans had been quick to defend their own interests. 'Russia, Germany and France were worried about the power Japan might possess after the invasion, so they interfered, forcing Japan to compensate China.' But Japan still made considerable gains. In 1904 war broke out between Japan and Russia. Japan's victory, after destroying the Russian fleet in the straits of Tsushima, was widely celebrated. 'We were ecstatic about the outcome, and held a great festival that lasted for three days,' recalls Mohei Tamura. 'Because of the great victory over Russia, we had no fear of foreigners. We felt that Japan was the land of the gods and would therefore never lose a war in the future.'

Japan's success brought confidence and pride to its people.

HATRED UNLEASHED (RIGHT) *The Boxer Rising was characterized by the violent killing of foreign missionaries and traders by Chinese nationalists. The Chinese regarded the establishment and control of railways and telegraph services by Westerners as economically exploitative, and zealous Christian missionaries threatened the traditional social framework.*

In many other countries there was good reason to fear foreigners, and to hope for change. In China Guo Jingtong remembers how people felt about the way their Manchu emperors had allowed Westerners to penetrate the country. 'The foreigners wanted to control us. They burned down our historical sites and bullied our China. In any decent-sized village or town they set up Catholic churches. The Church paid the Chinese who were prepared to convert.' In 1900 long-standing resentment at Western intrusion exploded into a violent rebellion known as the Boxer Rising. Both Europeans and Chinese Christians were killed by Chinese nationalists, and foreign legations in Peking were besieged. It took a large international military force to reimpose control.

White masters also exercised control over African peoples. In the newly formed Union of South Africa, Bob Ngwenya grew up working on a farm in the Orange Free State. 'The Boer was the king. Nothing else. He could do whatever he wished. They told us that blacks were nothing – and we accepted it.' Dorah Ramothibe also grew up on a Boer farm. 'They used to punish us. They'd make us lie on the table and whip us – even the men. Our fathers weren't happy about the way we lived. But there was nothing we could do, there was no alternative. So we had to stay.'

The United States had escaped from European colonization and tended to criticize European governments for their empires, but minorities within their own country were also oppressed. By 1900 most American Indians had been forced to live in designated reservations. There were concerted efforts to make them conform to the government's vision of what proper Americans should be. Indian children were forced to go to government schools, most of which were more like army camps: they were given uniforms and made to drill or set to work. They were ordered to speak only English, and were punished for talking in their own language.

Slavery had been abolished in the United States at the end of the Civil War. But thirty-five years later a comprehensive system of segregation still kept black people quite separate from the whites. Equality existed only in theory; blacks were not allowed to use the white man's restaurants, buses, railway carriages or schools. John Morton Finney, whose father had been born a slave, was eleven years old in 1900. He remembers that segregation

"We couldn't talk our language, we got punished for that, and if we did they took you and they whipped you...they forced us to go to school....We had already been here before the white man ever came, we've suffered for five hundred years."

HARRY BYRD

HOPI INDIANS *in Arizona, which had been taken from Mexico by the United States. As settlers moved westwards after gold was discovered in California, fierce Indian resistance to the incursions of the whites onto their traditional lands was crushed. Centuries of European migration greatly reduced the population of American Indians, who were expected ultimately not to survive at all.*

IMMIGRANTS QUEUE *patiently in the Register Room on Ellis Island on arrival in the United States after their journey across the Atlantic. Yetta Sperling and her family had endured a rough ten-day voyage in an overcrowded ship. She recalls their reception by the authorities. 'Every family was put in a cubicle, with bars like a prison. We slept in it that night.'*

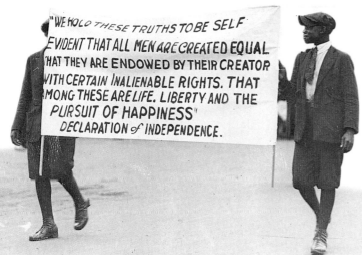

CREATED EQUAL *Liberty and the pursuit of happiness still seemed to be remote aspirations for most blacks in the United States. John Morton Finney learned when he was still very young that 'the blacks had nothing, and the only way they could survive was to work for the whites'.*

was not the worst thing that blacks had to face. 'There was no limit, it extended to everything. In many places black people could not even go to the polls to vote, though the law said they had a right to do so. If they did they could be killed, shot down or beaten to death.'

In Russia the hardship took a different form. Like black American slaves, the peasants had been liberated from serfdom in the 1860s, but by the early twentieth century their lives had changed little. The Russian monarch, the tsar, was venerated with almost religious fervour, and the great landowners still effectively controlled the lives of the peasants, who endured grinding poverty. Sergei Butsko grew up living in primitive conditions in a hut; eight of his brothers and sisters died from dysentery, and the whole family had to work for the local nobleman. 'All the tools were wooden. Almost everything was made by the family itself. The floor was earth....We had a loom where we used to weave all our linen for clothes.' For Sergei Butsko and for millions like him all over the world, the new opportunities that the twentieth century offered were still far out of reach.

A NEW LIFE IN THE NEW WORLD

'**G**IVE ME YOUR TIRED, YOUR POOR, your huddled masses yearning to breathe free.' This invitation, inscribed on the base of the Statue of Liberty in New York, welcomed millions of European immigrants to the United States in the first two decades of the twentieth century.

Potential immigrants, many of them young, were drawn by the advertisements placed abroad by employers and by the managers of steamship and railroad companies. Most people went in search of work, particularly those living in southern and eastern Europe, where the industrial development that had brought jobs to people in northern Europe was slower to develop. There were other reasons to seek a new life: to escape persecution, to avoid military conscription or to regain religious freedom. By 1920 a third of eastern Europe's Jewish population – many from Poland and Russia, where anti-Semitism was increasing – had migrated, 90 per cent of them to the United States.

Nellie Gillenson was the tenth child born to Jewish parents in Galicia, Austria. 'We had a poor life,' she remembers. 'My mother and father had to worry every day about our food....There was no way of making a living.' After a traumatic parting from her parents, who she never saw again, she sailed to the United States with her sister. Her spirits soared when they arrived there safely. 'When I made my first step on the ground of America I felt like I wanted to kiss it, and I said "God bless America" even then.'

By 1910 a third of the population of the twelve largest cities in the United States was foreign-born. While some of the immigrants returned to Europe, unable to adjust to the new country and new way of life, the great majority learned a new language and new skills, and also brought their own habits and experiences from Europe with them. Surrounded by their fellow immigrants, they set up new communities that were not the same as those they had left behind nor exactly imitated the American way of life. Many immigrants did enjoy more freedom than they had ever known, with the chance to work, live and worship as they pleased. Nellie Gillenson remembers, 'We felt that we were welcomed. They let us go wherever we wanted to go. They let us live the way we wanted.'

YETTA SPERLING (RIGHT) *was still a child when she sailed to join her father, who had migrated to the United States to avoid compulsory military service in the German army. Shipping lines offered advice to 'every intending emigrant to Canada or the United States' (RIGHT). Those who made the journey were given a medical inspection as they embarked (ABOVE) and when they arrived. Only healthy immigrants were allowed to stay.*

FLIGHTS OF FANCY
(OPPOSITE) *became a reality when Louis Blériot flew across the English Channel. Jeanne Plouvin (BELOW) was among the crowd watching him take off.*

STRIKING OIL (BELOW) *meant big business in the rapidly growing economy of the United States. Both industry and the internal combustion engine relied on oil for fuel.*

New idols

Technology, the fruit of science, was the great new force expected to transform people's lives. Many people had moved from the land to the cities since the nineteenth century, and it was there that the promise of the new century was felt the most strongly. 'In a city like Chicago,' says the American Elmie Steever, then a young girl, 'everything was modern. We had modern equipment, we had running water, we had bathrooms and the houses were well heated or cared for. And of course we didn't have those conveniences in the country – we couldn't have.'

Before 1900 people travelled by horse, bicycle, boat and train, but most often on their own two feet. The new century pioneered and popularized other means of transport. In 1900 the first electric tram appeared on the streets of New York. The first rigid airship, the zeppelin, was launched in Germany, and the first French underground railway, the Metro, opened in Paris. The new vehicle that had the most immediate impact was the motor car.

It was still an event to see a car when the first aircraft were also being built. In December 1903 the Wright brothers achieved the first controlled, powered flight in a heavier-than-air machine, a biplane, on a beach near Kitty Hawk, North Carolina. Then the French aviator Louis Blériot stole the limelight when he flew in a single-winged craft from Calais to Dover in 1909. Jeanne Plouvin, a young French girl, was there. 'When we knew that Blériot was going to leave, all the children in the district – everyone, from the smallest to the biggest – gathered in a field along the road. We heard him start to move forwards and begin to take off. Everyone clapped and waved, everyone shouted "Bravo!"....There was immense joy when we heard he'd landed on the cliffs of Dover.'

The inventions and new conveniences rapidly followed one another. People could get to work more quickly, and work faster when they were there. They could travel more and learn more, earn and spend more money. One of the most dramatic domestic changes came when electricity was introduced. For Elmie Steever, 'It was very exciting when we got electricity into the church, and the man just touched a button and the church lit up. It was just beautiful. Then of course they had electricity in the stores, and a few put it into their homes. My first experience with an electrical appliance was an iron. I thought it was the most wonderful thing to stand there and just iron, and not have to keep your irons on the stove, and keep the fire going to keep your irons hot.'

Another change came when the telephone was introduced. Jean Eloy was growing up in Paris, and his family thought it was a 'marvellous, magnificent invention....You had to turn the handle again and again until the operator finally deigned to answer.' He recalls his father's impatience when he had to wait for a response. 'When my father's shouting got too much, she'd get her own back on him by not putting him through.'

As a young woman Elmie Steever worked at the telephone exchange in Stromsburg, Nebraska. She recalls how long it took for people to get used to the telephone. 'People were supposed to look in the directory, find the number and give that number to the operator. But lots of times people just picked up the telephone and said "Give me Mr or Mrs so and so".' There were at first so few telephones that operators could memorize their numbers.

Technology was increasingly able to establish links across the world as well as between individuals. In 1901 the Italian scientist Guglielmo Marconi transmitted the first transatlantic radio signals; only two years later regular radio news services were set up in New York and London.

WINDOW SHOPPING (RIGHT) *Electric lighting installed by shopkeepers to light up their window displays at the beginning of the century was many people's first experience of electricity. In the industrialized world the range of goods on offer in the busy shopping districts was matched by the numbers of city dwellers able to afford them.*

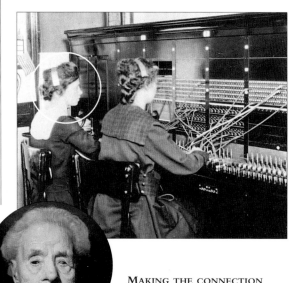

MAKING THE CONNECTION
*Elmie Steever worked shifts with a
team of women at the Stromsburg
telephone exchange. 'It was busy every
minute, there was just no let-up at all...when your shift
changed you had your headset on, and as the girl slid out to
the right, you slid in behind her. There was never a pause.'*

SELLING THE NEWS *was
an increasingly competitive
business in the early
twentieth century. As
education helped more people
learn to read, many of them
became eager for information
and gossip. The tabloids
offered headlines in large
print and stories of foreign
atrocities, and promoted the
latest fads and crazes.*

The age of the masses

For many of those who led privileged and protected lives, the most dramatic – and threatening – aspect of the new century was the growth of the new industrial class swelling beneath society's civilized and apparently stable veneer. For the twentieth century was to be the age of the masses.

There were now more people alive than ever before, and they were multiplying fast. Millions of people were on the move, drawn to the cities in the search for work. Industrialization in Europe and North America had created a new demand for factory workers, clerks and labourers. On trains, in cafés and parks, at seaside resorts, concerts, theatres and spilling over the streets there were crowds of people. Rural communities, closely knit and in many countries still based on feudal relationships, were in decline. The urban population was on the rise.

The press and later radio encouraged political awareness. The typical newspaper of the nineteenth century, which was densely written and highly informative, was read by very few. It was being superseded by the new tabloids: the *Daily Mail*, the *New York World* and *Le Petit Journal* were among the newspapers that were designed to be read by millions. They included photographs, which helped to sell copies and gave the public a new familiarity with prime ministers and presidents; advertisements alerted readers to the possibilities of life with more money. The new journalism, deliberately aimed at the new industrial class, gave them a more conscious sense of society and their position in it.

As people's expectations rose, so did their demands. And with each new gain they rose further. Strikes and protests were not a twentieth-century invention, but the extent and variety of the new organizations that led them was new. And for every benefit or reform granted to one person in the nineteenth century there were ten times as many people with ten times as many demands in the twentieth. Many people's working life began in childhood and ended only when they died. Edith Corcoran worked in a New York knitting mill from the age of fourteen. 'When I went into the mill, everyone was much older than me. It was a lifetime thing. There was no retirement. You worked until you couldn't get to your job any

more.' Arthur Whitlock was born in London in 1891. He too remembers the advantages of the rich. 'I only had an elementary education because in those days education belonged to the upper classes. You either had to find the money to go on to that further education, or it was impossible.' At the age of fourteen he found work at the prestigious Army and Navy Stores. Although he enjoyed his work – he was a telephonist and messenger boy – he was aware that all the employees were vulnerable. 'There was really no security in employment. If a customer complained, you were likely to get dismissal at a moment's notice.'

Minnie Way had begun work in a Scottish jute mill at the even younger age of twelve. She remembers how common the strikes were. 'They would go down the street singing: "We are out for higher wages/As we have a right to do/But we will never be content/Until we get the ten per cent/For we've a right to live as well as you".' Most industrialized countries were swept by strikes in the early years of the century. From 1900 to 1905 half a million American workers were fired each year because of their involvement in unions and strikes; Belgian workers paralysed the country in 1902, demanding electoral reform.

WAVES OF WORKERS *at the Belfast shipyard where the* Titanic *was under construction; more than 11 000 workers were employed to build the world's largest passenger liner. The ship's advanced safety features did not prevent disaster: as the* Titanic *crossed the north Atlantic on her maiden voyage in April 1912, she struck an iceberg and sank.*

ARTHUR WHITLOCK (ABOVE) *found that changes in retailing such as the mail-order catalogues were not matched by better job security for employees: 'There was no redundancy or anything like that,' he recalls.*

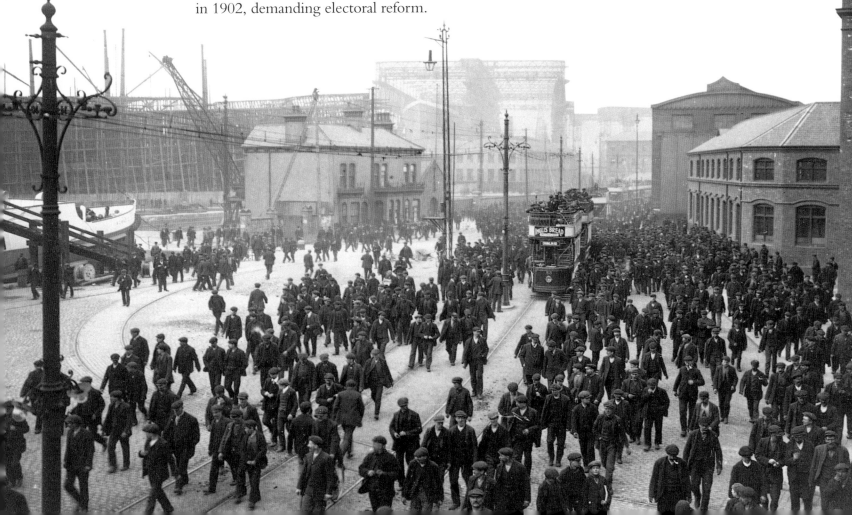

NEW INHABITANTS
thronged the streets of large cities such as New York at the turn of the century. It was in the world's cities that political upheaval and social change began.

ROWS OF CLERKS
(BELOW) *maintained the accounts and kept records up to date. As industry expanded, the need for administrative staff grew. Employment in offices was highly respectable; while men became clerks, educated women found work as shop assistants or typists.*

In many countries working people were already organizing themselves politically and campaigning for change. The German Social Democratic Party had been set up in 1875 when two workers' parties combined. It received only 500 000 votes and gained twelve seats in the Reichstag, the German parliament, at its first election; by 1912 it was the largest parliamentary party. Across Europe, new workers' parties were established on the German model. The British Labour Party was formed in 1900, and by 1906 there were twenty-six Labour members of parliament.

There were some who would not wait for peaceful change. Anarchists, ultra-nationalists and secret revolutionary societies were

WOMEN VOTE FOR CHANGE

'I WAS ASKED IF I WOULD AGREE TO BE CHAINED to Buckingham Palace gates and I said yes....I would agree to anything if it would help women.' Gertrude Jarrett worked in a British pottery factory; she was determined to help the Suffragette movement in its struggle to gain women the vote, even if it meant violent and sometimes dangerous demonstration.

At the beginning of the twentieth century women's lives were changing as more women went out to work, not only in factories but as typists, clerks, bookkeepers and postal workers. There was a growing demand for teachers and nurses. As more women gained financial independence, their social status improved. But economic power was not matched by political power. In 1900 the only countries in which women could vote were New Zealand, parts of Australia and the state of Wyoming in the United States.

Mounting pressure to grant women the right to vote had been growing in the United States and in Europe. In the United States the campaign for women's suffrage had at first been linked to the movement for the abolition of slavery, but although black Americans had gained voting rights after the Civil War, women had not. However, by 1915 a further fifteen states had followed the example set by Wyoming.

In Britain the first effective women's movement was launched in 1903: the Women's Social and Political Union. The suffragettes, as they became known, led a campaign to bring the issue of women's rights to the fore. Their tactics included public speeches, protest marches, civil disturbance, heckling politicians, and hunger strikes by demonstrators when they were imprisoned.

As women's associations became established in other countries, from France to India, the suffragette movement gained an international perspective. Women in Germany were denied the right to join any political organizations until 1907; that year, Finland became the first European country to give its women the vote. Suffrage was granted in Norway in 1913, Denmark in 1915, revolutionary Russia in 1917 and Canada in 1918. In some countries it was the First World War that precipitated a change in attitude, as women proved the value of their skills and resilience in a time of crisis. British women over thirty were granted the right to vote in 1918; postwar reconstruction brought voting rights to women in Austria, Czechoslovakia, Germany and Poland. In 1920 the right to vote was extended throughout the United States.

VOTES FOR WOMEN

(RIGHT) *American suffragettes take to the streets to publicize women's right to gain a public voice. Gertrude Jarrett remembers how in Britain, 'If it got too rowdy the police would come and move us off. We still used to say what we thought....I believed that women were equal to men and should have a say in things.'*

prepared to stop at nothing, and assassinations were reported in the newspapers almost as regularly as were strikes: the king of Italy, the president of the United States and the head of the Russian secret police were all killed by an assassin's bullet or bomb.

Socialism was also on the march in eastern Europe, and in Russia unrest and dissatisfaction led to revolt in St Petersburg in January 1905. Alexander Briansky remembers, 'People hoped the tsar could make their lives better, and would force capitalists to do something for the people, to ensure that they were not so oppressed....After 1905, when thousands of women and children had been killed, revolutionary ideas began to penetrate deeper into the people.'

Beyond Europe and the United States, it was even more difficult to achieve change. When the Herero people rebelled against their German masters in South-West Africa, the Germans responded with a massacre that killed several thousand. Other movements were beginning that would grow during the century, and eventually triumph. In South Africa blacks began to organize to press for peaceful change. Dorah Ramothibe was at one of the early meetings in the Orange Free State: 'We also wanted to be treated all right. We also wanted to live a better life like the white people, and have money and to be paid for the work we did, instead of being given a piece of bread.' In 1912 the various local groups merged to form the African National Congress. 'Just after the formation of Congress there was light, there was hope.'

In the years before the First World War, all the seeds of the twentieth century were sown. They included anti-Semitism, mass propaganda, government repression, and in the Boer War the first concentration camps for civilians, alongside democracy, equal rights and peaceful prosperity. Schools, mass literacy, newspapers and new communications were used to build up the power of the state: people taught to read and vote were also taught to obey. By 1914, poised on the brink of a war that would shatter the old world for ever, the masses who demonstrated for greater freedom were being marched to their deaths with barely a murmur.

POVERTY IN PUBLIC
Poor families gathered in the back streets of many of the world's cities and towns, where industrialization brought wealth to a few but continued poverty and hardship to many of those who sought work in them.

THE WORLD OF LEARNING (ABOVE)
Education was seen as the key to the future. Those who had access to the schoolroom, girls as well as boys, would become part of a better educated and better informed workforce who would learn to demand change rather than just enduring it.

WAR GAMES (RIGHT)
A gymnastic display demonstrates the fitness of young Frenchmen. Their mettle, and that of young men all over Europe, would soon be tested in a real war.

2

Killing Fields

THE EXPERIENCE OF THE FIRST WORLD WAR

EARLY ON THE MORNING OF 1 July 1916, just as the first waves of British soldiers climbed out of their trenches and advanced towards the German lines, the German troops scrambled out of their deep bunkers and opened fire. The British troops were heavily laden with the ammunition, grenades, rifles and barbed wire that they would need when – or if – they reached the German lines. Even under heavy fire these well-disciplined men continued to walk steadily forward across no-man's-land, to almost certain death. A German gunner remembered: 'We were surprised to see them walking...we just had to load and reload. You didn't have to aim, you just fired into them.'

The British soldiers had been told that the huge artillery barrage would already have killed most of the Germans, and that those who had survived it would have been buried alive. One battalion was told: 'You can slope arms, light up your pipes, and march all the way to Pozières before you meet any live Germans.' They had also

been told that the Germans' barbed-wire defences would all have been flattened. But neither assurance was true. The men of many battalions were trapped by uncut wire entanglements, then raked by machine-gun fire. The men had been betrayed by poor planning and muddle; they were, as one German said, 'lions, led by donkeys'.

This was to prove one of the most gallant and disastrous days in the history of warfare – the first day of the battle of the Somme, in northern France. In a war characterized by the remorseless slaughter of young men, it achieved a dreadful fame as the day on which there was the heaviest loss of life. In the four-month battle more than a million soldiers were killed or wounded.

The First World War was to sweep away empires, to cripple both the victorious and the defeated nations, and to leave a dangerous legacy of hate. It brought the United States into Europe, and ended European world supremacy. In 1914 going to war seemed like an adventure; by 1918 it had become a nightmare.

GOING OVER THE TOP *This photomontage of battlefield images captures the experience of the war.*

27

For king and country

The mood in which the world went to war in 1914 was one of naive patriotic fervour. It was your duty to serve your country. In four years of combat, sixty-five million men from more than twenty countries were called up. At first they did this with real enthusiasm. Margarethe Stahl, who worked in the press section of the German war office, saw the soldiers march through the streets of Berlin in August on their way to the front. 'There were flags everywhere, flowers everywhere. People were throwing flowers at the soldiers, and they had flowers in the muzzles of their rifles. They were given cigarettes and chocolate. Their mothers or wives

ran along beside them and everyone was singing.' Carl von Clemm, who was in the German artillery, remembers how it felt: 'It is normal all over the world with young fellows who see the war as just an adventure, and it is patriotism and it is partly to get decorations...and you get away from family and so on, you are all of a sudden on your own at eighteen or nineteen, which is great.'

In Vienna and in St Petersburg there were the same excited scenes. And also in Paris, where, as Hermine Venot-Focké remembers, everyone 'really believed that the French army would perform miracles; that it would reach Berlin in forty-eight hours – no more than that.' They too left with flowers in their rifles.

In Europe, only Britain did not impose compulsory military service (conscription), but many young men were eager to join up. One of them, Norman Tennant, was excited because he had already enlisted in the Territorial Army and had a uniform. 'The atmosphere was certainly electric,' he recalls, 'but it seemed almost unbelievable because we thought that it really couldn't affect us, not in this country, we were well protected, we'd got a good navy....The country was overrun by volunteers, in such numbers that I don't think the government could deal with them for a long time.' Walter Hare joined up because he thought the country was 'worth fighting for and we

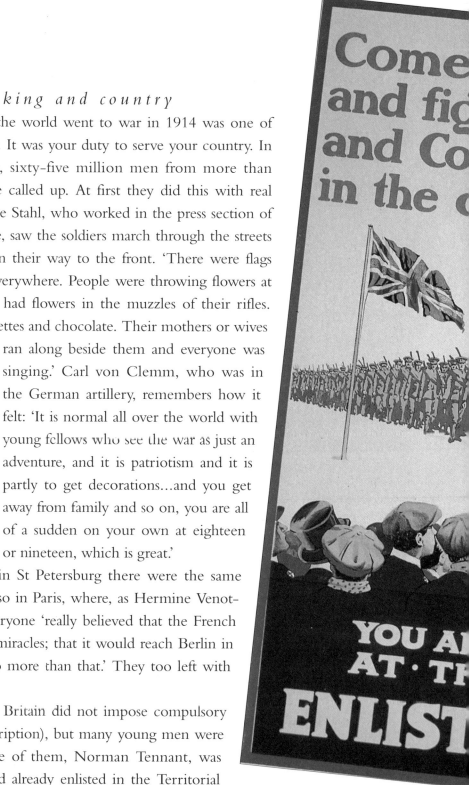

Come and fig and Co in the c

YOU A AT · T ENLIST

AN ENLISTMENT POSTER urges British men to do their duty and join the army. At first Britain relied on the patriotism of its citizens to volunteer for military service, before the compulsory call-up was introduced.

THE WORLD GOES TO WAR

Six GREAT EUROPEAN POWERS dominated most of the world at the beginning of the twentieth century. Years of diplomacy had established a fragile balance of power between them. Germany's rise to power alarmed its neighbours, particularly France; the alliance between France and Russia and the Anglo-French entente were an attempt to ensure that Germany could not dominate Europe. Feeling threatened by these three great states, Germany tried to strengthen its position through its alliance with the Austro-Hungarian empire and Italy. All these powers were rivals in industrial and military importance at home and abroad, so European stability was easily threatened.

The Balkan states of southeast Europe were of particular interest to the European powers. In the second half of the nineteenth century some Balkan provinces of the Turkish Ottoman empire – Bulgaria, Montenegro, Romania and Serbia – gained their independence. Bosnia and Herzegovina, two more Ottoman provinces, came under Austro-Hungarian rule. As their lands bordered the Balkans, both Austria-Hungary and Russia were closely involved with events in this unstable region. Russia encouraged the Balkan League (Bulgaria, Greece, Montenegro and Serbia) in its attempts finally to expel the Turks from Europe. In 1912 and 1913 two wars reduced Turkish territory in Europe to a toehold, and increased the lands owned by the members of the league. Serbia almost doubled in size; the upsurge of nationalism that followed found expression in a desire to 'free' the Serbs' fellow Slavs living under Austro-Hungarian rule in neighbouring Bosnia.

On 28 June 1914 the heir to the throne of Austria-Hungary, Archduke Franz Ferdinand, and his wife Sophie paid a state visit to Sarajevo, provincial capital of Bosnia. The Bosnian Serb extremists who assassinated the royal couple that day lit the fuse that led to world war. There was a tense pause, while Austria–Hungary sent a humiliating ultimatum to Serbia. Serbia was unable to meet all the Austrian demands; their counter-proposals were also regarded as unacceptable. On 28 July the Austrians prepared for war against Serbia.

It might have stopped there. But Russia was committed to come to Serbia's defence, and at once mobilized its troops. Germany felt obliged to make war on Russia if Austria was attacked, and believing that France would come to Russia's aid, invaded Luxembourg and Belgium and declared war on France. Britain had long promised to guarantee Belgian sovereignty, and entered the war against Germany. Lastly, Austria-Hungary and Russia went to war with one another. The system of alliances designed to keep the peace among powerful states had taken years to establish; it took only a few days for them now to lead to war.

ARRESTING THE ASSASSIN (RIGHT) *Gavrilo Princip, the Bosnian Serb nationalist who killed Archduke Franz Ferdinand, was one of a group of young extremists who were opposed to Austro-Hungarian rule and sought freedom for Bosnia to unite with Serbia.*

THE GREEDY BRITISH SPIDER *traps the whole of mainland Europe in its web – a German view of British intentions aimed at a French-speaking audience. Both sides used propaganda as an extra weapon of war, depicting the enemy as barbarous and evil. False stories were leaked to newspapers, and film, the newest art, was also used to spread myths about atrocities perpetrated by the enemy.*

ought to do our bit towards fighting for it. But we weren't fighting for king and country because we'd never met the king. I think it's because there was a war on and everybody felt that was something we could do. There was an army opposed to us and we didn't want them to get into England, and we thought the best way to stop them was to keep them where they were, in France.'

Everyone believed that the war would be over quickly, and that they were in the right. As Carl von Clemm says: 'We believed God was on our side, and we had it on our belts: "*Gott mit uns*"....After the shots at Sarajevo, we definitely thought that we were being attacked...the fact that the Austrians started their mobilization...the encirclement of Germany was being talked about...we certainly didn't feel we were out of a clear sky attacking others, we felt we were defending ourselves and I was very anxious to be a normal patriot and help defend my country.' Hermine Venot-Focké recalls: 'We didn't think that the war was going to be so long and so cruel.' She explains that the French regarded the Germans as 'uninvited guests who were depriving us of the joy of life, who were taking our men – our fathers, our brothers – and we resented them for it'.

A GERMAN TROOP TRAIN *at a station in Berlin prepares to take soldiers to the front in France. Chalked on the wagon is the boast Auf zum Preis-schiessen nach Paris – 'Off to Paris for a shooting prize'. Like their opponents, the Germans expected the war to be a brief and victorious one.*

War by timetable

Plans for mobilization in the event of war had been made by each of the European powers some years before. In every country mobilization was like a gigantic machine. Once it was switched on it simply poured men into their units and shipped them off to the front by train with the speed and efficiency of a factory production line. In the first month after war had been declared in August 1914, nearly sixteen million men were mobilized.

The speed of mobilization generated its own momentum. In Russia, with its millions of peasant soldiers, it was so vast a movement it could not be stopped once it had started. The same was true in Germany: when the Kaiser suggested that the march to the west be called off, he was told that there would be chaos if any attempt was made to stop the 11 000 trains that were carrying men, horses, supplies, artillery and ammunition. During the first six days of the war the German regular army of 70 000 men was augmented to nearly four million. Britain's war plans were detailed in the 'War Book'. Copies were kept in army depots and police stations; it took just a telegram to put the plans into motion. In one week 80 000 men and their horses were shipped to France. Horses presented a particular problem. They took much longer to train than the men, were difficult to load onto ships, and their oats and hay took up twice as much space as ammunition or food rations for the troops.

Outmanned by the Germans, France turned to its overseas empire to make up the numbers. Half a million soldiers went to fight in Europe from the French colonies in Africa, and another 150 000 volunteered from Indochina. Britain made a similar appeal. More than 300 000 Australians volunteered. 'It was the thing to do,' for Edward Smout, who left Sydney with the Australian Medical Corps for the Western Front in 1916. 'We were very loyal to Britain, and apart from that, if you had stayed a year or two longer you would have got a white feather from the girls.' Others volunteered from Canada, New Zealand and South Africa.

AN APPEAL TO SPORTSMEN *in Australia made the war seem like an adventure. Soldiers from Australia and New Zealand, as well as from other British colonies, fought for the Allies in Egypt, Mesopotamia, Palestine and most notably Gallipoli, where they suffered terrible losses in the unsuccessful attempt to inflict a major defeat on Turkey.*

FRENCH COLONIAL TROOPS *from Africa on a route march during training. All the major combatant countries looked to their overseas territories to contribute to the war effort, so both the impact of the war and the conflict itself extended far beyond the boundaries of the states that had started it.*

ALBERT POWIS (ABOVE) *joined the US Marines to fight in the Europeans' war. Fresh American troops arriving in France were keen to 'clean this goddamned thing up and get it done with', as he recalls.*

NEWLY DRAFTED US TROOPS (BELOW) *queue up to receive their equipment. American soldiers were told that their participation in the war was essential to the future of democracy.*

India contributed 1.3 million soldiers and labourers to the war effort, including 100 000 men who were shipped to France to fight on the Western Front. Cha Kunga volunteered to join the Indian Labour Corps. 'I wanted to fight in the British government's war. I wanted to see Western countries for myself. We were told they were healthy places.' But this was his first experience of very cold weather. 'I'd not seen snow before. It was unbearable. Some people just froze up and had to be carried away. We put on four layers of clothing, then a big coat on top of that. But with all these clothes on we couldn't work very fast.'

In 1917 the United States joined the war. The immediate reason was the threat to American lives, shipping and trade posed by the German submarine campaign. But the United States also changed the purpose of the war: it was presented as a crusade for democracy. Many of the four million young Americans who were drafted were also keen to go. Albert Powis was one of these. 'I guess I was patriotic,' he recalls. 'Every time I heard the band play a good marching song I'd have cold chills run up and down my back! We were fighting because they said that if the Germans whipped the English and the French they'd be over after us next. We knew the Germans wanted to rule the world. So we were fighting because they'd sunk our boats and we were fighting for injustices the Germans had done.'

With little idea of what they would have to face, the troops leaving New York harbour laughed off their fears. One of them was infantryman Tela Burt. He remembers coming up on deck and seeing the Statue of Liberty. 'One comic said, "Can you hear what that statue is saying?" They said no. "It's saying, 'That's your ass, big boy! That's your ass. You ain't never coming back!'"'

Like Tela Burt, a substantial number of the American soldiers were black, but they were often not trusted to fight; he had to stay behind the lines to help bury the dead, and 'never knew what the hell I was fighting for. I'd never heard of democracy before. All I knew was I liked the uniform and I wanted to be in the army.'

AN AMERICAN TROOPSHIP *arrives in Europe. The United States stayed neutral for as long as possible before becoming involved in the war. From 1917 the huge quantities of modern equipment, weaponry and ammunition, as well as the millions of extra men available to fight, turned the tide of war in the Allies' favour.*

A new kind of war

Few of the millions of soldiers converging on the battlefields knew how warfare had been transformed in recent years. They were ill-prepared for the reality of the front line. Walter Hare recalls his training with derision. 'It wasn't a scrap of good. I learned how to salute officers, which seemed to be the main thing in the army. I learned to slope arms and present arms, which you can't do in a muddy trench. I fired five rounds before I went out to France. I never saw a grenade, never saw a machine gun.'

The machine gun was born of the technology of the industrial revolution; it could be described as a machine tool of death. The counter to it was a tool of far more ancient date: the shovel. Both were to prove crucial to the character of the war. The battles of the early months demonstrated that the only defence against artillery bombardment and machine-gun fire was to dig a hole.

THE MACHINERY OF WAR

ECHNOLOGY TRANSFORMED military tactics during the First World War. New combat strategies were needed: cavalry could not charge against artillery fire, and infantry advancing in line towards machine guns proved suicidal as men were mown down in their thousands. In the early part of the war all sides used the Maxim machine gun. Capable of firing 600 rounds a minute, they were heavy, needing two or three men to operate them. Recognizing the need for mobility, the British introduced the Lewis gun, which could be carried and fired by just one man. Towards the end of the war the Germans developed the Schmeisser machine pistol, the first one-man portable sub-machine gun.

Deadly though the machine guns were, the worst injuries were inflicted by artillery fire, whose shells left huge craters in the landscape or exploded in the air, scattering deadly shards of steel – shrapnel.

New ways were sought to overcome the difficulties of advancing through barbed wire and over broken ground under fire. The most promising innovation seemed to be the tank. Introduced by the Allies in 1916, its initial success was in shocking German troops. But these slow, heavy vehicles were unreliable and often broke down, and their primitive tracks proved no match for the mud and shell craters of the battlefield, where they became easy prey for the German field guns.

Submarines were introduced for the first time in the challenge between Britain and Germany for supremacy at sea. With its naval fleet bottled up by the British blockade of the North Sea, Germany's retaliation took place beneath the waves. It was Germany's unrestricted use of the *Unterseeboot*, the U-boat, against merchant shipping as well as warships that brought the United States into the war in 1917.

Aircraft were another innovation. In 1914 they were new and untried but were soon adopted by all the main combatants. Their initial role was reconnaissance and helping to direct ground artillery. As both sides increased their air forces, dozens of aircraft fought for control of the skies above the battlefield. The aircraft brought another kind of terror. For the first time there were bombers and airships that began to threaten not only the troops and transport of the enemy, but their families and homes far away from the war zone.

Pilots were seen as glamorous heroes, but it was generally hard to maintain the romantic myths of the chivalry of war. Some of the new weapons were used in a way that was despised: U-boats, for example, were used against unarmed and neutral shipping, and the Germans viewed the use of armoured tanks as lacking in honour. There was one more new and terrible category of weapon: gas. Poison gases, first used by the Germans and soon adopted by the British and the French, added a new dimension to the horror of war.

THE NEW WEAPONS *both shaped the character of the war and were shaped by it. Powerful artillery pieces could fire enormous shells over great distances* (ABOVE); *aircraft brought a new dimension to the battlefield* (LEFT); *and tanks were developed as a new device to break the defensive conditions of trench warfare* (BELOW).

The battles were more like long sieges, as both sides established elaborate defensive positions and tried to inflict maximum damage on the enemy's defences only a few hundred yards away.

By the end of 1914 the Western Front ran for hundreds of miles, from Switzerland to the English Channel. It was not to move more than 16 km (10 miles) either way for the next three years. The opposing trench systems were not single lines, but webs of frontline trenches, support trenches and communications trenches, wired with telephone lines, protected by belts of barbed wire, and studded with gun pits and dugouts. The Germans dug the most elaborate trench systems, strong enough to survive heavy bombardment. German trench lines were often better established than the Allied lines, with concrete machine-gun emplacements scattered at intervals. All trenches ran in zigzags, both to minimize the effects of a direct hit and to prevent a successful storming party from firing along the trench at the defenders.

The troops mostly huddled in the trench, keeping their heads below the parapet and peering through spyholes in steel shields. They stood on the firestep only at the dangerous moment just before dawn, when on sentry duty or before going 'over the top' to assault the other side's trenches. The fire, support and reserve trenches were all linked with communications trenches. Telephones, radios, runners and carrier pigeons, and in the German army dogs as well, were all used for communicating. Light railways were sometimes laid to bring in the vast quantities of food, stores and ammunition needed by densely held sectors of the front.

The trench war, with millions of men who rained millions of shells and tens of millions of bullets at each other, was a battle not only between two great armies, but also between the new industrial might of the two great alliances. The general staffs had to cope with military logistics on an unprecedented scale. In the logistical contest, in spite of the scale and efficiency of German industry, Britain and France had the advantage, for behind them they had the growing productivity of American steel mills and ordnance factories as well as their own. The contribution made by American industry was to be decisive in the outcome of the war.

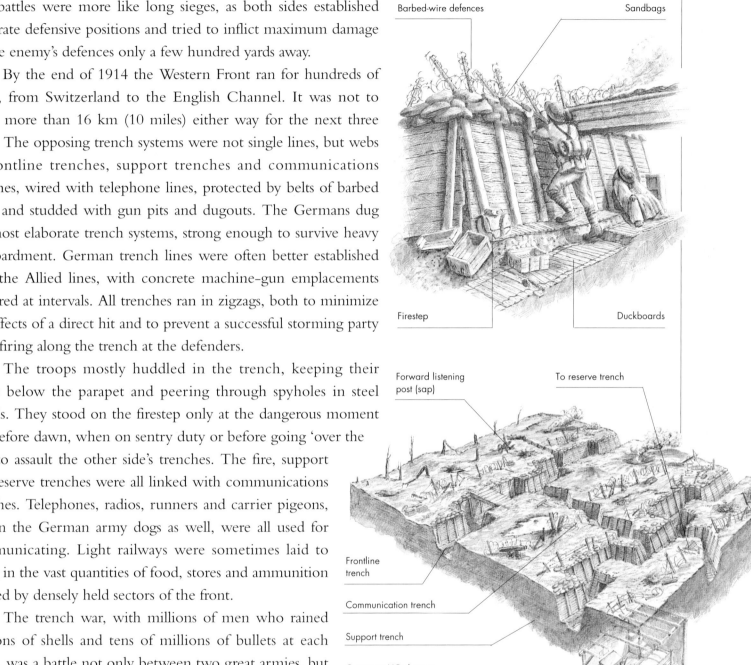

Barbed-wire defences — Sandbags

Firestep — Duckboards

Forward listening post (sap) — To reserve trench

Frontline trench

Communication trench

Support trench

Company HQ dugout

THE TRENCH SYSTEMS *of the opposing forces were constructed to meet similar needs: to provide safe defensive positions over long periods for the troops stationed at the front. Trench warfare took place not only on the Western Front but also on the Eastern Front in the conflict between the Germans and Russians, and in the Balkans between Austro-Hungarian and Serb forces.*

**BRITISH TROOPS
RESTING** *in the trenches.
Some parts of the front were
quiet for months at a time.
There were long days of
boredom and discomfort,
when in these cramped
conditions the men just
waited – waited for their
next meal, waited for the
post, waited for orders.*

A MOMENT OF RELAXATION *for Ernst Weckerling in a
German dugout. He remembers periods when 'No food could
get through to the front, and nothing to drink. We used to take
the water from the machine guns, but then the guns weren't
usable any more. We had very good discipline. Whether an
order was pleasant or unpleasant, we just had to carry it
through, we had to follow it. We just fulfilled our duty.'*

Life in the trenches

The Germans were relatively well equipped in their underground
quarters, which often contained kitchens, hospitals, electricity and
a water supply. 'They were better organized and harder working
than we were,' concedes Marcel Batreau, who was in the French
infantry. 'We were an offensive army whereas they wanted to hold
on to what they'd got. They'd built tunnels which we saw when
we advanced. They were really cushy.' It was different for the
Allied forces. 'Our trenches were miserable little scratchings,'
remembers Norman Tennant. This deliberately enforced the
British commanders' view of the duty of the British soldier in the
face of the enemy. A soldier able to take refuge in a trench or
dugout might want to stay in it rather than join in an attack.

The German soldiers, however, envied the Allied troops'
food supplies. Carl von Clemm helped to capture a British trench.
'The English had so many cigarettes, Player's Navy Cut, and it was
wonderful they had so much condensed milk, it was sheer luxury.'
The Germans were so hungry that if the troops passed a dead
horse, within ten minutes there would be nothing but the bones
left. Horse meat was specially welcome to accompany 'barbed
wire', as the German army's issue of dried vegetables was called.

DREAMS OF HOME

(ABOVE) *were a source of comfort
for men at the front. There was a brisk
trade in sentimental postcards. It was often
difficult both for the soldiers and for their loved
ones at home to be honest about how they felt or the
real conditions of the war. Not only was soldiers' mail
censored, but to protect their families and try to maintain
morale they often just wrote cheerful platitudes. Their relatives
and friends did the same for them. This card was written to the
Englishman Walter Hare at the front by his mother.*

NORMAN TENNANT (BELOW) *filled periods of inactivity by
sketching. He explains the idea for this sketch: 'The listening
patrol would be sent out to get as close as possible to the
German trenches and pick up information from Germans
talking among themselves, and one just thought of a German
chomping away.'*

Karl Henning Oldekop remembers that there was plenty of turnip
and potato soup, but 'the best things, like meat, the English had
and we didn't.' The Germans ate a sort of dripping that was so disgusting they called it 'ape fat'.

When the Americans joined in the war, they did not dig
trenches. 'They were too dirty,' explains Albert Powis. 'Every time
it rained your latrine would overflow, and the rats that went in
there were as big as tomcats.' Trench life was indeed unhygienic,
and the soldiers were plagued by lice. This was humiliating as well
as annoying. Edward Smout found that the steam laundry that
cleaned his uniform failed to kill their eggs. They had to be
burned off with a cigarette. His recipe for getting rid of lice was a
mixture of jam and sulphur. He kept this secret, so the lice would
move on to his neighbour.

Lice, dirt, heat, cold, rain, mud, rats, foul smells, days of
boredom punctuated by periods of intense fear – this was life in
the trenches. Conditions were so unpleasant that the troops were
rotated regularly between the front line and the reserve trenches.
Censorship prevented soldiers from telling their families how bad
life was. Even if their mail had not been censored they would have
found it difficult to describe how they felt. Marcel Batreau saw his

TELA BURT (ABOVE)
*discovered that being a black
American in Europe made
him popular – at least with
the women. He played
Dixieland jazz in a forty-
two piece band to entertain
fellow American soldiers.*

AN AFTERNOON'S PEACE
(RIGHT) *at this fashionable
French café offered a rare
chance for officers of the
Allied forces to leave behind
the horrors of the front line.
For the other ranks the
village bars also provided a
chance to relax and enjoy
local hospitality.*

mother when he went on leave, but he never told her of the really horrible things he had to endure. When he was at the front he would just write on a postcard, as he did on 17 September 1918, after years of horror: 'Dear mother, I'm in very good health and I hope the same can be said of everyone at home.' Another French soldier, Henri Auclair, was once so thirsty that he lapped water like a dog – from a crater with three dead bodies in it. He can still remember wishing, 'If only I could be dead by tomorrow'. Yet when he wrote to his mother he would invariably write just *RAS – Rien à signaler*, 'Nothing to report'.

On leave from the trenches, men wanted to forget the war, not to describe it, and many of them took to alcohol to keep them going. 'I was nineteen years old,' says Ernst Weckerling, a German infantryman. 'You cannot describe how terrible it was. Sometimes we found alcohol and just sat and drank together. Then it was easier to bear.' The American Albert Powis recalls: 'After battle the officers would tell us: now go out and get drunk and forget it. So that's what we'd do. We'd go out and we'd get into the cafés and we'd get drunk and have a good time....That's what they wanted us to do – forget the battle and get ready for the next one. After the war I had a problem – I'd come damn near being an alcoholic.'

Tela Burt found he was specially popular among civilians. 'The French people seemed to like black people, the blacker the boys were, the more they would go for them. We taught them a lot of dances and they liked our music.' Seventy years later, he still keeps a picture of a French girl he met on leave.

THE MAIN THEATRES OF WAR *surrounded the territories of the Central Powers. In the early months it was a war of movement, with the German invasion through Belgium into France in the west, and the Russian advance into Germany and Austria-Hungary in the east. But the new tactics developed in response to new weaponry led to the stalemate of trench warfare and high casualties. Many people were killed in the campaign by German and Austrian forces against the Serbians and their allies in the Balkans. The Italians also endured appalling casualties in the mountainous region near their border with Austria-Hungary.*

THE LOST GENERATION

THE TRUE NUMBER OF LIVES *affected by the war will never be known. Some countries kept accurate records of military casualties; for others they can only be estimated. These figures are chilling enough. No detailed records of civilian casualties are available, but there were probably as many civilian deaths — in excess of thirteen million people — during the war as a result of starvation, disease and military action. The influenza epidemic that swept the world in 1918–19 claimed another twenty million lives.*

Allied forces	Total mobilized	Deaths	Total casualties
Belgium	267 000	13 716	93 061
British empire	8 904 467	908 371	3 190 235
France	8 410 000	1 357 800	6 160 800
Greece	230 000	5 000	27 000
Italy	5 615 000	650 000	2 197 000
Japan	800 000	300	1 210
Montenegro	50 000	3 000	20 000
Portugal	100 000	7 222	33 291
Romania	750 000	335 706	535 706
Russia	12 000 000	1 700 000	9 150 000
Serbia	707 343	45 000	331 106
USA	4 355 000	116 516	323 018
Total	**42 188 810**	**5 142 631**	**22 064 427**

Central Powers			
Austria-Hungary	7 800 000	1 200 000	7 020 000
Bulgaria	1 200 000	87 500	266 919
Germany	11 000 000	1 773 700	7 142 558
Turkey	2 850 000	325 000	975 000
Total	**22 850 000**	**3 386 200**	**15 404 477**

Alliances

- Allied countries at outbreak of war
- Countries joining Allied forces
- Central Powers at outbreak of war
- Countries joining Central Powers
- Neutral countries

Major battles

- ✳ 1914
- ✳ 1915
- ✳ 1916
- ✳ 1917
- ✳ 1918

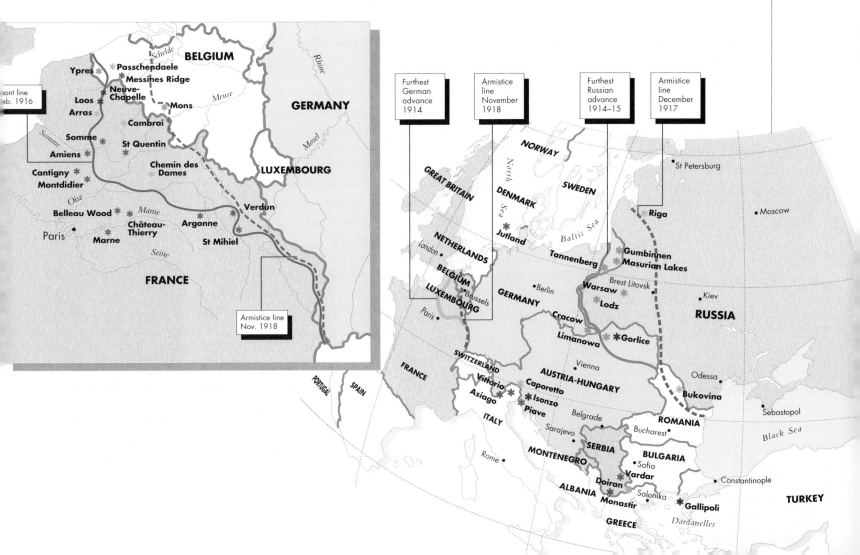

Going into battle

By 1916 soldiers were caught in a deadly war of attrition, as each side tried to wear the other down. The two major offensives of that year on the Western Front provide vivid examples of the character of the war as a whole. The great German effort to end the stalemate took place at Verdun in northeastern France. The Germans were convinced that if they could cripple the French army, Britain would also be defeated. They intended to 'bleed the French army white', and came close to success. Preparations moved with secrecy and speed, until by the beginning of February 1916 more than 1200 German guns were in position for an assault along a front less than 13 km (8 miles) long. The bombardment was heavier than anything the soldiers had experienced before, but the French high command was determined that this important fortress-city must not be surrendered, whatever the cost.

As French reinforcements were strengthened with their big guns, it was the Germans' turn to endure the terrible bombardment of the artillery. 'It was hell,' says Ernst Weckerling, who was pinned down in a shell crater. 'The air was full of smoke and fumes from the constant firing of the French guns. The crater I was in was so deep that the breeze couldn't blow the fumes away. The air was so bad that we were parched with thirst and breathing was very difficult.' He remembers with disgust the awful task of removing his dead comrades' belongings. 'I had to find the ID tags on their chests and remove them. I felt like a butcher sometimes as I rummaged around in all that blood. On some corpses the whole torso had been flattened by mortars, and pieces of flesh were hanging off everywhere.'

At Verdun, as at many other battles, the fighting was often so fierce that there was no opportunity for the dead to be buried. Marcel Batreau describes vividly how 'the rats would start eating their faces. First they'd gnaw at their lips and their noses, then get into their coats and start eating the rest.' The soldiers used their dead friends as duckboards. 'We had to jump from corpse to corpse,' he recalls. 'If we stepped in the mud on either side, we'd get stuck. We had to use the dead face-down because if we stepped on their stomachs our feet would sink in. It was disgusting. It was terrible. We were surrounded by death.'

Flower of remembrance

THE POPPY *was the first plant to emerge from the mud of the Flanders battlefields. Its blood-red flowers became a potent symbol of those whose lives had been lost where the flowers now bloomed.*

The Somme offensive was launched by the Allies at the beginning of July. It was partly intended to make the Germans divert forces from Verdun, and was also the French and British attempt to end the stalemate and drive the Germans out of France. The plan was to concentrate a massive artillery barrage on just one section of the German lines near the river Somme. One and a half million shells were taken up to the gun batteries in preparation.

As the guns thundered and the shells exploded above their heads, the Germans stayed in their deep dugouts. After 20 000 tonnes of shells had rained down on the German positions during the seven-day onslaught, the British prepared to attack. Fresh troops waited to rush through the gap they expected to have opened up in the German lines. Some 100 000 soldiers set out. But their commanders were wrong. The barrage had failed; it had neither demolished the barbed-wire entanglements nor destroyed the German positions. As the British advanced towards the enemy lines, the German gunners simply mowed them down.

Walter Hare managed to get to the German lines. 'I kept going, I got to the German barbed wire, I got through that all right, and jumped into a German trench. We stayed there all that day and the following night, with no food, no water, dead short of ammunition. One of our chaps contacted headquarters, then came forward to us and said, "I've got orders for you. You've got to retire to the trenches you left as best as you can, get back as best as you can." So I finished up there, where I left. I think there were 230-odd casualties and we never gained a yard of ground. I'd lost a lot of my pals...and we needed them. I thought how stupid it was.'

The experience was similar for the German soldiers when they were ordered to go over the top. Karl Henning Oldekop recalls: 'You felt it was your duty to advance with the others, not to leave them in the lurch. You only feel fear when you hear enemy mortars whizzing right past you, and then without thinking you automatically throw yourself down on the ground.'

Twenty of the sixty British battalions committed to the first wave of that attack on the first day of the Somme offensive were cut to pieces by machine guns in no-man's-land, the devastated area between the lines. Others were killed by artillery or in the hand-to-hand fighting in the German trenches. Machine guns and

GERMAN TROOPS (ABOVE) *at the Somme defend their trench against the enemy with hand grenades and machine guns. Despite the dreadful effectiveness of these weapons, some of the advancing soldiers still came through.*

artillery gave an overwhelming advantage to the defence, especially a defence as well dug in as the Germans. One German regiment lost 280 out of 3000 soldiers that first day on the Somme; the British division attacking them lost 5000 out of 12 000. German losses over the whole period, however, were also great.

After the repulse of the first British attack, the generals kept up the offensive for several months after it had become plain that a breakthrough was impossible. Between July and November there were over one million casualties; 380 000 soldiers lost their lives. The heroic sacrifice achieved little or nothing, except marginally to relieve pressure on other fronts. The entire operation penetrated at most 8 km (5 miles) into the enemy's lines.

The worst casualties of all were caused by shells. Shrapnel shells released lethal pieces of flying metal; high explosives could tear off limbs or head, or even destroy a man's body completely. When shells were fired in your direction, there was nowhere to run to. Norman Tennant describes how it felt. 'The only thing you could do would be to drop flat on the ground and stay there…and wait for the shell which was going to hit you…they seemed to get closer and closer until you thought, the next one's going to get you, my lad, you've had it this time. And it came over and burst and it didn't get you and you were so grateful for that.'

But he also recalls the horror. 'Things were dropping out of the air, unspeakable things. Once, a book, with a hole torn right through the middle of it. One arm, part of a body, dropping. A man had been blown to bits and I just saw this remnant falling through the air.'

WALTER HARE *on leave in England with his girlfriend. He was wounded in the battle of the Somme and taken prisoner. Looking back on the war, he says: 'It meant three years of my life were wasted.'*

GOING OVER THE TOP (BELOW) *was a perilous scramble out of the trenches and into the dangerous territory between the lines. Many soldiers were killed or mortally wounded before they even reached the enemy's positions.*

YOUR COUNTRY NEEDS YOU

THIS WAS A NEW KIND OF WAR, one in which civilians were mobilized. In previous wars, people caught in the track of fighting armies endured famine, disease and barbarous cruelties; this was the first time states mustered all their resources for war.

As more and more able-bodied men went off to fight, the people who remained at home had to devote their entire energies to the war effort. For the first time, civilians were as important as troops, women as important as men. Several civilians were needed to keep each soldier in the field supplied with equipment, ammunition and other essentials.

The shortage of men meant that women were needed to take over jobs they had never done before. Throughout Europe women ran public transport, did clerical work and operated machines in munitions factories. They worked not only in their traditional roles as nurses and cooks, but also as plumbers, electricians, shoemakers, farmhands, undertakers and even police officers. Their lives were hard; they often worked twelve-hour shifts, seven days a week, and were paid less than the men for doing so.

Before the war, women had already begun to work in paid jobs in large numbers. In France, for example, women made up 35 per cent of the labour force in 1914; the figure rose to 40 per cent during the war. The greatest change came in the kind of work that women undertook. Old prejudices were challenged as women proved that they could succeed in highly skilled, traditionally male occupations – as doctors and engineers, for example.

All the wealth of the combatant countries was diverted to one end. People were encouraged to invest in the nation as an act of patriotism by buying war bonds, loans to help their government meet the huge costs of war. Bonds were seen as an alternative to raising taxes; it was assumed by both sides that when the war was won, the enemy would have to pay reparations in compensation.

Everywhere, food was scarce and prices were high. Food rationing was introduced. Germany and Britain were both heavily dependent on imported food, and the war threatened their vital supplies. 'People's kitchens' sprang up in cities as governments struggled to keep their people fed; food riots became common as the hardships increased. In Britain more than 800 000 hectares (2 million acres) of pasture were ploughed up to grow cereal crops, and growing vegetables in allotment gardens became a patriotic activity.

In Germany one observer said, 'The whole empire is being turned into a field,' yet Germans were driven to use ersatz (substitute) foods that were more ingenious than nutritious. After the potato harvest failed in 1917, the Germans had to endure the 'turnip winter' – there was almost nothing else to eat. By this time many Germans and central Europeans were seriously undernourished, while in Russian and Polish cities many people were close to starvation.

Coal was in short supply, and the private use of electricity was restricted. The lack of food and warmth, the fear and loneliness drove many people to seek other forms of comfort. 'Drink is doing more damage than all the German submarines put together,' said the British prime minister, David Lloyd George. Britain and Germany introduced alcohol licensing laws, and in France alcoholic drinks could be bought only at mealtimes.

There were few opportunities to forget the war, though in the cities the need for escape was met by music halls and the cinema. The most chilling reminders were brought daily by the casualty lists carried by the newspapers. The thousands of names listed represented the lives of sons, brothers and husbands killed, wounded, captured or missing in action. Every family dreaded the arrival of a telegram bearing news of another life sacrificed in this terrible war.

WOMEN AT WAR *Women took over the jobs of the men who had gone to fight, directly contributing to the war effort in munitions factories. They worked in many previously male civilian activities, as well as nursing the wounded.*

THESE WOMEN ARE DOING THEIR BIT

LEARN TO MAKE MUNITIONS

Treating the wounded

As a stretcher-bearer collecting the wounded from the battlefield, Edward Smout saw more than his share of terrible injuries. 'You were frightened, there was no doubt about that. I was, I think everyone was…I lost weight, I became nervous. I was a complete nervous wreck and so I got leave…nobody understood shell shock. Looking back at it now,' he reflects, 'I feel it more than when I was there because you develop, not a callousness but…a certain indifference towards it because you couldn't carry on otherwise.'

Those who survived the perilous journey back across no-man's-land were treated behind the lines. The wounded were taken first to the field dressing station, where their injuries were assessed and they were given one of three different coloured tags, according to the type and seriousness of their wounds. Slightly

The stretcher-bearer (ABOVE) *was often in as much danger on the battlefield as the comrades it was his job to rescue.*

This devastated landscape (BELOW) *had been a pleasant wooded valley set in fertile French countryside before the war.*

Dying for freedom and honour

A MEMORIAL PLAQUE *was given to the family of every Briton killed in the war, including nurses and other civilians as well as members of the armed forces, to remind them of the value of their loved one's sacrifice.*

wounded men were moved to the casualty clearing station; the general hospital dealt with more serious cases; and soldiers with the worst injuries of all went to the big base at Etaples and then on to England. There were no painkillers except chloroform pads and morphia, and they were only for the seriously wounded. A very big shrapnel wound would be stitched, bandaged and tidied up before the patient was taken away. A shattered arm would not be amputated, but the man would be marked with an urgent tag.

Edward Smout reflects: 'Our two doctors at the field dressing station...I would say they learned more surgery in forty-eight hours than they would have learned in twenty years at home.'

Major surgery was undertaken at the general hospital. An exhausted surgeon recorded his day: 'The operating room starts at about 8.30 a.m., and four tables are going steadily until one o'clock at night. We've done 273 operations in four days.' One badly wounded British soldier was comforted by a young Frenchwoman. 'He was hoping for his mother,' Hermine Venot-Focké remembers, 'which was of course quite impossible. He must have felt someone beside him, because he stretched out his hand, which I took in mine. I thought, "He's waiting for his mother, and I'm going to give him the kiss he's waiting for." I kissed him, and he died. I never found out his name, but I never forgot him.'

Max Nathanovich Kleinman was in the Russian imperial army on the Eastern Front. Poorly led, the peasant armies of the tsar suffered terribly. The inadequate army medical services were supplemented by private hospital trains run by the great ladies of the court, who were more willing than skilful. He was taken to one of the trains after being wounded in the chest, he was also infested with lice. 'The nurses came from upper-class families,' he explains. 'They were all white-skinned, pretty blondes, wearing headscarves. One could enjoy looking at the nurse, but she was afraid to come close to me as the lice were running all over me, so it was up to the male nurses to do the dirty jobs.' These genteel nurses were also not permitted to treat wounds inflicted below the soldiers' waists.

TREATING THE WOUNDED (ABOVE) *was a seemingly endless task. While the battle rages, at this field dressing station behind the lines orderly rows of injured men await transport. Their destination will depend on the severity of their wounds.*

BLINDED BY GAS, *soldiers support each other as they shuffle painfully forward. Both sides used poison gases, first chlorine and then phosgene. Many victims of gas attacks died by drowning in the fluid that collected in their lungs. Later mustard gas, which blistered the skin, was also used.*

BEYOND THE CALL OF DUTY?

THE MEN WHO FOUGHT in the First World War experienced a new level of human endurance, both in the scale of the war and in the conditions in the trenches and on the battlefields. Harsh measures were taken against soldiers on both sides who could no longer bear the sights and sounds of death all around them. Some three hundred British soldiers were court-martialled and shot. One of them, Private Arthur Earp, was suffering from shell shock when he was found in June 1916 crouching in a dugout when he should have been in an attack. The court's recommendation that he should be shown mercy 'owing to the intense bombardment which the accused had been subjected to and on account of his good character' was overridden. The only choice for soldiers was between probable death if they went forward, and certain death if they went back.

In most armies there were mutinies as well as individual protests. On the Western Front the French had suffered the most. Those who had survived the bloodbath of Verdun were sent into an assault on the Chemin des Dames in spring 1917. Once again the infantry were hurled against strongly fortified positions. An advance of only 548 metres (600 yards) resulted in 120 000 French casualties. Some units began to bleat like sheep as they passed senior officers. 'We are men, and not beasts to be led to the abattoir to be slaughtered,' they objected. At the end of April one unit mutinied, and then disaffection spread through two-thirds of the French army divisions. Of the 3000 mutineers sentenced, 600 were to be executed; only about fifty executions were carried out.

On the Eastern Front, where more than two million Russians had been killed, discipline completely collapsed in the chaos following the fall of the tsar. Mikhail Abramovich Rosental was in the artillery. He remembers: 'It was chaos. The people who were supposed to give us logistical support ran away first. We began to go hungry. We were all very dirty....At the end of the war there were few people left who could give orders. Our division didn't exist. We were very happy that we were free to run away.' There were defections in the Austro-Hungarian infantry, and mass surrenders in Czech units.

Morale in the German army remained high; it was the navy that became disaffected. There were hunger strikes because food on board naval vessels was so poor. In June 1917 the crew of the *Prinzregent Luitpold* mutinied; two of the leaders were executed. In October 1918 the crews of the German fleets at Wilhelmshaven and Kiel received orders to sail into battle. Some refused to weigh anchor; others refused to return to their posts. Rebellion and insubordination spread rapidly through the fleet. The officers might have been prepared to launch a final attack as a display of honour, but the men made it clear that they had had enough.

A SENTENCE OF DEATH (BELOW) *was passed on Arthur Earp, who had disobeyed orders at the front. The plea for mercy was rejected by the British commander in chief, Sir Douglas Haig, who wrote: 'How can we ever win if this plea is allowed?'*

"*I didn't feel like fighting any more, there was no one to fight for when Nicholas gave up the throne.*"

Mikhail Abramovich Rosental

Russian and German soldiers (above) *on the Eastern Front after Russia's withdrawal from the war in December 1917. After the fall of the tsar earlier that year, one of the promises that brought Lenin to power in the Soviet Union was that he would make peace with Germany and end the Russians' suffering. In the chaos surrounding the revolution in Russia, military leadership and organization disintegrated. The starving troops felt abandoned by their leaders, and no longer knew who or what they were fighting for.*

Burying the dead (opposite) *French soldiers near Reims in July 1918 identifying some of their dead comrades, who fell in one of the last major battles of the war. Many soldiers did not have the dignity of burial.*

The war ends

As the war dragged on, the atmosphere increasingly became one of exhaustion and despair. The Germans were given new hope when the Russian tsar was overthrown in March 1917. When the United States declared war in April, the German leaders knew that they must deploy as many troops as possible on the Western Front before the Americans arrived. As the Russian armies disintegrated, German troops were transported from the east to help those in the west. But the American declaration of war had given the Allies fresh hope too, and they held on despite war weariness, mutiny and the desperate desire for the war to end.

At last, in the summer of 1918, it began to dawn on the German general staff that the war was lost. Europe's reserves of manpower may have been almost exhausted, but now there were also four million Americans under arms, two million of them in Europe. By October 1918 the German generals had had enough. They marched their armies under perfect discipline back to the fatherland. Many Germans found it hard to understand why their armies, which they believed had not been beaten in battle, had capitulated. It felt more like betrayal than defeat.

Flanders, Ypres, Tannenberg, Gallipoli, Isonzo, Verdun, the Somme: these and many other less notorious places were the killing fields. The mud, fear, pain, death and futility there set new standards for what was imaginable in the scale and intensity of human suffering. The people of every nation that fought in the First World War experienced dreadful slaughter. For everyone involved the war had been an unparalleled catastrophe. Sixty-five million men, many of them hardly more than boys, spent up to four years in discomfort, misery and terror. Nearly nine million of them died. Every one of the sixty-five million represented a job unfilled, a family deprived, a woman husbandless, children fatherless. Each of the nine million deaths inflicted a bitter tragedy on a wife, a mother, a friend. For most of those who waited for the men who did not return, the war was the worst thing that had happened in their lives. The men who did come back brought with them their injuries, their nightmares, their rage, their new contempt for once revered authority – and their determination that it must never be allowed to happen again.

Red Flag

COMMUNISM COMES TO RUSSIA

IT WAS AT NINE O'CLOCK ONE autumn evening in 1917 that three blank shots were fired from the battle cruiser *Aurora* over the river Neva in Petrograd (as St Petersburg was then called). At this signal the Red Guards moved in to take the Winter Palace. The great wave of unrest spreading through the Russian capital was about to break into revolution.

Alexander Briansky was one of the guards. 'When the *Aurora* fired everyone rushed forward shouting "hurrah". I was at the front, I ran up the stairs and stumbled into a big hall where there was a detachment of officer cadets with their rifles at the ready. I shouted to the defenders, "Throw down your rifles!" and they threw down their weapons as if to order. They'd seen how angry we were.' There was confused scuffling. A few shots were fired along the corridors and staircases inside the enormous building, and some nervous telephone calls were made between the opposing sides.

Ministers of the Provisional Government, which had ruled Russia since the tsar's abdication eight months earlier, were hiding from the danger of bombardment in a back room of the palace. One of the men leading the operation to take control in Petrograd suddenly burst in and announced to them: 'In the name of the Military Revolutionary Committee, I declare you under arrest.' The ministers were taken across the Neva to the fortress prison of St Peter and St Paul.

This supreme moment of the revolution was an almost bloodless coup d'état, an anticlimax. One eyewitness described it as little more than a changing of the guard. Nevertheless, what took place that night was a turning point, perhaps *the* turning point of the twentieth century.

The communists who had seized power promised change, liberation and equality for the oppressed Russian people. Alexander Briansky, like many others, was full of hope. 'I thought the future of Russia would take a different path: the people would be free, and there would be work without exploitation.' But before long the very people the revolution sought to liberate would become victims of the new system.

STORMING THE WINTER PALACE *A dramatized portrayal of the moment of revolution.*

War and revolution

It was war that frayed the fabric of autocratic rule in Russia and paved the way for the revolution. First the Russians were humiliated in 1904–5 in the war against Japan. In 1914 Russia entered the First World War as France's ally against Germany. This enemy was both more deadly and closer at hand. Many Russian soldiers were sent into war without weapons. Hurled at German machine guns by aristocratic officers using obsolete tactics, sometimes ordered to charge armed only with bayonets and hand grenades, the soldiers responded with courage that exposed them to fearful casualties: well over a million men were killed, more than four million were wounded (of whom 350 000 died of their wounds), and a further two and a half million were captured. The soldiers' hardships were compounded by inadequate supplies, and disease spread among both the fighting men and those supporting them behind the lines.

Life was also very difficult for the civilian population. So many men had gone to the war that both farming and industry were crippled. By January 1917 the transport system had broken down, and the bread and fuel needed by people in the cities failed to reach them. Tens of thousands of workers, already politically aware and made increasingly restless by revolutionary propaganda, were out of work or on strike.

Alexander Briansky remembers those times. 'We lived very badly. It got so bad one day there wasn't even a piece of bread,' he recalls. He decided that he would join the revolutionaries. 'There were many reasons: hatred for the tsarists, the shooting of ordinary strikers, this endless war that didn't show any mercy to people.'

Driven to desperation, huge crowds came out onto the streets to demonstrate. When garrison officers tried to restore order, the soldiers proved reluctant to fire on civilians. In late February, when the last few strands of authority snapped, the government lost control of the capital. In March Tsar Nicholas abdicated, and authority was passed to a Provisional Government.

A SOLDIER COMES HOME
Some fifteen million Russians fought in the First World War. Many of those who survived had only further hardships to look forward to when they returned home. For them, the revolution offered a new alternative to despair.

REVOLUTIONARY GUARDS *on patrol in March 1917, waiting with fixed bayonets for any challenge from the tsarist forces in the streets of Petrograd.*

THE FALL OF THE TSAR

'TO THE EMPEROR OF ALL THE RUSSIAS belongs the supreme and unlimited power. Not only fear, but also conscience commanded by God Himself, is the basis of obedience to this power.' This declaration in the Fundamental Laws of Imperial Russia describes the absolute rule of the Romanov tsars, under which the Russians lived for nearly three hundred years.

From the middle of the nineteenth century there had been some gradual changes. In 1861 serfdom had been abolished – two years before the emancipation of slaves in the United States. Until then, many of the peasants had also been little more than slaves of the great landowners, labourers tied to the land where they worked. Russia's long-established feudal structure did not easily yield to change, and for most peasants conditions did not improve much; their life was often still very harsh.

Improvements in farming took second place to industrial development. In the late nineteenth and early twentieth centuries the Russian economy began to grow. People left the land to seek work in the towns. Here too life was hard, but many city workers learned to read, and as they came in contact with new ideas discontent began to spread.

In January 1905 a procession of workers presented a petition for political reform to the tsar, Nicholas II. Soldiers fired on the demonstrators; at least two hundred of them were killed that day, which was remembered as Bloody Sunday. There was turmoil elsewhere, too. Workers went on strike. Peasant mobs burned landlords' houses and seized their land. In Odessa the crew of the battleship *Potemkin* mutinied. Russia seemed to be on the brink of anarchy. In October the tsar reluctantly made some concessions. He signed a manifesto that agreed to grant civil liberties, including freedom of speech and assembly, to the people. It also established an elected assembly, the Duma, with some administrative power.

This was in effect Russia's first constitution. The new prime minister, Baron Peter Stolypin, recognized the urgent need for modernization. He encouraged a 'dash for growth' financed by foreign investment, carried out land reform in the hope of giving peasants an interest in improving their land, and improved the education system. Stolypin was assassinated in 1911; with his death Russia's chance to make a peaceful transition into a modern state perhaps disappeared.

The pace of change seemed to be too slow. Many political groups were opposed to Nicholas's government, and with the outbreak of war in 1914 the unrest grew. Over the next few years, as soldiers were killed in their thousands and civilians suffered further hardships at home, strikes, riots and rebellion increased. The Duma was ordered to dissolve, but instead set up the Provisional Government. The tsar, finally realizing that he had lost control, abdicated in March 1917. The monarchy had ended.

TSAR NICHOLAS *in captivity with his wife and children. After the abdication they were imprisoned in the town of Ekaterinburg in the Urals. But the tsar still posed a threat to the revolutionaries, who felt he could provide a focus for anti-Bolshevik resistance, and one night in July 1918 he and his family were shot by their guards.*

LEADING THE PEOPLE

LENIN, LIKE MANY OTHERS among the best-educated and most socially aware Russians of his generation, had long despised the tsarist regime, and sought new, radical solutions to his country's problems. He had become a revolutionary in 1890 at the age of twenty, after his brother had been hanged for his part in a conspiracy to assassinate the tsar. Born Vladimir Ilyich Ulyanov, Lenin took his name from the river Lena in Siberia, where he was exiled in 1897.

For thirty years Lenin's life was punctuated with danger, periods of imprisonment and exile. He studied and then practised law before moving to St Petersburg, where he was prominent in a revolutionary group. Lenin's ideas developed from those of Karl Marx, the nineteenth-century German philosopher. Marx declared that change had to come through struggle rather than gradual development, and that progress required the overthrow of capitalism to make way for socialism. Lenin saw imperialism as the last stage of capitalism, and this led him to call for world revolution. The armies of the First World War should not fight each other, but turn their rifles on their own officers and the ruling classes.

In a series of powerful pamphlets Lenin developed and explained his ideas. Insisting that the revolution should be led by professional revolutionaries, he opposed democratic voting out of fear that the votes of workers and socialists would be swamped by those of millions of peasants still in favour of monarchy. His later policies towards the peasants continued to reflect this mistrust of them.

From 1900 to 1905 Lenin lived in Switzerland. He returned to Russia to take part in the 1905 revolution, but was again forced into exile. In March 1917, learning of the fall of the tsar, Lenin knew his time had come. The Germans, hoping to undermine their enemy's war effort by contributing to its unstable political situation, permitted Lenin to cross Germany in a sealed train on his way back to Russia. On his return he threw himself into coordinating the revolution.

Lenin brought new hope to millions of angry and frustrated Russians. He offered a new vision to people who had suffered a long history of oppression – to the soldiers exhausted by war, to the peasants who knew only work and poverty, to the city workers whose lives seemed to be a new kind of serfdom. He assured these voiceless people that their voice would at last be heard.

SPREADING THE REVOLUTION *Lenin believed that the revolution in Russia would ignite similar upheavals throughout Europe, setting the scene for the overthrow of capitalism and imperial rule everywhere. Many shared his belief, and waited with joy or dread for world revolution.*

LOOKING TO LENIN
Alexander Briansky (ABOVE AND RIGHT) *fought for the changes promised by Lenin (seen in the foreground of this photograph). 'I loved Lenin,' he explains, 'because he struggled for peace against blood-letting of any kind.'*

'Peace, land and bread'

Now a new contest began, between the Provisional Government and the revolutionary soviets, the councils of workers' and soldiers' representatives. The most powerful of these was the Petrograd soviet, led by Leon Trotsky. One young Russian, Valentin Astrov, reflects how many people felt at that time. 'There seemed to be no other way out of the crisis than going over to the soviets. The bourgeois would never be able to cope with the difficulties that were facing the people. I decided that's what I would struggle for.'

In the early years of the twentieth century there was a bewildering number of political groups, each of which claimed to offer the best alternative to absolute rule by the tsars. Among them were the Bolsheviks, a group of extreme socialists led by Lenin, who wanted a radical new system of government. After many months of political ferment, Lenin's conviction that the time for revolution had come took the Bolsheviks to the centre of the Russian political stage.

Under his leadership, the Bolsheviks' victory was sealed by the 'changing of the guard' at the Winter Palace. Karl Rianne, like Alexander Briansky, took part that autumn day in 1917. 'There were 90 000 of us, and when we arrived in Petrograd we were all sent to different areas. We were told to occupy the telegraph and the post office. There could have been blood spilt, but thanks to Lenin's orders we managed to cut all the means of communication of the Provisional Government in the Winter Palace in good time.'

That evening Lenin made an excited speech to members of the revolutionary soviets at the Smolny Institute, once a finishing school for the daughters of the nobility. Now its wooden floors echoed not to silk slippers in the waltz, but to the heavy boots of factory workers and peasant soldiers. He promised that the oppressed masses would themselves form the government. A new workers' state must be created. The war must be ended. Workers in Europe would come to the help of their Russian brothers. Landed property would be abolished, and the land given to the peasants to win their cooperation. 'Long live the worldwide socialist revolution!'

The slogan of the hour was 'Peace, land and bread'. It was a formula that would bind together behind the tiny clique of

The party card

EVERYONE WHO JOINED *the Communist Party had a party card – even Lenin. Between 1917 and 1921 three quarters of a million people became members; by 1940 there were almost two million. At first membership was a matter of patriotism, but it became increasingly necessary for those with political or social ambitions, and came to symbolize access to a ruling elite.*

FIGHTING FOR COMMUNISM *The people of Russia helped the revolutionary leaders to establish Bolshevik rule. Detachments of Red Guards were formed among many groups of workers* (BELOW). *But White armies resisted; a White army officer drew this sketch of a fellow Cossack with the two peasants he had just taken prisoner* (RIGHT).

CELEBRATING THE FIRST YEAR *of the 'dictatorship of the proletariat'* (OPPOSITE). *In this anniversary poster a worker and a peasant stand together triumphantly at the gate leading to the prosperous future world, the symbols of the power they have overthrown lying at their feet. The tools of their trade – the hammer and the sickle – became the emblems of the new Soviet Union's national flag.*

Bolshevik leaders the three great forces that would build a new Soviet society: peace for the soldiers, land for the peasants, and bread for the city workers. 'The ideals of the revolution inspired very many people. It seemed that life would open up in all its fullness and beauty,' explains a painter, Boris Smirnov-Russetsky. 'We believed that socialism was the path that would take our country to prosperity, to a new more complete form of society.' What Ella Shistyer, a member of the Communist Party from 1918, liked was 'the promise of a happy, classless society in the future, in which everyone would enjoy all the good created by the society.'

In the meantime, Russian soldiers demanded an end to the fighting that continued to claim lives in the war. Lenin gave them the peace he had promised by concluding the Treaty of Brest-Litovsk with Germany, though it was peace at a price as the terms further damaged the Russian economy. But the time for peace at home had not yet come.

Opposition to the revolution led to three more years of fighting, this time in a bitter civil war. In addition to their usual hardships, people who had already endured a foreign war were now exposed to the terror unleashed both by the Bolsheviks (the Reds) and by their opponents, the Whites, who were fighting to put an end to the revolution and to restore the monarchy with help from abroad. There was growing international involvement in Russia's revolutionary struggle. Troops of a dozen nations fought and pillaged their way across Russia, adding to the suffering. By December 1920 a further million people had lost their lives.

Taking revolution to the countryside

In this unpromising, even desperate time Lenin pushed ahead with his revolution. In March 1918 he moved the capital to Moscow as Germany threatened Petrograd. The Bolsheviks put themselves at the head of soldiers and urban workers. In Moscow and then in other cities and towns they took over shops, factories and other property, and set up revolutionary institutions, including the Red Army and, from the start, a secret police – the Cheka.

The most crucial test of the revolution was to come in the countryside. Lenin believed that the rural population were natural

ГОД
ПРОЛЄТАРСКОЙ
ДИКТАТУРЫ.
ОКТЯБРЬ 1917 — ОКТЯБРЬ 1918

'reactionaries' who would have to be taught to become good communists – whether they liked it or not. Everything depended on 'the dark people', as the peasants were called. Still making up four-fifths of the population, the peasants suffered for the most part in silence. Often with little or no education, and living in an enormous country with poor communications, they could know almost nothing about the world beyond their village or district. The revolution had to be brought to them.

The Russian peasantry had traditionally 'repartitioned' their land at intervals, reapportioning it so that no one would hold the best land permanently. However, much of the best land still belonged to the rich landowners. For the peasants, the revolution simply offered hope of a new and bigger repartition, in which the landlords' property would also be redistributed. In fact even before the 1917 revolution this 'grand repartition' was under way. Groups of peasants had been taking matters into their own hands, and seizing the estates of great landowners.

For the Bolsheviks land policy was a matter of tactics: Lenin knew that it was essential to win the peasants to his cause if the revolution was to endure. At the same time he was convinced that class struggle must be brought to the villages, and that class antagonisms were needed to help spread the revolution. To this end, Lenin invented new distinctions among the peasants, setting the poorer ones against their wealthier neighbours, who were labelled 'kulaks'. The word *kulak* means 'fist', and was used in a derogatory sense to imply greedy money-grabbing. Although it was not a term that the peasants used among themselves, the Bolsheviks adopted it as though it denoted an established class of society.

Force was also used against the peasants. From 1918 the Bolsheviks sent armed gangs to confiscate the harvest; the peasants fought back fiercely. Propaganda was used: special trains were sent to remote areas to demonstrate the achievements of the new state. At the same time, the rural population continued to be harassed, while inflation eliminated their savings. Decrees were ruthlessly enforced, and resistance mercilessly punished. Even in the early years after the revolution, the Russian people were being forced as well as led into Lenin's new world.

PEASANT PROSPERITY
Not all the peasants lived on the brink of starvation; some fared much better. But the wealthier peasants were also to suffer, as scapegoats in the communists' campaign to bring class struggle to the Russian countryside.

ENEMIES OF THE PEOPLE
(BELOW) *A revolutionary cartoon issued during the civil war reminded the Russian people who their traditional oppressors were: the aristocracy, supported by the capitalists, the Church and the rich peasants (the kulaks) – all typically depicted as fat, smug and greedy.*

SPREADING THE NEWS (ABOVE) *Crowds flocked to hear the new messages of hope, possibility and achievement brought by the trains from the bureau of agitation and propaganda – Agitprop. Through plays, films and leaflets the ideas of communism were spread to the people in a very effective propaganda campaign. In a country where so many people could not read or write and had little access to the world beyond their own village, the impact of the Agitprop activities was enormous.*

The New Economic Policy

By 1921, when the civil war came to an end, the Communist Party (as the Bolsheviks were now known) emerged victorious, but the economy was in ruins. As a result of the war, and during the subsequent famine, millions of people had perished, and in many parts of the country the peasants were literally in arms against food requisitioning. Then a dangerous mutiny erupted in the Kronstadt naval base, once a citadel of revolutionary fervour. It was violently crushed. As a result of the unrest, however, Lenin made a tactical shift by introducing the New Economic Policy. He abandoned 'war communism', with its almost military conditions of work, replaced food requisitioning with a money tax, and allowed a degree of private enterprise, especially in retail trade. In the middle 1920s the people of the new Soviet Union were at last given a breathing space.

This was a time of hope and excitement. The ideals of the revolution were brought to the people: factory workers would take control and make decisions, and profit would be abandoned. The new benefits would come from hospitals, housing, schools. 'For a large number of people, perhaps the majority, it wasn't the

ideology that was so important as the promise of a better life,' explains Lev Razgon, who was a young communist at the time. 'For most people this gave colour to their daily, ordinary, difficult, often unbearable existence.' Hopes rose as real change suddenly seemed possible. Literacy was one of communism's main aims: learning to read offered new possibilities to the millions of people trapped at the bottom of society. Before the revolution many people could not read or write, and among the peasants few had even seen a book. A campaign was launched to make lessons available to all, in every village.

Anastasia Denisova was seventeen years old in 1924, and worked in a local literacy programme. At first the men said, 'No, you can't teach us anything, you are too young'. But they soon changed their minds. One pupil was a woman who could not go to the class because she had to look after her baby, so she was taught at home. 'She held her baby in one arm and wrote while she rocked him. She studied so keenly. I'll remember that for ever — that striving for knowledge, for enlightenment. It was immense.'

This was a particularly exhilarating time for women, as new laws were passed to give them equality with men. They had the same opportunities in education and in work. Ella Shistyer taught Muslim women in Uzbekistan, one of the southern republics that had been incorporated into the new Soviet Union. 'At the same time as teaching them to sew we told them about equality,' she explains. 'They were real slaves....The revolution brought these Uzbek women into the world. It gave them the opportunity to get education and culture.' It brought Ella Shistyer herself new opportunities: 'The revolution gave me the right to feel equal with any man. It gave me the right to work, to study as I wanted.' She decided to become an electrical engineer. 'I didn't want just to draw up plans, I wanted to build an electric power station. That was my mission, and I achieved it.'

People who remembered life in the old Russia — unjust, poverty-stricken and illiterate — felt things were really improving. Lev Razgon remembers, 'There wasn't political freedom, but there existed cultural freedom. In the middle 1920s there were years of extraordinary blossoming, a renaissance of culture, triggered by the revolution.' There was a wave of artistic and musical experiment as young artists and designers put their creativity to work for the Party. The painter Boris Smirnov-Russetsky was one of them. 'We were carried away by a feeling of freedom — freedom to create, freedom of opportunities to work in whatever direction, whatever form we wanted,' he explains. 'That's how I understood communism — as the development of a new consciousness in people, a consciousness that would allow people to see all that was going on around them more broadly and more deeply.'

Izo Degtyar, a violinist, experienced the revolution as an orchestra with no conductor. In the 1920s he played in a Moscow orchestra in which the musicians were all regarded as equals, and made decisions collaboratively. 'If you didn't like something, you all had a vote. For instance, if you couldn't hear the clarinets, you told them the truth: "You're behind", or "You're not coming in on time. Who's in favour? Who's against?" This wouldn't happen in an orchestra with a conductor. It was a real innovation.'

Tatiana Gomolitskaya worked with the Moscow Theatre of the Proletariat. It was led by Sergei Eisenstein, who later became a great film director. 'All the actors were workers and peasants,' she says. 'We had very little to eat, but we didn't think about it. We were working for the future. The aim of the theatre was to bring culture to the people, and of course propaganda.'

New art for the people

'BEAT THE WHITES WITH THE RED WEDGE' *urges this civil war poster by El Lissitzky. The art movement known as Constructivism used new materials — plastic, glass and steel — to reflect the challenge of the times. It encouraged Soviet citizens to gain a new way of thinking for a new way of life.*

MASSACRE ON FILM *A woman flees with her injured child in a scene from Sergei Eisenstein's famous film,* The Battleship Potemkin. *The cinema was important to revolutionary Russia. Newsreels and feature films brought new ideas to the people, reflecting the hopes and opportunities communism offered, and celebrating its achievements. Films were an effective tool for propaganda, and film-making an exciting way to contribute to revolutionary fervour.*

"I loved Stalin from my whole heart. I would work enormously long hours and I gave all my strength, all my soul into this."

ELLA SHISTYER

THE NEW SOVIET WOMAN *was encouraged to work on equal terms with the new Soviet man. Ella Shistyer, seen here with the team she led, contributed by qualifying as an electrical engineer. She also helped other women, both by her example and through her work as a teacher.*

Mobilizing the people

During the 1920s the ideas of communism polarized politics and society around the world. In Europe and also in the United States, where democracy was struggling against alternative ideologies in the post-war years, many people were excited by the 'Soviet experiment'. Boris Smirnov-Russetsky firmly believed that 'Russia would show the path for other countries'. But people also felt threatened by the uncertainty and cruelty of revolution. Many ordinary citizens in democratic countries were afraid that their world might be invaded by godless thugs who believed in free love and common property.

Such fears in the West were matched by the attitudes of the rulers of the Soviet Union. With the Cheka, Lenin had recreated the secret police of the tsar, and despite all his promises of equality he ruled the Russian people with full party authority. When he died in 1924 he left the tools of control in a one-party and one-ideology state. Armed with this legacy his successor, Joseph Stalin, assumed supreme power and immediately set out to protect his dictatorship and that of the proletariat from potential enemies at home and abroad.

After Lenin's death many of the revolution's aims remained unfulfilled. Stalin was convinced that to make communism work in practice, and to defend the Soviet Union in a hostile world, a powerful modern economy needed to be created as quickly as possible, so he launched the first Five-Year Plan (1928–33). The Soviet Union was fifty, perhaps even a hundred years behind the industrialized countries and had to catch up. 'We must make good this distance,' he declared, 'or we shall be crushed.' So he took a traditional peasant society, just beginning to modernize before the setbacks of war and revolution, and hurled it into a programme of breakneck industrialization. The production of pig iron, coal, steel, electricity and machinery rose remorselessly.

To storm these heights, Stalin called for a 'new Soviet man', and the people responded enthusiastically to the call. For Tatiana Fedorova, who worked in construction, it was like something out of a fairy tale. 'Stalin's greatest achievement was that he united the people,' she explains. 'Wherever the Party called you, everywhere there was a response from the heart. Stalin set a task: build this or

BUILDING THE FUTURE

I T WAS CALLED the Magnetic Mountain because of its vast deposits of iron ore. In 1929 it drew thousands of people to a desolate corner of the Urals. They were inspired by Stalin's decision to build a huge steel works. Industrialization was to liberate the people. One volunteer, Valentina Mikova, remembers why she went: 'My heart summoned me to the great construction site of socialism.'

The plans were modelled on those of the United States steel plant in Gary, Indiana. But Magnitogorsk was built by hand, as Valentina Mikova explains. 'One takes the earth, and throws it to the level above. The second person throws it to a third, the third to a fourth, up five or six levels. That was how we got the earth out of the trench. Then it was taken away in wheelbarrows.' Working in sub-zero temperatures, many people died.

After 1930 the volunteers were joined by at least 20 000 kulaks sentenced to forced labour. They lived separately, under police surveillance. But one of them, Mikhail Arkhipov, still remembers that in spite of the hardship and the shame, 'we caught the enthusiasm, we too were fanatics'. After three years it was finished, the biggest steelworks in the world, a monument to Stalinism – and to the ideals, beliefs and suffering of the people who built it.

MOVING THE MOUNTAIN *It took only three years to complete the Magnitogorsk steel works, though they were largely built by hand. Thousands of men and women lived at the site, inspired by their belief in Stalin and his drive to turn the Soviet Union from a backward agricultural country into one of the greatest industrial powers in the world.*

build that, and thanks to the fact that young people believed him, trusted him, this enthusiasm made it possible. Remember this was a country where people were illiterate, lived in virtual darkness, wore birch-bark shoes.'

The heroic productive feats of these workers, who came to be called Stakhanovites after a particularly successful coalminer, were publicized until they became the equivalent of film or sports stars. Tatiana Fedorova led a team of Stakhanovites who helped to

ALEXEI STAKHANOV *(in the foreground) with a group of his fellow coalminers. They were hailed as heroes for their hard work in the cause of Soviet industry. They helped to transform their country into a leading industrial power in little more than a generation.*

build the magnificent Moscow Metro. 'No one forced you to do it,' she says, 'everyone wanted to be a Stakhanovite. It is very hard to explain, but it was a time of enthusiasts. Everyone was trying to do the best for the motherland. It was such a good time. There wasn't much to eat, we weren't well dressed, we were simply very happy.' They felt they were making an important contribution.

The achievements of Soviet society in the 1920s continued into the 1930s. Workers who kept out of trouble were rewarded with paid vacations, free medical care, and for the lucky ones there was improved housing. Even sceptical Western visitors were impressed, as they compared the energy, idealism and achievements of the Soviet Union to the stagnation and hardship that economic depression was then inflicting on people in the West. Charlie Nusser was one young American profoundly influenced by the contrast. 'In the Soviet Union they were advertising for workers – that really struck me because I was out of high school and had no job and millions of others had no job.' Inspired by this example, he decided to turn to communism. 'Stalin was leading the country in a very difficult period to build socialism....I felt he was leading in the proper direction.' After a visit to the Soviet Union one American journalist, Lincoln Steffens, wrote in a letter to a friend, 'I have seen the future; and it works'.

Collectivization and famine

The land of hope that these Western visitors saw was in reality quite different for the people of the Ukraine and southern Russia, who now experienced the worst famine ever recorded outside China. In 1932 Stalin set out to complete the process Lenin had begun in the countryside, where peasants were still farming their own land and had largely remained outside the communist system. He moved to bring them into it by collectivizing agriculture.

Stalin blamed the kulaks, the better-off peasants, for the grain shortages and for opposing his plans, and adopted a ruthless policy towards them. Izrail Chernitsky, who was a member of the Komsomol, the communist youth movement, was among those who carried out Stalin's orders in the Ukraine. 'If Stalin decided to start dekulakization to start creating collective farms then it was what we needed. I thought it should be done, so I didn't think

COMMUNISTS OF THE FUTURE *From the beginning, the communists sought to mould the minds of Soviet children. All ages were catered for: the youngest groups of children were known as Little Octobrists; nine- to fourteen-year-olds were called Young Pioneers, and through political education and recreation were prepared for joining the Komsomol, the All-Union Leninist Communist League of Youth. Membership of these organizations was essential to get on in life professionally and politically, and an important step in being admitted to membership of the Communist Party.*

about my feelings towards these people.' One of his tasks was to prevent anyone leaving his local village meetings who might then warn kulaks that they were in danger of being eliminated. Thousands of people died in exile in Siberia or were shot.

The peasants' agricultural equipment was requisitioned by the state, and the land was taken over to be farmed collectively, in large units. The poorer peasants were also targeted, and many resisted by killing their livestock in protest. Piotr Shelest, also in the Komsomol, took the machinery, horses and cattle from the peasants. He remembers their responses well. 'Some cursed their fate, others gave statements, there were those who even helped us. We asked them, "Do you want to go into the collective farm?" Several agreed and transferred their possessions to the collective farm – cows, horses. Some of them went very angrily. There were episodes when the father murdered his son because he had told the brigade that there was more. It was a very hard struggle....The elimination of the kulaks was to do with changing the social status among the peasantry. They did everything to put the brakes on giving up their meat or their products. That's why they were liquidated.' Like Izrail Chernitsky, his faith in Stalin and in the system prevailed. 'I was convinced that this was necessary and my feelings were on the side of action.'

Izrail Chernitsky went to one kulak's house with his commission. 'They had just built a very big new house and they lived well, were quite rich. There were no men at the house. The head of the commission said to the women and children, "No hysterics! Nobody's to leave the house. Put your valuables, earrings, rings on the table." I'd never seen so many valuable things. They made a list of goods in their house and they were told not to touch these things any more because they were to be taken by the state. The next morning people would come and take these

PERSUADING PEASANTS *of the advantages of new farming methods was no easy task. Thousands of meetings and rallies were held to try to convince them that working on large-scale collective farms would benefit them. Any resistance to the changes was brutally suppressed.*

> **"T**he corpses were piled up like bales of straw. The men took the cart to a big hole and tipped the bodies in – regardless of whether they were dead or alive. **"**
>
> PELAGAYA
> OVCHARENKO

things and in one or two days all these people were taken to a railway station to be transported to Siberia…or perhaps to be killed.' But, Izrail Chernitsky remembers, 'Everyone lived with the hope of a radiant future. And apart from that, we really trusted the Party. If Stalin said "Do it", then it was necessary.'

In a year of poor harvest, some 12 per cent below average, the government increased its demands of food by 44 per cent. It took all the grain, including what was being kept as seed to sow for the following year. The result was famine. While exports of grain and other farm products actually rose, over five years some seven million people died. As a child Pelagaya Ovcharenko was a victim of the famine. She remembers the terrible hunger. 'I would climb a cherry tree and would eat cherries, green cherries. My body swelled up, and I survived eating only grass and leaves. That was all my food.' One day three men came to the house with a cart. One of them looked after the horses, while the others piled up bodies on the cart. 'They threw on my mother. Then they

POVERTY AND PLENTY
Reality for this ragged band of undernourished children (ABOVE) *was a very different experience from propaganda that reported well-stocked granaries* (RIGHT) *and a wide choice of food and other goods in the shops during the years of famine. Many children died of starvation and disease; many of those who survived were orphaned when their parents succumbed.*

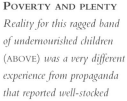

THE CULT OF STALIN

ON STALIN'S FIFTIETH BIRTHDAY in 1929 *Pravda* broke all its own rules and published a full-page portrait of Stalin. For five years he had been general secretary of the Communist Party. Now he became the *vozhd*, the 'power', the 'boss'. To celebrate his seventieth birthday, Stalin's portrait was suspended from an invisible balloon and transfixed by spotlights, shimmering in the sky over tens of thousands of worshippers in Moscow's Red Square. In the intervening twenty years Stalin had ruthlessly eliminated all rivals, real or imagined, and deported millions of prisoners to the labour camps under the Gulag system. He had also become the icon of a quasi-religious cult.

Born Joseph Vissarionovich Djugashvili, the son of a shoemaker in the Georgian mountains and intended for the priesthood, Stalin attained an almost divine stature for many ordinary Russians. He was accorded the ancient religious epithet of 'Father of the People'. Painters in the different Soviet republics gave him the features of their own people – Georgian, Kurdish or Uzbek. Kazakh mothers crooned:

> *Go to sleep, my Kazakh babe,*
> *Knowing hands will care for you.*
> *Stalin peers from out his window,*
> *Keeping our vast land in view.*

Stalin established his revolutionary legitimacy by persuading people that he had been Lenin's chief collaborator, even creating a false 'historical memory' by doctoring photographs. Every school, office, factory and collective farm in the land had his picture on its wall, and he used hoardings, newspapers and radio to propagate his image.

No flattery was too great. He was called 'the greatest man of all time'. Cities were given his name: Stalingrad,

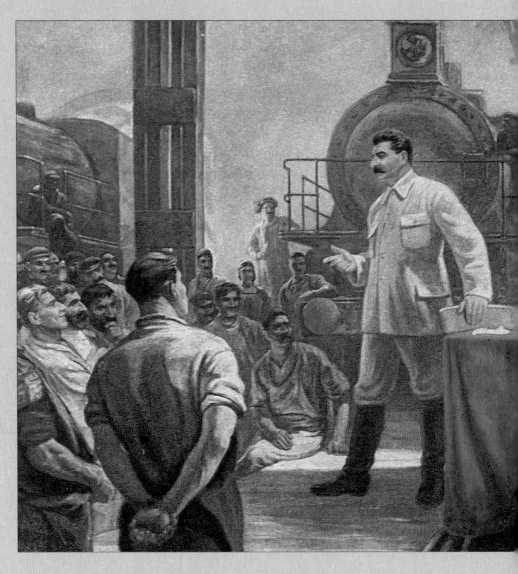

Stalino, Stalinabad, Stalinsk. Climbers carried his bust to the top of peaks named after him. The veneration that many people genuinely felt for Stalin reached back into both religious and monarchical tradition. Many prisoners refused to believe that he had any hand in the purges, and millions of people clung to the illusion that if only he knew what was happening, Stalin would himself put an end to the terror.

It was said that Stalin received such long ovations because nobody dared to be the first person to stop clapping. 'What could we do?' asked Nikita

Khrushchev, who was later to emerge as his successor. 'You only had to look at him and the next day you lost your head.' Not until several years after Stalin's death was the cult of his overpowering personality challenged.

The most bizarre aspect of Stalin's rule is that when his propaganda spoke of modernizing an entire economy and transforming a backward country into a great modern industrial and military power, and when his critics spoke of him as an insane tyrant who was guilty of crimes on a scale never matched before, both were telling the truth.

threw on my father. My father gestured to me, but the man said, "He's almost ready, he's almost dead." When my father gestured to me I knew that I had to go and hide. I crawled away on my hands and knees. And that's why I survived.'

One source of strength and comfort to the peasants was the Russian Orthodox Church, but it represented the old regime and was now also relentlessly attacked. The communists declared that there was no God. All over the country, priests were ridiculed and harassed, and forced publicly to renounce their faith. Izrail Chernitsky saw how one village priest was treated. 'The priest came to the meeting. He took off his cassock, and put it on the table. The barber came and cut off his hair. And the priest proclaimed, "There is no God, I have lied to you." Men began to shout, "How could you lie to us? We built a house for you, and now you are saying there's no God!"'

The years of terror

Not even the horrors of the famine and the murder of the kulaks in the early 1930s, however, matched those of the Great Terror later in the decade. Now it was not just the peasants who suffered. It began in the Smolny Institute, where Lenin had inspired the victorious workers' and soldiers' deputies with talk about 'peace, land and bread' in 1917. There, on 1 December 1934, an assassin sent by Stalin murdered Sergei Kirov, head of the Communist Party in Leningrad. This set off a chain reaction of purges — of the party, of the army, and of innocent people caught up in the machinery of terror. Stalin was obsessed with destroying all potential opponents and resorted to brutal methods. The terror was to continue until Stalin had eliminated every scrap of opposition that spying could detect or paranoia imagine.

To root out those he called 'enemies of socialism' among people throughout the country, Stalin controlled and conducted the terror himself. When the purges were over, by the best estimate at the very least twelve million citizens had been arrested

CHEERFUL RAILWAY WORKERS *listen with the eager attention of disciples to the 'Father of the People' in this stylized painting. The engines symbolize the strength of the modern Soviet Union.*

DESTROYING THE CHURCH *All over the Soviet Union churches and monasteries were pulled down, damaged or given over to other uses. The Russian Orthodox Church represented a challenge to the new orthodoxy of communism, and was not to be tolerated. It made no difference that religion could give meaning to the lives of many Russians.*

FORCED LABOUR
(RIGHT) *made up a large
part of the Soviet workforce
by the late 1930s. Many
prisoners died, 'under the
complete and utter control of
people deprived of any
human feelings whatsoever,'
as one of the survivors still
bitterly remembers.*

LISTING THE VICTIMS
*Stalin's purges were carried
out from lists of arbitrary
quotas for every town and
region, guaranteeing fear
throughout the country.
Stalin himself scribbled
additions to the quotas; this
one reads: 'Give a
supplementary quota of
6000 people in the first
category to Krasnodar'.
Category 1 meant death;
category 2 meant the camps.*

and sent either to prison or to the harsh labour camps of the far
north and far east of the Soviet Union. At least a million of them
were executed; a further two million died of illness, exhaustion or
maltreatment. Even those who had been early enthusiasts for communism could become victims. Karl Rianne, who had stormed
the Winter Palace twenty years before, was among those arrested
and imprisoned. The electrical engineer Ella Shistyer, who had
worked so hard for Stalin, was sent to prison in Siberia. During
the long winter journey there, with nothing but salt fish to eat, she
developed a huge thirst. 'I remember when there was a hard frost
how I used to lick the ice off the metal screws and bolts inside the
wooden cattle truck, fearing only that my tongue would stick to
them. That's how we travelled for nearly a month.'

By the end of 1938 there were about nine million people in
captivity, a million of them in prison and the rest in the camps,
where at least a tenth, perhaps as many as a fifth of the prisoners
died every year. These arrests and executions had come about as a
result of a system of spying, informing, torture and trials in which
false evidence was used. The whole of society was infected with
corruption, and tens of millions of people lived in agonies of fear.
'The most terrible thing was understanding that I was deprived of
any rights,' explains Lev Razgon. 'They could do whatever they
wanted, and if it were just me that would be one thing, but they
could do whatever they wanted with people who were close to
me as well.' After his colleagues and close relatives were arrested, he
lived in terror until his own arrest. 'When finally the doorbell rang
one night there was a feeling of relief. When I was taken into the
cell the elder of the cell said to me, "Sit down. Breathe in the freedom. You don't have to fear any more. Your arrest is over." He
expressed what we all felt.'

Stalin called himself an 'engineer of human souls'. Fear was
not his only tool; loyalty could also corrupt, and so could belief in
the party and its ideology. Valentin Astrov, a journalist on the
newspaper *Pravda*, gave evidence against Stalin's rival, Nikolai
Bukharin, in 1936. He reflects: 'Of course I sacrificed general
human values, as well as my conscience, to class and proletarian
values. Soviet power demanded this; I did it. If the party asked me
to say that I was an English spy, I would agree to it. If the party

**THE MAD DOG OF
FASCISM** (BELOW) *A
cartoon drawn by Boris
Yefimov to Stalin's order
shows a two-headed creature
whose heads are Trotsky
(despite his having been
disgraced and exiled) and
Bukharin who had dared to
criticize Stalin.*

wanted to take my life away, fine. If it wanted to take my honesty, well, that was fine too.'

Boris Yefimov, whose brother had been shot in the purges, was the official cartoonist at Bukharin's trial. Stalin himself dictated the subject for each cartoon. 'I felt like a fowl that would be glad if it woke up in the morning at home and not in a cage...especially because Stalin's unwritten law said that a wife must answer for a husband, a son for a father, a brother for a brother.' And yet Boris Yefimov's feelings about Stalin, like those of many others who experienced first the revolution and then the dictatorship, were ambivalent. 'We lived in a kind of nightmare. We saw his despotism, his autocracy. And at the same time you just had to lower your head, because Stalin must know best. It was like a terrible god who ruled us. We had to obey. We didn't judge. We didn't argue.'

THE MIDNIGHT KNOCK

THE RUSSIAN TSARS had all relied on secret police and their cruel methods to protect themselves. Lenin recreated this force, the Okhrana, with his own, the Cheka. Its role was to seek out all counter-revolutionaries. Its victims included political opponents, the nobility, the bourgeoisie and the clergy; its methods were murder, torture and the camps.

When Stalin succeeded to supreme power, he immediately set out to protect his dictatorship from his perceived enemies by equally ruthless methods. Under a succession of names – Cheka, GPU, OGPU, NKVD, MVD and KGB – the secret police exercised immense power in Soviet society. Every citizen came to dread the midnight knock.

During the years of collectivization the OGPU carried out the deportation and murder of the kulaks. Its chief, Genrikh Yagoda, staged the early purge trials, but was removed from power by Nikolai Yezhov, and condemned to death. As his successor, Yezhov lent his name to the Great Purge of 1936–38 – it was called the Yezhovshchina – only to disappear in his turn in 1939.

Lavrenti Beria, who took over in 1938, managed to survive for longer than his predecessors. He even survived Stalin, but was tried and executed in 1953. The following year the functions of the MVD were taken over by the KGB (Committee for State Security), which was responsible for border control and foreign intelligence as well as internal security.

SECRET SERVICE BADGE *A memento of the sinister power of the OGPU.*

TELLING THE TRUTH

People all over the Soviet Union read Pravda *('The Truth'), the official newspaper of the Communist Party. Its daily circulation reached some ten million copies, despite the fact that reading its six dense pages was said to be 'like eating dry noodles: no flavour'. Despite its title,* Pravda *was recognized as an organ of propaganda rather than information.*

A new superpower

In the very years when Stalin was terrorizing the people of the Soviet Union, communism's prestige and influence around the world was at its highest. In the 1930s it seemed that only the communists, allied with socialists and liberals, could be an effective force standing between democracy and the threat of fascism. The perception of the Soviet Union as the last protector of pluralism and human rights was reinforced by awe for the sheer strength of the Soviet state. It seemed as though the communist dream had come true. Almost everyone in the Soviet Union could now read; people had opportunities in their work that had never before been possible. By 1939 the Soviet Union had become the world's second industrial power after the United States, and was frantically manufacturing warships, tanks and aircraft in its bid to become the world's foremost military power. In that year, visitors to the New York World Fair were dazzled by a huge map of the Soviet Union, a mosaic made out of precious and semi-precious stones. Few realized that the stones had been mined under atrocious conditions by political prisoners and by the victims of Stalin's purges.

The wonderful promise Lenin had made in 1917 that 'the oppressed masses would themselves form the government' had not been fulfilled. Soviet citizens found themselves not liberated but subordinated, in a country where decisions were still imposed from above by a leadership that had shown its deep distrust of the very people in whose name it ruled. For Lev Razgon this was its fundamental defect. 'The right to choose is the main right, the main distinguishing feature of a human being…communism deprived people of this right.'

As the Soviet Union was brought into the Second World War in 1941 it was still the world's only communist state. After the war more than a hundred million people in eastern Europe would come under communist rule, the great majority of them against their heartfelt wishes, as the Soviet sphere of influence extended westwards. In China in 1949, and elsewhere in Asia, genuinely popular uprisings created new people's republics under the red flag of communism. But they too would eventually be transformed into ruthless party dictatorships on the Russian model, each under its own 'terrible god'.

Lost Peace

THE

INTER-WAR

YEARS

I T WAS THE ELEVENTH HOUR of the eleventh day of the eleventh month of 1918 when the guns on the Western Front fell silent. Dazed men climbed out of the trenches from which, for so many months, they had been trying to kill each other. Now, hardly able to believe what was happening, they staggered towards each other and shook hands. The fighting had ended.

Away from the battlefields, Armistice Day turned into a carnival for the winning side. In towns and cities people poured into the streets to celebrate. In France, which had suffered most in the war, the rejoicing was not just for victory but for survival. Georges Clemenceau had led the French to victory; his grandson Pierre remembers that day well. 'Paris was fantastic, everybody was in the streets, everybody was kissing everybody. My brother had the sense to tell a policeman that we were the grandsons of Clemenceau. So we got into his residence and went upstairs, and my grandfather looked at us – he was surrounded by all sorts of great people, of course – and he said,

"What are you doing here? You should be in school!" And then he took us in his arms and kissed us and said, "All right, it is a special day!"'

In Britain, when the ceasefire was declared, the church bells of London began to peal. Doors banged. Feet clattered down corridors. No more work was done that day as all London ran into the streets to celebrate peace. It was the same in New York. For the gleeful crowds on Broadway the war had been shorter, but no less glorious. The Americans knew that their intervention had been decisive in gaining victory for the Allies, and they celebrated enthusiastically their part in the war whose ending would surely make the world safe for democracy.

Whether celebrating victory or having to come to terms with defeat, everyone was relieved that the war was over. But the atmosphere of idealism and hope that surrounded the armistice was soon to change to one of disappointment and bitterness. The war itself had ended, but the world was not yet at peace.

JUBILANT CROWDS *of Parisians take to the streets to celebrate Armistice Day.*

The trauma of war

The end of the war left Europe in a state of deep shock. The Great War had been more destructive than any other, both in its scale and in its human toll, leaving in its wake an entire generation of people affected by its horrors. About nine million men had been killed and millions more mutilated in body or mind. The whole economic, political and social structure of the continent, which had taken centuries to develop, had been shaken to its foundations. The great empires of Austria-Hungary, Germany, Russia and Turkey had been destroyed, and the focus of economic power in the world had been moved from Britain and France to the United States. The countries on whose soil the war had been fought – France and Belgium in the west, Italy, Serbia, Poland and the Baltic states in the east – had been flayed by high explosives and machine-gun fire. Their peoples had been assailed by hunger and by the diseases that follow armies and the refugees they drive before them.

Soldiers of all the nations that had experienced the terrible reality of war were determined that it should never happen again. Captain Donald Hodge, who had witnessed the deaths of many of his fellow soldiers, was one of them. 'Their mothers didn't have those sons to be blown to pieces. It was a blasphemous waste, throw-

SHOULDER TO SHOULDER, *members of the Allied armed forces celebrate victory. The end of the war meant that those who had survived could at last return to their homes and families.*

ing back in the Creator's face all the goodness that He has given us.' Donald Hodge's fervent hope that 'all the awful horror and waste we'd endured would never be repeated ...that it was a war to end wars', was shared by millions of people across the world.

Karl Nagerl, who grew up in Germany during the war years, was relieved that they were over and wanted life to return to normal. 'I was happy that my father was home...we expected a manageable peace. A peace that would give the German people a chance to work again, and to lead the kind of life that any normal citizen can expect....We expected

Austria's agony 1919-20

THE DESPAIRING CIVILIANS (LEFT) *in this poster highlight Austria's plight after the war. As Germany's ally, Austria was also forced to pay reparations, despite its crippled economy and its people's suffering.*

a just peace.' But many people in the victorious countries wanted recompense for their great loss and suffering. They felt that the Germans had caused most of the damage and now looked to Germany to pay for it. Walter Hare, who had fought with the British army in the First World War, felt no pity for the Germans. 'I felt that they'd brought it upon themselves, so they had a right to suffer.' Others, like Maurice Bourgeois, who had served in the French army throughout the war, felt more pride in victory than horror at its price. 'What was important for us,' he recalls, 'was that we had beaten the Germans. They had wanted to wage war against us, and so they had to be punished.'

DISPIRITED GERMAN TROOPS (ABOVE) *make their way home after the armistice has been signed. For Germany, relief that the war was over was tinged with the bitterness of defeat.*

CLEARING A PATH

through the crowds (BELOW)
for Woodrow Wilson (centre,
in top hat) as he leaves the
palace of Versailles after
signing the peace treaty. The
Fourteen Points contained in
his 'Program for Peace' made
an appeal on behalf of the
'silent masses of mankind'.

THE SIGNING OF PEACE

(OPPOSITE) *took place in the*
ornate grandeur of the Hall
of Mirrors at Versailles after
six months of negotiations.
In this painting by Sir
William Orpen, the Allied
leaders look on while the two
German delegates (in the
foreground) sign the treaty.

Program for the Peace of the World

By PRESIDENT WILSON, January 8, 1918

I. Open covenants of peace, openly arrived at, after which there shall be no private international understandings of any kind, but diplomacy shall proceed always frankly and in the public view.

II. Absolute freedom of navigation upon the seas, outside territorial waters, alike in peace and in war, except as the seas may be closed in whole or in part by international action for the enforcement of international covenants.

III. The removal, so far as possible, of all economic barriers and the establishment of an equality of trade conditions among all the nations consenting to the peace and associating themselves for its maintenance.

IV. Adequate guarantees given and taken that national armaments will reduce to the lowest point consistent with domestic safety.

V. Free, open-minded, and absolutely impartial adjustment of all colonial claims, based upon a strict observance of the principle that in determining all such questions of sovereignty the interests of the population concerned must have equal weight with the equitable claims of the government whose title is to be determined.

VI. The evacuation of all Russian territory and such a settlement of all questions affecting Russia as will secure the best and freest cooperation of the other nations of the world in obtaining for her an unhampered and unembarrassed opportunity for the independent determination of her own political development and national policy, and assure her of a sincere welcome into the society of free nations under institutions of her own choosing; and, more than a welcome, assistance also of every kind that she may need and may herself desire. The treatment accorded Russia by her sister nations in the months to come will be the acid test of their good will, of their comprehension of her needs as distinguished from their own interests, and of their intelligent and unselfish sympathy.

VII. Belgium, the whole world will agree, must be evacuated and restored, without any attempt to limit the sovereignty which she enjoys in common with all other free nations. No other single act will serve as this will serve to restore confidence among the nations in the law which they have themselves set and determined for the government of their relations with one

another. Without this healing act the whole structure and validity of international law is forever impaired.

VIII. All French territory should be freed and the invaded portions restored, and the wrong done to France by Prussia in 1871 in the matter of Alsace-Lorraine, which has unsettled the peace of the world for nearly fifty years, should be righted, in order that peace may once more be made secure in the interest of all.

IX. A readjustment of the frontiers of Italy should be effected along clearly recognizable lines of nationality.

X. The people of Austria-Hungary, whose place among the nations we wish to see safeguarded and assured, should be accorded the freest opportunity of autonomous development.

XI. Rumania, Serbia and Montenegro should be evacuated; occupied territories restored; Serbia accorded free and secure access to the sea; and the relations of the several Balkan States to one another determined by friendly counsel along historically established lines of allegiance and nationality; and international guarantees of the political and economic independence and territorial integrity of the several Balkan States should be entered into.

XII. The Turkish portions of the present Ottoman Empire should be assured a secure sovereignty, but the other nationalities which are now under Turkish rule should be assured an undoubted security of life and an absolutely unmolested opportunity of autonomous development, and the Dardanelles should be permanently opened as a free passage to the ships and commerce of all nations under international guarantees.

XIII. An independent Polish State should be erected which should include the territories inhabited by indisputably Polish populations, which should be assured a free and secure access to the sea, and whose political and economic independence and territorial integrity should be guaranteed by international covenant.

XIV. A general association of nations must be formed under specific covenants for the purpose of affording mutual guarantees of political independence and territorial integrity to great and small States alike.

Wilson's grand design

The man to whom all looked to build the foundations of a lasting peace was the president of the United States, Thomas Woodrow Wilson. Born in Virginia, he had been a professor of history at Princeton University and was a Democrat who had been elected to the presidency in 1912.

While the world was still at war, in January 1918 Wilson drew up a fourteen-point programme outlining his ideas for a peace settlement. Some were general aspirations, like the proposal for a world organization of nations to prevent future wars and the call for open diplomacy. Others took specific political positions, such as the return of Alsace-Lorraine to France. These Fourteen Points seemed to many to encourage the peoples of the Austro-Hungarian empire to form their own independent nations, and to others to promise the end of old grievances. Wilson's group of young advisers on postwar settlement plans was much influenced by nationalist leaders, such as the Polish virtuoso pianist, Ignace Paderewski, and the Czech, Dr Thomas Masaryk.

By October 1918, with the Eastern Front collapsing, the Germans knew that they must lose the war. Their new chancellor, Prince Max of Baden, asked the United States for an armistice, indicating Germany's willingness to conclude peace on the basis of Wilson's Fourteen Points. This skilful move bypassed Britain and France, who would have demanded harsher peace terms. Negotiations took place for several weeks; the end was hastened when on 3 November Austria signed an armistice with the Allies. Germany now also had to capitulate, signing just eight days later.

Woodrow Wilson, ambitious to bring peace to the world, insisted on crossing the Atlantic to France to lead the peace conference in person. When he landed in Europe on 13 December, power was in his hands. Edward Bernays, one of his advisers, watched from the crowd in the Champs Elysées near the Arc de Triomphe while the audience gave Wilson an ecstatic welcome to Paris, cheering him as a saviour. To Edward Bernays the people's faith was not surprising. 'After all,' he points out, 'if it hadn't been for the United States it's doubtful whether the Allies would have resisted the Germans, and it was Woodrow

PAYING THE PRICE OF DEFEAT

Under the terms of the armistice, Germany agreed to pay reparations – compensation for the damage caused by its occupying armies. These included 5000 locomotives, 150 000 railway wagons, 5000 lorries and other goods to help restore ruined land, towns and cities. The principle of reparations had been set by Germany itself in 1871 after the Franco-Prussian war.

The great bitterness among the people of France and Britain for the suffering the war had brought was indirectly acknowledged by a clause in the peace treaty drawn up at Versailles expressly stating – for the first time – that the defeated states alone were responsible for causing all the loss and damage of the war. The resulting demand that Germany should be made to pay for the entire cost of the war led to far heavier penalties being imposed than those already agreed in the armistice. German objections that the terms of the treaty inflicted an unbearably heavy burden were overruled.

Details of the payments were drawn up by a reparations committee in 1921. Germany pleaded that it simply could not comply with the demand that over the next thirty years it should pay the equivalent of 132 billion gold marks in money and goods, and 26 per cent of the proceeds of German exports. The humiliation added to the Germans' despondency in defeat. As Karl Nagerl explains: 'The reparations meant that Germany was destined to be completely ruined. We expected to have to pay something, we had lost the war, but we certainly did not expect that the German population would be enslaved.'

German insistence that it could not meet the schedule of payments was proved right, and during the 1920s a series of conferences was held that gradually reduced them. There were also many practical problems. It would have been possible for Germans to help rebuild the homes and other buildings destroyed in Belgium and France during the war, but local people would not receive them. German industry could produce more goods than there was transport available to deliver them. France had twice within fifty years been invaded by the Germans; the French wanted to ensure that Germany's capacity to wage war was permanently reduced, and its trading power weakened. Yet if reparations obligations were to be met, German industry had to be rebuilt.

Before the war, Germany and Britain had been each other's best customers; British prosperity after the war was held back by Germany's inability to buy British goods. The widespread sense of betrayal and anger in Germany at the burden of reparations, and at the hardships they inflicted on the nation, were to contribute directly to the economic depression that affected the whole world during the 1930s, to the rise of Hitler, and eventually to the Second World War.

Wilson who made the world safe for democracy.' Winners and losers alike looked to him to impose a just and lasting peace.

From January 1919 the peace conference met in the great Hall of Mirrors in the palace of Versailles. President Wilson tried to take the moral high ground, but he was tenaciously opposed by the leaders of the two powers that had borne the heaviest burdens during the years of war: David Lloyd George of Britain and Georges Clemenceau of France. Clemenceau demanded a peace that would for ever deny Germany the power to invade France again, and was unimpressed by Wilson's idealism. 'God gave us ten commandments,' he observed, 'and we broke them. Wilson has given us his Fourteen Points – and we shall see!'

Wilson failed to gain support for his peace terms. The European leaders insisted that Germany accept full blame for the war. On 28 June the German delegation was summoned to Versailles, and with great reluctance signed the treaty, with its 440 clauses. They had no alternative but to make peace. Nevertheless, they resented the harsh terms of the treaty, which condemned Germany to pay huge sums in compensation to its enemies. As a result of the settlements, Germany lost Alsace and Lorraine to France, more land to Poland, Belgium, Lithuania and Denmark, the port of Danzig and the rich industrial area of the Saar.

For the losers the peace treaty seemed to have been designed to satisfy the vindictiveness of the victors. Paul Quirin was living in Bonn in the 1920s. He remembers how people felt that the reparations were 'like a mortgage which was eventually going to ruin the economy. The amount we had to pay bore no relation to economic prospects. We weren't going to be able to cope with this for long.' In Germany bells tolled in mourning when the treaty was signed, and newspapers appeared with black borders. The German leaders felt bitterly that they had been tricked. They had agreed to an armistice on the basis of the idealism of the Fourteen Points, but the treaty that followed was not in accordance with Wilson's ideals. These had included national self-determination of peoples, yet the treaty expressly forbade the German-speakers of Austria to join the German Reich.

The German leaders had recognized that their only option was to sue for peace, but most of the German people could not

A BEDRAGGLED AND PENNILESS GERMANY (LEFT) *stands alone in this cartoon as other countries reveal their empty pockets. The refusal by nations of the world to recognize the hardship that the reparations caused Germany added to the widespread bitterness among its people.*

FRENCH SOLDIERS *march into Strasbourg* (BELOW), *provincial capital of Alsace, in November 1918. The two French provinces of Alsace and Lorraine had become part of Germany in 1871 after the Franco-Prussian war. Now their citizens, many of them German-speakers, were once again to find themselves part of France under the terms of the Versailles treaty.*

believe that the war was fairly and squarely lost. Their armies had still been fighting on foreign territory; they had not been defeated in battle. The *Dolchstosslegende* thus took root – the legend that Germany had not been defeated by its enemies, but had been stabbed in the back by traitors. The hunt for scapegoats began.

An integral part of the Versailles treaty, and of subsequent treaties between the Allies and the other defeated powers, was the establishment of a new kind of international organization, the League of Nations. Its express purpose was to prevent future wars. This was intended to be Woodrow Wilson's master stroke: the league would bring the blessings of New World democracy to the feuding nations of old Europe, and replace their traditionally secret diplomacy with a new and open system of collective security. But Wilson, who had been the principal architect of the peace, now found that he was unable to rally public support for the treaty and the league in his own country.

Many Americans believed that the only way to maintain peace on American soil was to isolate themselves from the conflicts between other nations. Edward Bernays explains how many people felt: 'Most of the American public at that time had either been immigrants or the sons or daughters of immigrants…they had wanted to leave Europe and discover a new home. Any attempt of a president to make America international was not well regarded…there was no great feeling for any internationalism as a basis for peace and prosperity.'

Without United States support, the league was established in January 1920. Membership was limited to the Allied states and their supporters; Germany, like other former enemy nations and neutral states, was not yet included. The league at first had some successful interventions to its credit. It supervised the division of Upper Silesia between Germany and Poland, settled a dispute between Finland and Sweden over the Aaland islands, and for a while held in check the mutual hatred of Germans and Poles in Danzig. Only time would show how illusory was its real power.

DANCING FOR JOY *in the streets was one way for people in the victorious nations to celebrate the signing of the peace treaty. Life was returning to normal as men took up civilian life again, and women left their war work in the factories.*

NEVER AGAIN! *declares this anti-war cartoon* (RIGHT) *depicting soldiers marching into the jaws of death. It appeared in a Tacoma daily newspaper on the same day that President Wilson visited the city on his tour of American states to win support for the League of Nations.*

AMERICANS TURN THEIR BACKS ON EUROPE

ITHIN THREE MONTHS of the Versailles treaty being signed, it was in trouble in the United States. Opposition to it was woven from many strands of opinion. Among them were those of German-Americans who resented the harsh peace imposed on Germany, and Irish-Americans who were hostile to Britain. Many people felt that the United States had been manipulated by France and Britain into fighting the war, and wanted to prevent the possibility of this happening again.

Opposition among the American people was reflected in the attitudes of their political leaders. The Senate was now controlled by the Republicans and was split into three factions: those with minor reservations, those – led by Senator Henry Cabot Lodge – who had strong reservations, and those who would not have the treaty at any price. Lodge believed that the treaty robbed the United States of its sovereignty. He was willing, he said, to ratify the treaty without the League of Nations, and even to accept its covenant provided that Congress had the right to vote before the United States went to war; without these conditions, he would oppose it.

At each of several stages Woodrow Wilson could have saved his treaty and kept the United States in the league, in which case it might have been strong enough to resist the dictators in the 1930s and keep the peace in Europe. But Wilson insisted that the Senate ratify his treaty as it stood, and made this a party issue between Democrats and Republicans. The exertions of a 13 000-km (8000-mile) speaking tour to seek support for the treaty exhausted him. He was already a sick man, and his health now deteriorated dramatically.

In March 1920 the treaty and the covenant of the League of Nations as proposed by Wilson were defeated in the Senate by fifty-three votes to thirty-eight. Lodge proposed a compromise that also failed to win the two-thirds majority needed under the constitution to ratify a treaty.

For the next twenty years United States foreign policy would reflect the belief that it was best not to intervene in European affairs.

ELATED SOLDIERS *wave goodbye to their military camp on their way back to civilian life. This was the first generation of Americans to have been involved in a war abroad.*

*"**M**y mother was weeping, and of course I asked, 'Why are you weeping? Everybody is so happy!' And she said, 'We have freedom.'* **"**

ANNA MASARYKA

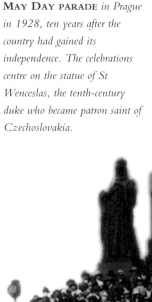

MAY DAY PARADE *in Prague in 1928, ten years after the country had gained its independence. The celebrations centre on the statue of St Wenceslas, the tenth-century duke who became patron saint of Czechoslovakia.*

The springtime of nations

Apart from Austria and Hungary, seven new states came into being as a result of postwar settlements. Poland was re-established from the provinces that had been taken by other states – Austria, Prussia and Russia – in the eighteenth century. The Croatian, Montenegrin, Muslim, Serbian and Slovenian peoples merged their national identities uneasily in the new south Slav kingdom of Yugoslavia. Four new republics emerged in the Baltic: Estonia, Finland, Latvia and Lithuania.

The republic of Czechoslovakia was first proclaimed in the United States on 18 October 1918, before the war had actually ended. Andrew Valucher, from a family of Czech immigrants in the United States, was seven years old at the time and was taken to Philadelphia for the event. 'There was this gentleman with a beard talking and telling the people that Czechoslovakia would be free, so there was tremendous excitement.' A few weeks later, the schoolboy Jiri Stursa heard the republic being proclaimed in Prague. 'My aunt took me down to the main street. There was a big crowd there and we met our neighbour, a police inspector. He asked my aunt, "Madam, have you heard the news? We have no Austrian empire any more, we have our own state."'

The bearded gentleman who proclaimed the republic of Czechoslovakia, first in Philadelphia and then in Prague, was Dr Thomas Masaryk. His granddaughter, Anna Masaryka, remembers that day very clearly. 'There were many, many people, all screaming, cheerful, embracing each other, and my mother was weeping, and of course I asked, "Why are you weeping? Everybody is so happy!" And she said, "We have freedom."'

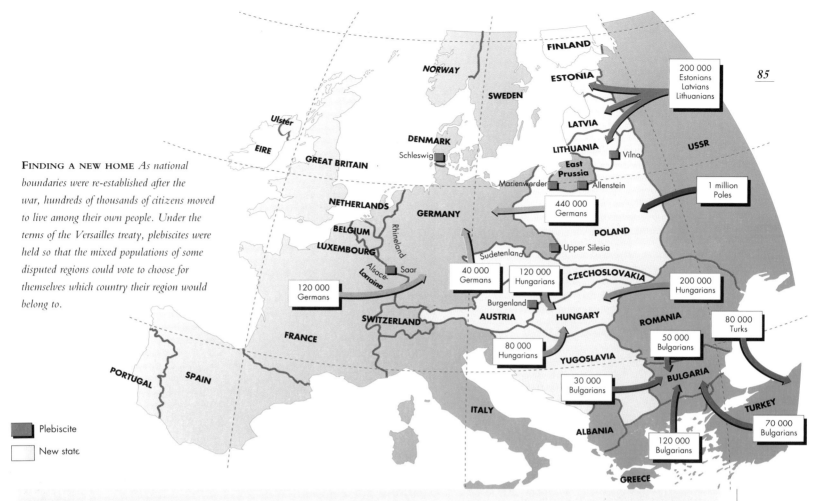

FINDING A NEW HOME *As national boundaries were re-established after the war, hundreds of thousands of citizens moved to live among their own people. Under the terms of the Versailles treaty, plebiscites were held so that the mixed populations of some disputed regions could vote to choose for themselves which country their region would belong to.*

Plebiscite

New state

NEW BEGINNINGS FOR ARABS AND JEWS

TENS OF MILLIONS OF PEOPLE were affected by the disintegration of the Ottoman empire after the First World War. Before the war, though its European and African possessions were greatly diminished, Ottoman rule had still held sway over a huge Asian territory.

During the war Turkish soldiers fought bravely at Gallipoli and in Mesopotamia. After the war ended old feuds with Italy and Greece continued – both countries sent troops to Turkey in 1919. They were repulsed by the Turks under their new leader, Mustafa Kemal Atatürk, who had led the revolution against such humiliations and established a secular modern republic in Turkey. The substantial Greek minority living there were expelled: more than a million Greeks were forced to 'return' to a homeland their ancestors had left up to two thousand years earlier; in retaliation some 410 000 Turks had to leave Greece.

Already by 1917 much of the Arab world had been in revolt against Turkish rule. In the postwar peace settlement the Allies divided the Arab territories of the Turkish empire among themselves. Some became independent (Saudi Arabia); others were administered under League of Nations auspices as 'mandates' to Britain (Iraq, Palestine and Trans-Jordan) and France (Lebanon and Syria). In 1917 the British

government had promised to establish in Palestine a national home for the Jewish people, many of whom cherished a dream of returning to their ancient homeland. Jews had begun to settle in Palestine in the late nineteenth century; by 1925 there were 100 000 settlers living there.

As nationalist fervour grew, the Arab states gradually began to achieve independence from their European governors. Palestinian Arabs became increasingly resentful of British plans to divide their country as Jewish refugees from Nazi persecution in Germany poured into Palestine during the 1930s. As the Second World War began, Britain was trying to maintain its influence in a Middle East that was modernizing rapidly; that was bitterly divided over Jewish immigration; and on which, because of its vast oil resources, Italy was casting covetous eyes.

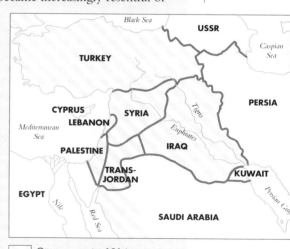

Ottoman empire 1914

League of Nations mandate

THE PLEASURE PRINCIPLE

THOSE WHO HAD SURVIVED the dark, sad years of war wanted to rebuild their lives, put the pain behind them and make the most of the peace. Among the well-to-do in the 1920s to be modern was the thing. In music, dance, fashion and behaviour the old rules were challenged. Jazz became the rage, and lively dances accompanied it.

The hard-working independence women had found during the war was now expressed in a new way of dressing. Layers of long, smothering garments were abandoned in favour of simple clothes; the more daring even wore trousers. Women challenged the demure, ladylike manners expected of them; drinking and smoking in public became more common, and more women began to wear make-up and go to restaurants without a chaperone. While some celebrated the new freedoms, others complained bitterly of decadence and immorality.

The search for pleasure sometimes seemed frenzied. Contestants collapsed at dance marathons, clubs stayed open all night long. Risky plays were staged, erotic film stars were admired. On gramophone records and radios the latest dance music crazes could be heard in millions of homes, and advertising increasingly reminded people of what they could aspire to. Sports cars brought speed and freedom; travel brought adventure. Newspapers and magazines fed the public's appetite for sensational stories. People worked hard at having fun. There was a spirit far removed from the austerity of the decade before.

DINING OUT IN STYLE (ABOVE) *For those who could afford it, like the fashionable Parisians in this contemporary print, there was gaiety and entertainment on a new scale in the 1920s. Young people in particular wanted to enjoy themselves and forget about the war.*

It was a strange experience to live through, this dismantling of empires and birth of new nation states. Gerhard Stütz, a German-speaker growing up in the little town of Gablonz, once part of Germany and was now in Czechoslovakia, remembers the day the Czechs arrived. 'My mother wanted to go shopping in the market and she came back quite shocked because there were Czech soldiers and they refused to let the people go to the market ...the Czechs had laid down for themselves a preferential status. In Gablonz, for example, which had 85 per cent German population, all the street signs had to be in the Czech language and beneath the Czech name was the German translation in small print. The grotesque situation was that all our streets were named after German writers – Goethe, Schiller – so the street signs read Goethovadice, Schillerovadice, or Eichendorffovadice.' Changes like these took place in towns and villages all over Europe.

No more war

In all the countries that had fought in the war, many people remained preoccupied with their memories of sacrifice and death. In the late 1920s a stream of people visited the war cemeteries, where hundreds of thousands of men lay buried. Great memorials, like the marble Menin Gate outside Ypres, in the Flanders battle-fields, were dedicated to the simple proposition: no more war. Films, poems and books about the war reinforced this theme. In Britain a play set in a dugout at the front, *Journey's End*, became a huge popular success.

Young people, too, were aware of what war was about, and the need to avoid it. Growing up in the United States, George Watt and a friend were deeply affected by reading a German book, later made by a Hollywood studio into one of the first sound films: Erich Maria Remarque's *All Quiet on the Western Front*. 'It was the most realistic presentation of war, it was filled with humour, it was filled with gruesome brutalities of war, and also sadness...we both swore that we would never go to war.' Later, at Columbia University, he took a peace pledge.

George Watt and his friend were part of a new, international peace movement that was beginning to influence the politicians. The financial collapse that began with the Wall Street crash in New York, and triggered the economic depression of the 1930s, threw millions of people out of work across the world. In poorer countries, social conflicts also sharpened and demagogues profited. Governments in industrial countries were troubled by mounting unemployment, and turned to economic protection in the vain hope of escaping disaster – and so embittered relations with their own best customers. There was renewed anger at the resources wasted on armaments.

To reduce the threat of war, it was necessary to reduce the weapons used to fight war. Germany had been almost completely disarmed; in the early 1920s wartime stockpiles of munitions were reduced; Britain, Japan and the United States had agreed to limit their fleets. Not until 1932 did the League of Nations organize the first disarmament conference, in Geneva. By that time peace was already threatened by the rise of extremism in Germany and of militarism in Japan. Ramsay MacDonald, Britain's Labour prime

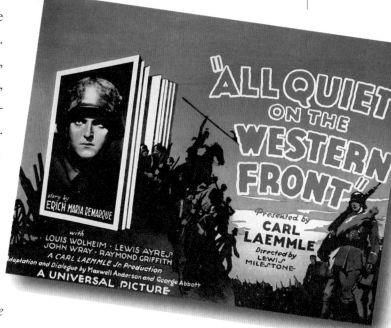

THE HORRORS OF WAR *were portrayed in films such as* All Quiet on the Western Front. *A new generation learned through entertainment that war was not glamorous and heroic but tragic and brutal. When the film was shown in Germany there were demonstrations against it, and the film was eventually banned there.*

PETITIONING FOR PEACE *at the Geneva disarmament conference. Millions of signatures were collected from people all over the world, putting pressure on governments to respond to popular demands for arms reduction and the end of war. Women were particularly active in the peace movement, gaining a new voice in world affairs.*

minister, said he would go to Geneva to reduce what he called 'this enormous, disgraceful burden of armaments'.

Jenifer Hart, a British peace campaigner, was present at the opening session of the Geneva conference. 'People came from all over the world,' she remembers, 'petitioning for disarmament.' One of the conference organizers put the nub of the question before the delegates: 'No one doubts that disarmament is possible, but the common man wants to know whether the governments with great military, naval and air forces are really in earnest in their desire for peace.' If they were, the whole international atmosphere would change 'as if by magic'. Although it was not a member of the league, the United States (where over a million signatures had been collected for the petition) sent a delegation to Geneva, and hopes rose even higher.

They were to be disappointed. It was one thing to announce a high-minded desire for peace, quite another to take the political risks associated with reducing a country's defence. As Ignace Paderewski, now Poland's prime minister, explained: 'It's a very good intention, a very fine idea, but a very difficult task. Everyone expects the other fellow to disarm, but he's not ready to disarm himself.' And by the 1930s there were leaders in power who made it quite plain that they saw the other fellow's disarmament as mere weakness, to be exploited without mercy.

Fading hopes for peace

The League of Nations had no power to impose peace. When Japan – a member of the league council – was formally criticized for invading Manchuria in 1931, it left the organization. Adolf Hitler came to power in Germany at the beginning of 1933, and one of his first actions was also to take Germany out of the league, which it had joined in 1926. In Italy, the fascist leader Benito Mussolini promised not peace but a sword. Italy's invasion in 1935 of Ethiopia, a fellow member nation of the league, dealt a serious blow to international peace.

The league's failure to deal with the dictators in Africa, the Far East and Europe weakened people's confidence in its potential as a keeper of international peace. Of the great powers, Germany, Japan, and Italy had left, and the United States had never joined.

IMMOBILIZED BY THE SNAKE'S GAZE, *the rabbit is rendered powerless in this political cartoon illustrating the weakness of the League of Nations. The league had been set up to provide a voice for weak as well as strong nations, but was increasingly unable to fulfil its potential peacekeeping role in the face of growing international aggression in the 1930s.*

ITALIAN TROOPS *being reviewed by their leaders. Mussolini sought to solve Italy's economic problems by seizing Ethiopia. The Ethiopian emperor, Haile Selassie, made a dignified appeal for help to the League of Nations. 'I must fight on until my tardy allies appear,' he said, warning that 'if they never come, I say to you without bitterness, the West will perish.'*

THE JAPANESE IN MANCHURIA

O N THE NIGHT OF 18 SEPTEMBER 1931 Japanese troops guarding the South Manchurian Railway to the north of the town of Mukden set off explosives along the track, and accused the Chinese of the sabotage they had themselves inflicted. The Mukden incident provided the pretext for the Japanese army to take over Manchuria, a strategically important region of China bordering the Soviet Union, with major mineral and industrial resources.

The powerful military elite of Japan had watched with mounting anger as the Chinese government worked with other leading world states to establish peace – to Japan's military disadvantage. When the Depression affected world trade at the end of the 1920s, Japan's economy was badly hit, as it had been dependent on the United States market for rice, silk and silk products. The impoverished farmers of Japan, and increasing numbers of unemployed urban workers, had little faith in the new democratic style of government that brought them so much hardship. The time was ripe for nationalist extremists to influence public opinion.

Secret associations were set up to work towards establishing military government. By 1931, as unrest grew, ambitious young officers turned to Manchuria as an opportunity for action. The government learned of their intentions and felt compelled to warn the emperor, who forbade any operations against China to be undertaken. It was too late. The Japanese army stationed in Manchuria went ahead with its plans. While most members of the government were shocked by the news, it was welcomed with patriotic delight by many Japanese people, who were aware that to have the assured market and the resources of the region at their disposal would ease their problems.

The unprovoked aggression that the invasion represented in the eyes of the world was just the kind of incident that the League of Nations had been established to contain. A commission was sent to investigate. The report of its findings so offended the Japanese that in March 1933 they withdrew from the league in protest. A puppet regime under Japanese control was set up in Manchuria (renamed Manchukuo). This was an important step in Japan's long campaign to change power relationships in the Far East in its favour. It was also the first public evidence that the league could do nothing to prevent international aggression – a failure that the German and Italian leaders observed with particular interest.

VICTORIOUS JAPANESE OFFICERS *toast the success of the Manchurian invasion with cups of saki. The invasion was used as a springboard for Japanese expansion into the Chinese mainland during the 1930s.*

A PEACE PLEDGE UNION *card was filled in by each member as a declaration that they denounced war. At first only men could join the union, but later women became members too.*

DONALD SOPER (BELOW) *addresses the crowd to rally support for the Peace Pledge Union. Pacifist values were based on a belief that peace and love could triumph over violence and hatred. As the threat of war became more real, the popularity of pacifism grew.*

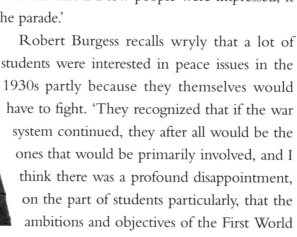

Collective security began to seem a naive illusion. As governments once again feared war, they prepared to rearm. Ignoring the restrictions of the Versailles treaty, in 1935 Germany also began to rearm. There was much disappointment, confusion and anger. Some people still clung to the ideal of peace, and continued to look to the league to enforce it.

There seemed to be no answer to this question, so others turned to a more radical position: pacifism. They wanted each country to renounce war altogether. In Britain, pacifism reached its height in 1936. The Peace Pledge Union persuaded 130 000 concerned men and women to sign a declaration that they would renounce war. A Methodist preacher, Donald Soper, was one of the leaders of the campaign. 'It was comparatively easy,' he recalls sixty years later, 'to persuade an audience of the rightness of what you were asking them to believe, and also dangerously easy to ask them at that point to sign on the dotted line. We had a great deal of immediate conversion. The problem was to maintain the ardour and spirit of it when workaday problems became more difficult and more complicated.'

In the United States there had also been a strong movement for peace since the 1920s. A number of 'no more war' marches took place in New York. Robert Burgess was sixteen years old when he joined the Green International march. He enjoyed taking part in it. 'I remember my pleasure when I signed up for this and received in the mail my green shirt…like any parade the people line up on the kerb, some of them sympathetic, encouraging you, some of them opposed, throwing words at you…it was a mixture. My feeling at the time was that if a few people were impressed, it justified the parade.'

Robert Burgess recalls wryly that a lot of students were interested in peace issues in the 1930s partly because they themselves would have to fight. 'They recognized that if the war system continued, they after all would be the ones that would be primarily involved, and I think there was a profound disappointment, on the part of students particularly, that the ambitions and objectives of the First World

War, which after all was billed as a war to end all war, the war to make the world safe for democracy, had done quite the opposite.'

For a large number of Americans, isolationism was a more attractive response to the new rumblings of war from Europe. The press took a strong line, influencing many people. In Chicago, the Bone family read the intensely anti-interventionist *Tribune*. Hugh Bone was no more than nine years old when his brother had come back from France with bitter memories of the war. 'The family of course…wanted to know about what he did in the war, his exploits. He literally refused to answer. He had told us time and time again, "I don't want to talk about the war." That influenced my thinking that never again, never again are we going to send our boys overseas.'

KARL NAGERL *rode into Austria on horseback. He was among the German troops welcomed by some 300,000 civilians when Austria was united with Germany in 1938. He remembers clearly how 'the barrier was lifted, our regiment's musicians marched ahead playing away, behind the border the Austrians were standing in crowds with swastika flags and they cheered out to us loudly: "One people, one empire, one leader". Finally the brother nation was reunited again with the brother nation.'*

The threat of war

When civil war erupted in Spain in July 1936 it increasingly became clear that nationalism and dictatorships were more than just threats to peace. For some, like the American George Watt who volunteered to fight in Spain, it meant an end to pacifism. 'We began to realize that an oath not to fight no longer had much validity with the rise of Hitlerism....When I came back from Spain I felt that the United States had to get involved in what was going on in Europe...we couldn't stick our heads in the sand.'

In March 1936, five years after the Allies had withdrawn their troops from the Rhineland, it was reoccupied in breach of the treaty by the Germans, who illegally 'remilitarized' it. Two years later Hitler reunited his native Austria with Germany, ignoring the explicit terms of the Versailles treaty. The people of Austria welcomed the union (*Anschluss*) and gave the Germans a rapturous welcome. Britain and France did nothing. Hitler now turned his attention to Czechoslovakia, claiming that the Versailles treaty had given two million Germans to the new Czechoslovak republic.

Strong feelings were aroused by the new national borders and minorities. Gertrud Pietsch was one of the Germans who lived in the Sudetenland, the area of Czechoslovakia lying on the border with Germany. 'A new Czech school had been built in Marienbad....It was a very nice modern school, but because the Czechs didn't have enough children they needed more pupils and approached my father, asking him to send his two daughters to the Czech school. He refused to do this because he thought we should learn German first and then Czech. Half a year later my father was dismissed, they told him they were cutting down on his job. Later on my father found out that a young Czech with two or three children got his job.' Relations between the Pietsch family and their Czech neighbours were strained. 'There was a strong feeling of resentment in our family towards the Czechs in general – and we children were aware of this.'

The Czechs, who had made a success of their young and independent republic, knew they were threatened by a strong Germany under Hitler. To support their large, well-equipped army they built a line of fortifications along the German border, and looked to Britain and France to come to their aid. At last the

REBELS AND CAUSES IN SPAIN

THE SPANISH CIVIL WAR symbolizes the conflicting political affiliations of the 1930s. Throughout Europe, people were nervous about the rise of fascism and the growing threat of war. For many politically aware young people the civil war had an intense emotional impact. Some 35 000 foreigners from fifty-four countries chose to fight for the republican side in the International Brigades, so called because their members volunteered from many different countries; smaller numbers supported the nationalist cause. Their principles led them to regard the war as, from one point of view, a fascist conspiracy to destroy democracy; from the other, a communist plot to overthrow law, order and religion in Spain.

The war was a bitter fight between the democratic government of the republicans, supported by the political left and trade unionists in Spain and the communist government of the Soviet Union, against Spanish conservatives, military rebels and the Falange party, backed by the Roman Catholic Church, monarchists, and the fascist leaders of Germany and Italy.

There had been military coups in Spain before. This one, led by General Franco in 1936, failed to overthrow the government; it took three years, the devastation of the country and the deaths of half a million people before fascism triumphed in Spain.

In a war characterized by massacres and bloody reprisals, civilians were badly affected. In April 1937 the small market town of Guernica was bombed by aircraft of the German Condor Legion. There was widespread horror at the devastation caused, which was to prove a grim portent of the war to come.

FLEEING FROM WAR *Spanish civilians leave their homes to seek refuge in France from the fighting.*

REDEFINING GERMANY *by reclaiming the Sudetenland had been as easy as moving a border post. The German people living there had been denied a plebiscite after the war, but now they had what they wanted. Karl Nagerl, who took this photograph, remembers how the Sudeten Germans hurried to the border with tears in their eyes to welcome the German soldiers as 'liberators from the suffering they had had to bear under the Czechs'.*

ANGRY CROWDS (OPPOSITE) *express their fear and dismay as German troops drive through Prague. Having gained possession of the Sudetenland, it was easy for Hitler to invade the rest of Czechoslovakia. But here, as Karl Nagerl recalls, the people 'threatened us, they waved their fists in the air... they made it quite clear that they didn't want us there.'*

impotence of the League of Nations was recognized, and Britain and France took matters into their own hands. In September 1938 Neville Chamberlain, the British prime minister, and Edouard Daladier, the French premier, went to Munich to discuss the Czechoslovakian crisis with Hitler. The three leaders agreed that the Sudetenland would immediately be transferred to Germany. When Chamberlain flew back to Britain and announced that he had brought 'peace in our time' the crowds rejoiced, believing that peace really had been secured by giving Hitler the Sudetenland. Chamberlain had brought back a paper with Hitler's signature on it, and declared that settlement of the Czechoslovak problem was only the prelude to a wider peace.

Daladier was greeted with a similar response by the French public. Etienne Crouy Chanel, who flew with him, saw a huge crowd waiting; he thought people had come to hiss and boo, but instead there was a wave of applause and enthusiasm. Daladier had none of Chamberlain's illusions. 'These people are mad,' he said.

The Czechs understood all too well that their country had been sold to Hitler. For Josef Beldar this was 'a terrible betrayal, a horrible treachery of our country by the Western powers, and especially France and England. We thought that this should never have happened, and even then we somehow felt that it was to be the beginning of some horrible world conflict.' On 3 October German troops crossed the Czech border, and the Sudetenland became part of the German Reich.

Czechs living in the Sudetenland had to choose between remaining in Germany under Hitler or leaving their homes as refugees. The British journalist Iverach McDonald was in Prague, and witnessed the Czechs' reactions to the Munich pact. 'The people were out demonstrating...but they were not speaking, they were just utterly crushed and were weeping with grief, despair and utter sorrow.' One of them came up to him and said, 'Every night I pray that God may forgive France for her infidelity and Britain for her blindness.' The Czechs celebrated their country's twentieth anniversary that autumn with deep foreboding.

The Sudeten Germans were the only people with cause to rejoice. In Gablonz on the river Neisse, Gerhard Stütz remembers, 'the whole village went spontaneously to the biggest square in town and just cheered and cheered "*Heil!*" We were immensely relieved that it had not led to any war. We were very glad that the oppression of the Czechs had ended and we had achieved self-determination for our people.' Gertrud Pietsch and her family were overjoyed that they could remain German, and that her father was reinstated in his job. 'We cried,' she remembers. 'We were so happy that we cried, we scattered flowers on the streets.'

The Munich agreement bought only six months of peace. In March 1939 German troops marched across Czechoslovakia into its capital city, Prague. Jiri Stursa, who had seen the Austrians leave in 1918, now watched the Germans arrive. 'My uncle came to us that morning and said, "Those bastards have marched into Prague". We went into town and saw that the German armoured vehicles and troops were there. What could we do? Nothing. We couldn't fight them with our bare hands. The fact is, though, that people shook their fists at them. The Germans seem to have felt that they were hated, they must have seen it.'

Voice of the world

RADIO BROADCASTING *was in its heyday during the 1930s. An increasingly familiar feature in the kitchen or sitting room, it brought not only entertainment but also local, national and world events into people's homes. Listeners could be both informed and misinformed – radio offered an ideal outlet for propaganda.*

Back to war

At last the veil was lifted from the eyes of the people in Britain and France. Neville Chamberlain posed the now unavoidable question: 'Is this the last attack upon a small state, or is it to be followed by others?' Hitler's answer was to embark within months on the next phase in his plans for conquest by invading Poland.

For another two years, Americans were to cling to the belief that, unlike the people of the European democracies, they could stand apart. The issue, Franklin D. Roosevelt said, 'is whether our civilization is to be dragged into the tragic vortex of unending militarism punctuated by periodic wars, or whether we shall be able to maintain the ideal of peace'. While President Roosevelt argued with the isolationists in the United States, all over Europe young men were opening the brown envelopes that contained their call-up papers.

The Frenchman Marcel Batreau had managed to survive the First World War, though twenty-five of his thirty classmates had been killed. He explains: 'It was hard to believe it could all happen again. To have peace, you have to be well-protected and always in a state of readiness. We needed to be armed, and we needed the Germans to be scared of us. The Germans took advantage of our sleepy state. I am not a military man, but I am a patriot.' He was prepared to fight again. Another First World War veteran, the Englishman Walter Hare, felt disillusioned as war loomed once more. 'I felt that what I'd done had been a waste of time. I was concerned because my son would soon be of military age, and I didn't want him to go through what I had gone through.'

In Geneva, the great white palace of the League of Nations stood empty. It had represented the belief that international cooperation and open discussion could put an end to war. The chance of lasting peace had seemed to be in humanity's grasp, but for the present it had been lost. Six years later, this ideal would be tried again, but by then some fifty million people would have died in another world war.

AT THE CROSSROADS *of war and peace, German troops prepare to invade Poland in August 1939. As Poland's allies, Britain and France were then obliged to declare war on Germany. As the war began, Karl Nagerl remembers, 'We thought back to the end of the First World War and hoped that it would not be repeated again, that this incident in Poland would be a short-lived tension and that the war would not become more widespread.'*

ENLIST, RE-ENLIST *urges this French war ministry recruitment poster (ABOVE) in 1938. Soldiers stand at the ready on the Maginot Line, a permanent defensive fortification. It had been built in the 1930s to prevent the Germans from advancing into France as they had done in the First World War. French soldiers who had fought in that war were now being asked to re-enlist, together with the young men of the new generation.*

WAR WAS DECLARED *(RIGHT) on 3 September 1939. At the final meeting of the League of Nations, its president warned: 'We do not know what the future will bring. We cannot even foretell tomorrow. We leave this assembly in grave anxiety for every nation.'*

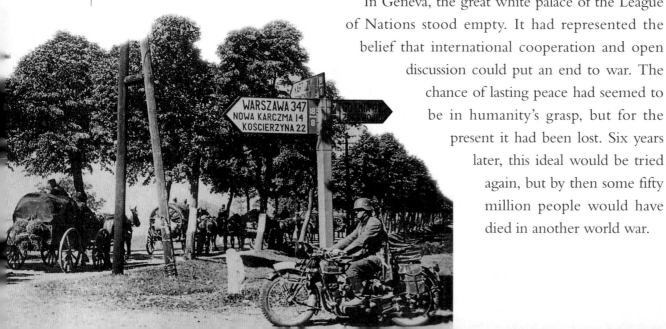

On the Line

THE EFFECTS OF MASS PRODUCTION

ONE HOT DAY IN AUGUST 1913, at the Ford Motor Company in Detroit, a young worker picked up a rope and slowly pulled a car chassis past the mechanics who fitted the various parts onto it. Instead of workers moving to the job, the work was moved past the workers. The following year, Henry Ford applied to car manufacture the technique he had first seen in the slaughterhouses of Chicago: he hooked the chassis onto a continuously moving chain.

As the car chassis moved down the assembly line, the workers had to perform their set tasks before it had passed by. The most important skill now was speed, as anyone could learn the simple, repetitive tasks in a matter of hours. Ford could produce more cars in less time and at less cost.

Other factories followed Ford's example. The moving assembly line dramatically increased production. Arthur Herbaux, who worked on the Renault line near Paris in the 1930s, found the new rhythm of work almost unbearable. 'You had to assemble so many parts per hour....No sooner had you finished one part than the next arrived. No stopping allowed. The workman was just part of the machine. At the flick of the switch the machine went into action and the workman had to keep pace with it. It was worse than hard labour...it was no better than being a galley-slave.'

This new way of making things transformed the lives of those who made them and those who used them. It brought within many people's reach products once luxuries only for the rich, from cars to fountain pens and electric stoves to vacuum cleaners. Ever higher production targets were set for the new mass markets as living standards rose with better wages. But the pressure of work also increased. Huge industrial complexes sprang up that employed tens of thousands of workers who were expected to become just as standardized and interchangeable as the parts that they bolted and welded together. As the discontent spread, more of them joined trade unions, and took part in the sit-ins and strikes that would eventually set new work standards for many of the world's workers.

MOVING WITH THE TIMES *Changing methods of assembly will transform the lives of industrial workers throughout the world.*

Early mass production

Many of the principal features of mass production already existed well before the assembly line was introduced. Firearms were assembled from standardized parts; sewing machines and railway engines were made in large factories. As mass production spread to other industries – shoes, clothing, clocks, typewriters, bicycles, and agricultural machinery were made in large quantities – the new processes increasingly reduced the role of those who worked in manufacturing. Semi-skilled and unskilled workers were not eligible for membership of the craft unions, and were refused the right to join new trade unions by their employers. They had no voice, no way to make their feelings clear.

It was in car manufacturing, one of the newest industries, that the greatest innovations took place, leading the way for the transformation of industrial production throughout the world. When cars were first made in France and Germany at the turn of the century they were individually built, costly works of craftsmanship. The early car industry in the United States began to use new techniques: the Olds factory made its cars using a trolley system, Cadillac used interchangeable parts, and the new General Motors Corporation brought out several new models. By 1908 the Ford Motor Company in Detroit was producing a hundred cars a day at its Highland Park factory.

Henry Ford wanted to go further. He spent six years planning a light, cheap car for a mass market; when he launched the Model T it was an instant success, not only in the United States but also in Britain. The Trafford Park plant in Manchester began making cars for Ford in 1911, and became the largest single car producer in Britain. When most British cars cost more than £300, a Model T was only £135. As orders for the 'Tin Lizzie' continued to flood in, Ford was unable to produce enough cars cheaply to satisfy the growing demand, and sought new ways of speeding up their manufacture.

ILLUMINATING INVENTIONS *The increasing use of electricity brought with it a growing demand for light bulbs. New technologies created new possibilities, boosting the market for many mass-produced goods and bringing new jobs for women – here working in a German light-bulb factory in 1910 – as well as for men. Electricity also powered the machines of mass production.*

LINKS IN THE INDUSTRIAL CHAIN (ABOVE) *Skilled workers in a metal plant in the United States producing parts needed in other manufacturing industries. With the use of new machine tools and standardized parts there was a gradual shift to semi-skilled and unskilled labour. The craftsman's pride in making something using his skill and training was no longer part of working experience.*

THE FLOW OF MASS PRODUCTION

IT WAS NOT THE MOVING ASSEMBLY LINE alone that revolutionized the way goods were produced. In factories of every kind, systems of organization such as the division of labour and the use of specialized machinery and equipment were all central to mass production. Improved transport networks meant that both raw materials and finished products could be taken over greater distances. Stronger, faster machine tools with greater precision and the use of lighter, more reliable metals made it easier to make standardized parts. Instead of skilled workers fitting metal parts that had to be cut to the right dimensions and then individually fitted with a hammer and file, unskilled workers could now simply assemble ready-made, interchangeable parts. The skill and long training of craftsmen became superfluous: now the skill was in the machine rather than in the coordinated eye and hand of human beings.

The workers and the way they worked came under scrutiny, and were also standardized. Believing that rationalization was the key to efficiency, F.W. Taylor developed a system he called Scientific Management in which the way people worked was analysed and reorganized. Complex tasks were broken down into simple, repetitive, timed jobs. This was designed to let man and machine work together to maximum capacity.

Instead of grouping general-purpose machines in separate buildings, under the new system the specialist machines were grouped around the point where they would be needed on the assembly line. Sub-assembly lines, like tributaries that flow into a river, fed the main assembly line with parts. The logic of flow production and the assembly line created factories on a scale the world had never seen before. Massive new industries were born – processing rubber to make tyres and glass for the windows. Everything possible was done to speed up and cut the cost of the manufacturing process.

WAR WORK *in a British munitions factory during the First World War. New manufacturing techniques were important in mass-producing weaponry. The war also brought thousands of women into factories for the first time to undertake jobs previously done by men. When peace returned many European factories adapted the techniques to make new consumer products along American lines.*

"If you had to build that car by hand, each piece, you couldn't afford to pay for it. But mass production, that's where the profit was, and that's where our jobs were."

TOM JELLEY

BEFORE AND AFTER *Large, hand-built touring cars like the six-cylinder Ford model of 1906 (ABOVE) were costly: this model was priced at $2500. It was mass production combined with simpler design and finish that dramatically reduced the price; the new Ford Model T (BELOW) was a more rugged car which came only in standard black. By 1913 nearly every American town had a Ford dealer, and by 1915 there were over a million Model T cars in the United States, where a huge, widespread rural population boosted the market.*

Time and money

It was the assembly line that proved to be the real breakthrough in cheap, efficient mass production. In 1913, when the Ford Motor Company already employed 25 000 men making 500 cars a day, cars were still assembled on wooden 'horses', and the men moved from car to car. It took them twelve-and-a-half hours to finish each one. When the moving assembly line was installed, that time was reduced to an hour and a half. The Highland Park factory was transformed. Few of the assembly line workers took the time to think about the changes; they were too busy worrying about how to keep pace with the moving line.

One Ford worker, Jim Sullivan, sums up the changes. For the economy, he says, the assembly line was good. 'But if you were on that line and you had a certain job to do and the cars came by as fast as they did, and you didn't get your part on there, you were in trouble.' The new pace of work was relentless, monotonous and fast. The workers were expected to make more cars in the same time, and for the same wages. After a very short time no one wanted to work on the moving line; the men complained that they had become little more than servants of the machines. Only a few weeks after the assembly line first creaked into motion, ten workers were leaving for every one who stayed.

Henry Ford then came up with an idea as revolutionary in its way as the assembly line that had made it necessary. The new way of making cars was proving so profitable that he could afford to double the workers' pay by including them in a profit-sharing scheme. Further changes soon followed. On 5 January 1914 Ford reduced the working day to eight hours and added a third shift, instantly creating thousands of new jobs. And for those eight hours of work Ford paid an unheard-of $5 a day. It was more money for less time than anyone had ever paid factory workers.

Tens of thousands of new immigrants arrived in search of a job at Ford. 'They were coming here from all over the world,' remembers Tom Jelley, who worked at the Ford factory as a tool and die maker. 'All the different nationalities...they were piling

in here for the five or six dollars.' Detroit rapidly became a boom town. Archie Acciacca's family left Italy to seek a new life in the United States at that time. With some reluctance, his father got a job at Ford, where the high wages made even the unrelenting, back-breaking work of the assembly line worth it, at least for a while. 'At that time, five dollars a day was very big money....We were able to have a respectable, decent living. They put food on the table, had a rented place...with five dollars a day they were able to raise seven children.'

Ford had realized that his well-paid workers would in due course be able to buy his cars themselves. By paying more for a stable work force, he also guaranteed a new market among people who had never before dreamed of owning a car. Erv Dasher, who was twenty years old when he got his job at Ford, was delighted with his new pay packet. 'You were in the bucks – you could afford this, you could afford that and you could afford a new car.' Etta Warren became the first black woman to be employed by the Ford Motor Company. 'People here, they made money and they put it to good use. They all bought homes and bought cars and educated their children.'

PEER PRESSURE *was intensified as each worker had to keep up with the production line in order to safeguard the job of the worker next to him. As the assembly line, built at waist-height for maximum efficiency, brings these flywheels to the workers it regulates their pace.*

LINING UP *for work (RIGHT). Many immigrants who settled in the United States found work in the new industries. But Archie Acciacca (ABOVE) remembers that his father soon left his job at Ford. 'The monotony of working that production line, day in day out, was too much for the man.'*

Life on the line

In 1924 Ford made its ten millionth Model T; by 1925 half the cars in the world were Model Ts. In the late 1920s the Ford Motor Company had established its assembly plants in parts of Asia, Australia, Canada, Europe, South Africa and South America. This was also a time when many other new goods – radios, irons, refrigerators, vacuum cleaners – were also being mass produced in factories where assembly lines had been introduced.

The European automobile industry, which had been slower to develop, also began to adapt to the new production methods. The heads of major European companies – André Citroën, Louis Renault, Giovanni Agnelli of Fiat, William Morris and Herbert Austin – all visited the United States to learn about the American methods. After adopting them, the French firm Citroën was able to make 400 cars a day. The largest French car factory of all, at Billancourt, belonged to Renault, which also set up plants in Britain and Germany.

In Italy Giovanni Agnelli also modelled his new factory in the Lingotto district of Turin on the American pattern of mass production, realizing that success in the market depended on it. 'Senator Agnelli and also the plant managers…were often in America, and they were on good terms with Ford. So what would happen there, we would try, if it was progress, to bring it over here,' remembers Giovanni Gobbi, who worked for Fiat.

In Europe, as in the United States, for the workers on the production line 'progress' meant working to rigorous new rules under strict controls, changes that were resented by workers at the Fiat Lingotto factory. When they decided to go on strike in 1922, the management responded by bringing in the army. Felice Gentile, posted to Turin, was one of the soldiers involved. Four machine guns were positioned around the plant, though they were not loaded. 'It was just to frighten the workers,' he says.

When Fiat installed new assembly lines in 1926 conditions in the plant became even more difficult. Felice Gentile, now out of the army, found himself on the other side when he himself took a job at Fiat. 'The atmosphere, the control, everything would go according to plans,' he remembers. 'The moulds, the timings, the pay – everything was programmed, and so we just had to submit

AROUND THE CLOCK *that regulates their working lives, Italian auto workers at the Fiat Corso Dante plant in 1916 punch their time cards as they begin and end shifts. This rational organization of the workplace was adapted from the American model.*

FACTORY OF THE FUTURE (OPPOSITE) *A poster illustrating plans for the new Fiat works on the outskirts of Turin in 1917. Its test track for new cars was on the roof. Giovanni Gobbi remembers how highly people spoke of it. 'A factory like this one, with a track that was so high up, was a bit of a marvel in those days.'*

WORKERS' LEISURE

HAPPY WORKERS WERE PROFITABLE WORKERS. While conditions in the factories were sometimes stressful, the management of large companies in most industrialized countries did attempt to encourage their workers' leisure-time pursuits – football pitches, gyms, swimming pools and halls for leisure activities were often provided. Les Gurl was very impressed by the 'wonderful sports facilities' that Morris provided in Oxford. 'Every sport that a man or woman could take part in was supplied by the company.'

In the intensely political atmosphere of the 1930s governments also became involved in the efforts to give people something enjoyable to do after work, especially in Germany and Italy. In Nazi Germany a new movement called Kraft durch Freude, 'Strength through Joy', was launched with slogans such as 'Happiness on the bench means higher productivity'. German workers were offered cheap excursions to the Bavarian Alps and Italy, and sea cruises to the Norwegian fjords. In 1936 six million people took advantage of these facilities.

By that year two and three-quarter million workers in Italy were enrolled in the Opera Nazionale Dopolavoro (National Afterwork Agency), which held that 'greater well-being of personnel would have favourable effects on output'. What began as a social welfare agency had become a national movement to support the economy.

At Fiat Dopolavoro provision was extended after 1932 to reduce the level of discontent among workers. The aim was to transform a class-conscious workforce into an elite, isolated by its privileges from other groups of working people. Fiat workers' sense of being a close-knit, privileged community was bolstered by sports facilities and cultural events, including opera performances, symphony and band concerts, choirs and drama, and a 10 000-volume library. Fiat also published its own newspaper, *Bianco e Rosso* (white and red); it took its name from the colours of the leading professional football club, Juventus, which had emerged at Fiat.

When he worked there Giovanni Gobbi enjoyed the activities, though the uniformity required of factory workers was never far away. 'When we were in the Dopolavoro building the uniform was shorts or long white pants, and then a red jersey with Fiat written on it.' He remembers how the Fiat complex housed a film theatre, and rooms for 'reading, language lessons, music lessons, table games, chess and billiards'. In 1933 it became compulsory for all Fiat workers to join the Dopolavoro. The advantages of these facilities were genuine, even if they were provided as much in the interests of the factory as in the interests of the workers.

YOUNG EXPLORERS (LEFT) *on an outing in 1925, organized by the Fiat employees' association for their children before the Dopolavoro was introduced.*

to these norms. There were never any discussions. If someone did not follow the rules they would be punished, or moved away or given a different position.' Felice Gentile understood the pressures that had driven the workers to act. 'On the job, we would work and you couldn't smoke and even when you went to the toilet they would check to make sure the worker was sincere or if he was going for a chat. But if he stopped for a chat and a guard were to come by, or the foreman, or even a director and find him there in the toilets he would fire him.'

American time and motion study was used in the European factories too. Fifteen-year-old Giovanni Gobbi was told to time the men at work. 'My boss put a stopwatch into my hand and said, "Go and measure how long it takes to do that job".' He felt awkward. 'One of the first people I had to time was a man who could have been my grandfather....The poor man was working away and I was the young kid having to time him. It was awful.'

In Britain, the Morris car plant at Cowley, outside Oxford, introduced many of the techniques of mass production during the 1920s, though like other British factories at the time it did not yet use a moving assembly line. Instead of pacing production by speeding up the line, the Morris factory increased its output by continuing to pay workers on a piece rate system: in addition to an hourly wage they earned a bonus for getting ahead on production; falling behind the given quotas meant lower earnings.

Unlike their American counterparts, British workers were sometimes still able to use their initiative. As a teenage boy Les Gurl worked out a new way of supplying hinges so that the men could fit more of them in a given time. They were so grateful that one of the workers came up to him and said, 'Put your hands together.' And he poured nearly a week's wages into Les Gurl's hands, saying, 'If you can keep this up, we'll have a whip round for you every week.' Les Gurl was delighted. 'It allowed me to give my pay packet to my mother and still have a load of money. I could live like a lord.' The benefits of higher wages were set against the drawbacks the workers had to' contend with: strict working conditions and management that assumed total control. They had no voice in the way the factory was run or the speed at which the line operated.

PIECE WORK *at the Morris car factory in Britain opened the door to prosperity for workers whose mastery of a particular task earned them higher wages. After the moving assembly line was introduced in 1934 the pace of work was transformed, as Les Gurl* (ABOVE RIGHT) *remembers. 'Say you have got twenty cars going up the line; you have only got a minute and a half, two minutes to do your job. If you are hanging a door, you have got to put three hinges on with nine screws in two minutes. You don't find any time to leave the job. You don't even get time to take a sandwich into work and eat it.'*

> *"If you had a job at Ford, you were made for life...they would say you have got the best job that is going in the country, no matter what you did. "*

LEN SMITH

INDUSTRIAL GIANT *The ambitious Ford River Rouge plant became the hub of a national and international economic empire. By 1927 it had 145 km (90 miles) of railway track to link its ninety-three structures housing 53 000 machine tools and a huge workforce.*

Symbol of affluence

The Ford emblem represented not only the achievements of the tycoon whose name it bore; it also acted as a badge of identity for the thousands of factory workers who wore it on their overalls. It gave the Briton Les Holder, who worked at Ford, a measure of respect in the community. 'It was one of the main sources of employment in the area, and once you got the Ford badge,' he remembers, 'you were treated very highly by the shopkeepers in the area because the rate of pay was superior to any other at the time.'

For workers in the United States, discipline in the factories grew even tighter as competition among major car manufacturers increased the need to step up production even further. 'They were dictatorial, slave-drivers,' remembers Warren Hart, who started working at Ford in 1919. 'You had a set figure to produce...and if you didn't do that, then you were criticized or maybe moved to another location.' John DeAngelo was sixteen years old when he and his father went to work at Highland Park. He stayed at Ford for the rest of his working life, but his father lasted less than a day. 'Look,' he told his son, 'if you want to stay here, you stay here. I think these people are crazy. I wouldn't work here.' He found it so bad that he did not even go back to collect his pay for the three hours he had worked.

In 1927 work was finally completed on a new Ford factory on the River Rouge in Dearborn, Michigan, and in December of that year Ford introduced a new car, the Model A, to replace the now outmoded Model T. The River Rouge plant was the biggest factory complex in the world, employing some 80 000 people. It included a foundry to make steel for the car bodies, an electricity generating plant, a glass works, a railway and a port – all the manufactured and raw materials needed to make the cars were owned by the company. Iron ore, coal, sand and rubber went in at one end, and Model As drove out the other.

THE COMPANY TOWN

L OW-COST COMPANY HOMES were provided for workers in the mill towns and villages of industrial Britain and the United States long before the days of mass production. Pioneered for textile workers in Scotland and in the United States, the company town continued to flourish until the 1930s.

Some companies experimented with model communities. In addition to housing set in attractive landscapes and green parks, workers and their families were offered education, recreational and sometimes cultural facilities. In the town of Bourneville, built by the British firm of Cadbury, employees were offered gardening classes as an antidote to the tedium of the factory; medical care and social reforms were also introduced. At Port Sunlight in Britain, a model industrial village built for the workers of the Lever Brothers soap and detergent company, residents had access to clubs, a theatre, a church and an art gallery; houses were built there until 1934. N.O. Nelson, a manufacturer of plumbing equipment, went even further, providing residents of Leclaire, Illinois with a library, dance pavilion and cooperative stores. The town's population grew from 400 workers in 1890 to 2000 in 1934.

Company towns were not always appreciated by those who lived in them. The paternalistic policies of employers were often reinforced; they took responsibility not just for people's jobs but for the homes and personal lives of their workers. Workers could not own their homes, and had little say in local affairs. In some towns there were even rules governing behaviour. Residents of some of the mill villages redesigned for the growing textile industries of the southern United States from 1917 were not allowed to smoke or drink; their children, who left school at an early age to work in the factory, received instructions in industrial discipline. Strict guidelines for cleanliness and hygiene in the home issued by Johnson & Johnson in its factory town in Chicopee, Georgia were enforced by company nurses.

Some company towns were isolated from the outside world, and the constant presence of the factory and its pollution could shadow domestic life. Irene Keyser, who worked for Westinghouse Electric in the United States in the 1920s and grew up in its factory town, remembers how 'people worked very hard on their homes to keep them clean...the porches we had to clean every day because the smoke, little black cinders, would come right up to the porch.'

From about 1925, while mill villages declined as a result of changing social conditions, several companies in the American West – Climax in Colorado, DuPont in Washington and Trona in California – continued to build new towns around their factories. From the 1930s, however, workers increasingly resented the dependence the company town imposed, and changing industrial relations brought a revision of company responsibility.

WORKING COMMUNITIES *Not all families benefited from the improved housing companies could provide. Attracted by employment prospects in local industries, families such as this one in Pennsylvania in 1938 often put up with poor living conditions because of the need to live close to where the work was to be found.*

MAN AND MACHINE *are
the focus of* Modern
Times, *a phenomenally
successful Charlie Chaplin
film made in 1936 about the
manic nature of factory work.
It brought the message of the
overpowering character of
modern industry to many
people who had never
experienced the inside of a
factory for themselves.*

Following in his father's footsteps, Archie Acciacca got a job at the River Rouge where he was put in the stamping plant. He had been raised on a farm in the countryside and this was his first experience of factory work. 'When I first went in there,' he describes, 'I saw people working rather fast and I was wondering if I could do that.' Like most people, he got accustomed to it. 'Once you start that production going…you have just got to think, I have got to keep up with this line, because if you didn't keep up with the line, you're in trouble.' As John DeAngelo remembers, 'You have got to make that production for them. If you weren't feeling good you couldn't say, I don't feel good so let me rest a couple of minutes, that was out of the question.'

In Britain plans were progressing for a scaled-down version of the River Rouge plant to replace the Manchester-based Ford factory, now unable to keep up with demand. The chosen site was at Dagenham, east of London. It was to be three times the size of Trafford Park, and like the Rouge, fully integrated, with access to the river Thames and a railway to bring in materials.

NEW CAR MODELS
(RIGHT) *like the highly
successful 1928 Chevrolet,
which outsold its Ford rivals,
were a sign of the
increasingly competitive
nature of the motor industry.
General Motors came to
include not only Chevrolet
but also – in ascending order
of cost –Pontiac, Oldsmobile,
Buick and Cadillac,
establishing it as one of the
United States' leading car
manufacturers. By 1930 the
United States dominated the
world car market.*

Work at any price

As the world economic depression of 1929 began to have an impact on the car industry, profits fell. The Model A Ford, outsold by rival cars, was discontinued. As sales plunged the River Rouge factory no longer needed to take on more workers. 'Thousands and thousands of people had been invited to come to this area, to work here,' as Paul Boatin remembers. 'They were being lied to.' Those lucky enough still to have a job needed to keep it at all costs. Mass unemployment in other industries meant that there were always new workers ready to fill the place of anyone who was dissatisfied, failed to keep up with the pace of production, or complained when wages were reduced.

Paul Boatin and his father joined the large crowd waiting for a job outside the Ford gates, across Miller Road. 'The majority of people just stood and stood, and waited and waited. You had a bunch of strangers, expressionless, looking down at the ground. They looked like they were half dead, hopeless. And when you looked into their eyes you thought maybe that is what you looked like too.' Espedito Valli, whose father already worked at Ford, remembers how cold it was waiting there. 'We stood out there in the yards, in a parking lot, like cattle out in the yard....We had to put newspaper under our coats, under our jackets, under our shirts, in order to stay warm....We stood in the severe cold for three, four hours at a time.'

There were similar queues outside the new Ford plant at Dagenham. When it opened in 1931, Britain too was in the depths of the Depression. The new factory brought much-needed work. Fred Ferguson grew up in Dagenham, and had seen the factory being built. Now he watched the influx of people in search of work. 'Two thousand workers with their families, which amounted to 7000 people, descended on Dagenham,' he recalls. Les Holder got a job there, and had to adjust to the new rhythm of work on the line. 'Start at half past seven. Finish at 12 noon. Half an hour lunch. Back on the job until 4 pm. These operations were very quick. So it was pick up, put it in the machine, clamp, press the button, drill the holes, retract, unclamp, and that is how it went on the whole time.' He made a hundred parts an hour.

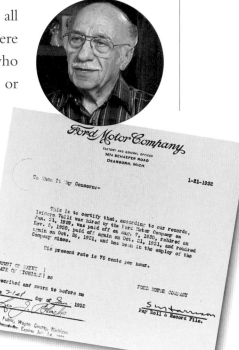

HIRING AND FIRING
employees at short notice was one direct effect of the Depression. Espedito Valli (ABOVE) remembers how his father 'was laid off about three times from 1929 to 1932' by Ford, which wrote him this letter confirming his fluctuating employment for tax purposes. When Espedito Valli finally got a job at Ford he wanted to leave. 'It was work, work, work – like a slave. You couldn't even move away from the assembly line where I worked without getting reprehended for it.'

VEHICLE OF CHANGE

MASS PRODUCTION on the land as well as in industry was made possible with the development of a new source of mobile power for the farm – the tractor. For hundreds of years farmers had depended on their own muscles and on horse power to plough their land and harvest their crops. It was at the turn of the century that tractors first began to replace horse and human power, and gradually took agricultural production to new heights.

The first tractor was made in Illinois in 1889; soon manufacturers in Canada and the United States began to design mobile machines, some with wheels and some with tracks, for ploughing. More farms adapted to new machinery, while many farm workers and their families were ·

leaving the land to find new jobs in factories and cities. Tractors enabled the farmer both to save labour costs and to cultivate land that had once been needed to grow fodder for the horses.

The first large market for tractors was in North America. In 1907 there were some six hundred tractors in the United States; by 1950 there were 3.4 million. The Fordson tractor, first made in 1917, was a huge success, and Ford quickly monopolized the home market. The Canadian manufacturers Massey Harris were eventually to become the world's largest tractor manufacturer.

In the 1920s, as agricultural production in Europe was picking up after the First World War, tractor sales to prosperous farmers increased there too. Adapting to the new tractors was not always easy. Len Sharman, who worked on a farm in Britain, can remember how the Fordsons were 'real demons to start in the cold mornings.... There was no cab. I've had two

overcoats on, two pairs of gloves, a pair of leggings, and still been so frozen I could howl with cold.'

As the rest of the world faced economic depression in the 1930s, the economy of the Soviet Union was expanding. Tractors began to play an important part in the attempt to meet the demanding new agricultural production targets. Thousands of tractor machine stations were set up to hire out tractors to collective farms. As well as importing thousands of machines from the United States, and the spare parts and expert advice needed to operate them, the Soviet Union began to produce its own tractors: the Stalingrad works alone were making 50 000 tractors a year by 1930, and within ten years there were more than half a million tractors at work. In just one generation, the tractor had transformed the age-old patterns of farming and brought mass production to agriculture.

TIME FOR TRACTORS
It was in Germany that stationary gasoline engines were first adapted for use in agriculture. Lanz was one of several companies that began to manufacture tractors at an early stage. By the late 1930s there were 60 000 tractors in Germany, which was also beginning to mass produce its highly successful version of the people's car – the Volkswagen.

The workers were under constant pressure to keep up, and men from the security lodge would walk along the overhead catwalk to ensure they did. 'If you were eating a sandwich or an apple, or not paying attention, or talking, that would be put down as a misdemeanour,' Les Holder recalls. 'There was always a queue of people outside the gate waiting to come in. You were paid by the hour, but you were dismissed by the minute.' It was the same at the Morris factory, as Les Gurl remembers. 'The foreman had absolute power over everybody who was in his shop, to hire and fire....You knew that those men were waiting outside the gates, so you never gave them a chance to get your job.'

In the United States the effects of the Depression were at their worst by 1932 in most manufacturing industries. David Moore, still waiting for a job at Ford, noticed a change in the atmosphere. 'The momentum was gaining every day. People were taking action. The people were in motion and it was all because of hunger, denial, disease, unemployment.' Discontent in Detroit

grew as, with no prior warning, the assembly lines came to a halt and the mighty Rouge plant was shut down. Anger erupted in Miller Road. Ford had promised work, but there was none. The men felt betrayed. Paul Boatin remembers, 'Ford said, "Anybody that wants to work, unless he's lazy, let him come," so we marched down towards Gate 3, the heart of the Ford Motor Company.'

As the workers in their thousands marched down Miller Road, they encountered a cordon of armed police. David Moore describes what happened. 'None of us were armed, we didn't come there to confront anyone. But you can imagine 80 000 people marching down a road, and for no reason at all on a cold day in March, six below zero, the water hoses are turned on you. And to see your friend being shot, blood running on Miller Road. All hell broke loose and that made people more determined than ever to do something. Out of that came a bond of brotherhood.' As Paul Boatin says, 'Instead of getting jobs, we got lead, we got bullets and blood. The workers had made their point, even though they didn't get any jobs.' Four men were killed at Miller Road that day. It marked a turning point for the men and women who worked on the American assembly lines.

STRIKING WORKERS
scuffle with police outside a Cadillac plant in Detroit. One of them struggles to hold aloft a placard bearing the slogan: 'This line is rough on rats'.

PAUL BOATIN (ABOVE) *and his fellow workers were featured in a mural based on the River Rouge plant by the Mexican artist Diego Rivera, commissioned by the Detroit Institute of Art. Paul Boatin describes its impact. 'The muscles, the brows, the strength that was shown in the faces was intimidating to some people because if they ever came off the wall they might prove dangerous.'*

Industrial action

The United Auto Workers (UAW) now began to recruit members among the workers of Detroit's car plants. The union offered hope of change to workers who had few means of bargaining with their employers over conditions, pay and hours of work, and who were under constant threat of dismissal. 'It was born out of desperation,' says Charlie White, who worked at the Fisher Body plant, part of the General Motors group. 'We'd just as soon there wasn't a need for a union. If they would give us what they rightfully should give us, there would be no need for it. But they couldn't see it.' Jim Sullivan, who worked at the Rouge, remembers how in the 1930s unions were associated with the radical element, and at first were treated with suspicion. But as they became more dissatisfied, the workers began to pay more attention to the union movement.

At first people often joined secretly, and did not necessarily tell even members of their own family. Jim Sullivan discovered that his father was a union member only during a discussion at the Sunday dinner table. 'I said to him, "Dad, if I stay at Ford's it's going to be a miracle. I don't like the way they are treating the people." So he said, "Well, Jim, you've got two things you can do. You can either quit or join the union." And I said, "Well, Dad, I belong to the union." And he said, "Thank God," and with that he flipped his collar and there was his union button.'

It could be dangerous to join the union. Ford's Protection Department employed strong-armed security men who watched union organizers carefully, intimidating and even assaulting them. Workers were scared of losing their jobs, and scared of the power of the Protection Department. Tom Jelley remembers how the department's boss, Harry Bennett, 'had the whole say of running the plant. And his goons, they would go into the toilets and you were sitting down there, and they would say, "Out!" – just like that. No dignity at all. So far as I'm concerned, that was one thing that brought the union in here.'

At the Morris factory in Cowley working conditions also deteriorated after four assembly lines were installed there in 1934. Some of the Morris workers decided to protest; in 1935 there was a stoppage in the B block trim shop. Lord Nuffield, as William Morris was now called, was as hostile to the unions as Henry Ford

A UNION MEMBERSHIP CARD *Joining the union was an important step for Steven Richvalsky, who worked at General Motors from 1935. But he remembers that the management's refusal to recognize or tolerate the unions made it necessary to be secretive. 'We were organizing clandestinely… no one was aware of it because if you got caught talking unionism at that time, you were automatically fired. You were finished. No questions asked, nothing.'*

TAKING A STAND *A crowd of strikers' families gathers outside New Bedford Mill in the United States in 1928 to listen to the president of Workers' International Relief. Powerful craft unions had long been established in the textile, engineering and coal mining industries. Public meetings helped to inform workers about their rights.*

WORKERS FIND A VOICE

THE NEW INDUSTRIES of the early twentieth century created a great mass of unskilled workers. Trade unions had originally been established to protect the wages and working conditions of skilled artisans and craftsmen; in the changing industrial climate a new 'industrial' unionism came into existence, not just to protect workers but to demand industrial power and also protection from the state.

Britain's old craft unions were supplemented by the rising number of unions recruiting unskilled or semi-skilled labourers, and transformed by their adoption of socialism. The union movement was represented by the Trades Union Congress (TUC).

During the First World War unions supported the war effort and accepted wartime controls. Shop stewards were elected to represent their fellow-workers' interests in discussions with management. After the war industrial relations deteriorated, coming to a head in the General Strike of 1926 when workers went on a sympathy strike in May after miners were threatened with pay cuts and longer working hours. During the 1930s more people joined the unions, which adapted in response to the changes in working conditions as mass production methods became more widespread. By 1935 there were four million union members in Britain.

In France, Germany and Italy the growth of unions was disrupted and concealed by wars, revolution and foreign occupation. Only after 1945 did powerful industrial unions, in some countries organized in communist, socialist or Roman Catholic federations, transform industrial relations. In the Soviet Union the communists succeeded in doing what the Italian fascists and German Nazis had also tried to do – making the trade unions subject to the ruling party and the machinery of the state.

In the United States the craft unions that formed the American Federation of Labor (AFL) had two million members by 1914, but here too the majority of unskilled workers, especially immigrants, women and black men, remained unaffiliated to unions in the booming industries of the 1920s – automobiles, steel, glass, electrical manufacturing. In 1935 John L Lewis led the way for unionization of these industries by forming the Committee for Industrial Organization (CIO). Soon workers in many mass production industries began to join CIO unions in large numbers, donning union badges and carrying membership cards.

Auto and steel workers strengthened their voice through the United Auto Workers (UAW) and the Steel Workers' Organizing Committee. By 1945 union membership reached an all-time high of almost fifteen million, more than 35 per cent of the non-agricultural workforce. Four million people were members of the CIO, which was eager to recruit black workers, and the rest belonged to the AFL. Many workers, especially new immigrants and black migrants from the South, were helped to join the mainstream of American economic and social life through their unions.

in Detroit and Giovanni Agnelli in Turin. 'Lord Nuffield reacted very quickly,' Les Gurl remembers. 'He put up large notices saying that he would not tolerate the union in his plant, and if the feeling in the plant among the people working there became strong enough to form a union, then he would shut the plant down.' Despite this threat, union leaders in Britain also recruited widely.

In the mid-1930s, as the Depression lifted, business at Ford was booming again. In 1935 alone Ford produced a million cars. Paul Boatin, David Moore and Espedito Valli finally managed to get jobs at the Rouge and a chance to earn a living, but at a price. 'We had to become complete strangers. You were being turned into a dead weight...worse than being a cog,' says Paul Boatin. 'Forget all the people that you had met out there. Forget all the bonds that you had established, forget all the new understandings, the little things we had told to one another. You felt complete frustration and isolation.' As they became angrier, workers began to talk in whispers about joining the union. David Moore, who was working in the foundry, met someone who said, ' "We're going to get a union in this place". He gave me some literature, and said, "Don't let anybody see you. Just put it in your pocket and read it when you get home." ' In mass production industries throughout the nation workers began to respond to greater drives for unionization made by the American Federation of Labour. Factory workers in their thousands began to join the newly formed Committee for Industrial Organization.

It was in France that the alienation and frustration of life on the line first boiled over into organized protest. Against a background of political turmoil a series of strikes erupted in 1936. They began in the aircraft and car factories, and then spread all over the country to different kinds of industries – to workers in department stores, hotels, restaurants and on farms. In May 35 000 auto workers in the Renault factory decided to stop working, incensed by speed-ups on the assembly line caused by higher production targets. 'We went from assembling 100 parts an hour to 110 and from there to 120,' remembers Arthur Herbaux. One day something snapped. 'We'd had enough. We weren't machines.'

The Renault workers downed their tools and occupied the factory. Their families brought them food. Management called in

"You couldn't tell a white man from a black man in the foundry – dust, smoke, the iron, sweat, the toilets....No consideration for an individual's health....The conditions in the plant at that time were almost unbearable."

DAVID MOORE

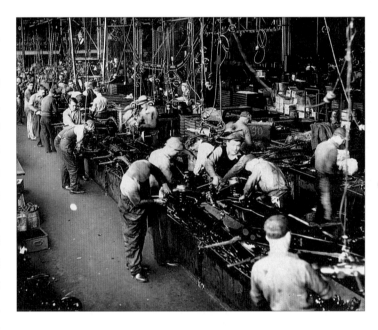

HARD AT WORK *Factory workers were often surrounded by loud and sometimes dangerous machinery. As Archie Acciacca remembers, 'When that press would come down and hit that die and there's thousands of machines operating at one time, it was very, very noisy.'*

DWARFED BY THE MIGHTY MACHINE (OPPOSITE) *A worker at the Fiat factory in Turin in 1934 poses beside the huge press from which he is pulling a red-hot steel crankshaft. During the 1930s the Fiat press office released a number of publicity photographs that glorified the power and beauty of machinery. Under fascism people were servants of the state as they were servants of the enterprises for which they worked.*

"You have no idea what a tremendous joy it was for everybody to get paid holidays. The whole of Paris, all the workshops, all the factories, everywhere people went crazy."

RACHEL LALLEMENT

ZENAIDE PROVINS
(ABOVE AND LEFT), *who worked at a plastics factory in France, took part in the workers' strikes in 1936. 'The men occupied the factories and the women would go there every day,' she remembers. 'We were pretty organized really. We played cards, we danced — we managed to have some fun too, it wasn't all bad.'*

the police. The workers locked the doors to keep them out. 'That's how the fight started,' Arthur Herbaux remembers. 'People hurled bolts, bits of wood, chairs...at the police to stop them from getting into the factories....I'm not saying it was right to occupy the factory,' he reflects, 'but it was necessary. The way we lived, the money we earned, it wasn't right. It had to change. We had to strike to get it, we had to get angry.' And it did bring changes. Social reform bills were passed through parliament. As well as a statutory forty-hour week they won holidays with pay. One factory worker, Zenaide Provins, took her very first holiday at the seaside. 'Although I was a Breton and I'd grown up just thirty kilometres away, I'd never seen it.'

The Renault workers had successfully demonstrated the vulnerability of the assembly line in the face of collective action. At the Rouge, union organizers also grew bolder. Jim Sullivan began secretly recruiting union members in his welding booth away from the watchful eye of the security men. David Moore was arrested for passing out union literature. In 1937 John DeAngelo also joined the UAW; many others were doing the same. But Ford retaliated. 'They started to fire people because they were active in the union, so then at Ford's it died out,' John DeAngelo recalls.

In 1937 another confrontation over recognition of the union erupted. This time it was between workers and management at the General Motors plant in Flint, Michigan. Howard Washburn remembers how it began. When he went to his workstation, 'The foreman said, "Let's go to work". We said, "No, we are not working, we are on strike".' For several weeks workers controlled the Fisher Body Plant No. 2 in a sit-down strike, resisting the police and soldiers of the National Guard until the company finally agreed to recognize the union.

For Howard Washburn the success of the strike meant that the workers now had a new voice. 'If you had a grievance you could have somebody to take it up for you...and they set up a seniority system, which they never had before.' He realized that the workers at General Motors in Flint were lucky compared with their Ford counterparts. 'Ford was terrible. He was the biggest anti-union person in the world....They had some terrible times.' The victory of workers at General Motors inspired others to act.

STRIKING FOR CHANGE
United Auto Workers picketing the Ford plant in St Louis, Missouri in 1937 during a strike. The workers showed that collective action could give them the power to stop the assembly lines and halt production.

FACTORY OCCUPATION
(BELOW) in the form of sit-ins gave the workers at General Motors power over their employers. But management sometimes retaliated with tactics of its own. Lock-outs were designed to prevent workers from entering the factories.

In 1941 union organizers at the Ford factory tried again. Paul Boatin saw one union official assaulted by company service men for speaking publicly to the workers. 'They pulled his coat over his head and they broke his ribs. They were trying to teach the union a lesson.' The assault had the opposite effect. The spark that set off the final explosion was a fight between a foreman and a worker; at this, the workers decided to strike. 'Force was going to get us what we wanted,' says John DeAngelo.

The Rouge was shut down again, but this time the workers were in control. When David Moore pushed a red button to stop the assembly line, his foreman immediately rushed over to him.

'Strike is settled' *announces the newspaper headline to the delight and relief of the workers at the Fisher body plant who had put their jobs at risk in the struggle for better working conditions. Now these men, many of whom had remained in the factory throughout the weeks of the occupation, could return home to their families.*

Industrial mobilization (OPPOSITE) *became top priority as the United States prepared for war in 1941. As civilian car production was set aside for war production, women filled the places of the workers who had gone to war. Britain's factories had begun making weapons in 1935; after 1939 factories in France, Germany, Italy and the Soviet Union were relocated to remote sites to avoid air attacks. By 1945 a fifth of the United States' military output had come from its automobile factories.*

'"What the hell do you think you're doing?" I said, "Strike! Strike!" Everybody went out hollering, "Strike! Strike!"' All they had to do, Jim Sullivan remembers, was shout, ' "We're on strike!" I felt real good. I was jigging and dancing. I made history, I shut down the Ford Motor Company!' Archie Acciacca was working the afternoon shift when he heard what was happening, and he shut down his press. 'Masses of people got together. Some of them went over there with crowbars and what have you, and busted the windows....The whole plant shut down that afternoon.' John DeAngelo recalls how 'a big march went to Gate 4 and all around. And we picketed there, until seven days later Henry Ford said, "Get these people in here and give them what they want".'

Working together

Ford signed its first contract with the UAW in July 1941. The contract guaranteed the assembly line workers a seniority system, health insurance and a pension. It also gave them something more than that. Jim Sullivan sums up what he felt that was. 'You got a little bit of human dignity,' he says. 'You had someone standing with you. Before, you had nothing to say about anything. In order to make progress you have got to learn to walk. In order to walk, you have to get off your knees. And that is what we did in 1941. We got off our knees, and we took some giant steps.' For Archie Acciacca things went from one extreme to the other, 'From almost being a slave to being the guy that is running the plant.'

After the conflicts between mass production workers and management, which had been centred on the car industry, both sides came to realize that it was in their interest for factories to run smoothly. The workers gained greater recognition and were able to participate in decisions about what they did and how they did it, even if management stayed in control; the workers recognized that ultimately their pay depended on efficient production. Trade unions continued to grow as the United States entered the Second World War, and its factories concentrated on war production as those in Europe had already done. The war became more than a military conflict; the speed and efficiency of industrial production became part of the international struggle, and an essential element in the effort to defend democracy and freedom.

Sporting Fever

THE GROWING APPEAL OF SPORT

THE CENTENARIO STADIUM in Montevideo, Uruguay's capital, was so new at the start of the 1930 World Cup that the concrete was still soft. The Uruguayans were proud to be hosting this new event, and to be welcoming European teams to their country.

In the final the Uruguayan team met their neighbours and arch-rivals, the Argentinians, who had beaten them just once a few years before. When its team crossed the River Plate to Uruguay a popular Argentinian newspaper boasted, 'The World Champions Return to Montevideo'. A Uruguayan football coach, Ondino Viera, recalls the reaction this provoked. 'This was a declaration of war, and the championship developed into a great war between Uruguay and Argentina.'

On the day of the final supporters began to fill the stadium in the early hours of the morning. Some 90 000 fans managed to get in; a multitude had to stay outside. At half-time the Argentinians led by two goals to one. Gradually they gave way before the storm of sound from the stands and the sheer will to win of the Uruguayan team. Two-all.

Three-two. Four-two to Uruguay.

All through the night church bells rang, car horns blared, and ships' sirens wailed down at the waterfront, and the following day was declared a national holiday. Ondino Viera joined in the celebrations in Montevideo with some friends. 'The scene was almost indescribable...the celebrations began at the stadium and extended through all the streets of Montevideo. The enthusiasm included everyone: men, women and children....The parties lasted all week.' In Buenos Aires the defeated Argentinians raged; mobs took to the streets, even stoning the Uruguayan consulate, and diplomatic relations between the two countries were broken off.

Football was one of the many sports that both brought people together and divided them during the twentieth century. Sport could bring new opportunities, becoming a road to fame for poor children; it developed into an enormous industry, and reflected the competitiveness and pride of nations. It attracted millions of people, both as players and as spectators, as sporting fever spread across the world.

EMBRACING VICTORY *Triumphant Uruguayan players rejoice in their success in the first World Cup.*

Amateurs and professionals

By the time the 1930 World Cup took place in Uruguay, English football had already become firmly established as a professional sport played for mass audiences. At the turn of the century it was played in many countries throughout the world – from Austria, Belgium, France, Germany, the Netherlands, Russia, Sweden, Switzerland and Turkey to South America. It was introduced by the British, whose children played football, rugby and cricket in the private schools and who as adults continued to play for personal enjoyment rather than for financial gain. Similarly, in Canada and the United States baseball, boxing and American football, which developed out of college rugby, were played at an amateur level. By 1900 there were also professional footballers and cricketers in Britain, and professional baseball players and boxers in the United States. Separate organizations catered for professionals, who needed to play for money, and for amateurs, who could afford to play for pleasure.

The amateur ideal of playing for enjoyment of the game and the desire to win, rather than for money, inspired the revival of the ancient Greek Olympic Games by a Frenchman, Baron Pierre de Coubertin. The first modern Games, held in 1896, also took place in Greece. The amateur ethic was at first rigidly enforced. At the 1912 Olympics in Stockholm, an American athlete forfeited his medals after it had been revealed that he once accepted payment for playing baseball in a minor league. At this stage the talent and skill of individuals was regarded as more important than national pride and prestige, though from the 1908 Games competitors entered as members of national teams rather than as individuals.

National pride became all too real during the First World War. When it ended and the troops returned, people could begin to settle back into peacetime life and interest in sport revived. In the 1920s the number of hours in the average working week was reduced, and at the same time wages were increased. There was a hunger for excitement among those who had more leisure time to enjoy and more money to spend, and by the 1920s sport began to attract larger and larger audiences. Sports journalism ensured that people could read about their favourite game in the new sporting magazines and newspapers, while sport itself offered exciting

CROWDS LINE THE STREETS *to watch the cyclists flash by. Local and national press follow the progress of the great Tour de France all over the country. Launched at the beginning of the century as a publicity venture to improve sales of a new sporting newspaper, the race quickly became popular. Initially covering more than 2000 km (1250 miles), its route soon extended over 5745 km (3570 miles).*

LEADING MARATHON RUNNER *Dorando Pietri in the 1908 Olympics. In a gesture characteristic of the times, when he collapsed at the finishing line officials helped him across it.*

TURNING TO TENNIS

THE YOUNG FRENCH TENNIS STAR Suzanne Lenglen caused a sensation when she appeared at Wimbledon in the 1919 British championships. She was a formidable player who, wearing a simple, calf-length, sleeveless dress that attracted as much comment as her sporting prowess, successfully challenged not only her opponents but also existing attitudes to women in sport. She fuelled women's sporting aspirations by winning six championships in Britain, six in France, and two gold medals at the 1920 Olympic Games. The press, devoting more space to sport as its popularity grew, needed players who could be fashioned into sporting personalities, and Suzanne Lenglen gained worldwide fame.

At the turn of the century tennis was one of the limited number of sports that were regarded as suitable activities for women. It was possible to play badminton, croquet and golf, to dance, ride and skate in the long, heavy clothes and restricting corsets that women were accustomed to wearing; but it was difficult to be more active until new freedoms were expressed in new fashions.

At a time when women were struggling for political recognition and for better opportunities in education, their participation in many sports was also deliberately obstructed. The arguments against higher education – that too much study would damage women's health in general and their ability to have children in particular – were also given as reasons for discouraging women from playing any but the most genteel sports. Field sports and team games were both deemed unsuitable, and only non-competitive gymnastics were acceptable. At the 1908 Olympic Games there were only three events in which women could compete. Both gymnastics and track and field events were excluded from the 1920 and 1924 Games. In defiance of this policy, separate Women's Olympics were held at four-yearly intervals between 1922 and 1934; they attracted competitors from many parts of the world, and drew many spectators too. Gradually, women's place in sport began to be accepted as it was in other fields.

entertainment to people looking for ways to enjoy themselves. John Cracknell, a cricket and football enthusiast, remembers how important sport was when he was growing up in London. 'There weren't the activities in those days that there are now....Sport was the great thing in your life.' As public interest grew, commercial interest in sport also gained momentum.

LEAPING TO VICTORY
Suzanne Lenglen competing at Wimbledon, where she dominated the Centre Court for six years.

JOE LIGUORI *outside the butcher's shop where he worked. Of the Dempsey–Carpentier match he remembers that 'the excitement of all the people and the stadium that they built was unbelievable'.*

A growing audience

Professional boxing showed the direction in which sport was now heading, by demonstrating how much money could be made. It had always attracted money; betting on the outcome of a prize-fight had been popular ever since boxing rose above the level of street brawls. An American boxing promoter, Tex Rickard, was one of the first to capitalize on its great money-making potential. In 1921 he staged a match in New Jersey between the American fighter Jack Dempsey and a French war hero, Georges Carpentier. Dempsey had been a professional boxer since 1914, and became world champion at his first attempt in 1919. To accommodate the huge crowd he intended to draw, Rickard built a temporary wooden stadium in an empty plot in Jersey City. Joe Liguori, who was twelve years old at the time, lived just down the street. 'I used to come and watch them build the stadium,' he remembers. 'It was a very exciting thing to see. And they built it in such a short time. Within a matter of weeks they had it up.'

Before long the novelty and scale of Rickard's plans and the unprecedented media promotion he obtained promised to justify his claim that this would be the fight of the century. Fans came from as far away as California and even Europe. Joe Liguori was

THE HUGE ARENA (RIGHT) *that Tex Rickard had ambitiously conceived to stage the 1921 world heavyweight boxing championship was built within weeks. By filling it to capacity he demonstrated sport's great potential for entertaining huge audiences.*

taken to the match by his boss. 'I was all excited about it – at that age I had never been to a fight. On the night of the fight you couldn't walk the street there were so many people around. The whole downtown area of Jersey City was just cluttered with cars. It was one of the biggest events I remember....It put Jersey City right on the map.'

Hundreds of reporters and telegraph operators arrived to relay the news to the world on live radio. More than 90 000 people poured into the stadium, the largest crowd ever assembled for a sporting event. Admission prices rose to as much as fifty dollars, the highest ever charged. The audience included celebrities whose presence gave a new stamp of social approval to this once renegade sport. The fight of the century was a short one. It was all over by the fourth round: Jack Dempsey won, and rose to superstardom overnight. Tex Rickard became a rich man; altogether Dempsey made him over $10 million. Boxing was now mainstream popular entertainment for thousands of people. The purpose-built stadium was dismantled shortly afterwards, but the big business of mass sport was here to stay.

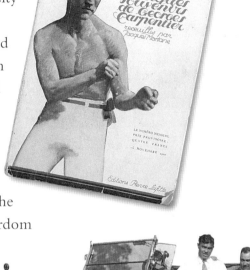

THE LUXURY LIMOUSINE *beloved of Jack Dempsey – he owned six of them – symbolizes the affluent lifestyle his boxing success brought him. Winning the world heavyweight championship against French boxer Georges Carpentier (*TOP*, featured on the cover of a monthly magazine) established Dempsey as a popular hero who had risen from obscurity to fame and fortune.*

Spectator's passions

The Dempsey–Carpentier fight proved such a successful business venture for Rickard because it provided wonderful entertainment. People were prepared to pay to watch the spectacle. The 1920s were not as prosperous in Europe as they were in the United States, and people had less money to spare than their American counterparts, but in Britain too people now worked fewer hours a week and sport played an important part in their lives. Billy O'Donnell grew up in Liverpool; he remembers the times as 'bad days – squalor, disease, vermin…it was terrible.' In the summer he played football barefoot in the street. 'We'd make a ball out of rags, old clothing or paper, with string, and we'd be playing till eleven or twelve at night.' For him and many like him, sport, and football in particular, provided a welcome escape from the poverty and hardship of the postwar years. For Sidney Garner, a loyal supporter of the London team West Ham, football provided 'relief from work, from war…it was a way out. In the late 1920s the times were very hard.'

The enthusiasm that drew large crowds to watch boxing, and the even more popular baseball, in the United States, had also taken root in Britain. Football had become a passion, especially among people in the industrial north of England and in Scotland. Before 1900 a handful of professional teams had attracted huge crowds in Liverpool, Manchester, Newcastle and Glasgow, and public support for the game grew rapidly throughout the country. By the 1920s there were more than eighty professional football clubs. When he was a little older and could earn some money, Billy O'Donnell went to watch his local team play every Saturday. 'It was always football in Liverpool. Nothing else. That was the only recreation at the weekend. There was very little on at the cinemas. Football was the main thing for most lads my age. You looked forward to Saturday coming. There was an old-time fruit market where I lived, and I'd go there at six o'clock in the morning to earn a few coppers. If I earned a sixpence I'd give half to my mother and

STREET FOOTBALL, *unlike many other sports, required no special equipment or location. Wherever adults had established football, children too could be found playing the game, reflecting football's fast-growing popularity.*

I'd put the other threepence away so I could go to the match on a Saturday. Everything, as far as I was concerned, was football on a Saturday. I sold papers as well to boost it up. Things were really bad in those days.' He could not afford a seat in the covered stand, so with his friends he would stand on the open terraces, following the game in all weathers, one week from the Kop, the cheap end at Liverpool football club's ground at Anfield, the next week at Goodison Park, home of Liverpool's great rivals, Everton.

The football industry was growing quickly and becoming increasingly commercial, but the ritual gathering of fans and their passionate team loyalties remained. Sidney Garner would turn up at matches to support West Ham wearing a hat and scarf in the team colours, brandishing his rattle. Football became a focal point for whole communities, with friends meeting regularly at the weekly match to enjoy themselves together. 'I would go with most of my footballing pals….Saturday or Sunday we'd all go together,' Sidney Garner recalls.

As more and more fans flocked into the spectator stands, new and larger stadiums were needed to accommodate them. In 1923 a new stadium complex opened at Wembley, in the London

Football cards

COLLECTING CIGARETTE CARDS *was a popular pastime for football fans. As Billy O'Donnell explains, 'If you got ten cigarettes you got a picture….That's if you could afford to buy the ciggies. They went in sets of about fifty. If you didn't have one or two, you could swap them with your friend – maybe he'd have what you didn't have.'*

SIDNEY GARNER (BELOW, *in the top hat*) *and his friends followed their team around the country, jubilant when it won and broken-hearted when it lost. Thousands of supporters turned up for every match, following the game and enjoying the shared excitement.*

(BELOW) *The Littlewoods pools were started in 1923. After an initial distribution thirty-five coupons were returned, and the winning dividend was £2.60; by the 1930s about ten million people participated, with winnings of up to £30 000.*

suburbs. It catered not only for football matches but for other events including tennis, boxing, ice hockey and greyhound racing.

That year a huge crowd flocked to Wembley to watch the Football Association Cup Final. 'All everybody wanted to see was the big game. It was the first cup final played at Wembley,' recalls Sidney Garner, who went to the match with his friends. So many people were trying to get in that the crowds overflowed onto the pitch. 'We made our way towards the main gates, and there were literally thousands of people. We couldn't go where we wanted to go. We had to go where the crowd pushed us....All of a sudden there was a great surge at the back, fences went down...a lot of people fell, got trampled on.' Mounted police, led by just one policeman on a white horse, managed to push the crowds back off the pitch so the match could begin. Nothing like this had ever happened before, and it confirmed the enormous popularity that professional football had now acquired.

CROWDS FLOOD THE PITCH *at the first cup final to be held at Wembley Stadium. As Sidney Garner explains, 'It was made to hold a hundred thousand. Well, that day there must have been two hundred thousand.' It took three-quarters of an hour to clear the pitch before the game could begin.*

The fever spreads

As interest in football spread it had a similar effect on other European nations, arousing in many people around the world more passion than any other sport. By 1929 there were more than 3500 football clubs in France, while in Austria a wealthy Austrian businessman and an English coach had produced a *Wunderteam*. Publishing and broadcasting helped the sporting fever to spread: in France *Le Vélo* kept sports fans informed; Italians could follow their favourite team in the daily *La Gazzetta dello Sport*; thousands of enthusiasts bought the German weekly *Der Kicker*. International governing bodies were established to regulate the game in different countries, and to set uniform rules as professional leagues were introduced.

Popular passion, national fervour and commercial investment were also extending beyond Europe, to South America and later to Africa and Asia. Football had been introduced to South America by the families of British administrators of the mines, railroad, waterworks and telephone companies in Uruguay. Diego Lucero, who played for Uruguay in the 1920s, describes how the game developed: 'It was a novelty…they called it the game of the crazy English, because they wore short pants….It was a strange game, and very difficult to understand, but the local kids watched them play, and they imitated the players, and began to think they were better than them.' United by the game, locals began to play in the English teams, and eventually formed their own. 'In 1915 we founded our football club,' Diego Lucero recalls. 'In 1916 we joined the league to play championships, and we were born. We were big, we were strong, we were proud. So, there the journey of football had begun.' The local style of play evolved differently. The English, in heavy boots, played a hard, physical game, with long, high passes, while the South Americans played the ball along the ground, a subtle, athletic game; in their soft, flexible shoes they soon outplayed the big boots.

Organized championships were held in Uruguay, and soon extended to neighbouring countries. Diego Lucero remembers how the great rivalry that soon developed between Uruguay and Argentina made matches particularly important. 'The international games between Argentina and Uruguay were, at first, great social

FOR DIEGO LUCERO *in Uruguay football was an opportunity to establish a sense of community, increasing people's pride in themselves and their country. 'Football was a great benefit…from the social and economic point of view, it held extraordinary importance. Without a doubt it was a great thing football players did for the country.'*

The World Cup

THE MOST COVETED TROPHY *in football was named after the Frenchman Jules Rimet, who proposed the tournament. Held every four years, it was the first official international competition and provided a showcase for the world's best players.*

NATIONAL HEROES *in international sport. The players of Uruguay and Argentina's rival football teams became famous names and faces at home, and ambassadors for their countries – little known outside South America – when they competed overseas.*

gatherings. The ladies came all adorned, the president of the Republic, all the ministers....The times were changing, and the upper class was losing its affection for football. The popular flood was taking its place, and converting it into a more rugged, rustic, people's spectacle.'

Football in South America not only provided a new spectacle for the people, it also brought new opportunities for wealth and fame to players, strengthened national identity and enabled poorer countries to compete on equal terms with rich industrial nations. In the international arena the Uruguayan team dazzled the Europeans at the 1924 and 1928 Olympics, winning two gold medals. When the team arrived in Paris for the 1924 Olympics, they found that their opponents had never even heard of Montevideo. In Diego Lucero's view, football completely changed the Europeans' attitude to his country. 'The people of the world began to look at their maps to see where Uruguay was. They became interested in its population of 1 800 000 inhabitants; interested in the products of its land, especially in the meat.' When Uruguay hosted the first ever World Cup in 1930, and went on to win it, the country gained even greater renown.

PRESENTING THE ITALIAN AND HUNGARIAN TEAMS
By the time the World Cup was held in Paris in 1938 the rites and ceremonies of football were well established. Playing the national anthem of the competing teams before a match began reminded both players and spectators that national pride was at stake.

Sporting heroes, sporting fans

While sport brought new status to the nations of South America, in North America it elevated individuals to the status of heroes. People's passion for the sport meant that players could now make a living from it. In no sport was this more true than in baseball, the national pastime of the United States. Like football in Britain, baseball had long been an important part of American life, growing in popularity since the first professional teams emerged in the 1870s. It was cheap to play, it was fun at any skill level, and it required no elaborate playing field or equipment. In the new sporting environment of the 1920s baseball thrived, its audiences grew, and national heroes soon emerged.

William Werber, who went on to play with the New York Yankees team after graduating from college, grew up playing baseball in the Washington DC area. It was *the* game for him and his friends, who played on unused ground. 'Our cities didn't have as much concrete on them as they've got today,' he explains. 'They had vacant areas where people would scrape off the grass....Every spring a whole mess of kids at agreed upon times would come there with lawn mowers and hand scythes and hoes, and we'd scrape out the infield and get it in shape and then cut out the outfield....And that's where we played, all summer long.'

Close to the newly built Yankee stadium in the Bronx area of New York, an immigrant family from Germany ran a steak restaurant. Anna Daube Freund and her sisters grew up with the game. 'Baseball and everything that had to do with getting you out of the whole Depression feeling was important, so sports were still a good outlet....We would go to ball games rather than the movies. And my worst punishment was to be told, "You cannot go to the ball game".' Anna Freund got to know all the Yankee players, including William Werber. They were all well-known stars, but the biggest star of all was Babe Ruth. She remembers walking home to the restaurant from her grandmother's house and finding the street full of people. 'They were all saying, "Babe Ruth's in there!" When we went in actually the whole 1927 team was there, but Babe was the calling card.'

Babe Ruth, a self-styled 'bad kid' who had been brought up in a home for 'incorrigibles' in Baltimore, joined the Yankees in

The baseball cap

THE PEAKED CAP *worn by baseball players to shield their eyes from the sun was soon adopted by fans of the game. Designed in team colours and carrying team emblems, it became a badge of loyalty, and eventually a popular piece of headgear among fashion-conscious youngsters even in countries where baseball was not played.*

PLAYING BASEBALL IN THE STREET *was almost a national pastime for American children. All that was required was a ball, a bat and possibly a mitt. For William Werber, 'It was not organized ball. It was not sponsored by anybody.' In the United States baseball crossed social barriers as football did in other parts of the world – anyone could play.*

THE FREUND GIRLS
played baseball with anyone
who wished to join in. Anna
Freund remembers that there
were 'Germans, Italians,
Polish, Jewish, Irish and we
all seemed to get along very
well. There wasn't any
discrimination about
who was going
to play.'

1919. His combination of skill, strength and coordination brought him an unprecedented numbers of home runs – when a player gets round all three bases and back to the plate with one great hit into the stands. Those hits (made possible by the introduction of a harder, livelier ball), soaring into excited crowds, transformed the face and popularity of baseball. No one ever bettered Babe Ruth's record: sixty home runs in the summit season of his career, 1927. He was the biggest commercial draw in the history of the game, and it made him rich. 'He was the first eighty-thousand dollar ball player,' recalls Anna Freund. 'It was really incredible because most of them were making five thousand dollars a year. And that was, for some, a lot of money.' It was largely due to Babe Ruth that the Yankees built a new stadium to cater for the growing numbers of spectators, and became baseball's most popular team.

Even in the hard years of the 1930s baseball's popularity continued to grow, and players could still earn a fortune. The Freund family was just one of the many immigrant families for whom baseball was part of the business of becoming an American. It crossed national boundaries too. Organized baseball had been played in Mexico and Cuba since the nineteenth century, and in Japan it was elevated to the status of a national sport.

Britain's bat and ball game was cricket. It too produced popular heroes; it too was a spectator sport with a mass following, and one that everyone could play. From the age of eight John Cracknell would join the older boys on Saturday afternoons at their local ground, the Oval in south London, specially to watch the outstanding batsman Jack Hobbs. 'I lived about a mile away from the Oval. And once it came through that Hobbs was batting

SPORTING MAGAZINES
(RIGHT) *were published that*
were aimed specifically at
young people, who rushed to
buy the new range of
newspapers and magazines,
hoping to read about their
sporting heroes as well as
glean tips on how to improve
their own game.

SUPPORTERS JOSTLE
THEIR HERO, *Babe Ruth.*
As Anna Freund describes,
'He never refused any child
his signature...when children
were around and they were
accessible to the players, the
players felt that they were
our idols, and they were...
Babe Ruth had that kind
of charisma'.

TIP TOP WEEKLY

"An ideal publication for the American Youth"

Issued weekly By Subscription, $2.50 per year. Entered as Second Class Matter at the N. Y. Post Office by STREET & SMITH

No. 170.   **Price, Five Cents.**

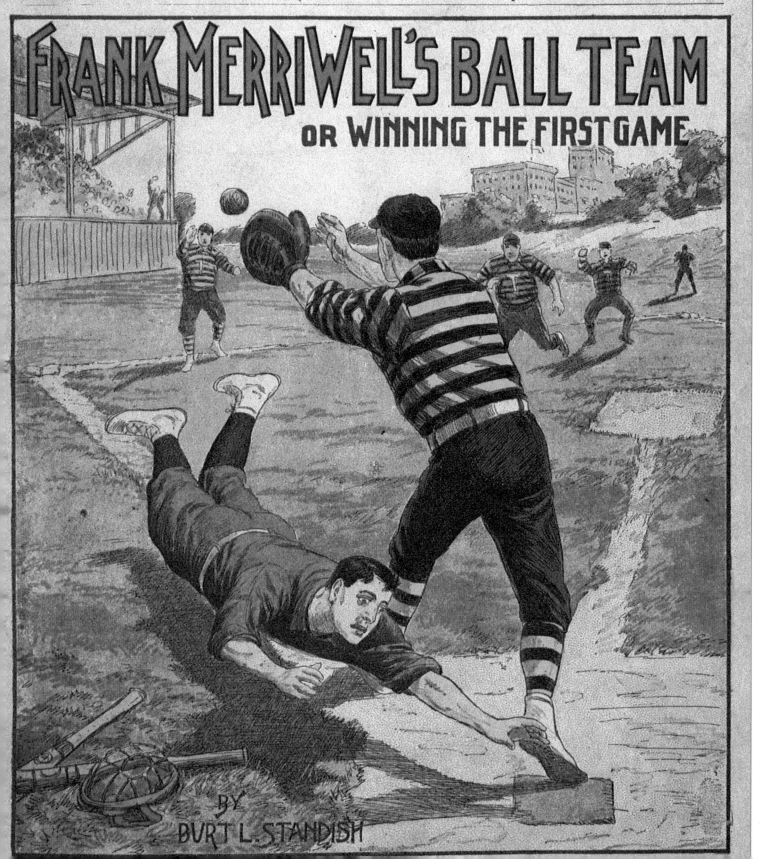

FRANK MERRIWELL'S BALL TEAM
OR WINNING THE FIRST GAME

BY
BURT L. STANDISH

we would go indoors, get some money from our parents and run all the way up to the Oval, just to see Jack Hobbs bat. He certainly drew you there.'

Jack Hobbs was England's greatest cricketer, scoring 197 centuries in his long professional career. He played for England in sixty-one test matches and scored a record 61 237 runs. Like Babe Ruth, Hobbs drew the crowds. 'I thought he was tremendous,' John Cracknell remembers, 'his technique was so good and he was always very composed...an absolute hero. People would go to see Jack Hobbs bat, that's what they went for.' Another fan, Bert Culver, also remembers the crowds at the Oval. 'It was amazing, the enthusiasm in those days....We were really squashed...and it was most uncomfortable really, but we didn't notice that because we were so enthralled.'

In cricket it was the international games, the test matches, that drew the largest crowds of all. John Cracknell was not allowed to watch the matches himself, but he does remember the queues. 'Crowds used to line up all night long outside the Oval for the test matches, the place was packed....They queued up from, say, seven or eight o'clock in the evening till the following morning.' As Bert Culver, who did go to watch, explains, 'It was a different game in those days. It's not the same today, the cricket...test matches were very important.'

A test series in the 1932–33 season between Australia and England proved just how important cricket had become. The Australian team had a particularly brilliant young batsman from New South Wales, Don Bradman. The English had noticed his one weakness: he did not like really fast bowling. The English captain, Douglas Jardine, planned to exploit the speed of his fast bowlers, especially Harold Larwood, by adapting an old tactic – bodyline. Bowled with great accuracy, the balls would reach the batsman fast, high and in line with his body. As the ball reared up off the pitch the batsman would try to defend himself, and be caught out by the ring of close catchers surrounding him.

Among the Australian crowd at the third test, held at the Adelaide Oval, was eighteen-year-old Cec Starr. 'People were anticipating something would happen, and they didn't have very long to wait. Woodfull was hit just below the heart by a sharply

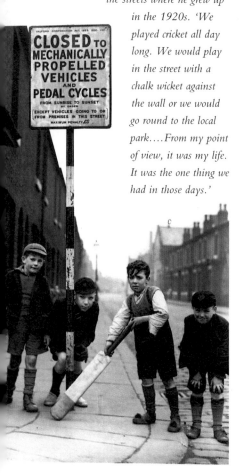

AN IMPROMPTU GAME OF CRICKET *In the 'playstreets' children could practise their favourite sport in peace. John Cracknell and his friends did little else in the streets where he grew up in the 1920s. 'We played cricket all day long. We would play in the street with a chalk wicket against the wall or we would go round to the local park....From my point of view, it was my life. It was the one thing we had in those days.'*

IT'S JUST NOT CRICKET *Douglas Jardine's bodyline bowling strategy, also known as leg theory, provoked unprecedented outrage during the 1932–33 tour and even threatened trading relations between Australia and England. It was seen as the end of cricket's gentlemanly tradition. As Bert Culver recalls, at that time test matches were 'always a life or death struggle, particularly with Australia'.*

IN REGRETFUL MEMORY OF CRICKETING IDEALS

PA?

LEG THEORY

rising ball and fell to the ground, dropping his bat, and some of the players went to his aid....The air became volatile, electric...the crowd really got terribly upset.' Two Australian players were hit that day, and the Australian press and public were vociferously hostile. The Australian Board of Control sent a telegram to the cricketing authorities in London, claiming that the England team's tactics were 'unsportsmanlike' and warning that friendly relations between the two countries were in danger. 'England were not very responsive,' Cec Starr explains. 'It was probably the first time in the history of the game that politicians had been requested to do something about the conduct of the game.'

The power of sport to stir the feelings of an entire nation affected other countries, too. Cricket, which had become popular all over the British empire – in India and the Caribbean as well as in Australia and New Zealand – gave whole communities a new sense of their collective worth, and would not be dominated by the privileged white world for much longer.

HEROES ON THE ROAD

IN 1900, ONLY TWELVE YEARS after the very first automobile was bought in Paris, thousands of people lined the route from Paris to Lyons to watch cars race by, excited by the rumour that there was one car capable of speeds as high as 80 km per hour (50 mph). A glamorous new sport had been born.

From the outset motor racing was a sport in which few could afford to participate but that attracted many spectators. It was also dangerous. On the first day of the 1903 Paris–Madrid race more than two million people stood to watch, some witnessing the accidents that caused the death of two drivers, two mechanics and several spectators. In Europe races were at first held on public highways over long distances. On roads built for horse-drawn vehicles, all except the leading driver were enveloped in a cloud of dust, and accidents were very common. To reduce risks, roads were closed to traffic while the race was held. Road racing dominated for about fifty years – races such as Le Mans, the Mille Miglia and Targa Florio.

In Britain road racing was banned, but special circuits were built instead: Brooklands opened in 1907. In the United States the Indianapolis Motor Speedway circuit opened the following year. These provided grandstands with a clear view of the circuit for the growing number of spectators. Motor racing soon became a commercial enterprise rather than an adventure for the rich. Early road races were not profitable, but the purpose-built racetracks, and in particular the circuits built in the 1920s and 1930s that combined the convenience of the racetrack with the demands of road racing, drew large crowds. Prize money attracted professionals who drove cars designed specially for racing. The skill of the driver was as important as the speed of the car; these masters of machines were much admired by the people who flocked to see them race.

LAP OF HONOUR (ABOVE) *Crowds applaud the Fiat team, winners of the Italian Grand Prix at Monza in 1923.*

The colour of sport

White supremacy was also being challenged in the boxing ring. In the United States boxing offered new opportunities for wealth and fame to successive waves of poor immigrants, who literally fought their way out of the slums of New York, Chicago and other big cities. First Irish-Americans dominated the ring, then they were challenged by Jewish, Polish and Italian-American boxers. But black boxers were often treated with hostility.

In 1910 the powerful middleweight Stanley Ketchel was knocked out by the black boxer Jack Johnson. In that year Johnson fought the retired champion, Jim Jeffries, and beat him as well. The publicity surrounding the fight was unprecedented, and so was the money paid to the fighters: $117 000 to the white loser; only slightly more, $120 000, to the black winner.

White America bitterly resented Jack Johnson's seven-year reign as heavyweight champion, and thereafter blacks were banned from championships until 1937. When one black champion did emerge who was capable of regaining the heavyweight crown, his backer warned him never to have his picture taken with a white woman, never to go into a nightclub alone – and to 'keep a solemn expression in front of the cameras'.

His name was Joe Louis Barrow, the son of poor Alabama farmers who had moved to Detroit. As a young man Eddie Futch, who had given up amateur boxing to become a trainer, belonged to the same boxing club as Joe Louis. 'Now imagine me...feeling that after Jack Johnson I would never see another black heavy-weight champion. I was standing shoulder to shoulder with Joe Louis, with this thought in mind, that I would never see one, that I'd never live that long.'

Eddie Futch remembers that Joe Louis 'had so much ability, and by the boxing writers coming up with their opinions on this great-looking prospect, the promoters in New York began to get the idea, "Why not use this talent? It's sensational". And so it was.' He was happy to have been proved wrong when Louis did eventually become the world heavyweight boxing champion.

CHALLENGING PREJUDICE *Jack Johnson (centre) became the first black world heavyweight champion. Despite the appearance of racial harmony, the white sporting community was intent on maintaining its supremacy and produced numerous 'Great White Hopes' to challenge him. But it was seven years before Johnson conceded the title.*

MONTREAL ROYALS (RIGHT) *meet the Dodgers in Daytona, Florida. Jackie Robinson (seen here with another black sportsman, Johnny Weight) was the first black player to be signed up for a major International League club, heralding the end of segregated baseball.*

RAISING THE FIST
*Flanked by his trainer and
manager, and surrounded by
officials and well-wishers, Joe
Louis celebrates his victory
over James Braddock in the
eighth round of the world
heavyweight championship in
Chicago in June 1937.*

IN A LEAGUE OF THEIR OWN

BASEBALL WAS PROMOTED as a sport open to all, but black players were excluded from the big league teams. The stage for black talent was the Negro National League.

The NNL was a big success. The teams toured the nation, playing to huge mixed-race crowds in big league stadiums at big league prices. The high point of the season was the East–West All-Star Game in Chicago, which drew crowds of more than 30 000 people.

Although players earned half the wages paid to their white counterparts, the Negro leagues were among the largest black-owned businesses in the United States. They also helped sell thousands of copies of black newspapers to a white as well as black readership. The all-star teams were chosen by readers voting through the two largest black newspapers.

Professional black baseball stars were symbols of achievement for black people: they had excitement, glamour, and more money than most blacks could ever hope to earn. Yet life was still hard. They played every day of the year, and up to three matches a day. In the winter players went south to Florida, Cuba or Mexico, where they could enjoy the warm weather and mix with white people both on and off the baseball diamond. One player, Willie Wells, told a reporter in Mexico, 'Not only do I get more money playing here, but I am not faced with the racial problem. In the United States everything I did was regulated by colour. Here in Mexico I am a man.'

The NNL implicitly recognized segregation, but its founders hoped their teams would make it to the major leagues. Although that did not happen, their huge popularity paved the way for individuals to win acceptance. As white sports columnist Dan Parker wrote, 'There is no good reason why, in a country that calls itself a democracy, intolerance should exist on the sports field, that most democratic of all meeting places.' When Jackie Robinson signed with the Montreal Royals in 1946 it was just the beginning; within a few years, a high proportion of all major league players would be black, as their skill became more significant than the colour of their skin.

FEB 14   FIGURE SKATING CARNIVAL
SAT MAR 17 K OF C TRACK MEET
...IN WRESTLING ALL STAR CARD
CIRCUS OPENS HERE EARLY IN APRIL!

DAILY NEWS A.A.

TRINITY CLUB

Joe Louis had fought his first professional match in 1934; within a year he defeated the Italian heavyweight champion Primo Carnera, who had recently killed an American boxer in the ring. Another twelve months later Louis suffered one of his rare defeats: he was knocked out in the twelfth round of a fight against the German heavyweight Max Schmeling. These fights began to take on a new political significance as in both Italy and Germany fascist governments began to issue their challenge to democracy.

A SEA OF SPECTATORS *surrounds the ring at Madison Square Garden. This enormous sports arena was built on the site of a railway station principally to provide a venue for boxing contests in New York.*

The political arena

By the 1930s people's passion for sport – whether baseball, boxing, football, cricket or athletics – had firmly established it as an activity to be exploited for commercial gain and national prestige. As national identity became increasingly linked with sporting success, winning or losing could unite or divide not just communities but entire nations. The desire to win international sporting events at any cost intensified as political tensions across the world were heightened. In the turbulent atmosphere of the late 1930s politital leaders took advantage of people's sporting passions, manipulating their feelings to build up nationalistic fervour and increase hostility towards regimes and peoples in other countries.

Football was adopted both by the communist government in the Soviet Union and by the fascists in Italy, whose national team dominated international competition in the 1930s. In the Soviet Union sport became an important instrument in creating the new Soviet man and woman. In Italy it was included as a weapon of foreign policy with the intention of arousing both fear and respect, and added to the determination that resulted in two successive victories in the World Cup, in 1934 and 1938. The Nazi ideal of populating Germany with a new Aryan super-race was also promoted through athleticism and sporting achievement.

It was against this background that 70 000 people entered the Yankee Stadium in New York in June 1936 to watch Joe Louis fight Max Schmeling. Protesters denounced Schmeling as a Nazi, while the Nazis criticized him for demeaning the white race by fighting a black man. Despite his colour, Louis won the support of the American public; for black people he had become a symbol of their faith in democracy and their hopes for fair treatment within the American democratic system.

Sam Lacy, who worked as a journalist for more than fifty years and paid close attention to sports involving black athletes in the 1920s and 1930s, recalls that when Jack Johnson fought for the heavyweight title the press was against him, but when Joe Louis, 'with his squeaky-clean self, proved he could fight, the whole nation embraced him.' In his judgement, 'Joe Louis and Jackie Robinson had a greater impact on social life in America than any other individual, including Dr Martin Luther King'.

POLITICS IN THE RING
Despite what the match between Joe Louis and Max Schmeling in 1936 came to stand for – political hostility between Germany and the United States – the souvenir issue of the boxing magazine The Ring *offered the public genuine sporting statistics on the two contestants.*

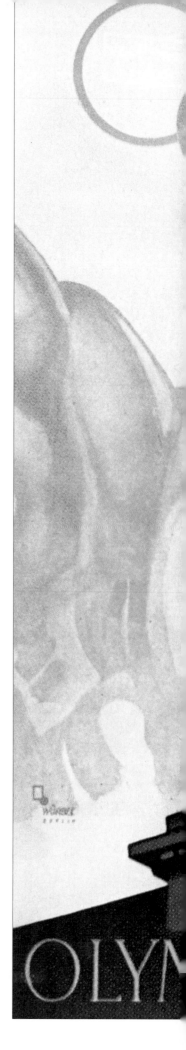

Max Schmeling's victory was seen as a significant political triumph for Germany as well as a sporting one, and the Nazis who had criticized him now honoured him with a hero's welcome. For American fans and followers, as Eddie Futch recalls, 'It was like a great president had died. That's how mournful people were...this was a very sad day.'

After Joe Louis lost, support for him was strengthened rather than diminished. 'When Max Schmeling defeated him,' Sam Lacy remembers, 'that galvanized the whole American public behind Louis. "We can't have this. We'd much rather have you, despite your complexion, than have this German."' Sam Lacy's mother, a fervent Joe Louis fan, used to follow the fights by listening to them on her crystal radio set. 'When he got beat, she never listened to another fight...he was held in such high regard that it was a blow to all of us, including myself, and I'm supposed to be objective because I'm a newspaper man. But I, like everyone else, had felt that he was indestructible, that he was the best, absolutely the best.'

A political Olympiad

No one exploited the political power of sport better than Adolf Hitler. Despite protests, the International Olympic Committee declared Berlin the setting for the 1936 Olympic Games. The ideal of the amateur spirit, on which the modern Olympics had been founded, was far removed from this Olympiad. The size of the audience had changed dramatically, as had the nature of the competition itself, which was transformed by Hitler into a mass propaganda event. The games were the first to be televised – to more than 160 000 people in and around Berlin.

The Olympic village had been designed on an enormous scale and for maximum effect. Thousands of athletes and 100 000 spectators from around the world converged on Berlin in August. The athlete Helen Stephens from Missouri was eighteen years old when she was selected to represent the United States. 'It was a sort of shock to go from peacetime America and a depression time, and to go over there to Germany and find that they were seemingly living pretty good.' The Uruguayan Diego Lucero, who attended as a journalist, was equally impressed by the spectacle. 'They organized a festival that was truly luxurious.' But he also

"The climate was right for Louis...after he proved he could fight the entire nation embraced him."

SAM LACY

OLYMPIC POSTER
(OPPOSITE) *The setting of the 1936 Olympic Games in Berlin provided Adolf Hitler with the perfect opportunity to promote Germany and the Nazi Third Reich, and to prove the superiority of Aryan athletes in front of an international audience.*

BERLIN·1936
1–16 AUG.

PISCHE SPIELE

HELEN STEPHENS *set a new world record when she won the 100 metres for the United States. She was received by Hitler in his glass box overlooking the stadium.*

SPRINTING TO VICTORY *The son of sharecroppers and the grandson of slaves, the American Jesse Owens distinguished himself and his country by winning four gold medals at the 1936 Olympics. Unlike Helen Stephens, he was not invited to meet Hitler privately, an omission that was widely interpreted as a deliberate gesture intended to snub Jesse Owens because he was black.*

MA OWENS SITS AT RADIO A
DAY LONG TO HEAR ABOUT JESS

THE AFRO AMERICAN
456 Year, No. 45   BALTIMORE, MD., AUGUST 8, 1936   Price: 6 Cents

LATE CITY
BALTIMORE

"I'm Afraid W
Jesse Jumps

"ADOLF" SNUBS U.S. LADS

Hitler Won't
Shake Hands

Intentional Discourtesy Is
Shown Owens, Johnson

By WILLIAM H. JONES
Staff Correspondent

Stockholders
of Bank Must
Pay $30,000

John R. Hawkins Sued
for $3,840, Tally
Holmes $2,780.

PRUDENTIAL BANK
FAILURE SOAKS 20

George Robinson Bar-
ber, to Be out $2,500.

Longest Legs
Longest Stride
JOHN WOODRUFF
U. of Pitt. six-footer steps
10 feet at a time to win the
800-meter Olympic final.
(Tuesday).

Joe Louis and
Sharkey in Gay
Good Humor

Meet at Commission-
er's for Coming Bout.
Kid and Jake.

BROWN BOMBER IN
TRAINING CAMP

Reporters Flock to
Look Fighters Over.

Democratic
Leaders Are

understood very clearly just what Hitler and the Nazis were hoping to achieve. 'Everything was organized towards a political end...to show a brilliant Germany....Their effort was a triumph for them because people left enchanted with the country and the treatment they had received. This Olympiad deserved the title of a political Olympiad.'

The German athletes did not fail their leader, winning most gold medals throughout the games. But to Hitler's dismay, black athletes in the American team dominated events on the field and track. The success of Jesse Owens, who won four gold medals for the United States – the 100 metres, the 200 metres, the last leg of the 4 x 100 metres relay and the long jump – spoiled Hitler's careful plans for turning the games into propaganda for his ideas about Aryan superiority.

End of an era

All the forces that were beginning to define sport – promotion and money, nationalism and propaganda – now came together in a single event. In June 1938 a second fight between Joe Louis and Max Schmeling took place at the Yankee Stadium. The world heavyweight title was at stake, but sport played little part: this was racial and political confrontation. Beyond the ring, the stakes were even higher, as Hitler had started on the road to war. Eddie Futch believed that now 'Louis wasn't just a black American...he was the representative of all America'. And Joe Louis did not his let his country down. He demolished Max Schmeling in the first two minutes. The symbolism was not lost on the watching world.

When the real war began both boxers still had their part to play. Louis was drafted into the United States cavalry, and the government made the most of his huge following to boost the war effort. The Germans used Schmeling, serving as a paratrooper, in the same way. They were just two among many sporting stars and heroes who fought alongside their fellow countrymen.

In the years after the war sport was taken up again with even greater enthusiasm. Millions of people played, and millions more thrilled at the exploits of their heroes. Commercial interests and politicians continued to use sport's power to move and motivate, and television brought live action to those who stayed at home.

GOING FOR GOLD

Winning an Olympic medal in 1936 was as much a symbol of political supremacy as it was a reward for sporting achievement.

JUBILANT AMERICANS (RIGHT) *in Harlem, New York, celebrate Joe Louis' victory over Max Schmeling in 1938. The fight had epitomized the links between sport and politics, involving participants and spectators in the struggle for power.*

Breadline

THE YEARS

OF

DEPRESSION

O N THE MORNING OF Thursday 24 October 1929 at the New York Stock Exchange on Wall Street the unthinkable actually happened. Wall Street was the financial heart of the modern world – and on that day the heart missed a beat. The market had been nervous for days, but on the Thursday, as chaos turned to panic, it collapsed. On that day nearly thirteen million shares changed hands, at prices that transformed dreams of wealth into a nightmare reality of poverty.

Thomas Larkin was a trader on Wall Street. He remembers the crazy days of the boom, and then the suddenness of the crash. 'Before 1929 everybody would be calling me up buying stocks, and they never asked what price they were going to pay...you just bought them, and you couldn't believe it but the market still kept going up and up. Then one day I couldn't sell the stocks any more...the ticker tape didn't stop all night...I couldn't understand the amount of selling that was being done. It was almost like somebody opened an enormous faucet and let everything through it. I worked three straight days without taking my clothes off. Everything was just down, down, down, there didn't seem to be any bottom at all....We saw all kinds of people walking around as though they were zombies. They thought they were rich one minute, and the next minute they weren't rich any more – if they had anything left at all.'

The stock market had become the focus of the prosperous, eager years of the 1920s. About a million people in the United States had caught the fever of investment and speculation, which reached its height in the first six months of 1929. But the boom could not last; instead, the impact of the crash of 24 October would be felt for years. It triggered a period of unemployment, homelessness and hunger not only in the United States but throughout the world. The crash was the beginning of an economic disaster on such a large scale that governments were shaken and millions of people's lives were shattered.

BEWILDERED NEW YORKERS *throng the streets in the chaotic days after the Wall Street crash.*

147

From riches to rags

The Great Depression was so traumatic partly because it came so suddenly. During the previous few years there had been a period of unprecedented prosperity, a mood of optimism and confidence, particularly in the United States. The American economy was, however, more vulnerable than it seemed, because its banking structure was weak and the organization of business unstable.

Few investors realized that the boom could last only for as long as new speculators or new money from established investors were entering the market. As soon as the pace of demand to buy shares slowed down, confidence began to wane, and the whole unsteady edifice tottered and collapsed. It was not just ordinary investors who were deluded in thinking that the boom years would last for ever; businessmen, politicians and economists all continued to proclaim their confidence in the capitalist system and also appeared to be taken by surprise when disaster struck.

One of New York's telegraph boys, Bill Bailey, had the unenviable job of delivering telegrams bringing news of their ruin to many stock market investors. 'Most of the telegrams said the same: "Things are bad…give us more money to haul up your interests or else you are kaput." It was sad, because eventually not only did we deliver to the same door three or four times a day, but the people wouldn't even answer the door. They were so afraid of what was taking shape, and so bewildered. It was shortly after that we found out that people were jumping out of windows, going bananas…and figuring that was the best way to go, head first.'

Bill Bailey shared the bewilderment of the people who responded so dramatically to the news he brought. 'Nobody had any idea what was going on, that was the funny part of it. Why would the stock market have such a bearing on everybody else around us? We couldn't understand why it was the stock market played a role in us losing jobs, warehouses left full of stuff, people thrown out of factories.' Only later did he understand the way everything was affected. 'We had no idea because we didn't understand the system…until we found out that the stock market was the main aorta of the system, and that how the blood flows through it has a big bearing on everything else.'

BALANCING ON THE BEAM (OPPOSITE) *A construction worker guides a steel girder into position on New York's Empire State Building. It eventually rose to 102 storeys, even taller than the Chrysler building behind it. Skyscrapers symbolized the ambition and confidence of the 1920s.*

THE DREAM OF WEALTH (BELOW) *turns to a nightmare of debt for the speculator who once proudly drove the car he is now so desperate to sell. As the stock market crash brought havoc to the lives of thousands of investors, it became harder to find buyers for once valuable possessions, however attractive the price.*

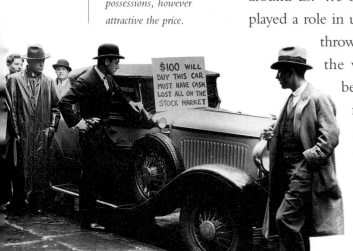

TRADING ACROSS
THE WORLD

PEOPLE EVERYWHERE were becoming part of a global manufacturing machine during the 1920s, a time of rapid economic growth. Plantation workers in the British and French colonies in Southeast Asia tapped rubber for the tyres for automobiles that were made with steel from works in Britain, Germany and the United States. In the mountains of northern Chile, men mined copper ore that was shipped to the Renault factory in France, where the workers wore overalls woven from cotton picked by Egyptian workers or American sharecroppers. These workers all came to depend on each other for their living.

The first steps towards a global economy had been taken a long time before; the pace had accelerated during the nineteenth century. Britain was the first nation widely to export manufactured goods and coal, importing raw materials and cheap food from its colonies and from the United States. From about 1870 American, German and later Japanese manufacturers began to export to the British markets in Africa, Asia and South America.

After the First World War the United States had more spare capital than the exhausted European states, and not only invested in the railways and factories of developing countries but also poured money into Europe. Gradually the centre of gravity of the world's financial system shifted from London to New York.

In the thriving economic climate of the 1920s many people's expectations rose, and the idea became widespread that almost everyone could make money. But all those who benefited from the prosperity of the 1920s – the individuals, the companies they worked for, and the countries in which they lived – were now dependent on the state of the world economy.

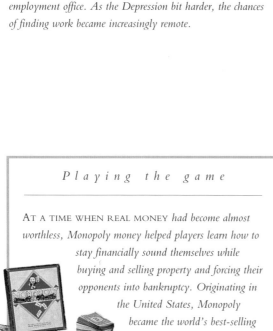

BESIEGED BY THE UNEMPLOYED *Desperate Americans try to attract the attention of the overworked officials in an employment office. As the Depression bit harder, the chances of finding work became increasingly remote.*

Playing the game

AT A TIME WHEN REAL MONEY *had become almost worthless, Monopoly money helped players learn how to stay financially sound themselves while buying and selling property and forcing their opponents into bankruptcy. Originating in the United States, Monopoly became the world's best-selling privately patented board game.*

Shock waves

When the stock market collapsed other disasters soon followed. Many investors had bought stock 'on margin' – with borrowed money. As the value of their shares fell, they could not pay back their loans. But it was not only investors who were affected. Panic-stricken depositors hurried to remove their savings, and banks were forced to close. As investment dried up and demand collapsed, the crash soon turned into a slump. The consequences were devastating: prices rapidly fell, trade withered, goods were stacked up unsold, factories closed, wages were cut, millions of people lost their jobs. Both individuals and nations faced similar problems – they could not pay their debts, and were unable to borrow to see them through the hard times.

For many, life now became a grey, discouraging struggle for mere survival. Millions of people found themselves in absolute want. With no public welfare provision such as unemployment benefit to help them, hundreds of thousands of Americans found they had no alternative but to line up for the free soup that churches and private charities began to provide. Many survivors

ONE DOLLAR A WEEK is all the payment being asked by these labourers and firemen. Both skilled and unskilled men endured the humiliation of having to beg for work in a country that had recently been proud of its growing prosperity.

A GOOD TIME FOR BEER

URING THE DEPRESSION, at a time when many Americans might have wanted to drown their sorrows in drink, alcohol was banned in the United States. Prohibition was hailed as a great experiment at the time, but it was in fact a disaster. Millions of Americans became criminals simply because they continued to buy beer, wine or whisky.

The National Prohibition Act, known after its congressional sponsor as the Volstead Act, had become law in January 1920. It banned the manufacture, transportation, sale and consumption of alcohol. Its unintended consequence was the temporary creation of a vast illegal network of liquor smuggling, serving thousands of 'speakeasies' – illegal drinking places.

The drive for prohibition had been coordinated nationally by the Anti-Saloon League. It originated not only in the religious and ethical beliefs of the Protestant churches but also in the prejudices of 'old stock' Americans of the Middle West and the South against the cities and their German, Irish and Italian inhabitants. These newer immigrants were seen by the Anglo-Saxon Protestants as drinkers prone to immorality and crime.

It was in fact prohibition itself that triggered a national crime wave. By 1927 drunken driving offences had risen by 467 per cent, and deaths from alcoholism by 600 per cent. Attempts to legislate morality offer new opportunities to criminals in the evasion of the law; what is forbidden may become more desirable. And so it proved.

There were twice as many illegal bars in New York as there had been legal ones before the Volstead Act. Bootleggers (named after seventeenth-century smugglers who had concealed bottles of liquor in their boots) smuggled liquor into the United States across the Canadian and Mexican borders, from the Bahamas and from ships anchored outside territorial waters.

In most major cities rival criminal gangs fought over the huge profits being made from the illegal drink trade and from the prostitution and gambling associated with it. The income bought cars and machine guns, increasingly used in self-defence and to eliminate rivals. And it also bought people: police forces were corrupted, and political influence brought the gangsters immunity from the law. In Chicago between 1927 and 1931 there were 227 gang murders – and not one conviction.

Chicago was called by one of its aldermen 'the only completely corrupt city in America'. One of the first gang bosses was murdered; his successor was shot by his bodyguard and his empire of illegal breweries, distilleries, truck fleets and speakeasies was eventually taken over by the most notorious gang leader of all, Al Capone. He drove around Chicago in an armoured Cadillac; both feared and admired, he was said to have ordered some 400 murders.

A commission reported in 1931 that prohibition was unenforceable. Although organized crime continued to flourish, the stream of money that had flowed into the coffers of the criminals slowed to a trickle as the Depression advanced. Prohibition was repealed in December 1933 as part of Roosevelt's New Deal. He himself observed: 'I think this would be a good time for beer.'

A WAISTCOAT OF WHISKY *finds ready customers in a speakeasy during the years of prohibition.*

remember the helplessness, the shock of sudden poverty, the acute sense of loss and failure being almost worse than the experience of hunger and the new physical hardships they had to endure.

When the pink slip came to tell them they were out of work, many people at first felt ashamed. Bill Bailey remembers the humiliating effort to find another job. 'I would get out and maybe hustle fifteen places a day, banging on warehouse doors, trying to find a job – but it was impossible. I ended up selling apples on Wall Street.' Others tackled the helplessness they felt by finding quite different kinds of work, sometimes in circumstances for which their upbringing had not prepared them. For a few of those who would compromise, it was still possible to earn large sums in unexpected ways, such as performing in the new nightclubs, while most people were queueing for hours each day in the soup lines.

'There was nothing that struck the imagination more than seeing a soup line of five hundred people,' explains Bill Bailey, 'and two days later a thousand people in the same line. It kept on growing until they went all around the block....To stand in line at any place like soup kitchens where you are trying to get something free is very humiliating. Of course later on it becomes a way of life, you don't care any more because everybody else is there.'

A young economics student, Robert Nathan, wanted to understand the processes that had led first to speculation and then to depression. He already knew that the difficulties of the 1930s lay in what had taken place in the 1920s. One of his professors explained away the crisis. 'He said, "Business cycles are part of the capitalistic system", and I remember he took a rubber band and pulled it way out and said "Boom"; then he let go and it collapsed back and he said "Bust". Capitalism is bound to have booms, which are prosperity, and also have busts, which are recessions and depressions.'

Robert Nathan was taught that this cycle of boom and bust was inevitable and that nothing could be done about it. This was what most economists believed at the time. But he thought it was wrong, that inertia was unacceptable and that something should be done, because the economic theories did not take into account the effect the cycle had

THE AVERAGE CITIZEN (LEFT) *often struggled to understand the forces that could make him rich or reduce him to poverty, and became bewildered by the complexities of economics and the jargon of financial affairs.*

A Chicago soup line
*set up and supported by the
gangster Al Capone.
Without any federal social
security system, American
citizens were dependent on
charity to alleviate hardship
during the Depression.*

on people's lives. 'The hardship was something you couldn't escape from. The lectures and the writing it off as an inherent element in the free enterprise system made less and less sense to me, because I saw that here were the plants closed down, here were the people wanting to work, here were the people who couldn't afford to buy anything, so you had a kind of vicious circle operating and nobody was prepared or willing to undertake major measures.' This sense of helplessness was a reality very different from the

THE DUST BOWL

THE CATASTROPHE of the American Dust Bowl was the result of some fifty years of inappropriate farming. The Great Plains, which had been opened up towards the end of the nineteenth century by the railroads, could be cultivated with the new steel ploughs, which were strong and sharp enough to break up their tough grasses. They were ploughed up to grow wheat, though the topsoil was thin and the climate semi-arid, with recurrent droughts.

The 'sodbusters', small farmers who bought a 'quarter section' of 65 hectares (160 acres) for about $200, and larger commercial farming enterprises ignored the difficult conditions. They set out to tame the land. They learned to survive prairie fires and plagues of grasshoppers, and to produce crops despite a continental climate of heatwaves and blizzards, drought, hail and flash floods. During the First World War the grain and cotton of the Great Plains fed and clothed the Allies, and production was further increased after the war, when Russian grain exports were no longer available to the European cities.

Farming methods that had been successful in the rich farmlands back east were eventually to prove unworkable in the Plains, with their thin, fragile soils from which the protective grass cover had been stripped. Single-crop farming and increasing mechanization worsened the problems, exhausting the soil. During periods of drought the bare earth turned to dust that was whipped by the prairie winds into huge dust storms.

In April 1933 there were 179 dust storms. These were black, brown, yellow, grey or even red according to which county's soil was being blown away. In one storm in May 1934, 350 million tonnes of dust from the southern Plains blew over Boston, New York and Washington. City dwellers woke up to find dust covering their floors. Dust was blown out to sea onto the decks of ships almost 500 km (300 miles) offshore. The storms caused breathing problems, derailed trains, and destroyed half the wheat in Kansas and a quarter of the Oklahoma crop.

Loye Stoops was a young woman on her family's farm in Oklahoma, and she remembers the storms well. 'We planted crops but those storms would come...and the sand would just cut them off at the ground....The dust was everywhere, you would have to sweep it out, shovel it out. The dust storm would come every few days. You couldn't see – it was like smoke, only it was red. We held out and kept trying to farm until the water level dropped and there was no water in the wells. I think it had been about three years that it had not rained.'

Loye Stoops and her family were among the half million 'Okies' (as they were called whether they came from Oklahoma or not) who decided to leave. Most had little left to lose. Long lines of cars filled with dispirited, exhausted families travelled slowly west in search of work. Some 300 000 people journeyed to California, where life in the fruit-picking camps was almost as tough as it had been in the Dust Bowl.

FAMILY LIFE *for many American farmers was reduced to pitiful levels of deprivation. In the grip of economic forces beyond their control or understanding, millions of families had to choose whether to stay at home and risk starvation, or abandon their homes and seek a better way of life.*

WAVES OF SAND *cover the land around an isolated Texan farmhouse during a dust storm.*

public image of the United States. During the early years of the century millions of Europeans had emigrated to the United States, full of confidence about their prospects there. John Takman reached Chicago from Sweden only weeks before the Wall Street crash. 'I saw the misery all around me, tens of thousands of people evicted from their apartments, whole families and old people sitting in rocking chairs on the sidewalk, nowhere to go, no food, nothing except the small things they had with them, and I couldn't stand it.'

John Takman decided to go west, as he had heard that 5000 jobs were available picking apples in Washington state. Seasonal farm work paid little, but drew many. When he arrived he found 25 000 people also hoping to get a job. 'I saw families with haunted eyes, men probably starved for a long time in order to give the children something. We knew that when people didn't have the money to buy bread, the wheat was burned; if they didn't have money to buy meat, the mounds of meat were destroyed with kerosene. There was huge destruction of food in the United States at the same time that millions were starving.' Farm prices had dropped so low that it was not worth the farmers' while to pick their crops. In Idaho wheat was even priced at minus three cents a bushel. So while hunger threatened the unemployed and homeless in the cities, good food rotted in the fields or was used as fuel.

Bill Bailey travelled around the country in search of work by rail, by boxcar. 'You have to pick the car up when it is doing five or ten miles an hour. After that you are taking a chance of losing a leg. Some of the cars were full of dirt, filth and slime – it was almost impossible to lie down and get any rest. We are talking about thousands of people on the rail every single day.' But there were hardly any jobs, however far afield they travelled. 'So they found themselves drifting around aimlessly, cursing at themselves, becoming more demoralized and wondering where the hell they are going to go from here. It was sad to see humanity in this state.'

KEEPING A LOOKOUT *Riding for free on trains was a risky way to travel, but was often the only option for those who had no money and no possessions.*

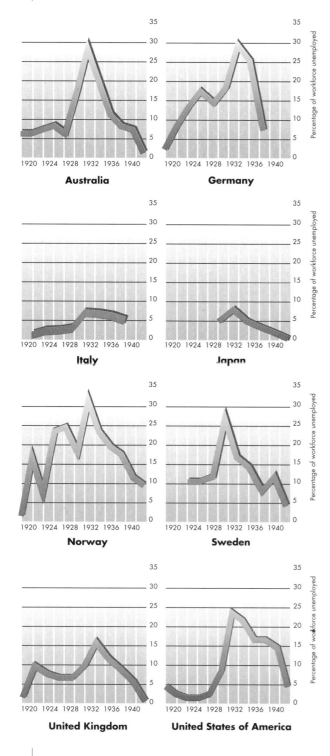

PEAKS OF UNEMPLOYMENT *followed similiar patterns in all the world's industrial nations as the Depression took hold in the early 1930s. Detailed statistical evidence is lacking for the countries that supplied raw materials – such as Chile and other Latin American states – but their working people were equally badly affected.*

Collapsing trade

The shock waves of the Depression began to be felt throughout the world. Measures taken in Europe and the United States to protect their economies brought the volume of international trade down even further, and in 1931 it virtually collapsed. Disastrous as this was for the industrial countries, it was even more catastrophic for the nations that depended on supplying their raw materials – copper, cotton, rubber and wool.

In independent countries such as Australia, New Zealand and the South American republics, prices, output and trade all declined steeply. The powerless peoples of the British, Dutch and French empires were even worse hit. In January 1933 the gold price of sugar, for example, was half what it had been in January 1929; the price of cotton fell by two-thirds over the same period, and that of rubber by 87 per cent. Manufacturers, processors and even consumers complained vociferously; the sufferings of those most badly affected, the plantation workers, went unheard.

In Chile prosperity was new and fragile. It largely depended on just one product, copper, and for that copper largely on one source – the American-owned opencast mine at Chuquicamata in the Atacama desert. The price of copper dropped by 29 per cent in only four years. For tens of thousands of miners, like Fernando Liborio Suazo, 'The crisis took us by surprise. It was as if you were walking in the street and something hits you and you are simply stunned. New York was far away, but when your own patron tells you that you no longer have a job, that the work's over, well that's the moment you go into shock. As he was a humane person, he gave us one year more, working there. He didn't sell that copper, he just stored it there. He didn't have a buyer.'

As an engineer, Eugenio Lanas understood the importance of the copper: without it, the city dies. He explains: 'The bakeries work for those hundreds of miners who come on donkeys or in light trucks to buy bread, the workshops work for the miners who need an engine fixed. The whole activity of the city is for the benefit of these people. The moment these rocks disappear, the cities themselves start to disappear.' That is just what happened.

The Chilean economy also depended on its 'white gold' – nitrates that were exported to North American farmers. Claudina

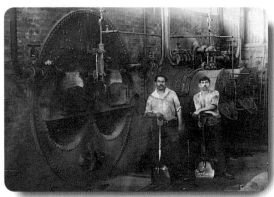

MAKESHIFT HOMES
(LEFT) *in Valparaiso, Chile.*
In the 1920s expanding
industries attracted people
from the countryside to the
towns in search of a better
way of life, but often the
only shelter available was
in shantytowns.

TWO STOKERS (ABOVE)
standing by nitrate boilers at
San Enrique, Chile. The
nitrate workers depended for
their livelihood on the
ability of American farmers
to buy the fertilizer. The
cartoon (TOP) *highlights*
their suffering.

Montaño Diaz lived in Humberstone, one of the many nitrate towns in the Atacama desert. It employed more than 150 000 miners and their families. 'It was our bread, our bread was the nitrate. That was our security and that was our life. We didn't have anything else. One day in December we knew that they were closing the works. They did not come to talk to the people. They just gave the orders. We didn't have anyone to complain to, though we had suffered this abuse, we had suffered a lot. It was very sad. The men of course were angry, because the workers were exploited and we were left with nothing. What could we do? Beautiful towns were abandoned. That was the crisis of the 1930s, that crisis was outrageous.'

Nearly 13 000 km (8000 miles) away in the northeast of England the crisis affected a town that depended on another once thriving industry: shipbuilding. With the collapse of world trade the shipbuilding, steel and coal industries all suffered: orders for new ships ceased, so the shipyards stopped buying steel plates, and the steel works stopped buying coal and iron ore.

Con Shiels's father worked at Palmer's shipyard in Jarrow on the river Tyne. In 1930, when he was fourteen years old, Con Shiels himself started to work there. 'Of course it was only natural for the sons to follow their fathers, which I did. He was working as a riveter and so naturally I started with him as a rivet catcher. You had to heat up your rivets, and carry them along the deck in a box of ash – and that was me with a job.' He started work hoping that he would be there for life, to learn a skilled trade and later to marry on the wages. 'But it didn't happen because one afternoon the foreman came round and said, "Con, you're finished tonight" – just like that. So that was me finished. Out. Got my books and money and away I went.'

He was just one among hundreds. Palmer's was closed as part of a scheme to reduce capacity in order to protect the more modern yards. When the Palmer's yard was demolished, many of the people who lived in Jarrow turned out to watch its twin cranes come down. They had been the town's principal landmark. Con Shiels speaks for many when he explains how he felt. 'They were just part of your life…honestly there were tears in our eyes seeing them go down, because we knew that if they came down the yard was finished. They were a symbol. Once the symbol had gone, that was it. A terrible day.' Almost overnight, in a town of skilled, hardworking men, the level of unemployment rose to 75 per cent. People called Jarrow 'the town that died', but Con Shiels would put it more strongly than that. 'It was murdered. A good town, just cut off like that, like a hangman dropping a noose. Once the yard was closed it was as though a blanket had dropped over the town…it was really very depressing for the future and for our children.'

IDLE SHIPS AND IDLE WORKERS (LEFT) *dramatically portrayed by the photographer Humphrey Spender. 'What I found on Tyneside was rather frightening,' he recalls. 'On the quayside I found despondent and idle men.' On his repeated visits to the hard-hit northeast of England his photographs became harsher as he depicted conditions with increasingly unsparing honesty.*

CON SHIELS *photographed with fellow trainees on a government scheme in 1936. His years of unemployment came to an end when he joined the navy.*

'WE MARCH AGAINST STARVATION' *declares one of the banners carried by the unemployed men of Jarrow, who walked to London in protest in 1936. Con Shiels's father was among the marchers.*

Years of deprivation

Between 1929 and 1936 deprivation spread across the world like a disease. The coal industry was one of the worst affected. Miners in Belgium, Britain, France and Germany were all caught up in the cycle. It was coal that provided essential power for industry, but with industrial production dramatically reduced, the demand for coal fell too. In the Borinage coal basin in Belgium there were 100 000 miners and their families living in appalling conditions. In the summer of 1932 the miners had gone on strike to protest against a 5 per cent cut in their wages. They were dismissed from their jobs, blacklisted from future work, and evicted from their company-owned homes. Two young film-makers, Henri Storck and Joris Ivens, found out what had happened and decided to publicize the miners' plight. 'We wanted to do a revolutionary film,' Henri Storck explains. 'We became totally indignant. Joris and I were sons of tradesmen, we didn't know much about workmen. We thought this was really impossible. These people were abandoned, they were treated cruelly by the colliery directors. It was something we couldn't tolerate, this incredible poverty – they didn't have any money at all.'

The Mouffe family were among those who were filmed to draw attention to the miners' hardships. The hunger and poverty they had to endure is vividly described by Yvonne Mouffe, who was a young child at the time. 'I can remember there being only one room. We used to cuddle up to each other to keep warm, it is much warmer that way if you are on the ground. There were nine children, and we slept on the floor. To get some coal they used to go to the slag heaps in the evening – otherwise we couldn't have any, we weren't authorized to have any. Father worked in the mines but during the strike they received nothing at all, so we had nothing but potatoes to eat and from time to time some bread, but apart from that nothing.'

There was worse to come. Yvonne Mouffe's father, who was a communist, was accused of being one of the strike leaders, lost his job and could not find another one. The children were taken from their parents and put in children's homes; Yvonne Mouffe was five years old when this happened, and did not see her parents again until she was forty-two.

LOCKOUTS AND STRIKES (OPPOSITE) *were a familiar feature in industrial communities as working conditions worsened during the difficult economic climate of the 1930s.*

EXPERIENCE AND EDUCATION (BELOW) *were no protection against unemployment during the Depression. The crisis affected professional people as well as the labouring men who were usually more vulnerable to fluctuations in the economy.*

I KNOW 3 TRADES
I SPEAK 3 LANGUAGES
FOUGHT FOR 3 YEARS
HAVE 3 CHILDREN
AND NO WORK FOR
3 MONTHS
BUT I ONLY WANT
ONE JOB

THE SAFETY NET

BEFORE THE DEPRESSION, the age-old assumption still held in most countries that families would look after their children, their invalids and the elderly. State provision, where it existed at all, was limited.

The first state system of social security for old age had been introduced in Germany towards the end of the nineteenth century. In 1911 Britain became the first country to provide state insurance for the unemployed; by 1927 twelve million British workers were protected by a contributory state insurance scheme that they had to join. But relief hardly lifted recipients out of poverty, and many turned for help to the poor law, still administered by parishes, and to charities.

Private insurance through companies was confined to higher paid workers, and often failed in times of hardship. Hundreds of thousands of people sought security by setting up their own insurance schemes through 'friendly societies' or trade unions.

Sweden was the first country to replace the poor law concept. By 1914 it had set up a national unemployment commission to provide jobs on public works projects. From 1925 it provided a nutritious daily meal to all schoolchildren. Sweden offered the best protection to its citizens during the 1930s, with unemployment benefit, pension provisions, subsidized sickness funds and medical care, and family allowances.

In the United States, where there had been no state-organized welfare, people could rely only on their families and on the support of community groups. It had been assumed that poverty was caused by personal inadequacy, until a quarter of the working population faced long-term unemployment. Only then, during Roosevelt's presidency, was there the political will to try to solve the problem by introducing the first social security provisions.

Fighting for change

Deprivation and despair led to rage, and rage sometimes led to rebellion. The cause was often simple necessity and desperation. But many people interpreted their own particular experience in terms of an abstract idea. They believed that the world economic system, the capitalist system, was at fault. Some thought it was fundamentally wrong, others that it had just gone horribly wrong. Millions of people concluded that radical change was inevitable. Few countries escaped bitter battles – between capital and labour, between the police, enforcing the existing law, and trade unions and other groups who were equally determined that the old rules should be changed.

In northern Sweden the wood pulp industry, a major source of wealth, was depressed by the collapse of world trade. The pulp and paper companies cut wages. Like the Borinage miners, the workers in the port of Lunde, near the town of Adalen, responded by going on strike. Strike-breaking labour was hired to keep the port functioning. As tension rose, the army was called in.

On 14 May 1931 the Swedish trade unions called their members to a big protest rally in Adalen. Tore Alespong was one of the trumpeters who led the union band on the march. The musicians were playing when soldiers opened fire. 'There was one fellow, who held the scores for one of the clarinettists, who had two shots through his hat. He found the bullets still in the crown. It was a miracle they didn't strike lower down. Some of the shots hit the ground, but most went high and hit people. A girl within touching distance from me began bleeding...she had certainly been shot. That's when I had the impulse to sound the ceasefire on the trumpet....They thought that it was their own bugler who had sounded.' By the time the shooting stopped, five people had been killed. Tore Alespong played the trumpet at their funeral.

People all over the country were shocked at what had taken place in Adalen. In Stockholm there was a mass protest against it. Göta Rosén, a young social worker, was 'devastated that something like that could happen. I went to the town square to attend the demonstration. It was frightening that this could happen to people in distress.' Swedes, like people in many other countries,

'THE SWEDISH PEOPLE'S PATH' *promises this election poster for the Social Democrats, 'is the path of people's freedom and democracy.' Their energy and vision helped to bring the Social Democrats to power.*

TORE ALESPONG (BELOW) *was among the bandsmen who led the march in Adalen that resulted in bloodshed. The tragedy 'did emphasize how people in power behave, people in government', he explains.*

NSKA
ETS

HJALMAR
BRANTING

HANS
HJÄRTA

ÄR

FOLK-
FRIHETENS

OCH

MOKRATINS

VÄG

ÖSTA
ED

TIET **SOCIAL-**
RATERNA

*"I believed in the Social Democrats'
programme. I am convinced that they defend
the young, the old, the downtrodden."*

GÖTA ROSÉN

GÖTA ROSÉN *with a
group of orphans. 'My aim
was to get away from the
communal care of children. I
tried to find people to take
care of them under the
slogan, "The right child in
the right family",' she
explains. She found the
Social Democrats sympathetic
to her ideas.*

became increasingly alienated from the ruling party. In the wake of Adalen, and the Depression that had triggered the incident, a new political movement emerged that regarded unemployment not as inevitable but as an outrage. Göta Rosén describes why it appealed to her. 'I saw unemployment as a terrible scourge. I understood that one must do one's utmost to remove that scourge from the people of Sweden, and I joined the Social Democratic party partly because I realized that they were getting things done.'

The Social Democrats were swept to power in the 1932 election. They saw their main priority as restoring confidence and getting the country moving again, rather than balancing its budget at all costs as governments elsewhere were doing at that time. It intervened by creating jobs and restimulating wealth, spending money both to invigorate the economy and to protect the needy.

GREETING THE PRESIDENT *American farmers gained confidence as a result of Roosevelt's policy to support farm prices. Many of them would have agreed with Loye Stoops, who remembers: 'I thought he was smart and I thought he cared and I thought he had people at heart because he was helping when nobody else could do anything.'*

DAIRY WORKERS ON STRIKE (OPPOSITE) *give vent to their frustration by overturning a milk truck in Toledo, Ohio, in 1935.*

Roosevelt's New Deal

Restoring confidence also became the key to challenging the Depression in the United States. In 1933 Franklin D. Roosevelt was inaugurated as president. Although he is credited with ending the Depression there, he did not at first have a clear strategy for recovery. He did, however, understand one very important thing: that part of the problem stemmed from lack of confidence. In his inauguration speech he gave new inspiration to the American people. 'Let me assert my firm belief that the only thing we have to fear is fear itself,' he assured them.

In the first hundred days of Roosevelt's presidency, thirteen major measures were passed by Congress to provide structure and support for recovery in banking, industry and agriculture, and to establish federal relief for the needy. Government projects were set up. Some of these, such as the Tennessee Valley Authority and the Civilian Conservation Corps, gave employment to millions of homeless unemployed men, while others were small self-help schemes. By 1936 a system of unemployment insurance and old age pensions had been instituted; in 1938 a new law established a minimum wage and maximum weekly working hours. Measures were also taken to protect union activities: collective bargaining, the right of labour to its own organizations. Employers often resisted these gains, and it took a series of bitter strikes for the changes to be accepted.

Roosevelt's action did not solve all the difficulties of the Depression. The economy did not really recover until war had broken out again in Europe in 1939 and the United States joined in the rearmament boom. But his greatest achievement was to raise people's hopes again, to convince them that something was at last being done to help – itself a major political turnaround.

The economist Robert Nathan describes the effect of the government's activities. 'A lot of the increased spending under the Roosevelt administration had to do with public works...when you put people to work building a dam, you have a lot of cement guys, pipefitters, a lot of guys running, cutting the big hole in the ground to put the dam up – you give a lot of people employment. What does that mean? It means there is more buying power. People have been unemployed and living on $10 a week, say, and

BILL BAILEY'S INTEREST *in politics began when he saw his mother standing in a soup line. The communists 'were the ones doing the driving, so you became influenced by what they were talking about, that the system wasn't working and nobody gave a damn.'*

ALTERNATIVES TO DEMOCRACY

WHEN THE ECONOMIES of democratic countries seemed to be failing them, many people were attracted by the certainties and apparent successes of communism and fascism. Democratic governments had always regarded economic depression as an inevitable feature of capitalism that could not be remedied. As the Depression fastened its grip, the slump in trade and the rise in unemployment brought desperation that led to tension and violence. Authoritarian regimes of both the left and the right seemed to offer solutions to the chaos and poverty so many people were suffering.

There was one country where there was no unemployment: the Soviet Union. Here the communist approach seemed able to defy the Depression; few people knew of the violence and coercion involved in the adoption of communist methods. At the opposite political extreme, in Germany from 1933 the fascist government also exercised tight controls over the economy to provide work for the six million people – about half the workforce – who were unemployed. And they were successful: by 1936 the figure had dropped to 1.6 million, and continued to fall.

In Italy, fascism was adopted in 1926; fascists came to power in Spain and Portugal too during the 1930s. In Britain and France both fascism and communism made some political gains in the 1930s. In the late 1920s and early 1930s thousands of American citizens applied for visas to emigrate to the Soviet Union, while others stayed in the United States but supported communist ideas. The Communist Party of the United States never became more than a tiny political minority, but in the desperate times of the Depression it had great influence.

After the First World War the expansion of self-determination in Europe and elsewhere was translated into genuine democracy only in a very few countries, such as Ireland and Czechoslovakia. In 1926 there was a military coup in Poland; in 1929 the Serbian king of the new Yugoslavia proclaimed himself dictator. In Hungary, after a brief communist revolution in 1919, the great landowners and smaller squires regained power and diverted attention from the poverty of the agricultural workers, among the most wretched in Europe.

Outside Europe, Kemal Atatürk modernized Turkish society, but granted only limited civil liberties. In India and other colonial territories mass movements for self-government had not yet shaken imperial rule, though the violence both of protest and repression was increasing. In China the nationalist Kuomintang movement was given an authoritarian structure. In alliance with the Chinese Communist Party, founded in 1921, the Kuomintang established its government in Nanking, and moved north to attack the warlords who controlled much of the country.

In Japan there was also restlessness. The Depression badly affected people both in the textile industries and in the countryside. This strengthened the hand of the militarists, who promised to tackle the problem, though their methods threatened Japan's young democracy. Political gangs collaborated with the security police to silence socialist and trade unionist activists, and there were many political assassinations.

In many other countries, too, even before the Depression had taken hold, political stability was threatened and a new culture of political violence was on the increase.

then suddenly they have $25 or $30...you had people that were at least ready and able to spend more, and anybody who suddenly had doubled their income, doubled their purchases.'

Robert Nathan most admires Roosevelt's ability to think of new solutions. 'When it got tough, he was willing to experiment with a whole lot of things that had never been done before. Masses of people really had a lot of confidence in this man because he talked about things that made them feel, "He is worried about me, he is concerned about me, he is going to do things for me". The result was that he was elected president four times.'

The confidence people had in their president was reflected in the growing confidence they had in themselves. The Reverend George Stith had become part of the changing times when he joined the Southern Tenant Farmers' Union as a young man. He can still remember the hardships of his early life. His family had slept three to a bed, and his grandmother had kept them alive on watermelons, wild onions, tomatoes and peas. 'You were in a land that grew cotton to make the best clothes in the world, clothes that we couldn't wear because we couldn't afford to buy them.'

George Stith was a sharecropper, working on a big cotton plantation in the South. The plantation owner decided how much he was going to pay them. 'You never got money. You got a coupon book, you could go to any of the plantation stores and spend them, but there was no money.'

Roosevelt's policies first affected the Stiths when the owner told them, 'We've got to plough up every third row of this cotton because the government says we're planting too much'. What he did not tell the workers was that the government had paid him to plough up the third row, and he had no intention of passing that money on to the people who actually did the ploughing. Joining the union was a dangerous thing to do, because agricultural labour had been excluded from the legislation passed under the New Deal to protect union activities. 'Everyone else had the right to organize, to bargain, but agriculture didn't have the right...they wanted it that if you organized you couldn't get a hearing because you had no right to organize, so we had to do it as best we could.'

In the South every plantation owner virtually made his own laws, and many were hostile to union activities. Meetings were

WAITING ON THE CABIN PORCH *surrounded by possessions, this family in the state of Mississippi in June 1938 is about to be taken to a new home, resettled with the help of the Farm Security Administration.*

OPPORTUNITY

FREEDOM OF religion – Speech

PRIVATE ENTERPRISE

Representative DEMOCRACY

NATIONAL ASSOCIATION OF MANUFACTURERS

e American Way

'IT'S THE AMERICAN WAY' boasts this poster reflecting renewed business confidence. For those whose lives had been reduced to wandering the streets with their possessions tied in a paper parcel, the freedoms and opportunities of the American way of life still seemed elusive.

raided by local law officers and plantation owners; union members were even whipped and beaten. Despite the harassment, the union continued to grow.

'I sometimes wonder why we did not give up,' George Stith says. 'But I guess we figured it this way: if you have nothing, you can lose nothing. The risk, for a lot of time, was death if they caught you. We had some organizers that did disappear, and we didn't know what became of them. I was very young at that time. They thought a union organizer had to be an older man, and I think that was an advantage to me, being a boy.'

Despite the danger, George Stith continued to believe that the fight for a better life was worthwhile. The Southern Tenant Farmers' Union provided both a fighting platform and a step to freedom for some of those whose lives were not affected by the vision of a prosperous future held out by Roosevelt's policies.

Someone else for whom the changing times brought new beginnings was Mancil Milligan, though his experiences were very different from those of George Stith. He and his wife had been teachers before the Depression and had put aside a little money in a bank, but when the bank failed they lost their savings. For several

Man of steel

SUPERMAN, THE GREAT HERO *of comic strips, reflected the thirst for social justice. He was both incredibly clever and extraordinarily strong. His superhuman powers were at first modest – he could leap hundreds of metres and only a bursting shell could harm him – but were later extended to include X-ray vision and the power to fly to the end of the universe. The strip appeared in four newspapers in 1939; by 1941 it was being syndicated to some three hundred newspapers reaching an audience of twenty million people.*

MANCIL MILLIGAN (ABOVE) *in his uniform as a safety officer at the Pickwick Dam, which employed up to 2500 people. As he explains, 'Everybody got a piece of the pie. When I got a job there I worked six days a week and I hired somebody to haul and chop wood for me, I hired somebody to paint the house' – tasks he had undertaken himself when he had been out of work. The dam brought electricity to the region; Mancil Milligan was proud of his refrigerator, his electric fan and his new radio.*

GETTING BACK TO WORK (OPPOSITE) *Men on their way to work at the Robins Dry Dock Company. As rearmament boosted the American economy, there were better employment prospects for people in many industries.*

years neither the state nor the county could afford to pay teachers. At one point he even had to take half a dollar out of their young daughter's piggy bank to buy a sack of flour. When Roosevelt's new measures began to take effect, Mancil Milligan finally got another job – as a carpenter working in a New Deal conservation corps camp for just $2 a day, 'from sunup to sundown'. Then the Tennessee Valley Authority started a huge project nearby to build the Pickwick Dam, and he applied for a job there. He has never forgotten the telegram that was brought round to his house. 'It read about like this: "Mancil A. Milligan, We are offering you employment at Pickwick Dam as a public safety officer for $1440 a year. Wire back immediately if you accept." ' And he did.

Rearmament

Mancil Milligan was one those directly helped by the New Deal. But there were many others who still continued to suffer, until rearmament put money back into people's pockets. After 1939, when Europe was once again at war, the United States was to become the 'arsenal of democracy'. Roosevelt described the new situation succinctly. 'Dr New Deal is off the case,' he said. 'Now it's Dr Win-the-War.'

By this time Robert Nathan was working for the Defense Advisory Committee. Part of his job was to find the raw materials needed for military production. Chilean copper for the jackets of bullets was one of these. Suddenly, he recalls, 'We started buying copper like mad from Chile'. Badly damaged by the recession in the United States, Chile now benefited from renewed industrial activity there, and prosperity began to come back into the Chilean economy too. The Americans were not their only customers. The Germans and Japanese, and later the British and the French, also came back into the market.

The middle way, the way of Swedish social democracy and of the American New Deal, would by different means both bring full employment to end mass poverty, and a standard of living that, even in the boomtime of the 1920s, only a few people in a few countries could have aspired to. But first, millions of steel bullets would leave their copper jackets, and many of them would tear their way into human bodies.

8

Great Escape

THE WORLD OF CINEMA

'WAIT A MINUTE! WAIT a minute! You ain't heard nothing yet!' declared Al Jolson to an enthralled cinema audience, but almost nothing could be heard above the cheering and the clapping. The audience were delighted. They had just heard the first words ever spoken in a feature fiction film.

It was 1927 and the opening night of *The Jazz Singer* in New York. Al Jolson's words were to prove prophetic. Once the technology had been developed to synchronize sound to film, the era of silent movies was over. Audiences around the world were thrilled by the introduction of sound, which brought a new realism to the movies. 'We felt we were really there when we could hear it,' says Kathleen Green, who saw *The Jazz Singer* when it was first screened in Britain. The idea of talking movies was so revolutionary that some people just could not believe they existed. 'We told my grandmother about the film when we came back,' Kathleen Green remembers, 'and she would not have it. Absolutely not...she would not believe you could hear them talking.'

The first sound systems were primitive yet highly effective, giving films a completely new dimension that could be used in many ways. Lisetta Salis, who went with her friends to see the film when it came to her home town in Italy, remembers the effect it had on them all. 'We were breathless,' she recalls. 'We kept saying to one another, "Let's watch it again".' And they did.

The introduction of sound was just one of several landmarks in people's experience of the cinema in the twentieth century. As they became increasingly widespread and sophisticated, movies made huge profits and created great industries and international stars. The power of film was so great that it was exploited for political ends. It fuelled people's aspirations, changing the way thousands of people thought about the world, and bringing new experiences, desires and ambitions to men and women whose horizons had previously been limited to their local communities. The cinema created a new, shared human consciousness. It not only showed people what the world was like but also offered them an escape into another one.

THE NEW MAGIC *of sound and screen attracts huge crowds to Warner's cinema.*

Silent beginnings

It was at a café in Paris in 1895 that the Lumière brothers first presented their moving pictures to a paying public audience. The programme of ten short films lasted twenty minutes, and the impact on the audience was immense. Sophie Monneret, whose grandfather was there that night, describes how he returned home 'absolutely marvelling', and exclaiming, 'It's extraordinary! The world has changed!'

At the start of the twentieth century people in countries all over the world paid to watch films of many kinds – comedies, fantasies, information ('actuality') and drama. These early 'movies' found their largest audiences among the poor. Mario Coarelli was growing up in Italy, and describes the first cinema he went to, in a poor suburb, as 'a place for the common people'. He remembers how the movies appealed to whole families. 'There were children, young and old men, women with babies in their laps, and all eating roasted pumpkin seeds.' Sometimes people did not pay much attention to the film itself, but 'when a dramatic film was shown, you saw people crying,' and if it was exciting they 'watched the film and they all started saying, "You swine. Look at that scum!" You started thinking, "Is he really dead? No, they're just faking it." The older people who were there, they were totally fascinated by the cinema.'

When he was only eight years old Luigi Cavaliere was the projectionist at his church theatre in Rome where local children attended catechism classes. 'They were more toys than projectors,' he remembers. 'There was a small crank that had to be turned to project the silent film. We had four or five films in storage, and we showed them over and over again.'

In India early films were shown in tents. When Rajam Ramanathan was seven years old her mother took her to see her first film. 'There would be sand poured on the ground where people could sit, and there were benches, and chairs without armrests, and finally chairs with armrests that were the most expensive seats in the house....There was a person standing in the front of the theatre who would say what the actors were supposed to be saying.'

MOBILE THEATRES *like this early Electric Theatre offering 'moral and refined' film spectacles to the American public were a growing feature of both town and country at the turn of the century. Travelling projectionists could easily set up their tents, bringing the new medium to fairgrounds and marketplaces. By 1905 these makeshift theatres were being replaced by permanent movie houses.*

FILM PREMIERE
With their newly invented Cinématographe, the Lumière brothers showed their films to audiences as excited as the one in this early film poster. Other pioneers of film techniques in Europe and the United States were quick to follow their lead. In 1905, after making thousands of films, the Lumière brothers decided to abandon film production.

INVENTION AND ENTERPRISE

IT TOOK A FLASH of inspiration for one man to jump the final hurdle in the race to develop moving pictures. Louis Lumière was that man. His brainwave was to install a mechanism to drive film through a camera, stopping it at intervals when a frame of film was in the 'gate'. The mechanism was based on a device called the presser foot, which shifts cloth through a sewing machine. This idea enabled Louis and his brother Auguste to develop the Cinématographe, with which they could both shoot and project films.

Although it was the Lumière brothers who found the key to projecting moving images onto a big screen, most of the technology needed for cinema, including colour and sound, was already available. Eadweard Muybridge, an English photographer employed by the Californian millionaire Leland Stanford, had broken new ground in the 1870s when he recorded a sequence of photographs showing a galloping horse. He succeeded in breaking down complex movements into a series of images taken at intervals of just a fraction of a second.

Another major breakthrough came in 1888 with the development of light-sensitive paper that could be placed on a roll – a film. The paper was soon replaced by celluloid and marketed by its American inventor, George Eastman, under its trade name Kodak. In the same year Thomas Edison, another American inventor and entrepreneur, also began to take an interest in the development of moving pictures. By 1891 one of his British employees, William Dickson, had built both a film camera, the Kinetograph, and a viewer, the Kinetoscope. By 1894 there were commercial viewing 'parlours' for the Kinetoscope in the United States, but the spectator had to peer into a little wooden box, and it was only possible to produce films of about a minute long.

Edison concentrated on selling the Kinetoscope to wealthy families for individual viewing, and paid little attention to the possibility of projecting the images onto a large screen. It was the Lumière brothers who were the first to recognize the enormous public appeal films would have. In the months that followed their first public showings in Paris in 1895 their representatives travelled the world showing films to excited new audiences.

MUSICAL ACCOMPANIMENT
*to silent films provided by
pianos (ABOVE), organs and
even orchestras, together with
the cheering and hissing of
the audience, meant that
the theatre was rarely
quiet while a film was
being shown. Danny
Patt (BELOW) used cue
sheets and imagination to play the piano at
his local movie theatre. Some cinema organs (ABOVE
RIGHT) came equipped with special
sound effects: drums, bells and
coconut shells mimicked
thunderstorms, sirens and a
trotting horse.*

The silent movies soon became one of the most popular forms of entertainment, eclipsing even the music hall and vaudeville. Many people went to the new movie theatres several times a week. Barry Johnson, who grew up in the country in southern England, remembers going to the cinema from the age of five. It was wonderful to be able to find something new and different to do. 'It was a great relief to be able to walk to the cinema at least once a week to get some amusement. We looked forward to it very much. It was a very small cinema, and had a solid floor with bench seats, and we as kiddies used to call it the "flea pit".'

It was the same in the United States, where the first cinemas were called 'nickelodeons' because the admission fee was just five cents, a nickel. They were usually concentrated in the poorer neighbourhoods, and became a central feature of many immigrant districts. Many of the theatre owners were themselves immigrants from eastern Europe, and some went on to play a major part in the great Hollywood film industry.

Although the films themselves were silent, music was often played to accompany them. Danny Patt grew up in Maine in the United States, and when he was just twelve years old he began to play the piano in his local movie theatre. He describes how he had to match the music to the films. 'A cue sheet was a very important part of the show because it told you what to play and when, and for how long.' No music was given to the pianists, so they had to build up their own collection. 'You had to have a good repertoire of mood music such as hurries, chase music, battle music, fight music, Indians and cowboys, marches and all that sort of thing.'

Part of the success of the early silent movies was due to their universal appeal. Without language, films could be understood throughout the world, and their stars shot to international fame. The first and greatest star was a comedian whose trademarks were a smudge of a moustache, a bowler hat and a cane. Millions of people came to love the exploits of the little tramp. He did not only appeal to adults, as Barry Johnson explains. 'Charlie Chaplin portrayed on screen the simplicity of funniness which the children easily understood, both in his actions and his pathos, the twirl of his stick, his little trip and mannerisms.'

Audiences all over the world understood and loved Chaplin's films. As a young girl in India, Nimmal Vellani watched every Chaplin film she could. She loved all of them, and 'especially *The Gold Rush*, because it's really beautiful that scene where he eats those boots of his – opens the laces and thinks it's spaghetti or something. It's really lovely.' *The Gold Rush* was the favourite film of Monique Guédant in France, too, who first saw it at a church film show in Normandy. 'When you are young and you see a movie by Charlie Chaplin, it is really enchanting. I remember especially that cabin at the top of the mountain, and the bear circling around the cabin with Charlie Chaplin. We didn't know if we wanted the bear to eat Charlie Chaplin or Charlie Chaplin to eat the bear!' she laughs.

CHARLIE CHAPLIN
(ABOVE LEFT) *or Charlot as he was known in Europe, captivated audiences with his sympathetic and comic portrayals of hardship and poverty. The British-born former vaudeville artist began his film career in the United States in 1913, and later wrote, directed and starred in his own films like* The Gold Rush *(1925), about the adventures of a prospector.*

ROOM FOR COMEDY
(ABOVE) *Some movie theatres showed only comedies, the most popular films of all. People went to the cinema above all to be entertained, and they could choose from a growing number of different types of comic films – from slapstick to chase films – at movie theatres devoted principally to comedy, like this one in the United States in 1915.*

"*These theatres had ceilings that were painted blue and special projectors that would project clouds and stars and sunrises on the roof....When the film started the curtain would part...the lights would go down and you would literally be drawn into this thing by your surroundings.*"

CY LOCKE

THE TOOTING GRANADA (OPPOSITE), *one of the opulent new cinemas in London, accommodated more than 3000 people at each performance. Len Smith remembers those picture palaces. 'They called them a palace and it was a palace...the hangings, the draperies and everything inside the cinema was absolutely wonderful...the cinema was the only place where I had seen this luxury.'*

LURING AN AUDIENCE (BELOW) *with exotic surroundings, live entertainment and star-studded film previews was Sid Grauman's answer to competition. At his ornate Chinese Theatre in Hollywood, built in 1927, movie stars were also invited to record their hand and foot prints for posterity in the concrete paving of the forecourt.*

The movie experience

During the 1920s shrewd theatre owners realized that they would increase their profits if movies could be made to appeal to a wider audience, the prosperous as well as the poor. One way of doing this was to make the audience more comfortable. In the cities new cinemas were constructed on a grand scale. Cinemas like the Roxy in New York, Grauman's Chinese and Egyptian theatres in Hollywood, the Gaumont in Paris and the Odeon, Marble Arch in London were designed in spectacular architectural style, and with extravagant and exotic interior decor. Luxurious cushioned seats replaced the old wooden benches, and pianos were replaced by mighty organs or full orchestras. These new cinemas became known as 'picture palaces', and offered a new taste of luxury.

John Anderson was a student in Boston in the 1920s, and got a job as one of more than thirty ushers at the Metropolitan, which seated 4000 people. He remembers the trouble that was taken to make movie-goers feel good. 'I was on the main floor, just inside the door. Outside, there was another usher all dressed up, with a dickey shirt front and a lovely jacket....The outside man had a swagger stick, and opened the door as the people were passed in to the second usher, who showed them to their seats.'

Cy Locke, who also lived near Boston, worked at pitching hay to earn enough money to go to the movies. 'It was really an experience,' he recalls. 'You would be treated like a king or queen. You were ushered into an enormous lobby of marble and gilt, with huge stairways leading up to the balconies. All the carpets were at least an inch or two thick. Everything was done in there to make you feel comfortable, to make you feel very important.'

In Scotland a young pianist, Rita Wooton, found work playing in the orchestra at the new Strathclyde cinema in Glasgow after passing her audition. She was impressed both by its size and by the facilities it provided. 'It had a very big balcony, a big vestibule too at the entry...and also a huge stage, of course. It had a grand piano for myself in the band pit. There were violins, cellos, saxophones, trumpets, trombones, drums, everything!'

NEWS HORIZONS (BELOW) *The Biograph Company produced weekly newsreels offering viewers the 'Latest events from all parts of the world'. These became regular features in cinemas, and for the first time people could see for themselves events that took place far away. For George Williams in Britain they were an important part of the show. 'The cinema was the only place where you picked up what went on elsewhere in the world, that's where we picked up most of our news.' The Pathé Gazette, produced by the leading French film company, also brought popular newsreels to international audiences from 1909.*

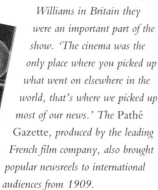

Barry Johnson's family decided to enter the film business in 1920. They bought a cinema in London. 'It was a medium-sized cinema seating about four to five hundred people.' He helped his father as projectionist, while his mother looked after the cash box. He recalls how after the shows, 'We had to go round and sweep up all the orange peel and the peanuts, with a screwdriver in one hand and a brush in the other, because the children would get so excited that they would literally shake their seats to pieces.'

One of the things that made the cinema so exciting was that it opened people's eyes and minds. As Danny Patt says, 'We didn't have radio then, there was no way for one town to communicate with another....By watching the silent movies we were able to see what was going on in the rest of the world. It was a wonderful thing for these small towns to be able to get that education.'

THE AMERICAN EPIC

THE WILD WEST, with its intrepid pioneers and heroic cowboys, became one of the most popular film subjects. First featured in Thomas Edison's first Kinetoscope show in 1894, the Western adapted to every shift in the fashions and fortunes of the movie industry. In the era of silent film, tales were told through cowboys such as Tom Mix, who fought black-hatted villains against a backdrop of breathtaking scenery. He was followed by singing cowboys such as Gene Autry, Roy Rogers and Hopalong Cassidy.

The essence of all Westerns was the conflict between good and evil, and the audience's enthusiasm to see the struggle resolved through action-packed drama. George Williams remembers his first experience of Westerns as a child in east London in the 1930s: 'When the film showed the white-hatted cowboys everybody cheered, when they flashed onto the bad cowboys, everybody booed.' The conflict could be set between white men and native Americans or Mexicans, between ranchers and homesteaders, or any individual against the community.

The first Westerns portrayed simple moral stories. By the 1930s some were beginning to explore more subtle types of conflict. *The Robin Hood of El Dorado* in 1936 and *The Oxbow Incident* in 1943 demonstrated the brutality of lynch law in the Old West, and asked searching questions about the racism and cruelty of Western expansion. In 1952 *High Noon* was interpreted by many people as an attack on the victimization of communist sympathizers at that time.

Above all, cowboys represented the most prized American virtues: independence, endurance, honesty and courage. These were epitomized by John Wayne as the classic hero in films such as *Stagecoach* and *She Wore a Yellow Ribbon*. Westerns, with their action-packed drama, spectacular settings, idealized heroes and moral resolution appealed not only to Americans, who could recognize the story of their own society on the screen, but thrilled cinema audiences in all parts of the world.

SETTING THE SCENE (ABOVE) *As the possibilities of film making grew more ambitious and challenging, directors began to explore new subjects and ways of dealing with them. Taking a lead from the Italian film industry, which began making historical, biblical and mythological epic films, Hollywood produced its own film extravaganzas.* Intolerance, *made in 1915, used elaborate settings like ancient Babylon to explore people's attitudes to others' beliefs. Although it was one of the most expensive films to be made at the time, it was not a commercial success.*

COWBOY STAR *Tom Mix, renowned for his skilful horsemanship, in a scene from* Rough Riding Romance.

A ʀᴏᴍᴀɴᴛɪᴄ ꜱᴄᴇɴᴇ *from the 1927 Hollywood film* Flesh and the Devil, *starring the Swedish actress Greta Garbo and John Gilbert. The cinema brought romance to viewers across the world, and millions of young men and women learned new ways to kiss by imitating lovers on the screen.*

People were even more delighted when talking pictures were introduced, though audiences accustomed to booing and hissing the villains and shouting when they felt excited had to learn to behave differently and keep quiet in order to hear what was being said. Now audiences in different countries needed the help of dubbing or subtitles to understand foreign language films.

Sound was not welcomed by everyone. The musicians who had accompanied silent films, which nobody wanted to watch any more, lost their jobs. It was a sad occasion for Danny Patt. 'When *The Jazz Singer* came out every little town throughout the United States...had a piano player or an organist or somebody playing for the silent movies....I realized that part of my career was nipped in the bud. I was full of grief.' Rita Wooton felt the same. 'The advent of the talkies was a tremendous blow to all musicians.... There must have been hundreds in Glasgow who were employed in the orchestra pits.'

Many of the small, older cinemas were also badly affected. They lacked the facilities and the space to show the new movies, and often could not afford the extra equipment. As Barry Johnson remembers, it meant 'all the average-sized silent cinemas closing down, one by one', including the one his family owned.

The cinema held a special attraction for young courting couples. Franco Ricci, who grew up in Rome, recalls, 'We didn't have cars...our refuge was the cinema. Nobody paid any attention to what other people were doing, no one was scandalized.' For the young Cy Locke in Boston, 'To go to the movies and not hold hands was absolutely out of the question. If you sat in the back row, that was fine, and it wasn't beyond the realms of possibility to try and sneak a kiss now and again.'

As well as being a refuge, the cinema was a school for lovers. Nimmal Vellani was shocked when she first saw people kissing on the screen. Most Indian films at the time were very chaste. She claims romance came into her life through movies. 'If there was one young girl falling in love with a nice-looking man, I would imagine myself doing the same thing. And it actually happened in my life that way. If I had not gone to the cinema so often, I would not have had romance in my life. I would just have been married off like an ordinary girl to the man of my grandfather's choice.'

Bʀᴏᴀᴅᴡᴀʏ ᴍᴜꜱɪᴄᴀʟ
With the new sound came a new kind of film — the musical. This first musical, Broadway Melody, *was made in 1929; it was also one of the earliest films to use Technicolor in some of its sequences. Experiments with colour film processes continued during the 1930s.*

The Hollywood dream

By the 1920s audiences around the world were flocking to see American films. The American film industry was not only making more films, it also exported them successfully, producing films that had enormous international popular appeal and subtly sold the view that American capitalism offered the best way of life. Like many others, Kathleen Green liked American films best. 'They were very lively and full of fun, and the British films seemed rather slow...not much in the way of chorus girls or happy times.' In Italy Lisetta Salis also remembers their fascination. She and her friends were struck by the great freedom that American girls seemed to enjoy, such as going out with their boyfriends, and she remembers their clothes as 'more revealing than what would have been worn in any other country'. She first saw a telephone, a car, and a skyscraper on the screen. 'Really the cinema was a great emotional experience! Of course later we became accustomed to these things, but the first moments were so exciting.'

Some people had mixed feelings about the wealth and luxury they saw in American films. Luigi Cavaliere remembers his mother's surprise that industrial workers in the United States owned cars, and Lisetta Salis feels that although people were very curious about American films, 'At the same time they were showing us how backward we were, because in the films they were wealthy...they were successful, happy, lively, well-dressed. The idea of being poorer and less elegant made us feel wretched.'

The American film industry was expanding from its base in Hollywood in California, where cheap real estate and reliable sunshine provided an ideal setting for massive film production. It was Hollywood and its stars that fascinated millions of people across the world, becoming synonymous with glamour, drama and romance. American fashions and new trends were successfully exported through its films.

In some countries attempts were made to resist the dominance of the American film industry. In Britain and Germany quotas were imposed, so film

THE STAR SYSTEM

THE FIRST MOVIE STARS were not names but faces. Actors and actresses in early silent films were not credited, so fans identified their favourite artists simply by their looks or by the studio that employed them. In 1909 Carl Laemmle, head of Universal Pictures, took the unprecedented step of naming the 'Biograph Girl' as Florence Lawrence. In a blaze of publicity he also hinted (untruthfully) that she had been killed in an accident. There was a public outcry. Studios began to realize the value of publicizing information about their actors, and a network of promotion and publicity was set up. The star system was launched.

Studios exploited the public's fascination with the stars by carefully feeding facts and gossip to magazines and newspapers. William Fox, founder of 20th Century Fox, promoted a tailor's daughter from Cincinnati as 'Theda Bara', an anagram of 'Arab death'. He circulated rumours that she was the daughter of an Arab sheikh, and portrayed her as a mysterious, exotic seductress.

There were also comic stars like Charlie Chaplin and the Frenchman Max Linder. The greatest, most romantic film stars of all were the swashbuckling swordsman Douglas Fairbanks and his wife, Mary Pickford; she became known as 'the world's sweetheart'. The couple were idolized by millions of fans. The cinema usher John Anderson remembers, 'Everybody was fascinated by movie stars, and especially by Douglas Fairbanks'. He recalls the public excitement when the star couple visited Boston. 'I stood there for hours waiting in line just to get a short glimpse of him when he went by in his limousine....He was my favourite movie star and I saw every single picture that he played in.'

While the stars were expected to parade the trappings of stardom – palatial mansions with huge swimming pools, limousines, and glamorous social lives – they were used by the studios as capital assets. A star's name would guarantee an audience, and would put a 'trademark' value on a film. But in return for astronomical wages, the studios imposed strict controls on their stars' lives. Stars could be loaned out to other film companies, or suspended without pay if they turned down a part.

The Hollywood system proved highly successful as a way of promoting films; the stars provided a dazzling diversion to their fans.

companies had to produce a certain number of home-grown films before foreign imports were allowed. This was only marginally successful because many of the film companies simply rushed through the production of cheap, poor-quality films in order to reach the quota. These films became known as 'quota quickies'.

Ever since the movies had first reached a public audience, church groups and other establishment figures had feared that they were immoral and that their influence would be corrupting. The liberated way of life portrayed by Hollywood films added fuel to this debate. Some people were scandalized by any suggestion, let alone portrayal, of sexual activity. Kathleen Green remembers the impact of one scene in a film she saw as a child. 'The man came out of the bedroom and there was an awful fuss.' She recalls that she and her friend were very innocent, and did not understand the sexual implications. 'We came to the conclusion that he had gone to bed with his shoes on.'

Pressure on Hollywood to improve its moral standards intensified, and a code of practice was established setting out what was and what was not permissible, both on the screen and off it. The Hays commission hoped to fend off state censorship through its new production codes, which were particularly concerned about sex. 'There could be no kisses with two people in bed together, even if they were husband and wife,' recalls Arthur Abeles. To counteract the adverse publicity arising out of scandals about the behaviour of Hollywood stars, a major public relations campaign was launched to emphasize the importance of the movies to American life. In other countries, which had their own censorship codes, concerns over film content varied, sometimes including portrayals of religion or politics. Whatever the moral dilemma, nothing seemed to lessen the grip Hollywood had on the public imagination. The popularity and power of its films remained undiminished.

GLAMOROUS STARS
Jean Harlow (LEFT) *and the celebrity couple Douglas Fairbanks and Mary Pickford* (BELOW LEFT) *were among the stars who captivated the attention of millions of fans. Their carefully shaped public image was often matched by their exotic private lives. But the fantasy did not last. Douglas Fairbanks and Mary Pickford divorced in 1936, as their careers were fading, and Jean Harlow died of ill health the following year.*

THE SMOULDERING SEXUALITY *of Jane Russell in* The Outlaw *proved too much for the censors. A cut version was finally released several years after the film was first made in 1943.*

RAJA HARISHCHANDRA
(ABOVE) *was the first Indian feature
film. Based on ancient Hindu texts, it tells
the story of a king who gives up his earthly possessions to gain
salvation. Its female roles were played by men. When Rajam
Ramanathan (ABOVE RIGHT) saw it as a young girl, she says,
'It was like God actually appeared in front of us....My
grandmother would even pat her cheeks as penance whenever
Rama or Krishna showed up on the screen.'*

EXPRESSIONS OF ANGST (BELOW) *in Fritz Lang's 1931
film – M – about a series of child murders. It was the first film
in which the leading director used sound. These nightmarish
scenes were characteristic of German expressionist films.*

National cinema

Hollywood exerted a powerful influence, but many countries had also been developing film industries of their own, with their own character. In India the film industry was begun by one man, Dadasaheb Phalke. Inspiration struck when he went to see a movie called *The Life of Christ*. 'I was mentally visualizing the gods, Shri Krishna, Shri Ramchandra and Ayodha. Would we, the sons of India, ever be able to see Indian images on the screen?' Spurred on by what he had seen, Dadasaheb Phalke worked day and night for six months with equipment he had bought in Europe until, in 1913, he produced the first Indian movie, *Raja Harishchandra*. He had laid the foundations for what would later become one of the world's most prolific film industries.

Indian movies soon found a widespread and enthusiastic audience. Older people were astonished by the new medium, and mythological films in particular had a huge impact. Vanraj Bhatia recalls how his great-aunt, who was ninety-two years old, reacted when she went to her first movie, which was about Krishna. 'She went absolutely berserk, she wept and prayed and she prostrated herself, and she thought God had finally arrived.' People took off their shoes before entering the cinemas, he says. 'It was as though they were going to a temple or something.'

PLAYING FOR POWER

FILMS WERE UNIQUE in their power to play on people's credulity and to manipulate their emotions. Almost from the start, the immense impact that films had on those who saw them was turned to political purposes: dictators and totalitarian governments used film for propaganda.

In Italy the fascist government exercised great influence in the film industry through subsidies. When people went to the cinema they became a captive audience for the documentary films that were screened as a regular addition to the programme. Some people enjoyed watching them, but others found them an imposition. Mario Coarelli's family lived in fear after his father had been attacked for his anti-fascist feelings. He remembers that 'All the movies were mainly propagandist….Whenever they spoke, it was all for propagandist aims: "Long live fascism!"…and you sat there and were taught what they wanted you to learn. You had to watch it.'

In Germany entertainment was used as the way to spread the Nazi message. Uninspiring feature films were superseded by sentimental 'waltz dreams', stories of mountain climbers, comedies and lavish historical films, all celebrating the pomp and splendour of Germany's past. Powerful documentaries promoted the Nazi ideals of supreme military order and the superiority of the Aryan race, and viciously anti-Semitic films were also made – all effective ways of shaping the minds of the German people.

During the Second World War the persuasive power of film was exploited in many nations. In the United States a series of seven documentaries was made to explain *Why We Fight*. Cy Locke was the projectionist at his army base and ran all seven of them, including *Know Your Enemy – Japan*. 'Its intent was to make us hate the Japanese,' he remembers. 'They were our enemy and we were supposed to destroy them, and the film certainly served its purpose….I have to fight with myself about that because I was really indoctrinated.'

While American soldiers were being taught to hate the Japanese, audiences in Japan were being shown 'national policy films' that taught them about their war responsibilities and the glories of military life. Nationalistic fervour in the Soviet Union was stirred up by documentary films such as *The Defeat of German Armies Outside Moscow*, which showed thousands of bedraggled, humiliated German soldiers, defeated by the Russian forces.

Film was also used constructively. Racial attitudes in the United States were helped to change by a highly influential film made in 1944, *The Negro Soldier*. Compulsory viewing for all soldiers, black and white, and shown to civilian audiences in 5000 cinemas across the country, it showed the most positive image of black Americans ever seen on screen up to that time – a positive result of film's power to change the world inside people's heads.

PROPAGANDA FILMS *Scriptwriter Carlton Moss recalls how the United States military authorities tried to boost morale among black soldiers in the army, who were still segregated. 'They had to do something on this black question…film was one of the things they were going to use.'*

In Germany the local film industry was also flourishing, especially in the studios that had developed out of the propaganda industry of the First World War. After the war German films reflected the prevailing mood of the time – they were full of pain and foreboding. In the Soviet Union, too, a vigorous film industry developed that reflected the political flavour of Soviet life. Films were used to support the revolution and its achievements, and played a vital part in mythologizing it for the people. They went to the cinema not for escapism or to canoodle in the back row, but to participate in the new socialist culture.

A world of make-believe

The harsh realities that were reflected in German and Soviet films soon became part of real life elsewhere. In 1929 the world was plunged into a devastating economic depression, and the next decade brought great hardship to millions of people. Cinema could offer a brief escape from the real world.

Arthur Abeles, who worked for the American film company Warner Brothers, recalls how competitive the cinemas had to be to draw in their audiences. 'Nobody had any money, so we had to attract them with gifts, things like that....Some people put on variety acts on the stage....But the only way really to get people into a cinema, and they'll come whether they're broke or they're not broke, is a good film.'

The films produced by Hollywood during the Depression were among the most extravagant and spectacular of all time, in dramatic contrast to most people's experience of life at the time. Kitty Carlisle Hart, who appeared with the Marx Brothers in their comedy *A Night at the Opera*, remembers how people responded to the glamorous films that were being shown. 'They were make-believe,' she says. 'They were the world that people didn't have, but that they wanted. And that's why they were so popular.... People were living in terrible circumstances; this was total escape.'

Although most people lacked money to buy warm clothes and struggled to pay the rent, they still flocked to the American movies to see film stars in elegant gowns and well-tailored suits, living in sumptuous apartments with expensive furniture. Cy Locke remembers what the Depression was like for so many people. 'The main square in the town would be filled with little kids shining shoes, selling papers, people wandering aimlessly around,' he says. 'I think that what movies did for these people and for us was to brighten what was virtually an intolerable situation.'

Comedy films were also very popular. Laughter was therapeutic, and as Mary Evelyn Hults, who grew up in New York, remembers, people needed it more than ever. 'It was very cheap to go to the movies in those days. But thinking about what kind of money

GOING FOR GLAMOUR *at the cinema in the 1930s provided relief from reality. Cy Locke (ABOVE) recalls how 'Many people would take what I assume was their last dime or their last quarter, and go see Ginger Rogers and Fred Astaire just to escape for a couple of hours.' The dancing duo, (BELOW) in the comedy musical* Carefree, *also initiated new dance crazes and fashions.*

"Just going and laughing for a little while at something that might be totally ridiculous was very important. It was a therapy really in many ways."

MARY EVELYN HULTS

HOLLYWOOD FANTASIES *offered audiences lavish ballroom scenes (*LEFT*) as escapism or the alternative world of horror in monster movies like* King Kong *(*RIGHT*). Large crews were needed for the elaborate studio sets and special effects, providing jobs at a time of widespread unemployment.*

GAME FOR A LAUGH (BELOW) *The Marx Brothers captivated audiences with their hilarious eccentricity in their 1935 hit* A Night at the Opera. *The American comic trio were originally part of a family vaudeville act with their mother and two other brothers, and staged successful plays on Broadway. Groucho's wisecracks and the chaotic activities of Chico and Harpo were at the heart of all their films.*

QUEUEING UP *for the Saturday morning cinema show in Britain in the 1940s was necessary if you wanted to be sure of a seat. 'You might have to go there half an hour or even an hour before it started, if it was a very popular picture,' remembers Ena Turnbull. 'We didn't mind how long we queued as long as we got in.' Cinemas continued to show films during the war to people who were much in need of entertainment. During air raids the screen would flash a warning sign at the audience.*

we didn't have, it was a very special treat. It was a difficult time for people....Just going and laughing for a bit at something that might be totally ridiculous was very important.' People loved the Marx Brothers, with their anarchic humour, and when Charlie Chaplin's latest comedies, *City Lights* and *Modern Times*, were released they were instant successes.

During the Second World War, too, films offered refuge from misery, and even provided inspiration. In German-occupied France the Nazi censors had approved a film called *The Night Visitors* as a simple love story set in the Middle Ages. To French audiences the heroine, Anne, represented France; the Devil, the night visitor, was Hitler. The Devil turns Anne and her lover into stone, but is finally defeated when he realizes that whatever he does, he cannot stop the beating of their hearts. The film's huge emotional impact helped to give Michel Lequenne the courage to join the Resistance movement, and fifty years later, as he re-reads that passage in the script – 'But it's their hearts that beat,' the Devil exclaims, 'That never cease to beat, that beat, beat, beat!' – he is still overcome with emotion: 'Look, I'm crying all over again'.

Boom and decline

Immediately after the war there was a boom in cinema attendance in Europe and in the United States. In Rome, Luigi Cavaliere remembers, 'Everybody wanted to have some fun, and the only thing available was the cinema. Television was not yet available. Everybody would eagerly wait for a new and beautiful film to watch. In these theatres, even if they were not well equipped, people would queue up anxiously waiting to watch the show.... Kids brought pans full of food from home while waiting for the theatre to open. Going to the movies was a party...everybody wished to forget about the ugliness of the war.' George Williams used to go to the cinema with his friends in London. 'The queues were so long, at times it was necessary to split ourselves up into ones and twos and just take whatever seats became available.'

During this time European film studios began producing better quality films than ever before, and local audiences started to identify with movies made by home-grown directors, first in Italy, then in Britain, France, Sweden and eastern Europe. International

ANIMATED IMAGINATION

WHEN A SMALL, mischievous mouse named Mickey first skipped across American cinema screens in 1928, animated film was catapulted into new realms of popularity. Walt Disney's *Steamboat Willie* was the first cartoon made with synchronized sound, and its star, Mickey Mouse, was to become an international celebrity.

Walt Disney played an enormous role in popularizing animation, but he did not invent it. Animation had existed before film itself, but moving pictures gave it a new lease of life. The camera could lie; film could bring life to the inanimate. Using a basic 'stop–motion' technique, films could record sequences of static images (drawings, puppets or models), each slightly different from the one before. When these images were projected in quick succession, the illusion of continuous movement was created.

Early cartoons tended to be short, commercial products designed to precede feature films, but a series of technical developments soon enabled them to stand as films in their own right. In 1913 Earl Hurd patented the use of a transparent medium bearing the moving parts of the cartoon over an opaque background. This technique used celluloid, and made the whole process of animation much quicker. Raoul Barre introduced the 'slash' system, which saved unnecessary drawing. The motionless parts of the characters were drawn only once, while the animated parts of the characters were drawn separately in many different positions. These drawings were then superimposed one at a time onto the background and photographed before the sequence was put together.

The arrival of sound in 1927 and the introduction of colour in the early 1930s allowed animators to create new worlds of magical fantasy. Walt Disney gave life to a cast of much-loved characters who became familiar all over the world to people of all ages. Cartoons were the ultimate escape, recreating a lost world of imagination for adults, and allowing children to revel in fantastic adventures that would be unthinkable in the real world.

MICKEY MOUSE *in his starring role as the sorcerer's apprentice in Walt Disney's phenomenally successful 1940 feature film,* Fantasia. *A whole generation of children were introduced to classical music by the film's cartoon figures, who were drawn to move to the music of Bach, Stravinsky and Tchaikovsky.*

PUBLIC SCREENINGS *at outdoor cinemas were held in postwar Europe at special festivals of international cinema. The huge screen in the courtyard of the Old Oberhaus Castle near Passau in western Germany needed new projection equipment, and special loudspeakers were used to relay films to the 40 000-strong audience. Film festivals awarded prizes and attracted distribution deals.*

film festivals meant that film makers could share new films and exchange new ideas and techniques. In Europe there was a move away from the glamour and fantasy of Hollywood. Italian 'neo-realist' films showed what real life was like. Mario Coarelli liked the new realism. 'They were so beautiful because they showed the same life we were leading,' he says. Franco Ricci appreciated them too, but felt that 'the majority of Italians did not accept this because they said that your dirty clothes should be washed in the family home and not shown abroad'.

Hollywood films were still popular, and as influential with their audiences. George Williams remembers that he learned from American films how to smoke, how to wear the collar of his overcoat pulled up round his ears, and how to kiss. He also remembers being impressed by the material comforts the Americans seemed to enjoy in the films. 'Their rooms always seemed so massive and the apartments so well lit, so luxururious. They had refrigerators, which I'd never seen....The cars were always

flash – great big limousines.' Children were encouraged to imitate the child star Shirley Temple. Ena Turnbull was one of them. 'Her hairstyle, her voice, her pretty little face – all mums tried to dress their little girls like Shirley.'

The postwar golden era for Hollywood was not to last. The monopoly of the big studios was challenged, and the film industry was shaken by accusations of communist influence. American movie audiences had reached their peak in the late 1940s, and gradually the fans began to drift away. Many of the sumptuous picture palaces closed and were refurbished as supermarkets or stores. Cy Locke remembers the changes. 'I still liked going to the movies, but there was a sadness...seeing half-empty theatres, and theatres that were starting to degrade in terms of upkeep.' In his view, cars contributed to the fall in audiences. 'Drive-ins were starting to flourish after the war,' he remembers. 'People could get out again, had enough gas to go places.' As people moved out to the suburbs they seldom went to the movies in town, and many young people tended to stay at home once they married and had

WIDESCREEN

processes like Cinerama and Cinemascope (ABOVE) *were the film industry's answer to television in 1953. Films such as* Tarzan *used new techniques to widen the audience's field of vision and give a heightened sense of movement and realism. This film poster also promotes the use of colour, gradually introduced in the late 1940s.*

PLANES, TRAINS AND CARS (OPPOSITE) *converge at a drive-in cinema in West Virginia, where people watch the big screen from the relative comfort of their cars.*

children. The baby boom spelled the end of the movie boom. Mary Evelyn Hults remembers, 'We had our first child and we seldom went out to the movies'. In Britain, too, as Arthur Abeles recalls, 'People got out of the habit of going twice a week, and they became more selective'. Cinemas and film companies introduced new tactics to draw back their audiences, from 3-D glasses to wider screens and even Smell-O-Vision, and an increasing number of films began to appear in colour.

These innovations were no match for the new entertainment medium. Television now caused a sensation that equalled that of 'the talkies' some twenty-five years earlier. For Ena Turnbull it meant the end of her cinema-going days. 'Television came in and that's when the cinema started to decline,' she says. All the cinema offered, and more, could now be enjoyed simply by turning a knob on the little box in the corner of the living room. People continued to watch films, but more often on television than at the cinema.

In countries where television was not yet available the film industry continued to flourish. India produced more feature films than any other nation during the 1950s. Many of these films, like those made elsewhere, were purely for entertainment, and the music in them was as important as the story. The film composer Vanraj Bhatia believes the songs were their lifeblood. 'With bad songs an Indian movie cannot succeed, no matter how good it is. But there have been bad films with good songs, and they have become hits.' The film industry in Japan was growing and also thrived during this period, as it did in China and South America.

Although the 1950s saw a decline in cinema attendance in some countries, it was still enriching many people's lives. Film had changed the way people saw the world, and to some extent the way they lived in it. 'It was everything,' declares Duilia Bartoli. 'It was about how to live, how to behave oneself, how to talk and walk and how to be courted....For me, it has been everything.'

WAITING FOR THE SHOW (RIGHT) *in Calcutta. While cinema queues in Europe and the United States were dwindling in the 1950s, the Indian film industry boomed.*

A NEW DIMENSION
Three-dimensional movies made during the 1950s required audiences to wear 3-D glasses, with transparent lenses, one red and one green to match the double image on the screen. The glasses, first introduced in 1935, had the thrilling effect of bringing the flat screen to life, but as Arthur Abeles describes, they presented practical problems. 'They had to be collected after each performance, cleaned and given out at the next performance.'

Master Race

THE NAZIS RULE IN GERMANY

WITH THE PRIDE AND precision of veteran soldiers, an apparently endless column of uniformed men moved through the dark streets of Berlin. They marched like conquerors under the Brandenburg Gate, then turned right into the Wilhelmstrasse, the heart of German government and German militarism. Yet these were not soldiers but well-drilled, fanatical supporters of national socialism. As they marched they carried flags and torches. The red and white banners displayed the symbol of the Nazis, the black swastika.

This was the night of 30 January 1933. The men were marching to the Chancellery, and there on the balcony to greet them was their leader, their Führer, Adolf Hitler. Above the blare of the marching bands rose the cheers of the watching crowds. Josef Felder, a socialist opponent of the Nazis, was among them. He remembers 'A sea of swastikas. We were out in the streets and went to the Brandenburg Gate, and watched the Nazis marching into power. People were drinking, there was a huge commotion. We were shocked by this incredible upsurge and the sudden swing to the Nazis' side.'

The Nazi propaganda machine beamed their victory throughout the nation. 'Like a blazing fire,' a radio announcer declared to his listeners, 'the news spreads across Germany: "Adolf Hitler is chancellor of the Reich!" A million hearts are aflame! The nation rejoices and gives thanks!' This was a colourful exaggeration, typical of the manipulation of public opinion that played such an important part in spreading Hitler's message across Germany.

Millions of Germans had opposed Hitler, millions had good reason to fear him. Yet it is also true that for many Germans at the time Hitler's strange grasping of power was a thrilling moment. After the First World War German pride had been badly wounded, and the country's prosperity shattered. By 1933 many Germans felt that only Hitler could give them back their jobs and their security, and restore the greatness and honour of the German people. He promised that he would make the world acknowledge the Germans as a master race, and many believed him.

ORDERED RANKS OF NAZIS *march triumphantly through the streets of Berlin.*

Democracy in crisis

Hitler rose to power in a period of chaos in Germany. In the early months of 1918, fifteen years before, imperial Germany seemed to be on the eve of a crowning victory against the Allied armies in the First World War. Instead, it was the German army that broke. Then the emperor abdicated and fled to Holland, and a republic was proclaimed. For the first time democracy was introduced in Germany under the Weimar Republic. But the country was on the verge of revolution. For a few weeks in 1918 and 1919, political extremists fought in the streets of Berlin, while the Allies imposed a vengeful peace that was to prove disastrous to the German economy.

The new government had to contend with grave difficulties arising from military defeat and a collapsing economy, problems that were not of its making but for which it was blamed. Moderate government seemed to be weak; democracy powerless. Then, with the help of American loans and investments, the economy began to revive. For five short years, from 1924 to 1929, in spite of everything, the Weimar Republic succeeded in restoring order. But the world recession was to bring further disaster. In each of the winters of 1930–31 and 1931–32 over six million people were unemployed; in one of every two German families the breadwinner was out of work. In their frustration and despair, many Germans turned to extremist parties for their salvation.

However, Hitler did not come to power as the result of an overwhelming popular vote. In the 1932 elections only a third of the electorate voted for the Nazis. Millions of people not only did not support what they stood for, but dreaded a future under Hitler's leadership. They had good reason to be fearful. As soon as Hitler took power, he quashed all opposition to Nazi rule. Political opponents were put in concentration camps, and trade unions were banned.

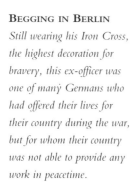

BEGGING IN BERLIN
Still wearing his Iron Cross, the highest decoration for bravery, this ex-officer was one of many Germans who had offered their lives for their country during the war, but for whom their country was not able to provide any work in peacetime.

SCAVENGING FOR FOOD
in the streets of Hanover. This was one way to get enough to eat – not always easy in the harsh reality of life during the economic crisis of the 1920s.

WHEN MONEY WENT MAD

THE HYPERINFLATION OF 1923 had a more profoundly disastrous effect on German society than any of the other hardships that befell the German people in or as a result of the First World War.

In 1914 4.2 gold marks equalled one United States dollar. By 1921 one dollar was worth 250 marks. The following year the rate was 1460 marks to the dollar, and in 1923 the inflation simply went crazy. In the summer the rate was 48 000 marks to the dollar. On 4 October it was 440 million, on 23 October fifty-six billion and by 17 November it was two and a half trillion. A solution was then found by issuing the new rentenmark, guaranteed against Germany's assets – land and railways. The government waited until the exchange rate was 4.2 trillion marks – in other words, until the old mark was worth one-trillionth of what it had been against the dollar in 1914. One trillion old marks could therefore be exchanged for one new mark, and the inflation disappeared overnight.

In its crazy course of little more than a year, the hyperinflation had done appalling damage. It reduced to nothing money hoarded during decades of hard work. Women could no longer save for their dowry, and worried about whether they could get married without one. Postage stamps were overprinted with seven, eight or even nine zeros. Banknotes were used as fuel for stoves. People paid for meals in restaurants before they ate because the price would have gone up before they had drunk their coffee. Others carted their savings to the baker's in wheelbarrows. Those with assets in land, in factories or in foreign currency became rich beyond their wildest dreams, while wages and salaries were worth almost nothing. Many Germans blamed the Weimar government, as malnutrition, hunger, fear and despair became the daily experience not only of those who already knew the effects of poverty, but also of many people accustomed to prosperity.

THE LAST STAMP
(ABOVE) *to be issued during the period of hyperinflation. Its value was 5000 million marks.*

BUNDLES OF BANKNOTES (LEFT) *may have been almost worthless, but they could still come in useful as building bricks.*

Hitler's new vision

Hitler skilfully manipulated people's desire to regain what they felt they had lost: pride in Germany's past, hope for its future, a sense of adventure, a sense of security. He would make Germany great again; all the German people were required to do was...do as they were told. Many people were relieved to find a leader with such confidence and strength, and were prepared to accept his belief that in the name of national unity and the restoration of order party politics should be abandoned, that only a strong government could take the harsh measures that needed to be taken. One of the

FROM FAILURE TO FÜHRER

BEFORE THE FIRST WORLD WAR, Adolf Hitler was a lonely, embittered, feckless young man. None who knew him then would have predicted his rise to power. A school dropout and failed art student, arrogant, lazy and aloof, he lived in a men's hostel in Vienna. He had squandered his inheritance, and had to paint picture postcards that earned him a pittance. Most children grow out of playing war games; in his teens, they were still Hitler's favourite occupation. The war offered him a chance to play these games for real: he could now become a hero. He was given the dangerous job of battalion runner and was decorated three times for bravery. He was regarded as an eager and dutiful soldier, but failed to be promoted because of his subservience to his officers and arrogance towards his fellow soldiers.

When the war ended Hitler, like the rest of the German army, was shocked by defeat and by the demoralized society he found when he returned. His own past humiliations and failures now became identified with Germany's fate. Many of the elite storm troopers (fast-moving, lightly but lethally equipped soldiers) joined the Freikorps, irregular units that were encouraged by the army high command to fight revolutionaries and communists, to invade Germany's lost eastern territories and to attack radicals and Jews.

After the war Hitler discovered his abilities as an orator among the disillusioned young men of Munich, particularly Freikorps members, anti-Semitic ideologues and right-wing plotters. He joined the German Workers' Party, the DAP, later renamed the National Socialist German Workers' Party (NSDAP or Nazis). Within a year he had become its undisputed leader. In November 1923 he leapt onto a table in a Munich beer cellar and proclaimed his plans for a coup. He was to march on Berlin and overthrow the Weimar Republic. Instead he was arrested and imprisoned.

While he was in prison Hitler wrote his political manifesto, *Mein Kampf*, 'My Struggle'. Many of his ideas had been gleaned from political pamphlets published before the war; now he infused them with his own hatred, anger and desire for revenge. The book was anti-Semitic, anti-communist, anti-Versailles, full of extreme nationalist sentiments. It laid out all too clearly this provincial politician's plans for taking over the state, reviving Germany as a power and destroying the Jews and all others whom he saw as his enemies. At the time, these ideas seemed so outrageous that few people took them – or their author – seriously.

Hitler undoubtedly had gifts: an extraordinary ability to influence and persuade, powerful appeal as a demagogue, a superb memory for detail, great skills as an actor who had total control of his voice. The extreme political and economic situation in postwar Germany provided circumstances in which these gifts, devastatingly combined with Hitler's complete ruthlessness and lack of compassion, were to sweep this unlikely leader to power.

REACHING OUT TO HITLER *An enthusiastic crowd surges towards Hitler, cheered by his promises to make Germany great again.*

ways in which Hitler gained support was to confirm people's view that the difficulties they endured were not of Germany's making, but were really the fault of politicians, the Allies, the communists, bankers, speculators and Jews. He offered them scapegoats – and promised to deal with them.

At the same time, Hitler seemed to offer a new vision, of Germany restored to all its former glory. His ideal was rooted in Teutonic myth, harking back to a time when German knights had been honourable and chivalrous, and their ladies beautiful and pure. Germans were flattered to be told that their Aryan ancestors had been a superior, uniquely cultured race. They were assured that they could regain this lost quality if they followed Hitler, who would lead the drive to turn the German people into the heroic race they deserved to be – the master race.

Hitler's rhetoric was an inspiration and a balm to those who shrank from the hardships, horrors and uncertainties of twentieth-century reality, with its wars and revolutions. They found refuge in the reactionary paradise Hitler offered them: an idealized German community that would be peopled only by pure, honest, beautiful, strong Aryans, unpolluted by the presence of modern ideas, or by Jews or Slavs. In particular, he drew on old hatreds, old jealousies towards the Jews.

A **vast crowd** *watches as massed troops parade in front of Hitler at a rally in Nuremberg. Deliberately magnificent in scale, and held in dramatic and imposing settings, the rallies reflected the Nazis' obsession with power and order.*

> *"Today our people know our will was stronger than the German crisis. After fifteen years of despair a great people is back on its feet."*
>
> ADOLF HITLER

An election poster (ABOVE) *for the Nazis depicts the misery of unemployment and urges people to turn to Hitler as 'Our last hope'.*

REINHARD SPITZY *and his wife fulfilled all the necessary conditions to marry and to breed Aryan children. The state gave loans to healthy couples to help them raise larger families, and even awarded medals to unusually productive mothers.*

THE IDEALIZATION OF MOTHERHOOD (OPPOSITE) *was part of the Nazis' reshaping of society. Posters such as this gave almost religious overtones to the important task of raising healthy Aryan children – against an idyllic rural background. Women were expected to fulfil only traditional roles as their contribution to the creation of the master race, and were discouraged from taking part in public life.*

Hitler convinced many people that he could make things better. Reinhard Spitzy, an officer of the SS (Hitler's elite bodyguard) from 1931, was one of them. 'What he said was what we all felt: he would get rid of the unemployment and the hunger of the Depression, and the injustice of the Versailles peace treaty and the reparations.' Flattered to be chosen for the SS, to be among those who would form 'the future, aristocratic backbone of the German nation', Reinhard Spitzy shared the Nazi dream of a new German kingdom, a Third Reich. He feels the resentment against the Jews was understandable. 'They were much slyer in business than the normal German and Austrian, and they were so excellent in literature and in theatre, and in cinema, and in science. More than fifty per cent of the medical doctors in Vienna were Jews, more than seventy per cent of the lawyers. Of course all that made for a strong and hardline anti-Semitism. But nobody thought that we would end by killing Jews and throwing them out.'

Walter Mühle, an Austrian who was also selected to join the SS, remembers: 'For us, the Führer was the highest thing that existed...people adored him. The people responded to him like a pop star today. My beautiful years were the peace in Berlin. That was the nicest time in my life...look how many apartments they built for the workers; industry was rebuilt.' It is true that as Hitler poured money into armaments, into housing and other public works such as roadbuilding, Germans became more prosperous. The number of people unemployed fell from the six million of 1932 to 0.3 million in 1939. Freedom was the price they paid for security. Trade unions were banned; instead all workers had to join the German Labour Front (DAF). No opposition was allowed.

Helping the farmers

The German Labour Front was only part of the drive for support in both the towns and countryside. Farmers had also suffered in the Depression, and were given financial assistance. They were also swept into well-managed demonstrations that brought people and party together. Harvest Festival became a mass celebration. Luise Essig, an education officer for the Nazi agriculture ministry, still remembers these occasions. 'Thousands of farmers...and young people from all over Germany travelled in special trains and then

Unterftützt das Hilfswerk

Mutter und Kind

TAKING TO THE ROAD

THE 'PEOPLE'S CAR', the Volkswagen, was Hitler's idea for a cheap, mass-produced vehicle that would make motoring available to all German citizens at a time when cars were a luxury for the rich few. Ferdinand Porsche, later famous for his sports cars, designed the car according to Hitler's specifications. It was to carry two adults and three children, and to look like a beetle. According to Hitler, 'You have to look to nature to find out what streamlining is'.

As part of his huge public works programme, Hitler aimed to build a road network that would be the finest in the world. His grandiose plan included 4000 km (2500 miles) of autobahns. The network eventually provided rapid links between cities, helping to boost the German economy. At first there was also a more immediate military purpose: to move troops and munitions quickly between the western and eastern borders.

The scheme gave work to thousands of unemployed Germans, whose energy and commitment was held up as an example to others – this was national socialism in action. Asked by a radio reporter to tell listeners about their work, one man replied enthusiastically, 'We're building bridges like you've never seen before. What we're building is reliable. We're proud of our work.' The workers' pride was shared by thousands of people who witnessed the opening ceremony as new stretches of motorway were completed, or who heard the radio reports heralding the work as a great German achievement.

In contrast to the willing German workforce whose skills were so widely celebrated, the gigantic Volkswagen factory was built and operated by non-Aryan labour. Seventy per cent of the workforce on the factory floor was made up of forced labour, adults and children, German and foreign. These workers were kept in labour camps, suffering varying degrees of deprivation and harsh treatment according to a precise racial

hierarchy. Discipline was rigorously enforced by SS factory guards.

Hundreds of thousands of Germans eager to acquire their own Volkswagen took part in the government savings scheme. They put aside five marks a week towards the purchase of their car. It was an exciting prospect. However, the factory was not ready until 1938, and it was soon converted to make military vehicles. The only 'Beetles' made before the Second World War were obtained by SS officers and other members of the Nazi elite. The people were cheated of their savings. Despite this, after the war the 'people's car' became extremely popular – a triumph of German design and manufacture.

marched for hours to get as close to the front as possible. We all felt the same, the same happiness and joy. The Harvest Festival was the "thank you" for the fact that we farmers had a future again. Things were looking up. I believe no statesman has ever been as loved as Adolf Hitler was then. It's all come flooding back to me. Those were happy times.'

Luise Essig put into practice the new ideal of the Aryan German as self-disciplined, fit, healthy and pure. She developed a training programme called 'Faith and Beauty'. Fitness and the revival of rural crafts were linked with racial purity and the sanctity of the soil. Thousands of young people in the Young Girls' League were taught through the scheme. Gradually a whole generation was taught to live the model life the Nazis prescribed.

Persecuting the Jews

Not everyone was part of this shared national 'folk' experience. The belief that held up pure-bred Aryans as the ideal Germans excluded Jewish people and condemned them as an inferior race.

Horst Slesina worked as a radio reporter. He still remembers how propaganda taught him 'that the Jews are in all the influential positions in the economy, in banks, in cultural areas'. At the time he was persuaded that 'they were ruining our Germanness'. Now he reflects: 'It was a process which developed gradually and took over whole sections of the population who had never thought about it before. A lot of them just talked about not necessarily believing it. But gradually their brains became fogged and they started to say "the Jews are our misfortune".'

Official persecution of Jews began as soon as Hitler took power. Children were excluded from the state education system. Simply because they were Jewish, many thousands of people were expelled from their jobs in law, in the civil service, in universities and elsewhere, or could no longer practise medicine. Both marriage and extramarital relationships between Jews and non-Jews were forbidden. These were not random acts but deliberate Nazi policy, formalized over several years in a series of increasingly harsh decrees, the Nuremberg laws.

'ALL GERMANY HEARS THE FÜHRER' *declares the poster advertising the People's Receiver (Volksempfänger). As Horst Slesina remembers: 'Propaganda gave people a big boost in confidence for the first time'; it played a vital part in Hitler's success. The development of broadcasting as an instrument of the state was masterminded by Josef Goebbels, who believed that 'A good government cannot survive without good propaganda'.*

'SAVE FIVE MARKS A WEEK (LEFT) *if you want to drive your own car' reads this slogan promoting the savings scheme for the Volkswagen.*

SALUTING THE FÜHRER (BELOW) *Construction workers drive past Hitler at the official opening of a new 1000-km (620-mile) stretch of autobahn.*

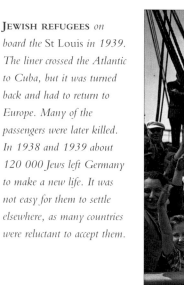

GERDA BODENHEIMER
*as a girl with her family in
their garden in Berlin in the
1930s. Only Gerda (with
her hand on her father's arm
and today, TOP) looked
Jewish. The family thought
of themselves as Germans. It
was thanks to the foresight
and courage of Gerda's
mother that the family
emigrated and survived.*

For most German Jews this sudden blast of official hostility was all the more bewildering and painful because, in spite of an undercurrent of anti-Semitism, they had always felt it was their country. A Jewish Berliner, Hans Margules, explains. 'We felt ourselves to be German before the Nazi time. We had German-Jewish beliefs, we were Germans.'

The critical moment, for Hans Margules and for millions of other German Jews, was Kristallnacht, the night of broken glass. On 9 November 1938, 'I was decorating the shop window with my boss and then we heard breaking glass everywhere, all over; it just didn't stop. We looked out into the street and saw a mass of people and we saw that the neighbouring shop, all the Jewish shops had been broken into. The people who were smashing the windows, they weren't even in uniform, they were just young boys with sticks who were enjoying themselves enormously. That was the end of Jewish business in Germany.' The owners of the 7000 businesses destroyed were never compensated; their insurance payments were confiscated.

As many as 30 000 Jews were arrested during Kristallnacht. Yet Hans Margules shows understanding towards the Germans. 'The German had to feed his family. He wasn't anti-Semitic, but he had to do what the party desired, he had to belong to the party to carry on his job, to feed his family, and as it was repeated that the Jews...are terrible, that must have gone into people's heads. They must have thought – well, maybe that's right. You can't judge all the German people...everyone had to speak quietly... fear...it was a dictatorship.'

JEWISH REFUGEES *on
board the* St Louis *in 1939.
The liner crossed the Atlantic
to Cuba, but it was turned
back and had to return to
Europe. Many of the
passengers were later killed.
In 1938 and 1939 about
120 000 Jews left Germany
to make a new life. It was
not easy for them to settle
elsewhere, as many countries
were reluctant to accept them.*

'JEWS NOT WANTED HERE'

JEWS HAVE BEEN PERSECUTED IN EUROPE for hundreds of years. Their history has been punctuated by hostility; their economic and cultural contribution regarded with suspicion, envy and superstition. In the late nineteenth century animosity towards Jews took a new form: it became an ideology. Jews were blamed for the assassination of the Russian tsar, Alexander II, in 1880. As a result the government officially reimposed restrictions on Jews and unofficially encouraged murderous pogroms. Jews were accused of ritual murder in Hungary in 1882. In that year an international anti-Semitic congress met in Dresden. The new anti-Semitism was also growing in the West. Jews excelled in many fields – as lawyers, writers, musicians, journalists, intellectuals, businessmen and bankers. Their success was often resented. An economic crisis in 1873 was blamed on 'Jewish financiers', and anti-Semitic politicians became popular in Germany and Austria.

In France and in Russia false accusations of Jewish conspiracy were widely circulated and believed. Many people were frightened by the rapid economic and social changes of the late nineteenth century, and some Jews seemed to represent the uncertainties of a bewildering future. Jews were also viewed with suspicion as both socialist revolutionaries on the one hand, and capitalists on the other.

In Germany the desperate situation after the First World War fed an angry search for scapegoats. First among them were the Jews, despite their patriotism during the war. Adolf Hitler drew on his own violent anti-Semitism to play on people's fears and whipped up the potential for hatred. As soon as he was in power, he ordered a national boycott of Jewish-owned businesses.

Further persecution was to come. Within two years the Nuremberg Laws had set out the exclusion of Jews from German society. They were deprived of German citizenship, their status reduced to that of 'subjects of the state'. They were not allowed to vote. More and more careers became closed to them; their children could not attend school; they could not employ domestic servants of German blood. Their passports were stamped with a distinguishing red 'J'. A decree in 1938 deprived Jewish communities of their legal status. The Nazis used the framework of the law systematically to remove from the Jews the protection that the law should provide for all its citizens.

COMING OUT OF SCHOOL *An illustration from one of the children's books published under the Nazis that were designed to help Aryan children identify Jews, and encouraged hostility towards them.*

Enforcing racial purity

The persecution of the Jews was only one aspect of the Nazis' determination to create the master race. They wanted to purge the German community of all those who they feared could weaken the Aryan breeding stock. This meant the persecution of people who offended social norms and were considered alien, degenerate and unproductive, including gypsies, homosexuals, prostitutes, criminals, alcoholics, vagrants, the workshy, the disabled and the mentally ill.

Many non-Nazi and even anti-Nazi social scientists at this time, in Germany and elsewhere, enthusiastically called for policies to 'improve' the genetic stock. What was different about the Nazis was the ruthlessness with which they pursued their own extreme version of these 'eugenic' ideas. At first the Nazis decided to lock away the 'genetically unhealthy' and sterilize them. By 1945 a total of between 200 000 and 250 000 people – gypsies, schizophrenics, alcoholics among them – had been sterilized.

Anna-Maria Ernst's family were gypsies living in Germany. She remembers her childhood in the early 1930s as a happy time. The gypsies had their caravans and horses, and they could wander wherever they liked, pitching their camps in a forest or by a lake. 'It was a beautiful life,' she reminisces, 'wonderful. There were happy celebrations, dancing – the women were full of vitality. Marriages were arranged. We had real gypsy weddings, which lasted for six or seven days. We loved living life as free as a bird in the sky.'

Gypsies had been roughly treated by the police before. But in 1935 they were described in a commentary on the Nuremberg decrees as aliens. To the Nazis they were an antisocial nuisance. They were now catalogued, categorized, harassed. Anna-Maria Ernst recalls sadly how things changed. 'Everybody had to sell their caravans and their things and move into flats. We had to settle down permanently and register....The wonderful life was over.'

When war began in 1939 the gypsies were rounded up and despatched to concentration camps. Anna-Maria Ernst was sent to Auschwitz. There too the gypsies danced: the SS would burst into their hut in the middle of the night and order them to dance and sing. Some gypsy girls were sterilized without anaesthetics. Many

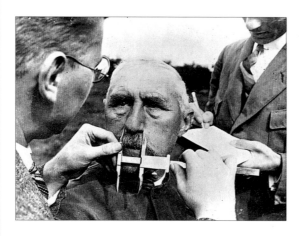

TAKING PRECISE MEASUREMENTS *of people's noses and noting other physical characteristics such as eye and hair colour were part of the pseudo-scientific categorization of individuals into more or less desirable racial types. Germany was not the only country in which questions of eugenics – race care – were being considered at this time. Darwin's ideas about the 'survival of the fittest' shaping the evolutionary process were applied to theories about the best way of ensuring healthy human populations. In Germany these theories were used to justify the Nazis' policies, which were designed to lead to the elimination of non-Aryan peoples.*

AS A LITTLE GIRL *Anna-Maria Ernst lived a happy life among her relatives. She lost almost all of them, the only one of her immediate family to survive the horror of the concentration camps.*

people died in the camps. At least 15 000 of the 20 000 gypsies in Germany were murdered, as were some 500 000 gypsies in other parts of Europe. Anna-Maria Ernst could not understand why they were treated so viciously.

In 1936 Hitler first challenged the other European states. He reoccupied the Rhineland, a demilitarized zone since the First World War. He offered two more challenges in 1938: he forcibly united Austria with the German Reich, and in the late summer annexed the Sudeten German fringes of Czechoslovakia. In 1939 he took over the rest of Czechoslovakia, and then invaded Poland. This time his bluff was called: Britain and France declared war. With the coming of war, Hitler's dictatorship became harsher, its methods even more grim.

Immediately before the war, the Interior Ministry sent round a confidential circular ordering the registration of children who suffered from congenital deformities. By early 1940 these children were being systematically killed or starved to death. In the summer of 1939 Hitler had personally ordered one of the leading Nazi doctors, Dr Leonard Conti, to organize what was called a 'euthanasia' programme (in fact a programme of mass murder) for adult patients suffering from a number of conditions, including schizophrenia and epilepsy. At first the victims were given lethal

A BEWILDERED WOMAN *is questioned by researchers. Gypsies, like other minority groups, were graded into categories. They were forced to register with the authorities and to settle permanently in one place.*

injections. In January 1940 the first patients were gassed, and thereafter the numbers executed increased steadily.

The reality of Hitler's racial policy was brought home to thousands of families, who learned with horror that a relative they believed was being cared for in a hospital or asylum had in fact been murdered. One of these was the Rau family. Marie Rau's mother suffered from depression and anxiety. Diagnosed as an incurable schizophrenic, she was eventually taken to a clinic at Hadamar. Here, in groups of sixty, patients were led down to a cellar and choked to death with carbon monoxide gas. The Rau family were told that their mother had died as a result of 'complications from a wart on her lip'. They learned the truth only after the war. As Marie Rau now says, 'The fact that these people were murdered is a disgrace for our whole society.'

Terrible suspicion hardened into certainty. Judges raised questions, but were told that the programme had Hitler's express authorization. A Protestant pastor objected in person to Hitler. Roman Catholic bishops also protested; Pope Pius XII published an order condemning the 'direct killing' of innocent persons. Count von Galen, bishop of Münster, preached a sermon against euthanasia. It is said that Hitler himself witnessed a demonstration against the transportation of mentally disabled children. In August 1941, when he ordered an end to the gassing, some 71 000 people had been killed; the programme continued by other means.

'The Jew will be exterminated'

In January 1939 Hitler had made a prediction that sounded to many at the time an ugly but idle threat. If 'Jewish financiers', he told the German parliament (the Reichstag), 'should succeed in plunging the nations once more into a world war, then the result will not be the Bolshevization of the earth, and thus the victory of Jewry, but the annihilation of the Jewish race in Europe.' Eight months later, Europe was at war and Hitler was in a position to put his bloodcurdling prophecy into effect.

As the Nazis moved into country after country, they isolated the Jews. News bulletins solemnly told Germans at home that in Poland 'the hardest task for the Germans is the Jewish question'. Their rhetoric represented a systematic policy of death. There

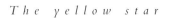

The yellow star

THE STAR OF DAVID *had traditionally signified God as protector of the Jewish people. When the Nazis forced all Jews to identify themselves by wearing the star it became instead a symbol of humiliation and a target for hatred.*

THIS DAILY NEWSPAPER *in Hanover carried an article on Wednesday 25 February 1942 written by Hitler himself. The subheading reads* Der Jude wird ausgerottet *– 'The Jew will be exterminated'. Hitler was confident enough to make his intentions public.*

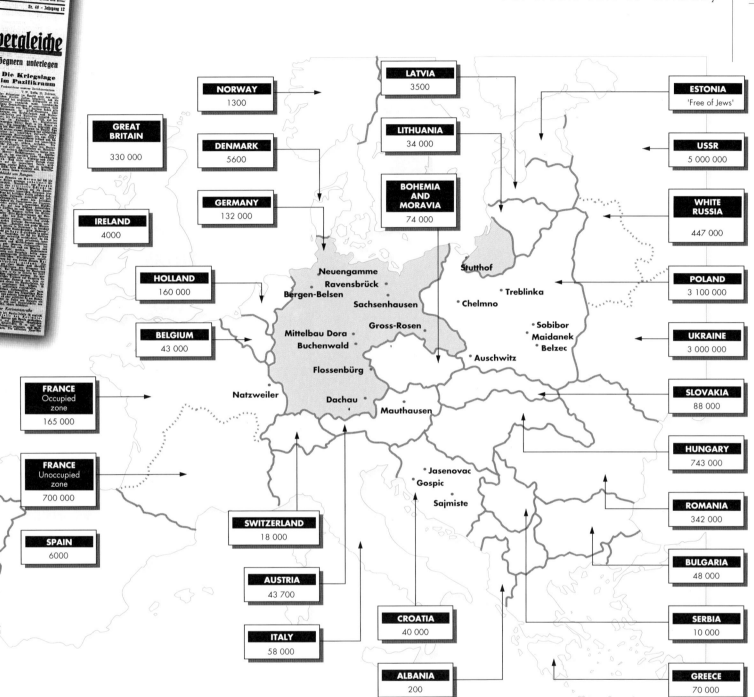

NORWAY 1300	**LATVIA** 3500
GREAT BRITAIN 330 000	**ESTONIA** 'Free of Jews'
DENMARK 5600	**LITHUANIA** 34 000
IRELAND 4000	**USSR** 5 000 000
GERMANY 132 000	**BOHEMIA AND MORAVIA** 74 000

WHITE RUSSIA 447 000

Stutthof

Neuengamme
Ravensbrück
Bergen-Belsen
Sachsenhausen

• Treblinka

• Chelmno

HOLLAND 160 000

Gross-Rosen

POLAND 3 100 000

Mittelbau Dora
Buchenwald

• Sobibor
• Maidanek
• Belzec

BELGIUM 43 000

Flossenbürg

• Auschwitz

UKRAINE 3 000 000

Natzweiler
Dachau

Mauthausen

FRANCE Occupied zone 165 000

SLOVAKIA 88 000

FRANCE Unoccupied zone 700 000

• Jasenovac
• Gospic

HUNGARY 743 000

Sajmiste

SPAIN 6000

ROMANIA 342 000

SWITZERLAND 18 000

BULGARIA 48 000

AUSTRIA 43 700

CROATIA 40 000

SERBIA 10 000

ITALY 58 000

ALBANIA 200

GREECE 70 000

EUROPE'S JEWISH
POPULATION *was listed
in detail by the Nazi leaders
at a conference in January
1942. The major
concentration camps are
named on this map. Most
of these were forced labour
camps; those in Poland
were set up specifically as
extermination centres.*

were three million Jews in Poland. Jews living in western Poland
were driven east and herded into ghettos in the towns, especially
in Cracow, Lodz and Warsaw, a process that was carried out with
the utmost brutality.

Tadeusz Pankiewicz, who worked in a chemist's shop in the
Cracow ghetto, saw what took place there. Thousands of people
were in the square waiting to be deported. The Germans searched
the empty houses, shooting anyone who had stayed behind. In the
silence, in bright sunshine, a young and elegantly dressed woman

> *"*T*he worst things that could possibly happen in the world happened in the ghetto... It was hell that those people lived through.*"*
>
> TADEUSZ
> PANKIEWICZ

CHILDREN OF THE GHETTO *shared their parents' suffering. In Warsaw the Germans allowed themselves 2300 calories a day. The Poles were allowed 900 calories a day; the ration for Jews was only 183 calories. This was deliberate starvation.*

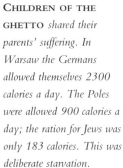

walked forward. 'I could hear her footsteps. As she approached the people who were to be deported she passed the Germans, Gestapo men, who were standing by with whips and pokers....They beat her in the face, in the eyes. All she wanted to do was to say good-bye to her mother, who was standing in one of the rows. She got to her mother, and they said their farewells. At that point the Germans pounced on her, dragged her back to the place she came from, beating her and kicking her mercilessly.' He speaks for all the ghettos when he observes, 'The worst things that could possibly happen in the world happened in the ghetto – unimaginable, indescribable murders.'

　　With the German invasion of the Soviet Union in June 1941, Nazi policy also crossed a line. Jews had been pitilessly mistreated; now their extermination was to be the final solution. At first the SS tried to get local anti-Semites to do their work for them, with some success. But it was not enough. Soon four special motorized SS murder units,

ROUNDING UP JEWISH FAMILIES *in the Warsaw ghetto. This was where the process of destruction began for Polish Jews. The frightened small boy in the foreground was the only one of the group to survive. One of the guards was later identified from this photograph and prosecuted for war crimes.*

each 1000-men strong, fanned out behind the advancing army. Their mission was to kill communist commissars by the hundred, and Jews by the hundred thousand. Sometimes they simply dug a grave, lined the Jews up in front of it, and shot them, in row after row, so they fell on top of each other into the grave. Sometimes they took them to nearby dunes or pits and shot them there.

Zvi Michaeli lived in Eishishky in Lithuania. Some 3500 Jews lived in the town. They were herded to the pits that had been dug in front of the old cemetery. Zvi Michaeli was sixteen years old; he went with his father and younger brother. He still weeps as he remembers that day. 'When we all undressed...when I saw Rabbi Zushe undressed, I thought this was the end. His glowing face...the verses from Psalms that he recited in our ears...up to then I'd been confident that we wouldn't die. And my father was

RESISTING THE NAZIS

'**W**HAT WE HAVE WRITTEN and said is in the minds of all of you, but you lack the courage to say it aloud.' These are the words of a twenty-year-old student, Sophie Scholl, who was executed for resistance to the Nazis. Although there was little effective opposition to the Nazis, a heroic minority of Germans from many backgrounds – Christians, both Lutheran and Catholic, socialists and communists, students and trade unionists, civil servants and army officers – did have the courage to resist. And it took courage: telling an anti-Nazi joke, hiding a Jewish friend or listening to a foreign radio station could lead to torture and death.

In 1936 and again in 1941 there were widespread demonstrations against Nazi orders to remove crucifixes in Roman Catholic districts, part of Hitler's campaign against religion. Clergy and doctors objected to the euthanasia programme set up in 1939 for patients with mental illnesses, and in February 1941 there was an uproar in Absberg, Franconia, as mental patients were being taken to their deaths.

Throughout the period of the final solution there was only one case of open protest by Germans on behalf of Jews, and incredibly, it worked. In February 1943 the Gestapo, cracking horsewhips and shouting 'All Jews out!', broke into homes and factories to round up the last 10 000 Jews in Berlin. Some 8000 of them were immediately sent to Auschwitz and the remaining 2000 people, Jews married to Aryans, were held at Rosenstrasse 2-4, a Jewish centre in the heart of the city. For ten days and nights their husbands and wives gathered outside, shouting 'Murderers!' at the SS guards. According to one witness, 'the accusing, demanding cries of the women...like passionate avowals of a love strengthened by the bitterness of life', could be heard above the traffic. Goebbels, fearing that the secret of the final solution might leak out, authorized the release of the Jews still being held in the Rosenstrasse centre.

saying, "You will live, don't be afraid. You will live and take revenge." My brother David...he clung so tight. And the shots of the machine gun....There was a mixture of voices, of people crying, and children, and the shots...and the dust...and everything mingled together...I found myself inside the pit. I felt my father give me a push and lie on top of me. He wanted me to live.' And live he did, escaping to the woods, covered with his own and his father's blood.

In the first year, the death squads murdered 750 000 Jews in the territories captured from the Soviet Union. Two German marksmen alone, helped by Ukrainian 'packers' who arranged the bodies of the dead, shot more than 33 000 Jews from Kiev in the ravine at Babi Yar. Over the next year, the SS were responsible for the deaths of one and a half million people. Altogether, two and a quarter million Jewish men, women and children were killed, either hanged or more often systematically lined up and machine-gunned so that their bodies fell into pits, where they were destroyed by fire or with quicklime or simply covered with earth.

Even worse was to follow. Although the Nazi leaders attempted to keep details of mass shootings secret, they themselves had no moral compunction about them. However, this way of killing people did cause psychological problems among the soldiers who carried out the executions. Some of the men in the firing squads became openly sadistic; others were overcome by fits of crying and suffered breakdowns in their health. Some of them even became deranged, and shot wildly at their comrades.

Mass shootings were not an efficient way to murder millions of people. As that was just what Hitler was determined to do, his dire purpose to exterminate the Jews was now transformed, with bureaucratic thoroughness, into an enormous operational plan: the extermination, not just of the Jews living in Poland and Russia, but of the entire Jewish population of occupied Europe, some eleven million people.

The SS turned to a more scientific weapon: gas, which had already been pioneered in the killing of mental patients in 1940. In December 1941 Jews were transported to the camp at Chelmno, in the German-occupied part of Poland. They were killed by being herded into vans that were then filled with exhaust gases. In

ON THE BRINK *between life and death, a gaunt victim awaits the bullet that will send him into the pit. In the wake of the advancing German armies, special murder units of SS men spread out across the occupied European countries. Their instructions were to find and kill Jewish people. Whole communities of men, women and children were rounded up and murdered in this way.*

March 1942 killings began at a camp at Belzec, this time in gas chambers filled with fumes. In May mass exterminations began at a new camp at Sobibor, and on 23 July at Treblinka the Germans started gassing the Jews from the Warsaw ghetto.

At Auschwitz in southern Poland a concentration camp for political prisoners had been extended to house forced labour for a large local factory. The commandant's deputy, ordered to execute political prisoners and Russian commissars, found that Zyklon B gas killed people with hitherto unattainable efficiency and in unprecedented numbers. Both Auschwitz and its adjoining camp, Birkenau, were linked to the main railway network. All was now ready for the greatest crime in history.

The final solution

Jews were being transported to the camps from all over occupied Europe. Hans Margules had earlier fled his own country, but he was caught by the Germans in Holland and forced to help with deportations. He explains his duties. 'At six in the morning we had to fetch the people who were on the transport list.…If they couldn't walk we had to take them on stretchers to the trains. No one had any idea that there were extermination camps, otherwise

CROWDS OF DEPORTEES *arrive at Auschwitz. The bustle gives the scene an air of normality, but for these passengers the destination meant death.*

HANS MARGULES *closing a railway wagon door. He was forced to organize the departure of Jews from a camp in Holland on their long train journey to the death camp of Auschwitz.*

MUSICIANS OF TEREZIN

IN JUNE 1944 A DELEGATION from the International Red Cross travelled to Czechoslovakia to visit the Nazi concentration camp at the walled town of Terezin (in German, Theresienstadt). The Nazis used Terezin as a show camp in an attempt to disprove international reports of the existence of extermination camps.

The entire town, built around its medieval castle, had been turned into a camp through which 140 000 Jews passed, most of them on their way to Auschwitz or one of the other death camps.

Conditions in the camp were so harsh that one in four inmates died. Yet they were allowed a degree of apparent freedom. As a result Terezin became at once a parody of Jewish cultural expression and a place of intense artistic activity.

There was a coffee house in Terezin and a café–concerthall. There was a symphony orchestra, several chamber music ensembles, and even a jazz band called the Ghetto Swingers. More remarkable still, music of lasting quality was composed in the camp by Jews who found the courage to work creatively under sentence of death. Viktor Ullmann, a pupil of Arnold Schoenberg, wrote over twenty pieces there. Other Terezin composers included Pavel Haas, a pupil of Leos Janácek, and Hans Krasa; his children's opera *Brundibar* was so popular in the camp that the jazz band played selections from it in the main square. The Nazis featured the band in a propaganda film.

CREATIVITY IN CAPTIVITY *In the Terezin coffee house a group of prisoners listens to music played on violin, trumpet and accordion. The sorrowful expressions of the listeners are a reminder of the reality that lies outside the café window.*

there would have been a panic and the process wouldn't have gone so smoothly. We had to shut the doors. The SS stood behind me and gave the orders. It was very difficult to say no. How could people in our position oppose an SS man?'

The train journey to the camps was itself a terrible ordeal. Norbert Lopper was a Viennese prisoner forced to work on the ramp where the trains stopped. 'We opened the carriages and the people fell out of them. They had just suffocated. Many had been badly wounded. With some of the transports, the SS went onto the roofs of the wagons and shot right into the carriages. Blood was all over the people. We had to get them out of the wagons and carry them to the trucks....This was the most dreadful thing I had to endure. These people were blue and puffed up...they had been crushed to death.'

As the prisoners arrived at Auschwitz in the trains, doctors divided them, some to the right, some to the left: those who were strong enough to go to the work camp, to live at least for a time; those who were to be taken straight to their death.

Dora Schwartz arrived with a group of mothers and their children; they were immediately sent to the gas chamber. 'When we arrived we didn't know where we were. We suspected this was a place of death. We saw the smoke from the chimneys. The sight made you shudder. This was going to be our fate. I was lucky. After the selection another official saw me and pointed for me to go with the others, with the ones who were allowed to live.'

At the time none of the prisoners realized the implications of the selection process. Those who were being sent straight to their deaths were told they were going to have a shower. Only when they had been lulled right up to the gate of the gas chamber, still clutching their towels, did the SS drive them in with beatings. Ten minutes after the gas was released, a doctor would look through a peephole. If everyone was on the floor, it was over. Gangs of prisoners then pulled the dead bodies out and loaded them onto trucks to take them to the crematoria.

Not all Jews went quietly to their deaths. People living in the Warsaw ghetto in April 1943 bravely resisted deportation to Treblinka, selling their lives dear for a month. There was also an uprising at Treblinka itself in August, and another in October at Sobibor. Almost a year later there was a mutiny among working prisoners at one of the crematoria at Auschwitz; they succeeded in blowing up the crematorium before they were overpowered. Riots were not uncommon, and on one occasion a contingent doomed to the gas chamber seized the guards' weapons and shot at them. This probably did not happen more often because of the prisoners' anguished mental state and dreadful physical condition by the time they reached the camp. Men, women and children, weakened by hunger and disease, and exhausted by the long journey crammed together in cattle trucks, were shepherded to their deaths with elaborate cunning by ruthless, heavily armed men.

BILLOWING SMOKE (LEFT) *from the crematorium chimney dominates this drawing by an inmate of prisoners under guard having to carry the bodies of their fellow inmates to be burned. As Wolfgang Gebhardt, whose father worked at the local factory, remembers, 'You could see the prisoners, and you could smell the crematoria. The question was, how did they kill people? Did they just leave them starving and burn them, or did they do something else? These people were starving, everybody could see that. My father was suspicious that people were killed. But he never asked because everybody was afraid to know too much.'*

A MOMENT OF ANGUISH *for a woman prisoner attacked by a guard dog in the camp, sketched by a fellow prisoner. The last words of several Jewish women were written down, and discovered years later hidden in a jar. One woman said, 'I am still so young. I have not really experienced anything in my life. Why should death of this kind fall to my lot? Why?'*

FACING THE TRUTH *When the concentration camps were liberated, Germans living nearby were brought in to see the terrible truth for themselves. These civilians confront the shocking sight of a trailer loaded with emaciated corpses in the camp at Buchenwald.*

RAISING THE SOVIET FLAG (OPPOSITE) *on the roof of the Reichstag, in Berlin on 30 April 1945. Within an hour, and less than a kilometre away, Hitler committed suicide. He had promised to rebuild Germany, but instead its cities had been reduced to piles of rubble.*

The terrible truth

The tide of war turned against the Germans in November 1942. In 1943 Soviet tanks began the long, bloody process of rolling the Nazi armies back, across Russia, out of Russia into Poland and back into Germany, while American and British forces fought their way towards Germany from the west. The master race was master no longer.

As the war ended, the true cost of the Nazis' delusion of a special racial destiny was exposed. On 26 January 1945 Auschwitz was captured by the Red Army. Just 7000 skeletal survivors were found. The SS had burned twenty-nine large storehouses before they fled. In the six that remained the Russians discovered, among other things, 836 255 women's dresses.

In mid-April British tanks entered the concentration camp at Bergen-Belsen. They found 30 000 prisoners in the last stages of starvation, and the remains of 35 000 more. Two weeks later the Americans liberated the camp at Dachau, where there were some 33 000 survivors. The emaciated bodies of the dead were piled 'like a heap of crooked logs ready for some infernal fire', as one witness described it. The American troops were so angry that they shot all 500 SS guards within the hour.

No one knows exactly how many people died in the war Hitler began. His insane venture was a disaster – not only for his enemies, but for his supporters too. He had promised to establish Germans as the master race. Instead, he had gambled with their country, and lost.

Years later, scraps of evidence were found, illuminating the human pain that was the price of the catastrophe. After the war, for example, in the ruins of the Gestapo headquarters where many hundreds of Hitler's opponents were interrogated and tortured, a piece of paper was discovered. On it, Harro Schulze-Boysen, an air force officer who had joined a left-wing resistance movement, had scribbled a poem. The last verse read:

Die letzten Argumenten
sind Strang und Fallbeil nicht,
und unsere heut'gen Richter sind
noch nicht das Weltgericht.

The final arguments
are not noose and guillotine,
and our judges today are
not yet the world court.

Total War

1 9 3 9 — 1 9 4 5

10

THE EXPERIENCE OF THE SECOND WORLD WAR

THE WAIL OF THE AIR-RAID sirens came at the end of a bright, sunny spring day in Plymouth on 20 March 1941. Betty Lawrence, a trainee midwife, was on night duty preparing for a difficult delivery when a bomb struck the children's ward next door. 'There was dead silence, and then you could hear these children crying. Then the next minute, a whoosh right down through the maternity block, and the lights went out and the debris was falling down.... I had to deliver this baby by torchlight, with muck and dirt and dust.'

The following day she walked through the devastated, skeletal city. 'The smell and the stench and the smoke and the fires still burning – I imagine that's what hell would look like....It was utter despair. I still remember the smell, an acrid, smoky smell....You couldn't even find the road. I felt my youth was gone.'

Margarete Zettel can still recall the confusion and horror of the air raid on Hamburg in July 1943, which produced a firestorm throughout the city. 'When we came out of the shelter it was just a pure inferno, chaos, an unbelievable storm, it's something that you can't really imagine....The first thing we noticed was this horrible smell, a smell I still have in my nose even today. The neighbouring house was just a pile of rubble. People were buried in it. There was the smell of blood and cement and burning all mixed together – it was horrible, revolting. It took me a long, long time to get over that.'

The Second World War was total war; a war in which civilians were targets and their homes became the battlefields. During the First World War soldiers had dug trenches at the front; now the civilians were doing the digging, preparing the shelters they hoped would protect them from aerial bombing. As the war escalated, the forces of both dictatorships and democracies mercilessly attacked each other's civilians. The years of fear became a grim test of endurance among whole populations; for many unarmed people it meant fighting for their lives against terrible odds.

BOMBED OUT *Civilians make the journey to work brick by brick through the smouldering ruins of their homes.*

219

Preparing for the worst

When Britain and France declared war on Germany two days after Hitler's invasion of Poland, no one knew what to expect. For people on both sides of the conflict, the shadow of the First World War still loomed. Margarete Zettel, a teenager in Hamburg, was too young to have experienced the first war, but shared her parents' memories: 'We felt very sad and really afraid at the same time...because in the First World War my family lost a number of people.' Horst Westphal, who was only nine, was aware that people in Germany were 'quite euphoric at trying to stop the Germans from being suppressed in Poland – that was the version presented to us in the media. But people were very unhappy that the war had started.' In Britain the news marked the end of distant negotiations by politicians abroad and the beginning of tangible fear at home. Betty Lawrence was at a dance in Plymouth when people started pouring onto the streets. She remembers, 'They were saying, "They're going to announce the war"....Everybody was very, very frightened.' She had heard about the First World War, but this time she felt it would be different 'because we knew there was going to be more bombing'.

During the 1930s there had been frightening predictions of what modern weaponry, and particularly aerial bombing, could do to civilian populations. Bombs had been used by the Japanese on Shanghai in 1937 and by the Germans at Guernica during the Spanish Civil War. Above all, people feared that poison gas would be used, as it had been in the First World War, but this time in bombs dropped over cities rather than shells in the trenches. Gas masks were issued to the entire British population, and in France to all those who lived in towns and cities. In Germany only civil defence workers, Nazi party members and civil servants were supplied with gas masks. People were instructed to carry their masks at all times of the day and night.

Other measures were taken to protect civilians. In France and Britain women with babies, and children both individually and as whole schools, were evacuated from Paris and London to unknown guardians

GAS ALERT (ABOVE)
An air-raid warden wearing a gas mask clatters his warning rattle during a civil defence exercise. Masks were issued for all adults, children and even babies, but people's fears of gas bombing were not realized: it was not used during the war.

VISIONS OF HELL
A baby screams desperately for help after the Japanese air attack on the Chinese city of Shanghai in 1937. Japan's merciless bombing raids provoked a sense of moral outrage and horror in the West, and the terrible reality of the Chinese experience fuelled the Europeans' fear of what the war would bring.

DIGGING IN (LEFT)
Families in Britain assemble their Anderson shelters. The shelters were issued free to those who earned less than £250 a year.

and destinations in the countryside. As the British government started to build large air-raid shelters, thousands of householders were issued with their own Anderson shelter. Donald Alder was a child living in Plymouth at the time, and remembers, 'My stepfather made ours up at the bottom of the garden. We put a bed in there, and I always felt safe in that shelter.'

The government also issued advice about how to protect homes from aerial bombardment, and instructions on how to seal doors in the event of gas attacks. People bought scrim, a fine canvas, to paste onto windows to prevent the glass shattering. Practising the air-raid drill became part of the daily routine in offices, shops and schools. Some areas were better prepared than others. Betty Lawrence recalls that at the hospital where she worked in Plymouth, 'We were told to get a wash bowl for each patient to put over the patient's head in case of an air raid'.

Throughout Europe a black-out was imposed so that cities and towns could not be identified at night. From the outset, people in Britain, France, Germany and Poland learned to manage in the dark. With no neon signs or illuminated shop windows, neighbourhoods were immersed in darkness after dusk and people relied on torches, which had to be pointed downwards, to find their way. Donald Alder remembers, 'Anyone who showed a light was taken to court and fined as much as two pounds....Even the cars, and there weren't many of them about, even the buses had half the headlamps blacked out and the light was made to show only on the ground.'

Despite the lengthy preparations, and the wail of sirens signalling only a false alarm within minutes of the declaration, aerial bombing remained a distant threat in Britain during the early months of war. Along the Belgian and French borders with Germany, British and French forces waited for German attack in concrete bunkers, but there was so little fighting on the Western Front that the period was dubbed the Phoney War. Elsewhere the picture was different. In Poland fears were borne out by the Germans' fierce bombing of Polish towns and the daunting reality of occupation; in October the Soviet army invaded Finland with air attacks on civilians. By spring 1940 western Europe, too, was in the firing line.

WAITING FOR THE TRAIN *A boy receives his destination tag as he waits with his school group in a queue of subdued young evacuees. At the start of the war the British government organized billeting for children from the cities with families in 'safe' areas. Country people were shocked by the condition of some young refugees from poor areas, who were unwelcome guests. Many were homesick, and returned within a few months to cities still free from raids. Two more waves of evacuation followed during the war.*

REFUGEES TAKE TO THE STREETS *in Belgium as their bombed houses burn. Those who went by car had to abandon their vehicles when they ran out of petrol. Most people went on foot or by bicycle, salvaging what they could and not knowing when or if they would return.*

UNEQUAL PARTNERS
A poster of 1941 urges Norwegian civilians to join the Waffen SS, Hitler's elite combat troops, 'against Bolshevism'. After Hitler's blitzkrieg campaigns German propaganda chiefs played on the patriotism of men in occupied Denmark, Norway and the Netherlands to form their own Viking Division within the SS, and in so doing attempted to gain support for the attack on the Soviet Union.

Living under fire

With the lightning war, or 'blitzkrieg', people in northern Europe experienced the full force of the Nazi war machine smashing into their towns and villages. In April 1940 German troops invaded Denmark and Norway. Denmark fell in a day; Norway, supported by Anglo-French forces, held out until June. In May the German armies invaded Belgium, Luxembourg and the Netherlands. German tanks and troops swept towards the English Channel, and by the end of May Hitler was ordering his troops to Paris.

Pierre Rondas was living in the Belgian town of Louvain. He had just received his call-up papers when a raid began, and he found himself in a long column of people trailing from the town to seek safety at the French border, under the threat of German aircraft. 'Most of the people walking on the streets were civilians with horses, trucks, carriages....The people fleeing had a lot of luggage with them, but along the way, as the trip was long and difficult, they were beginning to abandon it....There were lots of abandoned cars....What is happening behind you or next to you, you don't look at it and you don't remember. You just look forward. There was a lot of misery there.'

Exposed on the open road, everyone was a target for the German air force. 'You heard the noise of the planes and then the noise of the machine-gunning. We heard the whistling of the bullets and everybody rushed off the roads to find cover in the ditches. Once the planes had flown on, the people just crawled out of these ditches again...tried to grab all their things back together, all their suitcases and bags, and then they walked on....There were people who were injured falling off trucks. They had blood on their bodies and their clothes, but few people could help because they wanted to get away.'

When Belgium surrendered just eighteen days later Pierre Rondas began to feel safer. 'I heard it from a German army car radio that was stationed at some farm where I was sleeping....We were now part of Germany.'

In June 1941 Germany launched a new blitzkrieg on the Soviet Union, in one of the largest military assaults in history. The German army, supported by Finnish and Italian troops, swept across Belorussia and the Ukraine, heading for Moscow and

TOTAL GLOBAL WAR

THE SECOND WORLD WAR was the first global war, involving almost every continent in the world. Colonial links meant that many territories and sea-lanes far from the warring powers were also drawn in. Among the Allies, Britain included its empire, notably Australia, Canada and New Zealand, and for France the war involved its territories in West Africa and Indochina.

Among the few countries to remain neutral throughout the war were the Irish Republic, Sweden and Switzerland. Some countries changed allegiance during the war. Under the fascist dictator Benito Mussolini, Italy was a founder, with Germany, of the Axis powers ranged against the Allies, initially just Britain and France. Mussolini supported Hitler's invasion of France and then the Soviet Union, but after his fall from power and Italy's surrender to the Allies in 1943, Italy declared war on Germany. Northern France came under German occupation in 1940; the Vichy government there

collaborated with Germany until 1943, while the Free French army supported the Allies. The Soviet Union, unsure of British and French intentions, had agreed with Germany before the war on the joint division of Poland, and supported Hitler's invasion from the west with its own attack on eastern Poland. The Soviet Union also supplied Germany with raw materials until it was itself invaded in 1941.

The struggles between these countries were rooted in the domination and ambitions of powerful leaders. While Hitler embodied the most awesome totalitarian threat, ruthless expansionism also motivated Mussolini and the Japanese warlords. By the time war was declared in Europe, the Sino-Japanese war had already signalled Japan's territorial aims for its Greater East Asia Co-Prosperity Sphere, and the atrocities it was prepared to inflict to achieve them.

The war expanded dramatically when ambitions in the east collided with those in Europe, culminating in

Japan's attack on the American fleet at Pearl Harbor, Hawaii. As a consequence of the pact made weeks earlier between Japan and Germany, Hitler now declared war on the United States, precipitating active American support of the Allies.

A series of events marked the turning of the tide against Germany after its early successes in achieving a Nazi-controlled Europe. Among them were disastrous decisions made by Hitler himself, who kept personal control of his armies. His invasion of the Soviet Union started a war on a second front that he could ill afford, while his declaration of war on the United States – until then an unmobilized economic giant – gave massive impetus to the Allies. Decisive battles, especially in the Atlantic and the Pacific, and the Allies' re-entry into Europe gradually signalled the defeat first of Germany and then of Japan.

WORLDWIDE CONFLICT *The war was fought in east and west, on land, at sea and in the air.*

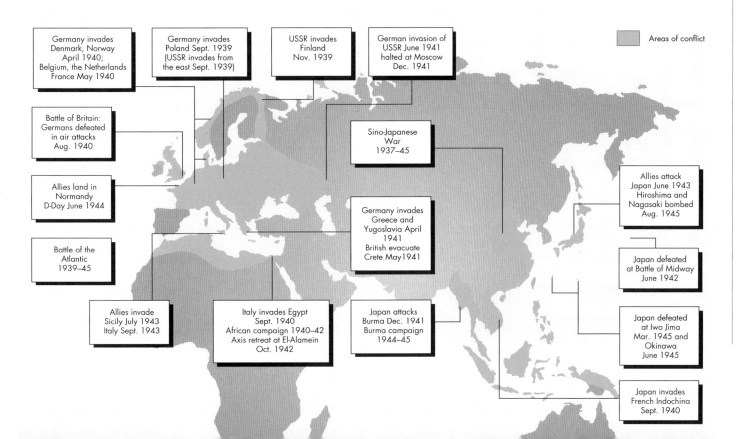

Germany invades Denmark, Norway April 1940; Belgium, the Netherlands France May 1940

Germany invades Poland Sept. 1939 (USSR invades from the east Sept. 1939)

USSR invades Finland Nov. 1939

German invasion of USSR June 1941 halted at Moscow Dec. 1941

Areas of conflict

Battle of Britain: Germans defeated in air attacks Aug. 1940

Sino-Japanese War 1937–45

Allies attack Japan June 1943 Hiroshima and Nagasaki bombed Aug. 1945

Allies land in Normandy D-Day June 1944

Germany invades Greece and Yugoslavia April 1941 British evacuate Crete May 1941

Japan defeated at Battle of Midway June 1942

Battle of the Atlantic 1939–45

Allies invade Sicily July 1943 Italy Sept. 1943

Italy invades Egypt Sept. 1940 African campaign 1940–42 Axis retreat at El-Alamein Oct. 1942

Japan attacks Burma Dec. 1941 Burma campaign 1944–45

Japan defeated at Iwo Jima Mar. 1945 and Okinawa June 1945

Japan invades French Indochina Sept. 1940

(RIGHT)

"Those who could tried to run away. I had five children with me...where could I run to, having so many children with me?"

SERAFIMA SCHIBKO

SHOCKING AFTERMATH
A woman huddles alone in the charred ruins of her home. Whole communities in the Soviet Union were the victims of arson attacks by German soldiers, who had been taught that the people they were killing were less than fully human.

Leningrad. In parts of the Ukraine the invading armies were welcomed as liberators from communism. But the Nazi view of Slav peoples as sub-human led to terrible atrocities.

Behind German lines Soviet partisans organized resistance, and paid the price of reprisals. Serafima Schibko lived in fear of both sides. She saw her village near Minsk burned several times. The men were taken away to execution or to provide forced labour for the Germans. In desperation people ran to take refuge in the woods. 'No one stayed in the village when it was burned for the last time,' she says. 'When we came back, we saw only burned ruins....We were glad to have survived....We weren't able to feel anything more, we were just trying to save our children.'

The early months of blitzkrieg had dramatically increased Hitler's gains in Europe. After advancing through France the German army had forced the retreat of British and French forces from the coastal town of Dunkirk in May 1940. France had been divided into the occupied north and west and the unoccupied south and east, with a puppet capital at Vichy. With the Germans just across the Channel the British prime minister, Winston Churchill, broadcast a sombre warning: 'The battle of France is over...the battle of Britain is about to begin.'

NO THROUGH ROAD
(RIGHT) *Fire erupts as German forces turn a street in the Ukraine into a war zone. Hitler's invasion of the Soviet Union, supported by the Finnish armies that had been victims of the Russian invasion two years before, was a repeat of his blitzkrieg tactics in Europe. But with the winter weather, the German army and its transport froze to a standstill and troops resorted to hand-drawn sledges. The German defeat at Stalingrad later confirmed the formidable capacity for endurance of civilians under siege.*

"We all hated the Germans at that time....An eye for an eye, a tooth for a tooth. I thought if they can do this to us, do it to children, we should do it to them. "

BETTY LAWRENCE

DAILY DEATH TOLL *People gather round a noticeboard listing casualties on the morning after an air raid in Plymouth, anxious to find out whether anyone they know has been killed.*

Under bombardment

In summer 1940 the aerial bombing of cities was becoming a reality in Britain. The Battle of Britain between the British and German air forces over the English Channel reached its peak in August; the German air force also began to attack urban targets. An all-night bombing raid on London on 23 August marked the beginning of the blitz. In September heavier raids began, and in mid-October nightly bombing intensified. During one of the worst periods, Londoners sheltered for seventy-six consecutive nights in the passageways and on the platforms of underground stations. Raids on other British cities followed. On 14 November the German air force launched a heavy raid on Coventry, an important centre of the war industry, destroying about a third of the city, killing about five hundred people and causing more than 1400 casualties.

Plymouth, with its large naval dockyard, was the most densely bombed city in Britain. More than one thousand people were killed there, and more than three thousand were injured. Sid Newham was at the cinema one evening when the noise became overwhelming, and people in the audience were advised to make their way home as best they could. 'When we got outside I had the shock of my life,' he remembers. 'The place was an inferno. Every other building seemed to be alight and the bombs were coming down.' Minutes later, a bomb hit the shelter in his back garden. He found himself staring at the open sky in a shower of dust. 'I could only free myself down to my waist, because there were big boulders resting on my legs. When I got the top part of my body free, I started pulling away at the rubble in front of me until I came across a woman's head. I smoothed her hair, cleared round her neck and patted her face. I said, "That you, Mum?" You couldn't tell because her face was just black. And she says, "Yes, it's me, Sid. I'm all right".'

Later that night Sid Newham was discharged from hospital with bandages on his injured legs and a walking stick to lean on; the beds were needed for the following night's raid. His grandmother and his sister died from the bombs, and his father, aged forty-two, was paralysed from the waist down.

Like the German air force, the British air force had tried to

COMMUNITY SPIRIT
(RIGHT) *Residents of
Islington, London, shelter
in a basement during an air
raid. For people without
a garden, church crypts,
cellars and coal holes became
places of refuge. The
frightening wait underground
was alleviated by determined
attempts to boost morale.*

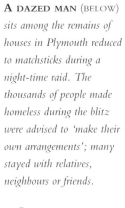

A DAZED MAN (BELOW)
*sits among the remains of
houses in Plymouth reduced
to matchsticks during a
night-time raid. The
thousands of people made
homeless during the blitz
were advised to 'make their
own arrangements'; many
stayed with relatives,
neighbours or friends.*

Decoration for heroes

THE GEORGE CROSS *recognized the heroic
efforts of civilians in living up to the defiant slogan
'Britain can take it' during bombing raids by
Germany. Introduced by King George VI in
1940, it was awarded mainly to civilians for 'acts
of the greatest heroism or of the most conspicuous
courage in circumstances of extreme danger'. The
honour ranked second only to the Victoria Cross,
Britain's highest military decoration.*

SIGNED UP *Sid Newham joined the Royal Air Force soon after losing his sister and grandmother in the blitz. 'I wanted revenge,' he says. 'I thought to myself, "This has got to stop, I've got to do my share".'*

SIGNING OFF *A member of a British air crew chalks a message on a bomb to his anonymous German enemy.*

hit strategic targets at first, but precision bombing had proved impossible and they too resorted to 'area bombing' to cripple industry and make workers homeless. Despite prewar concerns from leaders in both Britain and the United States that bombing should not be used against civilians, in 1942 Winston Churchill was boasting to his Soviet ally, Joseph Stalin, 'We hope to shatter almost every dwelling in almost every German city'.

The raid on Hamburg in July 1943 was unprecedented in its intensity. It created a firestorm, with hurricane-force winds and temperatures reaching 1000 degrees centigrade. Suction uprooted trees and flung people through the air over a sea of fire. About 42 000 civilians were killed in Hamburg – more than all the deaths during the blitz in Britain.

Horst Westphal immediately realized that the bombing was 'a completely different, new kind of bombing...flares were sent down by parachutes and lit up whole districts of the city...there were special bombs to break the windows, and then incendiary bombs came....The fire from the bombs was able to go wherever it wanted because there was no protection anywhere, there were no windows, no doors, everything had been blown out.'

Margarete Zettel remembers that during the days following the bombing, 'The sun never really managed to get through, you just saw a huge red fireball and there was smoke and this horrible stench, there was darkness everywhere, but not like night time. You could see the contours of the houses, it was very spooky. We were afraid from that point onwards....It was certainly a kind of total war. I can't imagine it being more total than that.'

People painted signs on bombed buildings to tell relatives where they had gone, while thousands more gathered at the railway station to be evacuated to areas where there were medical supplies and food. And the clean-up operation began. Horst Westphal recalls, 'An organization called Todt used to arrive with lorries; they piled the corpses on and took them to one of the mass graves at Ohlsdorf....Concentration camp prisoners were sent in with flame-throwers to burn the corpses, and the streets were walled up at the ends so no one could go in, because they were afraid of infection. It was a horrible chapter.'

SOLDIERING ON (LEFT)
Civilians carve a path through ruined buildings in Hamburg. Both in Britain and in Germany, people tried to maintain a pattern of daily life.

WAR EFFORT *Margarete Zettel* (ABOVE) *was awarded the Cross of Honour for her help rescuing people during the raids on Hamburg. 'After the attacks people were closer to each other but we were broken at the same time,' she says. 'Resistance grew a little bit against Hitler because people were saying, "What's the sense of it all?"'*

BOOSTING MORALE

ENTERTAINMENT was a valuable commodity during the war, and one that did not need to be rationed. It was also a vital means of strengthening morale, and the popular media of cinema and radio made it available to everyone.

Cinemas had closed at the start of the war in Britain because of the fear of bombing on such concentrated civilian targets. But when they re-opened they became oases of escapism and encouragement. Most people under the age of forty used to watch at least one feature film a week, and most of the films were American. After the entry of the United States into the war Hollywood began to play a more active role in morale-boosting, adopting the slogan 'Morale is mightier than the sword'.

In the United States, too, people flocked to see patriotic musical extravaganzas such as *Star Spangled Rhythm*, *This is the Army* and *Yankee Doodle Dandy*, a celebration of the American way of life starring James Cagney. There were dramas such as *Meet Me in St Louis*, a hymn to the good old days starring Judy Garland, and *Since You Went Away*, a tribute to the 'unconquerable fortress' of 1943 – the American family during the war. Hollywood

was more popular still among the troops serving abroad. In the United States armed services 630 000 men and women were watching a movie every night by 1943. Star performers travelled overseas to make personal appearances behind the battle lines, or to promote the sale of government war bonds.

The radio was a source of both information and reassurance. People in occupied countries risked their lives in listening to the British Broadcasting Corporation, while British civilians relied on it for Winston Churchill's speeches to the nation, and for the weekly edition of *Sincerely Yours*, hosted by Vera Lynn, whose signature tune became *We'll meet again*. The Japanese took advantage of her popularity to sap morale among British prisoners by announcing that she had been killed.

Entertainment also came direct to people at work and at play. Ousted from their grander venues by the threat of bombs, city musicians staged concerts in public parks, factory canteens and aircraft hangars, while provincial theatres declared with pride, 'We Never Close'.

MAKING DO *A harmonica player improvises for factory workers on a makeshift stage at a lunch-time concert.*

LAUNCHED INTO BATTLE *A Liberty cargo ship begins its journey from the West Coast to the open sea. A total of 2770 such ships were built in the United States in an effort to keep pace with their equally efficient destruction by German submarines during the war. As the war in the Pacific and the Atlantic raged on, thousands of troops lost their lives at sea.*

The war of production

A new chapter in the war began on 7 December 1941 when the Japanese attacked the United States Pacific fleet at Pearl Harbor in Hawaii. In 1941 President Roosevelt had banned the sale of raw materials to Japan because he wanted to help China in the war against Japan. By the following year negotiations were embittered and the Japanese were ready to take Pacific territories, rich in raw materials, by force. American volunteer pilots had already helped Britain's defenders during the Battle of Britain in 1940, but Pearl Harbor was the catalyst that turned the tide of American opinion from reluctance to indignant determination.

With the entry of the United States into the war, the world's greatest economy was converted to war production. It became the principal supplier to the Allies of machinery, aircraft and ships for the wars that were raging in the Soviet Union, North Africa, China and the Middle East. For people in the United States the Japanese invasion never came, but the war did change lives and landscapes as new factories were built and people found work.

California was one of the areas most affected. Shipyards there competed to produce Liberty ships in record time for the battle of the Atlantic. With the new urgency came innovation in manufacturing, as prefabricated parts and assembly-line production were introduced to keep pace with the demand.

Victor Cole worked at the Kaiser shipyard in Richmond, near San Francisco. He recalls the proud moment when a ship that had been built in a record few days was launched; there were 'people all over the shipyard and almost shoulder to shoulder, standing around and cheering and waving their hats. Everyone's mood was

ALL HANDS ON DECK *Victor Cole, pictured here with his wife Marge celebrating the completion of the '556th' ship, was part of the American battle of production at the Kaiser shipyard in Richmond, California. 'The mood there was, "We're winning",' he remembers.*

ROOTED IN SHOCK *Men at the United States naval base watch incredulously as a fireball erupts from the boats anchored on 'battleship row' in Pearl Harbor. About a hundred warships and 500 aircraft in the nearby airfields were sitting targets, and some 2500 Americans were killed in the attack.*

'WASTE NOT WANT NOT' *was the slogan of the home front in Britain, as household rubbish and iron railings were salvaged to make war machinery. There was an overwhelming response to the government's plea, 'Women of Britain, give us your aluminium…we will turn your pots and pans into Spitfires and Hurricanes.'*

"This is an impossible thing that we have done, and yet we can do it again, and so we have great pride".'

With every resource being poured into the war, the United States government introduced rationing for fuel and some foods. 'The things we normally thought would always be available were not,' says Victor Cole. 'It was hard to get whisky.…There was always enough rum around, so they would make you buy a bottle or more of rum every time you got a bottle of whisky.'

Food rationing was imposed everywhere. Goods that were usually imported from other countries were no longer available. The restrictions led to a flourishing black market. People in rural areas could grow more of their own food so they fared better than those in cities, who were dependent on the food supply. In Britain football pitches and lawn tennis courts were dug up to make way for vegetables and allotments sprang up on every available patch of suburban land. Everyone was given a ration book; as government intervention influenced the national diet, many families were eating better than they had done before the war.

Women were vital to the war effort. In March 1941 women in Britain were called to factories and farms to fill jobs previously occupied by men; in December national service was introduced for all unmarried women between the ages of twenty and thirty, and by mid-1943, 90 per cent of single women and 80 per cent of married women were employed in the armed forces or in industry.

In Germany the number of women working rose, but less dramatically. The Nazis were concerned that the 'psychological and emotional life' of women might be affected, and so might their ability to bear children. Even so, the 1941 Women for Victory campaign brought many German women into factories, and many more were called up for *Arbeitdienst*, work service.

The Germans also raided their conquered territories in Europe for workers to boost the war effort. There were three million foreign workers in Germany in 1941, and by 1944 there were seven million, 20 per cent of the workforce. They worked in aircraft and chemical factories, in quarries and on fortifications. Alexandra Sakharova was sent from Leningrad to a farm in Germany, where she worked fifteen or sixteen hours a day to help cut hay with a sickle, to harvest potatoes and to feed the piglets.

WOMEN'S WORK *in a German engineering plant. The war brought more women into factories, where they did highly technical work; onto the streets as postmen and transport workers; and onto the land as farm workers.*

She was paid a pittance, and given potatoes to eat. 'If anybody needed me, they just called out, "Russian Pig",' she says. 'Of course it was not very pleasant, but I was Russian. I was proud that I was Russian.'

The Japanese drafted children as young as ten from their own country to work in factories. Katsumoto Saotome was eleven years old in 1944. He had to work in a steel plant, shovelling scrap metal into trolleys and pushing them along railway tracks. 'The school wanted us to feel like military people,' he says.

Even unborn babies were regarded as part of the war effort. Yoshiko Hashimoto remembers, 'Before my first child was born I was issued with a maternity certificate....Where it should say "Scheduled date of birth" it says "Scheduled date of production". Looking at this, it makes me very angry, because the life of one person is considered as a commodity, an article. That's the way the government thought about people.'

Like the Germans, the Japanese wanted an empire and were prepared to consider other peoples as a mechanical means to that end. Japan imported one and a half million Koreans to work, mining coal, digging tunnels and building fortifications. The recruitment itself was brutal. Yan Pyun Tou was planting rice on his neighbour's farm in Korea when a stranger abducted him. He was locked in a prison cell and shipped to Japan, where he was put to work at a hydroelectric plant. 'Our bosses were very hard on us,' he says. 'We were beaten almost every day...they didn't see us as human beings.'

CHILD LABOUR *Children in many Japanese schools were sent to work in ordnance factories, where instead of schooling they were taught allegiance with the help of a military drill and patriotic slogans. Katsumoto Saotome paraphrases the wording on the bandanna he wore round his head. 'No matter what happens, Japan will win the war, because we are a land derived from the gods'. Children were part of the war effort in other countries too: in Germany members of the Hitler Youth went round their neighbourhood collecting bones from the Sunday roast to make explosives.*

"We were there twenty hours a day...we dug trenches in the ice. We lost people all the time because the Germans were constantly in the air bombing us."

LEONID GALPERIN

THE ROAD OF LIFE
Leonid Galperin worked around the clock to guard, maintain and improve the 56-kilometre (35-mile) route across Lake Ladoga. 'It was very difficult and very monotonous,' he says. An army of ten thousand civilians worked on the huge frozen lake, including nurses who helped drivers already weakened through hunger and injured by bombs.

Life under siege

As total war brought new privations to civilians in the combatant countries, no city experienced more hardship than Leningrad. By September 1941 the German and Finnish armies had encircled the city, and a thirty-month siege began. Rather than launching a full-scale attack, Hitler's tactic was now to starve the city out while continuing to bomb and shell its inhabitants. Civilians of all ages became involved in defending the city, and waging their own desperate battle against starvation as supplies dwindled. Elena Taranukhina, a piano teacher, helped to dig anti-tank ditches, and worked in a hospital nearby. As an exceptionally bitter winter set in, temperatures fell to minus 40 degrees centigrade, and she and her friends slept in their fur coats. There was no wood – they had burned all the furniture they had, and even their books – and no water. 'We couldn't wash ourselves,' she recalls, 'because we were only strong enough to fetch water to drink.'

The bread ration was cut to 125 grams a day – a slice and a half. When flour ran out, the bread was made from wood cellulose and sawdust, and soup was made from carpenter's glue. Elena Taranukhina would start to queue for something resembling food at four o'clock every morning. 'All the birds died because of the frost. We tried to catch them but it was very difficult....We ate grass, all kinds of grasses. We made soup. I brought the horse dung home, and I wanted to eat it.' Cats, dogs and mice disappeared from the city, and the sight of dismembered corpses bore haunting testimony to suspicions of cannibalism.

The deathly cold did bring one benefit: the huge Lake Ladoga froze over, creating a lifeline to the east. On 17 November two reconnaissance groups set out on foot, roped together and wearing life-jackets, to test the thickening ice. A few days later a 7-kilometre (4-mile) long column of 350 horses pulling sledges set out. The horses, which were also weak from starvation, were hardly strong enough to pull their sledges. But the convoy got through to bring back essential supplies.

Leonid Galperin helped to maintain the vital road across the frozen lake, and he

EXPOSED TO DEATH
Grieving civilians move through a silent landscape searching for their relatives after the retreat of German armies from a village in the southern Ukraine.

remembers, 'We called it the opening of the road to life. The road did not stop for a moment....When the ice became stronger, lorries and even tanks could get through, though they removed the upper layer of ice. At last Ladoga was working on a full scale.'

The road to life was under constant threat of death. Leonid Galperin remembers, 'We lost people all the time because the Germans were constantly in the air bombing us. Our anti-aircraft cannons didn't function but we were there around the clock and had no place to hide.'

Fragile epitaphs

SCRAPS OF PAPER *torn from an address book read as a litany of death, the names and dates recorded by an eleven-year-old girl in Leningrad as her mother, brothers and grandmother died around her.*

ACTS OF RESISTANCE

T HE RESISTANCE, the movement against enemy occupation, involved civilians in activities from spying and sabotage to guerrilla warfare. It was always risky. When activists were captured they were tortured for information, but the German army was often undiscriminating in its reprisals. In one of the worst incidents, German troops in Greece responded to the discovery of two murdered soldiers by killing thirty elderly villagers and thirty-eight young children in the village of Klissura.

In the Soviet Union the resistance forces, or partisans, were formidably organized, constituting a guerrilla army that operated in the forests, with radio links to its own army commands. Governments exiled in London helped to support partisans in other invaded countries, sometimes with dramatic results. In August 1944 the home army in Warsaw, supported by the Polish government in London, tried unsuccessfully to oust the German army and seize the city before it was occupied by the advancing Soviet army. But when the Soviet advance halted, German reprisals resulted in more than 20 000 deaths. General Charles de Gaulle also operated from London, and his volunteer army, the Free French, fought alongside the Allies. In France his emissaries vied with the communists in organizing sabotage campaigns, painting road signs black and planting ambushes.

Resistance was also a matter of individual courage. Volunteers landed by parachute or by boat in occupied countries, bringing with them escape route maps and forged identity cards hidden in chess sets, which they smuggled into prisoner of war camps. Others organized convoys to ferry prisoners home. All over Europe people were engaged in spying: railway clerks reported on goods being sent, while waiters picked up careless talk among German customers. People in Denmark and the Netherlands, horrified at the brutal treatment of the Jews during the German occupation of their country, held demonstrations in protest, and many Dutch families concealed Jews to prevent their deportation to concentration camps.

Yugoslavia was the one occupied country in which resistance succeeded in liberating the people. The communist leader Josip Broz Tito led a partisan army against Italian and German troops, and also fought a savage civil war against non-communists, capturing towns and establishing local governments in the areas they liberated. Here, as elsewhere, the price paid in lives and misery was very high.

A NEW IDENTITY *These false French identity papers were prepared for a British air force officer. Forged papers became a lifeline for pilots who had been shot down in occupied countries and for prisoners of war attempting to escape.*

The Germans failed to break the lifeline, but people in the city still grew weak and many collapsed and died of starvation in the streets. Elena Taranukhina, like thousands of others, dragged her dead mother on a sledge to her grave.

In the midst of all this horror, the people of Leningrad heard that the great composer Dmitri Shostakovich had written a new symphony dedicated to the city. The city orchestra's conductor searched for members of the orchestra and found that only twenty-seven were still alive: many of them had died of starvation. Determined to stage the symphony, he arranged special rations for the musicians and persuaded the army to release musicians to play with them. Each rehearsal lasted forty minutes – people were too cold, tired and weak to play any longer.

On the day the symphony was performed the Red Army created a diversion to draw away German fire. Lubov Zhakova was one of the hundreds of people in the audience. She remembers 'the feeling of enthusiasm, of celebration, in the fact that this Shostakovich symphony was devoted to Leningrad. Everybody realized that. People appeared here straight from the battlefields with their rifles.' At the end of the concert there was complete silence, and then tumultuous applause. Lubov Zhakova was pushed towards the conductor to hand him a bouquet of flowers, an astonishing sight during the war. She had picked them from her grandfather's garden in commemoration of the remarkable event. The symphony became an emblem of Leningrad's resistance, and marked a moment of human victory. The concert was broadcast across the country.

The siege was finally lifted in January 1944, when the Red Army broke the German stranglehold. By that time more than 630 000 civilians had died of cold, hunger and disease, and a further 200 000 had been killed by the German armies.

In June 1944 Allied armies broke into Hitler's Europe with an invasion that had been planned for more than a year. In the D-Day landings, forces of American, British and Canadian troops in an armada of 4000 Allied ships and 10 000 aircraft swooped onto the beaches of Normandy in France, beginning a series of battles towards Germany and the recovery of Europe. For civilians in Europe and the Far East, the battle of morale was not over.

RITE OF PASSAGE (OPPOSITE) *With bowed heads, a couple pulls a dead victim by sledge to the cemetery in Leningrad. In a diary written during the siege one entry reads: 'Taking a body to the cemetery exhausts the last vestiges of strength from the survivors. And so the living, in fulfilling their duty to the dead, are brought to the brink themselves.'*

REPRIEVE *Survivors of the Leningrad siege crowd round for tickets to hear the symphony dedicated to the city. 'We were carried away by the feeling that we were winning after the terrible winter…we hadn't expected to live,' remembers Lubov Zhakova. 'It was a real ceremony for us, a feeling of joy, a very serious victory.'*

Utter destruction

By spring 1945 the bombing of cities reached new heights. In February British aircraft launched an attack on the German city of Dresden that killed some 50 000 people, and resurrected debate about the morality of the indiscriminate killing of civilians. On 10 March American B-29 bombers, built to carry 'the greatest weight of death ever lifted into the skies', launched air attacks on Japan. Half a million incendiary bombs were dropped on Tokyo to force the Japanese to surrender.

Katsumoto Saotome, who was living in Tokyo, remembers, 'Nobody ever dreamed there would be such an air raid. We still believed we could put out the fires, that was what we were told, what we were taught....There was heavy punishment for the people who ran away from houses that caught fire.'

On the night of the Tokyo raid there was a strong northerly wind. Sumiko Morikawa, a mother with three young children, recalls, 'I was worried because of the wind....Later that night the sirens started going off continuously. Looking out from our window, I could see red. It was as if the clouds were burning.' When the bombs began to fall she strapped her twin babies on her back, took her four-year-old son by the hand, and with thousands of other desperate citizens hurried to the park, where 'fire just erupted everywhere around our feet'. She tried to put out the fire

A CITY LAID WASTE
Only concrete buildings were left standing in Tokyo the morning after the March raid. The city was a tinderbox of wooden houses and shops, which were reduced within minutes to funeral pyres. People fled from their underfloor shelters to the canals, but even the water could not quench the raging firestorm.

RAIN OF TERROR *An American B-29 drops its deadly load. In the same month as the Tokyo raids, kamikaze pilots flew suicide missions in planeloads of explosives to sink Allied ships off the Pacific island of Okinawa.*

with water from the lake but resorted to jumping in. 'Fire was actually coming into the pool,' she recalls.

Yoshiko Hashimoto ran to the river carrying her baby. 'There were people who had become fireballs themselves and were rolling over...it was like hell,' she says. 'I decided to jump into the river. As I jumped I saw my mother's face; it was very sad. I'll never forget that face.' Two young men pulled Yoshiko Hashimoto into their boat. 'We stayed overnight on the river. It was full of corpses....I was so tired I hardly knew whether I was alive or dead....In the morning the two men took me and my baby to hospital.' The Tokyo raids killed 120 000 people, more than any other single action in the war.

United States forces had seized islands in the Pacific in order to secure bases for their raids on Japan. Fighting lasted for weeks on Iwo Jima, and thousands died. On the island of Okinawa, some Japanese took their own lives rather than suffer the ultimate shame of surrender. Shigeaki Kinjo remembers, 'The men were given two hand grenades each....The sergeant who was passing them out explained that, if you came across an American soldier, you should throw one at the American and use the other to commit suicide... we were told it was an honour to die for the emperor.' He and his eighteen-year-old brother felt it was their responsibility to make sure that everyone in the family died. 'The first person we killed was my mother,' he says. 'We used a rope in the beginning. In the end we used rocks to stone her head. I was crying. It is a terrible, terrible experience to kill your own mother.'

Five months later, total war reached its climax. On 6 August United States aircraft dropped the first atom bomb on Hiroshima. It killed about 78 000 people. Those near the centre of the blast were vapourized; thousands more suffered horrific burns, and radiation sickness signalled the beginnings of lifelong illness. Three days later, a second atom bomb killed about 40 000 civilians at Nagasaki. Japan surrendered unconditionally on 15 August.

Some Japanese committed suicide, and Yoshiko Hashimoto recalls, 'There were many men crying because Japan had lost the war.' She felt differently. 'I held my baby, I held my sister with the burns, and I cried with happiness. I thought, "I never want to see another war".'

*"*T*hese aircraft were things that I'd never seen before....It was like a devil coming from somewhere out of this world. "*

KATSUMOTO SAOTOME

MAKESHIFT REFUGE *A lonely survivor sits in the blasted wasteland that was the city of Nagasaki.*

Coming home

By the time Japan surrendered, the war in Europe was already over. As troops returned to euphoric crowds and happy families, millions of refugees were starting the long, slow journey home, carrying their meagre possessions in bundles and hoping to find something left of their homes and their families. Alexandra Sakharova and her workmates had been freed in April 1945 when

American troops arrived at the German farm where she had worked. She made the journey home barefoot. When she reached Leningrad a month later, she found both her aunts and her mother alive. They had not expected to see each other ever again. 'Nothing else was left for me,' she says, 'just quite unbelievable joy.'

The war had cost more than fifty million lives worldwide. For the first time in the history of war, more civilians had been killed than soldiers. The Soviet Union suffered most losses, with twenty million deaths. Poland lost six million people, 15 per cent of the population, including three million Jews. The war cost Germany about four and a half million deaths, while 450 000 British people lost their lives and 120 000 died for the British empire. In financial terms, the United States had contributed almost half of the Allied war effort, and Germany had spent more than Italy and Japan combined. And the price of war continued to be paid by survivors now learning to live with the consequences.

As communists joined hands with capitalists over the ruins of fascism, the mood was for many people one of subdued shock rather than of triumph. The discovery of Hitler's concentration camps added to the known horrors of the war. The moral victory of freedom against totalitarianism, and the overwhelming relief that the years of siege and destruction had ended, was tempered by the knowledge of the terrible methods of the war and the means employed to bring it to an end. Many of those who had witnessed the use of complex technology and of fellow human beings as instruments of mass extermination now fervently hoped that in future the dread of such extremes in war would bring about peace.

WELCOME BACK *An ex-prisoner of war arrives from the Far East to a rapturous greeting from his wife and son in London. In Britain single-storey 'prefab' housing had provided a temporary solution to being bombed out. Soldiers all over the world returned to grown children, changed circumstances and unfamiliar surroundings.*

THE ROAD HOME (OPPOSITE) *Belgian, Dutch, French and Polish survivors edge their way over the river Elbe along a railway bridge destroyed by the Germans to halt the advancing Red Army. For thousands of refugees the journey home took weeks of trudging through landscapes mutilated by war.*

11

1 9 4 5 – 1 9 6 1

Brave New World

THE COLD WAR YEARS

'EAST AND WEST HAVE met,' declared the radio commentator excitedly. 'This is the news for which the whole Allied world has been waiting. The forces of liberation have joined hands.' It was on the afternoon of 25 April 1945 that soldiers of a United States army patrol first saw the Soviet lines near Torgau, south of Berlin on the river Elbe.

Alexander Silvashko and William Robertson were two of the first soldiers to meet. They both remember the excitement and comradeship of that moment. As Alexander Silvashko says, 'We met like brothers. We had defeated a common enemy. We were united in fighting fascism, and together we had won. The Americans gave us cigarettes and food. They gave us whatever they had, even watches, as souvenirs. The atmosphere was unbelievable.'

The Russians' exhilaration was equalled by that of the Americans. William Robertson recalls, 'There was the great curiosity of actually meeting Soviet soldiers. We knew they were a powerful army, but we didn't know them as individuals – and here they were shaking hands with us. It progressed to a great celebration of a very significant event. They were good people. There was the relief that the war was coming to a close, and that the Allies had won the war. We were just plain thankful that we were there and breathing.'

The photograph of the two lieutenants was seen around the world. It became a symbol of the victorious alliance between the communist Soviet Union and the capitalist West. However, within weeks it became apparent that fraternity was not to be the key to the postwar relationship between East and West; in the very moment of triumph a new conflict was being born. Popular hopes for peace were again to be disappointed. The Soviet Union and the United States, now elevated to superpower status, nursed a mutual hostility that divided most of the world into two armed camps. This led to a new kind of war – the Cold War – that was to have a profound effect on the lives of a whole generation.

THE WARM EMBRACE *between William Robertson and Alexandr Silvashko became a symbol of peace and hope.*

Emerging from the war

As the peoples of Europe emerged from the rubble of war and began to rebuild their lives, they knew that the victors represented two fundamentally different political systems. The differences had been buried in the urgency of the need to defeat fascism, but as soon as victory was assured, they resurfaced. The British, Soviet and United States leaders had met at Yalta in February 1945 to discuss the future of Europe, and particularly of Germany, when the war ended. At Potsdam near Berlin in July 1945 there were further negotiations, with the United States president, Harry S. Truman, and Britain's prime minister, Winston Churchill, both trying to restrain Joseph Stalin's demands for Soviet domination of Eastern Europe. The Soviet Union had suffered most during the war, with the loss of more than twenty million lives, and Stalin was determined to make sure that his country could never again be threatened by Germany. To allay his fears, he sought to extend communism to the countries of Eastern Europe, which lay on the Soviet Union's western borders.

The Allies agreed that Germany should be divided into four zones, administered by Britain, France, the Soviet Union and the United States. The capital city, Berlin (which was situated within the Soviet zone) was similarly divided. The trust and cooperation this arrangement required was soon to be tested, and the goodwill that had characterized the ending of the war did not last.

Anatoly Semiriaga, a Soviet army officer, was in Berlin in the early days after the war, liberating people from concentration camps and helping local townspeople to find food, water and shelter in the shattered city. He remembers his orders: 'I was told, "Captain, your job is to see to the population of this area, at least to find bread for them." People emerged from caves, from their hiding places to welcome us. You had to care for these people. They had to be lodged somewhere…you had to encourage them. They were under tremendous shock.' But within days the humanitarian effort was to be coloured by politics. 'We were called in by our officers and told: "Listen, the Germans were not solely responsible for

COMING HOME TO BERLIN *Many of Berlin's citizens had been evacuated from the city towards the end of the war to escape Allied bombing. When they returned they found their homes reduced to rubble, their ruined city in the hands of the enemy.*

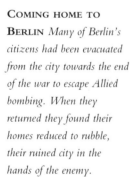

"A whole avalanche of these unfortunates were coming back to the east, and people were also moving to the west. These two currents were meeting. You had to care for these people. *"*

ANATOLY SEMIRIAGA

ANATOLY SEMIRIAGA, *an officer with one of the Soviet army units that defeated the German army near Berlin, felt compassion for the thousands of freed prisoners, refugees and homeless citizens he was instructed to look after in the early days of peace.*

REBUILDING WORK IN DRESDEN *being carried out by the patient labour of the city's inhabitants. The task of feeding, clothing and housing the bewildered citizens of Germany was a major concern of the occupying forces in the early years after the war.*

this war. It wasn't just Hitler, it was the imperialist system. And who are the representatives of imperialism now? The allies we fought on the same side as against Hitler." We were taught that the defeat of fascism was one important step towards the victory of socialism all over the world. Since the Red Army had liberated Eastern Europe, sooner or later socialism would be established there.'

Paul Nitze, who went on to become one of the United States' expert commentators on the Cold War, was also in Berlin when the war ended. He witnessed the Soviet efforts to gain compensation from Germany for the damage that had been done to the Soviet Union during the war. 'I watched what the Russians were doing. They were pulling up the railroad tracks and seizing every bit of everything they could find and moving it out of Berlin, straight back to Russia.' He was in regular contact with the Russians in Berlin, and remembers that 'Their unwillingness to compromise, to work out any workable deal, was something very frightening. You got the feeling these were difficult people who were going to be impossible for us to get along with.'

Soviet troops had freed the countries of Eastern Europe from the German armies. Now they introduced their ideology to

RETURNING HERO *A GI describes his wartime adventures to an admiring audience in his local store. For many Americans, this was an era of greater spending power and consumer choice than they had ever experienced before – as magazines (ABOVE RIGHT) and the advertising industry (ABOVE) were eager to remind them.*

these countries; Czechoslovakia, Hungary and Poland were all behind the Soviet lines at the end of the war, and were increasingly brought under communist control.

While Russians were helping the triumph of socialism, in Western Europe people's thoughts turned homewards, and their energies from survival to ways of reconstructing their lives. Americans, too, wanted to get home, to get out of uniform, get a girl and a job and put European conflicts out of their minds. 'With new cars and new tyres on the way,' boasted a newsreel, 'America will be rolling with a pre-war flourish. Yes, cars, radios, vacuum cleaners, nylons, juicy steaks – it sounds almost like a dream.' Gail Halverson, who had been in Europe as a bomber pilot, agrees. 'It's like a new life. It's like walking from one scene of a tragedy into a musical,' he explains. He was eager to get home, to 'go back to see my girl-friend, plan for what we were going to do after the war. All the worry and concern was just obliterated,' he remembers, 'and we disbanded our military. We just disbanded very rapidly. Now it was time for peace.'

'DADDY'S COME HOME!'
A newly discharged US soldier greets his happy three-year-old daughter on his return home to New York. For families on both sides of the Atlantic, peace brought reunion and the chance to rebuild family life.

From allies to enemies

By the autumn of 1945 it was becoming obvious to the strategists in Washington that the Soviet Union was already no longer an ally but a potential enemy. On 9 February 1946 Stalin made a speech in Moscow that sounded, as Paul Nitze recalls, like 'a delayed declaration of war against the US'. A few days later an expert in Soviet affairs, George Kennan, despatched from the United States embassy in Moscow what became known as the 'long telegram', arguing that the United States must 'contain' Soviet power.

The British were also concerned about Soviet intentions. Only a few days after Kennan's telegram had been received, the British statesman Winston Churchill visited the United States. At a small college in Fulton, Missouri, he sounded his own warning. 'From Stettin in the Baltic to Trieste in the Adriatic,' he growled, 'an iron curtain has descended across the continent. Behind that line lie all the capitals of the ancient states of central and Eastern Europe – Warsaw, Berlin, Prague, Budapest – and all these famous cities, and the populations around them, lie in what I must call the

Soviet sphere.' The Russians did not want war, he said; no, all they wanted was 'the fruits of war and the infinite expansion of their power and doctrines'. Churchill called upon the English-speaking peoples to adopt a policy of strength and a close alliance that would resist Soviet ambitions. There was a hostile reaction to his speech, but it helped to change the public mood. The press had once portrayed an alliance of three equals; now, Joseph Stalin was shown as a despot forcing whole countries into submission.

By the spring of 1947 Churchill's prophecy of a divided world was coming to pass. There was Soviet pressure on Iran, on Turkey and on Greece. Things were 'happening in a hurry', the United States president, Harry Truman, wrote in a private letter to his sister. On 27 February the president appealed to congressional leaders for a united effort. The secretary of state, General George Marshall, said: 'It is not alarmist to say that we are now faced with the first crisis of a series which might extend Soviet domination to Europe, the Middle East and Asia.'

To challenge the Soviet initiative, in March Harry Truman spelled out what became known as the Truman Doctrine in a solemn speech to a joint session of Congress. 'I believe that it must be the policy of the United States to support free peoples who are resisting attempted subjugation by armed insurgencies or by outside pressures. I believe that we must assist free people to work out their own destinies in their own way.'

TUG-OF-WAR IN BERLIN
Without a common language, this Soviet soldier and German woman have misunderstood each other's intentions. The money the woman has just been given was not a gift, but payment for the bicycle the soldier wanted to buy from her. Fellow civilians look on in some discomfort at this minor incident in a world that was filled with mistrust and misunderstanding.

THE IRON CURTAIN *that came down across Germany divided the countries of Europe into two very different political, economic and military groups. In 1949 the North Atlantic Treaty Organization (NATO) was founded in the West, matched in 1955 by the Warsaw Pact. In the postwar settlements the Soviet Union had gained substantial territories along its western boundaries, and absorbed the previously independent Baltic states of Estonia, Latvia and Lithuania. The peoples on either side of the Iron Curtain were taught to feel fear and hostility towards those on the other side.*

Members of NATO

Countries under Soviet influence

- - - Pre-1945 borders

PLANNING FOR PEACE

WHILE THEIR MEN were still fighting, leaders in the United States, the Soviet Union and the other 'united nations', as the allies against Germany were known, lay the foundations for the charter of a new international peace-keeping organization, the United Nations Organization. One of its goals was 'friendly relations among nations'. After negotiations in Washington and then at Yalta, the UN charter was signed in San Francisco on 26 June 1945, at a conference attended by representatives from twenty-six nations across the world. The United Nations formally came into being in October that year, with fifty-one members.

Like its predecessor, the League of Nations, the UN was founded on the principle of collective security for the peaceful settlement of disputes. It required its members to act together in a global effort to prevent war. Britain, China, France, the Soviet Union and the United States became the five permanent members of the UN's Security Council, which was responsible for maintaining international peace through collective security, economic sanctions or, as a last resort, military intervention.

As collective security depended upon agreement among the main powers, the UN charter ruled that decisions made by the permanent members of the Security Council must be unanimous. But with the increasing divide between the Western powers and the Soviet Union, the machinery of peace was weakened. When conflicts arose, the Soviet Union frequently exercised its power of veto, rendering the Security Council powerless. The only time the UN used military intervention in its early years, to settle the Korean conflict, the Soviet Union was absent from the council and therefore unable to veto the decision. The UN had been set up by the wartime victors to protect future generations 'from the scourge of war'. Now the conflicting interests of the two world superpowers prevented it from fulfilling this function.

The UN's principles of international peace may have been weakened by ideological and economic disputes, but it held firmly to its belief in equal rights and self-determination for people of all nations. It provided a new platform for the establishment of international humanitarian standards. Specialized agencies were set up. These initially dealt with postwar problems of refugees, rehabilitation and resettlement, and were then extended to cover issues such as slavery, religious intolerance and detention without trial.

Other agencies were set up to safeguard and promote better opportunities in employment, education, science and medicine. Through the newly established World Bank and the International Monetary Fund the UN was able to fund projects in developing countries, building roads and railways, and introducing telecommunications.

STARTLED BY THE UNITED CHORUS *from postwar leaders, the United Nations cradles the infant charter. This 1946 cartoon reflects the popular disbelief that the victors would be able to set aside their differences and work together for peace through the international organization they had themselves established.*

The changing relationship between the two former allies was demonstrated in an American newsreel at the end of the year. 'Soviet Russia was expansively stabbing westward, knifing into nations left empty by war. On orders from the Kremlin, Russia had launched one of history's most drastic political, moral and economic wars – a cold war. The United States was obliged to help Europe safeguard its traditional freedoms and the independence of its nations. Gone was the spirit of wartime unity that reached its peak on that historic afternoon in April 1945 at the Elbe river in Germany. Here two worlds actually met, but this coalition was to be torn asunder.'

The suspicion the West felt towards the Soviet Union was mirrored in Soviet fears about the intentions of the West. A Soviet feature film also recalled the meeting on the Elbe; in their version it was the Americans who were trying to take over Europe. Alexander Silvashko was now a schoolmaster in a remote village, and was disappointed when he went to see the film. 'I thought I'd find my character played somewhere in it. I was terribly upset when I realized that it was completely untruthful.' He remembers, too, that at that time 'there was an atmosphere of fear. Children liked my tales of the war but I never told them about the meeting on the Elbe. If I had discussed openly what had happened, I would have been in trouble. I would have been pulled in and questioned by the secret police.'

Ordinary Soviet citizens did not believe all they were told about the West. Nevertheless, as Anatoly Semiriaga explains, they did believe that Churchill's Fulton speech, the Marshall Plan set up to aid Europe's economic recovery, and the North Atlantic military alliance were designed 'to enslave Europe and set it against Russia'. Similarly, Westerners might not believe everything they were told about the Soviet Union, but they were still highly suspicious. One of the Americans who had met the Soviets on the Elbe was Elijah Sams. He appeared on a television programme, *Strike It Rich*, and decided to spend the money he won on visiting the Soviet Union to 'help peace efforts'. The State Department advised him not to go. His friends and neighbours 'thought we were kind of out of our minds'. When he returned he was questioned by the Federal Bureau of Investigation (FBI) on suspicion of being a communist.

Mutual hostility was reflected in political cartoons. Most Western cartoonists systematically dehumanized and demonized 'commies', 'reds' and 'pinks'. Their Soviet counterparts, who might have been banished to a forced labour camp if they failed to show enough enthusiasm in their work, understandably in their turn dehumanized and demonized Westerners.

'DARWIN CORRECTED' *reads the title of this cartoon from the satirical Soviet magazine,* Krokodil. *The ape is pointing to a picture of Heinrich Himmler, Hitler's deputy, emphasizing the likeness between him and the grim-faced, bloodstained American soldier.*

THE RED MENACE *of Stalin (*RIGHT*) looms over Europe. In this French cartoon he is poised to take over France, having already plunged the communist knife into the states of Eastern Europe and into China. The musicians accompanying his dance are leading French communists.*

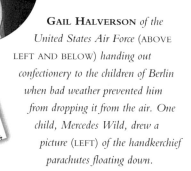

GAIL HALVERSON *of the United States Air Force* (ABOVE LEFT AND BELOW) *handing out confectionery to the children of Berlin when bad weather prevented him from dropping it from the air. One child, Mercedes Wild, drew a picture* (LEFT) *of the handkerchief parachutes floating down.*

The Berlin blockade

All the pressures of the postwar world converged on Berlin in 1948. The city was the spearhead of Soviet penetration into the heart of Europe, and at the same time a Western capitalist outpost deep inside the communist world.

In West Germany, the Western powers had introduced the currency reform that would shortly set off the *Wirtschaftswunder*, the economic miracle. They wanted to extend the reform to their sectors of Berlin. The Russians angrily refused permission. The atmosphere in Berlin was taut to breaking point when, on 23 June 1948, the Western powers announced that they were extending the currency reform to West Berlin anyway. The very next day the Russians began their blockade of Berlin.

Anatoly Semiriaga was now a Soviet liaison officer there, and remembers, 'The blockade was prepared weeks in advance. We had done everything we could to make the Allies leave West Berlin voluntarily, because it was a mote in our eye. So in the end we decided to force them to leave by making life intolerable for West Berlin.' They cut off the power, blocked the highways, stopped an American military train. But now the West, which had watched and done nothing as Stalin cemented his power across Eastern Europe, decided to act. Regardless of cost, they began to supply the city by air. The pilots who had bombed Berlin a few years earlier were now called back to feed its people.

Gail Halverson was one of these pilots. 'A telex came in and says we want four of your planes to leave Mobile, Alabama and go to Frankfurt within four hours, and we want crews for that. And I volunteered. We knew the dire straits that the people of Berlin were in.'

For many people in the West, the blockade confirmed all that they had been told about the Russians. To Gail Halverson it all came down to a simple comparison between good and evil. He was impressed to find that the children in Berlin spoke about freedom and did not ask him for anything. So he took to dropping them chocolate, fastening it to little parachutes made out of handkerchiefs. One young girl, Mercedes Wild, was at school when she saw the parachutes floating down. She did not get any chocolate, so she wrote to Gail Halverson: 'Dear Chocolate Uncle, Please

AIRLIFT TO BERLIN

THE CITY OF BERLIN, an island of capitalism well over a hundred kilometres inside the communist Soviet sector of Germany, became a besieged city as the blockade took effect. The Soviets were determined to starve Westerners out of Berlin; the Americans were determined to stay whatever the cost, and were instructed to respond as though the city was a beleaguered garrison.

The air corridor was the only remaining link between Berlin and the West. It became a lifeline for the two million inhabitants in the Western sectors. American aircraft – freighters and bombers – returned to Europe. The air forces of the United States and Britain flew round-the-clock operations that involved hundreds of aircraft. Berlin's two airports could not cope with the volume of traffic, so a third airport was rapidly built with the assistance of 19 000 volunteers.

It was dangerous and exhausting work for the pilots, who snatched sleep between flights on sacks in the aircraft hangars. There were so many flights, the aircraft were loaded to capacity, landing controls were primitive – it was a situation that could have brought disaster. But of the 272 000 flights that landed in the city in 321 days there were just twenty crashes. The most intensive flight schedule ever was a triumph of organization.

The skies above Berlin were constantly filled with the roar of aircraft; one landed on average every ten minutes bringing food, fuel and medical supplies. Most of these were everyday essentials, though the effort to maintain a degree of comfort was extended in December to Christmas trees and boxes of chocolates. The record delivery reached 13 000 tonnes of supplies one day in April 1949 – the average was 4000 tonnes a day for civilians and another 500 tonnes for military personnel.

The blockade was a political disaster for the Soviet Union, which failed to lure West Berliners into the Eastern sector despite offers of Soviet food and fuel rations. As a result of their endurance, the people of Berlin were seen to be choosing a future with Western values. The airlift continued until September, four months after the blockade was lifted. It hastened the division not only of Berlin itself but of Germany, and had highlighted the real dangers of the dangerous game of brinkmanship in the Cold War.

A CROWD OF WEST BERLINERS *watches an American aircraft, heavily loaded with essential supplies, flying in to land at Tempelhof airport during the blockade of the city.*

throw a parachute into the Hennelstrasse, you will recognize the garden because of the white hens.' He could not see the chickens, so he sent her some chocolate by post instead. The first piece, she says, was 'heaven on earth'; she put it on the windowsill and ate it bit by bit for a long, long time.

On 12 May 1949 the Russians finally gave in, and ended the blockade. By this time, the North Atlantic Treaty had been signed in Washington, and later that same month the West German Parliament voted through the *Grundgesetz*, the new constitution of a new sovereign West German state.

Life in the Soviet Union

The Soviet climbdown over Berlin turned a crisis for the West into a triumph. The Soviet people were told nothing. Their only task was to follow their leader. Millions were taught that central planning and collective work in unquestioning obedience to Stalin were the only ways to build a modern, just society. They sat through lessons where they were taught: 'We read the life of Comrade Stalin and we lift our heads. We clench our fists, we believe in our todays and our tomorrows. We believe in the battle led by Joseph Stalin.'

On Stalin's seventieth birthday in 1949 his people were summoned to celebrate the victorious march of socialism. Tamara Banketik, then eleven years old, was chosen to congratulate him. Among a group of children clutching bouquets, and in front of a huge crowd in Moscow, her voice rang out: 'We are the children of Lenin and Stalin. We strive to the summit of learning. Teacher, leader, beloved friend: Father Stalin, welcome!' She remembers now: 'I was transported into a fairy tale. He had such kindly eyes. It was as if he was my father.' Like the girl in the fairy tale, after the grand occasion Tamara Banketik had to give back her pretty dress. For her family, as for many others, reality was different. 'We lived in terrible conditions. It wasn't a house but a little shed. There was no running water or electricity. Each day I only had money for one ration of bread. I had to fight myself to stop eating it before I got home and shared it with my mother.'

From childhood, Russians were constantly reminded of the sacrifices that had been made in the Great Patriotic War, as the

A moment of glory *for Tamara Banketik as she makes her speech and presents flowers to Stalin. Like so many others, she bore the hardships because 'we always hoped that around the corner there would be a better life. Now I realize there was nothing around the corner.'*

Second World War was called, and of the economic sacrifices they must now themselves make in order to prevent the suffering ever happening again. More than 60 per cent of the country's budget was spent on defence, so the people endured continuing hardship while the armed forces were built up. Young Russians of Tamara Banketik's generation were brought up to see the West as decadent and dangerous. 'We knew our society was just and that capitalism was terrible. That's what we were taught. It did not matter how badly I lived now. I hoped it would get better.'

Russians lived in a closed world where all information about the West was ruthlessly controlled, and often distorted. Soviet newsreels painted the United States in garish colours, as a place where lynching was common, art and entertainment debased, and where millionaires kept their dogs in great luxury while the unemployed queued for food.

MAY DAY IN MOSCOW
The military might of the Soviet Union parades through Red Square in front of large crowds. A huge standing army was maintained to ensure the defence of the nation at a time when it felt under threat from the West.

"At that time everyone had to conform. Everyone had the same hairstyle, the same clothes. I never thought I would be a jazz man, but to me it was part of being a dissident. "

ALEXEI KOZLOV

ALEXEI KOZLOV *began to play the saxophone in 1957, when he was twenty-two years old. His interest in the culture of the West was dangerous, but nevertheless he listened to the Voice of America radio station and from it learned all the American and British songs. He also took the risk of approaching visiting Americans in the street so that he could acquire otherwise unobtainable American clothes.*

The spying game

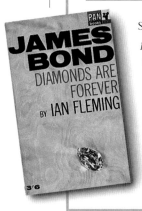

SPIES AND COUNTER-SPIES *infiltrated popular fiction during the Cold War. One of the most successful of them was the British secret agent James Bond, who pursued a glamorous career in espionage. Intrigue, adventure and suspense, as well as Bond's own flamboyant personality, made him a hero and the books an international success, selling millions of copies in a dozen languages.*

It was extremely difficult to gain access to Western ideas, though radio stations did broadcast over the Iron Curtain. Alexei Kozlov was one of the listeners. 'The radio was our only access to the West, and neighbours could denounce you for listening to those stations.' Like many others he had a special interest: it was not ideology, but jazz. 'I tried to learn English by listening. I bought myself a dictionary because I was so interested in what Nat King Cole was singing in "Walking My Baby Back Home". But you had to be so careful. If you said you loved Impressionism, or Louis Armstrong, you could be tried under the article "Idolators of the West".' In the Soviet Union jazz was banned, and the propagandists had a saying: 'Today he plays jazz, tomorrow he betrays the nation'.

Stalin did not rely on propaganda alone to maintain control over his people. All over Eastern Europe the new communist governments mounted show trials at which alleged 'traitors' were intimidated into making confessions, and their downfall then widely publicized. 'These curs planned invasions of the Soviet Union and Poland,' screamed a judge on a Soviet newsreel. 'I call for the death penalty. Crush him with an iron fist. There must be no mercy.' There was none. In Eastern Europe and in the Soviet Union itself, thousands of people were executed and millions more sent to suffer hunger and exhaustion in the forced labour camps.

Fear in the United States

Soviet propaganda against the West was matched by the hostility and fear with which the communist world was portrayed in the United States. Conventional Soviet military forces were far greater than those of the United States, and *Life* magazine devoted almost one whole issue to showing how large the gap was – 2 600 000 men in the Red Army to 640 000 GIs, thirty Soviet armoured divisions to just one American division. The military supremacy of the United States rested on its nuclear weapons. Even this was now to be challenged. On 18 September 1949 a United States aircraft flying over the North Pacific detected exceptionally high levels of radiation. 'Grim news,' a newsreel reported solemnly. 'The communist bloc also has the atom bomb. Behind the Iron

CONTAINING THE COMMUNISTS

THE PEOPLE of the Soviet Union were taught to fear and mistrust the world beyond their borders. The American diplomat George Kennan's analysis of this was reflected in the 8000-word message he sent from Moscow to the government in Washington. 'Wherever it is considered timely and promising,' he warned, 'efforts will be made to advance official limits of Soviet power....At the bottom of the Kremlin's neurotic view of world affairs is a traditional and instinctive Russian sense of insecurity.'

Kennan's view was very influential. In July 1947 he published an article in which he urged the United States to apply 'a long-term, patient but firm and vigilant containment of Soviet

expansive tendencies'. He urged that the United States should maintain their own forces wherever necessary to counterbalance the Soviet threat. Kennan, who admired and liked the Russian people though not their leaders, later insisted that his 'containment doctrine' had been taken out of context, and in particular that he had recommended political rather than military containment.

The more the United States sought to limit Soviet expansion in order to contain the threat of communism, the more the Soviet leadership felt justified in its fears of domination by the West. The more the Soviet Union built up its military strength so that it could resist the perceived threat from the United States, the more the Americans feared

Soviet power, and sought to limit it.

In April 1950 President Truman discussed with his National Security Council a proposal for a massive American military build-up if the containment of communism were to be more than a bluff. He was advised that defence expenditure would have to be more than tripled, to $50 billion a year, and was reminded that 'the Cold War is in fact a real war in which the survival of the world is at stake'. As more countries were gradually drawn into the superpower struggle, people throughout the world came to understand the nature of this new reality – that the activities of the two superpowers now shadowed the lives of everyone.

Curtain is the most sobering threat ever to menace free men.' To emphasize the real nature of this threat, the broadcast continued: 'The target area is our North American continent, but the bull's-eye of the enemy's target is you, your family, your home.'

Many Americans now succumbed to paranoia too. They believed J. Edgar Hoover, director of the FBI, when he declared: 'Communism in reality is not a political party, it is a way of life. An evil and malignant way of life. It reveals a condition akin to disease, that spreads like an epidemic and, like an epidemic, a quarantine is necessary to keep it from infecting this nation.' And Herbert Philbrick, an ex-communist who became an FBI informer, had this to say about his former friends: 'They are lying, dirty, shrewd, godless, murderous, determined...an international criminal conspiracy.' The United States became obsessed with the idea of communist infiltration, espionage and betrayal.

The official Committee on Un-American Activities had been investigating subversion by fascists and communists since before the war. Now a new figure, the senator Joseph McCarthy, entered the fray. For the next four years McCarthy occupied the

CONTAINING THE SOVIET UNION *was the key to United States foreign policy. As well as building alliances with friendly states on the borders of the Soviet Union, the United States also established a series of military bases in them.*

ON TRIAL FOR SPYING *The United States pilot Gary Powers, whose U2 spyplane was shot down by a missile over Soviet territory in 1960 while on a secret 'reconnaissance' mission at the height of the Cold War.*

spotlight, supported by other conservative congressmen and a whole cast of informers and denouncers. Many of their victims were highly placed officials, distinguished scholars, Hollywood actors and scriptwriters.

Others were caught in the whirling blades of McCarthyism. Manny Fried was a local official with the Machinists' Union in Buffalo, New York state. He was charged with being a traitor. He explains: 'Anything that was taking place, we were interfering and carrying out orders from the Soviet Union, which was nonsense, absolute nonsense. J. Edgar Hoover sent out a team of twenty-five FBI men to get me. They had decided I was a symbol of the left in the community and they must break me. They visited every single friend of my wife's, and one by one pressured them to break off their friendship with us. They wrecked my marriage. The difficulties in the union I could handle, but the difficulties they caused in my marriage were terrible, really terrible.'

Fear spread across the country. To alert citizens to the communist menace, civic leaders in the town of Mosinee, Wisconsin acted out a Soviet takeover for a day. Newspaper editor Bill Sweinler, who helped to organize the event, describes what happened. 'The Russian army came into the school, and burned school books there in a bonfire. I was arrested. They arrested all of the clergy – the community Catholic priest, the Lutheran minister and the Methodist minister; the mayor and the chief of police. They stopped a train. The people of Mosinee thought they had been invaded. Four of us actually broke into Dad's printing office and printed armbands with the hammer and sickle on them. Our school lunch that day was black bread and potato soup. The kids got an education that couldn't come out of a book. It was an education we saw first hand – that we had it pretty good as Americans!'

At the beginning of 1949 the Communist Party gained power in China. In the United States fears grew of Soviet world domination, while in the Soviet Union the news was greeted with delight. There people were assured that world revolution was inevitable. 'Now one quarter of the world is in the socialist

MANNY FRIED *was a union official persecuted for being a communist, and so for being, as this poster declares, an 'enemy of America'. He came under FBI surveillance – shown by this document authorizing the installation of a hidden microphone in the studio over the garage at his home.*

MOSINEE SEIZED BY REDS! *When the town enacted what could happen if communism took over the United States, the local newspaper joined in the exercise by reporting the events taking place that day.*

PERSECUTION IN POLITICS

'ONCE THE DOGS ARE SET ON YOU everything you have done since the dawn of time is suspect,' wrote Raymond Kaplan in a farewell note to his wife before he committed suicide. He was an engineer who had been summoned to give evidence to the Senate subcommittee investigating suspected communists. Another victim was Julius Hlavaty, a Czech-born mathematics teacher. He was being investigated because he had once broadcast over the Voice of America radio station, and the subcommittee feared communist influence there. Asked whether he had ever been a communist, he refused to give evidence, claiming his constitutional privilege against self-incrimination under the Fifth Amendment. As a result, he automatically lost his job.

The subcommittee's chairman was Senator Joe McCarthy. On 9 February 1950 he touched a nerve in the national psyche when he announced – quite untruthfully – that he had a list of 207 communists who worked in the State Department. McCarthy convinced himself that the United States was being undermined by a secret communist conspiracy. He was not alone. The Committee on Un-American Activities was already investigating the alleged influence of communists in Hollywood, in the State Department, among American experts on China and in the labour unions. Caught between the danger of prison for perjury if they denied communist connections, and the certainty of persecution if they 'took the Fifth', many innocent individuals who had joined the Communist Party in the very different political context of the 1930s now saw their lives ruined.

The background to this fear and the persecution which it encouraged was bewilderment. Only a few years before, Americans had returned from Europe after their victorious crusade for democracy. Now the world was apparently already under threat again, this time by the possibility of communist domination, and all American communists were regarded as traitors. It was on this mood that McCarthy capitalized.

After four years, McCarthy overreached himself. In 1954 he organized hearings to investigate the absurd possibility that the United States army was riddled with communist influence. On a live television broadcast he was humiliated by the challenge from Joseph Welch, an elderly Republican lawyer from Boston. 'Have you no sense of decency, sir, at long last?' Welch demanded. McCarthy was finished. He was censured by the Senate and in 1957 died of alcoholism.

RED SCARE COMES TO HOLLYWOOD *The fear of communism was played out in films such as* Red Planet Mars, *a thinly veiled story about communist invasion. When investigators became suspicious of communist infiltration in the film industry, some great Hollywood stars* (RIGHT), *led by Lauren Bacall and Humphrey Bogart, flew to Washington to protest.*

DIVIDING THE KOREAN PEOPLE

THE POLICY OF THE UNITED STATES to contain communist expansion faced its first real test in 1950 with the outbreak of war in Korea. Formerly ruled by Japan, the Korean peninsula had been divided between the Allied occupying forces at the end of the Second World War – the Soviets in the north and the Americans in the south. Attempts to unite the country failed, and the United Nations eventually recognized the newly created government of the Republic of Korea, established in the south in August 1948. A month later, the communist government of the Democratic People's Republic was set up in the north. However, each side claimed jurisdiction of the whole country, and thousands of soldiers were killed in border incidents.

On 25 June 1950, exactly a year after the withdrawal of United States troops from South Korea, the North Korean army, well equipped by the Soviet Union, invaded the south. It was as allies that the Soviet Union and the United States had divided Korea in the postwar peace settlement. Now they were political enemies, and another war was fought to keep it divided.

Fifteen countries sent forces to fight against the communist troops of the north after their attack had been condemned by the United Nations, but the United States was the principal contender. This was not just a conflict between North and South Korea, but a war between the United States and communism. When American troops penetrated deep into the north, approaching the Yalu river near the Chinese border, communist China intervened on the side of North Korea, forcing the United States troops to retreat.

The fighting continued for another two years. An armistice was finally reached in July 1953 after prolonged peace negotiations that were influenced by the United States' threat of using nuclear weapons against China.

The Korean war set a precedent for the use of intervention as a means of preventing communist expansion. In this, the United States had succeeded. Most of the 125 000 Chinese and North Korean prisoners of war did not want to return home. But after three years of fighting, cities had been destroyed and air bombing campaigns had devastated many of the industrial areas of North Korea, its transport systems and its housing. Millions of people temporarily became refugees, and more than three million people were killed, a million of them civilians. The people of Korea had paid a high price in the ideological conflict between East and West.

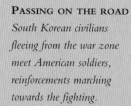

PASSING ON THE ROAD
South Korean civilians fleeing from the war zone meet American soldiers, reinforcements marching towards the fighting.

commonwealth,' declared a Soviet newsreel. 'Now one in three people lives under socialism. There are over a billion of us.'

Into this mood burst the news that forces of the communist republic of North Korea had invaded the south. Western newsreels portrayed the conflict as one between freedom and the Soviet push for world domination. 'It's a weary business,' one report put it, 'chasing Red bandits and liberating a country whose only wish is freedom from aggression. It also calls for sacrifice in lives and blood of Koreans and Americans who are grimly determined to

stop communist imperialism.' A Soviet newsreel painted a quite different picture, reporting that 'American imperialists declare war on peace-loving Korea'. Anatoly Semiriaga remembers that there was a war scare in Moscow, just as there was in Washington. 'The Americans were waiting to destroy us as an island in the turbulent seas of imperialism,' he says. 'We were told no more than that. So everything was simple. There were no doubts. They were our rivals, our enemies.'

Bids for freedom

Joseph Stalin died in 1953. Under the new leadership of Nikita Khrushchev the worst of Stalin's terror ended, though it would take several decades for his influence to fade. Khrushchev urged peaceful coexistence and competition with the West, rather than outright hostility.

Under the new policy Soviet citizens and the peoples of Eastern Europe were still not allowed to travel to the West to see for themselves the differences between the two ways of life. But foreigners could come and experience socialism. Tourism was encouraged. In 1957 the Americans were even allowed to bring an exhibition to Moscow. Thousands queued for hours to see what capitalist goods looked like. Alexei Kozlov, the jazz musician, managed to get into the exhibition. 'The Communist Party lost their hold over so many people by raising the Iron Curtain even for a month,' he says. 'It was as if we were discovering a new planet, stepping into the future. We were stunned. We couldn't believe that people lived like that.'

As the subject peoples of Eastern Europe realized that the tyrant was dead, they began to stir. A few weeks after Stalin's death, building workers in East Berlin rioted and were ruthlessly repressed. In October 1956 there was more trouble when Hungarian students in Budapest protested against Soviet rule. The authorities tried to stop them, but workers and soldiers joined in and a peaceful demonstration instead became a revolution.

Gergely Pongratz was a Hungarian farm worker who had been conscripted into the army, and now he found himself on the barricades. As the Soviet

'**THE END OF THE DEMOCRATIC ZONE**' *this damaged sign once declared. Taken from the border between the Eastern and Western sectors of Berlin, it is being carried by a worker during a protest march in 1953. The action, at first encouraged as a 'critical demonstration', was suppressed and martial law declared when real protests and strikes threatened to cripple industry.*

infantry followed the tanks through the city streets, darting from doorway to doorway, he says, 'I saw a Russian head looking out. I aimed and pulled the trigger, and saw the Russian soldier fall on the pavement. I started to cry; I had killed a human being.'

After just four days of intensive fighting the Soviet forces withdrew. For a week the Hungarians thought their uprising had freed the country. Talks were even held with the Soviet government about Hungary's independence. As Gergely Pongratz asks: 'Can you imagine how we were feeling at that time? We were in the glories, in heaven.'

Their joy was short-lived; the Soviets came back in force. Western radio broadcasts had talked of freeing those enslaved by communism, but now the West took no action on Hungary's behalf. After ten days, Gergely Pongratz recalls, 'We gave up because we saw we were not going to get any help and what we were doing was suicide'. There came one last despairing radio cry, monitored in the West: 'This is Hungary calling! The last remaining station....Early this morning the Soviet troops launched a general attack on Hungary. We are requesting immediate aid—' Then the voice was cut off. The people of Hungary felt that the free world had betrayed them. A quarter of a million Hungarians managed to escape to the West. Gergely Pongratz was among them, together with his mother and sister. Overcome with emotion, he describes their departure. 'We crossed the border, we went about fifteen or twenty metres and my mother turned around. She went a few metres back, under the flag, the Hungarian flag, and in a handkerchief she put earth. She is buried in the United States but that earth is under her head – Hungarian earth, Hungarian land.'

The Iron Curtain fell again, and the borders were more and more heavily guarded. There was only one gap – Berlin, where the German inhabitants were still able to move freely between the Eastern and Western sectors of the city. More than three million Germans voted with their feet for the West. But now this freedom was also to be denied.

BURNING PORTRAITS *of their hated prime minister, Matyas Rakosi, Hungarian freedom fighters take to the streets during the uprising in 1956. For a few exciting days it seemed that independence would be granted to Hungary; instead, Soviet forces returned and crushed the revolution.*

A HUMAN WALL *of East German soldiers on guard in Berlin on 14 August 1961. They are standing shoulder to shoulder on the western side of the Brandenburg Gate, 'protecting' the Soviet sector until the wall itself is built in this part of the city.*

A divided city

On Saturday 12 August 1961, 4000 East German refugees were registered in West Berlin, the highest number recorded. Early on the Sunday morning, 40 000 men began to seal off the Soviet sector. Two Soviet divisions were deployed in a ring round the city, ready to intervene if necessary. At first the 'wall' was a makeshift affair of barbed wire. It became an impenetrable concrete barrier snaking through the city on the line of ancient parish boundaries. On the Tuesday of that first week a photographer captured the moment that one of the East German border guards, Konrad Schumann, jumped for freedom in full uniform. Eventually hundreds more people escaped to the West, jumping from windows, swimming canals. East German guards were under orders to open fire on anyone trying to escape, and dozens of people were killed.

Anita Möller was one of those whose attempt to escape was successful. When the wall was first built she, like hundreds of thousands of other East Berliners, was in despair. 'We thought,

LEAPING TO FREEDOM
This photograph of Konrad Schumann escaping to the West became a famous symbol of the need to be free.

DIVIDED BY THE WIRE
Under the watchful eye of East German guards, a mother and daughter reach out across the new barrier. Many Berlin families suffered enforced separation from their relatives when the wall was built.

"We can't get out. It's all over." ' Her brother was already in the West, however, and he was determined to help her. He and his friends dug a 200-metre (218-yard) tunnel right under the wall. When they were ready they sent her a message to come with her husband and child to a café on the East Berlin side. 'We waited a long time in this café. It was like a spy film. There were secret signs: a newspaper, a party badge, a bag in the right hand. If things went wrong we could be shot. We all knew that.'

It was frightening in the tunnel. 'In the middle, right under the wall, someone had put a sign saying, "You are now leaving the Eastern Sector", and I thought, I'm in the West. Finally I got through and came up on the other side.' Anita Möller could not tell her parents she was leaving because she knew the secret police would interrogate them. Her mother was ill; she died without ever being given permission to visit her family.

In the West the Berlin wall was called 'the wall of shame'. In the East it was the 'anti-fascist protective rampart'. Less than twenty years after East and West had linked arms on the banks of the river Elbe in the moment of victory, they had become two armed camps, divided by two irreconcilable philosophies. The 'just and enduring' peace for which both East and West had fought, the brave new world they had both dreamed of, seemed as far away as ever.

ANITA MÖLLER (ABOVE) *escaped to the West with her family, but had to leave her mother (on the right of the photograph) behind. 'The West was portrayed as the evil capitalist enemy, but I had relatives in West Germany and I knew that wasn't the case,' she recalls. Accustomed to travelling across Berlin, she could not believe it when she heard about the wall suddenly being built across the city.*

A FAMILY IN FLIGHT (RIGHT) *The day before the bricked-up homes along the border were due to be evacuated, this family unblocked a doorway and fled to the West.*

A WATCHER ON THE WALL (RIGHT) *Protected by barbed wire and concrete, East German border guards maintained a constant, vigilant scrutiny of activities in West Berlin. For nearly thirty years the city was to symbolize the mutual hostility and contrasting ways of life under capitalist and communist systems.*

Boomtime

THE YEARS OF PROSPERITY

IN THE UNITED STATES A NEW era of prosperity had begun. When the Second World War ended Americans found that they were members of the world's richest, busiest, most confident nation. American servicemen returning home from Europe found dramatic contrasts: in the United States there was no rationing, cities and factories were undamaged, and shops were full of food and other goods.

In Europe life immediately after the war was very different. 'There was poverty and misery. There was nothing,' explains Gerardo Ciola, who lived in the mountains of southern Italy. 'The only work available was on the land. There were so many people and so little work.'

Life was equally difficult in France, where the orphaned Evelyne Langey was growing up. 'There were still soup kitchens,' she remembers. 'I'd queue up for four or five hours with my jug and come back with millet seed. You'd feed it to the birds now. I was so hungry that for the only time in my life I wanted to steal some steak from a butcher's stall. I could never pluck up the courage to do it. But when you had thoughts like that it just shows how desperate the shortages were, and continued to be long after the liberation.'

Throughout Europe there were refugees, homeless people, little work, little money, little food. By the winter of 1947 the United States government realized that the Europeans needed help. To prepare the public for this, and to draw attention to the Europeans' plight, a special train was sent across the United States collecting food parcels. The food this Friendship Train provided brought new hope to many Europeans at a time of desperate need; they had never seen such plenty. It was accompanied by the message that 'Prosperity makes you free', and allowed people a taste of the good times that Americans already enjoyed.

This was just the beginning. Many of the children of postwar Europe would grow up to a better life than anyone at the time could have imagined, and eventually caught up with their American counterparts. They too enjoyed this era of rapid economic growth and unprecedented opportunity – a boomtime.

THE AMERICAN DREAM *came true as prosperity brought a new suburban way of life to many families.*

New beginnings

At the end of the war the people of Europe were exhausted. Families were grieving for husbands and sons who had not come home. Cities had been devastated by bombing and by the fighting armies, and with factories in ruins there was little work.

In some countries there was a new mood of optimism. In Britain a Labour government had come to power, and it was promising dramatic change. It was part of Labour's vision to rebuild the bombed cities as fast and as well as possible. In a film about the reconstruction of Coventry, the planners announced that out of the ruins a great new city would arise, and they were not thinking only of its material prosperity. 'This is the people's city,' they declared. 'Coventry is going to be a place to live in where people believe that human life can be good and pleasant. In

PEDESTRIAN PRECINCTS *were an innovation in town planning that helped to make Coventry a popular modern city. It had suffered some of the worst bomb damage in Britain during the war, but with the growing postwar car industry Coventry became a boom town.*

QUEUEING FOR RATION
BOOKS *in London in 1951.
All over Europe food and
other supplies remained in
desperately short supply for
some years after the war.*

the days to come we must feel that it is not every man for himself,
but every man for the good and happiness of all people living.'

The road ahead, however, was a difficult one. As well as the
physical devastation that some of them had undergone, whole
countries had been reduced almost to bankruptcy, while their
weary people were impatient for the new society their leaders
promised. The winter of 1946–47 in Europe was the harshest in
living memory; in the icy conditions coal stocks ran dangerously
low. Rather than recovering from the war, Western Europe was
staggering from crisis to crisis. The United States government
became concerned, and sent an official to investigate. His report
was alarming. He warned that the wartime destruction to the
European economy had been greatly underestimated, and that the
political situation echoed the economic crisis.

The political situation did seem to be in a state of upheaval.
In France and Italy large communist parties enjoyed considerable
prestige because of the part they had played during the war in
resisting the Germans. Many working people believed that only
communism would bring a real improvement in their lives. Fear of
communist takeovers in Western Europe like those that had
already taken place as a result of the Soviet presence in Eastern
Europe helped to persuade the United States government that
something must be done. A huge programme of aid for the whole
of Europe was launched. Western Europe accepted the offer, but
the Soviet Union under Joseph Stalin would not tolerate the
countries of Eastern Europe becoming dependent on and grateful
to the Americans, and the aid was rejected.

The ration book

RATIONING OF SOME FOODS
*continued until as late as 1954 in
Britain. Everyone used coupons like
these to obtain their fixed allowance of
clothing and food.*

'**Free passage for the Marshall Plan**' (OPPOSITE) *is the message on this poster promoting American aid in West Germany. Marshall Aid brought hope and new opportunities to Europe as well as lifting the barriers of hunger and poverty in the aftermath of war.*

The Marshall Plan, as the aid programme was known, was both an act of generosity and one of enlightened self-interest. Its aim was simple: to make Western Europe prosperous again. The United States had learned some hard lessons in the economic depression of the 1930s, and recognized that in order to continue enjoying its wealth, it must share it. The United States was in need of overseas markets to export to – the healthier the markets, the more the United States itself would benefit. But the scheme was political and ideological as well as economic, as a prosperous Europe would be far less likely to embrace communism as an attractive alternative to capitalist democracy.

The British government took the lead in welcoming the aid, and went out of its way to allay fears about what it meant. In France the Americans were regarded with some suspicion. Wally Nielsen, an American on the staff of the Marshall Plan, thinks that 'the presence of these Americans was an embarrassment and a humiliation'. He describes their reception. 'The Americans came to France with probably quite romantic ideas that we were going to bring this economic help and we would be welcomed with open arms and that the wounds of war would be bound up. We were subjected to a number of jolts of reality. I remember that the first day I went to my office in the hotel I had to fight my way through a line of screaming pickets. They were members of the Communist Party in France. They were picketing the building because of their claim that the Marshall Plan was simply an American scheme to control Europe.'

Wally Nielsen acknowledges that the Americans' affluence might have been difficult for the French to accept, too. 'Most of us who staffed the Marshall Plan came from ordinary backgrounds, but once we got to Paris things were dramatically different. First of all the prices made everything just dirt cheap for us, so here we were having lunch in an elegant restaurant in the middle of Paris, that was pretty heady stuff. There was a luxury aspect of the thing that none of us had anticipated.' It was different for the French. Wally Nielsen remembers eating in a smart Parisian hotel soon after he arrived. 'I had a steak that was so tough I could only eat a little part of it...when I had pushed my plate away and the waiter

'GO BACK TO AMERICA!' (RIGHT) *declares this anti-American French Communist Party poster in 1950. Eastern Europe was not alone in its suspicions of Marshall Aid. Many people in Western Europe saw it as an attempt by the United States government to tighten its grip over Europe through dollar imperialism.*

DIVIDING THE AID CAKE (BELOW) *European recovery depended on cooperation, and the United States insisted on the submission of a joint plan for Marshall Aid by the countries that would benefit from it. After the First World War punitive reparations had been imposed on Germany; in the new spirit of peace after the Second World War American aid was offered to allies and enemies alike.*

Greece $694m

Austria $677m

Belgium/Luxembourg $556m

Denmark $271m

Norway $254m

Turkey $221m

Ireland $146m

Yugoslavia $109m

Sweden $107m

Portugal $50m

Trieste $32m

Iceland $29m

United Kingdom $3176m

France $2706m

Italy $1474m

West Germany $1389m

Netherlands $1079m

removed it, I noticed that he took the remains of the steak and wrapped it in a napkin and carefully put it in his pocket. The hardship of life in Paris at that time was really very severe.'

The Economic Recovery Plan (ERP) – the official name for the Marshall Plan – included both emergency aid to deal with the shortages of food and fuel, and development aid to help Western

European countries rebuild and modernize their agriculture, transport and other industries. Sixteen countries benefited, regardless of their wartime allegiance. At first shipments of food – grain and animal feedstuffs – were the most important priority; the first shipment, 9000 tonnes of American wheat, sailed from Texas in the spring of 1948.

The plan also helped European farmers to grow more food themselves. Raymond Jolivet was twelve years old when the tractor arrived on his father's farm – the first one in the district. There was great excitement. 'Lots of people stopped to see what was going on. They wanted to see what kind of work the tractor could do and to take a close look at it, because at the time we didn't see many in the countryside.' He remembers the difference it made. 'The tractor meant that production increased fivefold during busy periods like harvest time. It was easier because the tractor took some of the effort out of working in the fields. You no longer had to walk behind the horses – you always had to follow the animal when you were ploughing, you know, whereas with the tractor you were sitting down, and that made a big difference.'

Marshall Aid made possible some remarkable projects, including hydroelectric dams, land reclamation and irrigation. This was still an age of heavy industry: coal and steel, shipbuilding, and the manufacture of heavy machinery. Money was used to re-equip coal mines in Belgium, Britain, France and Germany, and to build modern steelworks in Britain, France, Germany and Italy. The Italian worker Giovanni de Stefanis recalls the excitement at the arrival of some milling machines from Cincinnati, Ohio. 'It was obvious where they came from. On the front there was a large badge divided in half: one half was the American flag, the other had the initials ERP. We knew it was part of Marshall Aid and we all worked happily. This wasn't second-hand machinery, and it was very efficient.'

In Douai, a town on the French–Belgian border, people turned out to line the streets and watch a giant steel press being delivered from Chicago. 'It was enormous,' says Jean Dubertret, an engineer who worked on it after it had been installed. 'When it was on its way from Le Havre teachers brought pupils of all ages to

A HELPING HAND FOR FARMERS *Tractors such as the one acquired by the Jolivet family had top priority in the early days of the recovery programme. As Raymond Jolivet explains, 'That was the beginning of progress in farming; farming expanded with the availability of high-performance equipment.'*

LOCAL PEOPLE GATHER (LEFT) *to learn how Italy can benefit from American aid, which also brings promise of better working conditions and higher wages. Meetings were held in towns all over Italy, featuring concerts, contests, variety shows and films in a huge propaganda effort to persuade Italians that aid was welcome and to ward off support for the communists.*

FRUITFUL TRADE (BELOW) *with distant countries brought back exotic fruit like bananas for the first time since the war. As European economies recovered, international trade links began to grow again.*

watch this monster go by. I'll never forget when it rolled into the factory. Most of the workmen stopped what they were doing to come and see this new toy. It was so different from what we'd known before that everyone was amazed.' The press was used to make the chassis for Citroën 2CVs.

Marshall Aid was immensely important to Europe. It totalled $13 billion (worth perhaps twenty times as much in the money of the 1990s) – 5 per cent of the gross national product of the United States at the time. And in addition to public money, the private American relief parcels that were donated to the Europeans amounted to a further $500 million – the equivalent of more than $3 from every man, woman and child

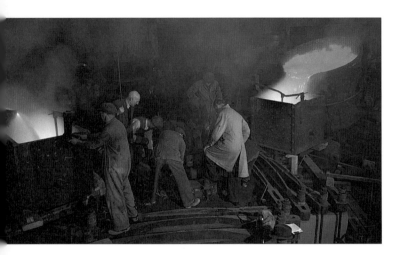

GETTING PEOPLE BACK TO WORK *in factories that had been rebuilt or had reverted to peacetime production, was an important part of the reconstruction process. American production methods helped European industries to modernize and become more efficient.*

in the United States. But Europe's postwar recovery was not solely due to American help. Their assistance made a major contribution to the work of reconstruction, while the Europeans continued to work towards prosperity for themselves.

The economic director of the British and American zones of West Germany, Ludwig Erhard, insisted on a drastic currency reform in June 1948. This produced almost immediate results. 'The black market suddenly disappeared,' he later explained. 'Shop windows were full of goods; the factory chimneys were smoking; and the streets swarmed with lorries. Everywhere the noise of new buildings going up replaced the deadly silence of the ruins.' Apathy was replaced by hope, in West Germany and elsewhere across Europe.

The reconstruction gradually led to industrial expansion, and was accompanied by social reform. Europe entered an age of political consensus; even in France and Italy, where communist parties were strong, the legitimacy of the system was accepted. Each Western European country introduced its own version of what, when it was pioneered in Britain by the Labour government between 1945 and 1951, came to be known as the 'welfare state'. Industrial productivity and social welfare, the components of the new 'social market' mixed economy, had a direct effect on the lives of tens of millions of people.

In the United States the postwar boom had already freed many Americans from the want and drudgery they had endured during the 1930s. The French engineer Jean Dubertret visited the United States to study American production methods in the early days of the Marshall Plan. He was interested in the American way of work; not just the analysis of costs and processes, which he had learned about from conferences he had attended, but the efforts to improve working conditions and to encourage good relations between the staff – attitudes that were quite different from his experiences in French factories. He was also astounded by the way Americans lived. After the austerity of life in Europe, it seemed almost like a dream. 'We were struck by the fact that everyone could have a car, a house and a garden. They had everything at the time – television, freezer, refrigerator, the lot. Our workers were astonished to find this was available to everybody.'

The American dream

The Americans were beginning to enjoy the new opportunities available to them. At the end of the war, Betty DuBrul had been living in New York with her mother as there were no houses or apartments for her and her husband Don to buy in the city. One day they drove out to look at a model house in Levittown. 'We came to the house, walked through it, and Don looked at me and I looked at him and he said, "Shall we?" "Sure, why not?" So we put a hundred-dollar deposit down and this is it, this is our house, this is what we wound up with. It was a perfect little house, and it came with a refrigerator and a stove and a washing machine. For so many young couples, with the men coming back from the war,' Betty DuBrul remembers, 'it was the answer to a dream.'

William Levitt was the Henry Ford of housing. He turned the idea of a detached house for every family from a dream into a real possibility. A house could not be moved along an assembly line, but the process of housebuilding could be broken down into twenty-seven separate operations, so twenty-seven separate teams of workers moved through the houses. Before the war, the typical builder had built five homes a year. Levitt built thousands. He could afford to sell them for $8000 each, and to add a swimming pool for every thousand homes. The men went off to work in the city, leaving the women and the children at home.

These families created a huge new market, and new ways of marketing soon followed them out to

BUYING A LIFESTYLE *not just a home* (ABOVE AND BELOW) *was only one of the benefits offered by the new suburban Levittown complexes, which had their own schools, shopping centres, churches, swimming pools, libraries and community centres. Of the 1400 homes bought on the first day the houses were for sale, some even came with a free television and vacuum cleaner. But the American dream home was not available to all: black people were excluded from them; the houses were for white American couples only.*

Pop-up toast

ELECTRICITY IN THE KITCHEN *brought many new gadgets to simplify domestic chores. The automatic toaster would make sure that 'bread becomes superb toast...not now and then – but always', as the advertisement for this gleaming Toastmaster promised.*

A REVOLUTION IN RETAILING *was introduced with new supermarkets, which appeared first in the United States and later in Europe. Shoppers took some time to get used to the confusing atmosphere of the huge shops with their wide range of foods and household goods at competitive prices, and to the new self-service method of retailing that they heralded. Supermarkets soon became a potent symbol of affluence, creating new patterns in people's lives and offering them greater choice than ever before.*

the suburbs. Discount stores such as E. J. Korvette sold the new labour-saving appliances for the new suburban way of life. One young housewife at the time, Louise Aber, explains why the stores were so popular. 'We were just starting out, and we had to fill the houses up with appliances, television sets, linens, you needed every little thing for the kitchen, you needed towels, you needed clothes for the children. Korvette was a terrific store, it was a discount house that everybody ran to. People came even to do their food

NEW REFRIGERATION METHODS (RIGHT) *enabled housewives to do all their shopping in a single weekly visit to the supermarket. Fridges and freezers quickly became a vital feature of the modern American household.*

BUY NOW – PAY LATER

THERE WAS A TIME WHEN the only people who could borrow money were those who did not really need it. The well-to-do middle classes could take out loans from the bank for major purchases, whereas those who had no money often could not buy what they needed. 'In God We Trust', declared the sign in many American saloons and shops, 'Others pay cash!'

Credit for all became an essential part of the postwar boom, assuring manufacturers of a growing number of purchasers. The American housewife Jackie Sunderland remembers what the new spending power felt like. 'It isn't that you had that much money,' she explains. 'You could charge everything. We didn't save like our parents did – we charged. You worried about paying the bills month after month, but you would spread it out. There is no question that shopping made you feel better.' Credit buying of consumer goods was first offered through hire purchase; then credit cards also encouraged many more people to buy on credit rather than waiting to save their money before spending it.

In consumer credit, as in consumer goods, the United States led the way. The housing boom of the 1950s was fed by easy financing. Car dealers advertised easy credit terms, and extended the repayment period from two years to three. Domestic appliances, televisions, consumer goods and even holidays were sold 'on the never-never'. In 1950 Diners' Club issued the first credit card in the United States. At first made of cardboard, it became plastic from 1955. American Express followed in 1958, and Carte Blanche in 1959. Under the headline 'What a Country!', *Fortune* magazine pronounced in 1956 that, 'Never has a whole people spent so much money on so many expensive things in such an easy way as Americans are doing today.'

For many people in Europe the idea of buying expensive goods in this way was alarming at first, but traditional financial caution was gradually eroded as customers lost their fear of debt. Hire purchase enabled buyers to take their new goods away as soon as the first instalment was paid, though they could be repossessed until one-third of the hire purchase price had been paid. During the 1960s credit cards were introduced in Europe, and rapidly became popular there as well. As people became more confident that their future was financially secure, they became more willing to pile up debts. Easy credit was not just a bubble on the surface of the new prosperity, but an essential part of it.

A TELEVISION *was one of the first items people were tempted to buy with the new credit offers.*

THE HIDDEN PERSUADERS

DURING THE Second World War the Coca-Cola Corporation persuaded the US military that the boys overseas needed a Coke to keep up their morale. Coca-Cola emerged from the war as a worldwide symbol of American culture. With its instantly recognizable red and white colour scheme, wavy writing and distinct bottle shape, Coke was also proof of the power of the sophisticated new advertising style that developed after the war.

Advertising created an appetite for goods and services on a new scale, and exerted a powerful image of Western life and Western values that would eventually spread throughout the world. Thirsty workers in Third World countries thought they were sharing in American prosperity when they bought a bottle of Coke; French intellectuals, wary of growing American influence, denounced 'Coca-Colonization'.

Using techniques borrowed from wartime propaganda and from social analysis, the advertising agencies clustered along New York's Madison Avenue identified new markets by targeting particular groups and creating new needs and aspirations. Advertising had once simply shown the product at its best, and given information about where it could be found and what it would cost. By the 1950s advertisements sold an image, pictured a lifestyle, created a mood, and exploited half-acknowledged desires.

Advertisements became increasingly influential, as Georgette

Braga explains. 'The commercial itself actually meant more to me than all these products they were talking about...they depicted all these lovely women – they were all so beautiful. They made you feel that if you bought this product, even though it was a floor cleaning product, you were going to turn into this wonderful creature. I think we were very gullible, and we bought into it because it was new.'

Sometimes the advertisement reassured potential buyers that they deserved to buy what they wanted. Cadillac showed 'the man who had earned the right to sit at this wheel'. The hamburger chain McDonald's slogans ended: 'You deserve a break today'. At the other extreme, admen found that the women who took four out of every five purchasing decisions about consumer goods could be influenced by guilt. To increase their own share of the lucrative washing powder market, Proctor & Gamble and Unilever vied with one another to make women feel their washing should be 'whiter than white'. Sometimes an 'expert' in white coat and horn-rimmed glasses would earnestly advise them...to choose the advertiser's product.

In the 1950s advertising was becoming a huge industry. As people became prosperous, the potential market grew. There were more and more consumers who could be persuaded that what they had never even thought they wanted was really what they needed to prove their success and bring them happiness.

Can you imagine a soda fountain without Coca-Cola—or an Amer... without the friendly invitation of this world-famous sign of g...

SIGN OF GOOD TA...

Someone's doing the **LOOK test!**

PERSIL washes whiter!
– and that means **cleaner** !

shopping because the food was discounted too.' Louise Aber can remember the evening Korvette first opened in her neighbourhood. 'We had never had anything like that before, and the first day that they opened up there were thousands of people there, the streets were packed, you couldn't get in, you couldn't get out. It was the beginning of a completely different era.'

It was indeed the beginning of a new era: one of prosperity based on cheap cars, cheap gasoline, cheap homes in the suburbs, cheap food and cheap appliances from discount stores. It was also based on the high wages that many more people could now earn, and boundless confidence in the American way of life. A cartoon called 'Meet Joe' spelled out the economic optimism on which the postwar politics of consensus were based. 'Hi folks! Joe's the king because he can buy more with his wages than any other worker on the globe. He's no smarter than workers in other countries. Sure, being an American is great, but how could you be superior to any foreigner when you or your folks might be any one of a dozen races or religions? So, if you're no superman, it must be the American way of doing things that makes you the luckiest guy in the world.'

The 1950s in the United States were a time of widely distributed affluence, of complacency and consensus, and of minimum dissent. In politics, extreme positions to both left and right were out of fashion. Big business and big labour unions worked together to increase productivity and wages. With the benign figure of General Ike Eisenhower as president, it was a period when American men worked for higher wages than they had ever dreamed of, and most American women stayed at home bringing up the big families of the 'baby boom' according to traditional values.

Caryn Pace's parents, like so many others who had lived through the Depression, gave their children what they themselves had missed. 'My mom was a housewife and mother, so she stayed

GOOD TASTE AND GOOD LOOKS *were sold alongside the products in advertisements. Women were used to help sell the goods as well as being targeted to buy them. Many women were intimidated by the new demands of advertising, and the role it imposed on them as keepers of the brightest, best and cleanest homes; they felt that their identity and independence were being undermined. As the American housewife Jackie Sunderland puts it, 'I was the extension of my husband. I was not me.'*

BARGAIN HUNTERS *examine the selection of toasters, irons, food mixers and hair dryers on display at a New York department store sale in 1951. These new domestic appliances met a growing demand for labour-saving devices in the home, and began to reflect people's increasing awareness of style, design and new materials.*

COLOURFUL NEW CARS
(OPPOSITE) *sold by General Motors offered their owners easier driving with automatic gear changing. It was important to the American economy for consumers to be able to drive easily and in comfort to the large new shopping malls.*

VEHICLE OF FREEDOM *for Bill Braga* (LEFT), *a lifelong car enthusiast. His 1958 Oldsmobile opened up new opportunities for himself and his friends: 'You could do what you wanted to do because you had your car, you could get the jobs that paid more money because you could get in the car and go to it. You could build yourself your own world.'*

GAS WARS (BELOW) *between rival stations reduced fuel prices further and further. As more people owned cars, generating new businesses, more gas stations appeared. But despite the cheap fuel, Bill Braga could not always afford to pay for it. Instead, he would sit and listen to his car radio. 'You could be ten minutes away,' as he explains, 'but you still had your own space, that car became your private space.'*

home; my father was a roofer, a blue-collar worker. I was his pride and joy, Daddy's little girl, and he couldn't do enough for me, and neither could my mother. Christmases were really great. I had five or six dolls, maybe four stuffed animals, three games, and a set of drums. One Christmas my cousins came over; they were three boys, and they were harder on things than I was, so all my new toys got broken. The next morning my parents went out and bought me all new toys for Christmas. My parents spent their money on giving me what they had never had.'

Not everyone was as content with their lot as Caryn Pace and her family. It was a time when rebellions of all kinds were beginning to simmer in American life that would boil over in the 1960s: against the authority of the middle-aged over the young, the dominance of men over women, the tyranny of whites over blacks. Like many housewives in the 1950s, Jackie Sunderland felt both happy and dissatisfied. As she recalls, 'I loved my husband, loved my children, I loved a lot about my life, but it was sort of empty. I was doing somebody else's work, and I wasn't doing what I wanted to do. I was a corporation wife. It was "shop until you drop", and this is what we did, with a few committee meetings and a few charity things on the side. We outfitted, we decorated, you know, we just bought.'

Nevertheless, many people found life in the 1950s exciting. Bill Braga was one of them. 'I worked after school in a gas station. I saw the cars come in and out, and picked the one I wanted – I looked for the shiniest, the biggest, the brightest car I could find. I bought myself a 1958 Oldsmobile. We used to ride down the highway with our flashy cars and a loud radio. The girls would turn and look, the car was bright and flashy, you had a date. The fifties were a great decade. Television was brand new. It was the first time that kids, the seventeen- and eighteen-year-olds, had their own music…it was theirs. It wasn't from your parents, it was your own.'

Bill Braga's wife, Georgette, remembers that girls did not have cars of their own, but still noticed the kind of cars the boys drove. 'I mean, who wanted to go to a drive-in movie in some guy's father's station wagon? So you did look for the guy with the flashiest car.'

GENERAL MOTORS HYDRA-MATIC DRIVE

a-Matic Drive will be offered at extra cost in the Futur-
Oldsmobile "98" and the Dynamic "60" and "70" for '48

400,000 Oldsmobile owners, who drive the Hydra-Matic way, are blazing the tra
tomorrow's motorists will follow. They go without shifting—without pushing a clutch
as Hydra-Matic Drive shifts the gears and does the footwork for them. During the pa
8 years, these 400,000 Oldsmobile owners have *proved* the day-after-day dependabili
of GM Hydra-Matic Drive. And today, as Oldsmobile leads the way into a new Gold
Era of progress and advancement, Hydra-Matic Drive is still *first* . . . *automaticall*

UTURAMIC **OLDSMOBIL**

'You've never had it so good'

In Europe ten years after the war all the investment and effort, both through American aid and the Europeans' own planning, was beginning to pay off. In West Germany the miracle was delivered by armies of businessmen starting up in improvised offices and workshops, while in France an almost equally dramatic economic boom was credited to the planners and technocrats. By the middle 1950s the battered French railway system had become the most efficient in Europe; the motor manufacturers Renault had been rebuilt, and at Sud-Aviation in Toulouse the Caravelle was being constructed, the first of a new generation of French airliners. In 1948 production in France had been at the 1936 level; by 1955 it was half as high again, and from 1955 to 1958 French productivity grew by 8 per cent a year.

In Italy the economic miracle came a little later and was even more dramatic; it was generated through both public and private enterprise. State enterprises such as AGIP in oil and IRI (a company with holdings in steel, shipbuilding, shipping, radio and television, telephones and banks, and the national airline Alitalia)

Badge of ownership

THE STRIKING SIMPLICITY *of the Volkswagen badge made it easy to recognize. Fixed to the bonnet of every Beetle, the VW logo became a familiar symbol of simple design and distinctive appeal among enthusiastic drivers of 'the People's Car'.*

A COMMUNITY OF EUROPEANS

THE DAY THAT SIX EUROPEAN NATIONS pledged themselves to build an ever closer union was a significant moment in European history. In Rome on 25 March 1957 Belgium, France, Germany, Italy, Luxembourg and the Netherlands set the seal on thirteen years of intensive efforts to create economic ties between the European states so strong that they and their peoples would never again try to destroy each other through war.

The postwar European movement had begun in the wartime Resistance against Hitler. In 1944 fifteen delegates from Resistance groups in nine countries, including German and Italian representatives, had risked great danger to meet in Geneva. There they passed a resolution declaring that 'Resistance to Nazi oppression...has forged between [the peoples of Europe] a community of aims....Federal union alone can ensure the preservation of liberty and civilization on the continent of Europe, bring about economic recovery, and enable the German people to play a peaceful role in European affairs.'

After three-quarters of a century of enmity, the French and the Germans came to recognize that it was in their mutual interests to find ways to end the era of hostility and try to build a future they could share. Their aims were supported by circumstances. For Western Europe to withstand the threat of communism, both from the Soviet Union and from the communist parties in their own countries, it was essential to repair the devastated European economies as quickly as possible; working together to achieve this was seen to be more effective than working alone. American insistence on economic cooperation among recipient countries under the terms of the Marshall Plan reinforced this view, and led to the establishment of the Organization for European Economic Cooperation. The OEEC, with its membership of eighteen European states, oversaw the fair distribution of Marshall Aid funds.

This was just the first stage in a long process leading towards European unity and eventually European union. The French continued to lead the way, establishing the European Coal and Steel Community with West Germany, and inviting other nations to join it. Those countries that chose to accept the invitation – Belgium, Italy, Luxembourg and the Netherlands – became the founder members of the European Economic Community (the Common Market) in 1957.

The founders of European union came from many nations, with different backgrounds and traditions of belief. What they had in common was their conviction that nationalism had led to devastating wars and the catastrophe of Hitler, and that the future of Europe must lie in greater unity. In later years, the European Community would grow both in the number of member countries and in its economic and political power. Some would say it also became cumbersome and bureaucratic. But it began as the dream of young idealists determined to create a new, strong Europe out of the ruins of the Second World War.

READY FOR THE ROAD
(BELOW) *Volkswagens at the West German factory, where industrial success was met by a growing demand from customers worldwide. Half of the 330 000 Volkswagens produced here in 1955 were exported.*

A GUIDE AT THE 1958 WORLD FAIR *in Brussels standing in front of the Atomium. Its molecular structure symbolized the newly linked nations of Europe.*

GETTING AWAY FROM IT ALL

For CENTURIES you could tell the rich by their white skin, evidence that they had no need to work. In the last years of the nineteenth century this began to change, as Russian aristocrats and rich English people discovered the winter sunshine on the French and Italian Rivieras. During the course of the century, sunshine was to become one of the goods that was marketed and sold to ever larger numbers of people.

When paid holidays first became law for French and British workers, they took their families to nearby seaside resorts. After the Second World War holidays in the sun were something many Western Europeans came to take for granted. In 1950 a million French citizens took camping holidays; by the early 1970s more than five million did so each year.

New travel companies were established to cater for new holidaymakers' needs. Kuoni was founded by Alfred Kuoni in Zurich in 1906, and after 1948 opened offices in Milan, Paris, Rome and Tokyo; eventually it had offices in all five continents. As early as 1951 Kuoni pioneered charter flights to Africa, and to the Mediterranean in 1959. In 1970 the first charter holiday flights to the Far East were introduced.

Another pioneer was Elif Kroager, pastor in the small Danish town of Tjaereborg. He could not afford to take his wife on holiday, so he offered to arrange a trip for a group of local people. In 1950 he took seventy people from the local school to Spain. The business quickly expanded, with package holidays by coach travelling throughout Europe. In 1959 Tjaereborg introduced air travel for its holidaymakers; in 1964 30 000 people applied for a holiday for which only 1000 places were available. By 1973 Tjaereborg had become the largest tour operator in Europe.

Club Mediterranée offered a different kind of holiday: an experience of 'simple village life' for people who lived in cities. Club Med was founded in 1951. Its camps were built on deserted stretches of the Mediterranean coast, in Morocco, Tunisia, Turkey and Yugoslavia. Visitors checked in their wallets when they arrived, and used poppet-beads to buy what they needed. They lived in grass huts near the beach, and newspapers and radios were banned. The recreation of a primitive utopia attracted more and more city dwellers, who were soon in danger of killing the very thing they sought. High-rise hotels replaced straw huts, and crowds polluted unspoilt beaches.

In May 1950 Horizon holidays pioneered the package tour in Britain. When the standard return air fare to Nice was £70, Horizon took groups to Corsica in chartered war-surplus aircraft for two weeks' camping at half that price. Escaping from the regulated atmosphere of package holidays, young people in the 1960s took the 'hippie trail' through Afghanistan to India and Australia; many young Australians and New Zealanders took the same route in reverse on their way to Europe.

Tourism spread Western money, Western fashion and ideas of personal freedom to countries as diverse as Indonesia, Thailand, Turkey and The Gambia. By 1974 tourists were spending $29 billion a year, 6 per cent of the total value of international trade. Generating income in convertible currencies, the world's fastest-growing industry had become a lifeline for the economies of many of the world's poorer countries.

A HOLIDAY IN THE SUN *was once the exclusive privilege of the rich. As tour companies organized more package holidays abroad at reasonable prices, they became increasingly popular.*

modernized rapidly. Family businesses such as Olivetti and Pirelli, and manufacturers of washing machines, motor scooters, clothes and shoes, and above all the giant Fiat car and engineering group, brought modern production techniques to the manufacture of stylish, imaginative new products. Italian industrial production grew at over 9 per cent a year between 1950 and 1958.

Throughout Western Europe the producers of all these new products were also becoming the consumers of what they helped to make. For working people this was a heady experience. The Jordan family, in the English Midlands, could speak on behalf of millions of industrial workers. George Jordan had experienced unemployment before the war. He moved from the Newcastle coalfield to work in a car factory in Coventry. 'It was unbelievable. You could go out, have seven or eight pints, go for a meal, and still have a few shillings left in your pocket. We used to go to the theatre, too. Whatever you wanted to do, you did. You wanted to go out of town, you went out of town.'

The car makers were some of the best paid workers of all. There were five big car factories in Coventry at that time. As George Jordan's son Ray points out, 'If your job didn't suit you, you could move to any one you wanted. I've known people who weren't happy, they'd move to another factory. The work was around. There was money to be had and to be spent. That's what I think money is for: earn a pound, spend a pound.' Easy credit made it possible to spend more even than you earned. And there were new ways to spend it, too – on foreign holidays, for example. 'The first time I went to Spain, when I was eighteen,' says Ray Jordan, 'I think I took £50 with me. I couldn't spend it all.'

Industrial workers in Germany, in the Netherlands and in Scandinavia were also earning incomes that would once have seemed unbelievable. It was the same in France. 'It was a bit like falling in love,' describes Monette Gaunt, who worked as a sales-woman in Paris. 'We called them the thirty glorious years after the war. It was a period of great expansion, of consumption, and there was no unemployment.'

In Italy the first symbol of liberation was not the car but the motor scooter, made by Vespa or Lambretta. Evio Barretti worked in the Vespa factory in the days when scooters were practically made by hand. In 1958 he bought his own. 'It wasn't possible for a working man to buy a car, but with a Vespa you could go to the mountains. I used to go with my wife and pick mushrooms. You could touch heaven with your fingers with your first Vespa.'

All over the north of Italy new factories were going up, and even with the new labour-saving machines they were still hungry for workers. Women as well as men were now needed as workers on the new assembly lines. Edda Furlan went to work in the Zanussi factory. The work was hard. 'They put me in the paint shop. We were spraying, and there was all the dust. We had to

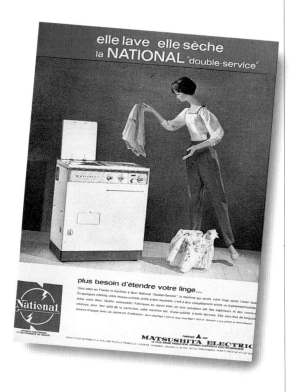

THE 'DOUBLE SERVICE' WASHING MACHINE *produced by the Japanese company National offered French housewives the extra convenience of dry as well as clean clothes. 'Washing machines, televisions with large screens, large refrigerators – all white,' lists Monette Gaunt as she remembers the consumer boom in France. 'It was a fairy tale.'*

FAMILY MOBILITY *in Italy was made possible by the addition of sidecars to the Vespa. In the United States a car cost the equivalent of a hundred days' work for an industrial labourer; in Italy it was equivalent to about a thousand days' work.*

wash from head to foot every day. You just had to put up with it, it was poisonous work, it was very hot, because once we cleaned the machines, they went into the furnaces at 600 degrees. But to have a washing machine is a huge advantage. In the winter I had to go and break the ice in the public wash-house...the washing machine is a great thing.' Edda Furlan regards herself as lucky. 'We found work, while the generations before us – you know how they were. I went into the factory and I worked my eight hours and then came home and did the housework...yes, I was happier.'

In the south there was an even bigger pool of labour eager to go to work in the new factories. Gerardo Ciola grew up in the Basilicata, where the only work was on the land. He did not want to leave. 'It was painful,' he recalls. 'We Italians are very attached to our families. But we had to go. We had to look for work elsewhere.' The first experience of factory work could be daunting. Lillo Montana migrated from Sicily to Turin to work for Fiat in 1969. 'The first day at work was traumatic,' he remembers. 'In our village there were no working rhythms or timetables. This sudden entry into the industrial world was certainly not a pleasant thing. Visually the place seemed to me like one of the circles of hell – there were sparks everywhere, noise, smoke, people running left and right who didn't speak.'

Giovanni Lano was a priest in Turin, and remembers both the sadness and the hope. 'One would see the trains arriving from the south,' he recalls, 'and unloading all these men with their baggage, and above all with their hearts full of expectations and hopes of a better life. Memories of these moments are always a bit sad...that crowd of people who would arrive with nothing and who would find themselves disoriented in a big city. It was the three Ms that made them come north: *mestiere*, a job, in order to get a *moglie*, a wife, and their last dream was a *macchina*, a car. They were not impossible dreams. People just wanted to achieve the standard of living they saw on television.'

GERARDO CIOLA *proudly driving his hard-earned new Fiat. 'I was so excited,' he recalls. 'I had worked and waited such a long time for this car.'*

Gerardo Ciola was one of those men. After a while he could afford a small flat. 'The first thing I wanted in the house was a television, and then the other household goods. Every month there was something else to buy.' Eventually he

MIGRATING WORKERS

FOREIGN WORKERS flocked into Western Europe during the boom years of the 1950s, attracted by far higher wages than they could have earned at home and the chance to learn new skills. They were prepared to do the boring, dirty or dangerous jobs that the prosperous Europeans were now reluctant to undertake themselves.

There were also 'internal' migrations within Europe. Up to nine million Italians moved from the impoverished region in the south, the Mezzogiorno, to seek their fortunes in the cities of the industrial north. Some twelve million Germans fled from communist East Germany to the West. The expanding West German economy was still not satisfied, and West Germany signed treaties with several countries allowing German companies to set up recruitment offices on their territory. Moroccans, Turks, and Croats from Yugoslavia responded by migrating in their hundreds of thousands. The millionth of these *gastarbeiter*, 'guest workers', was feted as a hero in the press and presented with a motorcycle.

Workers were also recruited in the former British and French colonies. The British National Health Service and London Transport, for example, were particularly active in the West Indies. After the Algerian war in the early 1960s some two million *pieds noirs* (Europeans from Algeria) and another two million Muslims from North Africa settled in France. Foreign workers made up about 7 per cent of the labour force in Britain, France and West Germany; the proportion in Switzerland was 30 per cent.

The newcomers' experience was often disappointing. Immigrants from the West Indies and the divided Indian subcontinent, arriving as full British citizens and expecting to enjoy the superior life they had learned was available to all in Britain, encountered instead cold weather, cold welcomes, discrimination, poor housing and sometimes racial hostility.

Elsewhere, foreign workers received limited rights and short term labour contracts. In West Germany the *gastarbeiter* were denied citizen's rights, could not vote and were often not allowed to bring their families, and in France they were not allowed to marry without permission. Everywhere higher wages were offset by the higher cost of living, so many immigrants felt they were no better off. Yet many of them did prosper. Their contribution not only made the economic expansion of the postwar period possible, it transformed Western Europe into a multiracial society.

ITALIAN WORKERS
(ABOVE) *at this Vespa factory worked night shifts producing enough vehicles to satisfy the huge demand. The extra shifts increased the number of jobs available, bringing prosperity to more workers who could then also afford to buy more products for themselves.*

was able to afford something better than a motor scooter. Fiat were making a tiny car, the 500 cc model known as Topolino, Italy's name for Mickey Mouse. Gerardo Ciola and his wife went to buy one. 'When I went to get it from Fiat...I felt so emotional my legs were shaking,' he remembers.

Giovanni Lano also bought his first car in the early 1960s. It meant a great deal to him at the time. As he points out, 'To tell an ordinary person living in Turin in the 1950s that he would have a car eight years later was like telling someone in 1500 that you would take them to the moon.' Yet for millions of people all over Europe the fantasy was coming true. Only twenty years after the war, they were part of the new Western prosperity, and for many of them the car symbolized their new wealth.

The oil crisis

Oil and petrochemicals were vital to the new Western culture. They generated power for industry and provided the basis for the plastics and synthetic textiles of the new consumer products. And they fuelled cars. In the 1920s, when Henry Ford had made the dream of a car in every garage a realistic aspiration, his T-models and A-models drank American oil. By the 1960s, however, not only Western Europe but the United States as well had become increasingly reliant on imports of oil from the Middle East – a dangerous dependence on an unstable region. Support for the Palestinians, driven from their homes after the establishment of the state of Israel in 1947, led to repeated attempts by Arab countries to recover the Palestinians' homeland. The Israelis, backed by money and weapons as well as diplomatic support from the United States and its allies in Europe, were able to defeat these attempts.

By 1970 the Palestinian Liberation Organization was openly at war with Israel and its allies; in 1973 Egypt launched another war against Israel. Again the Israelis won. In their frustration the Arab countries drew on their most formidable resource: oil. Oil supplies from the Middle East were reduced month by month; by December 1973 world production was down by about 9 per cent. An embargo was imposed on all supplies of oil to the United States, the Netherlands (a staunch friend of Israel), and later, in order to please the Arabs' allies in sub-Saharan Africa, to Portugal, Rhodesia and South Africa. As a result the official price of oil, which in 1970 was less than $2 a barrel and by 1973 had risen only to $2.90, in the summer of 1973 reached $11.65; in practice, prices went even higher than that. Western governments, together with the major oil companies, did their best to maintain supplies from other sources, with the result that, over the whole period until the embargo ended in April 1974, oil supplies fell by less than 20 per cent. Even so, fatal damage had been done to the carefree economic climate of the 1950s and 1960s.

Many people in the West had begun to assume that their new prosperity would last for ever. The oil crisis shook their confidence. It precipitated recession, growing unemployment and an unprecedented combination of inflation and stagnation, and heralded the end of the boomtime era.

RUNNING OUT OF GAS
Gas stations in the United States struggled to supply their customers, who were shocked by the sudden shortage of the fuel on which the American way of life depended.

THE OIL WEAPON
(RIGHT) *The desert kingdoms of the Middle East, realizing how dependent on Arab oil supplies their Western customers had become, began to play a powerful new part in international affairs.*

13

Freedom Now

THE STRUGGLE FOR INDEPENDENCE

IN MILLIONS OF INDIAN HOMES families gathered round their radio sets on the evening of 14 August 1947 to listen to their new prime minister, Jawaharlal Nehru, as he formally announced India's independence from British rule. Among them was Birenda Kaur's family. She can still remember the occasion vividly. 'When the speech came on, I don't know if any of us actually heard the words or not, but the atmosphere was so emotionally charged...and when he said, "At midnight, when the world sleeps, India will awake to light and freedom," we forgot about everything else, and we all sat up that night. And then when the dawn came I just cannot describe to you how heady that feeling was. It was as though the world was new...you felt you could do anything, that we were free now colonial rule was at an end.'

In the morning Birenda Kaur was among the thousands of people who went to Delhi's Red Fort to watch the ceremony. 'First the Union Jack came down,' she recalls, 'and then the tricolour of India went up; it is my happiest memory.' There were celebrations all over India. Satpal Sainai, who was a farmer, remembers how that day 'a wave of joy went through the crowd. Everyone was very happy because until then we'd been under the thumb of foreign rule, but now we were free.'

People had high hopes that there would be a brighter future. 'The man in the street thought all would be well for him – there would be schools, hospitals and all the things he ever dreamed of,' Birenda Kaur explains. Satpal Sainai hoped 'that we would become prosperous, that our children would get the jobs in government and that all business would be in our hands.'

When India gained its independence, much of the rest of the world was also still governed by remote states far away in Europe. India's success offered an inspiring example to other subject peoples in the fight for control of their own destinies. It was the start of a process that would continue for the next thirty years. Nobody at the time could have predicted the pace of change. There were in 1945 some seventy independent countries in the world; by 1975 there were a hundred more.

SEEING THE WORLD ANEW *Jubilant citizens take to the streets to celebrate the dawn of independence in India.*

The road to independence

Before the Second World War a fifth of the world's land surface had been under imperial rule. Both the plantations and the diamond mines of the Congo, in the heart of Africa, were controlled from Belgium. The populations of the East Indies, in all their ethnic and religious variety and with their oil, tin, rubber and timber, as well as islands in the Caribbean, were governed by the Netherlands. Portugal ruled Macao on the coast of China, Goa on the coast of India, and three territories in Africa – Angola, Mozambique, and the Cape Verde Islands off the west coast.

The French colonies encompassed Indochina and Syria, islands in the Caribbean and the Pacific, and vast African territories from the green equatorial jungles and the savanna grasslands to the Sahara desert and the rich cities and farmlands of the northwest. The British also ruled territories across the globe, administering the largest empire of all: it stretched from Hong Kong and Malaya to Burma and the Indian subcontinent, through much of Africa, to the West Indies and across the Pacific to Fiji. Power over the lives and welfare of all their peoples was wielded by governments in Paris and London.

Imperial rule had brought certain benefits to India: a railway network, new industries, efficient administration. What it did not do was to relieve the country's heavy burden of poverty, which was worsened by its ever-growing population. Protests against British domination were ruthlessly suppressed. Eventually one man, Mohandas Gandhi, convinced the people of India both that their economic conditions would not improve until they were themselves politically free, and that more would be gained by peaceful non-cooperation and passive resistance than by violent rebellion. Gandhi's inspired leadership offered a vision of a new future. He led Indians in a mass protest against British rule, and during the 1930s millions of people followed the strikes and boycotts he organized. He was himself among the 60 000 Indians who were imprisoned as a result of these activities. Yet the British government did finally yield to their demands first for self-rule and then for complete independence.

INDIA'S MIGHTY ELEPHANT, *deftly guided by the frail but indomitable figure of Mahatma Gandhi, defies the British lion in a German cartoon of 1933.*

WOMEN SPEAK OUT *in 1930 in Bombay. Some of them were seriously injured when the police resorted to using their lathis (long batons) to control the crowd. Gandhi inspired several such campaigns, and urged people to take non-violent action whatever their status in society.*

INDIA'S INSPIRATION

'GANDHI WAS a national institution, an inspiration, by his own example. He was almost deified by the Indian public in the years leading to independence,' says John Lall, an Indian civil servant. 'I met him, and saw him as a very saintly figure. One didn't feel fit to touch the hem of his clothes, as the saying goes. He created that kind of aura, though he was a very human person...and he had a sense of humour. His creed of non-violence is still an inspiration to freedom movements all over the world.'

Indians called Gandhi the Mahatma, the 'great spirit'. This fragile-looking man, whose public image was reflected in the home-spun cloth he wore, became a symbol of moral authority over manifest strength, and fostered a new confidence in India's village origins. Gandhi believed that the country's problems stemmed more from the shortcomings of the Indians themselves than from the power wielded by British guns. His great aims were to free India from British rule; to alleviate the oppression of the 'untouchables', some sixty million people in the lowest class of the Hindu caste system; to improve the status of women and the poor; and to turn India back from the pursuit of modernization to its traditional values and practices. He sought to inspire unity among Indians – rich and poor, high- and low-caste, men and women, Hindu and Muslim.

Early in his career, Gandhi experienced racism and intolerance for himself as a lawyer in South Africa, where he campaigned for Indian rights through the principle of *satyagraha* or 'truth force': non-violent resistance as a method of social and political struggle. For this deeply spiritual man there was no place for violence, conspiracy or guerrilla war. He emphasized the moral qualities of *swaraj*, or self-rule, for individuals as well as for nations, believing that there was a close connection between political freedom and personal discipline, which he himself tested with long fasts and periods of solitude.

Gandhi returned to India in 1915. He quickly became the dominant figure in the Indian National Congress, which he transformed from a middle-class debating society into a mass movement rooted in small towns and villages throughout India. Anti-British activities during the 1920s led to Gandhi's imprisonment. In 1930 he organized his first campaign of civil disobedience against the government's hated salt tax, with the simple act of walking to the sea to make salt from sea water. Thousands of people joined him in what became known as the salt march.

During the Second World War Gandhi supported the 'Quit India' movement, but he shunned political power for himself. He strove to heal religious intolerance, but became a victim of it: he was assassinated by a fellow Hindu in January 1948, at a prayer meeting. Nehru, after announcing his death, broadcast to a stunned and grieving nation: '...the light has gone out of our lives and there is darkness everywhere... and yet...a thousand years later that light will still be seen... for that light represented...the living, the eternal truths.'

Gandhi's vision led India to independence, but not to peace. Freedom from empire did not mean freedom from bigotry and hatred. No satisfactory solution had been found to the fear that the minority Muslim population had at the prospect of being ruled within a majority Hindu state. As independence approached, plans were made to partition the subcontinent between Muslim Pakistan, in the northwest and northeast, and non-sectarian but overwhelmingly Hindu India. Millions of people found themselves on the wrong side of the new borders as old resentments flared up

and hatred sought release in persecution. Altogether thirty million people – both Muslims and Hindus – fled from their homes, in what was perhaps the greatest forced migration in history. Some refugees travelled on foot, others went in convoys of bullock carts or crowded into and onto trains, clutching whatever belongings they could. The trains were often attacked, and thousands of migrants suffered from starvation or exposure.

The civil servant John Lall was posted to Delhi at the time of independence. He remembers that the atmosphere was at first 'absolutely delirious', but that 'the euphoria was very, very short-lived. The ugly fact was that killings were taking place in the newly created Pakistan and in India as populations moved back and forth from one country to the other. It was tragic. Whole trains would arrive from Pakistan that were empty. There was no one living left in them, no person alive in the whole train.' Hindus took revenge on Muslims, and when the Muslims fled they were treated with equal ferocity. During the weeks following Partition at least 200 000 people, perhaps as many as 500 000, were killed.

Rupa Gujeral grew up as a Hindu in Peshawar, in the heart of what is now Pakistan. It was a quiet town, with Hindus and Muslims living and working side by side. After Partition this changed. 'We could hear only murders, fires and noise. We were so scared. My family felt it would be safer to go away and come back when there was peace in the town again.' The Gujeral family's Muslim friends and employees escorted them to the station. An official who had been entrusted with some mail was a fellow passenger. Rupa Gujeral's mother was afraid of travelling with a single Muslim. 'But he said, "Don't worry, I am with you, and I have got a revolver," which as a child frightened me. When we reached Amritsar, it was his turn to be afraid. He said to my father, "Now you take care of me!"'

The tragedy of Partition was a very high price to pay for independence. But as Birenda Kaur recalls, 'I know there was the trauma of Partition: we lost a lot of property, other people lost a lot of relatives, lifelong friends became strangers overnight – but yes, it was worth it. You can't keep on being spoon-fed by some-body....Okay, we made mistakes, we will probably make bigger mistakes, but we are a country, not a colony.'

FREEDOM AND BLOODSHED *An Indian police officer receives help after violent clashes between Hindus and Muslims in the streets of Lahore in 1947. This one incident caused fifteen deaths and left 114 people injured. Partition intensified ancient Hindu–Muslim hostilities, and caused rifts between once peaceful mixed communities.*

"We could not sleep when we were in Peshawar because there was always noise. We could hear only murders, fires and noise."

RUPA GUJERAL

Freedom vote

INDIAN BALLOT PAPERS *carried symbols for each candidate, since the overwhelming majority of the population could not read or write. While all the images conveyed national progress of a kind, there was fierce competition among candidates for the most potent symbols. The Indian Congress Party was denoted by the twin bullocks, representing rural progress.*

THOUSANDS OF MUSLIM REFUGEES *seek sanctuary in the Purana Quilla Fort in New Delhi. At the same time Sikhs and Hindus make the journey south from the newly formed Pakistan. Millions of refugees from both sides fled to avoid becoming a beleaguered minority. The greatest forced migration in history was part of the price to be paid in forging the world's largest democracy.*

An example to follow

Gandhi maintained that if India could break free, others would be encouraged to follow its example. The European powers thought quite differently: they planned to hold on to their empires. But the Second World War had brought great changes in the status of the imperial nations, shifting the balance of power across the world. Japanese victories in the Far East had destroyed the prestige and apparent invincibility of the Europeans there, and the countries that emerged the strongest after the war, the United States and the Soviet Union, were both strongly anti-colonial. By 1947, as India went its own way, other Asians in Indonesia and Indochina were also fighting for their freedom. Indonesia gained its independence from the Dutch in 1949, and Vietnam from the French after defeating them at Dien Bien Phu in 1954.

The European powers were most determined to keep their African colonies. European needs often came first: much of the best land was used to grow crops for export rather than food for the local people. In the Portuguese colonies 98 per cent of Africans received no education, and instead of being self-sufficient on their own smallholdings were forced to work as labourers on the cotton plantations for low cash wages. In the Congo, Belgians used harsh discipline – including amputations – on the men who mined diamonds, copper and gold on their behalf.

About a third of the world's supply of cocoa beans was produced in the Gold Coast, in British West Africa where Anim Assiful was a cocoa farmer. 'There were a lot of British companies involved in the cocoa industry at that time,' he remembers. 'They sent their agents out to buy cocoa from the villages. We didn't have our own scales for weighing the cocoa, so we were really cheated by these agents. We had to accept the prices the British gave us. We had no say – our hands were tied.'

It was the Africans who had fought in the British army during the war who now began to loosen the bonds. Geoffrey Aduamah fought against the Italians in East Africa in 1940. On the way there he stopped in Durban in South Africa, where he met troops from all over the British empire. 'The Indians were very

A BUYER'S MARKET
(ABOVE) *Farmers on the Gold Coast deliver sacks of cocoa beans and collect their payment at a bush station. While farmers like Anim Assiful* (TOP) *resented the British price controls, they had no alternative markets for their crops.*

"Nkrumah came in his native clothes resplendent in his African attire, and he said, 'Africans should hold their heads up high'. **"**

EDDIE FRANCOIS

SONS OF AFRICA, ARISE *The father of African independence, Kwame Nkrumah (centre), is given an enthusiastic reception. He became a socialist and started to dream of a free, united Africa while studying in Pennsylvania and London. As leader of the first modern independence movement in Africa, he inspired Africans throughout the continent to take pride in their identity and demand a role in their country's future.*

political. They said they thought we were coming to help them fight the whites. We said, "We are fighting for white freedom." So they asked us, "Are you yourselves free?" We said no. "Well, fight for your own freedom first." This made a very big impression on the Gold Coast soldiers, and on me especially....I am fighting against somebody I don't know, and the person who is using me to fight is the same person who is oppressing me.'

When veterans returned home the struggle for freedom in the Gold Coast accelerated. Dismissed back to civilian life without pensions, they felt betrayed. 'We came back and saw that they were not doing anything to help us to get re-established in life.' Like many others, Geoffrey Aduamah joined an ex-servicemen's union, and took part in the early protests against the British. These were turned into a mass movement by Kwame Nkrumah, who had returned after twelve years in the United States and Britain, where he met other Africans against colonial rule. A charismatic campaigner, he urged Africans to take direct action themselves, and founded a new political organization, the Convention People's Party (CPP). He also organized a general strike and a boycott of British goods. The British regarded Nkrumah as a dangerous fire-brand, probably under communist influence, and imprisoned him. But far from quelling the campaign for self-government as they hoped, this gave it new impetus.

Geoffrey Aduamah joined the CPP as 'it was the only dynamic organization at that time. Those who brought Nkrumah from Britain, they were all lawyers, doctors and high-placed people; they didn't feel for the ordinary man like me,' he remembers. 'One of them even called us "verandah boys", and they didn't respect us at all. But Nkrumah said, "I am also a verandah boy. I will sleep on the verandah with you".... So we realized this man could do better for us. Nkrumah wanted self-government *now*. Self-government in the shortest time, we don't understand that; but we do understand "Now".'

VOTING FOR ALL *Africans vote for the first black African parliament in elections on the Gold Coast. Men and women trekked long distances to exercise their new right. The election was part of a gradual process, first of self-government under the British and eventually complete independence.*

While Nkrumah was in prison the party was successfully run by his friend Komla Gbedema. The British agreed to a general election in 1951, hoping that the CPP would lose. The result was a landslide victory for Nkrumah's party, and he was subsequently released. Komla Gbedema was there to meet him. 'Apart from my own personal feelings of joy, I didn't see very much because I was driving him, but the crowds were tremendous. A large area in front of James Fort prison was filled with people. It was a slow march, orderly singing and dancing and shouting, all the way to the arena where we held our meetings.'

The feeling in the party was that 'we prefer self-government in danger to servitude in tranquillity. We had to do things the way we wanted without showing that we didn't know what we were doing. By and large I think we did well enough, because in three years the Colonial Office of the British government said, "If you give evidence of your ability to manage the economy and control your finances, we will hand over power to you".'

A THIRD WORLD VOICE

TWENTY-NINE COUNTRIES were represented at the international conference held in Bandung, on the Indonesian island of Java, in April 1955. What was extraordinary about this event was that there were no Western European, American or Soviet representatives – the world's most powerful states were excluded. For the first time in modern history, recently independent states proved that they were now a force to be reckoned with. No longer could they be treated as pawns in an international game played by the great powers.

The conference host was the president of Indonesia, Achmed Sukarno, who told the delegates that their nations had 'arisen from a sleep of centuries', and promised that their

peoples 'would be able to mobilize the moral violence of nations in favour of peace'. The leaders of many Asian countries and several of the newly emerging African states had gathered to discuss issues of interest to them all such as racialism, colonialism and national sovereignty; the economic and social problems they faced; how they could contribute to world peace; and how to make the voice of their people – the majority of the world's population – heard in a world increasingly divided into the capitalist Western and communist Soviet camps.

The conference was held at a time when world peace was threatened by the hostility of the Cold War, and American and Soviet spheres of influence extended across much of the

globe. The gathering at Bandung was partly an expression of protest against the powerful states' failure to consider the points of view of the Afro-Asian nations in affairs that affected their part of the world. They were particularly concerned with the tension between the new communist regime in China and the United States. One of the achievements of the conference was that fear of Chinese communism among its neighbours, particularly Burma and India, was reduced.

The Bandung Conference both demonstrated and reinforced the new self-confidence of the emerging nations, and showed that when they stood together, they were now able to play a part on the world stage that could no longer be ignored.

Independence or assimilation?

The changes taking place in the Gold Coast were watched closely both by the rest of Africa and by the other European powers, who had no intention of following the British example of granting concessions. The colonial policy of France had in some ways been different from that of Britain. While the French and the British attempted to create an educated African elite, British efforts also focused on giving a minimum of education to a wider group. French policy after 1945 aimed at incorporating the empire into a 'greater France', and instead of independence the French offered 'integration': Algeria was legally part of France itself. In Senegal those born in the four principal towns were also granted French citizenship, which included the right to elect representatives to the parliament in Paris. Those who were intended to be leaders of French-speaking Africa were educated at the William Ponti Lycée in the capital, Dakar.

The special and privileged status of 'assimilation' did not necessarily satisfy those who qualified for it. One of them was Majhemout Diop. 'Being an *assimilé*: it meant everything and nothing,' he reflects. 'Everything, because your whole social status depended on it, and nothing because for all that, you never really felt like a Frenchman. The fact that I was born in St Louis, one of the special communes in Senegal, was what made me a citizen – I didn't choose to be one. The French wanted to transpose their culture: they introduced the French language and provided a good education for some people. But it was natural that as human beings we should want our independence and our freedom. We felt sure there was something unjust about our colonization which we had to overcome.'

Amadou Baro Diene, one of a group of radicals in Senegal, thought the leaders were too compliant. 'They were for independence, but more slowly and in a united Africa, whereas we were young and hot-headed, and we wanted independence at any cost and whatever the consequences.'

"From the cultural point of view, we were raised up to a higher level of development. But there were other sides to it, the sides of domination, of a foreign power in a foreign land. "

MAJHEMOUT DIOP

SHOULDERING THE BURDEN *The united efforts of French and African troops in the First World War are commemorated in a memorial erected in St Louis, Senegal, the first French settlement in West Africa. Thousands of Africans fought side by side with their colonial rulers, but their shared experience did little to encourage a lasting sense of unity.*

Fighting for the land

Some African colonies had attracted almost no settlers; the only Europeans were government officials and businessmen. In others where the climate was more favourable, there were plenty of new opportunities for settlers such as the tobacco farmers of southern Rhodesia, the train drivers and mining supervisors in the copper belt of northern Rhodesia, and those who lived in the highlands north of Nairobi in Kenya. Here in East Africa self-government seemed an even more remote prospect in the early 1950s.

A young Englishman, Peter Marian, had joined the British colonial service in 1939 after leaving university. 'I wanted to be an administrator,' he explains. 'There was a sense of dedication that you wanted to do something with your life, and there was also a sense of adventure. Colonialism was far from being a dirty word at that time, and you just felt that you might be doing some good for a country and for other people.' After the war he returned to Kenya and bought a farm, where he grew coffee and raised cattle.

A COLONIAL FAMILY (ABOVE) *in Kenya take afternoon tea with their pet leopard. Many settlers in Africa led a life they never could have expected, or afforded, to lead if they had stayed in Europe.*

Peter Marian loved the land he farmed. So did the Africans who had lived and worked on the land – 1.6 million hectares (4 million acres) of it – taken by the European settlers, who used them as servants and labourers, and denied them even limited political rights. There were 30 000 white settlers in Kenya; they were determined that they should be recognized as paramount, both then and, in the future, in a new East African Federation. But 75 000 Kenyan Africans had fought for Britain in the Second World War, and while British ex-soldiers like Peter Marian were encouraged to take up farming, the returning African soldiers were confronted by the restrictions of the colour bar, pass laws, unemployment, poor housing, and taxes that could be paid only by working on the plantations. Once again it was young men back from the war who were determined things should change.

The heart of Kenyan resistance lay with the Kikuyu people, with their traditional attachment to the land. One of them, Jomo Kenyatta, took up their cause, first in London and then, after his return in 1946, as leader of what became a popular nationalist movement in Kenya itself. Achhroo Kapila, a Kenyan lawyer who trained in Britain and knew Kenyatta personally, remembers that 'He had a tremendous following...he made an instant impression

A SEA OF SUPPORT (OPPOSITE) *for Jomo Kenyatta, who took up the cause of the Kikuyu people, and then of all Kenya's Africans.*

as a leader.' Achhroo Kapila also remembers the restrictions the colour bar imposed. 'We were not allowed to stay in a hotel or even go to a restaurant to eat a meal.' When the settlers pressurized the British to put down African demands for independence, the Africans' response was to form a secret organization calling itself a 'land and freedom army' – better known as Mau Mau. It attracted many thousands of supporters.

Assembly at gunpoint (OPPOSITE) *Mau Mau suspects wait to be taken to detention camps. British troops and civilian volunteer police raided Kikuyu villages and forest hide-outs for suspected supporters of the 'land and freedom army'. Women and children were taken to reception camps to await the result of the investigations, which could take as long as a month.*

Waihwa Theuri decided he would join the Mau Mau. 'It was because of hardships. The major problem was the fact that our land had been taken by white people. Before, we used to graze our goats in the settlers' farms and in the forest, but we were then informed that each family would be allowed to graze only fifteen goats. Then there was the question of education. The schools we used to go to started to be closed, and this is when people felt they had had enough of the persecution. We came together and took an oath that an African was your brother, but when you see a white man you should know that he is your enemy.'

The British used the police and army to round up suspects from Kikuyu villages. Like many others, Waihwa Theuri went into hiding in the forests. 'We were pursued, and we had no food, we had nothing. We could not go back to the emergency villages because we would be shot. To survive everybody had to work for himself...and there was nowhere else to run to. That's when we started to fight, attacking settler farms and stealing their cattle. We prayed to God for help because we didn't have the arms that the settlers had...we only had guns later, stealing them from the settlers.' The British dropped 50 000 tonnes of bombs to destroy the forest hide outs. Waihwa Theuri was arrested, interrogated and tortured for being a member of the Mau Mau.

A loaded rifle *accompanies the bedtime ritual for a white family in Nairobi* (BELOW). *Night-time raids by Mau Mau were an ever-present and alarming danger for settlers in Kenya, especially those living in isolated farmhouses.*

As the Mau Mau movement grew, fear became part of life for the settlers. Sylvia Richardson, who lived on a remote farm, remembers how she and her husband used to keep their guns with them all the time, and how their neighbours survived an attack. 'There was a bang on their door one night and this gang came rushing in. Kitty and Dot shot at these people and killed two of them....They shot a number of bullets, and one killed their dog.'

Jomo Kenyatta was among the many Africans opposed to the violence, but he was arrested and imprisoned for encouraging the rebellion. Altogether more than 11 000 Mau Mau rebels were killed and 80 000 suspects detained. Some 2000 loyalist Africans were killed by the Mau Mau. The terror they generated for white settlers, however, was not reflected in the death toll: just thirty-two whites were killed between 1952 and 1956.

The rebellion had a contradictory effect on Kenya's history. The violence alienated many Africans, including the Kikuyu, but by bringing in British soldiers to crush the Mau Mau the British

BRINKMANSHIP OVER SUEZ

WHEN PRESIDENT GAMAL NASSER announced the nationalization of the Suez Canal in July 1956, the Egyptian people greeted the news with delight. In both the Middle East and Africa his bold challenge to the Western powers was admired, while in the West there was anger and dismay.

The canal was one of the world's busiest shipping lanes. In providing a waterway across Egypt to link the Mediterranean and the Red Sea, it had shortened the distance between Mediterranean ports and Asia by as much as half. Intended both to serve and to profit from growing international trade, the canal had been opened in 1869 to all ships of all nations. At that time shares in the Suez Canal Company were held by Egypt and France; by 1875 the Egyptian shares had been sold to Britain.

Nasser's immediate reason for nationalizing the canal was to obtain for Egypt the revenue from tolls paid by ships using it. This would provide the huge sum of money needed to finance an ambitious national project to build a dam on the river Nile near the ancient town of Aswan. The dam would control the annual floodwaters, improve irrigation to boost agriculture, and provide hydroelectric power to support Egypt's industrialization.

The dam was originally to have been financed by the United States and Britain. But there were political strings attached to the promise of a loan, and as a result of improved relations between Egypt and the Soviet Union at the height of the Cold War, the West's offer was withdrawn. Nationalization of the canal would enable Egypt to go ahead on its own.

Britain and France were concerned that the canal would be closed altogether, cutting off Western Europe from access to vital oil supplies in the Middle East; they also feared Nasser's considerable following in the Arab world. To reinforce their own position, they secretly invited Israel (which had its own reasons to fear Nasser) to invade Egypt. Israel took action when its ships were prohibited from using the canal; a joint British and French invasion to 'protect' the canal against damage followed. However, the combination of Soviet threats, United Nations condemnation and United States disapproval forced the invaders to withdraw. Nasser had turned the tables on the European powers. Instead of being humiliated by them, he had inflicted humiliation on them.

Egypt's triumph for a time brought Nasser enormous prestige throughout the Middle East and in Africa. Nasser's bold initiative proved that new countries could outwit old masters on the international stage. It also showed that while the Soviet Union and the United States were world powers to be reckoned with, the European states were no longer to be feared. This realization boosted the determination of Africans fighting for an end to colonial rule.

THE SMOKING EMBERS *of Port Said, the Egyptian town badly damaged within a few hours by an Anglo-French bombing raid in November 1956.*

government had discovered how costly it could be to control the colonies, and its attitude was changing fast. Politicians of both parties became increasingly unsure that Britain could afford to maintain colonial rule, or that doing so could be justified.

There were European-born communities in French as well as British colonies. The largest community of white settlers — Italian and Spanish in origin as well as French — lived in Algeria, an overseas *département* administered as an integral part of France. In 1954 they too came under attack. Muslim Arab rebels took up the struggle against foreign control when a 1947 statute that would have allowed them a greater part in the political and social life of their country was not put into effect. Supported by the French army, the settlers resisted, and a terrible eight-year war followed. The military were given responsibility to deal with those who were involved in the rebellion, but extended their authority over the whole Muslim population. Their aggressive tactics against the villages and against their inhabitants increased support for the National Liberation Front (FLN).

As harassment and humiliation were stepped up, the rebels also became more violent, using guerrilla tactics that the army could not defeat. More than a million people died in the struggle, and millions more — both Arabs and Europeans — were driven into exile or suffered in the many other ways of civil war. It brought down the French government, and brought General de Gaulle to power. He was to preside over the dismantling of French colonialism, both in Algeria and in equatorial and West Africa.

SHOTGUN WAR *In Algeria women as well as men were recruited to fight for independence from France* (ABOVE). *This bitter colonial struggle, France's most costly conflict, lasted eight years and was a demonstration that the plan for 'integration' was unworkable. Soldiers of the French Foreign Legion often meted out harsh treatment to FLN rebels* (BELOW) *and supporters.*

The wind of change

The changes that were being so keenly resisted elsewhere were being put into practice in West Africa. The Gold Coast gained its full independence as Ghana in 1957, and Nkrumah was elected president. Komla Gbedema was there. 'We mounted a platform and we were all ready when the light went on at five minutes to twelve. Everybody was happy, cheering, there was total hysteria.' Nkrumah, moved to tears, declared: 'At long last the struggle has ended. At last Ghana, your beloved country, is free forever. From now on there is a new African in the world.'

Beatrice Quatey, who sold vegetables in the Accra market and was one of the traders who helped to maintain the Ghanaian economy, was thrilled that independence had been achieved. 'We were very happy...to elect a leader of our choice. When we heard that Nkrumah had won there was general merrymaking. We went on procession through the streets of Accra singing and dancing.'

WHIRLWIND CHANGES
The rush for independence in the 1960s in Africa was as rapid as the European scramble for territory had been in the 1880s, when frontiers were drawn up in Brussels, London and Paris. The colonial era left an indelible mark both on Africa's map and on its people. But as freedom arrived, expertise left and old tensions resurfaced; civil war and military takeovers followed in equally rapid succession.

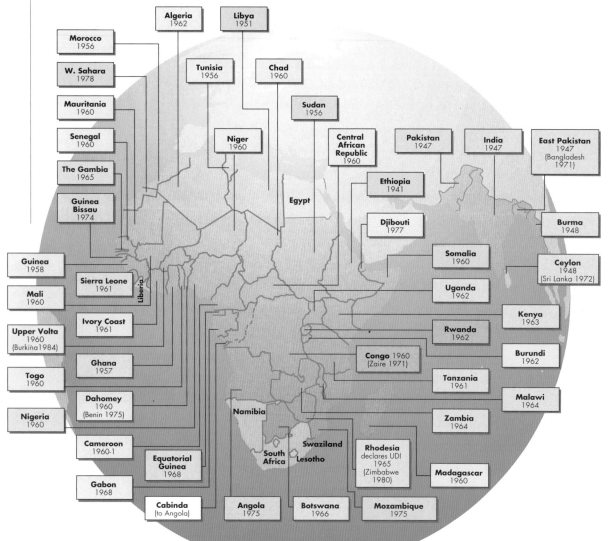

Algeria 1962
Libya 1951
Morocco 1956
W. Sahara 1978
Tunisia 1956
Chad 1960
Mauritania 1960
Sudan 1956
Senegal 1960
Niger 1960
Central African Republic 1960
Pakistan 1947
India 1947
East Pakistan 1947 (Bangladesh 1971)
The Gambia 1965
Ethiopia 1941
Guinea Bissau 1974
Egypt
Djibouti 1977
Burma 1948
Guinea 1958
Somalia 1960
Ceylon 1948 (Sri Lanka 1972)
Sierra Leone 1961
Liberia
Uganda 1962
Mali 1960
Kenya 1963
Ivory Coast 1961
Rwanda 1962
Upper Volta 1960 (Burkina 1984)
Burundi 1962
Congo 1960 (Zaire 1971)
Ghana 1957
Tanzania 1961
Togo 1960
Malawi 1964
Dahomey 1960 (Benin 1975)
Namibia
Zambia 1964
Nigeria 1960
Cameroon 1960-1
Swaziland
Lesotho
South Africa
Rhodesia declares UDI 1965 (Zimbabwe 1980)
Equatorial Guinea 1968
Madagascar 1960
Gabon 1968
Cabinda (to Angola)
Angola 1975
Botswana 1966
Mozambique 1975

Colonial territories and their dates of independence

- Belgian
- British
- French
- Italian
- Portuguese
- Spanish

TROUBLES IN INDONESIA

T HE EXPERIENCE OF INDIANS AND AFRICANS struggling for independence was matched in other parts of the world. In Indonesia, which had been ruled by the Netherlands since the seventeenth century, independence also failed to free the country from its reliance on foreign powers, and presented new problems.

During their occupation of the Dutch East Indies in the Second World War, the Japanese had hastened the process of decolonization by undermining Dutch prestige there and by releasing Indonesian nationalists from prison. Among them was Achmed Sukarno, who in 1946 became president of a new, self-proclaimed independent state. The Dutch fought back until 1949, when they agreed to a negotiated withdrawal and Indonesia became truly independent.

Indonesia is a vast archipelago consisting of over 13 000 islands, and its people belong to many different ethnic, religious and language groups. The conflicts that emerged between them were heightened by a crisis-ridden economy. Despite the wealth in the country's valuable rubber plantations, tin mines and oil reserves, there was chronic inflation and poverty. After independence, millions of Indonesians joined political parties and organizations hoping to effect change.

The huge support for the communists disturbed the powerful military elite, which believed that the foreign investment needed to rebuild the economy would be denied to a communist country. By 1965 Sukarno was discredited, and the army took control under General Suharto. In an attempt to wipe out all communist activity, he instigated a programme of mass murder, terror and imprisonment. More than 500 000 people were killed, and thousands more were imprisoned. Indonesia's links with China and the Soviet Union were broken in favour of Japan and the United States.

Indonesia had behaved aggressively towards its neighbours under Sukarno, and now the violence spread. Irian Jaya, formerly also part of the Dutch empire, was annexed in 1969. In 1975, a week after East Timor had gained its independence after five hundred years of Portuguese rule, Indonesia invaded and unleashed a reign of terror upon the people of the island: more than 100 000 men, women and children were brutally massacred, and a further 300 000 imprisoned.

PUBLIC RELATIONS *A smiling President Sukarno poses with troops' families in 1958 after suppressing an uprising in Sumatra. His rule was marked by corruption and conflict, and he eventually alienated even his former allies, the army.*

'RAISE YOUR HATS for the national anthem!' Komla Gbedema (ABOVE, second from left AND LEFT), at Nkrumah's side from the start, became Ghana's first minister of finance. He shares the pride and the glory as the newly elected president takes the podium on independence night. Fireworks and dancing followed in the old polo ground, where the song of the night was 'Freedom Highlife'.

CALL FOR FREEDOM *Followers of nationalist parties wait with banners and flags for de Gaulle in Dakar, Senegal, during his 1958 tour of French equatorial Africa. Some demonstrators ran along behind the president's car, waving their placards and shouting 'Independence now! Independence now!'*

S t a m p   o f   s t a t e h o o d

SYMBOLS OF NEW IDENTITY *were an important element in the changed status of nations at independence. In Ghana a commemorative stamp was issued to celebrate Independence Day, 6 March 1957. On that day, in a ceremony that was to be repeated all over the continent, the colonial flag was lowered and the new national flag – red, gold and green – hoisted in its place.*

This was just the beginning. Most European governments had recognized that independence could not be stopped, and had realized that they must compromise. In 1958 President de Gaulle toured France's African territories. His driver in Senegal's capital, Dakar, was Babacar Ndiaye. 'We drove in a convertible with de Gaulle standing up all the way, taking the airport road via the Corniche, which was crowded with people shouting "Vive de Gaulle!" But by the time we got to the Medina things had changed. People threw leaflets into the president's car, clamouring for independence. De Gaulle wasn't very pleased.'

Amadou Baro Diene, inspired by the activities of leaders fighting for independence elsewhere in Africa, was in charge of the placards for the demonstration. On the day of de Gaulle's visit, he remembers that 'Things were very tense. But we'd taken the precaution of hiding our placards. The moment de Gaulle arrived, we came forward.' De Gaulle's impassioned speech pleading for unity in the city square had little effect, and independence soon followed. By 1960 all twelve African members of the French Community had become independent republics.

In February 1960 Britain's prime minister Harold Macmillan also toured Africa. He told the South African parliament that 'the wind of change is blowing through this continent, and whether we like it or not this growth of national consciousness is a political fact.' Only eight months later Nigeria, the most populous state in Africa, was independent. In August 1961 Jomo Kenyatta was freed; within two years he had won a sweeping victory in a general election and was well on his way to power as president of an independent Kenya. Within less than three years, a total of twenty-five countries celebrated their independence.

The jubilation as new countries emerged was moderated by an awareness of the difficulties still to be faced. There were few administrators trained to run the new nations, and unity was hard to achieve with borders drawn up to suit Europeans rather than the distribution of different peoples and languages. For some countries the colonial legacy proved to be a bitter one.

Each of the main European powers had dealt with colonial power in Africa in a different way. The Belgians and Portuguese were the most reluctant to yield it, and bitterly resisted to the end;

the Portuguese held out in Angola and Mozambique until 1975.

The Belgians had kept the Congo as isolated as possible from the wind of change. While its mineral wealth, particularly in the province of Katanga, was vigorously exploited, most of the country was left virtually untouched by Belgian rule, and it was ill prepared to rule itself. In this huge territory of fourteen million people there were in 1959 only 137 Africans with a secondary school education, and just sixteen university graduates – only three among 1400 civil servants. Faced with violence, the Belgians got out as quickly as they could. With independence in 1960 came chaos, mutiny in the army, civil war, massacres and the secession of Katanga. Order was restored by a United Nations peacekeeping force, with the United States convinced that the troubles were the result of a Russian plot. Patrice Lumumba, the Congo's first prime minister, was dismissed, then arrested and murdered by the army. In 1965, the year after the United Nations left, Joseph Désiré Mobutu, with United States support, seized the presidency. His highly nationalist policies included the requirement that citizens take African names, and his one-party state was renamed Zaire.

WAR-WEARY REFUGEES (ABOVE) *in the Belgian Congo leave for home in the villages of Kasai province after staying in a refugee camp. The civil war following independence led to displacement, disruption and losses for many people.*

BATTLE FOR POWER (BELOW) *Soldiers of Colonel Mobutu's forces with Patrice Lumumba, former president of the Congo, shortly after his arrest. He was made to eat his words when the paper claiming his right to rule was forced down his throat.*

DIVIDED PEOPLES

THE STRUGGLE BETWEEN PEOPLES in countries seeking independence did not take place simply between the rulers and the ruled. Some of the societies over which Europeans imposed imperial domination had already been deeply divided before the Europeans arrived. In the Indian subcontinent, for example, a Muslim Mughal empire had ruled over a population still overwhelmingly Hindu. At independence India's Muslims insisted on creating their own state, Pakistan, because they did not trust the Hindu majority. Many Sikhs and Parsees in India, who had been persecuted before colonization, supported British rule, and other religious and ethnic minorities turned to the Europeans for protection.

During the colonial period the ruling powers had sometimes sent people from one part of their empire to work in another. Thousands of Indian labourers were sent to work on sugar plantations in the Pacific islands of Fiji, where they made their homes and brought up their families. By the time Fiji gained its independence in 1970 Indians made up nearly half the population, and there was considerable rivalry between the Indians and the indigenous Fijian people. In Guyana, on the northern coast of South America, colonial policy resulted in two different groups of foreigners, descendants both of African slaves and of Asian Indian labourers, dominating the nation's population; the original Amerindian people mostly lived in remote villages.

The colonial powers also relied on troops recruited from minorities or from abroad to help them govern: Sikhs from the Punjab and Gurkhas from Nepal were deployed in British India; Sikh police worked in Hong Kong and Shanghai; Indian troops were used in the British Middle East and black African troops in French North Africa. In Algeria a substantial proportion of the Muslim population joined the French army; after independence many thousands of them were killed for having done so.

The 'divide and rule' policies of the colonial powers were reflected during the independence process. In the newly independent nations many minority peoples continued to be exposed to the hostility of a more powerful majority – a bitter legacy of conflict and mistrust.

THE HUMAN TOLL *of civil war reached epidemic proportions in Nigeria in the conflict between the Hausa and the Ibo people of the Eastern Region, who attempted to secede as Biafra. Between 1967 and 1970 three million starving children were reduced to this pitiful condition.*

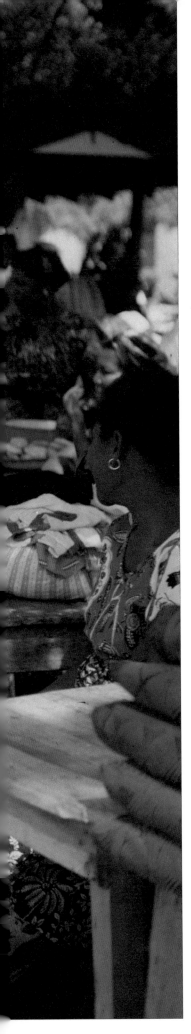

New hopes, new fears

Despite the difficulties they faced, many African countries began their life as independent states with high hopes. The Ghanaian cocoa farmer Anim Assiful remembers what Nkrumah helped them to achieve. 'We had very high expectations, and these were met immediately after independence. For example, he helped us in our cocoa industry, he gave us free education. Look at some of the facilities like dams, roads, hospitals, education. We realized that Nkrumah was living up to his promises.'

The changes that took place were particularly important for people in rural areas. Eddie Francois was assistant chief engineer in the public works department responsible for roadbuilding, and he too remembers how much Nkrumah was admired. 'He tried to unify all the various sections of Ghana. And he made sure that the women were a part of the political structure...in the early stages everything was just going right...he said Africans should hold their heads up high....I think his failing was economics.'

Like most of the new African governments, Ghana believed a socialist system and central planning could best improve life for its people. Nkrumah called his version 'scientific socialism'. But too much was attempted, too soon. A giant dam on the river Volta was planned that would produce enough electricity to supply the entire country. Huge silos were built to house the cocoa crop, but were not used. Eddie Francois became critical of the grandiose roadbuilding schemes that went far beyond the country's needs, but he was advised to keep his views to himself. There was also suspicion of corruption. 'The usual thing that was bandied around was that 10 per cent of every project went to the party. We supported independence movements everywhere in Africa – not just verbal support but

A VILLAGE WORKSHOP
(OPPOSITE) *At independence Ghana had a thriving economy in which women played an important part. Their prosperity was threatened by more grandiose enterprise schemes.*

NO MORE IDEOLOGY
Young people from the Institute of Journalism lead a protest against President Nkrumah, former hero of independent Ghana, whose 'scientific socialism' gave way to autocracy, self-idolatry and repression. Ghana underwent several attempted coups in less than a decade, and the president was finally overthrown by his own army in 1966.

financial support...until we actually went broke.' Beatrice Quatey explains how disillusionment set in. 'We started getting fed up with Nkrumah when he passed a law to declare a one-party state, and he introduced some socialist ideas. For example, he decided no one was going to get paid. Everyone was going to work for the state, and he organized points where you could get food to eat.... You were spied upon and bugged. Anything you said against Nkrumah, they would come and arrest you, and just send you to prison, and if you are there you die, you die.'

Nine years after the triumphant celebration of independence in Ghana, Nkrumah was overthrown in a military coup, which led to further changes. As Anim Assiful recalls : 'The soldiers neglected us completely. All they did was look after themselves. We were afraid to confront them or complain because they had the guns. You could be arrested or shot, so we just had to keep quiet and watch as they were amassing wealth and we were getting poorer and poorer.' Despite this, he is convinced that independence was worth while. 'When the British were here they did nothing....In anything you are beginning to do you are bound to have problems, and despite the problems it was very good because the local people also had opportunities to take things into their own hands.'

Many of the new African states experienced difficulties in the years after independence. Ghana's setbacks were repeated across the continent. Coup followed coup as armies claimed that only they could bring stability to countries in chaos. Most of the new dictators were cruel and corrupt, and for many Africans one kind of repression was followed by another. After all the suffering and the struggle to gain freedom from colonial rule, there were further freedoms they needed to gain: freedom from hunger, from poverty and from oppression. Peace and prosperity often seemed a distant prospect. Yet, as the Indian farmer Satpal Sainai points out, 'The price had to be paid. Who wants to be a slave? Everyone wants to be free in his own house.'

RULE BY THE BOOK
Holding aloft a copy of the Koran, Idi Amin is sworn in as military head of state in Uganda in 1971 after leading a coup. Eight years of notoriously brutal dictatorship followed. Amin was deposed by forces from the neighbouring state of Tanzania, which invaded Uganda in 1979 in retaliation for the Ugandan invasion the year before.

STATUES OF LIBERTY
(RIGHT) *Jakarta's extravagantly costly monument to freedom, a man breaking free of his chains, presents a stark contrast to the continuing poverty endured by many Indonesians. Despite this, many people here and elsewhere believed that independence was worth almost any price.*

14

Fallout

THE DAWN
OF THE
NUCLEAR AGE

THE LAST PEOPLE WHO COULD have prevented the test were the scientists who were monitoring it. But nothing went wrong; as they studied their instruments, at 5.30 in the morning on 16 July 1945 in the desert of New Mexico the world's first atomic bomb was tested. The secret experiment had been codenamed Trinity, and was the culmination of several years' research and development by nuclear physicists.

Berlyn Brixner was the army cameraman assigned to record the explosion. Inside a specially constructed lead and steel shelter, he listened as the countdown began. 'At zero,' he recalls, 'I was temporarily blinded by an intense light. Then I saw a ball of fire rising. It turned from white to a kind of yellow or an orange and then it changed to red before it finally went out amid a smoke cloud....I followed the smoke cloud on up. It was surrounded by a luminous blue haze, blue light due to the high radioactivity.'

The flash from the explosion was bright enough to be reflected back from the moon. No one experiencing the immense heat, the blast, the huge fireball mounting high into the sky could doubt that the test was a spectacular success. 'I was dumbfounded,' remembers Berlyn Brixner. 'I just sat there thinking about the fact that we had made the bomb and that soon World War Two would be at an end....I was extremely excited and elated....We would now use the bomb on Japan and they would have to surrender.'

Some of those who witnessed the test in the desert that morning had mixed feelings. Never before had humans possessed such devastating power. The mushroom cloud came to symbolize a new and dangerous age; the nuclear bomb was for years to cast a long shadow of fear and uncertainty over people's lives. The science that had brought about this momentous event was so complex, and developed in such great secrecy, that most people had no alternative but to trust what they were told by the experts, who predicted an end to the war and raised their hopes by promising that nuclear energy would bring great benefits in peacetime.

EXPLODING INTO A NEW ERA *Nuclear science unleashed vast new sources of energy to be exploited in war and peace.*

"It was like a sea of fire. The ordinary people of Hiroshima who were trapped under collapsed houses were being burnt alive. I could hear the scorching sound of burning flesh. People were calling their children's names. They were screaming for help....But the blaze was so intense that we could not do anything for them and had to abandon them."

AKIRA ISHIDA

DELIVERING DEATH AND DESTRUCTION *In an attempt to shock the Japanese leadership into realizing that further resistance was pointless, pilot Colonel Paul W. Tibbets (ABOVE, centre) and his crew were ordered to fly a specially adapted B-29 aircraft, the Enola Gay, to Hiroshima to drop an atomic bomb. With an explosive force greater than 20 000 tonnes of TNT, it destroyed two-thirds of the city instantly. The Museum of Science and Industry (TOP), gutted by the blast, remains a symbol of that destruction.*

A terrible new weapon

The nuclear age began with an arms race conducted in deepest secrecy. The possibility of building an atomic bomb was known to a few by the time the Second World War began; as it continued, the Allies became determined to produce one before Germany. An atomic weapon would be a major step towards victory.

Research in Germany was originally hampered by the departure of many nuclear physicists during the anti-Jewish purges in the 1930s. Some German scientists had misgivings about supplying the Nazi government with such a terrible weapon, and deliberately slowed the pace of development; this did not diminish the threat perceived by the Allies. The Manhattan Project was set up in the United States as a joint project with Britain specifically to produce an atomic bomb. The American physicist Robert Oppenheimer was appointed to lead it in September 1941, and huge resources – money and manpower – were poured into the project as laboratories were built and equipped. James Hill worked at Oak Ridge, Tennessee, one of the biggest research laboratories – it employed 78 000 people. 'A large proportion of us did not know exactly what we were doing,' he remembers, 'but there was this sense that what we were doing was important to the war effort, and if we succeeded it would make a change.'

They did succeed. Some scientists who worked on the Manhattan Project voiced concern about use of the atomic bomb. They suggested that a demonstration of its power in the desert would be enough to make Japan surrender, but the United States president, Harry Truman, and the British prime minister, Winston Churchill, believed that only a real strike on Japan could bring a swift end to the war. Harold Agnew was a young physicist working on the project. 'The war had been won, but it wasn't over and probably wouldn't have been over for quite a while,' he remembers. 'The emperor decided that they would fight to the last Japanese and they had been known to sacrifice themselves, the kamikaze pilots and all the rest.' Each day that the war continued, thousands more lives were lost.

Two atomic bombs were shipped to the Pacific island of Tinian and prepared for use by a team of American technicians. Harold Agnew, who was among them, recalls, 'When the bomb was being loaded we had some felt marker pens and almost every-body involved wrote their names on it with some nasty remarks for the Japanese emperor, Hirohito....There was this intense hatred of the enemy.'

At 8.15 a.m. on 6 August 1945 an aircraft called *Enola Gay* dropped the first atomic bomb on the port of Hiroshima. Some 9500 metres (31 000 feet) below, Akira Ishida and his brother were in a tram on their way to work in the centre of Hiroshima. The streets were full of people. 'I saw a bright flash,' he remembers. 'It was like lightning, a thunderbolt. It was so intense I was blinded for a second. I passed out immediately. When I came round my brother and I realized that we were buried under the bodies of all the passengers on the tram who died when the bomb went off. We were suffocating.' When the two brothers managed to crawl out of the tram they were met by a scene of terrible devastation. 'All the houses had collapsed...only a handful of tall chimneys and buildings remained standing....I could see that the entire city had been flattened. I couldn't see any of those people who had been walking in the street. I looked around me and saw slight traces of what looked like round heads, bodies and limbs, all completely burnt, and covered by dust and debris.'

In an instant, an estimated 78 000 people had been killed, and thousands more were horribly injured. 'Sitting on stone steps covered by blackened debris was a woman,' recalls Akira Ishida. 'Her entire body was burnt and her hair was completely charred. She was embracing a red burnt baby in her arms and she was trying to breastfeed it with her red burnt nipples, calling the baby's name again and again.'

Three days later Sumiteru Taniguchi was delivering mail in Nagasaki on his bicycle. He heard the sound of an aircraft and tried to look over his shoulder, but 'Suddenly I saw something like a rainbow, and the next moment I was thrown on to the ground.' A second atomic bomb had been dropped. At the moment of impact 40 000 people were killed. Everyone within a radius of 4 km (2.5 miles) suffered

The day that time stood still

PETRIFIED BY THE BOMB *This watch was found among the rubble and debris at Hiroshima. With its hands arrested by the explosion and still pointing to the moment of impact, it is an enduring reminder of one of the most cataclysmic events in the whole of human history.*

STUNNED SURVIVORS *of the Hiroshima blast. By the end of 1945 some 140 000 of them had died of their injuries or of radiation sickness. Among those who survived the blast in Nagasaki, 70 000 were to die within the next four months. The atomic bombs had devastated two major cities, and more than half the people living in them were either killed outright or doomed to a horrible death.*

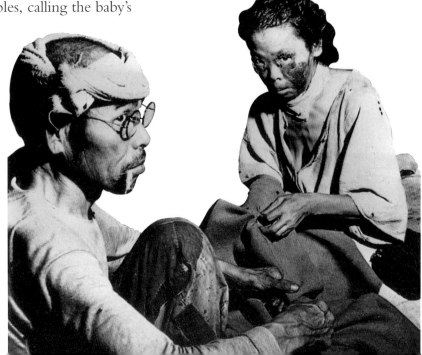

SPLITTING THE ATOM

THE DEVELOPMENT OF NUCLEAR power represents perhaps the greatest ever revolution in physics. For thousands of years the atom had been regarded as the smallest unit of matter in the universe; the Greek word *atomos* means indivisible. Yet atoms are in fact not solid matter but minute storehouses of energy.

It was the new understanding of the atom's structure in the early twentieth century that led scientists to explore its potential as a source of huge amounts of energy. Every atom contains a nucleus at its centre, composed of subatomic particles called protons and neutrons. Orbiting around the nucleus are particles known as electrons. All protons carry a positive electrical charge, and would therefore repel each other, but they are bound together by a type of energy known as the strong nuclear force. If the particles of the nucleus are rearranged, some of the energy that binds them is released.

This principle lies behind the development of nuclear power. The energy can be released in two ways: by fission and by fusion. Atoms vary in size and in how stable they are in nature; uranium, used for nuclear fission, is one of the largest, heaviest and least stable of all. It takes the addition of just one extra neutron, colliding with the nucleus of one atom, to start a process in which the nucleus divides and in doing so releases further neutrons that collide with further nuclei, this chain reaction takes place so fast that within seconds huge amounts of energy are released.

At the other end of the scale is hydrogen, one of the lightest and simplest atoms; at high enough temperatures – about one million degrees centigrade – hydrogen nuclei can be forced to combine, or fuse.

The new theories about atoms had been proved by scientists before the outbreak of the Second World War, and were well known. It took the terrible needs of war to apply the principles of nuclear physics to develop the technology of the atomic bomb, and later to harness the awesome power of the nuclear reaction to provide energy in peacetime.

NUCLEAR FISSION (LEFT) *releases enormous amounts of energy compared to other processes. One kilogram of uranium can yield more than 10 500 times the energy of an equivalent amount of gas; oil, coal and wood release even less.*

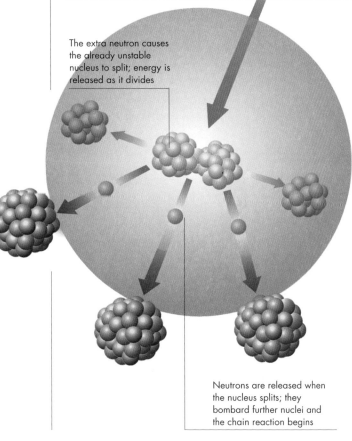

Neutron bombards nucleus of uranium atom

The extra neutron causes the already unstable nucleus to split; energy is released as it divides

Neutrons are released when the nucleus splits; they bombard further nuclei and the chain reaction begins

terrible burns from the intense heat and light. All the skin was burnt off Sumiteru Taniguchi's back and his left arm. 'I lay on my stomach unable to move for a year and nine months, waiting for the wounds to heal. I suffered throughout.'

The people of Hiroshima and Nagasaki had little under-standing of the new weapon that had been unleashed against them. Akira Ishida fell unconscious for weeks and later lost his eyesight. Over the following months and years the survivors suffered the debilitating, painful effects of radiation sickness from exposure to fallout, the radioactive debris from the bomb.

Five days after the Nagasaki bomb fell, the Japanese surren-dered unconditionally; the war was over. The news was greeted with intense relief and euphoria by many in the Allied forces. Sheldon Johnson was a young GI serving in the Pacific. 'I thought it was a beautiful, great thing....It saved my life. I was going to be involved in the invasion of Japan and I knew there was not a lot of chance of my living through that. I was elated. The atomic bomb saved my life and probably a million other soldiers' lives too.'

The race to arms

The bombs that brought the Second World War to an end made the United States the most powerful country in the world. They also brought the fear of another even more terrible war. In the Soviet Union Joseph Stalin, alarmed by the United States' formidable new power, accelerated the programme to acquire a Soviet atomic bomb. Ten secret cities, known as atomgrads, were rapidly built, and thousands of Soviet scientists, engineers and technicians were sent with their families to work in the new laboratories.

After having fought in the Red Army, Arkadi Brish went to work in an atomgrad situated in the industrial region around the Ural Mountains in the western Soviet Union. 'There was an irresistible desire to make a powerful weapon of our own and catch up with the Americans,' he remembers. 'Starting in 1947, my colleagues and I worked night and day to develop the new science and technology.' It was an exciting opportunity for scientists. Lev Altshuller, who worked in Arzamas 16, another huge atomgrad, recalls, 'The atmosphere was exceptionally fruitful…neither before nor after did I find such perfect conditions for scientific work as there.'

The Soviet scientists worked under intense pressure: as well as a demanding schedule, they were under constant surveillance by the secret police. As Arkadi Brish recalls, 'We were told not to discuss work matters at home. If I shared information with anyone I could be severely punished.' Lev Altshuller agrees. 'The regime of secrecy was very strict.…One of our colleagues was banned from work, transferred to the library first, then dismissed. We don't know why. When two men in civilian dress came to arrest him, he withdrew to a back room and shot himself.'

American scientists believed it would take the Soviet Union at least until 1954 to develop the atomic bomb. They were wrong: the Russians were fast approaching their goal by 1949, when the first test explosions took place. Arkadi Brish remembers waiting at the test site. 'We felt great responsibility because a lot of money had been spent and a lot of people were involved. We all realized that any breakdown would have tragic consequences for all of us and for our work.' The test was successful and the Soviet scientists,

WORKING FEVERISHLY *in the Cheliabinsk atomgrad, Aleksei Kondratiev* (BELOW) *was a laboratory assistant to Igor Kurchatov, the leading scientist responsible for the development of atomic bombs in the Soviet Union soon after the war.*

FIRED BY FEAR *the Soviet Union poured huge resources into the development and manufacture of ballistic missiles* (BELOW). *'We believed that the very fact of possessing nuclear arms was necessary to save Moscow from the fate of Hiroshima and Nagasaki,' remembers Lev Altshuller.*

THOMAS SAFFER *was one of 250 000 American servicemen exposed to fallout to test its effects. 'The ostensible purpose of our being there was to learn about a nuclear war,' he remembers. 'But I am afraid the enemy was our own government, who put us there without our knowledge or consent as to what the consequences would be and could be.' Years later, when thousands of the men began to suffer from radiation-linked diseases, the United States government still denied responsibility.*

including Arkadi Brish, triumphant. 'We were swept by a wave of such joy, of such pleasure, such self-confidence,' he remembers.

Now the arms race began in earnest. Both the United States and the Soviet Union, and later Britain, France and other countries, tested larger atomic bombs. The next goal was to develop the first hydrogen bomb (H-bomb), a weapon many times more powerful even than the atomic bomb. In the United States the project caused controversy among scientists, some of whom thought it should not be built. Edward Teller, who became head of the American H-bomb project, had no doubts about the moral issue. 'I believe that he who discovers has no right to make the decision how to use it. That belongs to the people.' But in the Soviet Union one leading nuclear physicist, Andrei Sakharov, publicly expressed his hope that the bombs would never be used; he was told by a senior Soviet politician, 'Your business is to produce. How to use what you produce we can decide ourselves.'

While the scientists concentrated on developing more powerful atomic weapons, the military practised the tactics that they believed would be needed in future nuclear wars. Despite the dangers of radioactive fallout – still not fully understood – they planned to use ground troops on the battlefield after a nuclear strike. Experiments were conducted on the troops to find out more about the psychological and physical effects of fallout. In the United States the army and marine corps competed to see how near they could get their forces to an atomic blast.

Thomas Saffer was a young lieutenant in the marines. Early one morning he and his fellow officers were taken by truck to a test site in the Nevada desert. 'Half an hour before the test was conducted a voice from an unseen loudspeaker said, "Good morning gentlemen, welcome to the land of the giant mushrooms. You are going to be closer to a nuclear weapon, or an atomic bomb, than anyone since Hiroshima." That left a very eerie feeling,' he recalls. Some 60 000 men took part in the exercise, all of them wearing standard uniforms without any special protection. Civilian scientists warned that they were too close, but the tests continued regardless.

Thomas Saffer remembers exactly what happened next. 'We were told to kneel, put our forearms over our eyes and close our

CLOUDED VISION
Oblivious to the danger, troops leave their trenches to admire the stunning spectacle of an atomic explosion from what they mistakenly believed was a safe distance.

WAITING FOR THE BLAST (BELOW) *troops line the trenches just a few kilometres from the point of explosion. After the blast their level of radioactive contamination was measured with a Geiger counter; dusting them off with a broom was expected to get rid of the radiation.*

eyes tightly. Then the countdown started: five, four, three, two, one....You heard a sharp click and felt this intense heat on the back of your exposed neck. The most shocking part was that you could see the bones in your forearm in a bright red light....Within a few seconds the shock waves from the bomb hit the trenches and I was immediately thrown from one side of the trench to the other....I was frightened beyond belief.'

Optimism and ignorance

While people were told little about the military experiments with nuclear weapons, their governments stressed the peaceful potential of the new energy. It was expected to transform medicine and transport, and provide limitless amounts of cheap electricity that would transform industry and bring new prosperity. Canada and France had been involved in the early stages of the Manhattan Project; immediately after the war they both decided to focus on civil nuclear research rather than on atomic weapons. The first Canadian nuclear reactor, at Chalk River in southeastern Ontario, went into operation in 1947. The first French nuclear reactor, near Paris, followed a year later, and by 1952 France had drawn up a complete programme for nuclear power. Britain, which also had ambitious plans for nuclear energy, began to supply electricity to people's homes in 1956. The Soviet Union constructed its first full-scale nuclear power station in Siberia in 1958.

In 1953 President Dwight D. Eisenhower made his 'Atoms for Peace' speech to the United Nations General Assembly. He proposed and later established the International Atomic Energy Agency, which would monitor and control the peaceful spread of nuclear technology. Two years later, when representatives from seventy-three countries attended a conference to discuss how atomic power could be used to enhance people's lives, Eisenhower pledged that the United States would 'find the way by which the miraculous inventiveness of man shall not be dedicated to his death but consecrated to his life'.

The conference was widely reported; within days people all over the world were reading about the benefits to be gained from atomic energy: atomic power would be a cheap, clean substitute for fossil fuels – coal, gas and oil – in the production of electricity; it would also enable countries that lacked other natural fuel resources to accelerate their development.

'DESERTS WILL BLOOM *through atomic power'* claimed the advertisement (OPPOSITE) *promising a new era of prosperity and plenty. Many people believed that atomic power would enrich even the most remote and desolate regions of the world.*

IN THE VANGUARD *of atomic technology in 1965, British workers* (BELOW) *pose before the nuclear reactor at Windscale. Despite potentially devastating accidents, governments continued to assure people that 'Nuclear generating plants are as harmless as chocolate factories'.*

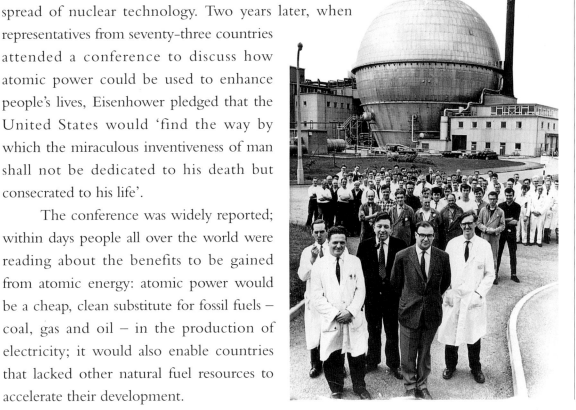

SHELDON JOHNSON
(ABOVE *with his family, and*
RIGHT *with his Down's syndrome
son) and his wife raised their children in St
George, building up a farm to give the boys work experience
and for the family to enjoy an outdoor life. Like thousands of
others, he was at first oblivious to the radioactive contamination
from the nearby test sites. 'We were exposed to the milk you
drink and the vegetables you eat and the radiation from the
outside atmosphere. We had ample opportunities to receive a
full dosage all the time.'*

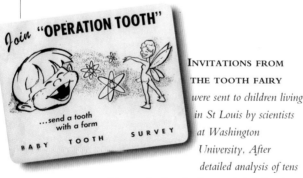

**INVITATIONS FROM
THE TOOTH FAIRY**
*were sent to children living
in St Louis by scientists
at Washington
University. After
detailed analysis of tens
of thousands of teeth, they concluded that the
radioactive substance strontium-90 had entered the food chain,
penetrating milk supplies and contaminating children's bodies.
The results were ridiculed by the AEC.*

Sheldon Johnson had come home after the war to the small town of St George, Utah. 'I was very thrilled to be part of this great effort to develop atomic energy for mankind's benefit. Atomic energy was going to give us cheap energy for electricity, for building dams and reservoirs and for building roads through mountains...we felt it was just a blessing in our lives.' The widespread optimism about the atomic age was based on ignorance about its implications. Governments did not tell people that the new power stations were also producing plutonium for bombs; nor did they make public the growing awareness of the devastating effects of high doses of radiation.

St George was some 250 km (150 miles) away from the Nevada test site. Although details of the tests were kept secret the inhabitants of the town, and its growing number of tourists, could see the flashes on the horizon. In 1953 they became concerned when the Atomic Energy Commission (AEC) issued a warning that because of a change in wind direction, a fallout cloud from a test bomb, Dirty Harry, would pass over St George. Reassurances were given that there was no danger, though people were advised to stay indoors. Sheldon Johnson heard the broadcast on the radio at his office. 'Most of the people in St George at that time totally trusted the AEC. They totally trusted the people in charge....Why would radiation hurt us? We were not knowledgeable about it at all.' Soon the truth about the dangers of radiation began to dawn on people. For Sheldon Johnson, 'The first time it really hit me was when, in 1954, we had a Down's syndrome son born to us....We found lots of others in the same situation....It came to me that for a small town we had an enormous number of children with mental retardation and various genetic defects who were born around 1954.'

The spiralling development of nuclear weapons meant a corresponding increase in testing, and concern grew about their impact. Barry Commoner was working in the United States at Washington University in St Louis, where his research alerted him to the effects of radiation both on people and on the environment. 'During the 1950s there were almost weekly explosions of nuclear weapons and they caused a great deal of fallout,' he recalls. 'Fallout circled the northern hemisphere, and when there was a heavy

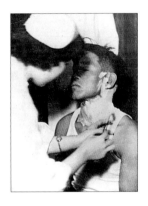

rainstorm it would come down and get into the food chain. It would come down on the grass, cows would eat the grass and it would get into the milk....In St Louis we made a serious effort to get powdered milk from Australia to give to the children.' The United States government still denied the danger, but Barry Commoner and some of his university colleagues felt, 'Here was an obligation that we in the scientific community had to the public to straighten out the complete confusion and lies that were emanating from the government nuclear programme.'

An incident in 1954 highlighted the danger, and forced the issue out into the open. A Japanese trawler, the *Lucky Dragon*, strayed close to the danger zone while the United States was testing its largest H-bomb on Bikini atoll in the Pacific. Matashichi Oishi was one of the twenty-three crew members who witnessed the explosion. 'My face came out in rashes and small blisters. Then after a week I started to lose my hair.' All the crew suffered the effects of radiation sickness – nausea, dizziness, diarrhoea and long-term liver problems – and one of them died. The accident provoked outrage and mass protests in Japan, where the truth was beginning to emerge about the numbers of people killed in Hiroshima and Nagasaki and the terrible suffering of the surviving victims. In 1955 a group in Japan set up the Council Against Atomic and Hydrogen Bombs, and demonstrators called on Western powers to stop their tests in the Pacific.

ILLUMINATED BY THE BLAST (ABOVE RIGHT) *A group of spectators at Cactus Spring, Nevada, photographed at night watching an atomic bomb test, 40 km (25 miles) from the point of explosion. Seconds ago it had been pitch dark, but the flash from the blast lit up the surrounding area as if it were midday. When daybreak came the atomic cloud could be seen drifting across the sky* (ABOVE LEFT).

BURNT BY THE RAIN *of radioactive ash from the American H-bomb, the crew of the* Lucky Dragon *receive basic medical treatment; no one could avert the long-term physical effects of exposure. Japan was later paid two million dollars in compensation by the United States government.*

THE SHADOW OF THE BOMB

'IN THE OLD DAYS, pre-nuclear weapons, the politicians could start a war, send out young people to kill each other, and nothing happened to them. It was a "no loss situation" as far as their own lives or families or properties were concerned,' Harold Agnew remembers. 'But with a nuclear weapon everybody was at risk.' He was just one among millions of people living in the United States, the Soviet Union and Europe after the Second World War whose lives were overshadowed by the terrible fear of a nuclear war.

In the United States a nationwide 'Alert America' campaign sought to reassure people that simple civil defence procedures would protect them in the event of nuclear war. Booklets and films offered suggestions on how to survive an atomic attack, and trailers and portable exhibits were used by the Federal Civil Defence Administration to familiarize people with images of the catastrophic effects of the atomic bomb, in the hope that this would forestall panic. Millions of comic books were distributed to schoolchildren, teaching them through a cartoon turtle called

Bert to 'duck and cover' in the event of an atomic strike. Metal identification tags were even issued in some schools. Towns were equipped with air-raid sirens, and evacuation procedures were also planned.

From 1953, as part of the civil defence programme, a series of test explosions took place in the Nevada desert, watched on television by millions of alarmed people who saw for themselves the atomic destruction of the model 'Doom Town' and its mannequins. But the development of the more powerful H-bomb rendered most measures totally inadequate, and during the 1960s the civil defence focus shifted to the construction of fallout shelters. Many families bought ready-made shelters and equipped them with bedding, basic food supplies and water. The assumption was that people could survive there until radiation had fallen to a safe level.

In the Soviet Union, where civil defence measures were introduced in 1955, people in factories, offices and schools received state training; articles, films and posters were widely distributed and drills were regularly held. An elaborate system of fallout shelters was constructed throughout the Soviet Union, and in Moscow many of the subways were equipped to shelter thousands of people.

The world's largest nuclear shelter was built in Stockholm in Sweden. Capable of sheltering up to 200 000 people, it could withstand any attack apart from a direct hit by an H-bomb. It was part of a highly sophisticated network of civil defence measures that would guarantee the safety of 20 per cent of Sweden's population.

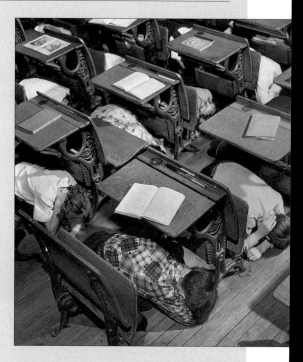

In Britain a shelter programme had been introduced in 1948, and civil defence volunteers were trained to deal with the aftermath. John Hunter was among them. 'We all thought we were going to save the world, initially,' he recalls. 'But after some time, as the years went on, seeing the increase in the power of the bombs, I think we realized that there'd be nobody surviving.' Increasing awareness of what conditions would really be like after a nuclear attack had only heightened people's fears rather than reducing them.

PREPARING FOR ARMAGEDDON *Schoolchildren were drilled in basic 'duck and cover' exercises* (ABOVE) *in case a nuclear attack took place, and many families invested in fallout shelters and survival suits* (LEFT). *Mail-order businesses advertised complete survival kits, which included protective suits, masks with respirators and filters, rubber gloves and boots, decontamination powder and handbooks.*

Protests and proliferation

Millions of people in the United States, in divided Europe and in the Soviet Union now lived in fear of nuclear war, and a new type of popular protest began to emerge, showing the depth of public concern about nuclear weapons as the arms race accelerated with the Cold War. Leaders of the superpower states acknowledged that each had the ability to destroy the other and could, in turn, expect to be destroyed. This strategy came to be called MAD – an apt acronym for Mutually Assured Destruction.

Britain's first H-bomb test was also carried out in the Pacific in 1957. With over a hundred American military bases, Britain was expected to be one of the first targets in a nuclear war. It was calculated that a third of its population, some eighteen million people, could be killed in the first few minutes of an all-out attack. At Easter 1957 thousands of demonstrators marched from London to a government nuclear weapons installation at Aldermaston. Some politicians called the marchers naive and subversive; in their own film, the campaigners stated, 'When politicians fail, people must give the lead. Not people of one class, or age, or country, for this is everybody's cause. These were ordinary people, not frivolous or eccentric, but ordinary people with a point of view.' Sally Doganis was one of the marchers. 'We were in at the beginning of history. It was a very simple idea: just no nuclear bombs,' she remembers. 'I suppose it was the people's march. It didn't have anything to do with party divisions, and didn't feel radical.'

MISSILE POWER *Moscow citizens watch a Soviet intercontinental ballistic missile being driven past in the annual May Day parade. Some onlookers were bewildered by the show of force. 'I can't explain, and I don't understand why so many bombs were made,' remembers Arkadi Brish. 'There was no need for so many – either for us, or for the Americans.'*

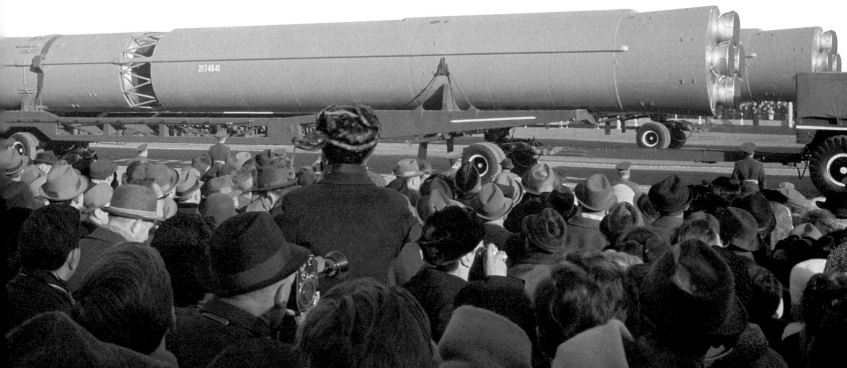

Symbol of hope

THE CND SYMBOL *was inextricably
linked with people's fight for nuclear
disarmament. With a design based on
the semaphore signals for 'N' and 'D',
the badges were originally made of
porcelain, thought to be one of the few
materials able to withstand the heat of
an atomic explosion.*

MARCHING IN PROTEST
*Fourteen thousand CND
supporters from many parts
of Britain join the
Aldermaston march.*

Winifred Howard also took part in the Aldermaston march; she too felt it was a turning point. 'It made many people aware for the first time that there was a problem, that it was a major problem, and that ordinary people had a right to stand up and be counted.'

The Campaign for Nuclear Disarmament (CND), whose organizers led the Aldermaston march, was founded in 1958 in Britain. Its symbol was soon adopted by protesters in Australia, Germany, Scandinavia and the United States, and eventually throughout Western Europe. A protest group also emerged in the United States: the National Committee for a Sane Nuclear Policy (SANE) held national marches and organized demonstrations. Despite all the public protest, governments pressed on with the race to acquire nuclear weapons and the power and status that went with them.

In 1963 the three countries that had first made nuclear bombs agreed not to test them in the atmosphere. In 1968 more than fifty countries signed a non-proliferation treaty intended to prevent the spread of nuclear weapons. It was not very effective. France had an atomic bomb by 1960 and an H-bomb by 1968; China had both types of bomb by 1967; India conducted an underground bomb test in 1974. Israel, Pakistan and South Africa were all believed to have secret weapons programmes, and many other countries were capable of using their nuclear technology to produce weapons.

Accidental fears

Although some governments had responded to their peoples' concern about nuclear weapons, competition to build the largest nuclear power stations was still growing. Increasingly aware of the financial and environmental cost of coal-powered electricity, governments persuaded taxpayers that investment in the nuclear future was essential. At enormous cost, by 1980 some 260 nuclear power plants were in service in twenty-four countries.

In the Soviet Union thirteen power stations were built in eight years. Many were situated close to major towns such as Kiev, Leningrad and Smolensk. Soviet citizens were reassured by government films: 'The station is absolutely safe for personnel and for nearby residents…no dust, no smog, no soot.' Supporters of nuclear power were just as confident elsewhere. 'Formed in the deepest recesses, eons ago,' argued the American Nuclear Society, 'our oil is being consumed at a heart-sickening rate. The nation needs more nuclear power plants. Reactors have proved to be safe, reliable and economical.'

This confidence was not justified; a succession of accidents brought renewed public concern. In 1957 a reactor at Windscale, Britain's first nuclear weapons production plant, caught fire and melted some of the fuel cladding, which contained toxic material. Surrounding farmland was contaminated by radioactivity, and the fallout spread to Belgium, Denmark, France and the Netherlands. The sale and consumption of milk in the surrounding area was banned for twenty-five days, and two million litres (half a million gallons) of it were dumped in local rivers. The following year there was an explosion at a nuclear waste site in the Urals. In 1976 Windscale was again the scene of danger after a leak of radioactive water from the plant.

In 1979 at the Three Mile Island nuclear power station in Pennsylvania radioactive steam escaped, bursting through pipes that contained radioactive water. Without coolant, half the reactor core melted. The radioactive materials were contained and the damage to the environment was minimal, but public awareness of potential dangers was increased further. Each new nuclear project in the West faced public opposition, while the scientists continued to maintain that people's fears were unfounded.

CONTAINING THE CONTAMINATION
(ABOVE) *Radioactive waste at a French reprocessing plant at Hague is packed ready for disposal. The transportation and dumping of lethal radioactive substances aroused acute public concern.*

DANGER SIGNS (RIGHT)
Increasing awareness of the dangers of radioactivity led to the adoption of an international symbol that alerted people to the proximity of nuclear installations or the transport of radioactive materials.

A DANGEROUS LEGACY

THE DANGERS OF RADIOACTIVITY are insidious. 'It is not like an electric current or a hot kitchen stove. You can't see or feel it. You can only see the consequences, which emerge some time later, and these can be tragic or even catastrophic,' describes the nuclear physicist Veniamin Prianichnikov. As more and more nuclear programmes for both civil and military use were established in Europe, the Soviet Union and the United States during the 1950s and 1960s, governments were increasingly faced with the difficult problem of how safely to store or dispose of the highly dangerous radioactive waste produced by atomic processes.

Some countries carelessly dumped nuclear wastes into the land and sea, believing that like other industrial wastes, they would in time disperse or dilute. Some of the waste, such as the gloves, overalls and laboratory equipment used in industry, was low level, and would decay in time, becoming less hazardous. But the radioactivity in some high-level wastes, such as the cancer-causing, man-made plutonium used in bombs, could take hundreds of thousands of years to diminish.

As the full extent of the dangers became more evident, new measures were sought to prevent contamination. In 1975 thirty-three countries banned the dumping of nuclear waste into the sea; Britain, one of the main culprits, continued to do so until 1983. Low-level wastes were stored in containers in concrete vaults; high-level wastes were stored in steel drums for temporary burial at the bottom of the sea or deep under ground. In some countries, the highly radioactive fuel rods used in nuclear reactors were reprocessed at plants such as that at Hague, near Cherbourg in France, or at Britain's Sellafield – but this was a process that created yet more waste.

In the new atmosphere of environmental concern in the 1970s and 1980s, the problem of nuclear waste became a political and moral issue as well as a technical one, as people's perceptions of nuclear power changed. Many took part in demonstrations, opposed to the waste dump sites threatening their communities. When plans were announced in Germany to build new nuclear power stations, there were large public protests.

In the United States intense public opposition successfully halted government proposals to use new sites as dumping grounds in 1986. The Swedish government, influenced by the strength of public feeling, decided to phase out its nuclear energy programme altogether by the year 2010. Yet in France the government embarked on a major nuclear energy programme, and by 1992 fifty-five power stations were supplying 75 per cent of the nation's electricity.

Alternative proposals for the disposal of plutonium have been put forward – detonation, combination with uranium for use as a fuel, conversion to safer substances, and even sending it into space to be dumped in the sun – all of which present further problems. Yet despite the failure to provide a safe long-term solution to the problem of waste, nuclear power stations continue to produce thousands of tonnes of radioactive waste. Matashichi Oishi, who was among the *Lucky Dragon* crew, believes, 'Only when we are certain about how to deal with nuclear waste should we use nuclear power for the advantage of mankind.'

FIGHTING THE FALLOUT
(OPPOSITE) *Firefighters at Chernobyl hose down buildings contaminated by radioactivity. Many of the firemen later discovered that they themselves were lethally contaminated. Trained to cope with minor accidents, they were ill equipped and unprepared to deal with such a major emergency.*

VALERY STARADUMOV
led army conscripts in clearing radioactive debris at Chernobyl. 'The soldiers had never had anything to do with radiation before,' he remembers. 'That's why a lot of time had to be spent on training them before they could fulfil certain tasks. A total of three and a half thousand soldiers worked on the roof in those perilous conditions....I don't know how carefully their health was followed up.'

RADIATION DISPERSAL (BELOW) *one week after the explosion at Chernobyl. The extent of the fallout partly depended on whether rain brought contamination back to earth from the atmosphere.*

It was in the Ukraine that public confidence in nuclear scientists' ability to control their technology reached a critical point. Chernobyl nuclear power station was 104 km (65 miles) north of Kiev; most of its workers lived in the new town of Pripyat, built just a kilometre away from the plant, which supplied electricity to much of the western Soviet Union. In April 1986 the accident that they had always been told was impossible did take place: an explosion blew the roof off the main reactor.

A helicopter pilot flew over the complex and saw exactly what the experts most feared: the orange glow of fire in the heart of the reactor. Scientists believed they could be facing meltdown, in which the core of the reactor would become so intensely hot that it would melt and burn through the foundations into the earth. If the water table became contaminated, the consequences for the environment would be catastrophic.

Engineers worked frantically to put out the fire and to find out what was happening inside the reactor. They cut through the 3-metre (10-foot) thick concrete lining; one person then had to undertake the most dangerous job of all: going underneath the reactor to see whether the radioactive core was burning through. The volunteer was physicist Veniamin Prianichnikov, who had watched the explosion from the window of his flat two days earlier and knew that a huge amount of radioactivity was being released. 'In my mind's eye I saw all the people of Pripyat, including my wife and my seven-year-old daughter, as living corpses,' he recalls. Now he climbed through the hole in the reactor lining, not knowing what he would find. 'When I pulled open the cover I felt something pouring onto my head. I was wearing just a thin protective cap. I immediately knew that I was in a dire situation, and I was probably finished. I shouted to the people who were

Radiation levels as multiples above normal

over 100
40–100
20–40
10–20
5–10
1–5
up to 1
normal

Chernobyl

Prevailing wind

with me to hand me the meter so I could measure the radiation intensity....The meter showed about two hundred units. It was then I realized that it was all right – I was alive.'

The dreaded meltdown was not taking place, but a massive radiation leak compelled the authorities to evacuate a 32-km (20-mile) zone round Chernobyl, including all the people who lived in Pripyat. As the families left, young army conscripts were brought in to help. The main task was to clear the reactor roof of highly radioactive debris from the core. With no special clothing available they could work only for a single two-minute period in the most contaminated areas. Valery Staradumov, who was in charge of the decontamination, recalls, 'It was clearly everyone's duty to reduce the dangers after the explosion....I am the father of two and I knew that the accident was particularly risky for our children because of the long-term consequences.'

Altogether 600 000 people were directly affected by the Chernobyl disaster. For months afterwards, radioactive dust drifted over western and northern Europe, threatening the health of millions more and contaminating livestock and farmland.

The fallout legacy

At the start of the nuclear age no one could have estimated the long-term effects of fallout. The learning curve was to prove costly in terms of both human suffering and environmental damage.

In the United States the desert tests had taken their toll. Many of the soldiers who had been there developed radiation diseases. Thomas Saffer believes, 'We were lied to. Even after the information emerged that these veterans were getting ill...caused by their exposure to radiation, millions of dollars have been spent to defend the government's position....We were sent to a place where no human being should have ever been without being briefed as to what the consequences could be.'

A large number of people living in St George, close to the Nevada test sites, developed cancers, and many of them died. Sheldon Johnson, who has suffered from numerous skin cancers, is well aware of the magnitude of the problem. 'The impact of all this has been enormous – in the sorrow and the pain and the discomfort and loss to many, many people. And I think the thing

"When the chiefs arrived they first played dare-devils, but after they had driven round the unit, few of them didn't turn pale. The sight they saw was shocking to all. We were absolutely unprepared to face such a tragedy, and we are not prepared now."

VENIAMIN PRIANICHNIKOV

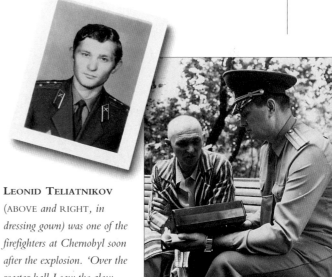

LEONID TELIATNIKOV (ABOVE *and* RIGHT, *in dressing gown) was one of the firefighters at Chernobyl soon after the explosion. 'Over the reactor hall I saw the glow, which was very rich in colour,' he remembers. 'You could see a shining column of white-blue light. You couldn't take your eyes away from it. You felt spellbound.' After just a couple of hours' work, Leonid Teliatnikov felt weak, was short of breath and began vomiting uncontrollably. All his brigade suffered acute radiation sickness; eleven men died.*

STANDING UP FOR PEACE (OPPOSITE) *Dutch anti-nuclear protesters march through the streets of The Hague. As the arms race accelerated and nuclear power programmes expanded, protesters in many countries resorted to mass demonstrations, marches, petitions and civil disobedience to make their views known. The strength of public protest and the ruinous cost of defence spending eventually forced most governments to review their nuclear policies.*

that I feel terribly bad about is that it has lost the confidence in our government. We really daren't trust them any more.'

By 1987 the Cold War had begun to thaw and the leaders of the superpowers, Mikhail Gorbachev and Ronald Reagan, signed an arms reduction treaty in Geneva, amid much celebration. But Arkadi Brish, who had helped to pioneer the Soviet bomb, still believed that a reversal of the arms race was impossible. 'You can never stop designing nuclear weapons, you can only start and go on continuously, perfecting them and moving forward.'

The civil, commercial use of nuclear energy still remained controversial, with governments having to set the strength of popular feeling against the long-term need for electricity. But Hiroshima victim Akira Ishida believed, 'The attitude behind the dependency on nuclear energy is laziness towards the conservation of energy'. He thought that other sources of energy should be developed further. 'If you look at solar energy, for example, there is still so much to improve in terms of both amount and efficiency.' Edward Teller, on the other hand, looked forward to the possibility of electricity being produced by atomic fusion, and claimed, 'Safe fusion will make reactors automatic and inaccessible, and will make the proliferation of weapons difficult'.

Whatever the long-term use of atomic energy, the effects of nuclear fallout still had to be endured. For Sumiteru Taniguchi, who still continued to receive treatment for his back injuries, 'The war ended fifty years ago, but not for us. We victims have been suffering ever since. And we don't know how it's going to affect future generations.' Despite fierce opposition to nuclear power in Japan, the government continued its nuclear programme, and by 1995 Japan's forty-eight nuclear power stations were producing a third of its power. The experts said that there was no other way of providing for people's needs, but here, as elsewhere, people were no longer sure that experts could be trusted.

NO TO NUCLEAR POWER
Public opposition, and the failure of nuclear power to fulfil its promise as a cheap, clean energy source, increased the need for research into other energy sources such as geothermal, solar, wave and wind power. Diminishing supplies of fossil fuels also forced governments to consider developing them.

IN REMEMBRANCE *Every year, in memory of those who died at Hiroshima, lanterns are lit and floated down the river past the remains of the Museum of Science and Industry in the city's Peace Memorial Park.*

15

1 9 5 0 – 1 9 9 5

Asia Rising

Economic boom
in
East Asia

IT WAS NOT UNTIL SEPTEMBER 1951, six years after the end of the Second World War, that representatives from the governments of Japan and the Western Allies met in San Francisco to agree the final terms of a permanent peace settlement. The Japanese agreed to pay huge war reparations to the countries they had invaded during the war in the Pacific, but regained their independence, bringing an end to the seven-year occupation by the Allied powers.

Since the Japanese emperor, Hirohito, had announced his nation's unconditional surrender in August 1945, hundreds of thousands of United States troops had been stationed in Japan. The future of the country looked dark. Miyoshi Ohba was then a public health nurse in Takaho, a small country village. 'We had lost everything,' she says. When the occupation formally ended on 28 April 1952 there were widespread celebrations in Japan. Under the terms of a separate security treaty, the United States would maintain military bases in Japan, but the San Francisco peace treaty heralded a new era. The Japanese needed to make up for the lost years of development; there was a sense of urgency and collective effort. As Miyoshi Ohba says, 'We had to catch up with the United States... a country that was flourishing. It was like a flea on an elephant.' Standards of living had slowly begun to improve, but cities still needed to be rebuilt, factories were poorly managed and raw materials were in short supply.

Yet Japan did rise again. By the 1990s its people were among the most prosperous in the world. Japan having led the way, prosperity soon spread to other countries in East Asia, whose economies grew faster than those of any other region between 1965 and 1980. Their success amazed people elsewhere, who wondered what it was about the Asian approach and attitude to work that brought them this growth. In what was soon being called an economic miracle they worked hard, ate better, enjoyed better health, lived longer and began to spend as much as, and to save more than, people in the West.

JAPANESE SCHOOLCHILDREN *are handed American flags to greet the Allied forces who had arrived to occupy their country.*

"We believed that Japan would win, but losing the war was the reality. It was midsummer, everybody cried because we lost. We were sad and we didn't know what Japan was going to be, we were worried about the future."

MIYOSHI OHBA

WARTIME DESTRUCTION *hastened Japan's urgent need to rebuild* (BELOW). *Nearly a quarter of its buildings and most of its major cities had been destroyed. When people returned to their homes in urban areas many of them, like this woman in what remains of her Tokyo house in 1949* (RIGHT), *found them in ruins. More than three million people were homeless.*

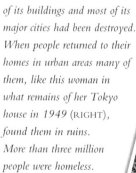

Recovery and reconstruction

The day after Japan surrendered on 14 August 1945, bringing to an end the war in the Pacific, a meeting was held in one of the few buildings in Tokyo that had not been flattened by American bombing – the offices of the South Manchurian Railway. A group of senior civil servants and economists were starting to plan how the ruined country could lift itself out of the ashes. 'The Japanese economy will be developed,' they predicted, 'through a high level of industrialization and a raising of technological standards.' Weeks later, Japan's first postwar prime minister, Shigeru Yoshida, noted his hopes for the future: 'After the rain, sky and land will become brighter,' he wrote.

Such prophecies seemed highly unlikely. Much of Japan was in chaos, its cities and industrial centres laid waste by devastating incendiary attacks, and by two atomic bombs. At least 2.6 million people had been killed during the war; the survivors, many of them wearing rags, were more concerned about finding food and shelter than mourning their nation's defeat. Yoshiko Hashimoto, who had been evacuated from Tokyo to the countryside, searched through paddy fields for locusts and roaches to feed her baby and her injured sister: 'Every day you woke up and you had to think about what to eat, how to keep your stomach full. I don't think I thought of anything else.' Under the direction of General Douglas A. MacArthur, the supreme commander of the Allied powers (SCAP), the occupation forces, most of them Americans, came to disarm and demilitarize Japan, and prevent it ever starting a war again. They believed they could do this by introducing the concept of democracy. But in the first months, what the Japanese needed most was food and medicine.

Unaccustomed to the sight of foreigners, at first many people were both afraid and fascinated by the Americans. The nurse Miyoshi Ohba recalls when they arrived in her village. 'We thought they were scary people because they had guns....But when we saw the Americans they were nice and generous,

COOPERATIVE SPIRIT
(LEFT) *An American soldier and a Japanese policeman stand side by side to direct the Tokyo traffic in the early years of the occupation.*

they gave chocolates to children, and they were smiling and saying "Hello". We were surprised.'

After years of war, Japanese civilians now faced the risk of epidemics, worsened by damaged water supplies and malnutrition. The occupying forces helped to treat the thousands of people afflicted with fleas and lice, intestinal worms and tuberculosis. 'These people were specialists in public health,' recalls Miyoshi Ohba. 'They were great. We were impressed by the democratic way of managing public health.' Hundreds of villagers went to the village hall in an effort to rid them of worms. 'There were so many people with stomach ache,' she says. 'So many worms came out. The largest number was one hundred and eighty. A child came up with the worms in a bowl and he showed it to me. They were wriggling – what a sight! But the child was so proud and happy.'

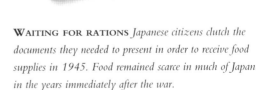

WAITING FOR RATIONS *Japanese citizens clutch the documents they needed to present in order to receive food supplies in 1945. Food remained scarce in much of Japan in the years immediately after the war.*

IN THE PLAYGROUND *of a new primary school, pupils take a break among the ruins of Hiroshima, which had to be completely rebuilt after the war. The Americans ordered the Japanese to overhaul their education system, and to stop teaching that the Japanese were a unique people.*

To prevent the Japanese being ruled by militarist leaders who could wage another war, the Americans said the country had to be 'democratized'. Obliged to renounce his traditional divine status, Emperor Hirohito urged the national parliament, 'We must endeavour to understand democracy'. A new constitution was drawn up in 1947. The state Shinto religion was discouraged, and American projectionists toured remote villages showing films about the history of the United States. Schools and colleges were remodelled on American lines. Equal rights for women, including the right to vote, were introduced. In the countryside peasant farmers benefited from land reforms, which broke up the property of landlords and allowed tenants to buy it at a reduced price. In the factories, workers were encouraged to form labour unions; within a year five million of them had become members.

Japan's formerly powerful economy had almost collapsed; the country depended on imported goods. Inflation and prices were high, and nearly thirteen million people were unemployed. There was an urgent need to modernize and rebuild industry.

EXPERT ADVICE (RIGHT) *At the Allied occupation offices of the Antitrust and Cartels Division of the SCAP Liquidation Branch, American officials consult a Japanese specialist over their plans to dismantle the powerful zaibatsu (financial clique), private business conglomerates that controlled Japanese commerce, finance and industry.*

The rush for growth

By the early 1950s things were slowly beginning to improve. The United States provided massive financial aid, and also launched a programme of economic stabilization designed to reduce Japan's dependence on foreign imports by helping its industries to develop for export. Instead of punishing Japan by breaking up its remaining heavy industries, with their long-term military potential, the United States increasingly realized that it should support Japan's economic recovery.

The worsening tension of the Cold War between the United States and the Soviet Union was a key factor in bringing this change in objective: as a strong and self-sufficient nation Japan would make a powerful ally against the spread of communism in Asia. American experts visited Japan to introduce modern principles of management and new techniques for industrial production. Funds from the United States helped to establish Japanese banks for reconstruction, development and export. People received vital training in new skills. And before they withdrew in 1952 the Americans gave Japanese industry a further boost: several millions of dollars' worth of orders for military equipment for the United States forces fighting the communist soldiers who crossed from North Korea into the South in June 1950.

In economic terms at least, the Korean war provided a valuable opportunity for the Japanese. The prime minister went so far as to describe it as 'a gift from the gods'. More than a thousand Japanese munitions factories rolled back into steady production of armaments. Building materials, military supplies, general provisions and transport were all needed. The Toyota company's output of trucks leaped from 300 to 1500 a month by 1951. People put up with poor wages, long hours, shortages of goods and difficult working conditions to help meet the growing demand. Yoshiko Hashimoto returned to Tokyo, and found work in a packaging plant. 'The plant started to set up and the work started to pick up. I think it was at that time that life got better,' she recalls. 'The orders were coming in, and as long as we worked hard that meant money would come in and we could eat.'

Japanese industry was privately owned, but government ministries intervened and guided companies in a way that was

EXERCISE REGIMEN
Men pause for T'ai Chi, an ancient Chinese form of exercise, at the Hamamatsu railway station on the Tokyo–Kyoto line. In the early 1950s many people still suffered from poor health in parts of the country; the average life expectancy was sixty years for men and sixty-three years for women.

unknown in Western Europe or the United States. Planners set targets, and used licences and foreign currency controls to divert investment to where it was needed most. The first priority was the development of heavy industry – coal, then steel, chemicals and shipbuilding. Suezo Uchida was a supervisor at a major shipyard in Nagasaki. It had escaped damage during the Pacific war, which had destroyed three-quarters of Japan's shipping. During the early years of the occupation they were permitted to build only small fishing boats. 'The size of those boats got bigger, and then they remodelled the whaling ship into a cargo ship. Then the real shipbuilding started again,' he remembers.

By the mid-1950s business at the shipyard was booming, and wages began to rise. 'An order for three ships came from the Philippines,' Suezo Uchida remembers, 'and orders came from other areas too....Maybe twelve ships were launched in a year.' Like everyone else, he worked extremely hard. 'I usually went to the company at eight o'clock. I continued working until nine in the evening. That was the usual day. On one day only – Wednesday – I came home at four o'clock. That was the working situation then. I was a workaholic, I worked almost all Sundays, too. I had no time to talk to my wife.'

Rapid expansion in the new car and electronics industries, accompanied by efficient management and production methods, soon followed. There was fierce competition between different companies. At the age of thirty, Akimoto Takehora joined a small new electronics company that was based in a modest two-storey house. 'We worked until seven or eight, and when we were very busy we worked until ten o'clock in the evening,' he recalls. 'We didn't even have a conveyor belt, so we had the product on the table and then it was passed to the next person. Each day we could make only five hundred units with thirty people working.' When they acquired a moving conveyor belt, production increased. More orders were coming in from abroad, and the renamed Sony Corporation quickly expanded. In

"The economy was growing in Japan, so maybe we played a part in it. At that time we only had Sundays off...that was a lot of work."

MASAAKI ICHIHASHI

HARD AT WORK *in a small Japanese factory. Alongside the key heavy industries that were being developed, small companies continued to manufacture goods for markets at home and abroad.*

LIFTING A PROPELLER (OPPOSITE) *at the busy Tsurumi shipyard near Tokyo. After receiving American technical assistance, the Japanese reorganized their shipyards and built large ships more cheaply than anyone else. By 1956 they had become the world's leading shipbuilder.*

September 1955 they released a transistor radio onto the market. 'I was sure this would sell well,' remembers Akimoto Takehora. 'We thought, "This will be the trend"....At that time portable radios were four or five times as big, so its small size had a great impact.'

From 1952 Japan's average annual rate of growth – more than 9 per cent – was the highest in the world. The economic 'miracle' was the result of hard work by educated, well-trained workers and managers in an environment moulded by the government to favour industry: low taxation, low inflation, high savings and high investment. In the early years left-wing trade unions tried to fight the companies for higher wages and more control. The showdown came in 1953, when the industry-wide car workers' union took on three car manufacturers; by 1954 the strike had been broken. From then on Japanese manufacturers created their own 'company unions', and averted further strikes by improving cooperation between management and workers.

In 1956 the Japanese government announced that the 'postwar period' was now over: living standards were back to prewar levels, and industrial output was reaching the high target set. Japan had overtaken both Britain and West Germany in shipbuilding; new offices and factories were being built; cameras and watches were being manufactured. In the towns people's standard of living had improved. As new industries began to develop, more labour was needed. The result was an exodus of people from the countryside: some four million young people left their homes in the space of five years to take up jobs in the new factories and offices. As the decade came to a close the Japanese were living far better than anyone had imagined would be possible only ten years before, and in 1960 the new prime minister, Hayato Ikeda, made a promise to the people of Japan that in return for their efforts their earnings would double within the next ten years.

Vogue product

THE TRANSISTOR RADIO, *first made in Japan by the Sony Corporation in 1955, was an innovation that played a major part in Japan's successful electronics industry. Four years later this compact model, the TR610, small enough to fit into a shirt pocket, was exported to the United States.*

LINES OF PRODUCTION (ABOVE) *in a camera factory. At first Japanese camera manufacturers concentrated on exporting their products, helping to establish a new reputation abroad for quality in Japanese goods. By 1964 half the Japanese population also owned cameras.*

TEAM WORK (RIGHT) *An early morning line-up outside the MK Taxi Company, one of many Japanese businesses that engaged staff in drills and routines designed to heighten their sense of belonging, loyalty and corporate commitment.*

WARRIORS IN BUSINESS

LONG HOURS OF WORK for six days a week were standard for Japanese workers, regardless of status, during the 1960s. Following the series of major strikes that shook Japan in the early 1950s, industry-based unions had declined and were partly replaced by 'enterprise unions'. Large companies offered their employees steadily increasing wages, lifetime employment, pensions and various fringe benefits. Strong corporate loyalty was encouraged: many employees were expected to wear company badges and to sing the company song before work each day. In return, companies avoided layoffs, and redeployed workers to other areas if orders fell.

Companies provided annual workers' outings and a range of benefits. Employees could eat in company canteens and sleep in company dormitories. Young married couples could move into company housing at greatly reduced cost. Holiday allowances were allocated according to seniority. Many factory workers looked to their company superiors to fulfil the traditional role of matchmaker in arranged marriages. As employees in large corporations were paid a salary that increased according to seniority and long service, rather than as a reward for merit, they had a strong incentive not to change jobs.

While large Japanese companies were good, if paternalistic employers, only a third of the Japanese labour force was employed by larger firms. Small companies offered less favourable terms of employment, and many temporary or part-time workers earned lower wages, with no bonuses or job security, and were deprived of the guarantees or pension rights offered to white-collar workers – the *salarriimen* – in bigger companies.

Women workers were paid less than men, and had far fewer opportunities. Of the sixty million people employed in Japan in 1990, twenty-four million were women, but only 1 per cent of them were in managerial positions. The majority of 'office ladies', or OLs as the young women were called, worked in junior office jobs for low wages; they were referred to as 'flowers of the office'. Several large manufacturing firms made it their policy not to hire women at all.

In 1986 an Equal Opportunity Law prohibited employers from forcing women to retire when they married or had children, though the practice was still quite common. As industrialization spread to other parts of East Asia, employers treated women in much the same way. In Malaysia women in electronics factories were encouraged to give up work after four years to get married – at about the time that their eyesight would start to deteriorate after constantly working with microscopes.

For their dedication and intensive working patterns Japanese men were called 'business warriors'. Only one in three workers expected to take a two-day weekend. In 1987 company employees took an average of only eight days' holiday a year, and by the 1990s the Japanese were working between 200 and 500 hours a year longer than their Western counterparts. It proved too much for some of them: cases of *karoshi*, deaths among workers as a result of stress and overwork, were on the increase.

The rewards of prosperity

The Japanese were delighted with their new prosperity and the new things it could buy. Soon almost every family had acquired the 'three sacred treasures' – a television set, refrigerator and washing machine. For Yoshiko Hashimoto, who had always washed her clothes by hand using cold water and a washing board, life became much easier. 'Among all the electrical consumer goods washing machines were the best, even better than television,' she recalls. 'When I bought the washing machine I was so happy, I couldn't stop laughing. At that time it was quite expensive, so you couldn't pay in one go, it was like a loan. But even so, I was happy.' Then there were fans and electric rice cookers, followed later in the 1960s by air conditioning units, colour televisions and cars.

The major Japanese car makers, led by Nissan and Toyota, were producing more cars than ever before, and more people were learning to drive. After working at the Toyota factory for six years, Chikara Abe could afford to buy a car at the age of twenty-four. 'I went up to heaven when I bought the car,' he remembers. 'I was single and I had an apartment and the parking place was a little way from the flat. Every day when I woke up I checked to make sure it was still there. Every day I washed the car with water.'

Japan's population had grown to 100 million, an increase of thirty million since the end of the war. As people continued to leave the countryside, where standards of living were lower, in the towns housing shortages and high rents became more common. To meet the crisis, new apartment blocks – *danchi* – were built in Tokyo and other cities with government funding. With their modern fittings and bathrooms they became very popular. People had to apply up to thirty times before they were allocated one of these small flats. Taisuke and Nobuko Sato applied eighteen times, and then won a new apartment in a Tokyo *danchi* through a lottery draw in 1965. They were one of the first families to move in. Their two children were fascinated by the number of light switches in their new home. 'In the old apartment there was just one light,' Taisuke Sato remembers, 'but in

SITTING EXAMS *Japan had high literacy rates and rigorous standards in education. Despite the pressure of so-called 'examination hell', the proportion of pupils who voluntarily went to high school after completing compulsory middle school rose from 43 per cent in 1950 to 55 per cent ten years later and 82 per cent in 1970. More than a hundred new universities and colleges were built during the 1960s.*

OLD AND NEW (BELOW) *These wooden homes were among those built in Tokyo immediately after the war to house the city's millions of homeless people. Work on the modern apartment blocks in the distance began in 1954, as the demand for housing increased in the overcrowded city.*

CHANGING LIFESTYLES
Car ownership spread in the 1960s (FAR LEFT, ABOVE), *and many of the* danchi, *the new apartment blocks* (LEFT) *included space for parking. When Nobuko Sato* (FAR LEFT, BELOW) *moved with his family into a new* danchi, *he was impressed by the amount of space. 'From one room to three rooms,' he says, 'and there was a bath in the flat.'*

SHOWCASE OF SUCCESS

THE TOKYO OLYMPIC GAMES signalled Japan's readmission to the international community after the Second World War. The city had been due to host the Games in 1940, but they had been cancelled. In October 1964 some 8000 competitors and about 80 000 spectators were among those who flocked to Tokyo to take part in or to watch the first Olympic Games ever to be held in Asia. Residents of Tokyo were actively encouraged to offer them a warm welcome. As the emperor declared the Games open, 10 000 coloured balloons were released and explosions of a thousand firecrackers could be heard.

The preparations had been immense. In the final hours before the opening ceremony was due to take place, bulldozers and an army of construction workers were still feverishly working to complete the Olympic sites and the new highways linking them to the airport and to the city centre. A total of £700 million was spent, some of it on building a 13-km (8-mile) monorail, on widening twenty-three newly designated Olympic roads, on 145 km (90 miles) of new motorway in Tokyo, on modern hotels and on the impressive Olympic stadia themselves.

The Olympic complex in Komozawa Park was the largest sports stadium in the region. It was designed by the architect Kenzo Tange around an open spectator area that featured traditional Japanese elegance in grey stone and pebbles. It included a soccer stadium with seating for 80 000 people under a petal-shaped overhanging roof, a £3 million swimming pool with enough space to seat 15 000 spectators, and an octagonal wrestling and martial arts hall. Here the Japanese sport of judo – which had been prohibited for a brief period as part of the drive to eliminate the military tradition in Japan – made its debut at the Olympic Games.

Japan had not been a particularly successful competitor in previous Olympics, but in Tokyo Japanese athletes excelled before the home crowd and the hundreds of millions of television viewers throughout the world. Tremendous enthusiasm was roused by the Japanese women's volleyball team, which played against women from the Soviet Union in the final. When the Japanese team won, many of the spectators burst into tears of happiness. In the end, largely owing to their successful performance in the martial arts, the Japanese tally of medals was exceeded only by those of the United States, the Soviet Union and West Germany.

As the final competitions took place, the veteran American president of the International Olympic Committee, Avery Brundage, called them 'the greatest Olympics ever held'.

this flat there were several switches.' Her husband was most thrilled with the bath in their new apartment. 'In the old days we used the wooden bath,' says Nobuko Sato. 'For the first time, it was my own bath, my own flat, and the bathroom was inside the flat.'

With growing industry and a powerful economy now established, more money could be allocated to the development of public services and utilities. In the cities new schools and universities, motorways and subways, as well as hotels and office blocks, were being built. In the countryside most villages had electricity, and television was now reaching them too. By 1964 Japan displayed its progress and new prosperity to the world when it hosted the international Olympic Games in Tokyo.

Between 1965 and 1970 Japan's economy grew at a startling average rate of 13 per cent – it was almost doubling every five years. Japan's economy had overtaken that of Britain in 1962 and of West Germany five years later, becoming the third largest in the world. Growth at such a consistently high rate fostered optimism, optimism encouraged investment, and investment first encouraged and then absorbed the world's highest rate of saving – more than 20 per cent of disposable income. People's earnings had already doubled – even earlier than Prime Minister Ikeda had predicted they would.

With their new wealth the Japanese began to spend more money both on consumer goods and on entertainment. They also began to adopt many features of the modern Western lifestyle – there were new fashions, new tastes in food and popular music. From the early 1970s many people chose to replace their traditional futons with Western-style beds, and spent more time and more money playing golf and taking holidays abroad.

BEACON OF PROGRESS
Yoshinori Sakai, who lit the Olympic flame at the start of the Games (LEFT), was born in Hiroshima on 6 August 1945, the day the atomic bomb was dropped there. In nineteen years his country had made enormous strides, and now proudly hosted an Olympics that reflected its achievements. The National Gymnasium (BELOW) was built on a site formerly used to house American troops.

RUSH HOUR SHOVE
Wearing white gloves, 'pushing boys' were hired to squeeze passengers onto congested commuter trains.

TAKUNORI NAGAOKA
was one of the drivers on Japan's new electric 'bullet train' or shinkansen. At a speed of 200 km (124 miles) an hour, it was the fastest express train in the world when it first ran in 1964 between Tokyo and Osaka.

NEW WAYS OF LIVING

Taisuke Sato can remember the first time she tasted meat at a Chinese restaurant in Tokyo, shortly after she was married in 1960. 'I had never seen so much meat before,' she says. 'Though I finished it all myself, I was shocked.' By the 1970s and 1980s, as the proportion of people working on the land in many East Asian countries dropped – in Japan from 50 per cent in 1945 to 10 per cent, and in South Korea and Taiwan from 60 per cent to 20 per cent – there were more imports of food and other goods from the West.

Among these meat, bread and dairy products such as cheese and butter were new to the Japanese diet, which previously consisted largely of fish, rice and vegetables. As the influence of the West became more pervasive in Asian countries, some people began to use knives and forks for the first time instead of chopsticks, and drank coffee and whisky rather than their traditional tea or *sake*, rice wine. Hisako Sugawara had her first taste of a cola drink at the Sony company where she worked. 'We were asked to try a cola, and it was a brown liquid, it tasted like medicine,' she remembers. 'I just couldn't finish it.' The American fast food chain McDonald's opened its first outlet in Japan inside Tokyo's Mitsukoshi department store in 1971, adopting the selling line, 'If you keep eating hamburgers you will become blond!'

With higher incomes more people could afford to eat out and to go on holiday. In 1985 more than 8.5 million Japanese travelled abroad, most of them to Hawaii, Hong Kong, South Korea and Taiwan. Traditional extended families were affected by overpopulation in the cities, which hastened an increase in small, single-family homes. The average number of people living in a household fell from five in 1920 to three in 1985. When birth control had first been introduced in country areas of Japan in the 1950s, health workers used special methods to overcome the shyness of village women. 'Until then,' says Miyoshi Ohba, 'women didn't know what a condom was....There was this 'love box' filled with condoms. You put money in and took one out without other people noticing.'

The best proof of the effect of improving diet and health care came in the statistics about the Japanese themselves: research in 1976 showed that the average height of a seventeen-year-old male had increased by nearly 7 cm (2.75 inches) since 1950. There was also an increase in life expectancy: by the 1990s the Japanese, with average life expectancies of seventy-four years for men and eighty years for women, were living longer than any other people in the world.

Dining out *in one of Tokyo's many restaurants catering for people's new tastes.*

By the 1970s there were visible signs that Japan's growth was causing problems. In the rush to industrialize, severe environmental damage had been inflicted by factories and chemical plants across the country. There was widespread pollution of the air, of rivers, and of the sea. And as Tokyo, Yokohama and other smog-filled cities went on expanding, people had to put up with cramped, expensive apartments and slower journeys to work.

Despite these hazards the economy continued to grow. By the 1980s Japan's Gross National Product (GNP) had overtaken that of the Soviet Union. As the yen continued to strengthen, the average Japanese income overtook that of Americans. In 1985 the United States, the world's largest creditor, became the world's largest debtor; most of that debt was owed to Japanese banks.

Years of austerity

Jang Chang Sun had wrestled for South Korea in the 1964 Tokyo Olympics and won a silver medal. When he arrived in Japan to prepare for the Games he had been very impressed. It was the first time in his life that he had used an escalator. 'Thinking about it now, it seemed like a paradise,' he reflects. 'There were a lot of tall buildings, there were highways, there were overpasses, there were things you couldn't see in Korea....People said that we were thirty years behind, but I felt we were behind at least fifty years.'

Despite its proximity to Japan and its status as a former Japanese colony, South Korea was still living in another era. If the Korean war had been a macabre 'gift from the gods' for Japan, for Koreans it was a tragedy, devastating their land, killing a tenth of the population, and leaving millions homeless. The division of the peninsula into two states within opposing spheres of influence – China and the Soviet Union for the communist north, and the United States for the People's Republic of Korea in the south – also divided millions of families, and cut off South Korea from the natural resources and limited pre-1945 industries in the north.

Most people in South Korea remained desperately poor throughout the 1950s. Under the corrupt regime of Syngman

STREET CROSSING *in the Shibuja district of Tokyo. The city's growing number of high-rise buildings, businesses and shops reflected Japan's economic success and status as a centre of world commerce. By 1986 eleven million of the Japanese population of 121 million lived there.*

"In those days there were no such things as refrigerators. You would put your food outside the window when it was cool, and sometimes it would rot because it was too warm."

YEON BONG HAK

BURDENS OF LIFE *South Korean basket weavers in Seoul in 1963, some with their babies on their backs, wait for the bus to take them to nearby farms, where they hoped to sell their baskets to rice farmers.*

Rhee the economy remained static, sustained by the American aid that paid for essential imports. There was no electricity in the countryside, where two-thirds of the expanding population lived, and many people still went hungry. Most goods were in short supply. Kim Bok Soon, who was then living in Inchon, a seaport city near the capital, Seoul, remembers how hard it was to feed her family of eight with the limited amount of rice available. She measured out a strict daily ration. 'I subtracted eight spoonfuls a meal,' she remembers. 'Because of our thrift we could live for one month on the rice that we would earlier have used up in only fifteen days....In the evenings we didn't eat a lot.' They used ashes rather than soap to wash their clothes, and walked or cycled long distances to work. While people in Japan were becoming more prosperous, in South Korea there were no televisions, few people owned cars, and even clocks, radios and watches were regarded as luxuries. Political instability led to a series of demonstrations and public disturbances.

Changes began to take place in 1961 when an army general, Park Chung Hee, seized power in May. Establishing a dictatorial and authoritarian regime, he launched a process of modernization and reform. Park's government adopted many of the methods that had successfully been used in postwar Japan. The government kept a tight reign on imports and foreign exchange, and concentrated on export industries. There were mass literacy campaigns for adults as well as children. People flocked to the towns and cities to work on ambitious construction projects. What was different from Japan was the speed and drive that came from above. General Park believed that the army was the most efficient force in the country. Generals were put in charge of building new roads, railways and ports, power stations and oil refineries. Most people worked for nearly sixty hours a week. 'Everyone was constructing,' recalls Kwak Man Young, who helped to build a new motorway between Seoul and Pusan. 'I worked day and night. I would work for a week with almost no sleep. There was no such thing as a vacation.'

Agricultural production was also boosted by government action. In 1971 the Saemaul Undong, or New Village Movement (NVM) was launched in the countryside. It urged people to improve farms, repair homes, install running water and electricity,

plant trees, build roads and bridges. Kang Sung Ro, a university student from Seoul, became active in the community movement in the village where he spent his holidays. In the morning they were woken up by songs and slogans beamed from loudspeakers. 'Each person would come out with a broom or a shovel and we would sweep or mend the road,' he recalls. Every morning there were group exercises. 'They were called "rebuilding exercises". And right after the exercises we would start cleaning the village.'

The NVM's policy of national self-improvement through individual self-discipline was echoed in its slogan: 'We too can live well if only we try hard'. In the interests of the nation's economy people were encouraged to eat coarse food grains instead of rice, and to give up alcohol. Women were urged to wear short skirts — not to show off their legs but to save cloth. 'You could make them faster,' says Kim Bok Soon, who became one of the community

BUILDING WORK (TOP)
On government orders, Korean workers clear away the remains of slum dwellings in the early 1960s to make way for new buildings.

TRAILER RIDE (ABOVE)
Mechanized cultivation methods in South Korea brought new means of transport to people living in the countryside.

movement leaders in her village. 'You needed less fabric.' To save money so that more would be available to invest in developing industries for export, the government reduced imports of consumer goods and discouraged people from wanting to buy them. 'We learnt that we should not use foreign goods and we should make our own. Although the quality might be poorer, if we used our own goods we would feel happy, we would feel proud,' says Kim Bok Soon. Everybody scrimped and saved and tightened their belts. Mass weddings were held to reduce the cost of getting married, and special awards were given to thrifty housewives.

South Korea, like Japan forty years earlier, began with light industries. Textile factories were built that could take advantage of cheap labour and find a ready export market. Yi Chong Kak worked at a textile factory in Inchon. Wages were low, and the working conditions terrible. 'The first day I got there,' she recalls, 'I thought, "This is hell itself". There were huge machines as big as houses, and there was so much noise you couldn't hear anything. You pulled thread out of cotton and that caused a lot of dust.' Yi Chong Kak worked ten, sometimes twelve hours a day. The women workers were scolded by the managers if they failed to keep up or arrived late. In the summer they worked in extreme heat under fluorescent lamps. As they could not stop to eat regular meals, many of them developed stomach ulcers, and constant exposure to the dust led to outbreaks of tuberculosis. Foot fungus, caused by wearing rubber shoes all day in the heat, was common. 'We all worked like machines,' says Yi Chong Kak. 'We worked to our full capacity, and we produced a lot.'

Heavy industry in South Korea had to be built from scratch. Much of the technical aid and vital materials needed for producing steel, building ships and later making cars came from Japan. Labour and construction costs were kept to a minimum. Yeon Bong Hak began work on the construction of a major new steelworks in Pohang in 1971. 'There were no buildings on the site. We didn't even have a place to change or eat lunch,' he says, 'and each time the wind blew, sand would fly all over the place and would get into my eyes.' As a shelter in which to eat his meals and change his clothes, he commandeered two large crates that had been used to transport machinery. The work was demanding: if

MATERIAL FOR TRADE (ABOVE) *Textiles and sports shoes were among the consumer goods made in South Korea for export.*

CAR BOOM (BELOW) *Hyundai Motors produced vehicles for export while people in South Korea could still only dream of owning a car. When wages increased, a 'My Car' campaign enticed people to buy cars, and banks offered 'My Car' savings accounts to help them.*

part of the foundations were found to be faulty they would have to be strengthened at once, even if it meant working a twenty-four-hour day. If workers complained to the foreman that they lacked the right tools, they were advised to make them themselves.

Since 1968 the government had poured $3.6 billion into the Pohang Iron and Steel Company, known as POSCO. When the plant opened in 1973 it had the capacity to make one million tonnes of steel a year. It could hardly have been a worse time: within two months the world economy was crippled by the oil crisis. Yet the plant was profitable from the start. People like Yeon Bong Hak created the economic miracle by the sweat of their brows. They were helped by the financial strength of the *chaebols*, conglomerates such as Daewoo, Hyundai and Samsung, many of which also profited from exporting the nation's prime asset – its disciplined labour force – to Middle Eastern construction sites.

YI CHONG KAK *and her fellow workers at the textile factory in Inchon* (BELOW) *encountered harsh opposition when they formed a women workers' union in the 1970s to protest over poor working conditions. 'In those days we were given just enough salary so that we wouldn't starve to death,' she recalls. 'I was so tired of the poverty, I just wanted to make more money. I thought if I worked hard I would be able to live well.' Following her arrest Yi Chong Kak spent nine months in prison.*

The government also decided that South Korea should go into shipbuilding. In 1973 Hyundai Heavy Industries started work on a new shipyard. The first ship to be built was one of the largest in the world – a supertanker. For the workmen pressure became intense as the launch date approached. Yi Sung Hwan from Ulsan was one of the team leaders: 'Work and sleep was the only thing. We didn't have time to take a break.' The deadline for completion was eight o'clock in the morning. At midnight they started welding the last plates into position; by four in the morning they had finished. Then they had to take X-rays, but the steel was still hot so the film kept sticking to it. 'The developing centre was behind the main office,' Yi Sung Hwan recalls. 'It takes twenty minutes on foot. I rode the bicycle as fast as I could.' By seven o'clock the hull was ready for painting. When they finished, on time, 'All the strength drained out of me,' says Yi Sung Hwan. 'I hadn't slept for three days, and I lost consciousness. When I woke up I was on the sofa in the office.'

For many people the relentless work and the lack of civil rights took their toll. Workers who joined a union or went on strike were dealt with harshly by the government. In the late 1970s there were more protests, and South Korea's economy came

SIGNS OF CHANGE *in 1984 in the Itewan shopping district of Seoul, where foreign influences and new consumer goods appeared as people's affluence grew.*

under threat as debts soared during the world recession. In 1979 another general, Chun Doo Hwan, took over. Martial law was imposed in 1980, and uprisings were brutally suppressed.

In the early 1980s a new generation of American-trained economists and civil servants began to liberalize trade and privatize banks to open up the economy. Political democracy did not come until 1987, under President Roh Tae Woo. By then the rate of growth was increasing rapidly. In less than ten years Hyundai had become the world's leading shipbuilder, and by 1983 POSCO was pouring 9.1 million tonnes of crude steel a year. Three years later it entered into a joint venture with an American company seeking to modernize one of its plants. Now it was South Koreans who were supplying the United States with capital and technology.

FACE TO FACE (ABOVE) *Students in Seoul confront the forces of power in 1987 to protest over the arrest of a student leader. There were widespread demonstrations in cities across South Korea as opposition to the autocratic rule of President Chun Doo Hwan mounted.*

As in Japan, South Korea's economic success began to be reflected by changes in people's lifestyles. More modern apartments were available; people had their own private bathrooms instead going to public baths, and they no longer had to carry gas canisters upstairs for cooking and heating. As incomes continued to rise, here too people could buy the televisions, refrigerators and washing machines now on sale. More people could afford to buy a car of their own. When the wrestler Jang Chang Sun began his career as an athlete, $300 a year was considered a good income. Now average earnings were more than $10 000. By the time the 1986 Asian Games were held in South Korea, as Jang Chang Sun says, 'We caught up with the Japanese and we won first place over all.' The next games to be hosted by Seoul were the Olympics.

KANG SUNG RO *worked as a door-to-door salesman for Hyundai Motors in Seoul. He travelled by bus for several years until he could afford his own car. 'In those days there were no other cars in the area, so I would honk my horn on the way home and my wife and children would know that it was me,' he recalls. 'People would all come out to see my car.'*

BUSINESS OF EXPORT *At one of the many manufacturing plants in Singapore, women workers produce electronic medical equipment to supply companies abroad. By the 1990s Singapore had become one of the richest countries in Asia.*

CONSTRUCTION ALL ROUND (OPPOSITE) *in Indonesia in 1995, the next country in line for economic growth.*

The Asian tigers

By that time the world was beginning to talk about the 'Four Tigers' following the trail Japan had blazed. Like South Korea, Hong Kong, Singapore and Taiwan had also grown at astonishing rates, partly stimulated by Japan's success and by foreign investment in their industries. By the 1990s they were followed by other newly industrial countries in East and Southeast Asia, especially Indonesia, Malaysia, the Philippines and Thailand.

Since the series of peace treaties had been signed between Japan and its former wartime enemies in Asia in the late 1950s, a Japan-centred economic system had developed in the Pacific region. Between 1982 and 1991 Japan replaced the United States as the biggest exporter to the Philippines, South Korea and Taiwan, and became the largest importer and investor in the region as well.

Such high success rates had dramatic effects on people's lives. In Malaysia the proportion of those living in 'absolute' poverty – lacking food, clean water and shelter – dropped from 37 per cent in 1960 to less than 5 per cent by 1990. That was achieved by hard work, especially by thousands of young, single women working in the garment trade or manufacturing silicon chips for computers.

As elsewhere, prosperity came at a price. Over-population and pollution threatened the quality of people's lives. In Taiwan there was concern about cancer rates, which had doubled since the 1970s; the number of cars in Hong Kong since the 1960s had risen by 700 per cent. The governments of Malaysia, Singapore and Thailand exercised tighter controls over their peoples.

For most people the benefits outweighed the drawbacks. Over half a century, first in Japan, then in Hong Kong, Singapore, South Korea and Taiwan, and eventually in almost the whole Pacific region, economic transformation was helped by people's frugality and hard work, by high-quality education and training, and by governments that protected their home industries until they could become fully competitive. The people of Asia had always known how to work. Now their efforts brought them a growing share in the wealth of the modern world. That wealth could be measured not just in the shiny products of industry, but in real improvements in the lives of millions of people.

16

1 9 4 8 — 1 9 9 4

Skin Deep

THE FIGHT AGAINST STATE RACISM

EARLY ONE AFTERNOON IN March 1960, thousands of men, women and children gathered at the black township of Sharpeville, near Johannesburg, in South Africa. They were staging a peaceful demonstration against the law requiring every black African to carry a passbook. These passbooks restricted the rights of blacks to enter 'white' areas, and were the latest in a long series of legal limitations imposed on black South Africans by the minority white government.

The demonstrators were unarmed, but as they approached the police station the officers of the white police force panicked, and began to fire at random into the crowds. Constance Maysiels was there. 'Shots started to be fired,' she recalls. 'People were running into houses....The shots flew right across the street, killing children, killing adults.' At least sixty-seven Africans were killed, most of them being shot in the back as they fled, and nearly two hundred more were wounded.

The following day images of the victims' coffins, lying in a row like piano keys, appeared in newspapers across the world. Shocked by the violence, many people expressed concern, and the United Nations Security Council urged the South African government to review its racial policies. For the black Africans themselves the massacre at Sharpeville was further proof that the minority white regime was determined to go on denying nine million people whose skin was not white the same voting rights, welfare, education and jobs as they wanted for themselves.

The belief that the law could still be used to legitimize racism was not limited to South Africa; the law still treated blacks and whites as different in many of the southern states of the United States in 1960. But the experience of American blacks and South Africans was to be very different. In the United States a massive popular campaign within ten years succeeded in securing radical changes to the law. For South African blacks the oppression worsened, and it would be another thirty years before the white government finally conceded the principle of equality and majority rule.

FLEEING FOR THEIR LIVES *Peaceful demonstrators in Sharpeville, South Africa, scatter under police fire.*

Segregation in South Africa

When the Nationalist Party gained power in South Africa in 1948, twelve million people came under its control. Two million whites of European origin dominated the rest of the population – eight million black Africans, one million Coloureds and 300 000 Asians. Despite the inequalities, many whites believed the Africans had a good life. 'I think the native, left to the people who know how to handle him, is a fine fellow,' stated one white farmer in a government film. 'If you can measure happiness,' said another, 'they are above us. They don't read the papers about the atom bombs and everything....They're children of nature.'

Millions of black Africans working for white employers saw things differently. Elizabeth Shuba worked for a white farmer for some twenty years. 'The white children always came around and smacked me for not doing things the way they wanted them done,' she remembers. 'Their father would come and finish the beating with a whip. We used to work from 3 a.m. to 10 p.m. with no break. We never received money. We were paid with over-processed milk.'

In the cities as well as in the country, every aspect of people's lives was defined by race. Nomathamsanqua Koha grew up in Johannesburg, where she was taught to make way for white people

BLACK WORKERS *packing grapes in a vineyard shed in Cape Province. There was no opportunity for the black men and women who worked for white farmers to share in the nation's wealth.*

BANISHED FROM THE TOWNS *Millions of black families lived in cramped, makeshift accommodation in shantytowns on the outskirts of cities. Unemployment and poverty contributed to a soaring crime rate.*

THE PRELUDE TO APARTHEID

SOUTH AFRICA WAS A NATION divided by wealth, power, laws and religion, and above all by race. It was a nation that, although it claimed its people lived in racial harmony, was a segregated society in which only those with white skins could enjoy freedom and acquire wealth.

There had long been divisions not only of race but also within the different racial groups that had settled in South Africa. The Nationalist Party drew its support from Afrikaners. They made up about 60 per cent of the white population, and were descended from seventeenth-century Dutch settlers (known as Boers) in the Cape. The remaining 40 per cent of whites were descendants of the British settlers who had come to South Africa after it had been declared part of the British empire in 1810. The discovery of diamonds and gold in South Africa during the second half of the nineteenth century had exacerbated existing tensions between the two groups, culminating in the Boer War of 1899–1902. Despite the legacy of mistrust resulting from the war, the white peoples attempted to bury their differences in 1910 when an independent Union of South Africa was declared. The new constitution gave even greater power to white South Africans.

The majority of Afrikaners were members of the Dutch Reformed Church, which argued that the Bible demonstrated the superiority of Afrikaners: as God's chosen race they were destined to rule over black peoples. Their view was supported by notions then widely accepted that different racial types had distinct physical, mental and moral characteristics and capacities.

Before 1910 there were already laws discriminating against black South Africans: pass laws to restrict their movements, masters' and servants' laws, special taxation. Further laws were enacted to ensure that blacks could not compete economically with whites: the 1913 Native Land Act prohibited Africans from owning land except in specially designated 'reserve' areas; the Native Urban Area Act of 1923 extended residential segregation to towns. In the 1920s white workers reacted violently when the mining industry attempted to use black Africans for semiskilled work, which might have threatened their own employment.

While the policies of various governments often differed, they had in common the deliberate maintenance of white supremacy. With almost complete power in their hands, the whites were able to lay the foundations for the legal structure of apartheid.

CLEARING RUBBISH *from a coastal street at Strand, near Cape Town, a black worker passes a sign reminding him that only white people could use this stretch of beach for recreation.*

MINING FOR DIAMONDS *in perilous conditions, thousands of Africans are employed on meagre wages and overseen by their better-paid white colleagues. As more black Africans worked in the mines, racial tension increased, particularly when black workers were trained to improve their skills.*

by stepping off the pavement and walking in the road. 'You would rather be knocked down by a car as you made room for the white to pass than bump into him,' she recalls.

In many parts of the world there were racial inequalities and conflicts; the South African government took this further by incorporating racial segregation into the country's legal system. Laws had already been passed to separate the races, but it was in 1948 that the Nationalist Party, led by Dr Daniel Malan, came to power in a general election for the first time. The Nationalists represented Afrikaners – whites originally of Dutch descent who spoke a form of Dutch called Afrikaans – and drew most of their support from among white farmers. The party's slogan was, 'The kaffir [African] in his place', and the new government pledged to consolidate legal divisions between different races. This doctrine became known as 'apartheid'.

To support apartheid a pseudoscience of racial theory was developed. Quentin White was made director of the South African Institute of Race Relations. Interviewed at the time, he

HITCHING A RIDE *to work (RIGHT). Black workers often had to travel long distances on crowded trains to get to work from the townships where they lived. Travelling on the couplings between carriages was a way to save money.*

said, 'Apartheid is intended to keep the races apart in all sorts of ways,' he said. 'The attempt now is to separate out your Coloured people (mixed bloods), your Indian group, your African group, so that they're residentially apart.' And not only residentially: Africans were soon to be prevented from living alongside whites in other ways – in schools and colleges, at work, in hospitals and in all other public places.

Within months of the election, a series of racial laws was passed by the Nationalist government to enforce apartheid: the Population and Registration Act labelled all South Africans by race, making skin colour the most important legal definition of a person; the Group Areas Act ruled that separate urban areas should be given to each racial group; the Immorality Act made sexual relations between the races illegal; and the limited voting rights of some Africans, Asians and Coloureds were abolished altogether.

The government left no detail unattended to keep the races separate. Even blood supplies for transfusions in hospitals were kept apart according to their 'racial origin'. Blood containers had to be coded: A for blood from Asians, B for Bantu (black Africans), C for Coloureds and W for whites. Nomathamsanqua Koha worked in Frear hospital in Johannesburg. 'Black blood would never, never be given to a white person,' she says. 'Black blood would be given to a black person, and white blood would also sometimes be given to a black person.'

Education also reflected apartheid. Tandy Gcbashi was one of millions of young Africans taught only domestic skills. 'The idea behind Bantu education at that time,' she says, 'was to teach young African women and men how to do the menial jobs in society – how to be good servants and good labourers.' Subjects such as mathematics and science were considered irrelevant to the lives of most African children.

In the 1950s the government consolidated the legal pillars of apartheid, and many whites were able to reap rich rewards from exports of South Africa's diamonds and gold, uranium, industrial metals and tropical crops. Meanwhile, blacks were systematically stripped of their political and civil rights, and without them found it increasingly difficult to challenge what was happening to them.

LASHING OUT (BELOW) *with her stiletto-heeled shoe, a white woman threatens an African in the street after a disagreement over a scooter. Retaliation by the African could lead to imprisonment or even death.*

Americans campaign for civil rights

In very different circumstances, the blacks of the United States – 12 per cent of the population – also faced legal discrimination. But while the black majority's plight was worsening in South Africa, American blacks were about to realize that it might be possible for them to shift the racial legislation that had kept them as second-class citizens, even after slavery had been abolished in the nineteenth century and despite the fact that the Constitution declared all people to be equal.

In most southern states racial segregation was enforced by local laws known as the 'Jim Crow' system. There was segregation in almost all public places and many private ones – the armed services, hospitals, housing and schools, drinking fountains, playgrounds and swimming pools, buses, taxis and trains, churches, restaurants and theatres. When the code of subordination – the taboo on sexual relationships in particular – was thought to have been broken, gangs of whites carried out beatings, burnings and lynchings of blacks while officials looked the other way.

With so much discrimination, the opportunities for young blacks were limited. By the mid 1930s in seventeen southern states only 6 per cent of students in higher education were black. For every seven dollars spent on the education of white children, only two dollars were spent on blacks, who had to go to separate schools and were prevented from attending whites' universities, technical institutes or military colleges. Laws discriminated against blacks becoming policemen or local officials.

After the Second World War many African-Americans who had travelled abroad during their military service were no longer prepared to tolerate legal discrimination at home. In the late 1950s new independent black nations were emerging in Africa, and in the United States itself the issue of racial discrimination came to the fore. Ann Pratt, a young black mother in Montgomery, Alabama, recalls the mood. 'I was boarding the bus downtown. I had my son on my arm and I was climbing on to the bus holding on with the other hand. There was a Caucasian coming behind me. He tried to swirl me around. "You don't go on the bus before I do, nigger," he says. And I said, "Watch me!" And I hoisted my baby on my shoulder and got on the bus.'

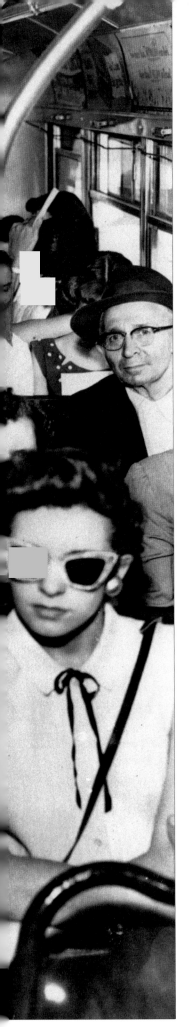

In 1954 the United States Supreme Court declared that separate education was unequal, and therefore illegal. All over the South, black people began to assert their newly declared rights, and to challenge local race laws more aggressively. Civil rights and church leaders in Montgomery called for a boycott of the city's segregated bus system. For maids such as Zekozy Williams, that meant walking to work or organizing a car pool. 'I would get up early,' she recalls, 'fix my husband's breakfast and get him off to work. Then I would set off in my car, picking people up and taking them to work.' As soon as she finished her own job, at four o'clock, Zekozy Williams would start driving again until everyone had been collected and taken home.

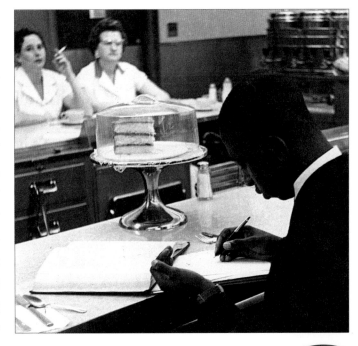

One of the leaders of the Montgomery bus boycott was a young Baptist minister called Martin Luther King, who had been impressed by the non-violent approach of Mahatma Gandhi in India. Soon ministers, students and many other black people in the southern states were putting non-violent protest into effect.

In Nashville, Tennessee, a group of students organized a workshop to practise self-discipline if they were subjected to racial violence. Bernard Lafayette was one of the students. He had his training put to the test when he entered the 'whites-only' lunch counter at a local department store. 'We took our seats quietly at the lunch counter,' he remembers. 'We were not to say anything until we were asked to be served. The waitress was very panicky. She was walking up and down, very confused about what she was going to do, but very clear that she was not going to serve us. And there were these fellows walking behind us. They would make cat-calls and say, "What are you doing in here, jungle-bunnies! Get out of here! You're not going to be served!" '

Another student, Frankie Henry, was very frightened. 'I was praying,' she says, 'when this white lady came and put her cigarette out on my arm. So I calmed myself down. While I was calming

SILENT TREATMENT
(ABOVE) *Waitresses at a 'whites-only' lunch counter would refuse to serve black college students. Bernard Lafayette* (RIGHT), *who was trained not to react to hostility from whites, recalls that, 'When we were finally served it meant that we were respected as human beings and as equals'.*

SITTING APART
(OPPOSITE) *in a Texan bus. The notice displayed above the rear window reminded black passengers that they had to occupy the rear seats while white people sat at the front. Anyone disobeying the regulations could be fined.*

'I HAVE A DREAM'

IT WAS THE POWERFUL RHETORIC of Martin Luther King that made his contribution to the American civil rights movement so formidable. His message, though rousing, was one of peace as he supported – and increasingly came to lead – campaigns of non-violent civil disobedience in the struggle to eradicate racial inequality in the United States.

The son of a prominent Baptist minister and teacher, King became a minister too. His first church was in Montgomery, Alabama, where he helped to organize the bus boycott that captured the nation's attention. Before long he emerged as the most eloquent of the new generation of black Christian leaders. In 1957 he founded the Southern Christian Leadership Council (SCLC), which was to become the focus of his civil rights activities over the following decade.

These activities culminated in the march to Washington on 28 August 1963. That morning the government ordered the National Guard to patrol the city's streets, as officials were nervous about what might happen when thousands of protesters descended on the capital. Its fears proved unfounded. By the afternoon some 200 000 people, blacks and whites, thronged the streets of Washington. They were disciplined and peaceful as they listened to Martin Luther King speaking from the steps of the Lincoln Memorial.

'I have a dream,' King declared, 'that one day this nation will rise up and live out the true meaning of its creed....I have a dream that one day sons of slaves and sons of former slave-owners will be able to sit down at the table of brotherhood....We will be able to transform the jangling discords of our nation into a beautiful symphony of brotherhood. And all God's children – black, white, Jews, Gentiles, Protestants and Catholics – will join hands and

sing "Free at last! Thank God almighty, we are free at last!" '

In 1964, after the Civil Rights Act was passed, King was awarded the Nobel Peace Prize. He continued to organize marches and demonstrations until the Voting Rights Act was secured.

Despite these victories, King faced many challenges to his leadership. Younger, more radical campaigners demanded black power, not shared power, and some believed that he was too conservative and too willing to compromise with whites. Nevertheless, his assassination in April 1968 provoked nationwide rioting. Bernard Lafayette remembers that on the day Martin Luther King was killed, 'He was telling us, "Whatever you do, don't abandon non-violence". He was telling us we must have confidence and stay the course, because non-violence will have its moment.'

LEADING THE PROTEST
*Martin Luther King (*ABOVE*, centre foreground, in a dark coat) leads an estimated 10 000 civil rights marchers in Montgomery, Alabama. He rallied massive support for the campaign, despite attempts by the Federal Bureau of Investigation (FBI) to discredit him.*

ERNEST GREEN (BELOW) *was among the first nine black students to enrol at Little Rock Central High School. 'We spent three weeks being barred from the school,' he remembers. His colleague Elizabeth Eckford (BOTTOM) was turned away from the school by armed soldiers of the Arkansas National Guard.*

down she lit the rest of her matches, pulled my poncho out and dropped the lit matches down my back.' Outraged by the group's daring, some of the white bystanders decided to make an example of one of the students. 'Paul La Pratt was pulled off his seat at the lunch counter,' says Bernard Lafayette. 'He was kicked and beaten on the floor....Ten minutes later they took us all to jail.'

In 1957, following the Supreme Court's decision that segregated education was unequal, nine young black students tried to enrol at the all-white Central High School in Little Rock, Arkansas. 'It was the premier high school in the mid-South, turning out large numbers of Merit scholars,' remembers Ernest Green, one of the nine students. 'But there was a barrier. Because I was a black kid, I couldn't attend there.' The state governor ordered soldiers of the National Guard to keep the black students out. But because of the Supreme Court's decision, President Dwight Eisenhower felt obliged to send in the army to escort the nine students in to school. Ernest Green was in a station wagon

"The most amazing thing was that through all the turmoil, the pain and the physical abuse that we took, we outlasted our enemy and we achieved something. I was able to stand there with my cap and gown, with my diploma, as a graduate of that school."

ERNEST GREEN

RESISTING CHANGE *White students in Pontiac, Michigan, protest against the court order to integrate buses, carrying banners urging their fellow students to join them.*

with one army jeep, mounting a machine gun, in front of him, and another behind. 'A cordon of soldiers surrounded us,' Ernest Green says. 'We went up those steps. It really was an exhilarating feeling that you had finally accomplished something. You could see the cameras and the people across the street. And all of it was focused on the nine of us going to school.'

Ten years earlier a group of radicals, blacks and whites, had tried to draw attention to segregation in the South by going on what they called a Journey of Reconciliation. Their leader had ended up on a Georgia chain gang. In 1961 their way of protest was revived. A civil rights group called the Congress of Racial Equality organized Freedom Rides. It sent two busloads of 'riders', some young black students and some older white pacifists, to test the segregation of southern bus stations. Jim Zwerg was one of the white riders. For much of the journey, the state police tried to protect the demonstrators from the anger of local white residents. 'As we looked out of the windows we were kind of overwhelmed at the force,' he remembers. 'There were police cars with sub-machine guns attached to the back seats, and planes overhead.'

Floyd Mann was an officer of the Alabama state highway patrol. He and his colleagues had arranged for sixteen car loads of state troopers to drive in front of the buses, with sixteen more behind. They also had air reconnaissance overhead. About halfway between Birmingham and Montgomery, Floyd Mann was told that there would be no police in Montgomery from the City Police Department to protect the riders. Anticipating this, he had arranged for a hundred state troopers to be ready there. 'I knew we were caught up in one heck of a dilemma,' he admits. 'We had a governor who had just got elected with the support of the Ku Klux Klan.' (The Ku Klux Klan was a secret, racialist organization of Protestant whites.) When the Alabama attorney general tried to serve an injunction on the crowd of white protesters waiting for the Freedom Rider buses, people began throwing bottles and bricks at him. Floyd Mann radioed for the troopers, but before they arrived the violence escalated, with the whites attacking the riders. 'They were hitting them with bats,' he recalls. 'I had to take my gun and put it to the ear of a man and say I would blow his brains out if he swung his bat one more time.'

Bernard Lafayette was at the Montgomery bus station. 'All of a sudden we saw this mob burst out of the doors....First they went straight to the reporters and started beating the newsmen and cameramen,' he recalls. The Freedom Riders began to sing the civil rights hymn, 'We Shall Overcome'. Within minutes they were attacked by the mob. 'There was a frenzy,' Bernard Lafayette says. 'They just went wild. It was absolutely out of control....They got a young guy, about eighteen years old, and they threw him to the pavement. They had this lead pipe, and they put a foot on his neck and they tried to force this lead pipe down his ear. They were so inhumane.' The Freedom Riders were taken to jail, but they had achieved their aim of bringing more publicity for the continuing evils of southern segregation.

Most white Americans, in the South as well as in the North, were outraged when they saw television reports of the violence used to suppress the protesters. Public opinion demanded that

FLOYD MANN (RIGHT *and* BELOW) *tried to contain the violence between blacks and whites. As clashes spread, violent incidents such as the 'arrest' (*BOTTOM*) of a photographer by troops of the National Guard in Cambridge, Maryland, became more frequent.*

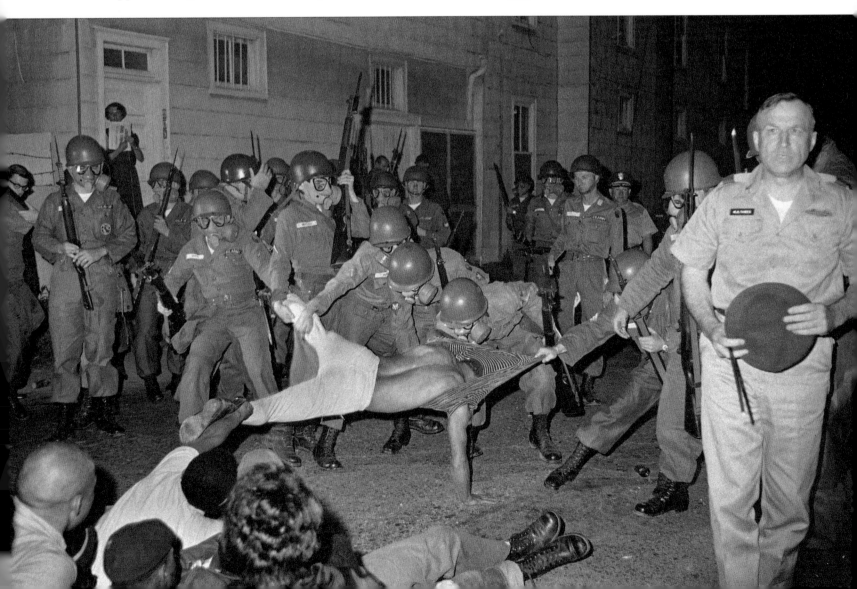

something be done. The march on Washington that took place in the summer of 1963 to pressurize the United States Congress into passing a civil rights bill proved to be the largest demonstration in the history of the nation. That summer President John F. Kennedy finally committed himself to asking Congress for new legislation that would guarantee an end to segregation in the South and make discrimination on the basis of colour an offence in law.

It was an exhilarating feeling for black Americans to see that the federal government seemed ready to keep its promise and use its power to attack the long-entrenched customs and practices that supported inequality. The following year a civil rights bill became law. As a result, voting rights were extended, equal employment opportunities were introduced, and segregation was prohibited in public facilities and in public education. It was huge step forward.

Some people were determined to resist integration. In many southern states white bureaucrats made it almost impossible for blacks to register for voting. Zekozy Williams tried to register several times. 'Every time you went down there, they would make you come back,' she says. 'People were told: "Come back in two months" or "Come back next year". They intimidated us so much that some people just wouldn't go back.' In Alabama a group of black teachers was barred from even entering the registration office. When the Reverend C. T. Vivien demanded justice from the sheriff he was dragged away and then attacked by the police. 'The idea was to beat people down, destroy them physically,' he remembers, 'to destroy their right even to work in a town if they had the courage to try and register to vote.' Many Americans, black and white, were horrified by the violence. Subsequent protest marches attracted widespread support, and in 1965, in response to public demand, Congress passed the Voting Rights Act, guaranteeing the vote to all black people living in the South.

The determination of African-Americans to acquire equal rights had proved stronger than attempts to suppress them. By 1965 the 'Jim Crow' system had been dismantled. Although full equality was to remain beyond their reach even many years later, at least the government had now acted to declare that as far as the law and the state were concerned all people should be regarded as equal, whatever their race.

BLACK CITIZENS *of Somerville, Massachusetts, queue up to register on the electoral roll. After years of oppression some black people needed encouragement to exercise their newly gained voting rights, but many were not deterred even when they encountered opposition.*

UNITED IN THE CAUSE (OPPOSITE) *More than 200 000 civil rights demonstrators from all over the United States gathered at Washington's Lincoln Memorial in August 1963 to hear Martin Luther King proclaim his vision for the future.*

The struggle against apartheid

While the civil rights movement in the United States gathered momentum, the white minority government in South Africa remained intolerant of opposition and continued to consolidate its power. But events in the United States did have an impact on South Africans. Michael Weeder was a Coloured boy growing up in Cape Town at that time. He understood even then that black Americans still experienced hardships in the United States, but he and his friends were excited and optimistic about the changes that were taking place there. 'We saw the examples of Martin Luther King, the examples of triumph,' he remembers. 'And for us, who were not very politicized or organized, those glimpses of black America made a very positive impression. It was the pop culture – the Jacksons, Stevie Wonder – that made me more positive about my own brownness. It gave me guts.'

For some white South Africans apartheid posed a moral dilemma. Hugh Lewin remembers being told by his father, an Anglican priest, that in God's eyes everyone was equal. 'But as a white South African,' he explains, 'blacks didn't exist for me other than as servants.' It was not until he began visiting Sophiatown, the black neighbourhood closest to white Johannesburg, that his ideas began to change. 'I saw people who were real, who were families and not just servants....There was colour there, there was noise, there was singing, there was life,' he remembers. 'And there were all colours, mainly black, and it was something that was tremendously powerful. For me it was a complete

LEAVING HOME (ABOVE) *Watched by armed police, a family prepares to move out of Sophiatown, the black neighbourhood near Johannesburg from which the government evicted the entire population from 1955.*

PLACARDS OF PROTEST (LEFT) *A crowd of demonstrators takes to the streets of Johannesburg to demand change.*

awakening, because there for the first time everyone was together. That was the beginning of my political awareness.'

Some of Sophiatown's inhabitants were quite prosperous and had bought substantial houses, but to the government the very existence of Sophiatown was an affront. The Group Areas Act had been designed to keep whites and blacks well apart from each other, with blacks living in distant, 'containable' townships, and being allowed into white urban areas only to work. Eventually the government simply closed Sophiatown. 'One morning the trucks came in,' recalls Hugh Lewin. 'Everyone was loaded into trucks, and the whole town was moved out. People were driven twenty-five miles southwest to Meadowlands and moved there.' Albertina Sisulu was a nurse in Sophiatown, and recalls the scene. 'We saw the people being bulldozed,' she says. 'It was terrible to see them being pulled out of their houses, their furniture thrown outside in the yards, and the children crying aloud. There were women with children on their backs who were lying dead. We saw it.'

By the early 1960s, after the massacre at Sharpeville, South Africa was in turmoil. Yet many whites appeared to be unaware of the daily despair the black majority had to endure. A reporter at the time asked a white woman on a Cape Town beach, 'Do you think the South African government's racial policy is right?' 'I really do,' she replied, 'because we cannot mix with the lower races.' A man on the same beach was asked, 'Do you feel that the white minority can continue their position?' 'Most decidedly,' was the answer. 'Forever.'

White confidence and complacency depended on the power of the police force. When David Bruce joined the police in Cape Town it was really a force just for the white community. He reluctantly found himself having to enforce apartheid laws such as pass control. 'I must say we felt pretty uncomfortable arresting a person two or three times our age – we were a very young police force.' When he arrested someone for not being in possession of a passbook, he would handcuff them and then, as he describes, 'you would trudge through the city until you found another person who had transgressed the law, and he'd be handcuffed too. At the end of the day you'd be walking with a whole string of a dozen people behind you.'

DAWN RAIDS *on black townships, such as the Durban shantytown of Cato Manor* (ABOVE), *became more frequent as levels of unrest rose. Documents were confiscated and arrests were made to prevent strikes and other protests. Detectives, security branch men and uniformed police were all involved. David Bruce* (RIGHT *and* BELOW) *felt it was his duty to uphold and enforce the law: 'In police work there isn't very much discretion'.*

As the grip of apartheid tightened, Africans found it even more difficult to express their opposition to it or fight it without breaking the white South Africans' laws. Unable to vote – and therefore to have an effect through parliament – they turned to the African National Congress (ANC), founded in 1912. One ANC member, the man who came to symbolize the black majority's yearning for freedom, was a young black lawyer, Nelson Mandela. In 1962 he was arrested with other black leaders and put on trial for conspiracy to overthrow the government. They expected to be given a death sentence. One of the others accused was Walter Sisulu, Albertina Sisulu's husband. 'When the trial began,' she recalls, 'everybody was angry. In fact when the judge came in, some of us did not even stand up. We were prepared to die in court that day, because we were so angry.' Nelson Mandela used the trial as an opportunity to state in public his own beliefs and the ideals of the ANC. 'I have carried the ideal of a democratic and free society in which all persons live together in harmony,' he said. 'It is an ideal for which I am prepared to die.'

The judge did not sentence the men to death. When he read out the sentence the wife of Dennis Goldberg, one of the defendants, could not hear it. She shouted, 'Dennis, what is it?' And he shouted back, 'Life! Life! To live.' For Nelson Mandela that meant twenty-seven years on Robben Island, a prison run by Afrikaner warders 29 km (18 miles) out at sea from Cape Town.

With the opposition apparently crushed, its leaders either in jail, in exile or dead, the white South African government was convinced that it could succeed in maintaining apartheid. But a new generation was growing up in the townships, one that would not accept that its enemies had won. All the old injustices rankled. Africans hated the pass laws and the Group Areas Act, which relegated them to the townships and added long hours of travelling to their working day. They resented their lack of voting rights, the

Symbol of segregation

ALL AFRICANS OVER THE AGE OF SIXTEEN *were compelled by law to carry a passbook issued by the Native Affairs Department. The pass stated where the bearer lived, who their chief was and whether they had paid the annual poll tax, which was levied only on Africans. White employers, policemen and civil servants could demand to see the pass at any time. Failure to produce one could lead to arrest and a heavy fine or even to imprisonment.*

CROUCHED OVER SLATES (RIGHT) *black schoolchildren struggled to gain a basic education without the facilities and funding enjoyed by young white children.*

BURNING INJUSTICE (BELOW) *Black protesters in 1961 defied the law by setting fire to their passbooks.*

poor-quality education given to their children, the restrictions on where they could live and what they could own, and above all the assumption that they were innately inferior to the white race.

In the townships into which black people had been herded a new wave of protest erupted in 1976. The latest grievance was the government's declaration that African children should be taught in Afrikaans instead of in English. Magdeline Choshane was at school at the time. 'Afrikaans was difficult as a subject,' she points out. 'We couldn't imagine having to do subjects such as history converted into *histidones*, or mathematics as *verskinde*. So we had to indicate that we didn't want Afrikaans. Initially our aim was not to destroy – the aim was a peaceful demonstration.'

VIOLENCE ERUPTS (ABOVE) *in Soweto in June 1976. Rioters used cars as roadblocks against the police, who retaliated by using firearms. The uprising triggered riots and student boycotts across South Africa.*

MOURNING THE MURDER *of Stephen Biko, supporters turn their grief into anger and energy. 'Don't mourn – mobilize!' became the rallying cry. Biko made a powerful impact on rebellious young South Africans such as Alaim Zende: 'They were preaching black consciousness, and this was the only power that appealed to us....We understood that we were being oppressed and we had to fight,' he recalls.*

In June 1976 students from Orlando high school in Soweto took to the streets to protest against being taught in Afrikaans. Soweto was a township that had swollen in size until it became a huge, impoverished African city, dwarfing nearby Johannesburg. Thousands more young people took to the streets. Suddenly the police fired tear gas to disperse them. Eric Rothele was among the crowd. 'We didn't understand what tear gas was. Tempers flared. We started throwing stones at the police.' Nomathamsanqua Koha saw what happened next. 'The children were running around, running away. The policemen were pointing guns at them, and we were shouting, "Hey! Stop it, stop it!" ' Twenty-five people were killed that day. Before the year ended a further 284 people had been killed and 2000 more wounded.

In 1977 Stephen Biko, an African youth leader, died in police custody after being tortured and beaten. By this time a new generation of Africans, bolder and more impatient with their elders' fatalistic endurance of apartheid, had concluded that violent rebellion was the only answer. With the ANC now committed to

ABORIGINALS AND MAORIS FIGHT BACK

IT WAS NOT ONLY in South Africa that the lives of the original peoples of the country were disrupted by the arrival of Europeans. In Australia and New Zealand, too, domination by whites brought discrimination and a long struggle against it.

The Aboriginals of Australia did not understand the European concept of land ownership, believing that they belonged to the land rather than that the land belonged to them. When British settlers arrived in Australia from 1788 they took what land they wanted, by force if necessary. Conflict and European diseases, to which the Aboriginals had little resistance, took their toll: the native population shrank from about 350 000 in the late eighteenth century to 40 000 by 1961.

As a society modelled on the West developed in Australia, the Aboriginals suffered increasing legal and social discrimination. They were herded into land reservations and denied the right to continue their semi-nomadic way of life; their culture was suppressed, and eclipsed by Western values; and they were denied many of the benefits enjoyed by the white settlers – good housing, health care and education.

By the 1960s some strong Aboriginal leaders were beginning to emerge who publicized the plight of their people, and forced the issue of land rights to the fore. It was not until 1962 that Aboriginals were able to vote in all elections; they appeared in the census for the first time in 1971. By 1975 public opinion had forced the government to set up the Land Fund Commission, which bought land and restored it to Aboriginals.

A similar movement took place in New Zealand, where about 200 000 Maoris lived when European settlement began in the early nineteenth century. The Maori chiefs had ceded New Zealand to Britain by the treaty of Waitangi in 1840. In return, they were guaranteed possession of their lands, forests and fisheries, and granted the same rights as British citizens. These rights were not always respected, and by the beginning of the twentieth century conflicts over land and the effects of European diseases had reduced the Maori population to some 42 000.

The Maoris began to recover their population and their rights only gradually. Some measure of self-government was gained before the First World War, and their cultural identity was strengthened by a new Maori religious movement, the Ratana Church. But it was not until 1935 that the Maoris could gain from welfare reforms in education, social benefits and land settlement. By the 1970s the Maori population had grown to 400 000, and a radical group of young Maoris, frustrated by the slow pace of change, embarked on a hard-hitting campaign to highlight their cause.

CAMPAIGNING FOR LAND RIGHTS *An Aboriginal protester wearing his protest on his T-shirt, depicting Ayers Rock in Australia. 'You are on Aboriginal land', it declared.*

"Many of those people were wanted for criminal activity...it struck me that it wasn't so much the political person that was rising up against the police but a person with a lot of grudges...lack of opportunity, lack of jobs, lack of decent housing...all those things that people want."

DAVID BRUCE

FIGHTING TO RESTORE ORDER *during the rioting in Soweto, white policemen try to arrest ringleaders among the protesting students. The ANC organizers joined the protest. Mass funerals for the victims of the violence later became further rallying points for resistance.*

armed struggle, some of them went abroad, to train as soldiers who would return to South Africa to fight for freedom. Alaim Zemde went to Angola. 'I didn't have a chance to say goodbye,' he remembers. 'My parents wouldn't have understood that I had to leave, because they thought I was very young, that I wouldn't be able to survive where I was going. So I arranged with some of my friends to come to my home, and I passed some of my clothes through the window. Then I told my parents that we were going to the cinema to watch a film. That's how I left home.'

Nomphiti Radebe went even farther from home – to the Soviet Union. 'We went to the armoury,' he recalls, 'to see the famous AK-47 and to learn the automatic and single-shot fires. We were all looking forward to going to the shooting range to use the weapon ourselves.' Many of the young rebels felt they were on a mission from God. 'I felt like Jesus,' recalls Alaim Zemde. 'I was coming to preach the word of liberation, and giving people the means of liberating themselves....Our presence really gave our people hope. This gun in my hand was my Bible.'

The government responded to the growing violence in the townships with a massive display of force. 'The police were always outnumbered,' remembers David Bruce, now a colonel in the police force. 'It meant you had to use firearms.' When tear gas and smoke grenades failed to disperse the crowds, rubber bullets were fired; when the police were fired on, they fired back with live ammunition. In Cape Town in 1985 young priests led a protest march. One of them was Michael Weeder. 'We were given two minutes to disperse,' he recalls. 'There were thousands behind us. We knelt down to pray. We were singing, "Our Father who art in heaven, hallowed be Thy Name". We didn't get any farther than that. We were about to sing, "Thy kingdom come, Thy will be done", when they were among us. I saw a nun being battle charged. The policeman was grinning as he hit her across the breast. They came with their dogs. They shot tear gas, they beat us up.'

The road to change

By the late 1980s the violence had escalated in the townships, not only between white policemen and black people, but also between supporters of the ANC and Zulu members of Inkatha, the Zulu movement headed by Chief Mangosuthu Buthelezi. To contain the violence, a state of emergency was declared in thirty-six South African districts. With the country now diplomatically isolated, many whites began to realize that South Africa could not continue with minority rule and apartheid, in defiance of the rest of the world. The economic sanctions that had been imposed by the international community harmed black Africans most of all, but together with anti-apartheid demonstrations in the West they did put extra pressure on the government to yield. The fears of white South Africans that they would be submerged by a communist revolution directed from Moscow were allayed when communism collapsed in Eastern Europe in 1989.

In September that year the parliamentary elections in South Africa were followed by a general strike in which three million

MY FREEDOM IS YOUR FREEDOM *Students demanding the release of Nelson Mandela demonstrate in Cape Town in 1988. Without the release of Nelson Mandela, the road to change remained blocked.*

CELEBRATING FREEDOM
Nelson Mandela addressing the audience at a concert held in his honour in London in April 1990, which was televised worldwide. He thanked all those opposed to apartheid who had worked for the release of political prisoners and had supported measures to end oppression in South Africa.

*"*G*oing to the voting booth was like going to a very private chapel. There was an element of great joy in knowing that this was the burial of something very evil. "*

MICHAEL WEEDER

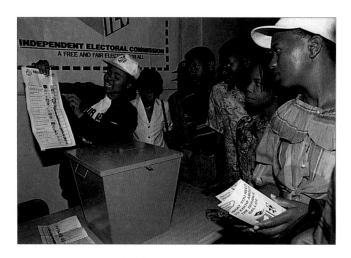

SOUTH AFRICA'S NEW VOTERS (ABOVE) *were offered special tuition to guide them through the voting procedure. The ballot paper listed each party, giving its symbol and a photograph of its leader. Nomathamsanqua Koha (*ABOVE LEFT*), now a hospital matron, began to believe after Nelson Mandela's release that change really might be possible. She was thrilled to be able to cast her vote for the first time.*

QUEUEING TO VOTE (OPPOSITE) *For the first time in their lives, black South Africans line up outside a polling station to cast their vote. A few practical problems with misplaced ballots and pirate voting stations did not diminish the excitement of election day.*

blacks stopped work. It was one of the country's largest protests ever. As more white people joined the protests, pressure for reform intensified. By the time F. W. de Klerk (who as education minister had unleashed the Soweto rebellion by imposing Afrikaans on African schoolchildren) became state president, the demand for action could no longer be ignored, and the worst excesses of apartheid began to be dismantled. On 11 February 1990 he lifted the bans on the ANC and other political organizations, and made an announcement that no one expected to hear: 'I wish to put it plainly that the government has taken a firm decision to release Mr Mandela unconditionally.'

The whole nation was watching on television as the arch-enemy of apartheid, aged seventy-three, made his first appearance for twenty-seven years. 'The day when Mandela was released,' one old miner remembers, 'nobody ate food in the house. Everybody was very, very, very happy – nobody felt like cooking.' Albertina Sisulu's husband Walter Sisulu had already been released. 'Sometimes,' she says, 'when you are excited it is accompanied by tears. It was just like that: it was mixed. You could feel the tears coming, and the joy stopped the tears.'

It took years of complex, tense negotiations between Nelson Mandela, F. W. de Klerk and the other parties before a route could be agreed to introduce one man, one vote, and a new parliament in which the black majority could exercise power. The first free, multiracial, democratic general election in South Africa took place on 27 April 1994. When the great day came, queues of people waiting patiently for their turn to vote stretched across the veldt and through the streets of the townships. Nomathamsanqua Koha describes her emotions. 'You went in, and when I was behind that screen I said, "I'm voting! Me! Voting!" I could hardly believe it. And you say, "Where is the ANC? I mustn't make a mistake. My 'X' must really go in the space provided"....It was wonderful!'

Long before the election results came in it was clear that the ANC would form the next government, and on 10 May 1994 Nelson Mandela became president. It would be a long fight to gain economic equality and equal access to education, housing and jobs, but at least all South Africans, of whatever colour, were now equal before the law, and state racism had finally been overturned.

Endangered Planet

CAMPAIGNING FOR THE ENVIRONMENT

THE MOST AWE-INSPIRING experience in space for the astronaut James Lovell came in December 1968 aboard *Apollo 8*. As the spacecraft first orbited the moon he put his thumb against the window and found that he was able to conceal the entire earth behind it. 'Now you had to think about that for a little bit,' he reflects. 'It gave you a feeling of just how insignificant we are on earth compared to the rest of the universe.' Later, as the spacecraft began its long journey back home, 'The earth came out of the horizon – and it was earthrise'. The astronauts' powerfully vivid photographs of the fragile planet floating in the darkness of space were brought to people around the world.

Richard Ayres, a law student living in the United States, was one of them. 'We were the first kids to see pictures of our planet taken by another human being. It made us feel how small the planet was.' For Bonnie Campbell, who grew up in the polluted industrial Midwest, seeing the earth was a turning point. 'You were watching TV, and here is a picture of the earth looking back at the earth. Here's a living planet, and the blue ocean,' she recalls. 'It really made you think, "Here we are; maybe this is the only place in the whole universe where life can exist, so let's take better care of it".'

The *Apollo 8* photographs fixed an image and caught a mood; they helped to focus attention on the earth and on its vulnerability as the dangers associated with industrial pollution became more evident. People's concern about environmental issues, which grew throughout the 1960s, was heightened in the following decades by a series of unnatural disasters and disturbing new discoveries.

Governments, politicians and industrialists were forced to listen as people around the world began to take direct action, joining new groups dedicated to protecting the environment and participating in mass protests. As local threats to the planet's health assumed global proportions, these people's commitment helped to spread a new awareness of the dangers of uncontrolled commercial exploitation.

EARTHRISE *Seen beyond the surface of the moon, the image of the fragile earth inspires a new environmental awareness.*

> "*We had no concern about industrial waste...there was no environmental ethic at that time. We were concerned and preoccupied with developing our industrial base and having jobs. The environmental concern was largely irrelevant because it was not even thought of.*"

CARL BAGGE

WASTED WATERS *of Minamata Bay, heavily polluted with over 600 tonnes of methyl mercury by the Chisso Corporation, were no longer safe for fishing. Hiroki Iwamoto was among the many local fishermen and fishmongers who were forced out of business. 'Our lives have always depended on the sea. The sea – which should be a great treasure for us to pass on to future generations – is damaged and we have lost our livelihood,' he says. 'My anger is beyond expression.'*

DIRTY BUSINESS (OPPOSITE, TOP) *Toshio Hanada, a resident of Minamata Bay, surveys the unhealthy scene of the huge Chisso factory complex from the top of a nearby hill. 'In those days, smoke and toxic gases would pour out of the factory,' he remembers. 'Even in the middle of spring, the lovely green leaves would turn yellow and the hill would become almost bald.' Smoking chimneys were a familiar feature of industrial landscapes everywhere.*

The dilemma of development

One of the first sinister episodes to prompt people's questioning of scientific progress took place in a little fishing port on the south coast of Japan. In the middle 1950s Japan was just beginning to rebuild its mighty industrial machine. A new factory belonging to the Chisso Corporation, a chemical company, had been built on the shores of Minamata Bay, where the fishermen continued to take their boats out on to the water to fish for octopus, squid, and other species of fish and shellfish as they had always done.

The first sign that anything was wrong came when the other fish-eaters of Minamata, the cats, began to behave in an odd way, staggering with what the fishermen and their families called 'dancing cat disease'. And then they died. Soon humans also began to be affected. Tsuginori Hamamoto had fished with his father since he was a child. At night they cooked bait made from wheat bran and dried bugs, and in the morning carried the heavy pots of bait down to the boat. But one morning Tsuginori Hamamoto stumbled and fell. 'I put the yoke back on my shoulders and put the bait-baskets back on the yoke, but as soon as I reached the beach I fell over again. Finally I realized what was happening: my whole body was trembling and numb.'

As more and more fishermen became ill, doctors from the local university came and filmed their shaking fits. They suspected that the cause was metal poisoning. Before long, babies were being born partially paralysed and suffering from other birth defects. Eventually it became clear that the disease was caused by methyl mercury discharged into the sea from waste pipes by the Chisso factory. The mercury entered the food chain: it was absorbed by the plankton on which the fish fed, and then by the cats and the humans who ate the fish. It damaged the nervous system, affecting people's ability to talk, see, hear and walk. Contamination from the fish eaten by pregnant women was absorbed by their unborn babies, causing severe brain damage. Soon no one would buy the fish at the local market. People's livelihood, long dependent upon the sea, was under threat.

At first the Chisso Corporation denied all responsibility. Tests confirmed that mercury was the cause of 'Minamata disease', but the company covered up the results. Hidenori Yamashita

worked in the Chisso laboratory at the time. 'The management didn't give a damn about pollution or about the environment, and the workers didn't give a damn either, and even if someone did they were just ignored.' Besides, he adds, 'Chisso helped the town a lot. People thought they might as well put up with it'. As the company continued to dump its highly toxic waste into the bay during the next ten years, more than seventy people died as a result of the poison, and thousands more suffered from its effects.

During the 1950s many people throughout the industrial world regarded smoke and dirt as an inseparable part of industry and progress – a price that had to be paid for the security of a job. Carl Bagge grew up next to a steel plant in northern Indiana. 'We accepted this as part of life in industrial America – the stench, the smoke, the absolute filth that filled our lungs. We thought this was the way life was, the way God intended, and the way prosperous America could survive.'

HIDENORI YAMASHITA
and his colleagues in the Chisso laboratory tested the water to try to prove that Chisso was innocent of the accusations made against it by the local press. 'One of my colleagues was in charge of the experiment that found poisonous mercury in the sludge,' he recalls. 'I saw it with my own eyes.'

Catalyst for change

In the United States many people could now afford to buy new consumer goods – domestic appliances that used more electricity, and cars that consumed more oil and polluted the atmosphere. Electricity was generated by nuclear reactors in new atomic power stations, and scientists countered public fears of radioactive fallout with assurances of their safety. On the land too, science offered progress in the form of agricultural chemicals, which were widely used during the 1950s. For farmers, new pesticides such as DDT offered an effective method for controlling pests, and so helped to increase crop yields. But the chemicals could kill birds as well as insects, and pollute land and streams as well helping crops to grow.

Trust in scientific progress was challenged in 1962 with the publication of a book entitled *Silent Spring*. Its author, the American biologist Rachel Carson, argued that far from being a harmless blessing, pesticides were inflicting irreparable damage on the environment. 'Unless we bring these chemicals under better control,' she proclaimed, 'we are certainly heading for disaster.' She asked whether anyone could believe it was possible 'to lay down such a barrage of poisons on the surface of the earth without making it unfit for all life'.

Despite attempts by industry and by science to deny and discredit her warning message, Rachel Carson succeeded in shaking public confidence and alerting the American people to the hazards of chemical pollution. Her prophetic book became a best-seller, and made many people aware of the way in which uncritical scientists in the service of business or government might damage the environment. At about this time Walt Patterson, a Canadian living in Britain, decided to become involved in campaigns to protect it. 'We thought things were getting out of hand,' he recalls. 'We thought that the people who were supposed to be in charge weren't in charge, they were actively aggravating the problems.' As public concern grew, an investigation into the dangerous side-effects of DDT and other pesticides was launched.

By this time petrochemicals had become the lifeblood of the modern world. The oil needed to power factories, fuel the growing number of vehicles and heat homes was being shipped across the seas from the Middle East and other oilfields in huge

SMOG SCREEN *Breathing problems were one of the consequences of the grey smog familiar to Londoners; it grew worse during the 1950s as traffic emissions increased. Some pedestrians covered their faces to protect their lungs from the thick smog – a mixture of smoke, fog and chemical fumes. After some 4000 Londoners died as a result of respiratory and heart problems in 1952, the British government passed a Clean Air Act.*

supertankers. In March 1967 the *Torrey Canyon*, fully laden with 120 000 tonnes of crude oil, hit the rocks off the south-west coast of England. Nothing like it had ever happened before. At first bombs were dropped in the hope of burning off the oil. Jonathan Tod, a British pilot, was part of the mission. As he flew south over the Scottish border, 'Looking up ahead of us we could see a large black cloud going up to at least thirty thousand feet...it made one realize very clearly the magnitude of the task that we had to undertake and the potential hazard that it could become for the environment as a whole. What we had there was in many ways an environmental time bomb,' he recalls. As his bombs hit the tanker, he saw a huge billow of smoke and a bright red flame leaping 300 metres (1000 feet) into the air.

The bombing did not succeed in burning off all the thick oil from the ship; it was washed onto the nearby beaches, polluting the water and sand, killing fish, shrimps, oysters and other forms of marine life, and fouling the seabirds. People moved by the plight of the birds struggled to rescue them. Olga Penrose was one of hundreds of volunteers who did their best to clean them. 'You looked in a box, and it

CLEAN-UP CAMPAIGN (BELOW) *on the coast of Brittany, where 100 km (60 miles) of beaches were affected by the* Torrey Canyon *oil spill. Volunteers such as Olga Penrose* (BOTTOM) *worked hard to rescue the oil-soaked seabirds.*

DISASTER AT SEA (LEFT) *A column of black smoke pours from the* Torrey Canyon, *the first super-tanker to run aground, and the first of many oil spills. Walt Patterson remembers it well: 'It was an image that was burned into the brains of people...that the industrial reliance on oil brought with it the possibility of this kind of environmental catastrophe.'*

"Earthday gave people all over the country an opportunity for the first time to express their concern, which they did in huge numbers. **"**

GAYLORD NELSON

EGG CURATOR *Lloyd Kiff made dedicated efforts to rescue the pelicans' fragile eggs on the island of Anacapa from reproductive failure as a result of DDT. It had taken some twenty years for the full extent of the damage caused by the pesticide to emerge.*

was a ball of tar and a beak sticking through. You literally had to scrape this ball of tar off until you got to the actual bird, and that was really horrific. You knew that the oil was burning the bird, so you tried to get it off as quickly as possible. It made you feel so inadequate, and very angry, to think that man had done this.'

The fate of a group of brown pelicans at Anacapa, an island off the Californian coast, brought yet more alarming evidence of the harmful nature of chemicals, though this time the cause was less visible. Lloyd Kiff was a member of an expedition sent to discover why the pelicans at Anacapa were not breeding. He climbed the steep cliffs to the pelican colony on the uninhabited island. 'It was an absolutely perfect scene, the gulls in the air screaming, the wind blowing, the ocean breeze, and five hundred pairs of pelicans, their nests all adorned with flowers. An untouched island. And then we looked into nests and all the nests contained broken eggs. And in that whole season, where there were twelve hundred nesting attempts by pelicans, they produced only two young,' he remembers. 'This was a horrifying scene to us. I can't describe how moved we were, that something so insidious could be changing the world like this.'

Lloyd Kiff had been aware of Rachel Carson's book, and he knew that DDT was now banned in several European countries, in Canada and in the North American state of Wisconsin. He also knew that when it entered the food chain DDT caused a decrease in eggshell weight. DDT had never been used on Anacapa itself, but minute traces of it had found their way from distant rivers into the pelicans' food chain, making the shells of their eggs too thin to bear the weight of the parent birds during incubation. It was just as Rachel Carson had predicted.

It was becoming clear that many of the products of modern industry – aerosols, fertilizers, pesticides, petrochemicals and other substances – were causing not just local problems but a threat to the whole planet. Maurice Strong, a Canadian industrialist with a deep commitment to environmental issues, sensed the changing mood: 'Industrial activities were giving rise to local air and water pollution, and residents were…increasingly sensitive to it. People saw some of their favourite recreational places – beaches, natural areas – being desecrated, waters being contaminated.'

CHEMICAL KILLERS *such as the DDT being sprayed in this orchard in northern Italy were at first hugely beneficial to farmers, but they were environmentally disastrous. As insects built up resistance to DDT it accumulated in their body tissues, and was passed on to predators. DDT was later banned in many countries.*

VISION OF THE FUTURE
A young demonstrator at Earthday in New York in 1970 adopts a gas mask as a symbolic warning message of the implications of continued urban air pollution for people and their environment.

A grass-roots movement

The growing concern for the environment was first shown on a national scale in the United States on 22 April 1970. Denis Hayes was one of the organizers of the demonstrations held on that day. 'Earthday was the most massive outpouring of human beings that had ever surrounded any issue up to that time,' he remembers. 'We had twenty million Americans drawn from all walks of life, turning out in these huge events in every major city and most of the minor hamlets across the country, to protest the direction that the world seemed to be headed.'

Earthday was devised and organized by Gaylord Nelson. 'I was creating an event in which the people at the grass roots could participate on their own,' he says. 'It worked because the grass roots responded and was interested and concerned.' Helped by the immense participation of the American public and the wide media coverage that it received, Earthday marked the beginning of the people's environmental movement, forcing the issue onto the agenda of American politics. The United States president, Richard Nixon, could sense the pressure. The great question of the 1970s, he told the nation, was 'Shall we make peace with nature, and begin to make reparations for the damage we have done to our air, our land, and to our water?' He announced the establishment of an Environmental Protection Agency, and persuaded a willing Congress to enact a Clean Air Act. An advertisement featuring American Indians echoed his pronouncement. 'Some people have a deep, abiding respect for the natural beauty that was once this country,' it ran, 'and some people don't. People started pollution, people can stop it.'

By the 1970s, people's new awareness of the dangers, and their impatience with the reluctance to act of industries and governments, was no longer confined to the United States. In India, educated campaigners for the protection of the environment joined voices with villagers concerned at the danger to their livelihoods posed by the pollution of forest, land and water. In Japan there was an equally new mood among the people of Minamata Bay. They had formed an association to take action against the company that had consistently denied responsibility for their plight. Still partly paralysed, Tsuginori

MAKING WAVES

I N 1971 A SMALL GROUP of men and women decided to join forces to oppose nuclear weapons testing by the United States in the Aleutian islands, west of Alaska. Twelve volunteers, armed with cameras and tape recorders, hired a small boat and sailed to the test site in the North Pacific. The resulting media attention triggered a tidal wave of concern over the testing, rallying public support for their cause. More than 177 000 people signed a telegram of protest that was nearly a kilometre long and took four days to transmit to the White House. Although one bomb was eventually detonated, the rest of the test series was cancelled. Robert Hunter took part in that first mission. 'As far as we knew it was the first time the anti-war and the environmental movements had found a common cause – thus the name Greenpeace.'

The Greenpeace movement began as an informal committee with few resources. 'There was virtually nothing, there wasn't a single typewriter, there wasn't an office, people just met in each other's living rooms or basements,' recalls Robert Hunter. 'There was nothing except everybody's common desire.' The

movement quickly grew, its campaigners seeking, among other goals, a worldwide ban on nuclear testing and an end to the dumping of dangerous waste at sea. Small groups of protesters, following a guideline of 'direct, non-violent action', risked their own safety by plugging industrial pipes to prevent the flow of toxic waste, spray-painting seal pups to render their fur worthless, and challenging large whaling ships in small dinghies. One American volunteer, Patty Hutchison, boarded a Japanese whaler in the Pacific Ocean, made her way to the massive harpoon, chained and padlocked herself to it and then, in full view of the ship's crew, threw the keys overboard. 'If you saw an injustice you could try to stop it,' she says. 'A small group of people, or even one individual, could make a difference.'

By 1995 Greenpeace had become one of the world's largest non-governmental organizations (NGOs) with a fleet of sea vessels, a research station in Antarctica, a steadily growing membership of five million people and a network of bases in thirty countries around the world. It offered a public forum for people who as individuals might have gone unheard, but collectively exercised increasing influence.

PRESSURE GROUPS such as Friends of the Earth, founded in Britain in 1971, and Greenpeace attracted widespread international support; they produced their own publications as well as organizing demonstrations.

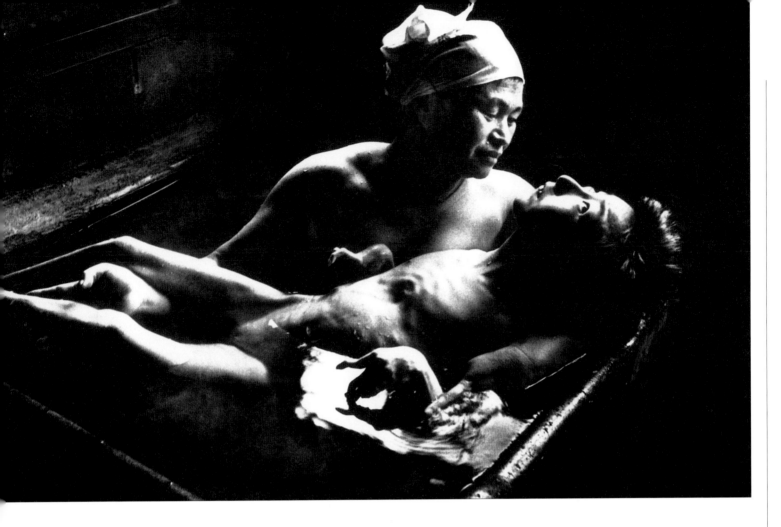

Hamamoto, the fisherman who had been one of the first to be poisoned, led a group of victims trying to reach a settlement. 'It was very tough, though we had doctors looking after us. They gave us injections and medicines while we stayed up all night negotiating with Chisso. We were exhausted, and felt absolutely disgusted with Chisso's uncompromising attitude,' he remembers. Under intense public pressure, the company was finally forced to make concessions. Its president performed the *dogeza*, bowing down to the ground in a formal gesture of submission, an act that would once have been inconceivable for a powerful Japanese industrialist.

Representatives from Minamata were invited to the first international conference on the environment, organized by the United Nations and held in June 1972. Delegates from more than a hundred countries met in Stockholm to describe and debate the damage that was being inflicted in and to their own countries. The meeting was chaired by Maurice Strong. 'This issue came from the grass roots,' he reflects. 'The issue of the environment really came from the growing perceptions of people that their lives were

THE CRIPPLING CONSEQUENCES *of Chisso's dumping of toxic waste were visible to all in the fate of Japan's thousands of poison victims. Born brain-damaged, deformed and unable to see or talk, one young sufferer* (ABOVE) *is bathed by her mother. Their plight helped to stimulate public outrage. Angry demonstrators in Tokyo* (BELOW) *demand justice from the company, which eventually yielded in 1971, awarding 664 million yen ($5 million) in compensation to the victims and their families after a fifteen-year battle.*

FOREST OF DOOM

Clearing forested areas helped many developing countries to reduce population pressure and economic difficulties by freeing land for farming and ranching, and providing timber for the world market. But as rich and delicate self-sustaining forest ecosystems were destroyed, the exposed soil became vulnerable to drought and erosion, endangering the survival of countless species of animals and plants as well as of indigenous forest peoples.

being impacted....Politicians didn't perceive this and then inform their people that this was a problem...it was quite the other way, this was always a people-based issue.'

As a result of the Stockholm conference, the United Nations Environment Programme (UNEP) and several national environmental agencies were established to monitor pollution levels and implement new policies. Popular involvement was still needed to effect change, as Anil Agarwal, a young Indian writer attending the conference, recalls. 'I did not come back with the impression that it was governments who were taking the issue very seriously.' He did have 'a very strong impression that the younger generation in Europe was taking it very seriously. Essentially it gave me the feeling of a new form of democracy beginning to emerge.'

EMBRACING THE FOREST

In THE HIMALAYAS, source of India's sacred river Ganges, villagers took a direct part in a campaign to preserve their livelihoods and their surroundings. For thousands of years the people, plants and animals of the forest lived in harmony, the mixed forest supporting wildlife and protecting the steep mountain slopes from the eroding impact of heavy rain, the local people taking from the forest what they needed without over-exploiting its resources and disturbing its fragile ecological balance. Like other forest dwellers, their way of life depended on trees to provide them with the raw materials for their tools and homes, and to supply food for themselves and their animals.

The forests became government property under British colonial rule, and were regarded more as a commercial resource to be exploited than as life-sustaining habitats. The programme of deforestation was accelerated after India's independence. Much of the remaining forest was 'developed' into cash-yielding pine plantations. Pine needles could not offer the umbrella-like protection of broad-leaved trees, which reduced the impact of falling rain. The result was torrents, flash floods and even landslides as the water ran rapidly down the bare hillsides. Within a century, the stability that had been sustained over thousands of years was being destroyed.

The peasant women living in the foothills of the Himalayas, whose job it was to collect essential fuel, water and fodder for their animals, were worst affected by the changes. In 1973, when the forestry department allocated the Chamoli district's ash trees – from which the villagers made their tools – to a large commercial company, they decided to take a stand. Inspired by Mahatma Gandhi's methods of non-violent resistance, the women flung their arms round the trees, shielding them with their bodies and challenging the woodmen from the logging companies to use their axes. The woodmen could not get past the Chipko (literally 'tree-hugging') people, and left without felling a single tree.

Inspired by this initial success, other villagers also began to resist, and the Chipko movement quickly gained momentum. Within five years it spread to eight districts in the Himalayas, covering an area of 51 000 square kilometres (19 700 square miles) with a population of nearly five million people. The landslides of 1978, which affected villages up to 500 km (310 miles) downstream, alerted the government to the scale of the destruction in the Himalayas, and helped to convince them that decades of rest and rehabilitation were now needed. A complete ban on the commercial felling of trees was imposed.

Although most of its initial demands had been met, the Chipko movement did not die out. Its intensive campaigning continued to spread environmental awareness in the region. Anil Agarwal, an Indian journalist, remembers, 'When the Chipko movement came in it gave us a very clear message, that if you destroy the environment you will inevitably create social injustice by affecting the survival base of the poor.' With the support of the Chipko movement, local people turned their energies to reforestation, continuing to play an active part in ensuring a future for the forest and for their descendants.

HUGGING THE TREES (RIGHT) *in non-violent defiance to protect them from loggers in the Himalayas. Although at first it was mostly women who took the lead, men joined the Chipko movement too. Its success inspired similar ecological movements in other parts of India as well as in Australia and the United States.*

Acting for the environment

New environmental pressure groups were being established that were concerned with wider ethical issues such as nuclear testing, the waste of natural resources and the treatment of animals. One of the issues tackled at the UN conference was the problem of species whose survival was being threatened by the continuing exploitation of wildlife. Many species of whale, for centuries hunted and slaughtered in huge numbers for their blubber, meat and oil, were now facing extinction. There were once so many blue whales that 100 000 of them were caught every year in the southern Pacific and Antarctic oceans by the factory ships of Japan, Norway, the Soviet Union and elsewhere. Yet in 1970 only twenty-three blue whales could be found. At the UN conference there were calls for a ban on the killing of certain species, but the international commission representing the whaling countries continued to allow the slaughter.

Now the Greenpeace movement adopted the whale as its new mascot, and decided to tackle what governments were failing to achieve. One of its early members, Robert Hunter, was sent as a reporter to cover Greenpeace activities; he stayed to become an activist, and led a Greenpeace expedition that tracked down Soviet whalers in the Pacific. The activists tried to get between the whale and the harpoon by using themselves as human shields. 'As these were 250-pound explosive harpoons with a steel cable we were obviously at risk,' he remembers.

Action was needed not just to prevent the possibility of new threats but also to force the authorities to rectify their past mistakes. Poisonous waste carelessly dumped in rivers, lakes and under ground all over Europe and the United States was now threatening the communities living nearby. At Love Canal, an industrial suburb in upstate New York, the Hooker Chemicals Company had buried 20 000 tonnes of highly toxic waste between 1942 and 1953 in the land surrounding the plant. A school was built on the landfill site, and a residential neighbourhood around it. Barbara Quimby grew up nearby. 'The chemicals and vapours would fill your house...it became unbearable in there....It would make you cough and choke and you'd have burning eyes, but it was just something people were used to, that's just how we lived.'

WASTE NOT WANT NOT *Recycling and conservation joined the environmental agenda. When the leading British drinks manufacturer, Schweppes, announced plans to abolish returnable drinks bottles in 1971, a small band of people from the new Friends of the Earth group dumped 15 000 empty bottles outside their London headquarters in a challenging media stunt.*

DEMONSTRATING THEIR CONCERN (OPPOSITE) *for whales at a Greenpeace protest rally in Glasgow, men and women of all ages take to the streets with badges and banners in a determined effort to stop the slaughter of whales.*

EXPORTING POLLUTION

SOME OF THE WORST environmental conditions in the Americas developed within a few kilometres of the United States–Mexico border. Dangerous chemicals leached into the soil, polluting water supplies and exposing people on the Mexican side of the border to metal poisoning and other serious health hazards. Yet the underlying cause of these problems was a process that boosted the Mexican economy.

From 1965 numerous foreign-owned factories were established in the border area. Most of these were run by American manufacturing companies taking advantage of low Mexican wage rates and avoiding the cost of increasingly stringent health, safety and environmental standards in the United States. The factory assembly plants, known as *maquiladoras*, imported components to be assembled into finished products such as cars, televisions and clothing for sale back to the United States, in foreign markets and later in Mexico itself. The reduced running costs enabled such companies to compete with low-cost Asian producers, while the Mexicans benefited from American technology and marketing expertise.

The *maquiladoras* provided badly needed jobs for hundreds of thousands of people. Despite low wages, there was never a shortage of labour, with hundreds of people arriving every day from all over Mexico, eager for a chance to work in an American factory. But the pollution of air, land and water and the degrading living conditions in the nearby shantytowns exacted a terrible toll. The growing number of people suffering from birth defects and rare cancers provided living proof of the serious damage being inflicted.

The explosion of the Mexican *maquiladora* industry was just part of the growing flight of heavily polluting industries from the developed to the developing world, the undoubted short-term economic advantages of these collaborations blinding both rich and poor nations to their potential human cost.

CONDITIONS OF LIFE *for the Mexican* maquiladoras *workers, housed in settlements often without proper sanitation or rubbish disposal, could be even more unhealthy than conditions within the workplace. Yet people living here were fortunate compared with those living in the disease-ridden shantytowns.*

In the late 1970s the steel drums containing the factory's waste began to rust, and the poison they contained seeped out. Children were burned after playing with explosive phosphorous rocks in the streets, and the rubber soles of their sneakers dissolved in the chemicals on the playground. The local postman drew attention to the dangers by wearing a gas mask to deliver the mail.

When Lois Gibbs moved to Love Canal with her healthy one-year-old son she thought she was buying into the American dream. 'That consists of a husband, a child, a house, a station wagon, a dog, a white picket fence. I had all of those things, and that's what I wanted to do: be a full-time homemaker, raise my children, take care of my husband.' Within five years her son had developed epilepsy, a liver disease, a urinary tract disorder and severe asthma. She decided to do something about it, and grew 'from a very shy individual to a very angry woman. My goals changed, my priorities changed...no longer did I care whether my floors were clean'.

The Love Canal residents, led by Lois Gibbs, organized themselves into a group and set out to persuade the government to relocate them to new homes. After resistance and repeated delays from state authorities and politicians, the women decided to take direct action. They took hostage several officials from the government's Environmental Protection Agency. Lois Gibbs called the White House and said, 'I'm calling to tell you we're holding these Federal officials hostage and we're not going to let them go until you release the Love Canal residents from these poisons'. She  gave them a deadline, noon the following Wednesday. 'At noon I was sitting by the phone praying – I'm not a big religious person, but I was praying they would call. When the phone rang we all jumped out of our skin. And it was the White House calling to say that all residents at Love Canal could be evacuated.' Nearly a thousand families were evacuated in 1978. Lois Gibbs had learned an important lesson. 'You don't have to be a scientist with a PhD, you don't

LEAVING TOWN (ABOVE) *A father clutches his children during the evacuation of Three Mile Island in Harrisburg, Pennsylvania, following an accident at a nuclear generating plant in 1979. The relocation of families from Love Canal was largely due to the determination of residents like Lois Gibbs* (RIGHT, ABOVE) *who helped to form community associations and organize protest meetings* (RIGHT, BELOW).

have to be wealthy, all you have to be is active,' she says. 'If you take one or two little steps you can change the world.'

By the late 1970s grass-roots campaigns were achieving results all over the Western world. In Europe the Green movement, focusing initially on nuclear energy, acid rain and pollution of the countryside and the rivers, entered mainstream politics. But not everyone benefited from the new environmental legislation. Some people felt threatened by the confrontational new style of those who wanted to save the earth. When a copper-smelting plant at Tacoma in the northwest United States was closed down after fears that it released arsenic into the atmosphere, hundreds of workers found themselves without a job. One of them was Chuck O'Donahue. 'They came, they attacked it and they cost us our livelihood,' he says. 'There are people from the smelter who haven't worked a day since that smelter closed down.'

Carl Bagge, who had been raised in the smoke and grime of Gary, Indiana, later became president of the National Coal Association; he spent twenty years attempting to save the coal industry from environmentalists who wanted to bring change. By the 1970s, he believes, 'This benign environmental ethic had mushroomed into a pervasive religious zealotry'. The government passed environmental legislation that damaged the producers of high-sulphur coal as well as the communities who were dependent on producing it.

Green goods

ENVIRONMENTALLY FRIENDLY *detergents and other household products appeared on many supermarket shelves during the 1980s, as people began to take more care over the effects of the products they used. Some of the names and colours chosen for these consumer products reflected the new environmental ethic. There was also a growing demand for used materials such as glass and paper to be recycled rather than thrown away.*

PLEASE DON'T PANIC! (RIGHT) *advises a banner displayed by protesters outside a nuclear power plant in Germany. As the dangers of radioactivity were more clearly understood, anti-nuclear campaigners became part of the wider effort to protect the environment.*

GREEN POLITICS

THE RELUCTANCE of established political parties to respond to environmental needs led some groups to seek their own political representation. Nearly a million people voted for the new Green party – Die Grünen – in the 1979 federal elections in West Germany. Although this fell short of the 5 per cent of the total vote needed to obtain seats in parliament, the voting did reflect the growing concern for environmental issues. In the 1983 elections the Greens passed the 5 per cent barrier, becoming the first environmental party to win representation in a national government. In another four years more than 8 per cent of the German people voted Green.

During the 1980s people throughout Europe began to look to politicians who would give priority to the environment. Green parties won national parliamentary seats in eight western European countries: Austria, Belgium, Finland, Germany, Italy, Luxembourg, Sweden and Switzerland. In the 1989 elections to the European parliament, too, the people of Belgium, Denmark, France, Germany, the Netherlands and Spain all elected Green party members; their voting system, based on proportional representation, reflected the number of votes cast. In Britain, which has a different voting system, the Green party succeeded in polling 15 per cent of the vote but failed to win a single seat. The electoral successes of Green parties depend upon proportional representation, where the support of individuals is not lost.

Public support for the new Green parties

was viewed with alarm by the major political parties, all of which were losing votes. They began to realize that to regain their voters they would have to include environmental issues in their own agendas. It was the votes of millions of individuals, who showed that for them the dangers to the planet's health were an issue of real importance, that brought environmental policies into mainstream politics.

COLLECTIVE CONCERN *for the environment is the focus of debate at conferences held by the German Green Party, which offered a new channel of hope to many young people. Founded by Herbert Gruhl in 1979, it became a national party the following year.*

For Carl Bagge, 'As a guy fighting for the coal industry it was a total, unmitigated disaster, because all the people who had been lobbying for environmental organizations were now in positions of power, they were the people I had to make my pleas to on behalf of coal. It was awful,' he says ruefully. 'I didn't want to get up to go to work in the morning. These guys were extremists, there was no balance at all.'

BLINDED AT BHOPAL
(ABOVE) *by a toxic leak at a chemical plant, local women wait patiently for treatment to relieve their painfully burning eyes.*

Drumbeat of disasters

The 1980s began with a backlash against the environmental movement, initiated by a new United States president who felt that concern for nature had gone too far. 'There is environmental extremism,' announced Ronald Reagan sceptically. 'I don't think they'll be happy until the White House looks like a bird's nest.' It was a much happier time for Carl Bagge. 'When Reagan came in and we had people that I would say were more balanced – from our standpoint, a balanced point of view,' he recalls, 'I didn't mind getting up in the morning. I would even bounce to work because I was talking to people who would listen to your story.' But a spate of disasters showed that the risks were as great as ever.

There had been leaks of poisonous gas at industrial plants in the past, but nothing could compare with the explosion at the American-owned Union Carbide factory at Bhopal in central India in 1984. The plant was situated in the middle of a poor neighbourhood of the city, and more than 2000 people were killed outright by the poisonous fumes. A further 20 000 were blinded or severely disabled. Eventually, in an out of court settlement between Union Carbide and the Indian government, the company paid $470 million compensation. (The question of responsibility and compensation arose again when the *Exxon Valdez* oil tanker ran aground in Alaska, causing devastating pollution in a pristine wildlife area. The clean-up operation cost Exxon $2 billion and, though nobody was killed, $5 billion in compensation.)

In 1987 there was another explosion at a chemical works, near Basle in Switzerland. Toxic chemicals were washed into the

TOXIC CARGO (RIGHT)
A train crashes in Livingstone, Louisiana in 1982, emitting hazardous smoke into the atmosphere. The risks of storing and transporting potentially dangerous substances increased as industrial production grew.

BUCKETS OF OIL (RIGHT)
are collected by relief workers after the supertanker Amoco Cadiz ran aground on the coast of Brittany, northern France in 1978. It had been carrying twice as much oil as the Torrey Canyon; the oil quickly spread over fishing grounds and oyster beds.

Rhine, and poisoned fish all the way down the river through Germany into the Netherlands. These accidents highlighted the now global effects of environmental damage. Lakes and forests in Canada and northern Europe were dying because of gases from power stations in other countries, hundreds of kilometres away. Pollution could no longer be seen as a local issue.

There was another new danger, one that could not yet be seen, felt or heard. Professor F. Sherwood Roland, a chemist at the University of California at Irvine, was carrying out research into chlorofluorocarbons (CFCs), chemicals widely used in aerosol cans and refrigerators. 'We were proceeding along with essentially an innocent problem, just trying to find out what happens to the CFCs,' he describes. Then he discovered that when the harmless CFCs pass through the ozone layer (a narrow band in the atmosphere that shields the earth from harmful ultraviolet radiation) they break apart. Highly reactive chlorine atoms are released, starting a chain reaction that would ultimately destroy the ozone layer. 'I came home one night,' says Sherwood Roland, 'and my wife asked me how the research was going, and I said, "I think the research is going fine, but it looks like the end of the world".' Satellites soon began to gather evidence establishing that the theory was becoming fact. In 1985 a hole – in fact a dramatic thinning – appeared in the protective ozone layer above Antarctica.

At about the same time scientists discovered that the level of carbon dioxide gas present in the atmosphere was steadily rising, threatening to change global climate patterns through the 'greenhouse effect'. The tens of thousands of hectares of rainforests being burned in Africa, Central and South America and Indonesia were partly to blame; the carbon dioxide released by burning oil, natural gas and coal in the power stations, factories, vehicles and homes of the West was the worst culprit.

Consumption of fossil fuels was rapidly increasing, and the

SUSTAINING A FUTURE

NEW DANGERS and risks continued to emerge in the 1980s, and demands on the earth also continued to increase as populations grew and their aspirations rose. Some people realized that the unlimited exploitation of limited resources could be permanently damaging to the earth.

The idea of sustainable development – managing the earth's resources so that present needs are met in ways that will not prevent future generations from meeting theirs – was introduced in 1980 by the World Commission on Environment and Development. A proposal for how this could be achieved – Agenda 21 – was put forward at the 1992 United Nations Conference on Environment and Development (UNCED) in Rio de Janeiro. It recognized the need for a global alliance to tackle the difficult problems of poverty, development and the environment.

At national and local levels, too, a new attitude began to emerge that encouraged efficiency, self-renewal and conservation alongside economic growth, as awareness grew that the use of recycled materials and renewable sources of natural energy (biomass, geothermal, hydro, solar, tidal and wind power), the reintroduction of traditional methods of farming that would replenish rather than deplete the soil, and the enforcement of restrictions on hunting and fishing, could all contribute to a gradual reversal of long-term ecological decline. Instead of building more power stations, nations could concentrate on ways of saving energy – reducing consumption levels, introducing local energy-sharing schemes, designing cars that consumed less fuel, and insulating buildings.

There were public demands for government initiatives to deter polluters and encourage 'greener' industries that would regulate their economic development in terms of sustainability. In Sweden, where a million people lived in communities devoted to sustainable living, the Natural Step programme established links with industry and education to devise new strategies for environmental change.

The need for sustainable development was also being tackled in the developing world, as countries with rapidly growing populations and few fossil fuel and mineral resources searched for affordable alternatives. By 1995 more than 90 per cent of the energy in Ethiopia, Nepal and Tanzania was supplied by burning vegetable matter, and in Brazil alcohol produced from sugar cane was used to fuel vehicles. The introduction of more efficient cooking stoves led to a 30 per cent saving in fuelwood in Sri Lanka, and reduced Kenya's demand for charcoal by the equivalent of one and a half million tonnes of trees a year. Nepal, a country highly dependent on its natural resources, established a National Planning Commission to integrate the need both for conservation and for development.

Conservation of the natural environment, economic development and the need to solve the problem of rising world population – growing at a rate of some ninety million people a year – could no longer be tackled separately; environmental needs would be met only if the huge problems of hunger and poverty were also addressed. Power elites, military aggression and a global market regulated by profit and competitiveness all raised obstacles to effective sustainable development, which required international agreement and an understanding that the health of the planet could not be separated from the well-being of all the people living on it.

HOLDING ON TO EARTH *A child clutches the hand of a walking exhibit at the Earth Summit that took place in Rio in 1992.*

problem of pollution could no longer be confined to the richer, industrialized nations. In developing countries, especially the nations of Asia, where more than half the world's people lived, there was rapid industrialization, and billions of men and women looked forward to the lifestyle already enjoyed by people in North America, Europe and Japan. To meet their needs would mean more cars and lorries, more power stations and more factories – all discharging more carbon dioxide into the atmosphere.

'We have a real dilemma,' says Maurice Strong. 'On the one hand, we have no right to impose constraints on the developing countries in pursuing their development, we have no right to deny them the right to grow....At the same time, if they follow the path that we followed, it's going to be disastrous for them and for us.' In India Mukesh Gupta, who was manager of a foundry in the outskirts of Delhi, saw the problem in more practical terms. 'About fifty men work in this foundry. Altogether they support probably four hundred people. The livelihood of these families depends on us,' he says. 'I'm sorry if our pollution harms the environment, but you must realize that we have to meet our basic needs.'

The fishing families of Minamata had their own answer to that. The mercury still lay on the seabed; they would never be able to fish in the bay again, and had to take their boats far out to sea to earn their living. Their experience was a microcosm of what was happening all over the world. Popular concern might have forced business and government to acknowledge the dilemma of progress, but the damage continued all the same. In the forty years to 1995 a fifth of all the earth's species of plants and animals either became extinct or were threatened with extinction. Half the rainforests were lost. Thousands of lakes, rivers and coastal areas were poisoned. Tomiji Matsuda, brain-damaged and blinded by the mercury at Minamata, understood the implications, and urged caution: 'I think people must be very careful about progress. It doesn't just bring benefits: it brings danger as well.'

TRYING TO BREATHE
Children in the Czech Republic wearing face masks on their way to school to protect them from the poor air quality. Eastern Europe became one of the world's most polluted regions as a result of rapid industrial development, and many people living there suffered from various pollution-related health problems.

DYING TREES *became common in Europe's forests, where millions of hectares faced destruction from acid rain falling as a result of pollutant gases from industry and vehicles collecting in the atmosphere. The severe damage caused to soils, lakes and rivers in Europe, in Canada and the United States continued to spread farther afield.*

Picture Power

THE IMPACT
OF
TELEVISION

IN FORT WAYNE, INDIANA, Elizabeth Fincher Dobynes had taken the day off work to make Christmas wreaths at home. With one eye she was watching the television set she had bought with her wages as an elevator operator in a local department store. 'Why were they pushing and rushing?' she thought. And then they announced that the president had been shot. 'I dropped everything and I found myself on my knees....I was praying. My eyes were bathed in tears.'

In every corner of the United States the assassination of President John F. Kennedy by Lee Harvey Oswald on 22 November 1963 in Dallas, Texas left an indelible emotional imprint. Within an hour some 90 per cent of Americans had heard the news. Millions of people grieved in front of their televisions as they watched the live coverage that followed. 'I think all our lives were centred round that four days. We watched the funeral and we watched the whole thing from beginning to end,' remembers Marjorie Brandt, who also lived in Fort Wayne. 'It was a very mournful thing to observe, and we realized history was being made and that we were a part of it. That was the beauty of television – we didn't have to read it, we saw it.'

People all around the world were similarly stunned as they shared the immediacy of the news of the president's death. 'It made me realize that the news belonged to television now,' reflects Conrad Frost, who had been a London newspaper journalist for most of his life. 'It didn't belong to newspapers any more. You could never get the impact that you got that night, you could never get that from a newspaper.'

On the day that Kennedy was assassinated, television was just over a quarter of a century old. In the decades that followed, it continued to grow to become the world's preferred source of news, information and entertainment, a giant industry and powerful global medium watched by people everywhere. It was no longer just a spectator or critic of the human drama: increasingly, television was becoming the stage on which a good part of the human drama was played out.

THE UNFORGETTABLE MOMENT *of the assassination of United States President*
John F. Kennedy is caught by the camera to be watched by millions.

An early spectacle

Technically, television had been on its way for a long time. As early as the 1880s scientists in parts of Europe and the United States had been developing the technology to transmit pictures as well as sound. By 1923 John Logie Baird was working on an early television set in London, and two years later the Bell Telephone Laboratories in the United States began research into television. By the end of the 1920s a number of inventors were hard at work on various television systems in Britain, France, Germany, Japan, the Soviet Union and the United States.

The world's first public television service was launched in Britain in 1936, with regular broadcasts of drama, game shows, music and sports programmes. 'At that time,' remembers Conrad Frost, who was one of the first people to buy a television set, 'people who had television regarded it as cinema. You put all the lights off to watch it, you had a special room for it – it was the television room.' Early televisions were designed as a piece of furniture and sold as complete cabinets that contained radios as well. Television was welcomed by those who could afford it; for most people it remained a novelty. When Tony Clarke first saw a television set at a neighbour's house, he tried to persuade his parents to buy one too. 'The first moments of actually seeing a live picture on a screen in somebody's house...that was a tremen-dous thrill,' he recalls. 'The television set was put smack in the middle of the room, the chairs were carefully arranged around it. It was *the* feature!'

PEERING AT THE SCREEN *of a television set displayed at a London exhibition in 1936. Like many early models it was contained in a wooden cabinet with the speaker below. By then, of the two main television systems competing in Britain, Marconi-EMI was favoured above that of Baird Television.*

At the electrical goods shop in Windsor, near London, where Harry Dix worked, they had been so busy selling radio sets that they hardly bothered with television at first. Eventually they decided to promote it by opening their showroom to customers during the evening. 'We used to provide as many chairs as we could, but often we had people standing as well,' remembers Harry Dix. 'People were really impressed by what they had

seen...so that did an awful lot for television sales.' By 1939 500 television sets were being sold in Britain each week.

Elsewhere, television was also making an impact – in Germany and in France, where television had been demonstrated as early as 1931, it was the star attraction at the Paris World's Fair in 1937. A regular French television service was launched in the following year. In the Soviet Union television broadcasts began in 1939; in the same year television transmissions in the United States made their debut at the New York World's Fair. Thousands of people caught their first glimpse of television among the stands and pavilions where the most modern scientific innovations were on show. 'It was absolutely amazing,' remembers John O. Brown, who visited the fair. 'They would take your picture in one room and then you could see it in the other room. And they said, "You know this is going to be something that we're going to have in every household soon." And I just couldn't believe it.' Don Hewitt, a picture editor at a news agency, was equally sceptical at first. 'I thought it was literally out of this world,' he says. 'I thought this is all a lot of experimental stuff, and it's great at a World's Fair and it's very amusing, but it's never going to be part of our lives.'

At the time of the World's Fair there were fewer than 200 television sets in the whole of New York, and sales remained low. Commercial television broadcasts began in 1941, only to be closed down a few months later as the United States joined the Second World War. Two years earlier, the picture had faded in Britain, too. 'I remember switching on one evening,' says Conrad Frost, 'and they said, "This is going to be the last television programme,"' and you suddenly realized that there was going to be a war....The first thing it meant to me was that I wasn't going to have television any more.'

VISION OF THE FUTURE *A crowd gathers at the site of a television exhibit at the New York World's Fair in 1939* (LEFT). *Three years earlier, television cameras brought live coverage of the Olympic Games* (RIGHT) *to Germans watching in twenty-eight halls across Berlin.*

PUBLIC VIEWING (ABOVE) *Customers at an American steak house pause to watch television. By 1953 half of American families owned their own sets at home.*

ESSENTIAL COMMODITY (OPPOSITE) *A German magazine featured television on one of its covers in 1952, the year regular broadcasts began in Germany.*

WINDOW SHOPPING *in Britain* (BELOW) *where 2 per cent of the population owned a television in 1950. Peter Robinson* (LEFT) *worked in a shop that sold televisions. 'People would come in just out of interest after seeing the set in the window,' he remembers. Sales swiftly improved by the mid-1950s.*

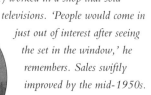

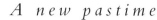

A new pastime

It was not until 1946 that television broadcasting was relaunched in Britain. The announcer jauntily introduced the first programme with the words, 'Hello. Remember me?' In the years immediately after the war, television was still a luxury. The national television service was run by the British Broadcasting Corporation (BBC), and funded through an additional licence fee charged to anyone who owned a television. At first it was confined to the London area. Peter Robinson was a schoolboy when the first television sets appeared in Preston, an industrial town in the north of England. 'We would go on the bus to town, have a wander round, and then see the television on in the shop window and stand there with the rest of the people,' he remembers. 'It didn't start until a quarter to eight in the evening and it closed at about ten past ten....We put up with the cold weather just to watch it.'

When Japanese television began regular broadcasting in 1953, with both public and privately funded stations, fewer than a thousand people had bought their own television set. Instead huge crowds gathered at street corners and in parks to watch it. Public viewing was also common in France and Italy; in the Soviet Union, where television was controlled and rigorously censored by the government, large monitors were installed in public places for collective viewing.

In 1947 there were only 60 000 television sets in the whole of the United States. When television did finally take off, though, it did so with tremendous speed and success. In the first half of 1950 alone, more than three million television sets were sold, most of them on credit. Unlike Britain, television in the United States was a commercial business, depending on advertising revenue and commercial sponsorship rather than public funding. By the mid-1950s there were more than 500 different commercial stations.

Fort Wayne, in the Midwest state of Indiana, was one of the last American cities to have its own television station. It caused a sensation. Until then, the few people who owned television sets had had to contend with poor reception from stations in distant cities. 'We were trying to put out as many television sets as we could,'

THE POWER TO SELL

ELEVISION PROGRAMMES were costly to make, and in countries where they was not funded by viewers or by government, commercial advertising and sponsorship provided the necessary revenue. In New York on 1 July 1941 people watched the first advertisement ever shown on American television: the Bulova Watch Company paid $9 for a ten-second spot. The need to attract large audiences and bring in the maximum income governed what programmes were made. They were interrupted by frequent spot advertising for the new consumer goods available after the Second World War. Television and advertising formed a mutually beneficial alliance. Manufacturers and businesses gained a unique advantage by selling their consumer products and services to a large and instantly accessible audience, and advertising revenue was used by television stations to produce and distribute programmes. From the start, the many competing television stations in the United States were supported by advertising and sponsorship.

In Britain television was seen as a public service that should not be driven by the need to deliver ever higher ratings. A licence system similar to that of the BBC was introduced throughout Western Europe – in France, Germany, Italy and the Netherlands – and in Japan. Only after a long political battle was a commercial channel allowed in Britain; when the first commercial channel, Independent Television (ITV), was launched it charged advertisers £438 for a fifteen-second, peak-time advertisement. People tuned in to the new station for the first time on 22 September 1955, and saw advertisements for beer, chocolate, margarine and soap.

As television ownership assumed global proportions in the 1960s and 1970s, it far surpassed radio and magazines as the leading medium for advertising, and advertising rates consequently soared. Specialized agencies were employed to create hard-hitting advertisements; market researchers and consumer experts analysed audiences to determine what brand of coffee or toothpaste they might be persuaded to buy. In the United States, where advertisers and sponsors were exerting a greater degree of control over programming content, advertising increased sixfold in financial terms between 1965 and 1985. For just a few seconds of air time, companies paid several thousands of dollars. By 1989 advertising expenditure worldwide had reached $250 billion.

As it developed, television advertising attracted criticism: television commercials were blamed for encouraging unnecessary purchases and creating social envy. When the same techniques began to be used to sell Western-made pharmaceuticals and powdered milk to poor people in developing countries, there were protests. Codes and standards to regulate what was advertised, and how, were introduced by most countries. In 1981 the United Nations and its World Health Organization established international guidelines for marketing products such as baby food. Alcohol and tobacco advertisements were banned from television in several countries. In Japan and the Netherlands advertisements for confectionery were accompanied by reminders to children to brush their teeth, and in Australia, Canada and New Zealand advertisements targeting children were limited to certain hours and certain days.

COMMERCIAL SET
(ABOVE) *A television advertisement for cigarettes being made by a New York film company. Thirty-second commercials could cost hundreds of thousands of dollars to make.*

remembers James Huhn, who was working at Rarick's, a local television store. 'Our advertising was such that we tried to entice people to buy them in the summertime at a special price and be ready when the station came on the air.' Everybody wanted to get a set, and as they did, everything in town was set to change in one way or another.

Marjorie Brandt and her husband had bought a television by the time WKJG Fort Wayne went on the air. 'Our first television set was a console set, and we also had to have an antenna and a rotor to be able to operate it. It dominated the room. Everything faced that set because it was an important part of our life in those days,' she remembers. 'It was our recreation and our channel to the outside world.'

As more and more people bought television sets, cinema audiences and library loans dwindled; radio and comic book sales decreased. As they stopped going to the cinema, young couples no longer needed to hire babysitters. 'We didn't call people on the telephone because it would interrupt a favourite show,' remembers Marjorie Brandt. The pastor of St Paul's Lutheran Church, Edwin Nerger, found that many of the popular programmes conflicted with church services. 'Services had to be changed, dropped. Some of the services were discontinued,' he remembers. 'The church had to do a lot of adjusting. Not only our church, but practically all the churches in town.'

Others, like Alex Azar, personally discovered the possibilities of commercial television. He decided to advertise his new 'Big Boy' hamburger restaurant on Fort Wayne's new station. 'When we first opened,' he says, 'we were lucky to do a couple of hundred dollars a day. We were brand new, people had never heard of us. They had never seen us.' The advertisement simply showed a well-known television announcer eating a Big Boy double-decker hamburger, with sauce and lettuce and mayonnaise. 'He just sighed that it was so good, and we all wanted one,' remembers Marjorie Brandt. Alex Azar's business boomed after that. 'The cars kept

SWITCHING ON TO TV (RIGHT) *An American advertisement of the 1950s compares the number of hours a person would need to work in order to earn a television: from 1224 in the Soviet Union to 1170 in Denmark, 529 in France, 513 in Britain and 136 in the United States.*

BARGAIN SALE (ABOVE)
Some people queued outside this London store all night to take advantage of the remarkable offer of a television set for only £1. Television sales peaked in Britain in the build-up to the Queen's coronation in 1953. Viewers in the United States were able to see a film recording of the ceremony, broadcast the following day.

coming and the people kept coming,' he says, 'and it continued for years. We had more business than we could accommodate.'

As more and more families everywhere bought television sets, their lives changed in much the same ways. They ate meals around it and rearranged their furniture around it. 'We didn't play as much because we watched the television,' remembers Wendy Vause. She was eight years old when she saw one for the first time, on a visit to her grandmother's home in Preston. 'Going to the theatre obviously stopped, going to the pictures some nights stopped....I stopped reading.'

Wendy Vause's grandmother was one of millions of people in Britain who decided the time had come to buy a television in the summer of 1953, shortly before the coronation of Queen Elizabeth II. 'They were selling like hot cakes,' remembers Peter Robinson. He now worked as a television dealer. 'In the weeks leading up to the coronation, things got very busy indeed. The rigger putting up aerials was working from the early morning until late at night....We were installing sets as fast as we could.' Those who could never have gone to London to watch the festivities in person took a renewed interest in the royal family. More than twenty million people saw the coronation on television at home, in pubs and clubs, or gathered in small crowds to watch through the windows of other people's houses.

By 1955 there were 37 million television sets in the United States and 4.7 million in Europe. 'Television was kind of a space-age thing then,' Joe Abrell had felt when he first saw one at a local store in Miami. 'Everybody would stand around the store window and look in and watch baseball games in the evening. I think that's when we really began to feel that television was here to stay and was going to become a part of our lives.' Within a year the number of sets outside the United States had doubled, and sales in Britain rose when commercial television was launched there. Television was launched in Australia in 1956, with commercial and national networks, in time for the Melbourne Olympic Games that year. As television reached many other parts of the world — from Algeria, China and India to New Zealand, the Philippines and Thailand — it had a similar impact.

A platform for politics

By the 1960s watching television had already become the main leisure occupation for most families in the developed world. As well as entertainment shows, millions of people watched the evening news, and news presenters achieved celebrity status. In the socialist bloc and in many newly independent countries, television was regarded as too important to be left to the market; it was seen as a tool for political control as well as mass education. In Cuba, Egypt and Eastern Europe, it carried speeches by party leaders and reports of record harvests and new industrial achievements. 'We had no freedom – we were under the constant control of censorship,' says Kamila Mouchkova, a news reporter in Prague. 'There was a man with us from the Ministry of the Interior whose job was to go through every news story before we went on the air. If he approved of it, he stamped the script and we could then broadcast it. Without that stamp, we couldn't broadcast anything.'

In the West, television was being used by politicians in an increasingly sophisticated way. It played a growing part in election campaigns, and politicians began to manipulate the news coverage by orchestrating 'picture opportunities' at which they were seen against helpful backgrounds. Speeches were written to include the soundbites that television used. American politicians spent millions of dollars buying themselves advertising space. Television became a

WAVING THE CZECH FLAG (ABOVE), *a man leaps onto one of the Soviet tanks that rolled into Prague on 20 August 1968 to reassert Soviet power over the country. Newsreader Kamila Mouchkova* (RIGHT) *was ordered at gunpoint to stop broadcasting as the TV studios were occupied.*

NEWS ANCHOR *Walter Cronkite* (BELOW), *the principal presenter in the United States, began to read the evening news on the Columbia Broadcasting System (CBS) network in 1962. He was held in such high regard that it was even suggested he should run for president. Television quickly overtook radio and newspapers as the preferred source of news.*

THE FIRST TV CONTEST *for the American presidency, held on 26 September 1960, was seen by millions of families across the country* (BELOW). *When Alex Azar* (LEFT) *watched the debate from his home in Fort Wayne, like many others he felt surprised by Nixon's appearance. 'It wasn't too inspiring. He looked tired and haggard, and Kennedy looked young and vibrant,' he describes. 'I came away thinking that maybe Kennedy was the better of the two.'*

main political forum when the first debate between presidential candidates was held on television. The Republican Richard Nixon appeared in a studio confrontation with Senator John Kennedy, the Democratic candidate. Don Hewitt, who now worked for a television company in Chicago, was the producer of the debate. He remembers the moment when Nixon, recently recovered from an illness, arrived: 'He came to the studio looking like the cat dragged him in – kind of green,' he says. Kennedy, on the other hand, had been campaigning in an open convertible in the California sunshine, and 'looked like Cary Grant'.

Elizabeth Fincher Dobynes, who would be voting for the first time, watched the programme in Fort Wayne. 'Before the debate I didn't know who to vote for,' she says. 'That was a turning point in my life. I was completely sold on that young man.' Most of the 115 million people who watched the debate felt the same. 'When it was over,' Don Hewitt recalls, 'people who heard it on the radio thought Nixon won, people who saw it on television thought Kennedy won....By the next morning everybody was saying, "Jack Kennedy is the next president of the United States". Nobody even waited for election day.'

Kennedy's television success helped to win him the election. Over the next three years his life, and then his death, were closely followed by the nation

on their television sets. 'We were all just fascinated,' says Dorothy Berger from Cleveland, Ohio. 'We had a real affinity for the Kennedy family – it was brought to us, right into our homes.'

Until the early 1960s television's development had taken place within national boundaries. Transmitters had a limited range, and viewers could follow events in distant countries only with filmed reports. This began to change when the first communications satellites began to allow direct links between continents. In 1962 *Telstar*, in orbit around the Earth, made it possible to receive and transmit television signals across the Atlantic. In Britain Peter Robinson watched the satellite broadcast from his local club. 'There was a tremendous cheer, and of course we had quite a few drinks after that,' he remembers. 'It was an exciting night to see those first pictures across the Atlantic, and it certainly reduced the size of the world.'

As the satellite system was extended, television organizations mounted a series of international programmes to demonstrate what was now possible. 'Our World' in 1967 linked The Beatles singing in London, folk singers in Mexico and babies being born in Japan. 'Town Meeting of the World' showed discussions about the future taking place between political leaders. The satellites made the most difference to news programmes, allowing pictures from distant places to be shown each day.

In the United States evening news bulletins were extended from fifteen to thirty minutes, and presented a less sanitized view of the world. One of the most significant events to be covered in the 1960s was the country's involvement in the war in Vietnam. Although television did not portray the full horror, it did bring disturbing images into people's homes, helping to turn public opinion against the war. 'I was against it,' says Dorothy Berger. 'We were all against it. If you watched television, you heard it every night and that was really gruesome.'

In the same way, television news reports of the civil rights demonstrations in the South helped to raise people's concern. 'I was so mesmerized with what was going on,' Elizabeth Fincher Dobynes recalls, 'and it was due to television.' Her local newspaper had failed to cover the events. 'Without television there would have been no civil rights movement, nobody would have known.'

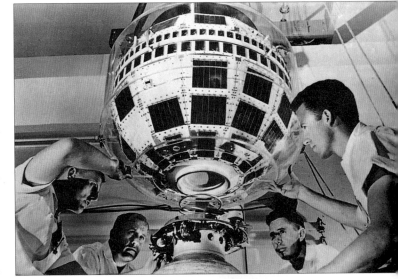

EXTRATERRESTRIAL COMMUNICATIONS
The pioneering Telstar *satellite* (ABOVE) *is inspected by technicians before being launched into space from Cape Canaveral in the United States in July 1962. Weighing only 77 kg (170 lb), the satellite orbited the Earth at the same speed as the Earth itself rotates, maintaining a stationary orbit above the Atlantic. Among the earliest transatlantic satellite pictures it beamed to television viewers across Europe* (RIGHT, *from top to bottom) were the American national memorial at Mount Rushmore in South Dakota, a Chicago baseball game and a view of the New York skyline.*

MOONWATCH (ABOVE) *Hundreds of people gathered in front of a giant screen in London's Trafalgar Square to watch the moon landing on 21 July 1969. Everywhere celebrations marked the historic moment, which had been preceded by four days of television coverage of the journey to the moon.*

COLOURED VISION
(LEFT) *A family gazes at its latest acquisition in a poster promoting colour television. Technically it was developed at an early stage, but was not widely taken up until the 1950s and 1960s. Through colour, television gained in impact. In Britain the TV licence fee was increased to take advantage of the change.*

Views of the world

By the end of the 1960s, progress in satellite communications meant that a much wider range of programmes could now reach people across the world. New colour monitors and transmissions in colour boosted television sales. 'When it first came and you first saw it, you kind of went "Oh!", remembers Wendy Vause. 'Once you had seen colour television you didn't want to go back.' And as television was introduced to more and more countries during the 1960s and 1970s – to parts of Africa, Asia, Central and South America and the Middle East – the numbers of television viewers everywhere soared. Before long, television cameras would even enable people to see live pictures from space.

In 1969 some 723 million people in forty-seven countries – a fifth of the world's population – watched the landing of the *Apollo 11* spacecraft on the moon. 'We had the television on the patio,' recalls Edwin Nerger, who was visiting his in-laws in Dallas that summer. 'It was a very clear night. The moon was just as big and bright as it could be. And we were looking up at the moon, and we were watching the moon landing on television....And when you realized that we were not the only ones watching, but the whole world was watching, it was a tremendous event.' All over Europe people stayed up into the early hours of the morning to watch their televisions. 'I couldn't believe the pictures were from the moon to begin with,' says Wendy Vause in Britain. 'That day I felt that I watching television for the first time....It was almost unbelievable.'

The same satellites were now increasingly used to beam sporting events, including international soccer and boxing, to audiences around the world. The largest audiences so far were expected for the Munich Olympic Games in the summer of 1972. 'There was an uplifting atmosphere,' recalls Hans Klein, a sports journalist who attended the opening ceremony. 'Everybody was aware that eight hundred million people via satellite were watching this fantastic event.'

In Cleveland, Ohio, Dorothy and Benjamin Berger had a special reason for watching the Games from Germany: their son, David, was competing in the Israeli weightlifting team. 'We came downstairs about eight o'clock for breakfast, which we usually do, turned on the television, and we saw one of the weightlifting coaches being interviewed,' remembers Dorothy Berger. 'Then we heard something about hostages.' They soon heard the news that the entire weightlifting team had been kidnapped by Palestinian terrorists demanding the release of prisoners being held in Israel.

What had begun as a major sporting event quickly became an international crisis covered live on television by the world's media. 'All day long we watched television to see what would happen,' says Dorothy Berger. 'We didn't hear from anybody; we didn't hear from the Israeli government. Pretty soon we began to realize this is not good. We just watched television all night....Nothing that day ever came through any source but television.' At 11 o'clock that night there was a

> *"I loved every minute of watching that man walk on the moon....When I thought my grandmother was in a log cabin and here I was seeing a man on the moon!"*
>
> MARJORIE BRANDT

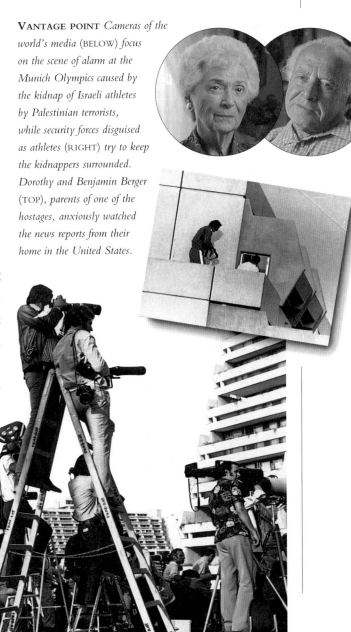

VANTAGE POINT *Cameras of the world's media* (BELOW) *focus on the scene of alarm at the Munich Olympics caused by the kidnap of Israeli athletes by Palestinian terrorists, while security forces disguised as athletes* (RIGHT) *try to keep the kidnappers surrounded. Dorothy and Benjamin Berger* (TOP), *parents of one of the hostages, anxiously watched the news reports from their home in the United States.*

REMOTE RECEPTION
Members of an Aboriginal family gather outside their home in central Australia to watch television. The sheer size of the country meant that its availability was limited in some places.

news flash. It announced that all eleven hostages had been killed. 'That's when we heard it,' says Benjamin Berger. 'We watched very briefly and then turned the set off.'

The hostages had been seized because members of the Black September group knew they would gain international attention. 'We were aware right from the beginning of the great influence of television,' says Abu Daoud. 'Our aim was to make the international community aware of the Palestinian cause....After the Munich operation, there was a great interest from the media in our cause and in the Palestinians.' And after Munich, where television itself had been hijacked, other terrorist groups found that they too could use the worldwide reach of television by staging incidents to draw attention to their cause.

Many people believed that television was not being used to its full educational potential, and in 1975 the boldest satellite experiment so far was launched. The United States agreed to loan a satellite to India as part of a national programme to improve the lives of millions of poor farming families. In India television was mainly available to people in towns and cities. Much of India's vast countryside was not covered by television transmitters, and many people had never even seen a television. With the new satellite, programmes could be beamed directly to remote rural regions.

The Indian government delivered television sets and satellite dishes to schools in 2400 villages, where families gathered each evening to watch programmes on better farming methods, family planning and health care. Madan Lal Joshi was a schoolteacher in the village of Bichoon. 'When people first assembled here we were not sure whether the programmes would appeal to them,' he recalls. They did take an interest: 'Like the farmers, who were taught about new agricultural implements and seeds. Whatever they were told they wanted to incorporate in their day-to-day life.' The programmes were broadcast to six states in six different languages. 'We were told about medicines, about pesticides for crops,' Radah Krishen, a cobbler, says. 'It was really a new thing!'

TELEVISION GAMES
A football match is being watched by sports journalists, not on the nearby pitch but on a multitude of television monitors. As well as reducing public attendance at games, television meant new competition for newspapers. 'Television was a great intruder,' remembers Howard Kleinberg, a sports writer in Miami since 1949. 'We had the locker room to ourselves, we had the post-game conference to ourselves, but along came this camera and this other person who always set up in front of us.'

SPORT ON SCREEN

BUSINESSMEN, SPONSORS and sports promoters soon realized that television, with its capacity to engage and thrill audiences, was made for the world of sport. 'You could listen to a baseball game if you were a sports fan, or listen to a heavyweight championship fight, but you couldn't see it,' Reese Schonfeld, then an American television reporter, recalls. 'The seeing of it was absolutely wonderful, it made it much more real.'

From the intricate detail of golf to the gladiatorial contests of tennis or boxing, and from the fast-moving action of football to the grand sweep of the Olympic Games, sport offered an immediacy that hundreds of millions of viewers could share, full of conflict, passion and drama.

The first transmission in the world of team sport was the Japanese broadcast in 1931 of a Waseda University baseball match. The 1936 Olympic Games, held in Berlin, were watched by 150 000 people on special demonstration sets provided in schools and halls around the city, and in the following year in Britain there was live coverage of the Wimbledon tennis championships.

As television ownership everywhere increased, so too did the variety of sports that could be watched from home during the 1960s – major league baseball, cricket, professional football, ice hockey, soccer, swimming and sumo wrestling. Players sometimes wore new patterned clothes so that they could be identified and distinguished on black and white televisions; rules were simplified; the timing of some sports was altered. Show jumping and snooker in Britain, and American football in the United States, became more popular as a result of television. Live satellite broadcasting attracted millions of sports

viewers, and television companies were paying first thousands, then millions of dollars for exclusive broadcasting rights of major international sporting events. In 1972 ABC secured exclusivity in the United States to the ill-fated Munich Olympics for the sum of $7.5 million; twenty years later, NBC broadcast the Barcelona Olympics for $420 million.

Televised sport had become big business. High-earning players and sports personalities doubled their incomes with sponsorship contracts, advertising, and personal appearances. Satellite and cable companies created sports-only channels for paying fans, and began to monopolize sports coverage. Tobacco companies, banned from advertising on television in several countries, poured money instead into sponsoring sports such as cricket, golf, motor racing and tennis. Television was transforming the world of sport.

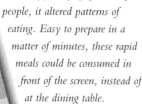
THE *TELENOVELA* (OPPOSITE), *advertised in a poster marking its appearance on German television, was popular with European viewers as well as South American audiences.*

ROLE PLAYING *Larry Hagman, who starred as J. R. Ewing in the American* Dallas *serial, distributes imitation dollar bills bearing his image. Soap opera characters were so popular that they sometimes acquired a life off the screen as well as on it.* Dallas *was dubbed into ninety different languages, allowing Steliana Stefonoiu (RIGHT) to watch it in Romania.*

Prime time viewing

By the 1980s television had become a global force and a powerful industry. By 1981 there were regular television broadcasts across 137 countries. One of the most popular programme formats, which captivated television viewers everywhere, was the 'soap opera'. Originating in the United States, where they had been used to sell soap powder by radio, and then adapted for television, these highly popular serial dramas drew huge audiences all over the world – in Australia, Germany and Japan, in India and Central and South America.

Brazilian soap operas, *telenovelas*, were among the world's most successful. Watched regularly by 65 per cent of the Brazilian population, these long-running narratives of romantic comedy, interwoven with historical, mythical or political drama, could be seen three times a day, six days a week. Diaz Gomes wrote many *telenovelas* for Brazil's TV Globo since they were first produced in the 1960s. At one time, he says, the ratings for one drama reached 'one hundred percent, which means that all of the television sets turned on at that moment were tuned to the same *novela* – to the same channel, the same story, the same scene,' he remembers. 'The *novela* stopped the country. You went out on the streets and the streets were deserted.'

They did not just appeal to Brazilian audiences. By exporting its *telenovelas* to more than a hundred other countries, TV Globo became one of the most successful television companies in the world. In much the same way, Australian soap operas were enjoyed by British audiences, and people in France and Italy watched American ones.

In the United States, *Dallas* was one of Elizabeth Fincher Dobynes' favourite soap operas. It was about the glamorous, feuding family of a Texas oil baron. 'I fitted my schedule to watch these shows,' she says. 'There was no VCR, nothing of that nature, I made sure I watched. I didn't have to ask anybody what had happened.' In Germany Alexandra Benes followed *Dallas*

EPIC VIEWING IN INDIA

ONE BRIDE WAS LATE for her wedding. Two ministers were late for their own swearing-in ceremony. All over India life had come to a standstill. The explanation was simple: everyone was watching *Ramayana*. 'The sale of televisions shot up at that time. People thought that they have got to watch this serial,' remembers Shyam Sunder Arora, a television salesman. 'There were instances when people asked trains to be stopped so that they could watch *Ramayana*.'

This thirty-minute, weekly television series that took the country by storm when it was first shown in 1987 was based on an epic poem taken from a classic Hindu text. The televised drama of the familiar and well-loved story of the life of the Hindu god Rama was shown every Sunday morning on the state-run television station, Doordarshan, and all over the country people stopped what they were doing to watch it.

When *Ramayana* began there were only about ten million television sets in India, but as many as seventy million people are thought to have watched the series. In some villages the television sets were placed in front of temples by the Brahmins, for all the villagers to watch together. For some among the millions of Hindu followers of the series, *Ramayana* became more than just a television drama. Believing the television actors to be incarnations of the gods they portrayed, many pious Hindus worshipped *Ramayana*, and burned incense or hung garlands around their television sets. While some of the actors were worshipped as gods, others were elected to parliament because of their popular role in the series.

As the potent force of the religious epic reached the villages and the urban streets it affected many people's lives. In the northern city of Jammu, angry *Ramayana* fans occupied a local power station after a blackout caused them to miss an episode. There were local reports of hospital patients being abandoned by doctors and nurses while *Ramayana* was being shown. As the

SOURCE OF UNREST *A scene from the* Ramayana *drama series, which had a far greater popular impact than any other programme shown on Indian television.*

end of the series approached, threats of civil unrest and strikes in some parts of India by people demanding that it should be continued persuaded Doordarshan to double the number of episodes. An appeal to extend the series had even been raised in parliament.

Ramayana had a powerful effect in politics. It boosted public support for the militant Hindu parties, especially the Bharatiya Janata Party (BJP). The series provoked religious riots, and some television stations were occupied and vandalized by extremists insisting that their Hindu festivals be broadcast on television. The wave of Hindu piety raised by the series led to criticism of Doordarshan by people who claimed that it represented a breach of the public network's commitment to avoid extended coverage of any one religion or political group. *Ramayana* was nevertheless the most successful series – commercially as well as in popularity – to be shown on Indian television.

GLUED TO THE SET
The number of television sets and transmitters in India grew as a result of government policy, and both popular series as well as educational programmes reached even larger audiences.

SESAME STREET
(OPPOSITE) *was launched in 1969 in the United States, becoming popular with young audiences all over the world. Puppets and games were used to teach preschool children about numbers and the letters of the alphabet.*

every week without fail: 'Everybody was talking about it in the office....so I thought, I just have to watch it.' In communist Romania, where food queues were part of people's everyday life and they could not enjoy the freedom to travel abroad, watching *Dallas* enabled some to catch a glimpse of life beyond their own country. It was a welcome change: 'There were lots of episodes,' remembers Steliana Stefonoiu, 'and as we watched we became acquainted with the American way of life: how Americans dressed, how they lived, how they managed their finances. Everything was new and special for us, and therefore there was a lot of interest in this series.'

Within a few years, however, Steliana Stefonoiu could no longer watch her favourite programmes from the West. In 1983, in an effort to reduce the nation's foreign debts, television transmissions were gradually rationed by the government, along with food and clothing, to only two hours of viewing a day.

A television revolution

After the Romanian president, Nicolae Ceausescu, had introduced rationing, television featured dull documentary programmes and news items interspersed with patriotic songs. 'There were shows worshipping the presidential couple in all aspects of their public lives,' remembers Badea Anghel, whose job was to sell televisions in Bucharest. 'There were very few programmes about science, professional training, or on life in other countries, not to mention movies. Everything went in one single direction: the worship and glorification of the dictator.'

For many people, television simply ceased to exist. Instead they read books, listened to the radio or, like Steliana Stefonoiu, took up needlework. Some resorted to other means. 'People watched Bulgarian, Yugoslavian and even Russian television, which showed different kinds of programmes,' says Badea Anghel. 'This almost turned into a large-scale industry – manufacturing aerials and other equipment to receive neighbouring television stations that could meet people's need for information, music, movies.' This was illegal, and it also meant that people had to follow programmes in foreign languages – still preferable to the constant propaganda of national television, and a source of information about what was going on elsewhere. And in Eastern Europe things were changing very fast in the last months of 1989, as communist governments began to crumble.

In December 1989 viewers were watching a live broadcast of Ceausescu making a speech when the audience in Bucharest's main square began to boo him. It was unprecedented. 'He was speaking from his rostrum and suddenly the transmission was cut off,' says Steliana Stefonoiu. 'We realized that something was going on. From that moment on we stayed glued to the television set.' Outside, a revolution was erupting as people demonstrated in the streets. They soon seized the television studios. 'It was sensational!' recalls Felicia Melescanu, who worked in the newsroom. 'We quickly organized a studio...and we started to talk. A colleague, who was principal newscaster and who had sworn to wear a navy blue suit only on the day that Ceausescu was overthrown, quickly went to put his blue suit on. He came back and started telling people, "Romanian television is free!" '

"We all experienced the joy of participating in history, and the awareness that we were making history, and that television was making history."

FELICIA MELESCANU

TRIAL BY TELEVISION *For five days Romanian television stayed on the air with live coverage of the dramatic fall of the communist regime. After twenty-four years in power, the dictator Nicolae Ceausescu and his wife Elena were shown on national televison in the last few hours before their execution.*

FILMING REVOLUTION (OPPOSITE) *A television crew in Bucharest records violent scenes between civilians and armed forces during the upheaval in Romania. Most people learnt of the revolution by watching it on television.*

Channel to the world

Television played an active part as the communist empire was dismantled. The new political situation was debated, and the new freedoms tested and demonstrated, on television. The entire course of the Romanian revolution was brought into living rooms around the world. Lightweight cameras and electronic methods of recording made live media coverage much easier, and round-the-clock international news channels such as the Cable News Network (CNN), founded in the United States in 1981, continued to bring people coverage of international events as they unfolded. Soon the letters CNN were as famous as any logo in the world: by 1990 it could be viewed in more than ninety countries

CNN was just one of a new generation of international broadcasters whose programmes could be picked up around the world, through domestic satellite dishes or relayed through the rapidly extending cable systems. Cable had once been used to give better transmission of broadcast television. Now higher capacity cable systems began to carry channels dedicated not to news but to cartoons, children's programmes, movies, sport and even shopping. In Miami Howard Kleinberg, who since the 1950s had watched television come of age, received several hundred channels. 'We've got a golf channel, we've got a food channel, we've got a travel channel,' he says. 'I can buy anything.'

In half a century television had become a formidable force: it was used to sell products to people, to educate, entertain and inform them. Elections were contested on it, votes were won on it, and leaders could be created or deposed by it. In the age of global television, it was harder for dictators to control what people watched, when with direct satellite dishes they could pick up international broadcasts from the sky.

By 1990 there was a television receiver in 98 per cent of homes in the developed world, and about 2.5 billion people in the developing world had regular access to one. From the start, people had instinctively understood that it would change all our lives. 'It has made all of us more aware of other nations, other people,' says Alex Azar. 'I didn't know a whole lot about areas outside the state of Indiana. And today – why, the world is part of our neighbourhood....I don't think the world will ever get along without it.'

THE CENTRE OF ATTENTION (OPPOSITE) *for these men in the Zambian capital of Lusaka is the football match they are watching on television. By the 1990s the advent of satellite broadcasts and the rapidly expanding global network of dishes and cables meant fewer and fewer limits to what people all over the world could watch.*

TELESHOPPING *on the QVC home shopping network was one of the numerous choices open to target audiences. With access to television, and with just a telephone and credit card number to hand, anyone could make a purchase from the wide range of products being advertised.*

MEDIA WAR *From its start in 1991 the Gulf War following the Iraqi invasion of Kuwait created instant and sensational news. As its full drama and horror unfolded in front of camera crews, televison viewers everywhere checked its daily progress.*

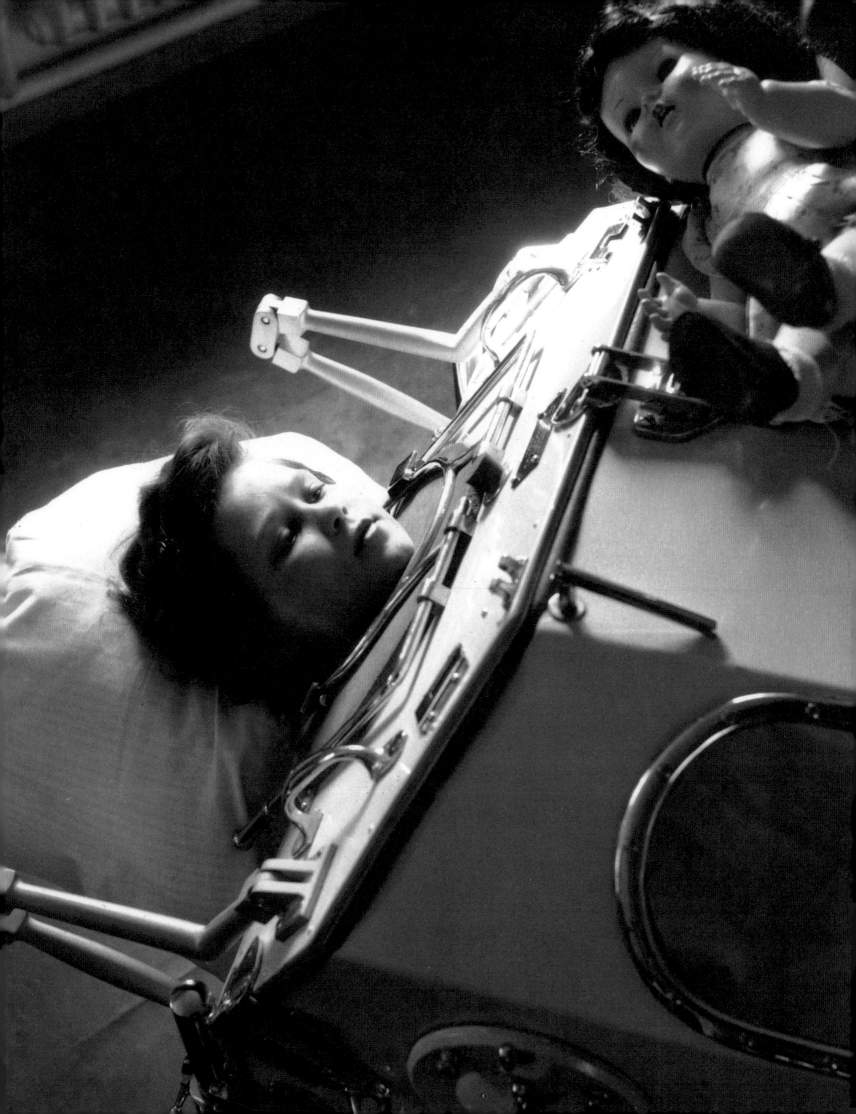

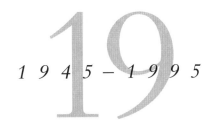

Living Longer

CAMPAIGNS
FOR BETTER
HEALTH

'IT'S 1954, IT'S BROOKLYN, trees, school, friends, the sun was still yellow, and suddenly that world ended,' remembers Sharon Stern. She was nine years old when she woke up one Friday morning in October with a severe headache. Her mother kept her home from school that day. A few days later she became extremely ill and was taken to hospital, and was diagnosed as suffering from polio. When her left leg became paralysed and she began to have trouble breathing, she was placed in an 'iron lung' – an airtight metal cylinder that enclosed her body right up to the neck, allowing her to breathe artificially. She was to spend the following nine months inside that machine. As she still vividly remembers, 'It's very frightening to a child, to be suddenly taken out of that little world that you're growing up in. I'm in this strange place, among strange people, and I have no control over my body or my breathing.'

Sharon Stern was just one among several hundreds of thousands of children all over the world who suffered from the debilitating effects of poliomyelitis right up until the 1950s. Within a few months of her own struggle with the illness, a preventive vaccine finally became available after many years of intensive medical research. It would relieve millions of parents and their children from the fear of infection.

In the three decades after 1945, medical science and improvements in public health care seemed to be overcoming one after another of humanity's oldest enemies. As more and more of the world's epidemic diseases were conquered, people increasingly began to rely on the successful methods of prevention and cure that scientists and doctors were now able to offer. Protected from many major diseases by immunization in their first year of life, millions of people could expect to lead longer and healthier lives. But as populations around the world began to increase ever more rapidly, unforeseen health problems as well as new diseases emerged, reducing the effects of the progress that scientists had brought as well as challenging them to find new solutions.

LIFE SAVER *A young polio victim rests, trapped in the iron lung that is keeping her alive.*

WAITING ROOM (ABOVE) *A mother prepares her children for a checkup in the Infant Welfare Clinic at Britain's first All-In Health Centre. Before the nationalization of health care, free medical treatment had only been available for the poor or homeless. After 1948 everyone became eligible.*

WARTIME WARD (RIGHT) *in northern Burma, where medical personnel of the United States army treat war casualties in a tent. American interest in the development of penicillin, stimulated after the Japanese invasion of Pearl Harbor, continued after the war when the United States became the largest producer of the new drug. Among the many infections it combated, penicillin proved remarkably successful in treating venereal diseases, a common wartime affliction.*

Health for all

At the turn of the century the millions of people throughout the world who suffered from the infectious diseases that threatened their lives could expect little by way of treatment. Only a few drugs were available to combat the scourges scientists were trying to cure – among them cholera, diphtheria, influenza, malaria, scarlet fever, typhus, yellow fever and whooping cough. Advances in antenatal care and obstetrics had begun to reduce the large numbers of women who died in childbirth. But millions of people were still afflicted by the often deadly viral and bacterial infections that spread ever more rapidly in the increasingly densely populated cities. At that time the number of years people could expect to live was relatively low: average life expectancy at birth in the United States was only forty-seven years, while in India it was as little as twenty-five years.

During the 1920s and 1930s several drugs were discovered, including insulin for treating diabetes, and new ways were found both to treat and to control viral diseases. In some countries mass screening was introduced to identify and control early outbreaks of disease. Vaccines were introduced to prevent diphtheria, influenza, tetanus and yellow fever. One of the most significant breakthroughs was made accidentally at a London hospital in 1928 when a British scientist, Alexander Fleming, spilled some mould onto a dish containing a bacterium, killing it. Further research in 1939 profited from that discovery to develop a powerful new drug – penicillin, an antibiotic agent that helped to fight infections.

By 1941 penicillin was being mass produced in Canada and the United States for military use, to treat soldiers wounded in the Second World War. It was used in large quantities to combat gangrene. James Lewis, an American army doctor, realized its value when he was working in an emergency operating theatre in northern France after the D-Day landings. 'I was treating serious abdominal wounds, chest

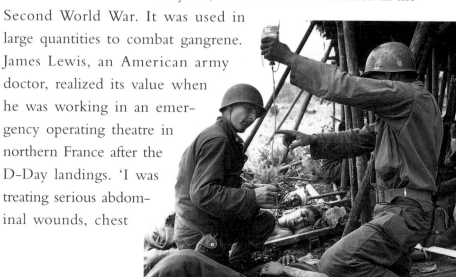

THE HEALTH OF THE PEOPLE

DURING THE CENTURY most Western governments saw that they had to take on responsibility for their people's health, and introduced new measures to improve access to health care. The earliest of these was Germany's Sickness Insurance Act, introduced in 1883, which became the basis for national health policy there. With money raised through contributions from employers and employees, the scheme began by offering medical care to those who were most vulnerable. It was later extended to provide health benefits for most of the population, and included dental care, maternity care and annual preventive health checks.

Japan turned to Western medical practice and introduced an Employee's Health Insurance scheme in 1922 based on the German model. At first limited to urban workers, it was extended during the 1930s and again in the 1960s to give compulsory coverage for the whole population.

In the Soviet Union, where people had suffered from frequent epidemics of cholera, typhoid, dysentery and influenza before the revolution, the new communist government undertook direct responsiblity for public health. The Commissariat of Health, set up in 1918, established compulsory health clinics, centres and programmes, improved standards of hygiene and sanitation, and offered free medical care to all. A similarly comprehensive approach was taken by Britain's Labour government with the establishment of the National Health Service. It took effect in 1948, offering free medical and dental care to everyone – regardless of age, race, income or occupation – in hospital and out of it. Private medical practice continued for those who could afford it, but thousands of hospitals in Britain were nationalized.

In the United States, federal grants for maternal and child health care and mass screening were introduced during the 1930s, but attempts to pass national health legislation through Congress repeatedly failed. Some companies that had set up workers' medical schemes during the war continued them in peacetime, but most people had to take out their own health insurance to pay for health care from private sector doctors and hospitals. In the 1960s national Medicare and Medicaid programmes were set up to care for the elderly, the disabled and the poor, but with the exception of some public hospitals, private sector health care was still more common.

Most developed nations chose national health provisions based on these methods, or a combination of private and public schemes. Their impact was considerable, setting new standards for millions of people who benefited from greater access to health care: a hundred years after the introduction of Germany's Sickness Insurance Law, Germans lived on average about twice as long; in Russia there was a sharp decline in mortality generally, while infant mortality had dropped by 90 per cent since 1913.

Developing countries had neither the money nor the trained medical workers to approach these levels of health care. By the 1990s even in wealthier nations the availability of treatment and hospital beds for larger and increasingly ageing populations was coming under threat as the cost of health care continued to rise.

wounds, amputations and head wounds, where the potential for infection was very great,' he remembers. 'I had one casualty who'd been hit by a shell that had blown his thigh open and blown manure into it, which had to be scraped out with a brush. These are potentially terrible infections, and penicillin played a big role. It was a miracle drug.'

After the war, millions of civilians were able to benefit from the new drugs that had saved the lives of so many soldiers. In 1945 many European countries were facing a public health emergency.

HEALTH POLICIES *of Britain's Labour government were a central feature of its welfare reforms after the war that promised social security and family allowances as well as free health care for the young, the old, the homeless and the unemployed.*

DRIVES TO COMBAT DISEASE (ABOVE) *Mobile X-ray units were used in 1951 to encourage people to come forward for tests in Glasgow, which had the highest number of tuberculosis cases in Britain, as part of the city's campaign to defeat the disease. X-rays helped doctors to discover the disease at an early stage by showing the shadow on the patient's lungs.*

A GERMAN CHILD, *displaced by the war from her home in Czechoslovakia, is deloused with DDT spray by a worker at a medical centre run by the United Nations International Children's Emergency Fund (UNICEF), before setting off to a new home.*

Millions of refugees were on the move. Food shortages and a lack of clean water made people particularly vulnerable to disease. Over pictures of bombed-out families taking water from a drain, a newsreel commentary warned: 'In biblical days his name was pestilence. His modern name is epidemic disease. His shadow is in the sewer water of a thousand towns. These people slake their thirst with typhoid fever and dysentery, with infectious jaundice and possibly with infantile paralysis.' DDT, a pesticide developed in 1944 to protect soldiers in the tropics, was now used to fight the spread of lice and ticks, typhus and malaria in the ruined cities.

In the postwar years, as standards of living began to improve, people in the West began to look to their governments and their employers for better health care. State-sponsored health provision and insurance schemes were set up, while insurance companies did their best to persuade those who could afford it to take out private health insurance. In 1948 a specialized agency of the United Nations, the World Health Organization (WHO), was established with twenty-six member states to promote better health for everyone. Internationally, the priorities were to continue medical research and to use the newly available medicines to stamp out old infectious killer diseases everywhere. In industrialized countries the worst of these was tuberculosis, known and feared as TB.

Cures for life

Fifteen-year-old Marjorie Cave grew up in the overcrowded East End of London. As her father was ill and her grandparents had come to live with them, she had to share a bed with her mother. 'My mother was very ill, and I saw her have haemorrhages and breathless attacks, fits of coughing in the night,' she remembers. 'It was very frightening.' After her mother died Marjorie Cave herself grew thinner, paler and more breathless. Then she also began coughing. 'I thought, "This is it, I'm the next," and I was right.'

Tuberculosis, a potentially fatal disease that principally affects the lungs, flourished where people lived in poor, overcrowded conditions. Hospitals were filled with its victims, and it had caused millions of deaths. 'The whole outlook was very bleak,' Marjorie Cave recalls. 'That is, of course, if you survived. They thought I wouldn't live three months.' She stopped going to school, and instead was taken first to a local sanatorium and eventually to Papworth, a sanatorium near Cambridge specially built to care for tuberculosis victims. It was five years before she fully recovered.

Until the 1950s there was no effective cure for people who were suffering from tuberculosis. They were instead encouraged to rest, follow special diets and spend plenty of time in the open air. Some patients received far more drastic treatment. When Les Ellis, who was serving in the British army, found it difficult to keep up with the drills, he was given an X-ray examination and was then referred to the military hospital. 'I didn't know what it was all about,' he remembers, 'but when I got there they said, "Well, you've got TB".'

Two months later Les Ellis was also moved to Papworth Sanatorium; the doctors told him he was to have a thoracoplasty. The idea was to collapse the lung so that it could rest. First they took out two of his front ribs, and when that did not work, they took out two at the back and one more in front. As he was given only a local anaesthetic, Les Ellis can remember the details of the operation. 'Dr Murphy, he was holding my hand as high as he could so he could get at the ribs. He made the incision and said, "You'll hear a crack. Don't worry about it, it's just one of your ribs". And there was this great bang, just like someone breaking a piece of wood.'

MARJORIE CAVE *feels fortunate to have recovered from TB. 'You were terrified of catching it. You couldn't mix freely with people, it wasn't very pleasant. You were very, very thin, pale, you sometimes had a horrible cough,' she says. 'Nobody really wanted to know you…except those who were very fond of you.'*

QUEUEING FOR PROTECTION (RIGHT) *Children await their turn at one of the emergency polio vaccination centres in Chicago in 1956.*

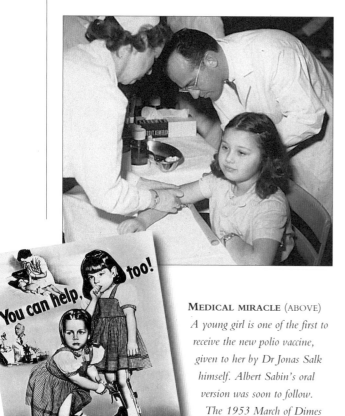

MEDICAL MIRACLE (ABOVE) *A young girl is one of the first to receive the new polio vaccine, given to her by Dr Jonas Salk himself. Albert Sabin's oral version was soon to follow. The 1953 March of Dimes* (LEFT), *organized by the National Foundation for Infantile Paralysis, urged Americans to make a donation to the campaign to fight polio. This poster, featuring two children affected by the crippling disease, was distributed throughout the United States.*

A few years later, once penicillin was in general use, new drugs specific to tuberculosis were discovered: Streptomycin in 1944, PAS in 1946 and INH in 1952. Together, they successfully inhibited the disease, curing all but the most advanced cases. 'It came a bit too late for me,' says Les Ellis. 'It would have been nice to have been saved all that surgery.' For millions of others, the 'white plague' of tuberculosis was no longer a threat.

People did continue to fear polio, a viral infection that destroyed the nerves, causing its victims – who were most often children – to lose control of their muscles and become paralysed, and in some cases to die. In the United States, where polio reached epidemic proportions in the early 1950s, 40 000 cases were reported each year. 'Everybody was frightened of polio,' remembers Deborah Runkle, who grew up in Minneapolis. 'The mothers were frightened and they made the children frightened.' In 1954 came yet another wonder drug, an anti-polio vaccine developed by Dr Jonas Salk at the University of Pittsburgh. It was followed two years later by one that could easily be swallowed on a lump of sugar.

The new vaccines could not cure polio, but they did prevent it from spreading, and immunization was introduced in several European countries, and in Australia, Canada and South Africa as well as the United States. In the early months, when supplies of the vaccine were still limited in Minneapolis, Deborah Runkle's father managed to reserve some for his daughter. It was a big day

"Polio was a sort of disease of the day. It was the top contender that everybody was frightened of getting, because it could strike anybody at any time."

VIRGINIA GRANATO

for them. 'We went and got the vaccine, and then it was over. That was the fix. There was no more polio. There was no more worry.' In Eastern Europe and the Soviet Union, where more than 115 million people were vaccinated, polio was almost completely eliminated by the end of 1960.

By the 1960s almost all children in the richer countries could expect to lead long and active lives. Western governments had the resources and the organization to make sure that everyone benefited from the new drugs. In developing countries, where more than three-quarters of the world's population lived, things were very different. In spite of the Indian government's efforts to improve health care for its people, poor sanitation, polluted water, poverty, overcrowding and hunger, and the lack of medicine to combat infection, left many of them vulnerable to disease. With a population of 500 million, basic resources were in short supply.

In Tegu Raghuvir's village in Uttar Pradesh, northern India, there was no hospital and no doctor. 'We used to go running to fetch a herbalist, but by the time we got back the patient would be dead,' he recalls. 'Smallpox, measles, cholera, plague, influenza – these were fatal diseases.' As many babies and children died, people tried to have large families, partly to help supplement the family income. Only six of Tegu Raghuvir's nine children survived. 'Some people had this fear that, "If I just have this one child, and if he dies, then my family will be finished". And some people kept having daughters hoping they would have a son.'

DEBORAH RUNKLE (ABOVE *and with her brother,* RIGHT) *was eight years old when polio inoculation began in her home town, Minneapolis. 'I remember it so very well,' she says. 'I think it took a year or two to get enough vaccine for everybody....At first, one day you could get it and the next day it was gone.'*

Search and containment

In India, as in much of Asia and Africa, smallpox was the disease people feared most of all. A potentially fatal viral infection, it affected people of all ages, causing high fever and making the body break out in pustules that gradually dried up, turning to scabs. After two weeks the scabs were shed by the scarred victims, and the infectious stage was over. 'The pustules were enormous,' remembers Dhanari Devi, who caught smallpox in his village of Rohaki. 'They were all over the body. It was a dreadful sight.' Another villager, Bi Karma, suffered such a massive attack that his eyes were forced shut by the pustules for eight days. 'When the pox receded, water oozed out of the pustules so profusely that I could wipe it down my limbs. The upper layer of the skin began to peel off. It was very painful. I felt I wouldn't live.'

The only protection against smallpox was vaccination. Immunization, begun in the nineteenth century, had succeeded in controlling the spread of the disease in many countries that had the necessary resources. But the virus was still rampant in every continent apart from Europe and North America, affecting more than ten million people a year and killing an estimated two million in 1967 alone. In India, where the government was determined to get rid of smallpox as other countries had done, a programme of mass vaccination was introduced, but there were still epidemic outbreaks. In 1966 an international campaign to eradicate smallpox from the entire world was launched by the WHO. It achieved considerable success: by the end of 1973 smallpox was restricted to the Indian subcontinent and parts of Africa. In India the WHO tried a new approach. Instead of trying to vaccinate everyone, teams of medical workers would search for individual cases, isolate them for the incubation period, and then vaccinate everyone within 3 km (1.9 miles).

Thousands of people set to work in villages and markets, the start of a long and difficult process. 'It was during the hotter season,' remembers Bohumir Kriz, a Czech doctor helping the Indian authorities. 'We were living in the villages, sleeping in the villages, eating in the villages, working for

THE FACE OF SMALLPOX *An Indian child is cradled by his mother, the disfiguring signs of his illness clearly visible. As well as a characteristic rash that turned into pustules, smallpox also inflicted on its victims fever, headaches, pains and sometimes vomiting and convulsions.*

SICK ROOM (BELOW) *With an earthen floor and corrugated iron roof, a smallpox emergency ward in the Pakistani capital of Karachi houses victims of the disease during the necessary incubation period. Despite often limited medical resources, many countries made huge efforts to combat infection.*

eighteen to twenty hours a day. Everybody was dedicated.' He and his colleagues would find an outbreak, contain it and move on to the next one. Every district health centre had a smallpox room, with a map to trace the spread of the infection.

Panchu Ram remembers the day a medical team arrived in his village. 'There was general excitement. The children and the women all came pouring out of their homes....Everyone, the young and the old, flocked to the village centre and arrangements were made for the vaccination of one and all.' There were some obstacles. In remote villages where smallpox had become an accepted part of life, people regarded the disease as a sign of the goddess Sitla Devi. Victims were thought to be blessed by her, and pilgrims came from all over India to worship at her temple in Varanasi. Many looked to prayer rather than medicine for cures. 'When I started to vaccinate a woman she was so angry she spat in

DANGEROUS GAMES
in Calcutta. Children's play could have catastrophic consequences, as poor sanitation and contaminated water contributed to the frequent epidemics of smallpox and cholera that claimed many lives.

MALARIA'S DEADLY BITE

IN 1939 SOME 700 million people in the world were suffering from the effects of malaria, an ancient parasitic disease that strikes at humans' internal organs. The parasites are carried by mosquitoes, and are introduced into people's bloodstreams when they are bitten by the female mosquitoes. The toxins released produce extremely unpleasant symptoms – shivering cold followed by chronic fever, sweating and vomiting. If the disease is untreated the spleen may be affected, and a quick death can follow.

The long struggle against malaria achieved its greatest success during the 1940s and 1950s. New drugs were developed that proved effective in both preventing and curing the disease. Until then, clearing swamps and marshes infested with mosquitoes had been the only method of controlling malaria. Chloroquinine was developed in 1943 by the United States army, and DDT was widely used during and after the Second World War, especially in subtropical areas, where it was sprayed in homes and in the mosquitoes' breeding grounds. By 1955 staff at the WHO believed that it would prove possible to eradicate malaria all over the world. It had already been banished from the middle west and south of the United States, and from both Greece and Italy.

By 1960 it looked as though this widespread disease had almost been conquered. But although most developed countries were malaria-free, the scientists had miscalculated. In those parts of the world worst affected by malaria – Africa, Asia and Central and South America – severe shortages of resources and equipment hindered the eradication campaigns. There were further setbacks when both the parasite and the mosquito itself developed immune strains resistant to medical and chemical treatment. Chloroquinine began to lose its effectiveness as a result of over-use, and DDT was found to be highly toxic, damaging to humans and to the environment. By 1976 a WHO official reported that 'the entire population living in the original malarious areas is now at malaria risk'. In the four years between 1972 and 1976 the number of reported cases of malaria in the world more than doubled – from 3.2 million to 7.6 million.

Malaria's growing resistance to once-effective drugs postponed hopes of its permanent eradication. In the meantime, alternatives being researched included the use of an ancient Chinese remedy and a trial vaccine developed in South America.

With ever greater numbers of people on the move as a result of political upheaval, famine and poverty, the disease continued to spread as it became more difficult to treat. In the tropical world tens of millions of people still suffered from malaria; more than two million of them died each year.

MOSQUITO NETS *treated with insecticide, first introduced in The Gambia and subsequently in Ghana, Kenya and Tanzania, offered effective protection from malarial mosquitoes, but in poor countries most people could not afford to buy them.*

my face,' remembers Zafar Husain, a paramedical assistant. 'I didn't say a word. But other people in the village were very upset by her behaviour. Later on everybody in the village was vaccinated.' In an attempt to overcome people's fear, rewards of ten rupees were offered to those who reported cases of smallpox.

The new approach worked: by 1974 the search had been narrowed down to the last few cases. One of them was a young girl living in Pachera, a small village in Bihar, north and west of Bengal. Zafar Husain was absolutely determined that she would be the very last case in his region, and spent fifteen days at her home, sleeping on the veranda to ensure that no one came into contact with her. 'I was completely confident that after this child the infection would not spread farther,' he recalls. 'The last scab shed in front of me and I destroyed it. Then I knew that the infection would not spread!'

In 1977, after two years of surveillance, India was officially certified as free from smallpox by the WHO. Bohumir Kriz was making plans to close his office in Delhi, discharge the staff and hand over the equipment, when he received a telegram asking him to report to Somalia, in eastern Africa, within a week. 'We hardly knew where it was, and of course we had no idea that there was smallpox there. We thought India was the last place with smallpox, that the whole thing had finished,' he remembers. 'We started again from scratch.'

The outbreak in Somalia proved to be a serious one, and the programme went on for several months. There were not enough medical staff in some of the more remote areas, and it was difficult to isolate smallpox cases among nomadic people moving from place to place. In this Muslim country some of the men refused to be vaccinated by women, and some women to be vaccinated by men. 'They were sometimes frightened,' remembers Bohumir Kriz. 'We assembled the whole village with the village chief, we talked to them, we explained to them what we would be doing, why we were doing it.' By October the virus was confined to one person: Ali Maalin, a twenty-three-year-old hospital cook. 'I never thought that I would live,' he remembers. His was the last case of smallpox in Africa. 'I saw it as a victory,' says Ali Maalin. 'The fear was no longer there. We realized that if enough effort was made against disease we would eventually be successful.'

In 1980 the WHO announced that smallpox had finally been eradicated from the world. Bohumir Kriz and his team could now return home. 'Our boss brought from Geneva a case of champagne. We were celebrating. We were happy. But later that night we were a little sad, because it was clear we would all be disappearing to all corners of the world. And at that moment somebody said, "Well, I wonder what mother nature will prepare for us next?"'

"The search started in 1973, and in 1975 we saw through the last case. A disease that had been going on for ages was eradicated."

ZAFAR HUSAIN

POINT OF RECOVERY
Malaysian children (RIGHT) line up for their vaccinations, supplied by the WHO in 1982. Berber tribesmen and their families (BELOW) in the remote valleys of Morocco are given antibiotic ointment for conjunctivitis. Since medical teams supplied with UNICEF drugs first arrived there in June 1953 they have achieved considerable success in keeping the seasonal infection at bay.

ONE FAMILY, ONE CHILD *'for today but especially for tomorrow', is the message on a Chinese poster promoting family planning. Reproductive rules for Chinese parents were introduced in the late 1970s, as mounting population pressure precipitated the urgent drive for national birth control in the hope that China's huge population of one billion would eventually be reduced to 700 million.*

A people's programme

The attacks on major killer diseases such as polio, smallpox and tuberculosis on a world scale, and the introduction of new public health measures, were proving successful – so successful that every year millions more children survived into adulthood, and millions more adults were also living longer. However, one result was a sudden, dramatic explosion of population that in some countries threatened to overwhelm food supplies, health care provisions, and even the survival of governments hard-pressed by the needs of ever more people.

Nowhere was the problem more acute than in China, where there were more people – including more babies – than in any other nation on earth. For centuries the Chinese had wanted large families, and in the countryside families with four children were common. In an effort to control the population, the communist government had launched several birth control campaigns in the 1950s and 1960s. In 1979 a new official policy of 'one family, one child' was announced. Women were forced to have abortions, and fines were levied on parents with more than two children.

In the Caribbean, South America, sub-Saharan Africa, and especially the Indian subcontinent, governments faced the same imperative: to control the mounting tide of births or risk all the progress that had been achieved through investment in economic development and improved health care. Between 1947 and 1975 the population of India grew from 350 million to 750 million. As a government film acknowledged, 'Fifty-five thousand babies are born in India every day – two births every three seconds, straining our resources of food, shelter, clothing, employment and welfare.'

In the early 1950s a series of programmes was launched in India to offer advice and information on family planning methods, but with little success. From the 1960s the campaign intensified. The prime minister, Indira Gandhi, announced, 'Family planning is an accepted official policy in India, but our programme will not succeed if it remains only an official programme. Family planning is truly a people's programme. Its success rests on individual citizens. They have to be approached, persuaded, prompted, and helped to practise family planning.' At local rallies the campaign elephant distributed condoms held in her trunk, and then set out

FUTURE REFLECTIONS *A boy gazes at a poster bearing the symbol of India's birth control campaign – the red triangle. The campaign was widely promoted through community education, at health centres and in family planning clinics. Some people resisted it. 'You had many children,' says Amravati Devi, 'because suppose you had four and each one of them contributes a penny, then you would have four pennies. They would help you on the farm.'*

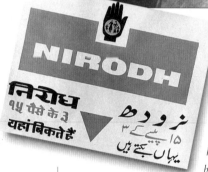

BEFORE AND AFTER

Women stand waiting to be sterilized (ABOVE), *while those who have already undergone the brief operation rest on the floor before returning home. Sterilization camps for both women and men were set up throughout India, and methods of contraception were widely promoted. Millions of condoms were freely distributed by the Nirodh campaign* (ABOVE LEFT); *the word means to stop or control.*

"Now people are going in for sterilization most willingly. They know that a small family is a happy family."

VASANTI SRIVASTAVA

to spread the message through thousands of villages. 'You have two, that will do' was the official slogan, similar to the message of the Chinese authorities.

India's democratic government did not feel it could use the same methods as the Chinese had done, but there were other ways of persuading people to have fewer children and even to undergo a sterilization operation, as one Indian doctor, Kalpana Bhatt, found. 'To attract patients,' she remembers, 'the workers would tell them that they would have a small injection, and they would go away walking, no need for rest or anything. And then the patients were given money – a hundred rupees – so they came for the money's sake. Sometimes they were already operated on, and they would come a second time. Even the bachelors would come sometimes.'

As the campaign was stepped up, millions of people across India volunteered. Dutta Pai, one of Bombay's leading sterilization doctors, was in charge of the Control of Population programme. 'Everybody worked hard. I remember those days – 1967 to 1974. The programme was being implemented with tremendous zeal, great conviction. A lot of effort was made to communicate the message to the minds of men and women, and we succeeded.' There were family planning clinics all over Bombay – at railway stations, in converted buses, and on street corners. Between 1971 and 1973 alone, more than five million sterilization operations

TOO MANY PEOPLE

I N THE EARLY 1930S the population of the world was about two billion; it had taken the whole of human history to reach that size. Since then there has been a dramatic explosion of population. In under fifty years the world's population doubled to four billion; by 1993 it had reached five and a half billion and was continuing to rise, being estimated to reach a peak of ten billion people by the year 2050 before beginning to level off.

Improvements in health care, nutrition and sanitation, the control of epidemic diseases and higher standards of living all contributed to the plummeting death rates and high birth rates that resulted in this population explosion by the early 1960s. Alarmed by the threat to food supplies, many governments increased funding for population control programmes, with a particular emphasis on family planning. Birth rates decreased in a number of countries, though the annual rate of population growth – some 100 million people – remained alarmingly high, with the greatest pressure in Africa, Asia and Central and South America.

The result was increased pollution, environmental degradation, and continuing poverty and hunger. In many developing countries there was concern that resources would be overwhelmed as millions more people needed food, health care, living space and work. In 1950 there were only three cities in the world with more than ten million inhabitants. By the end of the century it was expected that there would be twenty such cities, most in developing nations. In the 1990s many of the twenty-five million inhabitants of Mexico City lived in extreme poverty. With a land area roughly the same as that of the United States, China already had four times as many people, and far fewer resources of fertile land, fuels and minerals to support them. Its population was expected to rise to at least one and a half billion; some experts believed that the population of India, about 850 million, might exceed that of China within fifty years.

Billions of dollars were spent on population programmes in Africa, Asia and Central and South America. In 1994 the United Nations Population Fund initiated a world plan of action designed to stabilize population growth by the year 2050, through family planning and universal education. Experts were in no doubt that the population explosion would soon end; the question was whether it would come humanely, as a result of lower birth rates, or tragically through increases in death rates as a result of epidemics, starvation or war. By the 1990s many people had come to believe that the need to reduce birth rates, to increase food production while preserving the natural environment, and to distribute food and other necessities to all those who needed them, had become the greatest challenge of their time.

THE ESCALATING SCALE of the population problem was worst in developing countries, which were less able to cope with population growth, but it was the world's wealthier nations, where consumption was much higher, that placed the greatest strains on the earth's resources.

were performed, thousands of them by Dutta Pai. But, he says, 'Some people went too far, and this effort on the part of some misguided people led to a backlash....They tried to give greater incentives – people talked about giving away watches and this and that, so people who were not properly motivated came under the knife.' As more people claimed they had been coerced into having operations, the campaign became unpopular. 'In 1976 there was so much talk against male sterilization and family planning,' Dutta Pai says, 'that democracy won and family planning lost the battle.'

New epidemics, new diseases

In many parts of Africa, Asia, South America and the Caribbean, populations were rising almost as fast as in India. Now that viral diseases such as smallpox had largely been conquered, dangerous waterborne bacterial infections – typhus and cholera – posed the greatest threat to human health in poorer, overcrowded environments. The cholera epidemics that affected parts of Asia and Africa during the 1970s and 1980s, prompted by monsoon floods, famine and war, were an age-old problem.

In 1980 the WHO estimated that some twenty-five million people were dying every year from diseases caused by dirty water and lack of sanitation, six million of them children. Despite a drop

SOURCES OF INFECTION
Mexican villagers carry out their daily chores around their local water supply. Installing village pumps meant that people no longer had to carry water so far, and provided them with safe drinking water. This helped to prevent waterborne diseases from threatening many communities.

in overall mortality rates in many developing countries, infant mortality was still high and continued to encourage larger families. The only way to prevent the spread of infections such as cholera was to provide clean water and sanitation, and to improve public hygiene and health as well as curing disease. In 1981 the International Drinking Water Supply and Sanitation Decade was announced by the United Nations, an ambitious programme to provide clean water and sanitation for everyone by 1990. In ten years, thirty-five billion dollars were spent, mostly on local schemes. Villagers helped to drill wells, install hand pumps and dig cesspits.

In Peru, which had one of the highest birth rates, the size of the population was overwhelming the resources of the cities. Rubbish collection, water and sewage provision simply could not keep up. Standards of living and conditions of health and hygiene were poor. In the overcrowded shantytowns around the capital, Lima, people lived among their own rubbish and washed and cooked with water contaminated by untreated sewage. Cesar Queverdo Linares worked on a project to provide drinking water for the residents of Cajamarca in northern Peru. 'The drinking water system had been designed to supply the needs of places with 200 to 2000 inhabitants,' he remembers. 'The systems we installed there were calculated to last for twenty years, and our twenty-year

plan allowed for a fifty per cent growth in housing,' he remembers. 'But subsequently there was a population explosion and the drinking water system we'd installed proved inadequate.'

In 1991 a cholera epidemic broke out on the Peruvian coast, and quickly spread inland among people living in the Andes. In February, a month of carnival celebrations, Sennefelder Silva Marin was working at the hospital in Cajamarca, a town northwest of Lima. 'After the carnival we were surprised to learn that people had been admitted to the hospital with cholera, an illness none of us knew anything about, and which we'd never had to treat before,' he recalls. 'Never before in Cajamarca had there been an epidemic of such appalling proportions.'

In just over one year, 9500 people in Cajamarca caught cholera. Teams of emergency workers went out to treat them. 'It was an illness characterized by violent vomiting and diarrhoea,' says Sennefelder Silva Marin. 'It was a truly horrific illness.' When Maria Llana Rudas' husband fell ill with cholera, she had no idea what was wrong with him. 'His stomach hurt, his head hurt, he

BREEDING GROUND *for infection. Smoky Mountain in the Philippine capital Manila, where nearly half the city's inhabitants lived in poverty in makeshift homes with no sanitation or rubbish disposal. Here as elsewhere, deprivation and overcrowding contributed to disease.*

HONOURING THE DEAD (ABOVE) *A family in Lima visits the grave of a relative, one of the thousands of victims of the Peruvian cholera epidemic.* 'There were some who'd bury their dead straight away,' says Luis Correa Camacho, 'others who would refuse to bury them and who would leave them where they were because it was cholera.'

HELPING HANDS (ABOVE) *Western aid workers carry away the dead to prevent further spread of infection in the Kibumba refugee camp, where an epidemic outbreak of cholera in 1994 killed thousands of displaced Rwandans fleeing from the bloody ethnic fighting in their country.*

didn't speak to me, he didn't say a word. Even his faith seemed to have gone,' she remembers. 'My eldest son helped me take him to the hospital. We thought he might get better, but he didn't. We took him away dead.'

Part of the difficulty was to help people understand the infection so that they could avoid catching or spreading it. Although there was no cure for cholera, lives could be saved by quick treatment administered by trained staff, but both were in short supply. Sennefelder Silva Marin had the help of only three colleagues. 'Then we were joined by two more doctors sent by the Department of Health,' he remembers. 'So there were six of us fighting to save three and a half thousand lives....We treated people morning, noon and night, working in shifts.' Things were made worse by the local custom of holding a three-day vigil before burying the dead. Luis Correa Camacho, a former mayor of Otuzco village, attempted to persuade one family to bury their dead relative immediately. He even threatened to call the police.

MOUTHS TO FEED

ONE MILLION PEOPLE – men, women and children – seeking refuge from civil war died of starvation when famine broke out in Biafra, Nigeria in 1968. While epidemic diseases were successfully being fought, many people's lives in Africa, Asia and South America were still threatened by hunger and hunger-related illness, despite a steady rise in the amount of food being produced in the world as a whole. Many developing countries, with relatively weak economies, political instability and poor conditions for farming, became increasingly burdened with the task of feeding their rapidly growing populations.

Food production in industrialized countries soared during the 1970s and 1980s with new advances in agricultural science that enabled farmers to produce high-yielding, fast-growing crops. There were hopes that increased foreign aid to developing countries and the new 'Green Revolution' would solve the world's food problems: Mexico's wheat harvests increased threefold, and Pakistan stopped importing its wheat from the United States. But in the poorer countries most farmers could not afford the fertilizers, pesticides and modern machinery that were required by the new intensive methods of farming.

As people in developed countries enjoyed more food than ever before, there was less food available to many of those living in Africa and parts of Asia. By relying more heavily on foreign aid and food imports, the economies of

developing countries began to be overburdened by massive debts and soaring interest rates. To repay the debts, governments spent less on health services, housing and welfare, leaving their most vulnerable people, many of whom were too poor to buy or grow their own food, unsupported. In some countries farmers were encouraged to produce cash crops for export – coffee, cotton, sugar and tobacco – to help alleviate foreign debts, rather than growing food for local people to eat. Food shortages worsened as areas of once-fertile land turned into desert as a result of over-development.

During the 1980s a series of droughts in sub-Saharan Africa caused crops to fail, killed livestock and precipitated widespread starvation in the region. In Ethiopia five million people, many of them refugees from war, were threatened by famine; starving people fell ill after eating unfamiliar wild plants. Media attention, particularly to the suffering of the children, prompted a vast international relief effort in 1984 as the daily death toll rose. Aid arrived from European countries and from Australia, Canada and the United States, while charities and rock musicians banded together to raise funds and collect food and clothing.

The scale of the Ethiopian famine alerted the world to the sobering fact that in the face of drought and conflict, not even modern technology, greater food production and international aid could solve the problem of hunger. In 1991 civil war in Somalia left 250 000 people without food. Seven million people in Sudan faced hunger while the government used the country's resources to finance war. The physical and mental development of millions of children, and ultimately their whole future, was affected. By the 1990s, in a world of plenty, 800 million people continued to go hungry.

BARREN DESERT

(BELOW) *Weary from hunger, heat and exhaustion, refugees carry their few possessions on the long and difficult journey through the semi-arid Sahel region on the southern rim of the Sahara. Frequent droughts killed large numbers of cattle, devastated crops and brought widespread famine.*

'They ignored me. They kept vigil, chewing coca, and they prayed and chanted,' he recalls. 'Then suddenly – boom, the dead man exploded, faeces and guts all over the mourners, and by seven in the morning about eighty per cent of them had cholera. It was dreadful.' There were some 50 000 cases of cholera in the Peruvian epidemic, and more sporadic outbreaks continued elsewhere.

While the worst of the traditional killers were being driven back by vaccination and public health campaigns, a deadly new disease surfaced that was to threaten people in the developed and the developing world. Acquired Immune Deficiency Syndrome (AIDS) was first formally identified in the United States in 1981, though it had been spreading in some populations before then, particularly in parts of Africa, where it reached epidemic proportions in the 1980s. Caused by the human immunodeficiency virus (HIV), which damages the immune system and leaves its victims vulnerable to even minor infections, AIDS was easily transmitted through sexual intercourse and infected blood, and from mother to infant.

Everyone was frightened of catching the new disease. In Kenya Rowlands Lenya found that he was HIV-positive in 1989. 'I announced it to some friends, I went to the police and they took my photo, then the problems started,' he recalls. 'At my place of work, my colleagues did not want to share with me the usual office facilities. At home many of my friends stopped coming to our house. In school my children were abused by other children....So the situation became very difficult.'

By 1988 there were 120 000 reported cases of AIDS in 138 countries around the world; millions more people were infected by HIV. In the West, where major infectious diseases had long been brought under control and age-related illnesses posed the biggest threat, AIDS prompted a public health crisis. At first homosexual communities were thought to be most vulnerable to the disease, but it soon became clear that everyone was at risk. In

---

Ribbon of awareness

THE RED RIBBON *was adopted in the 1990s by AIDS campaigners trying to raise awareness about the disease. Part of the worldwide campaign against AIDS and HIV, the ribbon became a symbol of understanding and an expression of support and sympathy for its victims. Ten million ribbons, folded by volunteers, were produced for distribution all over the world – including China and India – through charities and other organizations such as schools and scouts clubs, in the army, at AIDS meetings and other public gatherings. The campaigners hoped that by prompting people's curiosity the red ribbon would help to save lives by giving more people accurate information about the disease.*

the United States 50 000 people had already died from the disease as medical scientists raced to discover new drugs for its treatment. Education, screening programmes and counselling facilities were set up, and many governments launched campaigns encouraging 'safe sex'. In 1990 the WHO reported that between eight and ten million people in the world were infected by HIV.

As the disease continued to spread, scientists were still unable to find a cure. 'My experience was that almost everything you could get was curable and easily treatable,' says Peter Staley, who became infected in 1985. He joined other sufferers in the United States, attending conferences, forming self-help groups and demonstrating in Washington. 'We had a sense of optimism that as long as we shook the trees of the scientific establishment, the cure would fall out,' he remembers. 'Unfortunately it didn't happen that quickly. A lot of people lost hope, a lot of people died. I don't know if science is going to be able to defeat this in time for me and my friends.'

AGAINST AIDS (RIGHT)
A French poster produced for a Paris AIDS conference in 1990 promotes the use of condoms to prevent the spread of infection. Angry at the failure of the United States president, George Bush, to initiate a national plan against AIDS (BELOW), crowds demonstrate in Washington in 1991. Peter Staley (LEFT) and his fellow AIDS sufferers took an active part in such demonstrations. 'I would survive the crisis just by shaking the tree, just by demonstrating, just by screaming,' he says.

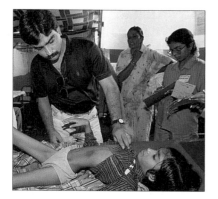

MEDICINE BY TRAIN
A doctor from the Life Line Express examines a young patient in a nearby tent. India's hospital trains brought medicines and medical care by rail to people living in remote areas.

THREE GENERATIONS *of a Japanese family pose for a wedding photograph (OPPOSITE). By 1993 life expectancy in Japan was the highest in the world. As elsewhere, the growing percentage of elderly people in the population created new social and economic burdens.*

New hopes and old fears

It was a discouraging thought that new diseases such as AIDS could arise, and age-old diseases that doctors believed had been conquered could reappear. Yet that is just what happened. After forty years in decline, tuberculosis was once again threatening lives. By weakening their resistance to infection, HIV made many people more susceptible to TB. The disease that struck Marjorie Cave and Les Ellis in the 1950s killed nearly three million people in 1990; by the mid 1990s, people were beginning to realize that the high hopes and ambitions of medical science in the 1950s and 1960s might have to be abandoned.

Deborah Runkle, who was among the first to receive the new polio vaccine in the United States, grew up believing that medicine held all the answers. 'I never knew anybody with a bad infectious disease. If you got sick, the doctor would prescribe something and it was over in three days.' But the spread of AIDS raised new doubts in her. 'I wonder, will polio come back? Are my children safe? What about my grandchildren?' she asks. 'I am not so positive any more. I think we had a lucky twenty-five years and I am not so optimistic about the future.'

From 1945, progress in twentieth-century medicine and health care was largely responsible for the threefold increase in the world's population. That success created new burdens, but it also improved countless numbers of lives. In India, Budu Harku was able to receive proper treatment for his cataracts. 'In the old days there were no eye operations,' he remembers. 'Once you were old, you became blind. But now, if you have even a minor eye problem you get your eyes fixed, and then you can look after yourself again.' Amravati Devi has also witnessed the dramatic changes. 'There is not so much disease now. Smallpox is gone. There is much less cholera and plague. People used to die of TB, that's also reduced. When the women came out of labour, they would get a kind of fever – and that's gone as well. Now there are doctors and medicines available in every village.' Since the early years of the century, average life expectancy everywhere had increased. In India by the 1990s it had risen to fifty-eight years, while in rich countries the average span of life was seventy-five years. For the majority of people, living longer was no longer a dream.

Great Leap

MOBILIZING THE PEOPLE OF CHINA

THE COMMUNIST SOLDIERS of the People's Liberation Army reached the city of Shanghai on 27 May 1949. Ma Gennan and her fellow factory workers rushed into the streets to welcome them. 'There was an endless stream of people, some playing military band music, some dancing,' she remembers. 'The great joy was indescribable.'

After the years of fighting, China's bitter civil war had at last ended, bringing victory for the communist forces. 'What the liberation meant to us was the collapse of the "three mountains"– feudalism, imperialism, bureaucratic capitalism,' recalls Ma Gennan. 'It was under the leadership of the Communist Party that we had succeeded in toppling the three mountains: in the countryside we had been subjected to the repression and exploitation of feudal landlords; in the factories we were suppressed by capitalists and foremen. Now we were to be liberated.'

Four months later, on 1 October, hundreds of thousands of people congregated in Tiananmen Square in the capital city, Beijing (Peking), to hear their new leader, Mao Zedong (Mao Tse-Tung), proclaim the People's Republic of China. Huo Buo was one of the official photographers there that day. The atmosphere was so electric that she found herself in tears. 'As soon as the broadcaster announced "Chairman Mao has arrived", the square was immediately seething with excitement. The crowd was chanting, "Long live Chairman Mao".' They listened intently as he declared, 'The People's Republic of China is now established. Chinese people are now standing up.'

This day had not come easily, but China's communist revolutionaries had proved to be an irresistible force. As a result, a way of life and a society that had continued almost unchanged for hundreds of years was about to be shattered. As their leaders set the Chinese to achieving their vision of a socialist utopia, and to building China into a strong power, people were to be swept into an unprecedented form of revolutionary mania, and subjected to new tests of endurance.

THE COMMUNIST FLAG IS RAISED *as people celebrate the triumph of the Chinese revolution in the city of Shanghai.*

"I wove cloth day and night to make ends meet....In the old days there was justice for the rich but none for the poor."

HU BENXIÜ

PLIGHT OF POVERTY *China's large population of illiterate peasants endured a life of continuing hardship and suffering. Many of them died of starvation or disease.*

The turning point

The upheaval had been coming for a long time. China had been ruled by its imperial dynasties for more than two thousand years. Millions of people endured harsh poverty, barely able to survive. Ninety per cent of the population still lived on the land; peasants were pushed into debt by government tax collectors and by their landlords, who imposed high rents. Child labour was normal, and women were subjected to forced marriage or concubinage.

A series of uprisings and organized rebellions had begun to challenge China's rulers during the nineteenth century, but the possibility of real change came with the death of the empress dowager in 1908. The Manchu dynasty was overthrown, and a republic declared in 1911; a period of instability and suffering followed, as rival political groups and regional warlords fought for control. By the late 1920s there were two major forces in the struggle for power: the Guomindang (Kuomintang) nationalist forces led by Jiang Jieshi (Chiang Kai-shek), and the Chinese Communist Party (CCP), which was founded in 1921.

During the chaotic years of the 1920s and 1930s there was little improvement in living standards. For many people, like Hu Benxiü, who grew up in the southwestern province of Sichuan, life in the old society was very hard. 'My mother looked after our three sisters. She had bound feet so she couldn't go to work in the field. Our life was very poor. As the landlord took away our land, we had to earn a living by spinning.' They were able to buy only a small amount of rice with their earnings. 'Struggling not to starve,' she says, 'we couldn't afford to take care of what we wore.'

China's cities were expanding as the country began to industrialize, but conditions there were little better. Ma Gennan's parents sent her from the village to work in a Shanghai factory. 'Once recruited to the factory we weren't allowed to return home and we had to live inside the factory,' she recalls. 'The place we lived in was a straw shed....We ate stinking vegetables and salted fish. At mealtimes, everybody fought for more food. Our monthly wage was only about twenty fen, not even enough to buy a roll of toilet

THE LONG MARCH

THE BITTER FIGHTING between the nationalists and communists intensified in 1930, when Jiang Jieshi launched a series of extermination campaigns against the Red Army soldiers. As they drew the noose tighter round the communist mountain enclave in southeastern Jiangxi province, by the summer of 1934 it looked as though China's communists were about to be wiped out. They decided to retreat.

On 16 October 100 000 soldiers, remnants of a far larger communist army that had been whittled away in the fighting, attempted a break-out. Joined by thirty-four women, including Mao Zedong's pregnant wife, and a few children, they began one of the most challenging feats of the century.

Over the next year they made their way in a great arc from southern China almost to the borders of Tibet, then north across great rivers, snow-covered mountain passes and vast, uninhabited, swampy grasslands. On the way they came under frequent attack from the nationalists, but were supported by the peasants, who responded to their disciplined, courteous behaviour. The communist soldiers' courage and endurance was often tested, as when they reached the Dadu river, a tributary of the Chang Jiang (Yangtze), where the only crossing was over a bridge, suspended by chains and laid with wooden planks, high above a deep mountain ravine. Many of the planks had been removed by the nationalist forces waiting on the other side.

The exhausted soldiers at last reached the sanctuary at Yan'an in the remote northern province of Shaanxi, 368 days after they set out. They had walked some 40 km (25 miles) each day, with little food, and fought many battles along the way. On the Long March – in all covering some 9600 km (6000 miles) – only 30 000 of them survived the hardships of the journey and the fighting. They formed a stronghold at Yan'an, building up power to continue their struggle.

What had begun as a retreat from an advancing enemy became a show of great strength and unity that safeguarded the communists and ensured their survival. The Long March also gave Mao new standing as the undisputed leader of the Party, and assured both Mao himself and the other campaign leaders of lasting prestige.

PEASANT SUPPORT (BELOW) *was a vital factor in the communists' victory, and a key aspect of Mao's revolutionary strategy. In contrast to the often harsh treatment meted out by nationalist soldiers, the communists treated the peasants well and even offered recompense for their hospitality.*

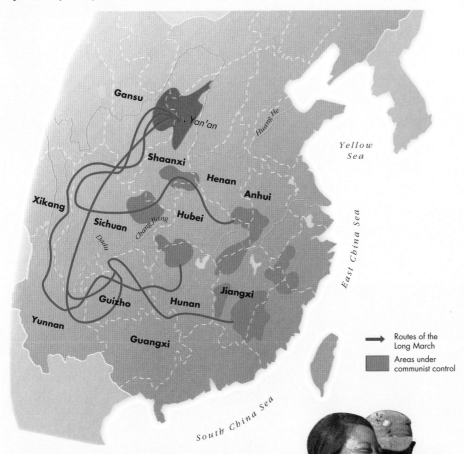

→ Routes of the Long March

▮ Areas under communist control

THE PERILOUS TRAILS (ABOVE) *of the Long March wound from south to northwest China. From three starting points the communist soldiers followed different routes through the harsh terrain, establishing communist bases along the way, until they reached safety at Yan'an.*

paper. If you didn't do your work well, the foreman would hit you with an iron rod wrapped in cotton flannel.' But for the wealthier middle classes life was very different, as Jin Jingzhi, whose husband ran an advertising company in Shanghai, remembers. 'We had many social engagements....My husband always paid great attention to his dress when going out....When he returned home in the evening, I made him really comfortable....I was very happy.'

It was to the huge peasant majority of the population that the communist leader Mao Zedong now looked for support. He believed that revolution would come through them. The communists promised them land and an end to poverty and oppression, and managed to establish local control in parts of the country they called 'liberated areas' as bases from which the revolution could spread. Pamphlets were secretly distributed among workers and peasants. 'We thought that what was said in the leaflets was right,' says Ma Gennan. 'We lived a bitter life, like beasts of burden, enduring hard labour but earning no money.'

The communists fought a fierce guerrilla war, both against the nationalists and against the Japanese troops who had in 1931 seized Manchuria in the northeast, and in 1937 launched an attempt to annex China itself. For a time the communists and nationalists formed an uneasy united front against the invaders, but after Japan's surrender at the end of the Second World War, full-scale civil war resumed in 1946. Victorious in Manchuria, and now armed with captured Japanese weapons, the strong, newly

"*We* saw the People's Liberation Army sitting by the road. They didn't even ask for a cup of water or food, they asked for nothing at all. They were very disciplined. **"**

REN FUQIN

CLASS STRUGGLE

Alarmed at the now real prospect of a communist victory, prosperous Chinese citizens jostle in a queue at a Shanghai bank in late 1948 to convert their savings into gold. When the communists took over, hyperinflation worsened China's already weak economy.

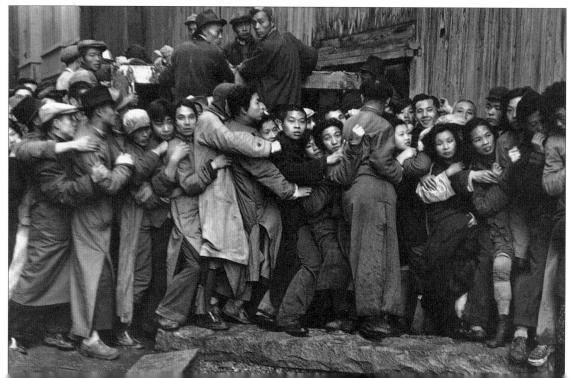

formed People's Liberation Army seized one area after another. By October 1949 Mao and his lieutenants were celebrating their final triumph in Tiananmen Square in Beijing, while the nationalists fled to the island of Taiwan.

When Hu Benxiü witnessed the arrival of the communist soldiers in Sichuan she was frightened of them at first, but as they visited people's homes they told them, 'We are your own people!' The general mood went from one of daunting fear to euphoric joy. 'We danced and paraded in the streets,' Hu Benxiü describes. 'We also sang a song which went, "The East is red, the sun is rising, and there is Mao Zedong in China, he creates happiness for the people".'

STANDING GUARD

Soldiers of the invading Japanese army watch over the citizens of Tianjin in 1939. 'Opposite our house there was a post where the Japanese set up checkpoints,' recalls Ren Fuqin. 'Any Chinese who went through it had to bow to the Japanese. If they forgot, the Japanese would make them kneel down with a heavy barrel of water on their heads.'

Mobilizing the millions

At first the revolution was widely greeted as a liberation. When the communists came to power China's economy was in ruins; most of the railways and main roads had been destroyed by the war, and disease and hunger were widespread. To implement the new socialist ideal and fulfil the promises of the revolution, productivity on the land and in the factories had to increase. It was the communist intention that the people should bring about the changes by their own efforts. Their energy and resourcefulness were to be tapped, and directed into building a healthier and stronger country.

"We would follow the Communist Party wherever it directed us, and would do whatever the Party instructed us to do. Now we were the masters, and our life was to be secured from the cradle to the grave. "

MA GENNAN

Mao had taken the decision to rely on the peasants, not on the urban workers, and they had fought for him. To reward them, land was confiscated from the landlords and given to the peasants. 43 per cent of China's land was redistributed to 60 per cent of the people. For the landlords, who became targets of blame and hostility, it was a frightening time. They were dealt harsh penalties at village 'people's courts'. The communists also organized 'speak bitterness' meetings, at which the landlords and the former village chiefs were publicly denounced before being imprisoned. Many were tortured or killed. Party activist Luo Shifa attended one of these meetings in Sichuan: 'We first asked the tenant farmers to make speeches denouncing the landlords.' The landlords were rounded up, bound hand and foot, and made to listen to the denunciations. 'We called it "eating bitterness",' describes Luo Shifa. 'Then it was time to chant slogans. We redistributed the land and farming tools. Peasants were very happy after the land redistribution as they could plant their crops in their own land.'

The communists also introduced a Marriage Law in 1950, which awarded equal rights to women and abolished child marriage and concubinage; people were discouraged from holding traditional arranged weddings. Prostitutes were cleared from the

VILLAGE SPECTACLE (ABOVE) *in the northern province of Henan, where a man is publicly tried for attempting to sell one of his relatives, the young girl seated on the stool in the centre. Under the communists, women's lives underwent dramatic changes.*

REVOLUTIONARY PYRE (OPPOSITE) *of former land deeds and other official documents seized by the communists in 1951. As many as a million landlords are thought to have been killed after the communists came to power, and much of their land was redistributed.*

THE GREAT HELMSMAN

FROM THE BEGINNING of the Chinese liberation, the nation's attention was focused on one towering figure: Chairman Mao, or the 'great helmsman', as he came to be known. Jiao Shouyun had been brought up to revere Chairman Mao. Each school morning she and her fellow pupils would stand in front of his portrait to recite passages from his writings. 'I had always cherished, since I was little, a feeling of great esteem for Chairman Mao, and dreamed that one day I could meet him.' A few years later, at a rally in Tiananmen Square, she did. 'I shook hands with Chairman Mao three times,' she remembers. 'I was simply intoxicated with great joy and happiness....I would follow Mao everywhere, do whatever he asked me to do.' Afterwards, everybody wanted to shake her hand, the hand that Chairman Mao had touched.

The man who cultivated this adulation, and who worked to use it to his own political ends, was born in Hunan province in south-central China in 1893, into a family of well-off peasants. Mao received a basic education in the Confucian classics before serving briefly as a soldier. In 1918 he qualified as a teacher from a school in the provincial capital, Changsha, where he came into contact with Western ideas and writings and began to shape his own ideas about revolution.

Mao realized that the time for profound change had arrived, and was determined to be one of its agents. From the 1920s he slowly emerged as a leading figure in the Communist Party. In 1927 he organized the Autumn Harvest peasant uprisings in Hunan and Jiangxi provinces. After the success of the Long March in 1935, he became chairman of the Party. A firm believer in Karl Marx's analysis of class and the need for class struggle, he tried to adapt the Soviet model of revolution to China's different circumstances by putting the peasants, rather than the workers, at the centre of his struggle, spreading his powerful guerrilla army among them 'like fish in the sea'.

After Mao led the communists to power, the entire country became steeped in his thinking. Young children were taught to sing, 'Father is dear, mother is dear, but Chairman Mao is dearest of all'. Adults learned that, 'All our victories are victories of the thoughts of Mao Zedong', and crowds of young people wished him, 'Ten thousand years of life!' The cult of Mao reached its height during the Cultural Revolution in the mid-1960s, when his image appeared on countless badges and posters, his quotations were broadcast on loudspeakers, and his thoughts were circulated in his published writings.

Through his mastery of propaganda and his personal charisma, Mao managed to dominate the Party and the nation until his death in 1976 at the age of eighty-three. Despite the ruthlessness and failure of some of his policies, Mao continued to portray himself as the father of the people, and many of them continued to adore him even though he had subjected them to great suffering.

LEADING THE CHINESE PEOPLE (BELOW)
Mao Zedong appeared at the centre of propaganda images encouraging people to devote their energy and enthusiasm to building a new China.

streets and given jobs. These changes were not easy to implement at first, and many people resisted them. But Hu Benxiü felt really inspired by the new opportunities. 'When my husband died, my child was only three and a half. As a woman nobody would want me. I had no way out in the old society,' she remembers. 'It was Chairman Mao and the Party who liberated me.'

Public health was one of the Party's top priorities. Mass inoculation campaigns were introduced all over the country, and people were urged to observe cleanliness and hygiene, and to spit in their handkerchiefs instead of on the ground. In occupation, the Japanese had referred to the Chinese as the 'sick men of Asia'. Now, Ren Fuqin remembers, 'We used this as an example to mobilize everyone to participate in the public health campaigns.' As a local public hygiene worker, Ren Fuqin and her colleagues brushed the walls with water and stuck up posters. One read, 'Everyone takes part in exterminating the four pests: bedbugs, flies, mosquitoes and rats'. Schoolchildren would proudly present their teachers with boxes of dead insects. Ren Fuqin also had to inspect people's homes. 'We would put our hands in the dustbins to see if they were clean. We mainly examined whether the table was dusty or not,' she remembers. 'Families that had done a good job would be given a little flag.'

There were campaigns for literacy, too. People were not only taught how to read and write, they were pressed into service to teach other people. One of them was Guao Xiuying. 'I used a wooden door as my blackboard. I wrote words on it and they copied them. Some of those who were learning had to carry their babies with them, breastfeeding them while studying.' People were encouraged to learn as they worked on the land or in the factories. 'I still remember what we learnt to read: "We are all Chinese; we are workers; we are peasants",' says Ma Gennan. 'I enjoyed studying. There were five girls in our family, all of us illiterate. Now, as

SHAO AI LING took this personal photograph of Mao at the moment of their meeting. 'When I was told that Chairman Mao was going to receive me, I was tearful and sleepless,' she describes. 'I felt that for the rest of my life I should serve the people better.'

FIELD WORK *A farm worker is treated for a minor injury by one of China's new 'barefoot doctors'. With a little training, a health manual and a few basic medicines, they set about providing health care for their fellow workers in often remote rural areas. Under the communists people received free medical care.*

a factory worker I had the opportunity of free classes, so I really wanted to learn.'

Private enterprise in the cities was allowed to continue at first (though it was closely controlled by the state) in an attempt to stabilize industrial output, but by 1952 people had to relinquish their businesses to the nation. Jin Jingzhi and her husband had to adapt to the new social order. 'I was very worried at the time,' she remembers. 'I thought that the Communist Party spoke on behalf of working-class people, and I didn't know how people like us would be treated.' She later attended a local residents' meeting, and then became involved in the household committee.

People were rallied into collective action by means of huge posters and banners, newspapers, loudspeakers or at public meetings that spread the communist ideology of class struggle and delivered a new political consciousness into the minds of millions of people. Mao's power and status quickly grew, and in 1954 he became chairman of the republic as well as the Party. Shao Ai Ling was a teacher in Shanghai. 'We constantly filled the minds of our pupils with Mao's political thoughts, and held him up as a figure of authority. To our minds Mao was our paramount leader, a great man. As a result the students soon came to realize that the changes taking place in our city, in our families, in the school, were brought about by Chairman Mao. They knew that Chairman Mao was our great saviour.'

Gradually the gigantic process of the revolution worked itself out in every corner of the country. Reconstruction, helped by aid from the Soviet Union, was under way. The bulk of the rural population was organized into cooperatives and collective farms; factories were taken over and run by state enterprises. The Party's will reached out into every village in the vast countryside, and every alley in the great cities; the Chinese people, some joyfully, some in fear and doubt, transformed themselves into revolutionary workers. By 1956 food output had grown by over 70 per cent. Yet Mao was not satisfied; by 1958 he was worried. China was not moving fast enough, and it was losing sight of its revolutionary goals. His solution was a new campaign for growth in both agricultural and industrial production.

HEROIC WORKERS *of Tachai are commemorated in a poster* (ABOVE) *following the successful completion of an ambitious project to build walls to control the annual flooding of a river. Several irrigation projects involving thousands of workers were launched* (OPPOSITE). *The Red Flag Canal project, begun in 1960 in Henan province, took more than 70 000 workers ten years to build. Numbers alone were not enough – China needed modern technology as well.*

NEW OPPORTUNITIES *A schoolgirl practises on an abacus, demonstrating her knowledge to her uneducated grandmother. In 1950 only one in five people could read. Many people benefited from the education policies introduced by the communists.*

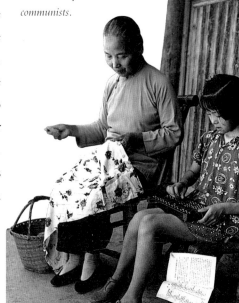

COMMUNAL LIFE *Children living on one of the large new communes are looked after while their parents are at work.*

'Greater, faster, better'

The new campaign was known as the Great Leap Forward. It called for renewed efforts in town and countryside alike. Banners exhorted the Chinese to work so hard that China would soon be able to catch up with the West. But behind this push for greater production was a second motive: to complete the revolution. Collectivization was speeded up and expanded. The family was no longer to be China's basic social and economic unit, as it had been for thousands of years. Instead, millions of people found themselves marshalled into enormous, unfamiliar and labour-intensive communes where they lived and carried out public works projects, manufactured industrial goods or farmed.

Twenty-four thousand communes were set up in the first two months of 1958 alone. Unlike cooperative farms, communes housed everyone, not just farm workers. In them, all aspects of people's lives were effectively 'collectivized' and regimented. Communal nurseries freed the women from looking after their children and communal dining halls fed their families, so they could devote all their time and energy to working under strict discipline. Instead of money, residents of the rural 'people's communes' were provided with six community services absolutely free: education, food, funerals, haircuts, health care and movies.

Zeng Guodong was a Party cadre, one of many officials assigned to implement policy and encourage others to do so. He participated in the transformation of eight agricultural cooperatives into communes in

NEW LINES OF COMMUNICATION *were opened in 1956 with the completion of a railway across a mountainous landscape to link the southwest and northwest regions of China. Workers applaud one other at the site of a monument to their labour, as a train makes its first journey towards the city of Chengdu.*

Tianjin. 'There were about two hundred and seventy thousand people in two big communes,' he describes. 'Big communes could deal with big projects. With several hundred thousand people to do a job, things were completed in next to no time.' One of Zeng Guodong's duties was to organize the dining halls. 'There was one big dining hall for every hundred households, and each dining hall catered for several hundred people,' he recalls. 'In this way, we managed to assemble the working forces and have food at the same time.' It was Qin Yongchang's job to serve the food in a commune in Henan province, where they were first established. 'When the village bell rang, people would return from the fields and come to the commune's dining hall,' she remembers. 'We would cook noodles, sweet potatoes, and bread made from wheat husks.'

All this was part of the policy called the General Line and the Three Red Flags: 'Go out, aim high, and achieve greater, faster and better results in building socialism'. One of the most extraordinary campaigns launched during the Great Leap Forward was intended to double China's steel production. Zeng Guodong helped to spread Chairman Mao's message. 'I didn't think China would be a powerful nation if it was without iron and steel. Building machines, ships and trains all needed steel,' he says. But instead of building new steelworks, Mao planned to mobilize the peasants once again. Small 'backyard' furnaces sprang up as people began to smelt iron and contribute to the target of ten million tonnes of steel a year. The demand for scrap iron was so great that peasants were persuaded to give up their cooking pots and tools to be melted down.

Shortly after He Jin Lua and Lian Tianyun got married in Henan province, they threw themselves wholeheartedly into the steel-making campaign. 'Those who were less productive would be seen as good for nothing,' He Jin Lua remembers. 'We were determined to follow the Party's instructions. We were willing to do whatever the Party asked us.' Her husband made a bag by tying up the legs of a spare pair of trousers, and filled them with all the scrap he could find to hand over to the factory. He Jin Lua cut off her pigtail, using her hair to reinforce the furnace, which was

"Other workers asked to rest, but I didn't want to leave the "battlefield" and continued to work by the furnace. "

LIAN TIANYUN

STEEL-MAKING COUPLE
He Jin Lua and Lian Tianyun (LEFT), who worked feverishly to outproduce one another in the steel-making campaign during the Great Leap Forward. As steel production targets continued to rise to meet China's growing industrial and agricultural needs, people in villages throughout the country were urged to contribute by using domestic 'backyard' furnaces similar to the idealized version depicted in propaganda pictures (TOP). In 1958 the Chinese claimed that steel production was more than double that of the previous year.

made of earth. Assigned to different work groups, the young couple competed furiously. 'If his group produced more we had to outdo them,' He Jin Lua remembers. 'I used to have sleepless nights after our tiring meetings discussing our strategy.' Steel-making took precedence over everything, even starting a family. 'How could we have time for children?' she asks. 'We didn't even visit our parents when they were sick, because we devoted everything to steel-making.'

The campaign at first appeared to achieve astonishing results: China's steel output was said to have doubled in a single year. Mao's attention again turned to accelerating agricultual output. To meet the absurd production quotas that were set, some people resorted to trickery. 'We removed all the ready-planted rice from the fields and replanted it in a show field so that we would reach our quota,' remembers Zeng Guodong. But the densely planted rice did not grow. 'Before long the rice rotted, and the peasants got angry. They said, "If you take all the rice and waste it, what will we eat in the autumn?" ' Extravagant targets also encouraged the tendency to boast. Many Party cadres and farmers falsified their achievements, exaggerating national production figures. Of the 375 million tonnes of grain said to have been produced in 1959, only 275 million tonnes were actually harvested.

Nothing was permitted to stand in the way of high yields – not even the birds. 'The word came down from above to mobilize the masses to kill the sparrows,' remembers Hu Benxiü, who helped to organize a 'kill sparrows' campaign in her village. 'Villagers old and young joined in. We were so busy that we even had to take turns to eat,' she describes. 'The trees were really high, and hard to shake, but everyone made an effort to do their best, so the sparrows could not land on them. We also used catapults to shoot them down. Some people used guns....Those who killed the most sparrows were praised and given rewards. Those who caught smaller numbers were criticized, and encouraged to do better the following day.'

Despite the nation's huge efforts the Great Leap Forward was a failure. Fewer sparrows meant more insects, which did more harm to the crops than the sparrows had. The steel that had been enthusiastically produced in backyard furnaces at low temperatures

turned out to be useless, and, as Zeng Guodong came to realize, the campaign to make it had diverted millions of agricultural workers. 'As a result, wheat and sweet potatoes were left to rot in the fields,' he admits, 'The loss was very great.' To make things even worse, a series of droughts, floods and typhoons beginning in 1959 caused immense damage. The excesses of the Great Leap, combined with these natural disasters and then the withdrawal of Soviet aid after a rift in Sino-Soviet relations, were followed by what may have been the worst famine in Chinese history.

Food was in desperately short supply. To avoid starving, people ate any kind of vegetable they could find, such as cabbage roots or sweet potato vines. Others lived on fermented earth dried into biscuits. Times were hard for factory workers in the towns. 'We overcame the shortage of food by tightening our belts. We ate the stem from a green vegetable – *won*. We called it "seamless steel pipe". We first smashed the stem and then mixed it with flour,' Ma Gennan remembers. 'Chairman Mao assured us at the time that all would be well after this period of natural disasters, so we must follow Chairman Mao's instructions to get over this hurdle.'

In the countryside the effects of the famine were far more devastating. 'We simply had nothing to eat,' remembers Ren Yangchen, a worker on the Red Flag Canal project in Henan province. 'We had to eat wild vegetables or herbs. We ate elm bark and leaves from the trees. We ate almost anything in order to survive.' When Luo Shifa made his way back to Sichuan from Beijing, he found that people were dying from dropsy, severe bloating brought on by starvation that was made even worse by the consumption of wild vegetables. 'In our commune sixteen hundred people were starving,' he remembers. 'Some people fell over from weakness and were lying in the road, others were already dead. When the peasants saw me they began to cry. I cried too.' In the three years after 1959 more than twenty million people are thought to have died in the famine.

HARVESTING HOPES
United by their efforts to produce ever greater yields, commune workers (ABOVE) deal with the rice crop, while young girls tend a sweet potato field on an agricultural cooperative (LEFT).

VICTIMS OF FAMINE
In China's long history there had been many disastrous famines and mass starvation. Under the rule of the communists, people did not expect to suffer a similar fate.

THE ABODE OF SNOW

O N 7 NOVEMBER 1950 the People's Liberation Army entered Tibet, known as the Abode of Snow. Its people differed greatly from the Chinese ethnically, in language and in religion, and did not welcome the communist 'liberators'.

Until the early years of the century the Tibetans, sheltered by the highest mountains in the world, had lived in peaceful isolation, though the Chinese emperors claimed that they were subjects of Beijing. People in this religious, feudal society lived under the rule of their king and spiritual leader, the Dalai Lama, working as serfs for Buddhist monasteries or for secular landlords. Trouble had begun when a British expedition crossed the Himalayas from India into Tibet in 1904. Tibet became caught up in quarrels between Britain, the Russian empire –

which was expanding into Mongolia – and China. The British accepted China's suzerainty over Tibet, which Tibet refused to acknowledge; with the collapse of the Manchu dynasty, Tibet tried to assert its independence.

When China's internal conflicts ended, Tibet was again drawn into China's orbit. After the invasion in 1950 the Chinese promised to respect its status as an autonomous region, and the rule of its lamas. But instead they treated Tibet as an integral part of the People's Republic. Collectivization was enforced on its people, monks were coerced into marriage and work, and monasteries were closed down.

Chinese rule was so unwelcome that in 1959 Tibetans organized a revolt, which was brutally put down. Thousands of people were executed, arrested and deported, and about 80 000 Tibetans, including the Dalai Lama, fled to safety over the mountain passes into India. Communist rule was forcibly imposed. Buddhism was outlawed and temples destroyed. Local people were forced to carry identity cards, and large numbers of Chinese settlers arrived. When the Red Guards came in 1967, during the Cultural Revolution, they set about ravaging any remnants of Tibetan culture and tradition.

The severity of China's attempt to transform Tibet into a province of China was relaxed during the 1970s, and tourism and economic development were permitted. But when the Tibetans rebelled again in 1987 many were executed, tortured and imprisoned. China was willing neither to leave Tibet alone nor to allow its people to live as they had for centuries. A poor and isolated country, Tibet's once stable agricultural economy was sacrificed to Chinese collectivist dogma. The Tibetans remained bitterly resentful that their religion had been slighted and their culture undermined for a period of almost fifty years.

THOUGHT REFORM (BELOW) *Students sent to work in the countryside pause to study the writings of Chairman Mao.*

Rekindling the revolution

In 1962 Mao had to admit defeat. The suffering and destruction caused by the Great Leap fuelled opposition to his policies both within the Party and in central government. He issued a public 'self-criticism' acknowledging the failure of his economic policies, and a programme of recovery was launched by the more pragmatic leaders: Deng Xiaoping, the former secretary-general of the Party, and Liu Shaoqi, who had been appointed chairman of the republic in 1959 following Mao's resignation from that post. Nevertheless, Mao was still a powerful figurehead. At the age of sixty-nine he retained the chairmanship of the Party and was still supported by hardline radicals and the army.

Mao did not stay in the background for long. To regain a tight rein over the country and re-establish his power, he began a campaign that turned into the Great Cultural Revolution. In its earliest stages, it seemed to reassert an ideological and cultural revolutionary spirit. With the help of the Gang of Four – a group of hardliners that included Mao's third wife, Jiang Qing – millions of copies of a 'little red book' containing selected *Quotations from Chairman Mao* were distributed, and the *People's Daily* newspaper reiterated the message. At first, tendencies that were thought to be

"There were several hundred Red Guards with their armbands. Some had scissors in their hands and wanted to chop people's hair. They regarded me as an anti-revolutionary reactionary simply because I didn't carry Chairman Mao's Red Book with me that day."

SHAO AI LING

TARGETS OF ABUSE *Three people accused of being anti-revolutionaries are paraded on the back of a truck through the streets of Beijing. Forced to wear dunce's caps that bear their names, they are publicly denounced as a crowd of jeering Red Guards looks on.*

Bible of the masses

THE 'LITTLE RED BOOK', *as the* Quotations from Chairman Mao *was popularly known, was published by the Chinese army in the mid-1960s to draw mass support for Mao's ideological Cultural Revolution. Hundreds of millions of copies of the book, containing a selection of Mao's writings, were printed and distributed to the vast Chinese population, who were urged to study and recite from its passages of Maoist doctrine. There was virtually no other reading matter available at the time. The pocket-sized version of the book was produced so that people could always carry a copy with them.*

anti-revolutionary in dance, in literature and in the theatre were targeted. By purging society of 'bourgeois' tendencies and abusers of power and privilege, Mao believed that a truly proletarian culture would emerge.

In 1966 the Cultural Revolution began to speed up. Backed by the army, Mao took the opportunity to denounce and discredit his political rivals, Deng Xiaoping and Liu Shaoqi, and assume power once again. This time it was young men and women to whom Mao appealed. They attended mass rallies and flocked to Beijing in their thousands to listen to his speeches, which whipped up their enthusiasm. With Mao's support, students who had begun to call themselves 'Red Guards' took the lead. The movement grew so fast that there were soon up to twenty million Red Guards in cities across China. Zhang Pingan was one of them. 'We thought we were spearheading the revolution, responsible for clearing all obstacles to the revolutionary cause. We felt we were the vanguard of the Party and of Chairman Mao, and we were proud of our role.' Mao told them, 'The Chinese future is with you'; they responded by carrying out his revolutionary will. They were provided with free food, accommodation and transport.

What had begun as an ideological campaign soon descended into a dangerous hysteria as the increasingly militant Red Guards set out to search for and denounce 'enemies' of the revolution. 'Anyone in power became a target, whether they were right or wrong,' Zhang Pingan confesses. 'Our teachers and the principal were not really bad people, in fact they were quite progressive, but we had to find a target, otherwise we would be in trouble. So we organized ourselves and targeted them. We ordered the principal to confess, but he said he had nothing to confess. We thought he was dishonest, so we began to beat him up. We dragged him from place to place until he had a heart attack.'

Shao Ai Ling, who had become the principal of Shanghai Number Six Girls' School, was also denounced by her students. Several hundred student Red Guards came for her, some wearing armbands, some military belts. 'They chopped off my hair and beat me with sticks,' she remembers. 'They told me that revolution means rebellion, and that it is not soft-hearted. They ordered me to produce the Red Book. But that day I was wearing a white

PEKING OPERA

THE CHANGES BROUGHT by the 1949 revolution were at first welcomed by China's actors and singers, who had lived humbly in the old society. 'Although we could earn quite a lot of money, our social status was very low, and people despised us,' remembers Tong Xiang Ling, who was a performer in Shanghai's Peking Opera. Under the communists, he says, 'We were told that we artists were the engineers of human souls. We didn't perform only to earn money, but had a serious responsibility to educate people through our art. We felt a strong sense of emancipation, not economically but ideologically.'

The Peking Opera was the finest of many provincial opera schools of this highly popular Chinese art form, which dated back to the thirteenth century. After the revolution the communists objected to many aspects of traditional opera, and began a programme of reform. Some operas were revised so as not to give offence to revolutionaries. The characteristic clashing cymbals, symbolic, stylized gestures, rich costumes and dramatic makeup were toned down in favour of a new simplicity and directness.

By the early 1960s Mao thought that social transformation in the arts was too slow in coming. 'Isn't it absurd,' he asked, 'that many communists are enthusiastic about promoting feudal and capitalistic art, but not socialist art?' Mao's wife, Jiang Qing, herself a former actress, took an active role in transforming the theatre. 'The grain we eat is grown by the peasants,' she said. 'The clothes we wear are made by the workers, and the People's Liberation Army stands guard for us. Yet we do not portray them on the stage.' Peking Opera's centuries-old plays about Chinese history and legend were replaced by new operas commemorating revolutionary feats and proletarian virtues.

During a national festival in 1964 more than seventy theatrical groups performed about 7000 shows of the 'revolutionary' operas to audiences totalling seven million people. The most famous of these was *Taking Fierce Tiger Mountain with Wise Strategy*, in which Tong Xiang Ling felt honoured to play the role of the hero. One night, Chairman Mao and Premier Zhou Enlai were among the guests of honour. 'We were told that the fate of the play would be determined that day,' he remembers. At the end of the show, as the curtain was lowered, the perfomers waited anxiously on the stage. 'My heart was beating really fast. When the announcement about Mao's approval was made, I couldn't help jumping up,' remembers Tong Xiang Ling. 'That night was the happiest moment of my life.'

Peking Opera faced its most critical test in 1966, as it fell victim to the Cultural Revolution's vengeful assault on traditional culture. During the convulsions that followed, the Red Guards were turned loose on actors and singers, no longer 'engineers of the human soul' but anti-revolutionary reactionaries. 'One morning my wife telephoned me, asking me to go to the Peking Opera troupe immediately,' Tong Xiang Ling remembers. When he got there he found huge denunciation posters that read, 'If Tong Xiang Ling doesn't surrender, he will be exterminated'. He could not understand what it was that he had done wrong. 'In the past I played emperors and feudal gentry, but now I played heroic revolutionaries. Even so, I was being targeted.' Many popular actors and singers were killed or committed suicide in a desperate last act.

TONG XIANG LING *the Peking Opera star, stands proudly next to Chairman Mao (TOP, left of picture in leopardskin costume). He was later branded an enemy of the people after being denounced as an anti-revolutionary and forced to attend gruelling denunciation meetings.*

ROLE REVERSAL
Uncharacteristically, the male parts in this Peking Opera production staged after the revolution were played by women. Chinese women traditionally did not appear on the operatic stage, so all the female roles had to be played by men.

shirt with no pockets, so I hadn't got the Red Book with me. They said, "If you are not carrying the Red Book, that means you are not loyal to Chairman Mao....You deserve to be overthrown!" It was December in Shanghai and very cold. They ordered me to stand outside the playground from morning to night. But then they thought the punishment was not severe enough, so they got a big blackboard and pressed it down on me. One of them stood on it on the right side and one on the left, like a seesaw, and I was squashed in the middle.' Shao Ai Ling survived the torture, but was left with permanent injuries to her face.

Many others did not survive. Thousands of people were killed or committed suicide; thousands more were relentlessly persecuted by the fanatical Red Guards. Luo Shifa had supported the Cultural Revolution, but he too was confronted. 'I knew I hadn't done anything wrong. I had always followed the mass line,' he says. 'I answered to whatever name they called me: landlord, anti-revolutionary, capitalist-roader....I knew it was just a routine I had to endure. At the denunciation meeting, they slapped my face and forced me to kneel down. Kneeling on hot charcoal and broken glass was almost a daily routine, so I put a soft pad inside my trousers and that made it easier when I was forced to my knees.' Luo Shifa was paraded through the streets with a denunciation placard hanging from his neck. Even the Party cadre, Zeng Guodong, was attacked. The Red Guards twisted his hands behind his back and forced him to bend over, sometimes for as long as three hours, while they denounced him.

As former capitalists, Jin Jingzhi and her husband were also sought out. Their home was searched for ten days. 'I was confined to one room and my husband to another. They didn't allow us any contact. They bombarded us with questions day in, day out,' she recalls. 'If they suspected that something was hidden in the ceiling, they would rip open the ceiling. All the trees in my garden were uprooted, but they found nothing and finally left.'

The Cultural Revolution affected almost everyone. The way people cut their hair or the clothes that they wore could easily give them away as 'bourgeois reactionaries'. A Red Guard slogan said that China had to be rid of the 'four olds' – old habits, ideas, customs and culture – so ancient temples, museum artefacts

CRITICAL TIMES (RIGHT) *Dazibao or handwritten 'big character' posters denouncing enemies of the revolution were a familiar sight on public walls in the late 1960s. The one in the centre accuses Mao's rival, Liu Shaoqi. Shao Ai Ling also fell victim to them. 'For a middle school principal, big character posters were mainly confined to the campus,' she says, 'but in my case they were put up in the People's Square, the Great Shanghai Cinema and the Great World Amusement Centre.'*

THE GANG OF FOUR (BELOW), *largely responsible for the upheavals of the Cultural Revolution, are the subject of a 1976 poster illustrating their downfall.*

and countless other examples of China's heritage, as well as signs of foreign influence, were destroyed. Books printed before 1949 were burned, scientists and scholars attacked. People argued in the factory and at factory gates. Husbands argued with wives, parents with their children. Everywhere people were debating, discussing, quarrelling, putting their thoughts into slogans on 'big character' posters for everyone to see. The country ground to a halt. Farmers stopped planting, workers stopped producing. Hospitals could not function without the doctors who had been discredited and sent away, schools could not teach without teachers.

By 1967 China had slipped into something like anarchy. The British embassy was burned down, and foreign diplomats were attacked. In some places Red Guards split into factions and fought each other with machine guns and artillery. Mao responded by calling in the army to restore order, and despatched millions of young people to the countryside to learn from the peasants.

From 1969 the zeal and excesses of the Cultural Revolution dwindled, but Mao still held on to power into the 1970s. He had purged both the Party and the government of his political rivals, and now ruled with the help of his lieutenant Zhou Enlai and the Gang of Four. In 1976, the Chinese year of the dragon – which was traditionally a time of great change – both Zhou Enlai and Mao Zedong died. 'I didn't know what would happen to China,' remembers Zeng Guodong. 'All those people who shared Mao's vision were gone. Who would lead the Communist Party now? Nobody had the power and the authority to unify China as Mao did. I felt at a loss.'

END OF AN ERA (BELOW) *Thousands of people publicly mourn the death of Mao Zedong at the Great Hall of the People in Beijing in 1976.*

> "*In the past we had been so cut off, the students knew nothing of the outside world. After the endorsement of the open-door policy, my former students have become liberal....They can judge, compare and decide what is right. They have enriched their experiences.* "
>
> SHAO AI LING

SCENE OF VIOLENCE
(ABOVE) *A wounded young demonstrator is hemmed in by armed soldiers in Tiananmen Square in 1989, as student demonstrations for greater freedom were suppressed by the military.*

A TASTE OF THE WEST
(OPPOSITE) *An American fast food restaurant in the southern town of Shenzhen in 1991 symbolizes China's new economic liberalization.*

The second liberation

After Mao's Zedong's death, China gradually began to move away from the undeviating revolutionary path he had mapped out. The Gang of Four were arrested and publicly tried, and in 1978 Deng Xiaoping became president amid calls for greater reform. The communes were disbanded, land was redistributed, and farmers were permitted to sell their surplus produce for personal profit. Foreign investment and even some aspects of Western capitalism, such as private ownership, were permitted. More consumer goods appeared in the shops, and attempts were made to modernize industry using Western expertise. With the free market, there were wider disparities in wealth between successful entrepreneurs and their workers in the rapidly growing special economic zones. Zeng Guodong saw these changes. 'Deng Xiaoping said, "Reform is China's second revolution". I was deeply impressed by his comment. It is indeed the second revolution, or second liberation.'

Some things did not change. People's hopes that economic liberalism would bring political freedom were dashed by the regime's relentless repression of any dissent. As students demonstrated for democracy and political reform in 1986, rioting spread across the country. In 1989 the government gave orders for tanks from the People's Liberation Army to disperse the crowds of young demonstrators in Tiananmen Square, killing and wounding thousands of people. After forty years the revolution had turned on its own children.

The Chinese now seemed to turn away from their great revolutionary adventure, emerging from years of sacrifice to focus on increasing prosperity. With its rapidly growing economy, China began to occupy a new place on the world arena. Huo Buo, the photographer who had captured the coming of the revolution in 1949, reflected, 'For the last forty-five years our country has continuously made progress. But there are ups and downs, many trials and hardships. It is like the growing up of a human being. There is a Chinese saying that "failure is the mother of success".'

21

New Release

CHANGING ROLES
FOR
YOUNG PEOPLE

On 14 JANUARY 1967 thousands of young people filled Golden Gate Park in San Francisco for an event that for many epitomized the mood of their generation: it was called the 'Human Be-in'. Ron Thelin helped to organize the peaceful gathering. 'We didn't know how many people would show up,' he recalls, 'and when ten thousand people, or maybe more, came out of the woodwork it was just breathtaking, it was earthshaking – this many people were having this experience. There was a sense that something was in the air, this was a new time, a new age.'

The generation of young people who made San Francisco their haven that year felt that the Human Be-In was the high point of what they described as a shared sense of unspoiled liberation. Martine Algier, who was living in San Francisco, took part in the public extravaganza of music and dance. The attitudes and ways of these young people were unlike anything anyone had seen before. 'We felt there was an awakening,' Martine Algier recalls. 'We even used the word among ourselves – mutants. We felt that there was a whole wave of people, specifically young people, who were coming into this awareness. And many of them were isolated in small towns across the country and didn't know there were others like them. We felt we needed to wave and say, "Hey, we're here, you're not alone. Don't be afraid, come on out and *be*, be who you really are".'

Elsewhere in the industrialized world, too – in Australia, Canada, Europe and Japan – young people gained new freedoms in the 1950s and 1960s. They did not all share the 'new age' ideas seen in Golden Gate Park, but almost all did use their new freedom and opportunities to question the authority of their parents, the attitudes and values of society and of the politicians who held power. In their efforts to find new and better ways of living, young people succeeded in challenging long-held conventions and traditional ways of thinking, and came to play a far greater part in society than the young had ever done before.

SHAKING OFF *old restrictions, people gather in the park for a festival of fun and dance.*

Breaking the mould

The world in which the immediate postwar generation grew up was one in which most children were taught to treat their parents and others in authority with unquestioning deference, and to imitate their elders' tastes and values when they themselves reached adulthood. But the dramatic changes of the 1960s had their roots in changes already taking place during the conservative 1950s.

More babies were born in the first ten years after the Second World War in the United States than in the fifty years before it. There were so many 'baby boomers' that school playgrounds and classrooms soon became overcrowded. 'We were the first class to go into a new building because of the growth,' says Bob Bossar, who went to school in Pittsburgh, Pennsylvania. 'I remember the schools, the Salk polio vaccine, how we had to wait in line to get our shots, schools being very crowded.'

In Europe economic recovery from the war was slower, but there too young people were growing up in a very different way from their parents' generation. Prompted by reforms that made education more accessible, young people stayed on longer at school. New schools were built and the number of pupils in them rose, though in the late 1950s only 4 per cent of young people in Britain went to university, 7 per cent in France, 8 per cent in the Netherlands and 11 per cent in Belgium, and as many as 20 per cent in the United States. Beyond Europe – in Australia, Canada, Japan – the same trend could be seen.

In the United States more young people had money to spare than in any previous generation, and they spent it on new leisure opportunities. There were new skating rinks and bowling alleys. There were magazines catering specially for young people. 'The cars were made for us,' says Bob Bossar. 'We had new highways, we had new clothes and music, new schools – just a lot of bright things were going on. Probably a marketer's dream, the baby boomers.' By the end of the decade some two-thirds of American nineteen-year-old males and half of all females were licensed to drive.

Despite the prosperity, as the Cold War between the Soviet Union and the United States intensified it was an anxious time. Living with the fear of a nuclear attack

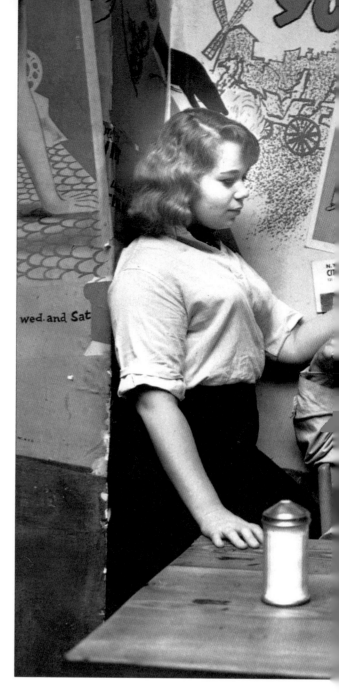

Musical box

JUKEBOXES *became popular during the late 1940s and 1950s, first in the United States – where they had been mass produced since the mid-1930s – and then among young people in Europe as well. Installed in cafés and clubs, they offered a selection of records chosen by the companies that owned them; the selection was regularly updated as new records were released and became chart hits. These coin-operated gramophones were one of the new ways in which the growing incomes of teenagers could be tapped. Wurlitzer jukeboxes, made in the United States, were among the most successful designs.*

raised questions among the young. 'It was scary,' remembers Martine Algier, who lived in a small town in Michigan before moving to the suburbs with her family. 'It was really crazy. It looked like the adults were going nuts – I mean here were these adults who were supposed to be running the world and taking care of us, and yet they'd obviously done something very crazy to put us all in a situation like this.' At school teenagers hid under their desks during air raid drills, and at home they watched their parents store food and dig bomb shelters in their backyards. 'After the Second World War our parents wanted, needed security,' says Ron Thelin, who lived in a small town in California, was an Eagle Scout and attended Sunday School. 'Things were programmed, your future was programmed out....It was like being in a trance.'

For the vast majority of young people everywhere, music helped to break through that trance. Most parents did not approve of the loud, provocative sounds of rock and roll music, which they associated with rebelliousness. Their children felt very differently. While he was still at school in 1955 Ron Thelin watched a film about juvenile delinquency, *Blackboard Jungle*, with its soundtrack featuring music by Bill Haley and the Comets. 'It was a revelation for me. I had never heard the beat before,' he recalls. 'It was totally unlike anything that I'd experienced in my life.'

Rock and roll music had a similar effect on teenagers everywhere who were beginning to question the values their parents tried to impose. 'It seemed like there were ways you were supposed to be and clothes you were supposed to wear, and people who were so concerned with status,' says Martine Algier. 'If you danced there was a way you were supposed to dance....I wanted to dance freely.' When *Blackboard Jungle* was shown in Britain the following year there were riots at some cinemas, and it was banned in certain towns.

Rusty Sachs grew up in a farming community in Norwich, Vermont. Then a rock and roll fan, he used to collect Elvis Presley records. 'The music and the performance were an example to us of how we should move, and how we should let the music dominate us, and be channelled by something other

BOY SCOUTS *in the 1950s were taught the same values – obedience and team spirit – as they had been since the movement was founded early in the century.*

LATEST DANCE MOVES *are demonstrated by a young American couple as West German students attending a dance at the Free University of Berlin in 1953 look on.*

TIME FOR LEISURE *at the Cock' n' Bull in New York's Greenwich Village, one of the centres of attraction for the young generation of 'beats' or 'beatniks' during the 1950s. Breaking with the traditional attitudes and the conventional dress worn by many young people, they were labelled bohemians.*

than the standard behaviour patterns that were around us,' he remembers. 'This was something new, this was very out of the ordinary. This was breaking the mould. And it was fun.'

As more and more young people listened to wilder, angrier sounds in music and watched the new films, they began to dance differently and to look different; many of them also felt different. There were some early signs of rebellion as young people began to challenge established patterns of behaviour. In Britain the Teddy Boys broke with postwar conventions of dress, wearing eccentric outfits of narrow trousers and long, tailored jackets. There were similar groups elsewhere: the *Blousons Noirs* in France, the *Halbstarken* in Germany, the *Taiyo-zoku* in Japan, the *Skinnnuttar* in Sweden and the *Stilyagi* in the Soviet Union. In the mid–1960s people in the United States would be shocked by the appearance and unruly behaviour of motorcycle gangs clad in leather, who called themselves Hell's Angels. By 1960 over half the people in the United States were under the age of eighteen, and increasing numbers of them were finding fault with the world around them.

> *"It was a time of prosperity. We hadn't known poverty....It was a particularly sheltered, very middle-class community. There wasn't a lot of questioning that went on."*
> —
> PARKER HALL

CULTS OF YOUTH
Many of Britain's Teddy Boys in the early 1950s came from poor backgrounds and were out of school or out of work. Some of them caused trouble; most just enjoyed wearing distinctive clothes as a way of shaping a new and different identity for themselves. David Sackett's brother was one: 'He used to dress up, he had the ties and the crepe soles....He was a little bit out of the ordinary.'

'TEEN PICS' *described films that were specifically aimed at a young audience. When the leather-jacketed Marlon Brando (far right) starred in* The Wild One, *filmed in 1953, he became an idol of youthful rebellion for teenagers, many of whom adopted a new attitude as well as a new look.*

The generation gap

As economic prosperity came to people in Western Europe at the end of the 1950s, so did the social freedoms and choices that those living in the United States enjoyed. In France, Italy, West Germany and elsewhere there had also been a surge in the number of babies born after the war, and teenagers were growing up in a time of great change. With greater prosperity, they were under less pressure from their families to leave school as soon as they could and start contributing to the family income, though there was plenty of work for those who wanted it.

When he was fifteen years old David Sackett, who lived in London, joined a fashion-conscious group calling themselves Mods. One of them owned a scooter. 'Now we had a bit of mobility,' he says, 'we could go where we wanted.' Every Friday night they watched *Ready Steady Go* on television. 'It was all about the Mod scene, the latest dance craze, the latest footwear, the latest hairstyle,' he says. 'That was a must – the new music, the new sounds, the new groups and the fashion.'

In 1960 compulsory military service in Britain came to an end. Another of the ways in which the values and discipline of the older generation had been instilled was now removed. 'They weren't going to take half a million of us off to France again and ask us to shoot one another,' says Rogan Taylor. 'There was a feeling that we'd had a bloody lousy time and it's about time we had a good time.' In his seaport town, Liverpool, sailors brought back music from the United States, and Liverpool was itself a thriving place to hear the hundreds of bands that performed at popular clubs and dance halls.

One of the bands featured at The Cavern club had changed its name from The Quarrymen to The Beatles. They were sought after by club owners. In 1963 they became hugely successful. 'The music was different from what we were used to,' remembers David Sackett. 'We were listening to something new, that type of music grew on you. We could hardly wait for the next single or album to come out.' Teenagers began to dress like The Beatles, and even copied their 'mop-top' hairstyles. 'Once their hair got long,' recalls David Sackett, 'everybody had long hair, that's what you did.'

THE CAVERN *in Liverpool* (ABOVE) *was a favourite music venue for Rogan Taylor* (RIGHT). *The club was a low-roofed, arched building converted from a warehouse. The noise and the heat under the low ceilings were unbelievable. 'Everything a youngster could want was in there,' he remembers. 'You felt you were at the very heart of it.'*

YOUNG MODERNS – *Mods – prepare for action near the Brighton seafront, scene of a number of sometimes violent confrontations between the scooter-riding Mods and their arch-rivals, the motorcycling Rockers, in 1964.*

YOUNG CONSUMERS

FOR PEOPLE IN THE WEST, the growing affluence of the 1950s bred a new consumer culture, first in the United States and then in Western Europe. For the first time, young people began to be targeted by advertisers and courted by manufacturers, who identified them as a new, potentially profitable consumer group with their own particular tastes, views and preferences.

It was easy for most young people at this time to find work, and they could earn more money than ever before. Businesses were quick to capitalize on their new spending power. Publishers and broadcasters introduced 'pop' columns, music magazines and chart shows, and clothing manufacturers and distributors of consumer goods began to cater for younger shoppers. Some retailers and department stores even despatched their staff on crash courses about the new culture of youth.

Shops were quick to reflect new trends among the young. There was an abundant choice of goods – the latest fashions, the most popular records, soft drinks and cosmetics.

In 1957 some 150 million pairs of blue jeans were sold in the United States, where teenagers were each spending about $400 a year – about $22 billion in total. They bought badges, cars, comic books and clothes as well as guitars, radios, music posters and tickets to attend pop concerts.

In Britain, the Netherlands, Sweden and West Germany teenagers spent between seven and ten times more than those in less prosperous European countries, such as Italy and Spain. By the late 1950s teenagers in Britain were spending about £830 million a year. 'I very much wanted some money to spend on myself,' remembers Penny Hayes from Britain, who left school at fifteen to work in a hairdressing salon. 'I would say ninety nine per cent went on clothes. We didn't have a very expensive social life, it was down the local coffee bar. If I bought a cup of coffee or Coke it was rare. You just went to meet friends, so it was all clothes....You all looked the same, and that was very important.'

From the late 1950s fashion stores in London's King's Road and Carnaby Street were making large profits by catering for this new fashion-conscious market. Leading boutiques such as Bazaar, Biba and Bus Stop mirrored the characteristic boldness of style that set young people apart from the older generations. There were daring new fashions, such as the ultra-short 'mini skirt', which appeared in Mary Quant boutiques in 1965; it was followed by ultra-long 'maxi skirts'.

Music was by far the biggest seller and teenage consumers, spending hundreds of millions a year on records, accounted for as much as 80 per cent of sales. The film, music and television industries all grew spectacularly, largely as a result of their skill in exploiting the youth market.

In their search for an alternative way of life, the 'hippies' of the 1960s openly rejected these consumer values. Yet despite their efforts to avoid materialism, the culture of consumption prevailed: it was not long before shops were selling the fashions, beads, handicrafts and macrobiotic foods so central to their 'alternative' lifestyles. The *Whole Earth Catalogue*, which set out to teach its readers how to adopt a self-sufficient way of life, sold millions of copies while making a fortune for its editor.

RECORD SALES *of two and a half million were reached in just three months after the release of the* Sergeant Pepper *album by The Beatles in 1967.*

The Beatles had much the same impact elsewhere. In the United States one and a half million people rushed to buy their single in the first weeks after its release in 1964. When the group appeared on the *Ed Sullivan Show* television ratings shot up. 'Everybody was glued to their television set,' says Bob Bossar. On their second tour of the United States, The Beatles performed some thirty-two concerts in thirty-four days across twenty-four American cities, and they caused pandemonium wherever they went, inspiring a whole generation to break with convention and adopt a new look that was unlike anything their parents had.

By the mid-1960s, as the baby boomers everywhere were coming of age, millions of them began to enrol at universities and colleges. With free or virtually free education in many parts of the world, student numbers soared. The number of students in France had doubled since 1945; in West Germany, Italy, the Netherlands and Sweden it was also proportionately larger than before. In the United States there were five million students in 1964, an increase of two million since 1950; they were a sizeable interest group in the country, outnumbering farmers, for example. 'This was a time when everyone went free to the community colleges, to the University of California,' remembers Parker Hall, who grew up in San Luis Obispo, a small town in California, one of the first states to implement new laws offering free tuition. 'Everyone could go.'

In Britain there were a million more people between the ages of fifteen and nineteen than there had been in 1951, and more of them went on to higher education. 'The local authority would pay a grant to allow you to go to university,' Rogan Taylor recalls. 'So bright working-class lads were getting into university and coming out three years later with a degree, and a profession.' The number of students rose by more than one and a half million, and twenty-two universities were built to cater for the explosion.

TEENAGE IDOLS
The Beatles' success in Britain soared after they appeared at the London Palladium (ABOVE RIGHT) *in October 1963. Before long they became the focus of unprecedented teenage adoration. Bitten by 'Beatlemania', teenagers bought glasses and mugs, badges, posters and T-shirts bearing the group's image* (RIGHT). *The police struggled to control the screaming fans* (BELOW).

Rebels with a cause

There were simply not enough universities to cope with the huge number of students, and many campuses became overcrowded. One of the most congested in France was the Sorbonne, the University of Paris. During the early 1960s a hundred thousand students crammed into its lecture theatres each day, and conditions and standards within them inevitably suffered. Many people found university a liberating experience, but it could also be an alienating one; it was there that many young people felt a growing difference between their own values and those of the rest of society.

In the United States, Vivian Rothstein won a scholarship to study at Berkeley – one of the eight campuses of the University of California, across the bay from San Francisco. Its sheer size added to its impersonality. Vivian Rothstein shared her psychology class with a thousand other students. 'Of all of us who went to Berkeley, many of us were first-generation kids who got to go to college, and we were a big deal in our families, and we'd all got really good grades in high school,' she remembers. 'There were twenty, thirty thousand kids in the school and nobody knew us. Nobody talked to us. We had no counsellor....I felt that I was part of this huge, massive community in which I was unimportant. I started looking for a place to belong.'

It was the same for students on other campuses, prompting the government to increase expenditure on education. Mounting tensions gave rise to new student groups and organizations. The Students for a Democratic Society (SDS) had been set up at the University of Michigan in 1960, and was fast becoming one of the largest student groups in the country. 'We are of this generation, bred in at least modest comfort, housed now in universities, looking uncomfortably to the world we inherit,' read its manifesto. In the United States a 1964 poll estimated that 5 per cent of those between the ages of twenty-one and twenty-five had joined a political group of some kind.

The civil rights movement was what triggered Vivian Rothstein's involvement. 'The whole civil rights effort and the people I met in the civil rights movement became the core of my life at Berkeley. It was harder and harder to stay connected to my studies,' she remembers. 'I had never belonged to anything like that in my whole life....The sense of urgency and community and common mission was very exciting.' At first she took part in local demonstrations outside shops and restaurants that refused to employ black people, and on one occasion she was arrested. In the mid-1960s Berkeley became the site of the first serious student protests for the civil rights movement, which then spread to other colleges around the country.

In many parts of the world, as students grew more aware of global events and issues or watched more television news reports, an increasing number of them began to take a new interest in political and social problems. New courses in the humanities became popular among students; in France the number of social sciences students multiplied by four during the 1960s. Although she was not a student herself, Penny Hayes was working at the University of London. 'It had quite an effect on me,' she recalls. 'It completely opened my eyes to another world. It had been a very closed society in which I had grown up. We didn't have much interest in what was going on outside our own small group. But

> "*Individually we felt that something was being born, was coming to the boil, and that was very strong.* "
>
> ROMAIN GOUPIL

Alternative reading

THE 'UNDERGROUND' PRESS *that thrived in Europe and the United States from 1966 became a channel for the younger generation to produce its own alternatives to the more conventional, mainstream magazines that were on sale. Popular magazines such as Oz, which was produced in Britain, featured humorous or satirical articles by young writers. There were also underground groups, films and festivals.*

the university really made quite a change.' Penny Hayes soon decided to join the Campaign for Nuclear Disarmament (CND). She joined in protests against the presence of American nuclear weapons in Britain. 'It was a terrific feeling of being a group of people together,' she says. She was also arrested, for her part in a demonstration outside the American embassy in London. As the police ordered the crowds to disperse, Penny Hayes ran right up to the embassy entrance. 'What I thought I was going to do when I got there I don't know,' she says, 'but it was the fact that I had that chance. I ran up the steps and screamed at the top of my voice, "Yanks go home!"'

In France the government's attempt to defeat the Algerian nationalists, which only ended in 1962, had aroused considerable opposition among young people. 'Everyone you met was liable to be called up if they were young,' says Romain Goupil, who lived in Paris and was still at school when he began to take part in peace marches. 'So there would be discussions about torture, about censorship. I remember some extremely violent demonstrations.' As well as joining in the opposition to the government, he and his friends increasingly challenged other authorities ruling their lives. When they grew their hair long, 'We were stopped at the school entrance by an official or a prefect, who said, "If you have your hair like that you can't come to school". From that one little detail,' he remembers, 'we started to question the discipline and the whole organization.' In retaliation they stood outside the school gates and distributed pamphlets that read, 'We aren't sheep, and we won't be shorn!'

The international issue preoccupying most young people was the war being fought by

VOICING OPPOSITION *to their government, a group of French students leads a street protest. More young people in France began to take an active interest in national and foreign policies; even school pupils took part.*

PARADING FOR PEACE
(RIGHT) *News of the full horror of the Vietnam war reached young people all over the world. Despite its remoteness, it had a direct impact on them. In October 1968 thousands of people turned out for this London peace march.*

the United States in Vietnam from 1965. By the end of that year the military call-up in the United States had doubled, and already 120 000 had been dispatched to fight in the war. Their average age was nineteen. 'We were really involved in a life and death movement,' feels Jeff Jones, who went to Antioch College in Ohio in the autumn of 1965. 'If you were drafted your chances of going to Vietnam and getting killed were very high.' Young men who had gained admission to university on leaving school were able to claim deferment from the draft, and because of this the number of students increased. So did the number of anti-war protests. Some people burnt their draft notices in defiance. 'Everyone you knew was affected by the Vietnam war,' says Parker Hall. 'Every male had some story to tell about the draft. If you were a female you had either a husband, a lover, or a brother – everyone was touched by it. It consumed our generation.'

Many students were arrested as demonstrations spilled over into open confrontations on city streets. In 1966 Parker Hall joined in an anti-Vietnam protest on the campus at Berkeley. 'It was just overwhelmingly powerful to have, in one place, 30 000 people who were opposed to the Vietnam war,' he remembers, 'and up on the stages, the rock and roll bands and great speakers, charismatic people, making a lot of sense.'

News of peace movements in the United States began to reach students in other countries. 'Suddenly I became radical,' says Romain Goupil. He knew what was happening at Berkeley: 'We had a sign that we were working towards the same end, or at least we had a common enemy. This applied to what was taking place in the United States, but also in West Germany, in Italy, in Japan.' Romain Goupil's parents tried to reason with him. 'The more they tried to be reasonable the more I revolted, and this wasn't just true for me, but for my whole generation. We knew that in other countries at the same time people were discussing the same things...that helped us realize we were not alone, and that we were probably right, because there were many other youth groups.'

Elsewhere students shared the same pressing opposition to the war. Some were drawn to more radical groups or left-wing politics, hailing revolutionary figures as heroes. It seemed as though the whole generation was rising against the establishment.

"There was a generational optimism....If The Beatles could become the most famous rock and roll band in the world — well, hell, I could go to Nepal if I wanted to, surely?"

ROGAN TAYLOR

CHANGING APPEARANCES
The hippie culture and lifestyle that produced unconventional 'psychedelic' posters (ABOVE), exotic new fashions and long hairstyles for both men and women, lured Martine Algier to San Francisco (RIGHT). Things had changed a great deal since the day she was ordered to leave a school dance because she had moved her pelvis too much.

TAKING IT EASY *in Amsterdam (OPPOSITE), which acquired a reputation in the 1960s as a European centre for young people looking for tolerance and alternative lifestyles. The availability of cannabis, a popular drug at the time, added to the city's attractions.*

The summer of love

Not all the 1960s generation concentrated on seeking radical political change. Many simply wanted to take advantage of their new social freedoms by having fun or enjoying the opportunity to study. Others who felt disillusioned with society looked for alternatives of their own making. For some, revolutionary politics and a revolution in lifestyle went hand in hand. When Bob Bossar first went to Kent State University it struck him as a college filled with 'baby boomers'. 'In the mid-1960s,' he remembers, 'people who were dressed a little differently were a little strange....But by 1967 and 1968 it became the norm.'

Changing trends and fashions among the young reflected the ever-widening gap between the generations. In the United States, perhaps more than anywhere else, young people had begun to look more and more distinctive. Their hair was long and untidy. They began to dress flamboyantly in brightly patterned, colourful clothes; some young women wore body stockings and beaded necklaces, and painted their faces and bodies.

'Hippies', as they called themselves, talked about love and peace and freedom. Martine Algier was instantly attracted by their lifestyle. She had read and enjoyed the works of the Beat poets and writers of the 1950s, who were in some ways the precursors of this new youth culture. On her way from Michigan to visit her parents she had hitched a lift in a car. Her journey took her to Haight-Ashbury, the district of San Francisco that became the centre of the hippie culture. 'There was music and dancing and people being free and being wild,' recalls Martine Algier. 'I think there was a consciousness that there was a movement happening. There was definitely a sense of being a part of a big wave of something that was coming up.' When her parents later visited her there, at first they were shocked by what they saw as they drove down Haight Street. 'I was just so ebullient and so excited and so thrilled with the whole thing,' says Martine Algier. 'I remember my mother bursting into tears as somebody wafted across the street in a cape with long, plumed feathers.'

A CULTURE OF DRUGS

ONE WAY IN WHICH young people demonstrated their defiance and their desire for new experiences in the 1960s was to take drugs. Although they were illegal, drugs were becoming much easier to obtain.

Several drugs were available. Amphetamines or 'speed', a drug that affected the central nervous system, could be bought at night clubs as 'black bombers', 'French blues' or 'purple hearts'. Hallucinogenic drugs such as mescalin, peyote (derived from 'magic mushrooms') and cannabis (also called dope, grass, marijuana, pot, tea and weed, or hash – hashish – in resin form) could be smoked at 'pot parties', brewed as tea, or baked into cakes.

Cannabis was the most popular drug among students. The hippies' favourite drug was LSD (lysergic acid diethylamide), which induced 'psychedelic' experiences in the people who took it – intense and vivid hallucinations.

LSD was a legal pharmaceutical drug. Discovered in Switzerland in 1938, it was introduced into the United States in 1949 to treat psychiatric patients. In 1960 a psychologist at Harvard University, Dr Timothy Leary, began to manufacture it in large quantities and distribute it to young people at parties, anti-war rallies and on college campuses, urging them to 'tune in, turn on, drop out!' By the mid-1960s LSD was being widely used for recreational purposes.

In California another LSD enthusiast, the novelist Ken Kesey, set out in 1964 with a group of 'Merry Pranksters' in a multi-coloured, dazzling bus to popularize 'acid'. For four dollars they dispensed the 'acid test', an extravaganza of drugs, lights and music to an estimated 10 000 people. 'I was one of those people that LSD had a huge impact on,' remembers Ron Thelin, who was living in San Francisco at the time. 'It was a great experience for me, it was an eye opener, a catalyst to a new awareness....It was an awakening.'

Together the psychedelic, mind-altering drugs became associated with colourful, swirling patterns of psychedelic styles in fashion, fabrics and mixed media entertainment. There was psychedelic art, literature, poetry and poster art. 'Acid-rock' bands such as the Grateful Dead produced chemically inspired lyrics, and a number of musicians died as a result of excessive drug use.

By the late 1960s many countries responded to the increased use of drugs by reinforcing legal restrictions against them. In 1968 a committee set up in Britain to campaign for the legalization of cannabis estimated that up to a million people were using it. In most countries LSD was not an approved drug and there were tight restrictions on experiments with it. It was declared illegal in the United States in October 1966, but by 1968 as many as a million people were thought to have taken it.

DRUGS FOR SALE *at the 1970 Powder Ridge Music Festival in Connecticut. For just a dollar anyone could experience the effects of LSD or 'acid', recently made illegal.*

FESTIVAL FANS (LEFT) *Despite torrential rain, the Woodstock music festival drew more than 400 000 people to a muddy farm in upstate New York in August 1969 for an event billed as 'Three days of peace and music'. Similarly vast crowds were drawn to pop festivals held at the Isle of Wight in Britain, at Rotterdam in the Netherlands and to hundreds of rock concerts.*

'It seemed like anything was possible,' reflects Ron Thelin, who had dropped out of college in San Francisco. 'Every kind of character in time seemed to appear on the street, because you could dress however you wanted.' The hippies rejected the social and moral values of their parents and teachers. They were anti-establishment, anti-materialism, anti-war. They were more open in their relationships. They took drugs and gathered at festivals and open-air concerts to listen to songs of protest, folk music, rock or the harsher, drug-induced lyrics of 'acid rock'.

Ron Thelin opened a shop in Haight-Ashbury, in which he sold books, crafts, drugs and records. The Psychedelic Shop even had a room for meditation and art shows. 'We put "free" in front of everything,' he remembers. 'We were exploring what freedom was, what a free society was.' There were free stores, free meals in

ITALIAN HIPPIES *in Milan staging a hunger strike for seventy-two hours in a cellar in 1967 over restrictions on the distribution of their newsletter, the* Mondo Beat *(Beat World), enforced by the Italian authorities. Youngsters such as these were known as* capelloni – *the 'long-haired ones'.*

the park, sometimes even a ceremonial burning of money. Their journey of exploration included alternative lifestyles and systems of beliefs. Relatively cheap and easy modern transport encouraged more young people to travel from Europe and the United States to the East in search of mysticism and drugs.

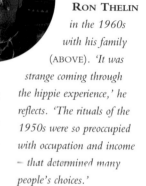

The East attracted Rogan Taylor in Liverpool, who remembers that 'Eastern traditions arrived in the West like a monsoon. Suddenly there was a massive flood of them...you could take your pick from a dozen gods and nobody would turn a hair.' He and a friend decided to set out on the long journey to India. 'The only way a working-class lad travelled before the late 1950s and 1960s was as a soldier or as a sailor,' he says. 'I thought freedom had arrived, coupled with this new kind of confidence, this new optimism – really there wasn't anywhere we couldn't go, there wasn't anything we couldn't do.'

By the summer of 1967 young people in their thousands were pouring into San Francisco to take part in what was called the Summer of Love. Many more conservative Americans were astonished by reports of the Human Be-In that they read in the national press. As it turned out, the earthly paradise had not arrived. With teenagers from the suburbs of an entire continent bearing down on them in pursuit of happiness, with the mainstream culture taking over their lovebeads and psychedelic clothes, and with the police closing in on their drugs, many hippies began to think their time was up. There were incidences of violence and rape, and the Haight-Ashbury police station appeared to have become a clearing house for teenage runaways.

Meanwhile, on university and college campuses as well as city streets across the world, many young people were becoming increasingly critical of society and of their place in it. In particular, the issue of the United States' continuing involvement in the war in Vietnam provoked a heightened sense of radicalism and anger that was about to reach a new pitch.

'DEATH OF THE HIPPIE'
Disenchanted with the materialism and false values he felt had become associated with the hippie movement, on 6 October 1967 Ron Thelin closed his Psychedelic Shop and staged a symbolic funeral procession in San Francisco: 'We carried a coffin down Haight Street, filled with beads and lace shirts...and burnt it in a pyre.'

RON THELIN
in the 1960s with his family (ABOVE). 'It was strange coming through the hippie experience,' he reflects. 'The rituals of the 1950s were so preoccupied with occupation and income – that determined many people's choices.'

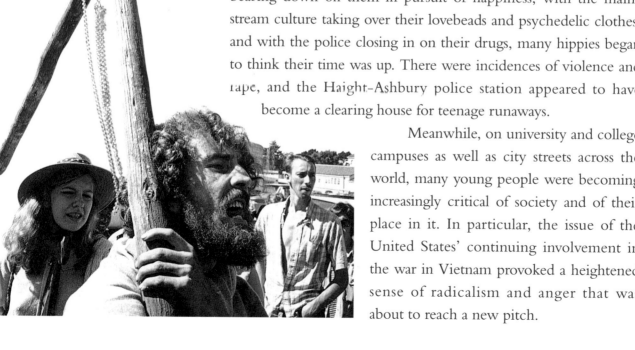

COMMUNAL LIVING

ANY OF THOSE who became part of the 1960s 'counter-culture' experimented with different ways of living and working. They rejected the conventional lifestyle of the suburban families in which many of them had grown up in favour of communal living.

The influx of young people in the Haight-Ashbury neighbourhood of San Francisco gave a powerful impulse to the setting up of communes in California. 'There was a sense of danger in the city, of things falling apart,' says Martine Algier, who decided to join a rural commune at Big Sur, overlooking the sea in the mountains south of San Francisco. 'In order to get on with making changes, we needed to get to places in the country where we could live together in groups in healthy ways, and have gardens and schools and create the healthy alternative.' In her commune there were seven or eight adults, five children, and a few goats.

In these communes the theory was that no one person was in charge. Instead people pooled their resources and shared ownership, money, duties and responsibilities – for housekeeping, for producing and cooking food, for irrigating land, collecting firewood, even for bringing up children. On most communes, instead of separating work and family life people grew their own food, baked their own bread and made their own clothes. The Drop City commune in Colorado was built of geodesic domes made from recycled materials. Some communes identified with Native Americans, and their members wore – and sold – moccasins and silver and turquoise jewellery. Other communes developed small enterprises such as alternative schools, bookshops or storefront law offices. There were also political communes inhabited by more radical activists. There were some on which people advocated nudity and practised 'free love'; others, set up by religious groups, were strict or even puritanical.

By 1970 there were about 3000 rural communes and a number of urban communes in the United States. Many of them failed. Some ran out of money, and found that they could not survive without some income. Others failed to sustain a free and healthy way of life. 'A lot of people didn't know how to survive, and they didn't know how to grow carrots and dig latrines, and they didn't know how to create alternative schools,' remembers Martine Algier. Some, such as the Hog Farm commune, foundered as a result of drug abuse, malnutrition and even violence.

Communes were also established in Europe. In Germany *Kommune Einz* (Commune Number One), set up in 1967 in West Berlin, was famous for leading radical political action. The idea also spread to Japan, where about fifty communes and hundreds of co-operative villages were set up in the mid-1970s. In Britain by 1972 there were a hundred communes. Some of them were extremely successful, like the Findhorn community; founded in northern Scotland in 1962, by 1972 it had grown into an elaborate organization with over a hundred members, and communal facilities that included a craft centre, a folk singing group and a theatre.

UNDER ONE ROOF *Commune members shared family duties as well as living space.*

Days of rage

As 1967 turned into 1968 youth protests were on the increase in many parts of Europe, both east and west, as well as in Australia, Canada, Japan, Mexico and the United States. The two issues – the Vietnam war and university conditions and organization – ran in parallel, and were often combined. The radical student activity that began in Australia in 1965 at the universities of Sydney and Queensland grew more frequent as students occupied buildings and staged demonstrations calling for reform. In Canada students demanded more representation on university governing bodies, equal access to research facilities, day care centres for their children and a louder voice in academic policy-making. At several universities – Montreal, Ontario and Toronto – students demonstrated, disrupted classes and started a fire.

PEACE OFFERING *Flowers became a symbol for young pacificsts opposed to the Vietnam war. At the 1967 peace march in Washington, they were used to confront armed soldiers.*

In the United States anti-war protests were also becoming more violent. One of the largest took place in October 1967, a few months after the government had sent a further 100 000 troops to Vietnam. A march was held in the capital, Washington DC, at the Defence Department, housed in the Pentagon. Jeff Jones, who had joined the leading radical student group, SDS, took part. 'When we got to the Pentagon,' he recalls, 'there were thousands and thousands of people there.' The army was sent in to control the crowd, some 100 000 people. 'Things had reached the stage where the government had to call out the army to protect the Pentagon from the people. It was intimidating,' feels Jeff Jones. 'It was also exhilarating, because the message of alienation and disagreement and contempt had apparently gotten through.'

Later that year the government announced that students who were arrested in anti-war demonstrations would lose their draft deferments. They were not deterred. There were continuing campus rebellions – at Antioch College, at Berkeley, Columbia, Cornell, Harvard, Kent State, Jackson State and others. Students had led many of the demonstrations, but the anti–war movement was now far wider, with an estimated thirty-six million people having taken part. The day after the Pentagon protest was held in Washington, 5000 people marched in London to demonstrate against the Vietnam war. Students caused disruption at universities across Britain – at Birmingham, Bradford, Bristol, Essex, Hull, Leeds, Leicester, Manchester and elsewhere – and the government launched an investigation into the causes of the protest.

Students were becoming harder to ignore. There was unrest in Czechoslovakia, in Poland and West Germany. In Italy there were riots and sit-ins at universities in Milan, Rome and Turin. In Denmark, where the number of students at the University of Copenhagen doubled in just five years, violent demonstrations

RUSTY SACHS (LEFT) *was initially excited as he enlisted in the United States Marine Corps in 1964. When he returned from Vietnam he felt differently: 'When you're twenty-four and you're coming home from a war with blood on your hands, you don't feel good about it.' He joined other war veterans in discarding his medals. 'It was a cutting of apron strings, a gesture of defiance.'*

PUBLIC OPINION *in the United States had shifted against the Vietnam war. Some still labelled student critics as communists and traitors, but many older people increasingly supported their efforts.*

took place in April 1968. In Japan, where the Vietnam war had fuelled existing anger over education policies, hundreds of students were arrested when they smashed the windows of the Foreign Ministry. Some shielded themselves with gas masks or wore cycle helmets and carried weapons made of sticks and stones as they formed themselves into compact human shields.

The greatest turmoil of all took place in Paris that year, where student demands included an end to the sexual segregation that still existed in university accommodation, wider access to higher education for working-class pupils, reforms in teaching methods, examinations and course content, and the right to appoint class representatives. In 1967 there were more than eight and a half million students in higher education in France. To house some of them, the Sorbonne had built a new campus at Nanterre, in the suburbs of Paris, but even there numbers swelled from 2000 to 11 000 in just four years.

It was there that disturbances began in the spring of 1968, triggered by student protests against the Vietnam war. On 3 May they spread to the Latin quarter in the heart of the city. The Sorbonne was closed and many students were arrested, sparking renewed moves as others, including Romain Goupil, joined in. 'It was an astonishing expression of solidarity,' he recalls. 'Between six thousand and ten thousand students went to the Quartier Latin to surround and open up the Sorbonne....We started to overturn cars,

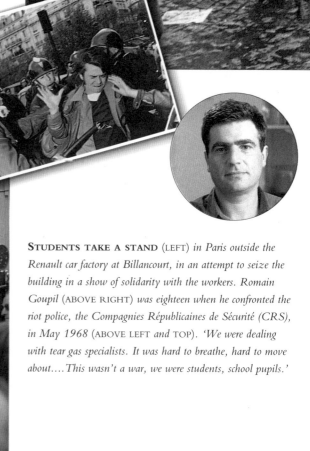

STUDENTS TAKE A STAND (LEFT) *in Paris outside the Renault car factory at Billancourt, in an attempt to seize the building in a show of solidarity with the workers. Romain Goupil* (ABOVE RIGHT) *was eighteen when he confronted the riot police, the Compagnies Républicaines de Sécurité (CRS), in May 1968* (ABOVE LEFT *and* TOP). *'We were dealing with tear gas specialists. It was hard to breathe, hard to move about....This wasn't a war, we were students, school pupils.'*

and to set up barricades around the students....We found ourselves behind the barricades saying, "We shall not be moved!" '

On 6 May the riot police were called in. At first they were wary of confronting the students, some of them secondary school pupils, but soon there was violence. 'We had learned a lot of lessons from the United States, from West Germany, from Italy,' Romain Goupil reflects. 'We defended ourselves, which led to a truly violent confrontation. For our generation, this was the first confrontation with the police.' The students prised up heavy paving stones from the city streets and threw a few petrol bombs. They too protected themselves by wearing cycle helmets, covering their faces with cloths soaked in lemon juice against the effects of tear gas. Within a week, 367 people had been injured.

The clashes triggered a nationwide movement, bringing the country almost to a standstill. Millions of workers who had already threatened union action over their own work grievances joined in a national strike, partly out of sympathy for the students. Public services stopped functioning: rubbish piled up in the streets, post was not delivered. Two friends of Charles-Henri de Choiseul Praslin, one of the students, were killed in the violence. 'For two months we demonstrated tirelessly, we spoke with everyone in the street, we fought against the police,' he says. At the height of the general strike nine million people took part. Some feared the country was on the brink of anarchy, but gradually people went back to work as the government reasserted control, undertook to modernize the universities and negotiated with the workers.

In the Netherlands trouble spread from Tilburg to campuses around the country in April 1969. In the United States Jeff Jones took part in a 'Days of Rage' protest in Chicago, organized in October by the radical Weathermen Underground group. 'The first night was the most terrifying thing I was ever involved in,' he says. 'We started down through the streets of Chicago and very quickly it turned into a riot of sorts....People started breaking shop windows and car windows.' As they broke through police barricades, hundreds of people were arrested and six were shot. By the end of the 1960s, says Bill Arthrell, 'It seemed as though every spring we thought the revolution was going to come, that we were going to profoundly change American society.'

WANTED FILE (BELOW) *For his part in causing 'riots and conspiracy', Jeff Jones was wanted by the United States Federal Bureau of Investigation (FBI). He had already been arrested many times on anti-war demonstrations: 'I was always under the jurisdiction of one court or another.' He went into hiding in 1970. 'Some of us had no choice but to go underground, just so we didn't have to waste time and money going on trial.'*

Testaments of youth

In the spring of 1970 two events dramatized how far things had gone. At Jackson State College, Mississippi, two students were shot by National Guard reservists. In May the National Guard fired into a crowd of student demonstrators at Kent State University in Ohio, killing four of them. 'It was a classic confrontation,' reflects Bill Arthrell, who remembers the whole episode. 'On the one side you had student activists, hippies and radicals, the new generation. On the other side was the National Guard, representing the establishment, though they were very young as well, and some of them were Kent State students and some of them were evading the draft, too.' Seventy-five colleges closed, and the students had to wait until December to graduate.

By the end of 1970 student rebellion had begun to die down. Young people no longer had an immediate, personal reason for opposing the war after the United States government began to withdraw troops from Vietnam, and abolished the military draft in 1973. In some ways the war had acted as a catalyst for them to speak out. 'It was a generational movement,' says Bill Arthrell, 'the first time in history that a whole generation actually stood up against the establishment.'

During the 1960s people under the age of twenty-five had outnumbered their elders. By challenging the old order, they shaped new ideas and brought many changes to society, politics and popular behaviour. Whether they had taken part in the protest movements or not, young people earned new opportunities and rights – to better education, to greater social freedoms, to a wider range of jobs and careers. They had also been admitted into the political mainstream: in many countries the voting age had been lowered from twenty-one to eighteen, and politicians now paid attention to the opinions – and the votes – of young people.

By the mid-1970s the tide was turning towards a new, populist conservatism, and the average age of populations began to rise. But the example of participation and involvement set in the 1960s remained: though the issues were different, people continued to speak out on the environment, nuclear power, equal rights. 'All of a sudden, it was the people who counted,' says Romain Goupil. 'That's what was so extraordinary about the sixties.'

FIRST IN LINE *at the polling station in North Newton, Somerset, a young woman exercises her right to vote in March 1970, after new British laws reduced the minimum voting age from twenty-one to eighteen.*

PASSPORT TO THE FUTURE (OPPOSITE) *Graduation day at the University of Notre Dame, Indiana. The number of universities in the world doubled during the 1970s to provide for the huge number of young people seeking further education.*

Half the People

WOMEN FIGHT FOR EQUAL RIGHTS

Just before she turned the the corner into Fifth Avenue in New York City, Jaqui Ceballos hesitated. She was there to participate in a public demonstration on 26 August 1970, organized by the women's movement. 'I was afraid we would have only two or three thousand women,' she remembers. 'I'll never forget when I turned the corner at the Hotel Plaza – I could not see to the end. There were thousands of women there!'

All over the city, women stopped what they were doing to join in the huge parade. Some carried placards and shouted out slogans. 'We'd say to the women, "Join us, join us!" ' describes Jaqui Ceballos. 'We just took over the whole avenue, and the horns were beeping, people were lined up on the side, some screaming at us, but most of them were looking at us in real amazement.'

More than 50 000 women are thought to have taken part in that demonstration. The day on which it was held marked the fiftieth anniversary of the constitutional amendment that had granted women the right to vote in federal elections, as men did. Now American women wanted a wider equality, beyond basic political rights. Although many women were better educated, whole areas of life were still closed to them. The equality march was the largest of many that were held throughout the United States that year, as more and more women discovered a stronger sense of identity and began to question their position. 'It was a consciousness-raising day,' remembers Jaqui Ceballos. 'It meant that the possibility of freedom was around the corner....It was the time that the women's movement became a movement.'

It was also the time when women across the world began to serve notice on men that they were no longer prepared to be regarded as second-class citizens. In their shared resolve for change, millions of women began to demand the same opportunities as men, and the right to make their own decisions about their lives. They began to assert themselves, and their collective cause, in society and politics, becoming more ambitious and more determined along the way.

MARCHING FOR EQUALITY *Protesters throng the streets of New York City in the summer of 1970 to demand equal rights for women.*

"During the war girls did all sorts of wonderful things.... They flew aircraft and could do almost anything."

GINNIE WHITEHILL

WOMEN AT WORK (ABOVE) *in a Japanese armaments factory in 1940. By 1945 there were more than three million Japanese women in the workforce. The Girls' Volunteer Corps was set up to draft those between the ages of twelve and forty for industrial work. Women who refused could be fined or imprisoned for up to a year. When the war ended women were awarded a number of new rights, including the right to vote.*

'ROSIE THE RIVETER' (OPPOSITE) *starred at the centre of campaigns to recruit women for wartime work in the United States in the early 1940s. Some 80 per cent of them trained in heavy industry.*

New roles for women

By 1970 the lives of many women in the world's developed nations had changed greatly since the beginning of the century. With their families, they had benefited from better health care, better housing and more mobility. They had the same rights to education as men, and many more were going to university. But deeply rooted attitudes and prejudices continued to shape the lives of women. Most women's activities remained confined to the home and family. Those who did go out to work – whether in factories, in offices, or in service industries such as catering or cleaning – were paid far less than men.

On two occasions, it was war that had, indirectly, done most to change the daily lives of women at home. As millions of men left to fight in the First World War, women were recruited into their factory jobs; they also worked in banks, the civil services and insurance companies. For the first time, women became streetcar conductors, carpenters, painters, stokers and tool setters.

Combined with the suffragettes' campaigns, it was women's war efforts that helped persuade many governments to give them the vote. By 1920 women in most northern European countries, in Canada, the Soviet Union and the United States could vote. They claimed new social freedoms, too: to dress differently, to wear makeup, and to smoke in public. In the Soviet Union the communist revolution ushered in reforms for women, and they were now expected to perform the same jobs as men. There were more women in Europe in paid employment than ever before, but in the 1930s both the economic hardship of the Depression and opposition from male-dominated unions meant that women came under pressure to give up their jobs.

During the Second World War, as in the first, the female proportion of the civilian workforce dramatically increased in the combatant nations. In the United States seven million women went to work, many for the first time. 'In the 1940s they called on women to leave those telephone operator jobs and to leave those clerk jobs and come in here and build this engine,' remembers Kay Foley, who grew up in the city of Lynn in Massachusetts during the war. 'They came in and they welded and they did all sorts of things that were typically men's jobs.' By 1942 thirteen million

women were at work in the United States, and more than half of them were married.

Women's status in the workplace changed fundamentally during the war. When it was over, the political advance of women continued – in Argentina, China, France, India, Italy and Japan women also gained the vote. In its charter, the new United Nations Organization declared that men and women's rights were equal, prompting its member nations to do the same. Principles of equality were contained in the new postwar constitutions of France, Italy and West Germany.

In the world's less developed nations, despite the principles of equality set out by the United Nations, continuing poverty, the lack of education and enduring social traditions meant that most women's lives did not change. Even in the industrialized world, within a few years traditional stereotypes and restrictions had again reasserted themselves; equal opportunities seemed to be in retreat.

Back to the home front

When the soldiers returned to the United States, four out of five women wanted to hold on to their jobs. But employers felt bound to give jobs back to the men who had left them to fight, and many of the girls who had taken their place married and settled down. 'I did what most girls did,' remembers Ginnie Whitehill, who grew up in a New York suburb. 'I married a war hero. That's what we were supposed to do. And I had children. Every woman was expected to have children. No woman would have ever dared not consider having children.' Hollywood films, radio soap operas and early television serials all reinforced the image of women as housewives and mothers. In some British schools girls were taught housewifery and how to do laundry as part of the curriculum. Television commercials often portrayed women as incompetent.

By 1950 a third of American women still went out to work, the majority of them in poorly paid, unskilled jobs: they could be a domestic maid or work in a textile factory. The better-educated could qualify as librarians or teachers. When Kay Foley left school in 1956 she went to work at an electrical goods factory as a key-punch operator. 'You had to be able to read and transmit that through your brain to the three tips of your fingers, and be able to

TAKING A BREAK *from work (BELOW) to admire a former colleague's baby is the image on an American magazine cover. The requirement that women give up their jobs on marriage reinforced a common view of women's work as temporary and unchallenging.*

keypunch numbers onto punch cards,' she recalls. 'It never occurred to me to look for something else, because there was nothing else.' A few years later, like most women, Kay Foley gave up her job, married and had a baby. Jaqui Ceballos, who grew up in New York, did the same. 'You could be a secretary for a while, or work in a store. A nurse maybe, a schoolteacher,' she says. 'In any career you took it wasn't really a career, it was a job until you got married.'

The nurseries provided during the war were closed; there were few remaining facilities to help working mothers. Lorena Weeks worked as a telephone operator in Georgia so that she could earn enough to support her three children. 'Telephone operators worked around the clock,' she recalls. 'I worked split hours so that I could be with my children in the afternoon....I'd go back and work from seven until eleven at night, and it was hard. Most men's jobs at that time were eight to five, plus the pay was so much better.'

Discrimination in the workplace was widespread. Whole professions were closed to women applicants. Women often could not be promoted above a certain level in the company hierarchy, and some women lost their jobs when they got married. Even after graduating from college, many women were unable to choose the careers they would have liked. Dusty Roads grew up in Cleveland, Ohio close to where the national aviation races were held every year. She had always dreamed of becoming an airline pilot, 'Until I was in high school and found out from my father, "You can't be an airline pilot, darling, they don't hire ladies". It broke my heart,' she says. Instead, when she was twelve years old she decided she would become an airline stewardess. 'I thought, well, if I can't fly in the cockpit at least I can ride in the back.'

REBUILDING RAILROADS *was a priority for these women living in devastated Poland. Until conditions improved in the late 1950s, European women played a key role in reconstruction after the war.*

Women's wake-up call

By the 1960s increasing numbers of women both in the United States and in Europe were frustrated with the restrictions on the way they could live. For much of the population, especially the young, this was a time of change: there were greater opportunities for education, more open relationships and new social freedoms.

But although it was becoming easier for single women in some countries to obtain various forms of contraception, abortion was still against the law. 'One mistake, and you were off in the suburbs, home having babies and starting a family,' recalls Amy Coen, who was a student at the University of Michigan, 'or you were risking your life in a back alley abortion.'

FOR MOTHER OF TWO
Anilu Elias (ABOVE) *the pill meant freedom. 'It was a long time before it got to Mexico,' she recalls, 'but when I read about the pill, I thought it was magic!'*

An important development came with the introduction of the birth control pill, by far the most convenient and reliable form of contraception to date. It was sold in the United States for the first time in 1960; six years later, six million women in the United States were taking the pill. Amy Coen's university was one of the first to offer it to students. 'It changed my life, and it changed the lives of my friends,' she says. 'We did not have to worry about being pregnant.' Women could now choose if, and when, they wanted to have children.

The pill transformed the lives of millions of women everywhere. When it became available in Mexico, Anilu Elias, who already had two children, took it secretly. Her husband wanted to have a third child. 'Without the pill he would have been able to control me,' she describes. 'Taking the pill meant breaking with tradition....It was like stopping the whole mechanism in the world against women and against myself.' Anilu Elias was more fortunate than most women in Mexico, who could not afford to pay for the pill or who had no access to it. In France, Italy and other Roman Catholic countries it was banned altogether.

Without access to safe, reliable methods of contraception, thousands of women still resorted to illegal, sometimes dangerous

STEALING A KISS
(BELOW) *in New York. Some people blamed contraception for changing social patterns.*

> ### *Prescription of choice*
>
> THE ORAL CONTRACEPTIVE – *known as 'the pill' – took five years to develop in the United States. It was tested on volunteers and approved by the Food and Drug Administration in 1960. It prevented ovulation, and thus pregnancy, by mimicking the body's hormones. The first commercial birth control pill was Enovid-10, produced by the G. D. Searle Company in Illinois. Although the pill was marketed as reliable and harmless to women, it was later discovered to have potentially dangerous side effects; despite this, by 1991 some 200 million women in the world were taking the drug.*

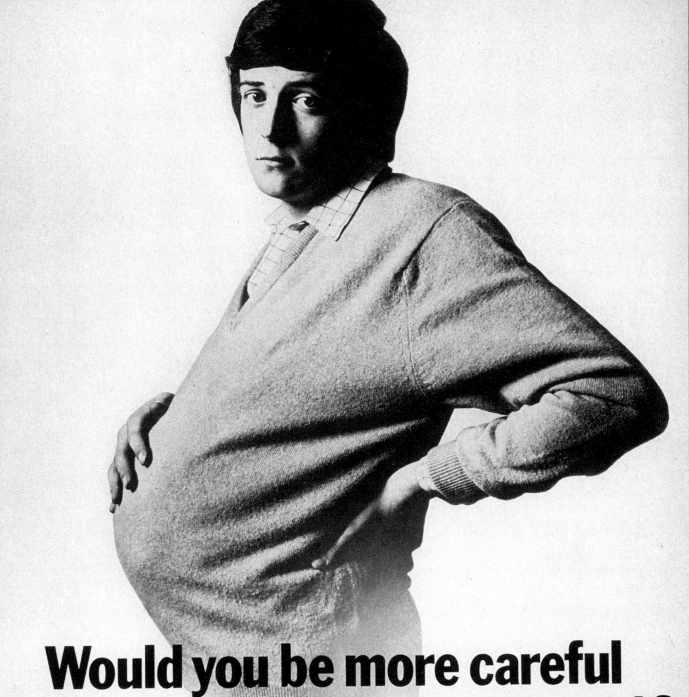

Would you be more careful if it was you that got pregnant?

operations. Even in the United States, women sought clandestine abortions. 'No other issue got women involved in the same way, because everyone had experienced something like that,' recalls Jaqui Ceballos. 'There were always thousands and thousands of women looking for abortions. There was such anger that men were dictating what women should be doing with their bodies.... Women began to think, "Why are we going through this?" '

These questions of contraception and abortion and the ethical issues that they raised, added to the less controversial issues of equal pay and equal rights at work. There

WOMEN'S MUTILATION

BY CHALLENGING traditional approaches to their fertility, women in the West gained new freedoms over their bodies and rights over their reproduction. But in developing countries millions of women still faced potentially life-threatening attempts to control their bodies, and all in the name of tradition. Shortly after Shamis Dirir was born in Somalia, her father left her mother. He had wanted a son. When she was seven years old, she was taken one morning to be circumcised. 'When the time came,' Shamis Dirir remembers, 'I ran away. I was caught and brought back.' They assured her that she was becoming a woman, that without the operation she could never marry and have children. 'I was circumcised with six or seven other girls,' she remembers. 'There was no anaesthetic at all. It was very painful.'

Some ninety million girls are thought to have suffered a similar fate. An ancient practice, female circumcision or 'female genital mutilation' (FGM) – a name used by campaigners against the practice to emphasize the fact that it is a far more radical operation than male circumcision – spread from Egypt to other countries across Africa. It was most widely practised in Central, East and West Africa – including Burkina Faso, Djibouti, Ethiopia, Eritrea, Mali, Nigeria, Sierra Leone, Somalia and northern Sudan – and to a lesser degree in some Muslim parts of Asia.

Despite its popularity among Muslim populations, traditional beliefs and social customs rather than religious rules pressurized parents into forcing their daughters to submit to the practice, in some cases out of fear that they might become social outcasts without it. Some communities believed that it cleansed women and freed them from impurities; others considered it mandatory before marriage, and sought to reserve women's bodies solely for procreation, not pleasure, to ensure their fidelity in marriage; some thought that uncircumcised women could not conceive. Millions of young African girls were victims of female circumcision. Most of them suffered from a host of long-term health problems as a result of the operation, including vaginal and urinary tract infections, pain and permanent scarring; many died in childbirth.

During the 1930s female circumcision was also reported in Australia, Brazil, India, Mexico and Peru, and later among some Christian communities in the Soviet Union. It was used in the United States until 1937 to treat women who had been diagnosed as suffering from 'hysteria' or 'nymphomania'. Female circumcision continued to be clandestinely carried out in the West. In Britain some 10 000 girls from predominantly Somali and Sudanese immigrant communities were thought to be at risk in the 1990s, though the practice had been banned in 1985. Legislation against it was also introduced in Australia, Canada, France, Sweden, Switzerland and the United States, though it often proved difficult to implement.

Women's health organizations and human rights groups around the world campaigned against the practice, which continued to mutilate millions of women in Africa alone. It was local people's efforts to challenge the traditions of their own cultures that offered the greatest hopes of preventing further suffering. In some countries, women's refuges were set up to offer escape for the victims of circumcision, and in Sudan, where an estimated 89 per cent of women were still being mutilated, women's groups began to provide honest information about it in the hope of eradicating the traumatic operation.

In Burkina Faso it was efforts by the government during the 1990s that achieved considerable success in influencing local people's views. National school campaigns, public awareness films, radio broadcasts and posters and village meetings began to transform their long-standing beliefs.

CALENDAR MESSAGE
'For my health I refuse circumcision' – the words on a poster against female genital mutilation, pasted onto the walls of a village health clinic in Burkina Faso. More than half of all women in the country underwent the dangerous operation before the government launched the campaign to phase it out.

were still many hurdles to overcome. When Dusty Roads began to work as an air stewardess, she discovered that it was not a career after all. The airlines viewed it as a temporary opportunity for single, attractive young women. 'They even called it the "charm farm",' she remembers. 'We were supposed to wear girdles, and of course we wore high heels. Occasionally they'd do a girdle check. They'd come up and give you a little tap on your rear end, and if you didn't have a girdle on you would be called into the office.' Stewardesses had to maintain slender figures and, unlike the male pilots, they automatically lost their jobs if they married. 'That made me angry,' recalls Dusty Roads. 'It also violated my sense of fair play that pilots could be fired at age sixty and we were fired at age thirty-two. Something was wrong there.'

With some of her colleagues, Dusty Roads decided to become a lobbyist, and in 1963 she began to protest against the compulsory retirement age for stewardesses. Many other women were also becoming more determined to pursue their quest for change; many of them were helped by an influential book that first appeared in 1963. When Jaqui Ceballos, unhappily married and now with four children, discovered *The Feminine Mystique* by Betty Friedan, she stayed up all night long to read it. 'I'll never forget the way I felt. It changed my life,' she describes. 'I realized that it wasn't my husband, and it wasn't me. It was the society, and the society had to change.'

The Feminine Mystique had the same powerful impact on numerous other women. In it, Betty Friedan drew attention to the way in which women had been thrust back into their traditional roles. She argued that, like men, women could only find their true identity in work that used their full capacities, and not in the dull routine of housework. Within seven years, more than a million copies of this feminist manifesto had been sold in Britain and the United States. It was also read by educated women in developing countries. In Mexico, Anilu Elias had been forced by her husband to give up her job as creative director at an advertising agency. When she read Betty Friedan's book she was overwhelmed. 'I put it away because it felt like keeping a bomb in the house,' she says. 'I knew that after reading that book the only thing I could or should do is to get a divorce.'

VIEWS OF WOMEN *as the weaker sex were reinforced by advertisements such as these – separated by more than a decade – portraying them as helpless if their cars broke down.*

SERVICE WITH A SMILE *Airline stewardesses were expected to be young and attractive. They lost their jobs when the airlines thought their 'charm' might begin to fade, as Dusty Roads (LEFT) discovered when she became a stewardess.*

Women's bid for equality

From the mid-1960s the number of women in paid work was on the increase, though they still continued to earn less than men. In Australia and Britain, 45 per cent of women worked. In the United States and Canada the proportion was 49 per cent, and in Denmark and Sweden it was 57 per cent. In the United States, where women were still not legally entitled to receive the same pay as men for doing the same work, the prospect of real change came in 1964 when the Civil Rights Act was passed. It banned job discrimination on the grounds of sex as well as race.

Lorena Weeks was still working long hours as a telephone operator, taking and transferring calls, when she heard about the new ruling. 'I'd watched these men, the toll test men, the switch men, all of them, in work that I felt I could do,' she remembers. 'It was much better pay. The hours were better, the overtime was better....I knew immediately that this was a chance for me to get one of these jobs.'

When she applied for a better job, Lorena Weeks was told that it was being awarded only to men. She then appealed to the union. 'The president told me that he didn't have anything against me,' she recalls, 'but that if I got the job it would mean other women would come into this type of work, and that I was not the breadwinner in the family, the man was the breadwinner.' Next Lorena Weeks decided to take her case to the law courts. The company's lawyer used an obscure ruling – originally intended to protect them – that women and minors should not lift weights in excess of 14 kg (30 lb) to prevent Lorena Weeks from getting the job she wanted. 'It was just foolish to use something like that against women to keep them from drawing these better salaries and having these better-paid jobs,' she insists.

Towards the end of the 1960s more women were beginning to demand changes to such laws. And as they launched a more vigorous campaign for equality, women began to extend their concern to a wider range of issues, such as the environment and nuclear proliferation. Their protests became more committed, and more angry. Jaqui Ceballos was among them. 'It was a fabulous time,' she says. 'It was like a fever of excitement of all the women changing their lives....What we wanted was to be

GRADUATION DAY (LEFT) *for Amy Coen and a friend at the University of Michigan. She first joined a feminist group to challenge double standards of admission at the college. 'We were very excited. That was one of the first feminist victories that I remember.'*

ROWS OF WORKERS (ABOVE) *in a clothing factory in Budapest, Hungary in 1980. In Eastern Europe, as elsewhere, the textile and clothing industries employed predominantly women in non-managerial roles. Women's groups in Eastern Europe were disbanded under communism; although many women were as well educated as men, there were fewer opportunities for them in senior positions.*

thinking human beings and take responsibility for running this world equally with men.'

Sensing the changing mood on her university campus, Amy Coen and her fellow students became involved in women's protest groups. 'We understood that women could get together and make a lot of noise and get change,' she remembers. 'We didn't know quite what we were doing in our relationships, but they were going to be equal. Equal was our word.' When they discovered that the university entrance regulations discriminated against women, they succeeded in having them changed.

In the courts, more sexual discrimination suits were being fought by women. After a five-year court case, Lorena Weeks was awarded the job she had wanted for so long. As women continued their individual battles against the establishment, a new women's movement was gathering momentum.

Group force

In 1966 a group of women in New York came together to form a new organization devoted to women's rights. The National Organization for Women (NOW) was the first of its kind in the United States. Jaqui Ceballos became one of the organizers of the group. 'We were beginning to learn how to do things. We did everything ourselves – we wrote our press releases, we put out newsletters, we learned to talk on the telephone, we learned to demonstrate,' she says. 'And so these shy, retiring women who only had their anger...were beginning to learn how to use their power to make changes.'

A CHAIN OF PROTEST *links members of the National Organization for Women as they picket the White House in Washington DC in 1969. The chain, decorated with flowers, was intended to draw attention to the oppression of women.*

PASS the EQUAL RIGHTS AMENDMENT N.O.W.
NATIONAL ORGANIZATION for WOMEN

Best kept secret since 1923...
THE EQUAL RIGHTS AMENDMENT
N.O.W. demands passage this year!
NATIONAL ORGANIZATION for WOMEN

REPEAL ABORTION LAWS N.O.W.
NATIONAL ORGANIZATION for WOMEN

The group forced women's issues onto the political agenda by dispatching telegrams to Washington and picketing government offices. The women called for an amendment to the US constitution to give them equal rights and equal pay. They demanded the enforcement of laws that banned sexual discrimination in employment, and repeal of the laws banning abortion. They lobbied for equality for women at work and for the provision of maternity leave and childcare centres. They also targeted newspapers that printed separate listings for women in job advertisement sections, and challenged airline companies over the unfair treatment of stewardesses.

Through the growing number of newspapers, magazines and groups devoted to women's issues, more women discovered that they shared similar problems and they began to organize themselves. 'We used to get together and talk and bare our feelings, which we'd never done before,' says Jaqui Ceballos. 'It was a catharsis, it was just a feverish movement going from meetings to demonstrations, to consciousness-raising groups.' Several of the feminist publications that appeared in Europe and the United States mirrored the enormous impact of Betty Friedan's book.

By 1968 the mushrooming women's liberation movement was becoming increasingly difficult to ignore. In that year NOW chose the Miss America beauty contest in Atlantic City, New Jersey – an annual event that had continued unchallenged since 1920 – as a focal point for its protest. Women arrived from all over the country to take part. 'There were about seven buses leaving from New York City,' recalls Jaqui Ceballos. 'There were buses that came from Canada, from Washington DC, from California, Florida – all these young women. It was really becoming a grass-roots movement.' Outside the hall where the contest was being held the protesters expressed their indignation in unconventional ways: 'We paraded a sheep and we crowned her Miss America. We threw our garments and cosmetics into the trash can,' as Jaqui Ceballos describes. 'We threw bras and girdles and stockings, high-heeled shoes, corsets, false eyelashes – they were oppressive items for women.'

SHOW OF ANGER (ABOVE) *Voicing their disapproval in public, women demonstrate outside the Miss America beauty contest in Atlantic City in 1968. 'The demonstration was against the idea of women being preened to be beauties,' remembers Jaqui Ceballos. Two years later, members of the women's movement in Britain stormed the annual Miss World contest at the Royal Albert Hall in London* (TOP). *They were dragged out by police after hurling stink bombs, smoke canisters, bags of flour and ink pellets onto the stage.*

"It was a feeling of power...that we all want to change society and we can do it."

JAQUI CEBALLOS

TAKING A STAND *The Statue of Liberty* (RIGHT) *in New York Harbour was used by campaigners to publicize the NOW equality march two weeks before it was due to take place. Jaqui Ceballos* (ABOVE) *recalls how they secretly carried two giant banners to Liberty Island and placed one of them on the balcony beneath the statue; it read: 'Women of the world unite'. 'We were so afraid that we weren't going to get people in the streets,' she says, 'this was a way of announcing it.' The striking images carried by the world's press the next day helped spread awareness of the event and of the women's movement.*

UNCHANGING WAYS *of life* (OPPOSITE) *for women washing clothes in northern Brazil. While women activists in industrial countries fought for equal rights, many poorer women in developing nations were also becoming more active in finding ways to improve their lives. As Serafina Soriana Gallardo, who fought for water to be supplied to San Miguel in Mexico, says, 'Everything has been a struggle. Who are the ones who have carried most of the weight for this struggle? The women.'*

The event was widely reported by the media, which helped to spread awareness of women's issues. The activists encountered some public ridicule, anger and even abuse, but by the time the equality march in New York took place in the summer of 1970, NOW's membership had steadily risen from just 3000 to 15 000. Thousands more women were joining all the time. Some men took part in the marches, too, in support of the women's movement. 'After the march it seemed that everything opened up,' remembers Jaqui Ceballos. 'And it was a worldwide movement – Britain, France, Italy – there were movements all over the world....There was a tremendous feeling of optimism in the 1970s.'

In some parts of Europe, where women's rights had been slow to progress since the 1950s, the women's movement was fuelled by the radical student and worker rebellions that were also taking place during the late 1960s. A French student, Gabrielle Dequesne-Cudenet, had been brought up to believe that women should drink sherry rather than whisky, and that they should smoke only when they were indoors. 'It was an education to mould you as an obedient housewife,' she says. She found that taking part in the student demonstrations that erupted in Paris in May 1968 opened new doors for her. 'Afterwards,' she adds, 'I was no longer the delightful little housewife that I could have been.'

Disillusioned with their low status in a society that still prevented them from divorcing their husbands or having the right to use contraception, Italian women also took to the streets in 1968. Women in Britain formed the National Joint Action Campaign for Women's Equal Rights, and organized an equal pay rally in London's Trafalgar Square in 1969. The following year they convened the first national women's conference. In West Germany women's rights campaigners defiantly hurled tomatoes at their male opponents during a conference, and in Paris women laid a wreath beneath the Arc de Triomphe in honour of 'the unknown wife of the unknown soldier'.

A STEADY PROCESSION (OPPOSITE) *of Italian women from feminist groups engulfs the broad avenues of central Rome. A series of public marches in the capital, involving 20 000 women in 1975 and 50 000 in 1976, finally succeeded in changing Italy's strict laws on abortion – a crime that had been punishable by heavy fines or even imprisonment – despite continuing opposition from the Roman Catholic Church. France and Spain were affected by similar upheavals.*

DIVIDED INTERESTS
Advocates of abortion confront a pro-life campaigner at a rally in Boston (BELOW). Reproductive rights were a constant source of dispute, and strengthened the resolve of lobbyist Ginnie Whitehill (RIGHT) to overturn the abortion laws.

The liberating years

The women's campaigns of the early 1970s led to a series of notable victories. In Europe and the United States it was a time of crucial change as women succeeded in overthrowing, one after another, old laws that had dictated their personal lives. Although in many places unfair attitudes to women still prevailed, new laws affected the lives of millions of women in many different countries and from different social backgrounds.

In Italy women were allowed to seek divorce from 1970, and following further demonstrations, they were able to use birth control legally for the first time in 1972. In Britain a woman government minister introduced an Equal Pay Bill to parliament in 1970. For working women in the United States, whose average earnings were still only 60 per cent that of men, the contentious issue of equal pay continued to be the focus of their campaigns. 'The majority of NOW and the big organizations concentrated on getting the Equal Rights Amendment passed,' remmebers Jaqui Ceballos. They partially succeeded: the conditional amendment to the Constitution, which would guarantee equal rights for women, was passed by Congress in 1972; it was given a seven-year deadline for the ratification by individual states that would bring it into effect.

The laws governing abortion, at that time still illegal in many countries – including France, Germany, Italy, Sweden and the United States – aroused even greater controversy. Demands for free and legal abortion, and outrage over deaths following unsafe operations, triggered local women's movements. In Mexico, Anilu Elias joined a small coalition group to fight for women's rights. 'Abortion was our first and our biggest battle,' she says. 'The first time we ever took to the streets was in a fight for abortion....The first marches were exhilarating. The streets had never been taken over by women's groups before.'

Despite their continued efforts, Mexican campaigners failed to get the laws on abortion repealed. In France and Italy, where thousands of

JUGGLING ACT (RIGHT)
A businesswoman reassures her toddler as she says goodbye at a daycare centre before beginning her professional working day.

CARING FOR CHILDREN

B Y THE LATE 1970S Western women had passed what many
regarded as an important milestone: the majority of them went
out to work. The highest proportion of working married
women were in northern Europe, particularly in Denmark and Sweden
where 57 per cent of women over the age of fifteen worked, and in
Australia, Britain, Canada and the United States. Many of the women
needing or wanting to work were mothers, who faced the crucial
question of how to look after their young children and earn a living.

One option was part-time work. In the 1970s and 1980s many
businesses sought to reduce labour costs by increasing their proportion
of part-time workers. Most of these jobs went to women, many of
whom welcomed the opportunity to combine working with bringing
up a family; part-time work gave them an income without their having
to pay for childcare. In 1986 some 90 per cent of part-time workers in
Belgium, Britain and Germany were women; in Denmark, France,
Luxembourg, Norway and Sweden the figure was almost as high.
Women in full-time employment usually had to find alternatives such as
daycare centres or nurseries for children too young to go to school.

In the Soviet Union falling birth rates rather than welfare concerns
prompted the state to offer maternity leave and other benefits to
working women during the 1970s. In Eastern Europe, state provision
for childcare was widespread, but low standards drove many women
wanting to work to seek part-time jobs, or to work at home.

Childcare varied widely in Western Europe, where it tended to
decline with the economic recessions of the 1980s. By the mid-1980s
the only countries in Europe where more than 5 per cent of children
under the age of five were in government-run childcare centres were
France, Belgium and Denmark. In Sweden it became the responsibility
of local authorities, not parents, to reserve places for children at the state
run daycare centres.

Equal opportunities also meant equal parental responsibility.
Northern Europe set a precedent in encouraging fathers to play a more
active part in looking after their children. In Norway more men took
paternity leave after the government provided them with two weeks'
paid leave following the birth of their child, and a Swedish law entitled
fathers to paid leave to look after sick children.

Japan offered more daycare facilities than any other industrialized
nation in 1991. In the United States working mothers suffered as a result
of stringency in public expenditure. Their need was met by a substantial
increase in private childcare. In Britain, where only 2 per cent of
children under the age of three were in public childcare by the mid-
1990s, the situation was worse. Some companies provided crèches, but
many working mothers had to rely on friends, relatives, community
groups, nannies or private nurseries. Some mothers had to reduce their
hours of work or, if they could afford to, give it up altogether.

women took part in demonstrations, the ban on abortion was eventually lifted, in 1975 and 1977 respectively. In 1973, when the last obstacles to legal abortion were removed in the United States, the news was greeted with alarm in some circles, but for the majority of women it represented a huge victory. 'We'd fought for years for the right to have an abortion,' says Lorena Weeks, who had undergone an illegal operation some years before. 'It meant that the pain that I had gone through was something that women did not have to go through any more. It was a big moment.'

By the mid-1970s, with the new sense that anything was now possible if only they felt able to reach for it, people of all ages challenged conventional rules or assumptions that stood in their way. Ten-year-old Fran Pescatore, from Richfield in New Jersey, loved baseball, and was good at the game, but the town had

LEARNING NEW SKILLS
Claudine Huck became France's first woman woodcutter in 1992. In the thirty years after 1954, the proportion of French working women who were wage earners rose from 59 per cent to 84 per cent, becoming higher than that of men in salaried employment.

refused to let her join the Little League team. 'Boys and girls in my town were treated totally differently in athletic sports,' she says. 'My dad said to me, "Frances, no one can tell you that you can't do anything just because you're a female".' In 1974 she won a lawsuit brought by her father, and became the first girl to play in the team. 'It was a big deal,' she recalls. 'People started throwing things at me, I remember being hit in the back with rocks and bottles....My brother said to me, "Fran, you don't have to go out there". And I remember saying to him, "No, I want to play baseball, I'm not going to let them stop me!" '

As the new legal framework helped begin to change people's attitudes, women found they had greater chances of pursuing new careers. Hannah Dadds applied for a job as a train driver in London. 'I was asked a lot more questions than any of the fellows I worked with,' she remembers. 'When I qualified, my friends, my family, all of them thought it was terrific.' When people first saw her in the driving seat, they stared in disbelief. 'Some of the passengers said that we were doing men out of a job,' Hannah Dadds recalls. As new laws were introduced in Britain in the late 1970s to protect working mothers, giving them new rights to

PRIME POSITION
Benazir Bhutto, elected prime minister of Pakistan in 1988, waves to a mostly male crowd. The first woman to head an Islamic state, she was one of a growing number of stateswomen; they were also to be found in Britain, France, Iceland, India, Ireland, Israel, Norway, Portugal and Sri Lanka. The Scandinavian countries had the highest proportion of women elected to parliament.

maternity leave and maternity pay, the number of women in the workforce rose sharply.

All over the world growing numbers of professional women were succeeding in areas that were once regarded as the exclusive domain of men. They became judges, lawyers, mayors, orchestral conductors, priests and politicians, even heads of government. 'I could be a doctor instead of a nurse, a pilot instead of a flight attendant, a senator instead of a secretary,' points out Dusty Roads, whose lobbying efforts had helped to change the laws on early compulsory retirement for stewardesses. 'It gave me a big thrill when I went up to that cockpit and I saw a girl there, and I knew that I had something to do with it.'

IN THE COCKPIT *of a Boeing 767 jet in Sydney in 1992, Sharelle Quinn was the first female pilot to become a captain on Australia's national airline, Qantas.*

526

RAISING THEIR FISTS (ABOVE)
*Indian women workers campaign
for change. The women's
movement had been gathering
strength since the early days of
India's independence movement,
and as they achieved greater
political and professional success
Indian feminists actively
campaigned against the violent
oppression of poor women.
Resistance to change was
strong: the forbidden ritual
of* sati *– suicide on their
husband's funeral pyre by Hindu widows
– still survived in some places. The poster of an Indian
women's liberation group* (LEFT) *announcing International
Women's Day, celebrated on 8 March, tells women: 'We will
rest only after having broken out of this prison.'*

A decade for women

Since the 1960s the women's movement had developed into an
international one. At the beginning of the century there were 200
international women's organizations; by 1986 the number had
risen to 18 000. In the developing world, women had long been
engaged in their own battles – for better living and working
conditions, basic health care and family planning, and education.
Women's issues were gaining more worldwide attention, and in
1975 the United Nations announced that it would host three
world conferences on women during the UN Decade of Women.
Jaqui Ceballos was one of thousands of women who attended the
first meeting, held in Mexico City. 'There were women from all
over the world,' she recalls. 'There were women from Third World
countries who were there to push for other things.'

In poorer parts of the world millions of women continued
to be affected by overriding poverty, hunger and illiteracy, but
there too they were challenging the systems that oppressed them.
Women in many countries had agitated with varying success for

BANKING ON WOMEN

OMEN IN THE developing world were the most likely people of all to be landless and to face absolute poverty. In 1995 the United Nations reported that of the 1.3 billion people who lived in poverty, 70 per cent were women. In Bangladesh, women in rural districts were among the poorest of the poor. Yet it was there that one of the most promising ideas emerged for helping them to overcome their plight.

In 1976 a Bangladeshi economics professor founded a new development project in the district of Chittagong, with initial funding from local banks. Within ten years, the Grameen or 'village' bank project grew to become a formal, independent bank, branching out to other districts in Bangladesh.

What was unique about the Grameen Bank was that its customers were mostly landless and extremely poor. And 94 per cent of them were women. With a firm belief in everyone's right to receive financial credit, the Grameen Bank operated a pioneering system of 'micro-loans'. Believing that conventional development economics failed because people who most needed cheap credit – the very poor, and especially very poor women – could not get it, the Grameen Bank began to loan money to impoverished, often starving women. They could then buy goats or chickens, perhaps a sewing machine, and use them to generate a regular income, instead of begging. Some could eventually afford to take out a mortgage to buy a small piece of land.

The Grameen Bank preferred to lend to women, who were more reliable borrowers. They did not drink, gamble or squander their money, and children came first in their order of priorities. The bank had remarkably low default rates. It did not ask women for collateral, charged lower interest rates (20 per cent a year compared to the money lenders' rates of up to 20 per cent a month), and offered a much safer alternative to borrowing from other sources.

The bank divided its customers into groups of five women, who encouraged and supported one another when repayment was difficult, and who also had a say in who received bank loans. Bank officials travelled to villages to offer advice to customers as well as to collect loans. When they signed the Grameen Bank's sixteen-point code, borrowers also pledged to keep their families small, to avoid child marriage and wedding dowries, to build and use pit-latrines and to plant as many seedlings as possible. The bank also encouraged more women to vote. It helped empower them in the fight against poverty, and to improve both their living standards and their social status.

By the mid-1990s the Grameen Bank was one of the largest in the country, with more than a thousand branches that loaned millions of dollars every month to two million borrowers living in 68 000 villages. As the micro-loan idea spread, similar institutions were set up in more than thirty countries – most of them in Africa and Asia. In 1995 the Grameen Trust also sponsored 170 worldwide development projects.

BAKING BREAD *outside their new home in Dhaka, one of the many Bangladeshi families who benefited from a local Grameen Bank project to help homeless people build their own houses using local materials.*

WOMEN'S DAY IN ALGERIA (ABOVE) *is marked by a march in the capital in 1994 to honour those killed by the Islamic fundamentalists who threatened women's freedoms.*

MOMENT OF JOY (LEFT) *for a newly ordained woman priest in Britain, one of thirty-six women deacons admitted into the Church of England priesthood in 1994.*

BREAKING INTO THE RANKS (OPPOSITE) *New arrivals from the United States army await orders at a Gulf port in 1990. More governments were prepared to admit women into their armed services, though their roles were restricted.*

the reform of laws that restricted them. They tackled difficult issues such as dowry murder in India and female infanticide in China. In Muslim countries such as Algeria and Iran, where an Islamic revival was taking place, the Western idea of progress was being challenged as traditional attitudes were restored.

Women's achievements faced a new challenge in the West, too, especially in the United States, where powerful religious groups reacted fiercely against the abortion laws. The Equal Rights Amendment to the Constitution had still not been fully ratified by all the states of the Union when the deadline – which had already been granted an extension – expired in 1982, so it failed to become law. Jaqui Ceballos was devastated. 'This was just the right, like men have, to be free and equal citizens, that was all,' she says. 'It was terrible. It was just like rolling up your sleeves and starting all over again.'

For the majority of Western women, many aspects of their lives had improved dramatically. More avenues were open to them both at work and in society in general. With marriage no longer an obstacle to professional advancement, women were able to reach new heights in their careers – as pilots, in the navy, as sports umpires, as union presidents, as astronauts. Nearly forty years on, Kay Foley was employed at her local factory once more – and as a chemical processor in the hard hat area alongside the men, rather than as a keypunch operator. 'It never occurred to me in that time frame that I could do what they were doing, that I could make the kind of money that they were making,' she remembers. 'And it came about because these doors were opened by the women who were the activists of their day.'

In 1995 thousands of women delegates gathered for the Fourth UN Conference to discuss women's status. This time they met in the Chinese capital, Beijing. It was a good opportunity for them to take stock. Although there was still much to do, and many women had not yet benefited from the progress made since the 1950s, for American campaigner Amy Coen it was a time to acknowledge what had been achieved. 'I realized that I made a very decent salary, I had a very responsible job, I had wonderful children. I realized how personally I had benefited from all the social changes I had spent my entire life trying to have happen.'

23

War of the Flea

THE IMPACT
OF GUERRILLA
WARS

IN A LAST BID FOR SAFETY, hundreds of men, women and children struggled to get past the armed guards who surrounded the American embassy in Saigon. Those who did manage to squeeze through the crush joined the scramble to board the tightly packed American helicopter. It was April 1975, and the final evacuation of South Vietnam was under way.

The South Vietnam government, which had been backed by the United States, had fallen. The Vietnamese most closely associated with it were desperate to flee the country, as the American withdrawal would leave them defenceless against the advancing communist forces.

One side's defeat meant triumph for their opponents – the communists of North Vietnam and their supporters in the south. For the Viet Cong troops entering Saigon it was the end of a long struggle: after thirty years they had finally achieved the victory they had been fighting for. Lam Thi Phan was an intelligence officer with the Viet Cong. When the Americans left at last, she recalls, 'I was extremely happy. I had sacrificed my whole life up to that time for the revolution. The Americans had withdrawn – and we had victory.'

The conflict in Vietnam was one example of guerrilla warfare, movements by groups of armed rebels that became increasingly common during the twentieth century. In Vietnam a guerrilla force had undermined one of the most powerful armies in the world. Like fleas on a dog, guerrillas could sap the enemy's strength while their own agility made them too elusive to be confronted.

In many parts of the world guerrilla methods were used to fight for political revolution, national independence or religious freedom. They claimed that they were fighting for 'the people', and grass-roots support was always vital to their success. Mao Zedong, leader of the Chinese communist revolution, believed that guerrillas should 'move like fish in water' among the people. 'With the common people of the whole country mobilized,' he wrote, 'one can create a vast sea of humanity and drown the enemy in it.'

FLIGHT FROM DANGER *Desperate South Vietnamese families clamber aboard an American aircraft in Saigon.*

Revolution in Cuba

Twenty years before the evacuation of Vietnam, and on the other side of the world, a small group of revolutionaries provided a classic demonstration of how an apparently strong regime could be challenged by guerrillas who used the appropriate tactics.

In December 1956 a band of exiles set out from Mexico in a boat called the *Granma*. Their leader was a former lawyer, Fidel Castro, and his aim was to start a popular revolution in Cuba. Arsenio Garcia was among the rebel force that waded ashore on the Cuban coast in the early hours one morning. 'We always think of the arrival of the *Granma* as a shipwreck,' he remembers. 'The boat was grounded, though it didn't sink completely because the water was so shallow. From there we could reach the land through the roots of the mangrove swamp....If one thinks of all the time we spent training, our journey in the boat, getting out of this place and even the two years in the mountains, the landing here was still the most difficult task.'

As they clambered through the mangroves, the guerrillas knew the difficulty of their mission. There were just eighty-two of them, and they believed it was their mission to free six million Cubans from exploitation, poverty and repression. Most Cubans in the countryside worked in the sugar cane and tobacco fields of wealthy landowners. They were poorly paid, and were forced to live in crowded, squalid shacks on their landlord's property. There

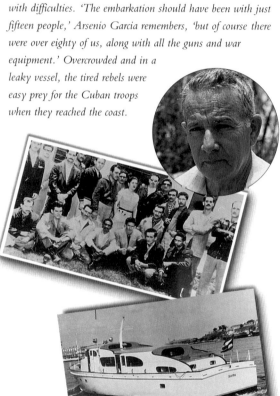

MEN WITH A MISSION (BELOW) *Arsenio Garcia was among Fidel Castro's rebel army on the journey from Mexico to Cuba in the* Granma *(BOTTOM). It was a voyage beset with difficulties. 'The embarkation should have been with just fifteen people,' Arsenio Garcia remembers, 'but of course there were over eighty of us, along with all the guns and war equipment.' Overcrowded and in a leaky vessel, the tired rebels were easy prey for the Cuban troops when they reached the coast.*

VIOLENCE ERUPTS (RIGHT) *at Havana University after a presidential decree gives special privileges to the Americans and British. Many Cubans resented American economic and political influence, but fear of military reprisals meant that few people voiced their anger in public.*

were few schools, so many people had little or no education. In stark contrast the capital, Havana, which was only 144 km (90 miles) away from Florida, thronged with American tourists. They used Havana as a playground, pouring money into casinos and clubs, some of which were controlled by the American Mafia. Much of the money being skimmed from Havana's gambling and prostitution businesses was channelled to Cuba's military dictator, General Fulgencio Batista, who maintained his regime with an army of 46 000 men.

When Batista heard that the guerrillas had landed he rushed convoys of well-equipped troops to the eastern province, confident that they could outnumber the rebels and easily overwhelm them. They intercepted and attacked the guerrilla force, showing their captives little mercy. Most of the rebels were killed, but Castro and twenty-one of his men managed to escape. They fled into the most remote and wildest part of the country, the Sierra Maestra mountains. There, deep in the forests, they established a hideout and began the task of rebuilding their forces.

Sergio Fuentes helped to protect the guerrillas and supplied them with food and arms. Eventually he joined them. 'Everything about being a guerrilla was hard,' he remembers. 'We were usually barefoot and had few clothes. We couldn't wash and we had no luxuries like soap. There is no material benefit to be gained from being a guerrilla. It's exhausting and full of hardship.'

But the Cuban peasants were not put off by the privations and dangers. Many were inspired to join the guerrillas when they witnessed the savage reprisals meted out to the rebels by Batista's army. Even some of Batista's soldiers, sickened by the brutality that riddled the Cuban army, deserted to join the guerrillas.

Castro's tiny rebel force soon swelled into thousands. Other underground groups fighting against Batista banded together under his leadership. A strict code of conduct was enforced to ensure that the guerrillas maintained the people's support. 'You had to be respectful to the peasants and their families,' remembers Sergio Fuentes. 'You had to have discipline, and respect what wasn't yours.' Shop owners who were sympathetic gave food to the rebels. 'Sometimes we needed much more than they gave,' recalls Sergio Fuentes. 'So we'd take everything without leaving

*"**B**atista's army were assassinating the rebels as if they were animals. That's what motivated me. I decided that I was not going to kill them. I was going to help them."*

SERGIO FUENTES

CUBAN PEASANTS *flock to join the rebel army, inspired by Fidel Castro (centre) and undaunted by the privations of guerrilla life. At first they were hindered by the shortage of arms, but once local sympathy was tapped the movement quickly grew into a force sufficiently powerful to challenge General Batista's army.*

"*It was a joyful moment when they said Batista had left. This was real satisfaction for us. We all hugged each other. We toasted each other.* **"**

SELESTINO SANCHEZ SANTO

JUBILANT CROWDS *in Havana, greeting the triumphant rebel army in 1959, listen to Castro's promises for a fairer and more prosperous Cuba. After his victory Castro gained massive popular support by executing Batista's supporters and instituting radical land reforms.*

any money, but we'd leave a note. When we got money we would pay them back.' Dishonesty was severely punished. When one of the guerrillas stole for himself, Sergio Fuentes judged him and condemned him to death, even though they were related. 'I was defending the honour of the guerrillas,' he explains. 'This man was creating an atmosphere that undermined confidence in us.'

The young Fidel Castro was an inspiring leader. 'He gave the impression that he was always looking after your needs,' recalls Sergio Fuentes. 'The guerrillas had nothing. Their families needed money and we always tried to send some to them....Fidel tried to help people. That's why we see him, and why we will always see him, as our leader. People who fought with Fidel were prepared to die with Fidel.'

At first the guerrillas were desperately short of weapons. In small, remote clearings camouflaged by jungle foliage they set up workshops to manufacture crude mines and grenades; the weapons were as unreliable as they were makeshift. The rebels depended on the peasants to supply arms. Selestino Sanchez Santo was eager to support Castro. 'He was here to liberate Cuba from the terrible dictator, Batista. That's why we started fighting....We began by looking for arms. We had to go to people who owned land and ask if they would cooperate. We had to try to convince them they should give us weapons.'

Women were also important. 'They would tell us this person's got a gun, or that person's got a gun. So that's how, very quietly, we started going to these places....We didn't get anything by force. It was more that we just had to convince people – and that's how we worked.'

One of Castro's most powerful weapons was the mimeograph. It was used to print thousands of propaganda leaflets, circulated throughout Cuba despite efforts by the secret police to stamp out the underground movement. In the cities Castro gained the support of many people, some of whom organized a series of sabotage and bombing campaigns against Batista's forces. These provoked such savage reprisals that local support for Batista diminished further. Gradually the guerrillas controlled more and more of the country, until by the end of 1958 they were fighting on the outskirts of Havana itself. The United States, having initially backed Batista's regime, withdrew its support and General Batista fled from Cuba.

In January 1959 excited crowds lined the streets of Havana to welcome the victorious Fidel Castro and his army into the city. 'We had achieved our aim, our dreams, our triumph,' Arsenio Garcia recalls happily. Fidel Castro was at first to establish a new government that enjoyed mass support from the Cuban people.

Revolutionary fervour spreads

The Cubans had made revolution look surprisingly easy. They had challenged and overturned an oppressive regime in less than two years. The victory achieved by the insurgents, the charisma of their leaders and Cuba's proximity to the United States meant that they had an enormous impact. In Central and South America and also in Europe other revolutionaries, inspired by their example, were encouraged to attempt the same feat, and a number of new guerrilla movements sprang into action.

Some guerrillas tried to adapt guerrilla tactics to the cities, merging into the urban workforce and using this cover to rock the streets with car bombs and stage kidnappings, hijackings and bank raids. Many of these rebels were well educated and from privileged backgrounds. This sometimes distanced them from the very people they believed they were fighting for, and made it difficult for them to gain mass support.

In Argentina from 1974 an urban guerrilla group known as the Montoneros fought a campaign against the radical dictator Juan Perón. Hernan (surname withheld) was an Argentinian who joined the Montoneros. 'We thought we could build a better country,' he recalls. 'It seemed the only way of actually breaking down a government we considered unjust....The great schemes were to nationalize the production and also to socialize great areas of the country. But they were very vague ideas. What we wanted was to end the hunger. We wanted to end the poverty.'

Some of the Montoneros were inspired by events in Cuba. 'The Cuban example was always there for us,' recalls Hernan. 'I

HITTING THE HEADLINES *The dramatic acts of violence by terrorist organizations such as West Germany's Baader-Meinhof Gang, also known as the Red Army Faction (*TOP*), and Italy's Red Brigades (*ABOVE*) publicized their cause and attempted to undermine state authority. Attacks in urban areas had the greatest impact, as more people were affected and public outrage ensured that their governments could not ignore the terrorists' demands.*

> *"Che Guevara was like Christ. He had a doctrine and he upheld it all his life. He sacrificed himself....He died for the poor."*
>
> ARSENIO GARCIA

believe it was the mother of all the revolutions in Latin America.... And the figure of Che Guevara influenced everyone. He was an example of somebody who was untouchable.'

The Montoneros followed traditional guerrilla tactics. 'Our strategy was not to have large battles, but to have small, precise hits at the establishment to wear away the enemy,' remembers Hernan. 'Then we hoped to increase the amount of propaganda so that the working-class people, for whom we were doing this, would begin to take notice and make decisions for themselves.'

Despite the dedication and courage shown by the guerrillas, they failed to win the support of the population. Many people were bewildered by them. Claudia Avila, who lived in the same block of flats as a general whom the Montoneros tried to assassinate (instead, they mistakenly killed his daughter) remembers the public confusion about the rebels' cause. 'I didn't know who the Montoneros were. I didn't know why they were killing people. The press said they were fighting for the workers. But nobody knew exactly why or what for.'

Ernesto Bareira was a member of the Argentinian military intelligence who attempted to infiltrate the guerrilla force. 'The Montoneros were a group of very intelligent, well-prepared men,' he recalls. 'They were of good social origin, and with a good education...but they should have operated with more depth and a political objective, not just with political theory....It was rather a romantic attitude,' he believes, and doomed to failure.

In an attempt to redistribute wealth, the Montoneros gave money to the poor in the cities, particularly in the capital, Buenos Aires. Yet there was no popular uprising in their defence when the army was ordered to annihilate the Montoneros in 1975. 'Most of the population did not help the Montoneros,' remembers Hernan. 'When the most violent time came the Montoneros themselves couldn't put up enough resistance, and the masses didn't back them. That is why revolution failed in Argentina.'

The failure of the guerrillas to bring about revolution in Argentina was echoed elsewhere in South America, as governments – often supported by the United States – learned how to crack down on insurgents, not all of whom were able to gain the allegiance of the very people they believed they were fighting for.

THE FACE of Che Guevara (OPPOSITE) on millions of posters, banners and T-shirts became a symbol for a whole generation of radicals who were inspired by his belief that individuals had a crucial part to play in bringing about world revolution.

CHE GUEVARA

ONE MEMBER OF the intrepid band of revolutionaries who clambered through the mangrove swamps in eastern Cuba in December 1956 was a fervent young Argentinian, Ernesto (nicknamed Che) Guevara. The son of an architect, and himself a qualified doctor, Che Guevara had spent many years travelling through Central and South America observing the wretched way of life endured by millions of urban slum-dwellers and rural labourers. Concerned about the social injustice he encountered, and shocked by the United States-backed invasion of Guatemala in 1954, Che Guevara became a passionate and committed revolutionary.

In Mexico Guevara met Fidel Castro, and joined his group of rebel Cubans. He became a close adviser to Castro, and after the revolution's victory was given the powerful post of president of the Cuban National Bank. In 1961 he became minister of industry, but his main preoccupation was still to attempt to set down the ideas and tactics of the Cuban revolution, and to propagate revolution in the rest of Central and South America.

In 1965 Guevara resigned from his comfortable position in government, and set off to lead a revolution among the poor peasants and tin-miners of the Bolivian Andes. Within weeks he was betrayed, ambushed and shot dead by the Bolivian army, with secret United States' backing.

With Guevara's death came immortality. Newspapers around the world carried photographs of him lying on a stretcher, and gave graphic accounts of his mission and his fate. The image of sacrifice for a revolutionary cause caught the imagination of rebels and protesters all over the world. Among them Che Guevara was elevated at that time to the status of a martyr, and he began to exert an influence far greater than it had ever been during his lifetime.

The struggle in Vietnam

In Asia, where 'people's wars' had been far more successful, Mao Zedong's revolution in China had inspired political activists who wanted to try and loosen the grip of colonial rulers or bring down regimes they opposed. It was in Vietnam that the longest, most bitter struggle took place. It engulfed the country for thirty years.

Since the nineteenth century Vietnam had been part of the French empire. After the Second World War the Viet Minh, a communist-led guerrilla movement named after its leader, Ho Chi Minh, launched a revolutionary war against the French, eventually defeating them in 1954. At an international conference it was decided that Vietnam should be formally divided into two states: North Vietnam, led by the communist Viet Minh and supported by the Soviet Union and China; and South Vietnam, which was committed to Western-style capitalism and backed by the United States. The communists declared that the anti-communist South Vietnamese government was just a puppet regime, and pledged to overthrow it by the same means as those they had used against the French. By 1960 at least 5000 communist guerrillas, known as the Viet Cong, had infiltrated into South Vietnam and were fighting against its government.

For the next twenty years a fierce battle was waged for the hearts and minds of the people of South Vietnam. It was at its most savage in the heavily populated Mekong delta. The government tried to convince the peasants that they should trust the rulers in the capital, Saigon, but the guerrillas told them that only revolution would release them from their poverty and oppression. Many peasant farmers worked in the fields during the day and fought for the Viet Cong at night. Among them was Phan Dinh. 'I followed the Viet Cong because the revolution promised to give

DRINKING PARTNERS (ABOVE) *In apparent harmony a young Vietnamese boy and an American marine take a break from building a bunker to drink Coke. Most American soldiers believed they were helping to protect the local people, but many of the Vietnamese regarded them more as enemies than as allies.*

LESSONS OF THE PAST *A veteran militiaman* (LEFT) *shares his experience, gained resisting the French, with fighters of a Viet Cong unit. Both forces successfully used guerrilla tactics, enabling them to defeat opponents far better equipped, financed and trained than themselves.*

TOWERING OVER VILLAGE LIFE (ABOVE) *Government security posts were erected to guard against Viet Cong activity. Built to protect the local people, the watch towers were often regarded with suspicion and resentment by the villagers, who frequently collaborated with the Viet Cong to sabotage them.*

us land, rice and clothes,' he declares. 'We were very poor.'

In Phan Dinh's village government forces, known as the ARVN (Army of the Republic of Vietnam), set up a security post to keep a lookout for rebels. The Viet Cong, desperately short of weapons, used trickery to capture the post. 'The soldiers' families all lived in the village,' remembers Phan Dinh. 'We told them they had a duty to call on their fathers, husbands and sons to leave the government post and to come home – and that if the soldiers refused, we would kill them. And we encouraged the villagers to demonstrate.…The soldiers gave up. They just handed over their rifles and marched out of the post.'

Thousands of local officials loyal to Saigon were murdered by the Viet Cong, and by 1963 the Saigon government feared it was losing the battle for its own survival. The United States sent 12 000 military and political advisers to stiffen its resistance. Earl Young was one of them. 'We were part of the Kennedy generation,' he says. 'We were prepared to do anything to save South Vietnam from being taken over by the communists.'

The Saigon government soon realized that the guerrillas were heavily dependent on local support, so they decided to move many of the villagers to new settlements. Thousands of peasants, regardless of their age or health, were forced to abandon their homes, gather up their possessions and embark on a long trek to new districts. On arrival they were organized into groups and given the strenuous task of building new communities, under the close scrutiny of Vietnamese officials and American advisers. The new villages were known as 'strategic hamlets', and were designed to be impenetrable by the Viet Cong. 'We provided the barbed wire,' remembers Earl Young. 'We provided the fence posts. We

AMERICAN ADVISERS *working with government forces. Their attempts to encourage peasant farmers to defend their land against the communist rebels failed. 'They moved the people away from their own land into these hamlets,' recalls Earl Young* (TOP), *'but it was like the Trojan Horse, because they also brought the Viet Cong infrastructure inside the hamlets.'*

provided training. There was to be a medical technician in every hamlet. It was our belief – if you will, our naivety – that the people would be so thankful for the new school and medical personnel, the drugs and the food, that they would support the Saigon government and cut off their allegiance to the Viet Cong.'

It did not work. The villagers, who felt they had lost their freedom, resented the enforced membership of the militia and the time required to train. Some of them, like Chau Van Nhat, fought in the militia one day and for the Viet Cong the next. 'When I was in the militia I would have one night on duty and then the next night off,' he recalls. 'When I was off duty, I'd contact the guerrillas....I helped them creep into the hamlet undetected.'

To many people in the West, aware that communist regimes had taken over in Eastern Europe after the Second World War, the conflict in Vietnam seemed more than just a local issue: the whole balance of power in the Cold War world was at stake, and they believed they had a duty to intervene to stem the further advance of communism. In August 1964 the Americans claimed that two of their destroyers had been attacked in the Gulf of Tonkin by North Vietnamese torpedo boats. This incident, and the Soviet Union's increasing involvement with North Vietnam, fired the United States into battle. In April 1965 President Lyndon Johnson ordered US combat troops into South Vietnam. At the height of the fighting they would number 600 000.

The Viet Cong now faced the armed power of the most technologically advanced nation in the world. The Americans and the ARVN set out to defeat the guerrillas using conventional combat methods: mobilizing huge numbers of troops in large groups equipped with heavy weapons, tanks and helicopters, and supported by the world's most powerful bombers, B-52s. But the Viet Cong used hit-and-run tactics, proving too elusive for the Americans to confront and eliminate.

Although short of weapons, the Viet Cong were ingenious in converting the scrap and debris of superpower arms into simple, lethal contraptions such as grenades and mines. They also used natural materials to make traditional fighting weapons. Whole communities were involved in equipping the guerrillas. At the age of eight, Nguyen Thi Be helped to sharpen stakes. 'I'd follow my

CHILDREN HELP *to make simple but lethal weapons for Viet Cong supporters using traditional local skills. These young boys are preparing a booby trap that would be strung up in the trees above a narrow pathway, and triggered to drop down on an approaching enemy.*

NEW WEAPONS FOR OLD (ABOVE) *Viet Cong guerrillas dismantle a dud American bomb. They would use its parts to make their own weapons.*

mother around and help her with her work,' she remembers. 'I also helped other people by bringing the bamboo sticks to where the traps were being made. The soldiers would often fall into them when they went on patrol.' Poison or excrement was sometimes smeared on the stakes to make wounds turn septic.

Trained to fight a different sort of war, the Americans were living on their nerves. 'The impact on the soldier was psychological,' recalls US army colonel David Hackworth. 'Every time you put your foot down, you didn't know whether you were going to lose a limb or your life. And this was played out for three hundred and sixty-five days going down trails, going down waterways – it took the fight out of you....I took over a battalion down in the delta. It was called the Hard Luck Battalion. In the six months before I took over it had six hundred casualties, all from mines and booby traps. It had never met the enemy.'

SOUTH VIETNAMESE TROOPS *were weighed down with American weapons and trained in conventional Western fighting tactics. They were ill equipped to challenge the speed and agility of the Viet Cong. Most recruits were posted far from their home villages, and desertion rates were high. Between 1954 and 1975 some 200 000 ARVN soldiers were killed.*

TRAN THI GUNG *fought with the Viet Cong for many years, living rough in the jungle. 'There were lots of dangers. There were many different kinds of snakes and deadly black ants.... When we were moving through the jungle we had to tie our legs with rubber bands, so that if snakes bit us the poison wouldn't penetrate far into our bodies. The temperature sometimes went up as high as forty-one degrees.'*

TUNNELLING FOR REFUGE (LEFT) *The Viet Cong dug tunnels to escape enemy troops, but the Americans often pursued them under ground. 'When they got into the entrance we threw grenades or shot at them,' remembers Tran Thi Gung. 'Then we would withdraw to another level.'*

FRUSTRATED AMERICAN troops (OPPOSITE) *try to launch an offensive against the Viet Cong, but are forced into defensive positions against their unseen enemy. Only when the American forces themselves adopted guerrilla tactics did they achieve any measure of success.*

Frustrated in their attempts to confront their opponents, the Americans tried to deprive the Viet Cong of refuge. Entire villages were destroyed and forests decimated. Hundreds of thousands of tonnes of napalm, high explosives, Agent Orange defoliant and phosphorus bombs were dropped. The scale of destruction made it difficult for the peasants to believe that the Americans were really liberating their country. More firepower was ultimately unleashed against the Vietnamese than had been used in all earlier wars put together, and more than a million civilians were killed.

To avoid the shelling and bombing the guerrillas went under ground. They dug a network of tunnels, which they constantly extended. Tran Thi Gung replaced her father in the Viet Cong forces when he was killed; she spent weeks hiding under ground. 'Moving through the tunnels was like crawling in hell,' she recalls. 'You went down and down. When we got really hungry we ate a little dry rice and drank a little water....It was particularly difficult for us girls. We had a lot of problems with hygiene in general because women's ways are different. For men, five days without bathing was fine, but it made us feel uncomfortable, like dirty dogs.' American patrols tried hard to find the tunnel systems and destroy them, but the entrances were well hidden and the tunnel network complex; when tunnels were found, many Americans were simply too large to get into them.

While much of the countryside was in Viet Cong hands, the capital remained the government's stronghold. But the Viet Cong were infiltrating the towns, and many families were split by the same ideological divide that cut across the country. Lam Van Phat had risen to become a general in the South Vietnamese army; his sister, Lam Thi Phan, was a communist. While she was staying with her brother in Saigon she took advantage of his position to pass information to the Viet Cong. 'If I had used my brother for personal gain, then it would have been wrong,' she declares. 'But as I used him for the benefit of the country, for the people, I was right. I am proud of what I did.' Suspecting her, Lam Van Phat reported his sister to the authorities. 'To inform on her like that tore me to pieces inside,' he recalls sadly. 'My heart was in pain because I had betrayed my sister....I was at fault with my family, but the nation's concern came before family.'

CLOSING THE DOORS OF CAMBODIA

GUERRILLA MOVEMENTS conducted in the name of the people sometimes had appalling consequences. Cambodia, like Laos and Vietnam, was a French colony until 1953, but independence failed to bring peace to this troubled region. The Cambodian leader, Norodom Sihanouk, was overthrown in 1970 and replaced by the pro-American military government of the Khmer Republic.

A communist guerrilla force, the Khmer Rouge, led by a group of French-educated revolutionaries, seized its opportunity. Already backed by China, they now allied themselves with Sihanouk, against whom they had rebelled in the 1960s, and launched a guerrilla war against the government. The United States invaded Cambodia in an attempt to suppress the Khmer Rouge forces. Nearly 100 000 people were killed in the fighting, which lasted for five years; millions more became refugees. In April 1975 the government collapsed. The Khmer Rouge quickly occupied the capital, Phnom Penh, and took control of Cambodia in 1976, placing Sihanouk under house arrest.

In the renamed Democratic Republic of Kampuchea the Khmer Rouge leader, Pol Pot, launched an idealistic revolutionary programme to establish a self-sufficient agricultural economy based on collectivization of the countryside. Millions of people were forced out of the towns and cities into rural areas to dig canals and toil in the paddy fields. Everyone, regardless of their particular professional skills or lack of farming experience, had to work on the land to further the agricultural ideal.

As contact with the outside world was cut off, the borders were closed. Foreigners were moved out. Money was banned and the postal system abolished. People were victimized and in many cases executed if they were well educated or bore even slight signs of what the Khmer Rouge condemned as Western influence. Any opposition was crushed. The reign of terror was characterized by mass murders and purges in which more than a million people were killed or died from hunger, illness or sheer exhaustion.

Relations with neighbouring Vietnam, which had already been marred by territorial disputes, grew worse in 1978. Border clashes culminated in a full-scale Vietnamese invasion of Cambodia, which succeeded in toppling the Khmer Rouge. Pol Pot fled, and people began the huge task of rebuilding their country under another new regime.

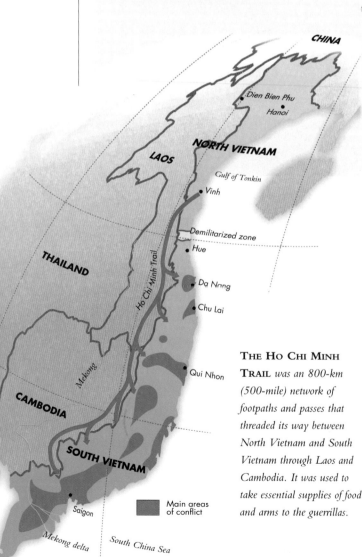

THE HO CHI MINH TRAIL *was an 800-km (500-mile) network of footpaths and passes that threaded its way between North Vietnam and South Vietnam through Laos and Cambodia. It was used to take essential supplies of food and arms to the guerrillas.*

Lam Thi Phan was captured and, like thousands of others, faced brutal interrogation. 'When they questioned me they attached electric wire to my ears, around my breasts, my feet and even in my vagina. Then they turned the power on so high I thought I was going to die. While the current was running they poured detergent into my mouth. My stomach swelled up and they kicked my stomach until I vomited.' Lam Thi Phan still suffers from the effects of the torture.

In January 1968 the Viet Cong believed they were strong enough to take the fight into the towns. Many soldiers in the South Vietnamese army were celebrating the new year Tet festival when the guerrillas launched a coordinated attack on cities all over the country. In Saigon the Viet Cong invaded the American embassy. Although United States troops and the South Vietnamese army quickly regained control, the attacks had a dramatic effect on American public opinion. Earl Young was back in Washington. 'I thought this was a total disaster, as psychologically the American people were already very uneasy about the course of the war. And when they saw this apparent victory of the communist forces, able to enter every one of the provincial capitals...the American people said, "With all the American troops there, everything we've done in South Vietnam, if we cannot prevent the American embassy from being captured, my God, what are we there for?" '

Television pictures of the savage reprisals inflicted by the ARVN shocked viewers across the world. As the number of American soldiers killed continued to rise – the total was 57 000 – the will to carry on fighting was eroded, and pressure to withdraw grew. In the United States the campaign to end the war intensified until President Richard Nixon signed an agreement with the North Vietnamese government in Paris in 1973, instigating the withdrawal of all American troops from Vietnam.

Triumphant communist forces entered Saigon in 1975. They had shown how a tenacious guerrilla force, with the help of local people and outside support, could defy a great superpower.

FRIGHTENED CHILDREN (ABOVE) *flee the napalm bombing of their village, their plight recorded by news photographers. This attack by South Vietnamese forces was said to be a mistake – it was claimed that their real target was a neighbouring village dominated by the Viet Cong.*

SMILING IN VICTORY (BELOW) *After nearly thirty years of war, Viet Cong troops pose triumphantly in the streets of Saigon, soon to be renamed Ho Chi Minh City. Tran Bach Dan, a leader of the Viet Cong there, had always believed the guerrillas would win: 'They were supported by the people around them, who took care of them, guided and protected them....They also knew what they were fighting for.'*

URBAN GUERRILLAS IN NORTHERN IRELAND

VIOLENT CONFLICT among the people of Ireland could be traced back over centuries, but the emergence of powerful, highly organized urban guerrilla groups was a twentieth-century phenomenon. A low-intensity civil war had festered ever since the Act of Union in 1801 made Ireland part of the United Kingdom. Its ferocity increased during the twentieth century, as opposing guerrilla factions resorted to terrorism and violence.

Religion was always a fundamental division among the Irish people. The majority of them were formally Roman Catholic, but a powerful minority of Protestants, descendants of English and Scottish emigrants, lived in northern Ireland, particularly in the province of Ulster. Early in the century Irish resentment of Britain's sovereignty and their desire for home rule culminated in the unsuccessful Easter Rising of 1916 in Dublin. Protestants in Ulster were already determined to oppose any severance from Britain, and pledged to fight it with force if necessary.

In 1922 the independent Irish Republic was formed; six of the nine counties of Ulster remained united with Britain. Northern Ireland's prosperity outstripped that in the south, but discrimination against the minority Catholic community in employment, housing and other areas caused much resentment and conflict.

Many civilians in Northern Ireland, including some Protestants, campaigned for equal civil rights in Northern Ireland. When violence erupted in 1969 British troops were sent in; they were to experience at first hand how difficult it was for a modern army to fight anonymous guerrillas who had merged into the community.

The soldiers' original task was to protect Catholics against Protestant aggression, but they soon became the focus of extreme Catholic resentment. The Provisional Irish Republican Army (IRA) and the more radical Irish National Liberation Army (INLA) embarked on a campaign of bombing and shooting attacks on British soldiers and security forces, both in Northern Ireland and on the British mainland. Frustrated by British policy, they aimed to bring their cause to international attention by targeting important members of the British establishment – in 1979 Earl Mountbatten was murdered, and in 1984 the IRA came close to killing the prime minister, Margaret Thatcher.

Many Roman Catholics in Northern Ireland claimed to be Irish nationalists, but only a minority supported Sinn Féin, the political party linked to the IRA. In the Irish Republic Sinn Féin was supported by less than 5 per cent of the electorate. The IRA did receive outside support and funding, much of which came from Irish sympathizers in the United States.

For twenty-five years thousands of British soldiers on duty in Northern Ireland patrolled without ever quite knowing who the enemy was, and in fear of ambush, booby traps and sniper attacks. Terror was returned with equal ferocity by extreme Protestant guerrilla

BURNING RESENTMENT *flared into violence in 1969. The suspension of the Stormont (Northern Irish parliament) in 1972 and imposition of direct British rule increased tension and bitterness on both sides.*

groups, who murdered hundreds of IRA and INLA members and other Roman Catholics. Altogether some 3200 people were killed during 'the Troubles', including 2224 civilians.

Late in 1994 tentative overtures were made between the opposing factions, and a slow, precarious peace process was begun.

Holy war in Afghanistan

Victory in Vietnam had come from a union of communism and nationalism. Conservative guerrillas could use the same tactics with equal success if they too had enough popular support. The clearest demonstration of this came in Afghanistan in the 1980s.

The fifteen million Afghan people had fierce tribal loyalties and were devout followers of Islam; most of them lived in the countryside in a very traditional society. In 1978 the communists seized power in the capital, Kabul, killing the former president. The new communist government was ruthless in its efforts to eliminate potential rivals: all non-communists in positions of authority came under threat, and thousands of religious leaders, teachers and political opponents were killed. The new regime attempted to impose some of the social and political reforms that had been welcomed in Cuba and Vietnam, including measures giving women equal status with men. But many people disliked the changes, which were forced on them with little sensitivity to their traditional beliefs and the customs that had evolved over hundreds of years.

After a popular uprising against the communist government in 1979, the Soviet Union sent in its own troops to support its client Afghan government. The soldiers were said to be there to help defend socialism; soon there were 100 000 Soviet troops in Afghanistan and, as the Americans had done in Vietnam, they greatly underestimated their enemy. To the Afghan guerrillas it was both a war against foreign intrusion and a holy war, fought to safeguard Islam against non-believers. They believed their cause to be worth every sacrifice and deprivation, and that to be killed defending it was an honour. They called themselves the Mujahideen (Soldiers of God). They continued to pray five times a day, and reverently kissed the Koran before going into battle.

Ahmed Shah Massoud was a leader of the Mujahideen, based in the remote scrublands of the Panjshir valley to the north of Kabul. He had read the teachings of Mao Zedong and Che

GREETING THE TROOPS
Children in Kabul line up to welcome Soviet troops to the city. In reality the majority of Afghans deeply resented the Soviet presence.

YOUNG MUSLIM REBELS (BELOW), *armed with old guns and sticks, prepare to take on the might of the Soviet Union. Ambushes* (OPPOSITE) *were one of the most effective strategies used by the guerrillas to weaken the Soviet troops, who were dependent on supplies of food, weapons and equipment transported by road.*

IDENTITY CARDS
(RIGHT) *belonging to Soviet soldiers captured by the Mujahideen. Fear of the guerrillas' brutality meant that many soldiers carried personal poison capsules and grenades – a quick death was preferable to torture.*

Guevara; their politics were anathema to him, but he was attracted to their tactics. 'Without mobilizing the people it was impossible to fight against Afghan communists or the Russians,' he recalls. 'We were, as they say, "like fish in water": when the people rally, the enemy doesn't have a chance. The communists were unbelievers and the Russians were invaders. Islam and the independence of Afghanistan were our main rallying cries.'

The Russians thought that their advanced technology would make it easy for them to defeat the geographically divided and poorly armed Mujahideen. But their weapons and conventional military strategies proved too cumbersome against the agile rebel forces, who constantly outwitted them and always had the support of local people. Oleg Blotsky, a young Soviet infantry lieutenant sent on two missions to fight in Afghanistan, found this out for himself. 'The first time I went for six months. I thought I was doing what was morally correct....I was shocked by what I saw. The second time I knew what was going on in Afghanistan. The officials were lying. In reality we had no friends in Afghanistan.'

Both sides committed appalling atrocities. Oleg Blotsky recalls how the Afghan children loved fireworks. 'Once some Soviet soldiers replaced the rocket fuel with explosive and gave the firework to some children who were running around. At night the children gathered to watch this rocket launch. One of them pulled the string and that was it. No boy, and no others.' He remembers how Soviet soldiers feared capture by the Mujahideen, who were renowned for their brutal behaviour. 'One person could be raped repeatedly by up to thirty men, then their stomachs were cut open, their skin pulled off and they were placed, still alive, under the sun to allow flies to settle on them....The Russians hated the Afghans for their cruelty, though at the same time they admitted they were no less cruel during the war.'

Within a few years the guerrilla forces had gained control of most of the countryside, with the Russians governing from heavily armed camps and from the cities. But Mujahideen sympathizers, many of them women, infiltrated the cities. Madar Shawall, whose two sons had been killed by the government

side, agreed to smuggle weapons across Kabul. 'Hidden under my clothes and tied to my body, I carried two kalashnikovs to my rendezvous....I was nervous because life is sweet and carrying guns

in that way was terribly dangerous.' Later, Madar Shawall also relayed vital documents to the Mujahideen; when she was caught she was tortured for three months.

The Soviet forces, like the Americans in Vietnam, tried to obliterate all refuge for the guerrillas. They pursued a scorched earth policy – bombing villages, attacking water wells and driving millions of people out of their homes. Regardless of their age or health, many civilians fled into the mountains for refuge, while others joined the flow of refugees trekking through the mountains to the Pakistan or Iranian frontiers. Altogether five million people were forced to flee.

Huge refugee camps filled with Afghans, and their hatred of the Soviets grew. In 1986 an eight-year-old boy described just one terrible catalogue of events: 'They shot my father with three bullets....My brother and his friend got very angry and fought with them. My brother jumped and grabbed one of the weapons. At this point more Russians came and my brother's fingers were

AFGHAN FAMILIES (ABOVE) *trek through the mountains in search of safety. Up to a third of Afghanistan's people were forced to flee their villages, leaving behind possessions, livestock and land. Three-quarters of Afghanistan's villages were abandoned or destroyed during the war.*

MOUNTAIN PASSES *on the frontier between Afghanistan and Pakistan provided a supply route for the guerrillas as well as an escape route for millions of refugees. Pakistan offered a safe haven for the guerrillas' families, and also provided a base for exiled Afghan political parties.*

STONE THROWERS OF GAZA

WHEN AN ISRAELI TAXI DRIVER carelessly drove into a crowd of Palestinian labourers on 8 December 1987, a powder keg of resentment and humiliation exploded. Resistance to twenty years of occupation by Israeli forces had brought no progress towards independence for the Palestinian people. The death of four Palestinian labourers that day proved to be the last straw, and the entire Arab community in the West Bank and Gaza Strip was quickly galvanized into action. The Intifada was launched.

The Palestinians were committed to bringing about the destruction of the state of Israel, which had been established as a result of the partition of Palestine by the United Nations in 1947. The Israelis' determination that it should survive spurred them to victory in armed conflicts with their Arab neighbours in 1948, 1967 and 1973. After winning the Six-Day War in 1967, Israel had taken control of the West Bank and Gaza Strip; in these occupied territories they subsequently demanded high taxes from the Arab population, confiscated much of their land for Jewish settlers, and made it illegal to hold press conferences without special permission. Flying the Palestinian flag was also forbidden. Years of discrimination and the apparent indifference of the rest of the world to their plight led to the Palestinians taking increasingly violent action on their own behalf.

The Intifada – in Arabic meaning uprising or shaking off – was a mass uprising that involved men, women and children, young and old, in a spontaneous outburst against the occupying forces. Few firearms were used, but there were violent demonstrations, street fighting with petrol bombs broke out, and gangs of children became expert at hurling stones and outwitting Israeli troops. Women played a vital part, often at the forefront of the conflict but also in intelligence work, providing safe houses for the wanted and injured, distributing food in often perilous circumstances and organizing boycotts of Israeli goods.

Faced with the anger of an entire people, and determined to resist any threat to national security, Israeli troops responded in a way that shocked many of their own people as well as the outside world. In the first four years of the Intifada more than a thousand Palestinians, a quarter of them under sixteen years old, were killed by Israeli forces. The reprisals intensified the hatred, and strengthened Palestinian resistance.

In November 1988 Yasser Arafat, leader of the Palestine Liberation Organization (PLO), made the first tentative steps towards peace by finally accepting the existence of Israel. Yet the conflict continued until 1993, when renewed efforts to establish a peace process were achieved through patient Norwegian mediation. Despite these initiatives, there still seemed little likelihood of an independent Palestinian state – the goal for which the Intifada had been launched – being established.

PALESTINIAN CIVILIANS AND ISRAELI TROOPS *congregate on each side of the crater made by a petrol bomb.*

cut off. They were cut off by a bayonet – so of course he was helpless. After all his fingers had been cut off they beat him. They shot him in one ear and the bullet came out the other.'

As in Vietnam, the guerrilla fighters were not self-sufficient. Money and support came both from other Muslim countries and from the United States. The path through the mountains from Pakistan was worn by the feet of heavily laden camels and mules in supply caravans bringing food and arms into Afghanistan for the guerrillas. In the final years of the conflict the animals carried the latest American Stinger missiles, designed to shoot down Soviet helicopters and other aircraft.

The Soviet troops transported their own supplies through Afghanistan by road in convoys of trucks accompanied by armed escort vehicles. They frequently had to pass through remote mountain areas that offered ideal opportunities for ambush. Gul Hyder was among the Mujahideen operating in the mountains. 'Once we hit an armoured vehicle with a rocket,' he remembers. 'It went straight through the vehicle and sliced through the heads of the two soldiers inside....Of course, I enjoyed killing Russians because they were invaders. When we were blowing up their tanks and when they were dying, I was really happy.'

By 1989, 15 000 Russians had been killed and a further 35 000 wounded. In the end the tenacity of the Mujahideen and the growing economic and political crisis in the Soviet Union broke the resolve of the government in Moscow. The Soviet leader, Mikhail Gorbachev, finally ordered the withdrawal from Afghanistan. For the second time in fifteen years, the guerrilla tactics of a poorly armed people's army had defeated a superpower.

In all the guerrilla wars, bitterly fought and won at such cost, the fighting left a poignant legacy of grieving families, scarred landscapes and bitter political divisions that would last for many years. And victory alone was no guarantee that guerrilla fighters would rule their people any better than the enemies they had fought so fiercely to defeat.

THE BEREAVED PARENTS *of a Soviet parachutist mourn their loss. The Soviet withdrawal was greeted with relief by Oleg Blotsky. 'It was clear to everyone that the war was meaningless and we all just wanted to leave....Everyone felt humiliated.'*

BRANDISHING THEIR WEAPONS (OPPOSITE), *the Mujahideen celebrate victory in Kabul. After eight years of war the guerrilla forces had fought the Soviets to a stalemate. Faced with the hostility of both Islamic and Western countries, and the opposition of its own fifty million Muslim inhabitants, the Soviet Union finally accepted defeat.*

God Fights Back

RELIGION ON THE RISE

ON THE EVENING OF 31 January 1979 in a suburb of Paris, Hadi Gaffari was among a group preparing for a long-awaited journey home. 'At midnight, those who were to return to Tehran with the Imam started gathering in the courtyard,' he says. The following morning they boarded an Air France 747 jet. 'We were very happy to return to Iran. All of us had a common feeling....I noticed that the Imam was leaning his head against the window and he had his black cape around him,' Hadi Gaffari recalls. 'As the pilot announced that we had passed the Elburz mountains everybody exploded in tears... everybody started chanting, "*Allah ho Akbar!*" – "God is great!"'

The figure in black at the centre of all this activity was the Ayatollah Ruhollah Khomeini, revered elder leader of the Shia Muslim faith, who had been exiled from Iran for many years. Now he was returning, and three million people poured into the streets of Tehran to welcome him home. Shakoor Lotvi was among them: 'The crowd was so huge that people had no room. They climbed the trees, anywhere they could just to get a glance of the Imam.' Moshen Rafigdoost drove the Imam from the airport. He was so full of emotion that his hands were shaking as he gripped the steering wheel: 'People were sitting on the car, the car was moving and people were being dragged along by it....Those hours are the best memories of my life.'

Khomeini and his followers were intent on carrying out an Islamic revolution that would radically transform people's lives. Yet much more than the fate of Iran was at stake. Across much of the world, religion was on the rise as growing numbers of people began to question the ideas and values of the West, rejecting modernity and turning instead to the alternatives offered by their faith. With mass popular support, increasingly politicized religious movements would challenge established governments. After a century in which progress and modernization had been identified with science and with the rejection of religion, God, it was said, was fighting back.

RELIGIOUS RETURN *Iranian Muslims in the city of Qom surround the Ayatollah Khomeini's car to welcome him back.*

555

Old ways and new

By the beginning of the twentieth century most of the world's Muslims had come under the domination of Europeans: the British in India, Russians in central Asia, Dutch, French and Italians elsewhere. Reform movements had swept through the Islamic world, from west Africa to the Indian subcontinent by way of Egypt and the Arabian peninsula, but only the Ottoman empire survived as a great Islamic power – until it was dismembered after the First World War. In Turkey, its former heartland, Mustafa Kemal, better known as Atatürk, created a secular, modern nation modelled on the ways of the West. People who were accustomed to living in a traditional Islamic society now also had to conform to these Western ways. Atatürk abolished the power of the clergy, substituted civil for religious law, introduced changes to the education system, and replaced the Arabic script – essential for reading the Koran – with the Roman alphabet. Hats were to be worn instead of the traditional fez. 'There was a distinct difference between the old Istanbul, the old way of life, and the new way of life,' recalls Altemur Kilic, who witnessed many of these changes. 'People learnt a new script, and street signs changed, shop signs changed ....My mother, who had worn a scarf all her life, threw it away.'

GROUNDS OF DISCONTENT *Iran's oil industry was nationalized in 1951, bringing a rich new source of revenue, but many people, such as these refinery workers in Abadan living in makeshift huts, were unable to share in their country's new wealth.*

DEEDS OF REFORM (BELOW) *A man proudly displays his land deeds, acquired under the shah's Land Refom Act of 1962. Land redistribution continued until 1971, benefiting millions of people but weakening the power of the Shiite Muslim clergymen from whom much of the land was taken.*

Similarly, Muslims in Iraq, Lebanon, Palestine, Syria and Trans-Jordan, now under British and French control, found their traditional way of life shaped by the culture of the West. Young people increasingly went to study not in the schools of Islam, but in the universities of the West. An Islamic state was established in Saudi Arabia, home of the holy centres of Mecca and Medina, but there too, the discovery of oil in 1938 was to bring with it many aspects of modern secular society. Britain's plans for the creation of a Jewish homeland in Palestine exacerbated Arab sentiment against Western interference, and strengthened Muslim unity and resolve for independence.

The tide began to turn after the Second World War as many Muslim nations asserted their independence. When British India

CODES OF DRESS (LEFT)
Following in Turkey's footsteps, the shah of Iran had decreed in 1928 that men were to wear Western clothes. Women were banned from wearing the veil in 1936. Moloud Khanlary had greeted the ruling with pleasure: 'We started singing songs and dancing.... Then we started kissing each other out of joy.' The policy was sometimes enforced by the police, but as the rules were relaxed in later years some women chose to return to traditional Islamic dress.

was granted independence in 1947, Pakistan was established as a new Islamic state. In the 1950s first Egypt and then Iraq threw off their British or British-imposed masters. Independence movements were also succeeding in Indonesia, Malaya, and north and west Africa. But although Western power over these territories diminished, much of its influence remained, and many countries maintained economic and strategic links with the West. Several reformist leaders, determined to create modern, secular states, pursued Western-style policies rather than returning to traditional Islamic ways. Islam was even deliberately suppressed in certain countries, such as Syria and Tunisia. While many people enjoyed the new social freedoms that came with a secular society, there was resentment among devout Muslims, who were dismayed by the path their countries seemed to be following.

This was particularly true of Iran, where the former army officer and self-appointed shah, Reza Khan, had initiated a process of Western reform during the 1920s and 1930s. Secular laws were imposed in the courts, and Western curriculums in the schools. The process of modernization was continued by the shah's son, Muhammad Reza Pahlavi, who initiated an economic and social revolution in Iran during the 1960s.

PUBLIC PARADES *were held all over Iran in 1977 to mark the fourteenth anniversary of the shah's rule. The prime minister reviews the Health Corps, sent to work in poor and isolated Iranian villages to help eradicate disease.*

'When the shah started his programme Iran was a backward country,' remembers Daryoush Houmayoun, a journalist at the time of the shah's reforms. 'Land reform, granting voting rights to women, bringing women up to the level of men in our society, literacy drives, bringing new ideas and technology to the villages. Iran was being covered with new factories and public buildings. And everywhere the pace of change was frantic. Iran was really being transformed.' Trade links with Western countries meant that there were many foreigners in Iran; architects and construction engineers from many parts of the world converged on Tehran in search of contracts. There were bars, cinemas and discos. Mashid Amir-Shahy, who came from a secular background, remembers: 'We used to go to cafés, we used to enjoy ourselves, we gave parties and we went to parties. We drank if we wanted to,' she says. Iran's rich oil industry brought new wealth not only for industrial and military development but also for new luxuries: French wines, German cars, Italian fashions.

For a few, the boom brought new wealth. But the dollars did not trickle down to the peasants in the villages, or to the poor manual workers who had crowded into the cities and shantytowns in search of their share in the new prosperity. The life they found was not better than it had been in the countryside – it was often all but unbearable. Grasping landlords, indifferent employers and the police force seemed to be protected by a corrupt political elite whose members used their wealth to import Western luxuries, and who adopted Western attitudes. To many people, Western films, songs and advertising encouraged immorality and blasphemy. Confronted by what they saw, people turned back to the religion of their ancestors; it was to this poorer majority that the religious parties made their appeal.

Most of the population of Iran were Shiites, followers of the Shia branch of Islam. Firm believers in the justice and struggle of Islam, they denounced the Western influences that threatened their Islamic way of life and offended their religious nationalism. The widely respected cleric Ruhollah Khomeini had criticized the shah's father long before for abandoning the traditional ways of Islam, and now denounced the rule of his son. In anti-government sermons and publications, Khomeini and his followers among the

THE PATH OF ISLAM

MANY PEOPLE THROUGHOUT the Muslim world felt uncomfortable with the introduction of a secular way of life because it was in direct conflict with longstanding Islamic tradition. Changing social patterns threatened to prevent them living as true Muslims in a society shaped according to the precepts of the holy Koran – the sacred text held by all Muslims (whether of the Shia or the Sunni branch) to be the word of God.

The Koran lists five basic duties for all Muslims that form the pillars of Islam. They must accept submission to God and the role of the Prophet Muhammad as his messenger. They must undertake to pray five times each day, at the mosque or at home, facing in the direction of Mecca; children are taught to pray at the age of six or seven, and many Muslim countries provide prayer facilities in offices, factories and at airports. The third pillar calls for an annual payment of alms for the poor and needy, which is determined as a fixed percentage of personal wealth and assets. During the holy month of Ramadan fasting from dawn until dusk, which includes refraining from smoking, drinking and sexual activity, is also compulsory, though the Koran excuses the elderly, the ill, young children, menstruating women and travellers. In the fifth pillar, Muslims are required to make at least one pilgrimage to the holiest site of Islam, the Kaabah, at Mecca in Saudi Arabia.

In addition to these basic tenets, Islam has its own laws under the *sharia*, the 'straight path' of Islam. Islamic law calls on all Muslims to defend Islam from aggression. Punishments are specified: lashing for the consumption of

alcohol, stoning for adultery, and amputation of hands or feet for theft, though these measures are seldom practised. As well as penal laws there are commercial laws guiding businesses, economic laws forbidding usury and the charging of bank interest, laws on gambling, inheritance, marriage, divorce and polygamy.

Family life is regarded as the basis of Islamic society, and although divorce is permitted, women must seek their husbands' consent and are liable to lose custody of their children. Islam does not exclude women from inheritance or property rights, though it does permit arranged marriages without their consent. Women are encouraged to wear the veil, and men as well as women are urged to dress modestly, according to the traditions of Islam. Islamic law also includes guidelines for eating and drinking, expressly forbidding the consumption of pork or alcohol, and ruling that livestock must be slaughtered according to traditional methods.

The application of Islamic law has varied widely in the Muslim world, and it often clashes with Western-inspired modern aspirations. Because of the Koran's sacred status, its principles and dictates have remained unchanged for 1300 years. Recited in the mosque and studied both privately and at school, it forms the bedrock of Islamic beliefs and way of life, and its doctrine continues to inspire Muslims throughout the world who wish to follow the true path of Islam.

GREAT PILGRIMAGE (LEFT) *Every year, about two million Muslims gather to worship at the great mosque in Mecca. All male pilgrims wear a simple white robe* (RIGHT), *symbolizing their equality before God.*

PARTY AT PERSEPOLIS *In 1971 the shah held a party to celebrate 2500 years of monarchy. Five hundred guests were flown in from sixty-nine countries to the ruined city of Persepolis, capital of ancient Persia. They were housed in tents containing several rooms – including two bathrooms – drank the finest champagne from crystal goblets, and ate food flown in from Maxim's in Paris. The estimated cost of the event was $200 million. The celebrations caused great resentment among the Iranian people. 'I saw that billions of dollars needed by our poor country – with no water, no electricity, no hospitals, no roads – was being spent on ceremonies for kings,' says Hadi Gaffari.*

"What was so difficult for people was the lack of democracy. Pressure was being imposed on them by the government. This laid the groundwork for establishing Islamic rule as a better hope for the people."

SAID GONABADI

influential Islamic community and clergy began to stir people against the shah, who used his secret police, the Savak, to suppress any opposition. Khomeini's arrest in 1963 sparked a wave of protests. As the military were called in to restore order, many thousands of civilians were killed. The following year Khomeini was forced to flee the country.

Fuelled by widening social and economic disparities and government repression, the determination to root out what were seen as corrupt and decadent customs of the West became a constant theme in the revival of Islam. Abdul Shah Hosseini was clear about what he felt was needed: 'Cease relations with the oppressive Western regimes, discontinue the flow of capital from this country to the outside, rid the country of American military personnel. We wanted no alcohol, no corruption among the young people.' A new, strongly political Islamic consciousness was taking shape. 'The shah's programme for modernization turned into an issue against Islam,' says Ebrahim Yazdi, who supported Khomeini. 'They thought that in order to succeed in modernization, they must combat Islamic resurgence. In turn, Islamic resurgence became a way to resist the oppression of the shah.'

Calling for revolution

Despite being in exile, Khomeini, who had attained the status of an ayatollah – a religious leader of the highest rank – still had a considerable following among Iran's Muslim population. He had established a base across the border in neighbouring Iraq, in the holy city of Najaf, from where he worked to gather momentum against the shah. 'We had a great goal,' remembers Hadi Gaffari. 'It was to liberate Iran from a regime that was associated with foreigners....We believed we must be independent, and independence meant we must struggle against the shah's regime. The best way to make the masses aware was to revolt against the shah. Religion and politics are the same thing.'

As Islam became more overtly political, so too did the local mosques where people gathered to pray. The mullah Hadi Gaffari translated Khomeini's words into political action. 'Young people and intellectuals came to the mosque, and it would turn into an ideological meeting, and this would be recorded,' he recalls. 'The courtyard and all the alleys leading to the mosque would be full of people. Some of them would bring pieces of carpet to sit on, and people would bring tape recorders, and it was rumoured in Tehran that the mosque of Hadi Gaffari had recordings of Khomeini's speeches.' Shakoor Lotvi distributed

DEMONSTRATIONS OF ANGER *continued throughout the 1970s. Inspired by Khomeini's leadership, people persisted in stirring unrest and openly displaying their resentment towards the shah's government* (ABOVE), *despite the potential dangers they faced from his secret police. Images of the shah and his queen* (BELOW) *are set alight and paraded through the streets.*

revolutionary leaflets. 'Anywhere we felt these bulletins and leaflets had not reached we would put them up – on the walls of the mosques, at bazaars, in shops and alleys.'

These activities could prove dangerous, but the mosques offered a kind of sanctuary. 'As a result of the brutality of the Savak, practically all the political parties were paralysed,' says Ebrahim Yazdi. 'However, the mosque was

"At that time we had no liberties, everything was at the disposal of the government....We can say that with our revolution we brought the rule of people over people."

MOSHEN RAFIGDOOST

BULDINGS ABLAZE *People gather at the site of a cinema that has been set alight by Muslims in the town of Tabriz in northwest Iran after weeks of rioting in February 1978. Many buildings throughout Iran were destroyed as anti-government demonstrations escalated.*

still alive.' Hadi Gaffari sometimes disguised himself as a woman in a *chador*, a cloak covering the body from head to foot. Soroor Moradi Nazari also took precautions. 'If there were even books about Imam Khomeini in our house we would be arrested by the Savak and tortured. I hid pictures inside the kitchen cabinet door.'

In 1977 people began to show their support for Khomeini more openly. 'Religious students took part in the demonstrations, and they started a systematic burning of government buildings,' remembers Daryoush Houmayoun. 'Khomeini became the focus of all the opposition groups. They turned to him more and more.' Not all Iranians supported the campaign. Many educated, liberal families who had welcomed the shah's reforms were alarmed by the Islamic movement for change. When Moloud Khanlary encountered thousands of veiled women marching in one demonstration she could not prevent herself crying. 'I thought of the catastrophe that was falling upon my country,' she recalls. 'If the day of unveiling was a day of joy and happiness, that day was for me a day of mourning and misery.'

The following year, at the end of Ramadan, the Muslim month of fasting, Khomeini was able to turn the protests into a mass movement. On 8 September 1978 a great crowd of three-quarters of a million people made its way towards the centre of Tehran. 'As we began going towards the city,' Hadi Gaffari describes, 'the people standing in doorways joined the crowd. It was the end of summer, above thirty degrees centigrade, and people were spraying water from their houses to cool down the demonstrators, and distributed refreshments and food.' As the crowd drew nearer they were confronted by soldiers. People tried to appease them with flowers, but their attempts failed. The shah ordered his troops to fire on a crowd of demonstrators in Jalah Square, close to Shakoor Lotvi's home. More than a hundred people were killed. 'As I reached the edge of the square, near the

hospital, I saw the injured being rushed to the emergency rooms,' he remembers. 'We queued up to donate blood for them.' Soon afterwards, martial law was declared in Iran. That day came to be known as Black Friday.

The following month, Khomeini was forced to leave his Iraqi sanctuary. This time he chose Europe as his refuge. Paris might be one of the centres of the alien culture of the West, but there he would have access to the Western media. Khomeini settled in a villa in the suburb of Neauphle-le-Château, while mullahs such as Hadi Gaffari travelled between Paris and Tehran. Others used the telephone connections between the two cities. 'When Khomeini had a message,' describes Ebrahim Yazdi, 'there were people in Paris in charge of reading his message down the telephone to people in Iran. There were more people in Tehran and in the provinces receiving that message – recording it, then transcribing it, publishing it and distributing it to people in the mosques through the various mullahs.'

As the street demonstrations in Iran continued, thousands of people were killed. 'They were using tear gas and bullets without any consideration for women or children,' remembers Shakoor Lotvi. 'Our streets were battlefronts in those days....We thought that the shedding of our blood would help the fruitfulness of the revolution.' Twelve-year-old Said Sharifi Manesh enthusiastically

DAY OF RECKONING (TOP LEFT) *On 8 September 1978 clashes between civilians and the military resulted in the loss of many lives. Hadi Gaffari* (TOP RIGHT) *witnessed that day. 'There were many soldiers, many commandos,' he remembers. 'They had anti-riot gear, they had clubs; they were prepared to beat people and kill people.' A poster showing the bodies of victims of Black Friday* (ABOVE) *directs blame at the shah's policies and at his links with the United States president, Jimmy Carter. Anti-American sentiment was to become a familiar feature of Iran's Islamic revolution.*

"When they were gunned down everybody was crying. The whole country was crying. That was the spark of the victory of the Iranian revolution. That was when it was proven that the shah had to leave, because of that day."

ABDUL SHAH HOSSEINI

LEADER IN EXILE *Khomeini and his circle of advisers seated in the garden of his villa in Neauphle-le-Château outside Paris, from where the Iranian revolution was begun. Ebrahim Yazdi spent some time there. 'We needed to have the commmunication with Khomeini in order to bring the body of the masses, ordinary people, into the political struggle against despotism and foreign domination in our country,' he says.*

THE TOWERING MONUMENT (OPPOSITE) *to Iran's Pahlavi dynasty is the site of its downfall, as millions converge there in December 1978 demanding the overthrow of the shah and the return of Ayatollah Khomeini.*

joined in the protests, together with his father, two brothers and one of his sisters. They were injured by the shah's guardsmen on several occasions. 'It was sometimes cold and difficult, but that wasn't important to me,' he says. 'During those demonstrations people were very united – the whole nation. It was like a miracle, all the young and the old. People were working for the triumph of the revolution and the Imam entering the country.'

The whole of Iran was affected. Radio and television both went off the air, and there were widespread industrial strikes that drastically reduced the country's oil production. For Daryoush Houmayoun it was a time of great terror. 'From the winter of 1978 the wave of demonstrations turned into small bands of people who burnt cinemas, offices, liquor shops.' There were instances of unveiled women being attacked by mobs, and demands for the expulsion of foreigners. The climax came in December during the religious holy day of Ashura, as the Islamic cycle of mourning culminated on the tenth day of Muharram, when Shiite Muslims mourn the martyrdom of Husain, grandson of the Prophet Muhammad.

On that day up to five million people converged on the vast square in Tehran where the shah had built the Shayyad monument to the Pahlavi dynasty. Abdul Shah Hosseini was standing on a crowded overpass overlooking the square when a messenger came with new slogans from the central clergy council. 'He asked me to shout these slogans because I have a loud voice,' he recalls. 'So I shouted out, "Why don't you shout what your heart wants, what every single cell in your body is seeking, why don't you shout what is Islamic, what God says? You should all shout, "Death to the shah!" And all the people started shouting, "Death to the shah!" That was the greatest joy of my life up to that time.'

The shah could have ordered his tanks to open fire, but he did not. The game was up. On 16 January 1979, after thirty-seven years of rule, he flew from Tehran airport, having said that he was going on holiday. Moshen Rafigdoost, who had earlier been arrested for supporting Khomeini, listened to the news that after-noon. 'The radio announced that the shah had left the country,' he recalls. 'People were clapping, they jumped up and down in the streets….That day I bought a lot of sweets and distributed them.'

Society under God

With the departure of the shah, Khomeini's return was only a matter of days away. Millions of people welcomed him back to Iran with songs and slogans. 'One of our slogans was a verse from the Koran which said that goodness comes and falsehood vanishes,' Said Sharifi Manesh remembers. When he saw the Ayatollah arrive at the airport he felt as though, 'My father had gone on a trip and was now returning. The shah was darkness to us; it is a Koranic verse – from darkness, we take you into light.'

Khomeini now declared his vision for Iran. There was to be no Western democracy, no socialism. In the few years of life still left to him, he began to build a thoroughly Islamic society. The revolution's enemies were rooted out; Islamic revolutionary courts dealt harsh verdicts to those who had supported the shah's regime. Many westernized Iranians joined the stream of foreigners and diplomats who fled the country.

Those who stayed found themselves swept up by changes that affected every aspect of their lives. Friday prayers were interspersed with political harangues about the Islamic revolution. Images of the Ayatollah were pasted everywhere – in offices, at schools, in people's homes. Street names were changed. Bars were looted, alcohol burnt, cinemas destroyed. 'There was a liquor store, and my friends and I went and closed it down and put a wall up in front of it so it couldn't operate any more,' remembers Said Sharifi Manesh. 'Gambling casinos, cabarets had been open all night long,' he describes. 'But when the revolution triumphed all of these vanished.' Western music was banned, as was alcohol. Women still had the right to work, but they were encouraged to stay at home and study the Koran. On buses they were expected to use separate doors and to sit at the back; and they were obliged to cover themselves with the *chador*.

Many of the middle-class women who had benefited from the shah's years were appalled by the changes. 'I refused to wear the *chador* to begin with,' recalls Mashid Amir-Shahy. 'I was so outraged that I didn't have time to be frightened of the mullahs,' she says. 'I felt terribly bitter about the whole thing and extremely frustrated. I thought that, after all, the freedom of choosing one's clothing was among the most preliminary freedoms.' But other

women, like Dowlat Noroudi, disagreed. 'Wearing the scarf would enable women to work actively,' she says. 'Socially it created an atmosphere in which you could really participate and express yourself...as a human being, not only as a sex object or as a woman.' Many Iranian men chose to stop wearing Western ties.

But Islam was not just about prayer and styles of dress. In the new constitution of the Islamic republic, which was adopted on 1 April 1979 Islamic law, the *sharia* – which governed every aspect of life – was reinstated. There were even Islamic business codes, which sought to prevent exploitation of the poor. 'Our lives changed a lot,' says Said Sharifi Manesh. Now schoolchildren recited the Koran instead of singing the national anthem. Girls' uniforms also changed. 'They were entering schools wearing veils and Islamic covering – the way we liked it, the Islamic way.'

REACHING OUT (LEFT) *to their new leader, who had won the overwhelming support of the Iranian people. 'Khomeini was the centre of the commotion,' describes Ebrahim Yazdi. 'The enthusiasm of the people was tremendous, almost hysterical.' Khomeini remained at the helm until his death in 1989.*

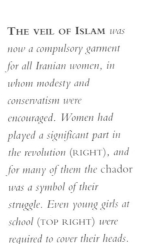

THE VEIL OF ISLAM *was now a compulsory garment for all Iranian women, in whom modesty and conservatism were encouraged. Women had played a significant part in the revolution (RIGHT), and for many of them the chador was a symbol of their struggle. Even young girls at school (TOP RIGHT) were required to cover their heads.*

THE IRAN–IRAQ WAR

THE LOYALTY of the Iranian people was put to the test only a year after the birth of their Islamic republic. In September 1980 Iraqi troops, under orders from their president, Saddam Hussein, crossed into Iran at four points along the border, from its northern frontier to the marshlands and rich oilfields of the Arabian Gulf. What followed was to become one of the twentieth century's longest as well as most destructive wars between sovereign states.

Its immediate causes centred on disputes over territory, oilfields and ownership of the Shatt-al-Arab waterway, which carried a large proportion of the world's oil. But there were underlying religious motives as well. Some 55 per cent of the Iraqi population, most of them in the south, were Shiite Muslims. Saddam Hussein felt threatened by the militancy of Iran's Shiite revolutionary leaders, who condemned his socialist Baathist regime, dominated by Sunni Muslims, and called for his downfall. As the war escalated, they appealed to the large Shiite presence in Iraq to defend their faith against the blasphemous tyranny of their president, who had dared to attack the Islamic republic.

Iran launched a series of successful offensives against the Iraqis, and by 1982 Iranian soldiers had entered Iraqi territory. As the fighting grew more intense, hundreds of thousands of Iranians volunteered to fight in what Khomeini declared a *jihad*, a holy war, responding to his calls for would-be martyrs. Many of them, like Said Sharifi Manesh, were boys who were keen to experience what they perceived as the glory of martydom. Although he was too young to fight, he managed to secure a place in the army by forging his papers. 'We were struggling against blasphemy,' he says. 'In the holy Koran it says that if you are killed you are martyrs on the path of God and you will reach high levels.'

After years of deadlocked trench warfare in which thousands of troops were killed, and the use of chemical weapons and long-range missiles by Iraq, Iran's army grew weaker. People suffered greatly from the shortages and misery brought by the war. Iraq succeeded in turning the war into an Arab–Iranian conflict by enlisting the diplomatic and financial support of other Arab countries, including Kuwait and Saudi Arabia. Iran grew increasingly isolated, and had to face the added burden of arms embargoes, while large quantities of arms were supplied to Iraq by Britain, France and the Soviet Union. The United States, keen to contain the spread of Iran's Islamic revolution, also poured billions of dollars into the Iraqi war effort.

The war entered a new phase in 1984, when the United States sent a fleet of warships to the Gulf. In August 1988 Iran reluctantly accepted the terms of a United Nations ceasefire resolution that finally ended the eight-year war. It had exacted a heavy price: both countries faced huge debts, their economies were severely weakened, much of their land was devastated, and there were enormous numbers of casualties. According to one estimate, 367 000 Iraqis and Iranians were killed and about 700 000 were wounded.

MARTYRS OF WAR
Iranian volunteers about to leave for the front in 1986, as the Iran–Iraq war intensified. They joined thousands of other young men willing to sacrifice their lives in war in return for the glory of martydom. Women were also encouraged to become revolutionary warriors.

Religious awakenings

At a time when millions of people – Christians and Hindus as well as Muslims – were turning to their faith in the search for answers to the moral uncertainties of modern life, Iran's revolution pointed to new possibilities for Muslims in other countries. Arab identity was becoming strongly aligned to Islam, and Islam to politics. A coup led by army colonel Muammar al Gaddafi in 1969 brought a new brand of Islamic socialism to Libya. When rival religious factions fought for control of Lebanon in the civil war of 1975, it was to the Hizbollah, the 'Party of God', that Iran pledged its support. In 1979, when Afghanistan was invaded by the Soviet Union, it was as 'Soldiers of God' that Muslim Afghan guerrillas of the Mujahideen fought. A series of Islamic institutions, world summit meetings and conference organizations had been set up. Millions of people living in the poor and crowded neighbour-hoods of cities faced the same social inequalities that had stoked the fires of revolution in Iran – and reached the same conclusions.

THE WORLD OF ISLAM
The Islamic Conference Organization first met in 1969, and was established two years later. It aimed to give political and Islamic unity to Muslim states throughout the world, uniting more than a billion people through their beliefs. About 80 per cent of them are Sunni Muslims. As well as its forty-nine member states, the ICO granted observer status to the unrecognized Turkish Federated State of Cyprus.

Members of the Islamic Conference Organization

- Majority Muslim population
- Minority Muslim population
- Observer status at the ICO
- Non-member states with more than 10% Muslim population

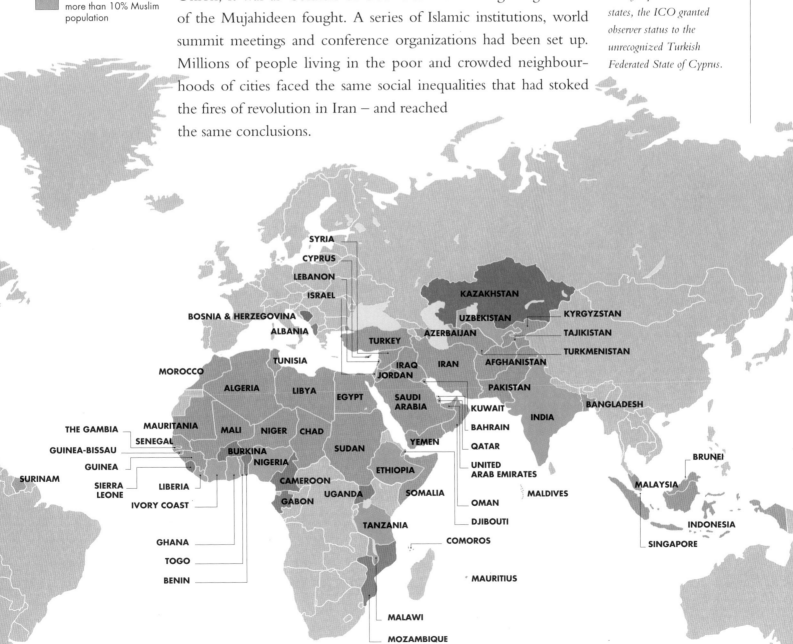

In the Islamic republic of Pakistan, the state established as a new nation for Muslims in 1947, people were in fact governed not by the Islamic laws of the Koran but by a wealthy elite of generals and politicians who pursued modern, secular policies. Seeking to assert the path of Islam as the way forward, Muslim groups succeeded in gaining mass popular support. Following months of rioting in 1977, the Pakistan People's Party was overthrown, martial law was imposed and a new leader took over.

General Zia ul-Haq won many people's confidence by announcing his plans to turn Pakistan into a truly Islamic state. 'We thought that he was a good Muslim,' remembers Hamid Subhani, who worked in a bank. 'Everybody in our family was happy…that at least in Pakistan we have got somebody at the top who was religious, who was a good Muslim, and who would probably deliver his promises to bring Islam to the nation and solve all our problems.' Islamic laws – and punishments – were implemented. Annual payments of alms to the poor, as stipulated in the Koran, were made compulsory. Fasting during the month of Ramadan was strictly enforced. Children

RIVAL FAITHS *In the Indian town of Ayodhya in Uttar Pradesh, clashes between Hindus and Muslims led in 1992 to the destruction of a disused sixteenth-century mosque by Hindu extremists. They claimed that the Babari mosque had been built on an important site of Hindu worship. More than 3000 people were killed in the rioting that followed. India's secular, democratic government faced a real challenge in reconciling its diverse religious communities.*

PRAYERS AND POLITICS (ABOVE) *The religious revival in the United States during the 1970s and 1980s extended beyond the churches to rallies and demonstrations in the streets, as thousands of Christians became increasingly vociferous about political and ethical issues.*

RALLYING TO JESUS

FOR MANY PEOPLE in the West, it was easy to regard the events taking place in Iran and elsewhere in the Muslim world as a result of Islamic 'fundamentalism'. But in other countries too there were signs of renewed religious fervour in the 1970s and 1980s.

In the United States many people were beginning to look to religion to solve society's troubles. It was largely, though not entirely, among American Evangelicals – Protestant Christians who accept Jesus Christ as their personal Saviour and believe in the absolute authority of the Bible – that Christian fundamentalism took hold. It had avoided involvement in politics as a manifestation of a flawed secular society, but by the mid-1970s the movement became increasingly political. Under the New Christian Right of the 1980s, politically motivated religous groups began to claim a large following.

Many Americans joined its ranks in response to what they perceived as growing social and moral deterioration, even decadence. 'You couldn't watch television or pick up a newspaper without realizing we were constantly, daily in violation of the word of God,' remembers Carol Owen. 'We felt there was real judgement on the nation because of this.' The movement was also fuelled by angry reactions to liberal movements for civil and women's rights; it looked for a return to Christian values, prayers at school, an end to abortion.

It was through the movement of the Christian Right that issues such as abortion, divorce, sexuality and drug abuse entered the political arena. There were mass rallies and public prayer vigils at which some people showed their anger by burning books, magazines and records. One minister, John Gimenez, organized a 'Washington for Jesus' rally in April 1980. 'We didn't know how many people would come. We went out there in amazement when we saw bus after bus after bus,' he says. 'They went home determined that they were going to have a voice, they were going to get involved.'

Church membership, which was especially strong in the affluent parts of the south and southwest, was growing. Membership of the powerful Southern Baptist Convention rose from 10.8 million in 1965 to 13.6 million in 1980. By that year, several surveys suggested that some 40 per cent of Americans regarded themselves as 'born again' Evangelicals, and a similar number attempted to convert others to Christian belief. Many Evangelical schools, and even several universities, were established. Religious groups such as the Moral Majority, established in 1979, used television or direct mail to gain the support of the public. As preachers rose to greater prominence through the media and won financial backing, they presented more of a challenge in the political arena.

The overwhelming endorsement of Ronald Reagan in the 1980 presidential election by Christian supporters who had previously abstained from voting may have contributed to his victory. In 1988 Pat Robertson, one of the leaders of the Christian Right, himself made what was to be an unsuccessful bid for the presidency. Anne Kincaid was one of millions of people who voted for him. 'What those people represented was a ground swell of people saying enough is enough. It is time to stand tall for what we believe. We are tired of watching America just turn its back on God,' she says. 'It was like recognizing that there really is hope – that maybe before the end of this century we could see a change in America.'

who had been taught in English at school were now taught in Urdu. Wearing the veil was compulsory in state schools and in government offices. Cabinet meetings and public ceremonies began with readings from the Koran. 'Zia introduced a law that people should pray while they are in their offices,' remembers Hamid Subhani. 'Normally people used their lunch breaks. Now it became your right.' Many people looked forward to a better way

Living by the book

THE KORAN *plays an important part in the daily lives of Muslims all over the world. Recited at prayer time and in schools, it has remained unchanged since it was revealed to the Prophet Muhammad in the seventh century. It was written and is still read in Arabic, the universal language of Islam; foreign translations of the word of God were traditionally discouraged. The message delivered in its thirty sections, comprising one hundred and fourteen chapters, covers all aspects of life and remains a constant source of guidance for Muslims.*

Copies of the Koran are usually wrapped in cloth, and are awarded a place of honour in people's homes. The holy Koran is also sometimes used to administer oaths.

of life. 'They pictured that everybody would be equally treated, they would be provided with food and shelter and education,' says Sheik Khwafa Irshad Razvi. 'They thought that Islam meant bread and butter, and shelter, and self-respect.'

In reality, the new military dictatorship was characterized by corruption and abuse of power under the guise of Islam. The charity payments collected by the government in the form of public taxes often failed to reach the poor. For most people life did not improve under Zia ul-Haq. 'Initially, we had very high hopes,' remembers Hamid Subhani, 'that he would bring changes to society and as a result we would be more Islamic at the end of his period. But later on, he delayed his promises and there were draw-backs in implementing Islamic laws....To remain in power he created a new way to get a vote of confidence from the general public – that if you like Islam, vote for me.'

In Egypt many more people were also turning to Islam. During the 1950s and 1960s President Gamal Nasser, champion of

CULTURE CLASH (ABOVE)
Egyptian Muslims kneel for Friday prayer on a busy Cairo street. Behind them are signs of the Western-style consumerism that provoked such resentment among many poorer people.

Arab nationalism, had led Egypt in an increasingly secular direction. He had abolished the Muslim Brotherhood, a long-established, influential religious organization, and the Islamic *sharia* courts, and ushered in a period of modernization. Cairo's Al-Azhar University, which had survived for hundreds of years as the Muslim world's most important centre of Islamic learning, became a modern state university. In 1967 Egypt fought a war against Israel in a continuing territorial conflict that had become the focus of much hostility between the Arab nations of the Muslim world and the West. Egypt's defeat heightened Muslim opposition to Nasser's reformist policies. When he died in 1970 a militant form of Islam was winning converts both in the villages and in the teeming neighbourhoods of Cairo.

Egypt's new president, Anwar Sadat, presented himself as a champion of Islam, sometimes joining in prayers at local village mosques. But he believed that the pressures of poverty made it urgent to modernize Egypt, and to do so he adopted an 'open door' policy with the West. He made peace with Israel, and invited Western businesses to invest in Egypt. The shops were flooded with Western consumer goods. For those who could afford them, it was an exciting time, but many people resented the advertisements showing American women using suggestive poses to sell them expensive products they did not need and could not afford. 'Poor people used to watch with regret the expensive suits and shoes in the shop windows,' remembers Aly Abdel Hamed. 'Ordinary people found it difficult to get their basic needs met. The gap between the rich and the poor was very wide....In popular areas there was a lack of educational and social facilities; prices soared....Sadat promised people years of welfare and prosperity after the peace with Israel. But none of those promises was fulfilled.' As they grew more dissatisfied, more people began to take part in anti-government demonstrations.

It was to the mosques that they turned for medical care, education, and other welfare facilities that were dispensed

MUSLIMS ABROAD
Children of North African immigrants in the French town of Dreux study the Koran at a local mosque. In 1980 there were about two million Muslims living in France, and new communities of Muslims were well established in other parts of Europe and in the United States. Some of them were treated with hostility by local people.

BEHIND BARS (ABOVE) *Muslims imprisoned as part of a government crackdown on Egypt's Islamic activists. 'These people were from all walks of life – doctors, engineers, people from trade unions, writers and politicians,' recalls Yasser Tawfiq* (TOP), *an Islamic teacher imprisoned in 1981.*

VOTING FOR ISLAM (OPPOSITE) *meant voting for change for the many thousands of Algerians who turned out to demonstrate their support for the Islamic Salvation Front (FIS) in the 1991 elections.*

in the name of God, and in return people pledged themselves to Islam. There they were taught the superiority of Islamic laws over the decadent, corrupt secular world. 'This is what we call *dawa*, missionary activity,' describes Yasser Tawfiq. A high school student in his last year, he also taught at the mosque. 'Our job was to teach people the Koran....Every neighbourhood would work to help people, the poor and the needy.' The Islamic awakening spread on student campuses as well as at the mosques. Mona Hamed noticed the changes at her university. 'Girls began to wear the Islamic dress, the *hijab*. Meetings were held at prayer times. Religious books spread in large numbers.' Many people felt inspired by the success of Iran's Islamic revolution. 'When a secular, non-believing regime like the shah's collapses, this brings great hope,' observes Yasser Tawfiq. 'We were hoping to have in Egypt an Islamic state as well.' Religious organizations, including the Muslim Brotherhood, were revived, some of them more radical than others, as Aly Abdel Hamed remembers. 'Members of the Islamic groups tended to describe their opponents as disbelievers, to tear away their wall posters, and use chains and knives to threaten them.'

As Egypt's Islamic movement grew more powerful, the government became increasingly hostile. 'The state wanted Islam to be just prayer and nothing else,' says Yasser Tawfiq. 'No awareness, no education, and no reformation.' In September 1981, following street riots in Cairo, President Sadat ordered the arrest of religious activists. Yasser Tawfiq was among the 1500 people who were detained. 'The only thing they hated me for,' he says, 'is for preaching to follow God.' Once in prison, he was out of touch with the outside world: he had no lawyer, no newspapers, no radio. A month later a new arrival to the prison brought him and his fellow prisoners the startling news that President Sadat had been assassinated by Islamic extremists while he was reviewing troops near Cairo on 6 October. The prisoners responded to the news by declaring, '*Allah ho akbar!*' – God is great!

Algeria's second bid for freedom

The Muslim movement failed to install an Islamic government in Egypt, but what had happened there highlighted how Islamic revivalism had emerged as a strong rival force in Arab politics. When Muslims in nearby Algeria made their formal bid for power, they did so not by militant or extremist means, but through an established democratic process.

As a former French territory, Algeria was one of the most secular Arab states. The Algerian Muslims had won their independence in a bitter, destructive war. But the autocratic rulers of the new socialist government, the National Liberation Front (FLN), failed to fulfil many of the promises of freedom. After an initial period of prosperity, Algeria's economy fell into decline during the 1980s. Oil and gas revenue was used to fund government reform programmes, but economic stability often failed to reach many parts of the countryside and overcrowded cities. People were faced with housing shortages and poor educational opportunities, and often had to queue for bread. 'We started to lose confidence in the government,' remembers Muhammad Ammatari. 'People grew more desperate. The price of oil went down, which affected our economic situation. This created unemployment, and unemployment created corruption, and corruption led to despair.'

In October 1988 thousands of people took to the streets to protest at the contrast between their lives and those of the leaders of the FLN's one-party state. 'They are eating and drinking in their beautiful villas,' one young mother shouted, 'and we have got nothing. We eat dirt in our food.' Another Algerian, Muhammad (surname withheld), watched the demonstrations on television. 'It was impressive for us, I hadn't seen that kind of thing before,' he says. 'Three or four days later it affected our town. At that time, it wasn't really just Islam, it was a revolt against corruption. I was fed up, the people were fed up.'

The Muslim groups among the demonstrators began to gain wider public support. But the government refused to tolerate any opposition, and began a campaign of arrests of the 'Islamists'. The result was popular unrest. Faced with grumbling revolt, continuing violence and mounting terrorism, the government announced its plans to hold what would be Algeria's first democratic elections for

DOWN WITH FRANCE (ABOVE) *Armed Shiite Muslim members of Lebanon's Hizbollah party display their views on foreign intervention, denouncing their former French rulers in a demonstration in southern Beirut in 1987. Heavily embroiled in the Arab–Israeli conflict and ravaged by civil war, Lebanon was divided by the political hostility between its many rival religious communities, and factional fighting continued until 1991. Western fears were heightened by the militant activities of some extremist groups, such as foreign hostage-taking and embassy sieges.*

FACING THE DIRECTION OF MECCA (OPPOSITE), *which is compulsory during prayer, Uzbek Muslims attend a mosque in the town of Termez. Uzbekistan was one of the five newly independent central Asian Muslim nations to emerge from the break-up of the former Soviet Union in 1991. Religion had been vigorously suppressed under the communists; now former Soviet citizens were free to worship again.*

thirty years. The Islamic groups founded their own political party, the Islamic Salvation Front (FIS). They delivered political sermons to thousands of people attending Friday prayer, transforming the mosques into campaigning centres. One of the Islamic leaders delivered a speech at Muhammad's school. 'There were twenty thousand people in the courtyard,' he describes. 'He started to talk about things that were real to us, things that no one had said before because they were afraid. That's the first time I had a feeling of being represented by someone. The people listened to him because he talked about people's problems, about their values, everything they had suffered, and he told them, "So follow me, create a multi-party system".'

Elections were to be held first for the legislature, then for the presidency. Thirteen million Algerians voted in December 1991. 'The whole family was thrilled,' Muhammad says. 'It was the first time in their lives they had voted. It was the first time they felt they were really free.' In the first round the FIS won 126 seats; the FLN, after thirty-two years in power, gained just twenty-two.

Despite this overwhelming victory, the Islamic party did not stand in the presidential election: the government cancelled it. Several thousand people, alarmed at the prospect of Islamic rule, took to the streets in anti-Islamic demonstrations. The FIS was banned, and its leaders were among the thousands of people who were arrested. Algerian society was torn apart, and thousands of people were killed, in the civil war that followed.

By this time the man who symbolized Islam's resurgence, Ayatollah Khomeini, had died. News of his death in June 1989 provoked frenzied public grief; on the day of his funeral hundreds of thousands of mourners thronged the cemetery south of Tehran where he was to be buried, and again when the new mosque containing his shrine was opened exactly one year later.

The revolution Khomeini had begun had acquired its own momentum. In some countries Islam now held unchallenged power; throughout the Muslim world, even in states not under Islamic rule, religion had become a formidable political force. As the century ended, God's followers – and not only Muslims but some Christians and Hindus as well – were determined to try to order the lives of others on religious lines.

People Power

COLLAPSE OF THE COMMUNIST EMPIRE

ON 9 OCTOBER 1989 journalists were refused entry to Leipzig, East Germany's second largest city. The huge rally described as 'peace prayers' being held that night was expected to attract up to 70 000 East German citizens; the security forces were under instruction to prevent any anti-government demonstration. Many casualties were expected, so hospital wards had been cleared and blood stocks increased.

Two days earlier, returning to Leipzig after visiting Berlin to join in East Germany's fortieth anniversary celebrations, Dietmar Passenheim had watched as lorries were driven into a crowd of demonstrators. On the Monday, 'Ninety-nine per cent of us expected violence,' he remembers. 'We thought the tanks would roll in and destroy us.... But along with the fear was the feeling that I had to go and be with these people in order to change and improve things. It's indescribable, I just knew I had to be there.'

While the crowds gathered in front of the Nikolaikirche close to Karl Marx Square, prayers were said before the demonstration began. In the meantime, military vehicles blocked the side streets, armed and poised for action.

The evening of 9 October proved to be a decisive moment in the history of East Germany, and had far-reaching repercussions. No shots were fired, no violence erupted. The Soviet president, Mikhail Gorbachev, had visited Berlin for the anniversary celebrations and had made it clear to the East German government that he would not support those who refused to accept the need for change. For the communist leaders in Berlin, the end was near.

The Leipzig demonstrations were part of a pattern of protest accelerating in Eastern Europe. Within a month the Berlin Wall, since 1961 a symbol of the division between capitalist Western Europe and the communist East, had come down. The power of the Soviet Union, which since the 1940s had held Eastern Europe in its grip, was now being challenged. The monolithic empire of Soviet communism was soon to be shattered.

WAVING BANNERS *of protest, the people of Leipzig demonstrate against communist rule in East Germany.*

Living under communist rule

In the early 1970s the world was still divided into the spheres of influence of the two superpowers that had dominated international relations since the end of the Second World War. Each represented a polarized ideology. The United States saw itself as the guardian of democratic freedom and the champion of capitalism, while the Soviet Union proclaimed the glories of communist society and the benefits of controlled economies. The Soviet Union dominated Eastern Europe; the United States jealously guarded its influence in the West. Conflict in countries outside Europe often drew on the resources and support of the superpowers, each eager to prevent an expansion of the other's influence.

The state continued to shape the lives of people living under communist rule. In some countries it decided how many children people could have, where they were educated, what job they could pursue, where they lived, what information they were exposed to, what allegiances they had and what opinions they were allowed to express.

Communist ideals were introduced to schoolchildren from a young age. Dasha Khubova, who later became Moscow's leading oral historian, remembers her education in the Soviet Union in the 1960s and 1970s. 'From your first day at school you were taught about your country and told that you must be proud of it. They told you about the revolution and you felt it was all for you....From when you were a small child you heard and read about it. There was no choice, no option, you believed it....This mania, this feeling that we were the best and that we had the best of everything – we never doubted it.'

Some people believed that the communist state justified its existence because of the security and welfare it provided. Harold Jäger, a border guard in East Germany (the German Democratic Republic, GDR), recognized the benefits this could bring. 'We enjoyed cheap rents, money for holidays, free education....Even if I hadn't been a member

THE COMMUNIST STATES (BELOW) *in Eastern Europe were – with the exception of Albania and Yugoslavia – for forty years dominated and largely controlled by the powerful Soviet Union, which was itself made up of fifteen republics. Eastern Europe provided a buffer zone between the Soviet Union and the capitalist nations of the West.*

NINA MOTOVA (ABOVE), *who worked in a ball bearings factory in the Soviet Union, was an ardent believer in the communist state. 'The work, the government and the Party are my life,' she says, 'and I am proud of them all.'*

OFFICIAL CELEBRATIONS (TOP) *were staged each year on May Day. The cream of the nation's workers and athletes, military personnel and weaponry, followed by cheering crowds, paraded before the Soviet leaders in Moscow's Red Square.*

of the state security, I would never have been scared of unemployment or of having too low a pension....I really appreciated that feeling of security.'

Others felt that they were having to live a double life. When Carmen Blazejewski was a child she believed, 'Socialism meant peace and no difference between rich and poor.' As she grew up her parents told her that they did not agree with everything they were told. This knowledge was dangerous. 'I had to learn from an early age not to let the kindergarten teacher know anything about the knowledge I had from my parents,' she recalls. Children in East Germany were tested at school to check whether they watched the forbidden West German television. Carmen Blazejewski's mother was a teacher. 'She warned me that we would have to draw a clock like the one shown on TV,' she says, 'and that I must draw the one on GDR television, not the one from the West.' One clock used dashes to display the minutes, the other dots.

Governments bombarded their citizens with evidence of the success of communism, but some Eastern European nations were close to economic collapse by the early 1970s. Millions of people still endured great hardship: food was often scarce; housing was desperately inadequate; people had to wait up to ten years for a flat or to buy a car; industry was inefficient and wages were low. Western clothes and consumer goods were highly prized, but were unobtainable except at huge expense through the black market.

Access to the West was strictly limited, and it was difficult to gain any information about the outside world, particularly in the Soviet Union. But many people yearned for something more than the hardships and the monotony of communist life. Natasha Kusnetsova lived in the town of Rostov. 'We didn't have enough food,' she says. 'All you could buy were carrots, cabbage and potatoes.' She became intrigued by the liveliness in Western music. 'I imagined the meaning of the words,' she recalls. 'I felt the sense of freedom even without the words ….Later I saw pictures, and was fascinated. I couldn't forget them; I wanted to know all about the world they came from.'

It was dangerous to try to find out about that world. Any communication with Westerners was strictly forbidden, and no criticism of the Communist Party was tolerated. Citizens were kept under close surveillance by the secret police, and informers were encouraged to report any deviation from the communist line by neighbours, colleagues at work, friends and even members of their own family. In East Germany there were 86 000 secret police (Stasi) agents, and another 100 000 people who were tempted – or pressurized – into acting as informers. Stasi files were kept on six million of East Germany's eighteen million citizens.

Dietmar Passenheim worked in Leipzig. He was a police informer who searched trains that ran through to West Germany, looking out for anyone who might be trying to escape to the West and checking on the passengers for 'subversive' intentions. 'We always made the assumption that every West German was an agent,' he says. 'He was an enemy, and we had to find out what he was doing here.' Suspicious-looking people were first identified on the station platform. Posing as an ordinary citizen, Dietmar Passenheim would get into the compartment with them. 'I would

A CAPTIVE AUDIENCE *Potential buyers choosing televisions in a Moscow store. Few consumer goods were available to people living under communist rule, but most citizens had access to television, which was controlled by the state.*

SHOPPING IN THE MARKET (RIGHT) *in Moscow. Buying food was a daily chore for many people in communist states. There was little choice, and people living in the cities sometimes faced shortages of basic goods such as bread and meat.*

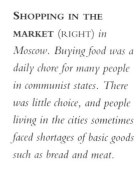

DIETMAR PASSENHEIM (BELOW) *was a member of a cooperative that assembled prefabricated housing (BELOW RIGHT) in East Germany as a young man. He was later employed by the transport police (BELOW LEFT), and then worked as an informer. 'A precondition of the job,' he says, 'was being a Party member… another was that we didn't have any relatives in the West.'*

just start talking to them and try to build up a bit of a relationship,' he recalls. 'Then I would ask what they were going to do in West Germany, and whether they enjoyed their time in the GDR....A superior officer walked up and down the corridor, and we had a sign language...if I pulled my right ear lobe it meant that I wanted to talk to him, and we would meet farther down the corridor.'

Some agents and informers had to work between twelve and seventeen hours a day. After ten years Dietmar Passenheim tried to resign, claiming that the hours were too long and the job too stressful. 'If I had told them the real reasons,' he says, 'I would have been imprisoned immediately. I would have been regarded as an enemy of the state.' His resignation was rejected.

Challenges to communist rule

Millions of citizens living in Eastern Europe resented and feared the regimes under which they lived. There were several occasions when people had tried to stand up to them. In 1953 there were riots in East Berlin, and three years later an uprising in Hungary. In 1968 the Red Army marched into Czechoslovakia to put an end to the reforms introduced during the 'Prague Spring'. In country after country forces of the communist regimes, backed by the Soviet Union, ruthlessly suppressed all signs of discontent or rebellion among their peoples.

The people of Poland had long resisted Soviet-dominated communism. Protests in 1956, 1968, 1970 and 1976 had all been crushed with the use of force. The disturbances in 1970, triggered by sudden price increases on many foodstuffs, were most serious in the Baltic ports and shipyards, and particularly in Gdansk, once the German port of Danzig.

Alena Borusewicz was a nurse in the Gdansk shipyard where her father also worked; her husband, Bogdan Borusewicz, became a member of the dissident group KOR (Committee to Defend the Workers). She realized the difference between the Polish government's propaganda and what was really taking place. 'The press was portraying the shipyard workers as hooligans and idle workers,' she remembers, 'but I knew that my father was a very different kind of person.' She started to write articles for the underground publications produced by the resistance movement; for the first time many workers were able to read uncensored material about health and safety at work, occupational diseases, and political and historical events in Poland and in the outside world. 'We wanted to give the people courage to do something,' she says. 'We tried to break the censorship so that people could read what they wanted.'

By early 1980 the Polish economy was close to collapse. with nearly half the state's budget spent on food subsidies. Foreign debts were crippling the economy, wages were low, and there were acute food shortages. When the government again announced an increase in food prices – the price of meat was almost doubled – spontaneous strikes broke out. As before, the centre of resistance was Gdansk. In the shipyards a strike committee was formed, led by Lech Walesa, an electrician. Strikers from all over Poland joined

the committee, which called for political as well as economic change: for freedom of the press, the right to form independent trade unions, the release of political prisoners and the right to strike.

Taking part in the strike was dangerous, and not all the Gdansk shipyard workers did so. But enormous numbers of people from other occupations did gather outside the shipyards to show their support. Alena Borusewicz remembers seeing a woman out walking one Sunday morning with two smartly dressed little girls. At first she assumed they were going to visit someone. 'I suddenly realized that this woman was taking her children to the shipyard gate,' she remembers. 'I felt like crying. I felt it was a symbol of support for those of us who were on strike.'

Henryka Krzywonos was a tram driver. Her fellow workers sent her to represent them at Gdansk. When the strikers in the shipyard considered returning to work, she stood on a truck and shouted anything she could think of that might persuade them to stay. 'I tried to explain that if they left, if they went home, they would be betraying all the other striking workers,' she recalls. Henryka Krzywonos was convinced that the strikers had a responsibility towards all Polish citizens. 'Beyond the gates were more than a million people,' she remembers. 'The square was full of people....Without them we wouldn't be able to do anything, but we knew we had their

JOINING FORCES (LEFT) *Workers inside the Gdansk shipyard, and their supporters outside it, united in their efforts to bring about change in Poland. The strikers were led by Lech Walesa (in the centre of the photograph, on the far side of the railings). Members of Solidarity, the federation of trade unions, included doctors, engineers, manual workers, shopkeepers and teachers, and some 900 000 former members of the Communist Party. Their demands included 'Work for bread', as the banner they are carrying declares (RIGHT). Most of Solidarity's demands were eventually conceded by the Polish government.*

A HOLY ALLIANCE

SPONTANEOUS CELEBRATIONS broke out all over Poland on 16 October 1978 when a Polish cardinal, Karol Wojtyla, was elected Pope, head of the Roman Catholic Church. He was the first Polish Pope ever, and the first non-Italian one for more than 450 years.

Seven months later more than 500 000 Poles gathered in Warsaw's Victory Square to listen to Pope John Paul II, as he was now known, address his countrymen. 'The future of Poland will depend on how many people are mature enough to be nonconformists,' he told them. His words brought inspiration to the deeply religious Polish people, most of whom were still practising Roman Catholics despite the communist government's attempts to discourage religious worship.

More than a quarter of Poland's population turned out to hear the Pope preach in public as he toured the country on his nine-day visit. Its enormous impact was played down by the government-controlled media, but there was a huge resurgence of religious activity, including services held in public. 'The mass united the people,' remembers Henryka Krzywonos. 'People were standing together and creating a kind of community....We were not afraid.'

The Church played a subtle but important role as the Polish people fought against communist rule. Its aim was to survive within the communist system that it wanted to see overthrown. At first it condemned the strike, but later supported Solidarity's demands. 'The Church's involvement with the conflict gave us extra security,' recalls Bogdan Borusewicz. 'The authorities allowed priests to enter the shipyards and conduct mass....It was an important experience for the community, and it consolidated us. We were convinced we were doing the right thing. If the priests were with us, we believed no harm could come to us.'

When martial law was imposed in December 1981 the Church continued to support Solidarity, providing refuge for hunger strikers and medical, economic and moral support to union members. Its part in the opposition movement made the Church a target for government attack. The abduction and murder of a popular radical priest, Father Jerzy Popieluszko, provoked worldwide condemnation, and increased the pressure on the Polish government to listen to its people.

support....The strike unified us. We started to be a nation for ourselves.'

After intense negotiations between the strike committee and the Polish government, on 31 August 1980 the Gdansk Agreement was signed. Workers were given the right to form trade unions and to strike; an economic overhaul was promised, including a rise in wages; and the Catholic mass was to be broadcast on the radio each Sunday. The strike committee formed the basis for a national trade union and political movement, *Solidarnosc* – Solidarity – which rapidly grew to have more than ten million members. It was an extraordinary victory for the workers. The confrontation between them and the leaders of the workers' state that claimed to represent them had been closely followed all over the world; many strikers believed this would protect them from reprisals by the Polish authorities. They were wrong.

The political crisis in Poland continued. In February 1981 the defence minister, General Wojciech Jaruzelski, took over as premier; he was appointed first secretary of the Communist Party in October. As union militants, advised and supported by the Roman Catholic Church, continued to press for change, further strikes caused upheaval throughout the country. They also began to have an impact further afield; governments elsewhere in Eastern Europe were extremely alarmed at the possibility of their own peoples following the Polish example. In December, under intense pressure from Moscow, Jaruzelski imposed martial law. Solidarity was banned, its members imprisoned or intimidated.

Henryka Krzywonos continued her work for Solidarity, but in secret. She knew that she would eventually be found out. 'The fear was indescribable,' she says. Eventually, 'They came and broke my door down. The fact that I was pregnant made no difference to them. They beat me, throwing me around like a ball, then left me bleeding.' She lost her baby. Her flat was searched, and she was forced to leave the area. Despite the fear and the harsh repression, Solidarity survived underground. Within six years – though only after a change of government in Moscow – it would re-emerge.

POPE JOHN PAUL II *addresses his fellow countrymen during his tour of Poland in 1979.*

LINED UP *against the people, the Polish militia in riot gear* (TOP) *oppose crowds of demonstrators. Zbigniew Lelental* (ABOVE) *was a trainee officer in the police when martial law was declared in December 1981. 'We didn't know what to expect,' he remembers. 'But we knew that if we didn't maintain order ourselves, it would end tragically for Poland.' Soviet military intervention was probably averted by the severity of the Polish authorities' action.*

"The Soviet Union was the Big Brother. We thought that if they can do things then so can we. We identified with glasnost and perestroika…it played a major role."

CARMEN BLAZEJEWSKI

Reforms and revolutions

It was not until Mikhail Gorbachev became leader of the Soviet Union that the situation in the communist world began to change. In 1985 he succeeded Konstantin Chernenko. Fifty-four years old, Mikhail Gorbachev was the youngest member of the Politburo, the Communist Party's ruling committee. Yevgeny Mahaev, who sold fish in Moscow, was among many people who welcomed the news of Gorbachev's appointment. 'When Gorbachev came, everyone said that because he was young and had a lot of energy life would improve,' he remembers. 'Life in the early 1980s had stagnated. We needed change.'

Within days of taking office Gorbachev was already talking about the need for change. The new policy came to be known as *perestroika* (restructuring): the whole Soviet economy needed to be made more efficient. Gorbachev put into practice his own belief that leading Party members should get closer to the people. He spoke openly about the dire economic crisis facing the nation, acknowledging the fact that the quality of its products was low, that management was riddled with corruption, and motivation among workers was poor. In a country where the state controlled everything, Gorbachev now encouraged a degree of free enterprise. Yevgeny Mahaev remembers: 'He said that we could work

FACE TO FACE *Mikhail Gorbachev* (ABOVE) *was the first Soviet leader to talk directly to the people. Yevgeny Mahaev* (LEFT) *was enthusiastic. 'We had hopes that there would be changes….I liked it.' Gorbachev's plain speaking and personal charm at first brought him popularity and widespread support.*

THE OLD GUARD *ended with the funeral* (RIGHT) *of Konstantin Chernenko, who died on 10 March 1985 after only a year as president of the Soviet Union. He and his predecessor, Yuri Andropov, were in poor health during their time in office. Chernenko maintained the hard line of President Leonid Brezhnev, who died in 1982.*

SUPERPOWER RECONCILIATION

WHEN MIKHAIL GORBACHEV became leader of the Soviet Union in 1985 few people foresaw that the appointment would spark off an explosion of change affecting not just the communist empire but the whole balance of international politics. There had been previous attempts to improve relations between the two superpowers – the Soviet Union and the United States – but they had foundered in 1979 with the Soviet invasion of Afghanistan.

Gorbachev was a pragmatist. He believed that communism must evolve and change if it was to survive. He recognized that one of the most vital changes was a scaling down of the arms race between the superpowers. The Soviet Union was spending a quarter of its total revenue on arms, and this was crippling the economy. Gorbachev injected new vigour into arms talks with the United States, and embarked on a series of summit meetings with President Ronald Reagan. The Cold War was beginning to thaw.

The first summit was held in Geneva in 1985, and despite mutual suspicion the two leaders agreed to continue cautious exchanges. They met again at Reykjavik in October the following year, though the talks broke down when President Reagan refused to give up his Strategic Defence Initiative (SDI). By 1987 the Soviet Union's need to reduce its arms expenditure had become urgent, and when Reagan visited Moscow in 1988 to sign an arms reduction treaty it was apparent that Gorbachev would pay almost any price to bring about an end to superpower competition.

Gorbachev was the first Soviet leader to acknowledge the cost of the communist empire. He knew that the Soviet Union could no longer pursue its interventionist policy in other East European states. Opposition groups within the Eastern bloc were encouraged by Gorbachev's abandonment of the 'Brezhnev doctrine', by which Moscow had justified Soviet involvement in the defence of socialism wherever it might be under threat.

This dramatic change in foreign policy, the scaling down of the arms race and the radical domestic reforms in the Soviet Union made Gorbachev a hero in the eyes of many people living in both East and West. Carmen Blazejewski remembers the excitement created by Gorbachev's visit to East Berlin. 'The news of the visit spread fast,' she recalls. 'Normally everything had to be organized: people were given flags to wave and had to take the day off work. But when Gorby came the state didn't have to organize anyone – people wanted to see Gorbachev anyway. They filled the streets, chanting "Gorby! Gorby!" ' Much of Europe was swept by 'Gorbymania'; in 1990 Gorbachev was awarded the Nobel peace prize.

and earn money for ourselves. The people believed him and soon founded their own small enterprises and businesses. I quit my shop and became independent from the state.'

Reforms within the Party structure enabled Gorbachev to push through new measures. In order to rally the public behind *perestroika*, Gorbachev introduced a policy of *glasnost* or 'openness', in which the media, the people and the state were all encouraged to be more open and honest. People found their newspapers full of stories about inefficiency, bad management and nepotism. Disturbing facts about current events, such as the devastating nuclear accident at Chernobyl, were matched by revelations about previous leaders and their policies. The works of banned writers were published, and many political prisoners were released. Some people found the revelations too much for them. Nina Motova was a factory worker in the Soviet Union, and had won awards for her work. She was intensely proud of the nation's achievements. 'When *glasnost* came they began to tell us things we didn't want to hear,' she recalls. 'They told us bad things about Lenin and how he ruined the history of the world. Well of course Lenin could make mistakes, but the life was good and we were moving towards a very bright future. Now I am ashamed to hear the criticism of our economy and our country.'

Gorbachev's reforms were soon extended to relations with other states in the communist bloc. The 'Brezhnev doctrine', which had been used to justify Soviet intervention in the affairs of other communist states, was replaced by the 'Sinatra doctrine' – they could do it their way. In Hungary opposition groups were legalized, and reformers within the Communist Party gained more power. Market reforms replaced the old centralized economy, and in early 1989 the Communist Party declared its support for the transition to a multi-party political system.

One of the most dramatic and welcome changes came in Poland. In January 1989 Solidarity's legal status was restored, opposition to the Communist Party was allowed, and parliament reformed. These initiatives swiftly led to multi-party elections; by the summer of 1989 a coalition government led by Solidarity was in power, the first non-communist government in Eastern Europe for forty years.

Encouraged by the changes initiated by Mikhail Gorbachev, opposition groups in East Germany also grew stronger. When Hungary opened its borders with the West early in 1989, thousands of East Germans made their way to Hungary, which they could visit legally, and from there left for the West. This mass exodus shocked some East German citizens. Bärbel Reinke, who was a waitress in East Berlin, thought that 'What these people were doing was leaving a sinking ship. I was torn in two about it... not everyone could run away, otherwise the country couldn't change.' The official press denounced those who left as enemies of the

DISMANTLING THE BARRIER *A barbed wire fence had separated Hungary and Austria since 1969. When Hungary opened the border in May 1989, large numbers of East Germans took the opportunity to escape to the West. In September Hungary declared all its borders open – the first Eastern European state to open its borders to a non-communist neighbour.*

THE WALL COMES DOWN (RIGHT) *Jubilant crowds at the Berlin Wall after the East German government announced the opening of the border in November 1989. The wall divided the city and people of Berlin for twenty-eight years; many people had died when they attempted to cross it to reach the West. Now people chipped away at the wall by hand before equipment could be brought in to demolish it.*

state. Bärbel Reinke recognized the consequences of the exodus: 'We didn't have a proper workforce any more. The doctors were leaving, and soon we didn't have enough nurses either.'

In October 1989 Mikhail Gorbachev came to Berlin for the GDR's fortieth anniversary celebrations. In a thinly veiled warning to the East German leader, Erich Honecker, he declared, 'He who is too late is punished by life'. It was a clear indication that Moscow would not back the East German government in repressing the people's call for reform. Reassured by this message and by the peaceful demonstration in Leipzig, protesters gathered in the other major East German towns; on 4 November half a million people rallied in East Berlin to call for an end to communist rule.

Faced by this overwhelming pressure, on 9 November the East German government announced that the border was to be opened. People were free to visit West Berlin. Andreas Höntsch, a film-maker in East Berlin, heard the news flash. 'We just couldn't believe it,' he says. 'Then we saw pictures on television showing people at the border crossing...they were waving...it seemed impossible.' At first there was confusion. Bärbel Reinke went to the wall immediately, and decided to visit West Berlin by walking through the Brandenburg Gate. 'Nothing would stop me,' she says. But when she arrived she found her way was blocked. 'I became terribly frightened,' she recalls. 'I thought they had tricked us and simply shut the wall again....I started to shout and panic.' Eventually she was allowed to go through; an officer escorted her. 'It was dangerous,' she reflects, 'but looking back everyone behaved very calmly.'

Carmen Blazejewski and Andreas Höntsch were also determined to see for themselves, so the next day they bundled their sleeping child into their car and drove to the border. They were concerned that it might be closed again before they could get there, but when they reached it the guards waved them through. 'People were getting out of their cars and giving flowers to the guards. It was a very peaceful sight,' says Carmen Blazejewski. 'Someone greeted us

with a bottle of sparkling wine, and chocolate for the child....We were in the West. I was shaking, I was so excited....The streets were full of people, and everybody was embracing each other ....There was a feeling of great joy.'

Harold Jäger was on duty at the border on 9 November. He was bewildered by what was happening. 'We had no instructions, no orders during that critical situation,' he recalls. 'That was proof to me that everything was lost....The desire and will of the people was stronger than the power of the state. It was the end of the GDR.' In October 1990 the GDR did come to an end. After an overwhelming vote for unification, the political boundary between East and West Germany was dissolved.

BÄRBEL REINKE (LEFT, with her children), like thousands of other East Berliners, regarded the Brandenburg Gate as a symbolic entrance to the West. When concerts were held and political speeches delivered in West Berlin close to it, 'We would go and stand at the gate and listen,' she says. 'We weren't allowed to, but we still did it.'

DESTROYING THE EVIDENCE *In January 1990 East German citizens broke into the Berlin headquarters of the secret police and tore up thousands of Stasi files. The Stasi had accumulated files on a third of the East German population and more than half a million foreigners.*

Revolution spreads

In Czechoslovakia the communist regime was also struggling against massive popular rebellion. Dissidents such as the playwright Václav Havel became increasingly prominent in the resistance movement. Andrej Krob had long been friends with Havel. He was a handyman and Havel's driver, and as a stage hand helped Havel to put on some of his controversial plays secretly in flats and barns. He continued to work with Havel in the underground movement. 'We knew it was no joke working for something that was disliked by the Bolsheviks,' he recalls. 'It could easily ruin our lives. But I had a sense of justice, so I had to make my decision, despite the consequences.'

In the late 1980s Andrej Krob began to work as a cameraman for an underground video journal. He recorded dissident meetings and protests, and some sympathetic people who worked for the official Czech television station helped to edit them. 'We would make a master copy, and then make multiple copies and distribute them,' he recalls. 'They would be screened in pubs and even factories, all over Czechoslovakia and abroad....We wanted to spread information among the local public. That way the people would come together and could become more organized.'

Petr Miller was a blacksmith working for a large company, CKD, in Prague. Like many others with an adequate standard of living, he was at first reluctant to join a revolutionary movement. People remembered the Soviet invasion of their country in 1968, and were afraid to risk change. Their fears were allayed when Mikhail Gorbachev made an official visit to Prague in 1987. Petr Miller was impressed by him. 'He started to talk about things in a new way,' he says. 'It was very engaging, and his new policies were widely discussed in the workplace....It was transparent that something big was happening in Eastern Europe. It seemed that the Iron Curtain was bound to fall.'

On Friday 17 November 1989 a peaceful crowd gathered in Prague's Wenceslas Square for a memorial demonstration in honour of a student killed by the Nazis fifty years earlier. Andrej Krob filmed the demonstration; he was expecting trouble. 'We saw the militia gathering,' he remembers. 'I carried my camera under my coat and mingled

ANDREJ KROB (LEFT, *talking to Václav Havel) set up an underground video journal in Czechoslovakia. His contact with Havel was vital. 'Havel's role is undeniable,' recalls Andrej Krob. 'He was the initiator, he put us together and made us think things through.'*

CANDLES OF HOPE (ABOVE) *in Wenceslas Square in Prague were lit as a symbol of peaceful protest against government policies in November 1989, while state riot police assembled in the side streets. There were daily demonstrations in support of political change.*

with the crowds....We knew the government would have to act.' The demonstration was violently suppressed. On the Saturday and Sunday some 200 000 people demonstrated in protest at police brutality. It was also on Sunday that Václav Havel and his fellow dissidents formed an official opposition group, Civic Forum, after a series of meetings. Petr Miller went to the Magic Lantern theatre to listen to their discussions. He asked Havel, 'Who is representing the workers here?' He remembers how Havel 'pointed his finger at me and said, "Well, you are going to".' Petr Miller was swept into the reform movement, organizing strikes and later participating in negotiations with the government. Members of Civic Forum, including Petr Miller, were pursued by a growing number of journalists. 'Suddenly there was a huge number of foreign press reporters, television photographers, film producers...all seeking our views. We were not groomed for this role. We tried hard not to let it show, we tried to present ourselves correctly, but we were really complete amateurs.'

The Communist Party had lost all hope of continuing. By the middle of December the old regime had been swept away, and was replaced by a newly elected democratic government. Change had come about in Czechoslovakia so quickly and peacefully it became known as the 'velvet revolution'.

BURNING THE FLAG *of the Romanian Communist Party, demonstrators in Bucharest give vent to their anger and bitterness during a memorial in January 1990 for victims of the violence.*

It seemed as though the entire edifice of communism might be toppled without bloodshed. But the revolution in Romania was to prove far from peaceful. Romanians were kept as isolated as possible from the events taking place elsewhere in Eastern Europe, and the regime there refused to countenance any changes. Nevertheless, on 17 December 1989 a crowd of Romanians demonstrated in the city of Timisoara, in Transylvania, demanding civil rights and political reform. The president, Nicolae Ceausescu, ordered his security forces, the Securitate, to fire into the crowds. More than a hundred people were killed that week, and many more injured.

Four days later Nicolae Ceausescu and his wife Elena appeared before a crowd of 80 000 people outside the Central Committee building in Bucharest. Instead of giving their usual organized ovation the crowds shouted, 'Down with the murderers!' Television cameras filmed the scene, but transmission was cut off so viewers did not see Ceausescu's bewilderment. He then realized that he had lost even the simulated support of his people. Soon the army went over to the opposition, while the Securitate started shooting. Ceausescu and his wife escaped by helicopter. They were later captured, tried and executed.

ABANDONED CHILDREN (ABOVE) *Many thousands of Romanian orphans were barely able to survive the terrible conditions in which they had to live.*

A CULT OF REPRESSION

THE PEOPLE OF Romania endured one of the most tyrannical regimes anywhere in the communist world. For a time their ruler, Nicolae Ceausescu, was regarded as a liberal in the West because of his attempts to promote nationalism and throw off the Soviet yoke; less was known about the ruthless domestic policies he inflicted on his people, sacrificing their welfare for national prestige and personal glorification.

In the early 1980s the Romanians suffered acute food shortages as Ceausescu increased food exports to reduce the country's foreign debts. Fuel was rationed so that oil could be exported; anyone who burnt fuel when the state declared the temperature to be above 10°C (50°F) was liable to prosecution. Ceausescu ruled the country with an iron hand: all the media were censored, contact with foreigners was strictly forbidden, faxes and photocopiers were banned, and every typewriter in the country had to be registered with the state so that any subversive printed material could be traced to its originator.

While the people suffered material deprivation and were denied any civil and political rights, public money was squandered on gigantic architectural projects. Thousands of Bucharest citizens were forced into slum housing on the outskirts of the city so that a large area could be cleared to build a new palace for Nicolae Ceausescu and his family. Any sign of resistance by the people was immediately quelled by Ceausescu's personal security forces, the Securitate. Numbering more than 100 000, the Securitate terrorized the Romanian people into submission. It was rumoured that every telephone was bugged, and that a quarter of the population were 'informers' working for the Securitate.

The regime penetrated every aspect of people's lives. When the birth rate dropped, abortion was made illegal and contraceptives were banned. All women under the age of forty-five were expected to have at least five children, regardless of their income, health or personal wishes. The legislation was enforced by compulsory regular gynaecological inspections.

The result of this policy was that women already struggling to feed and clothe their families resorted to illegal, often dangerous abortions, or abandoned babies they could not provide for. Hundreds of thousands of children were left in overcrowded, squalid orphanages run by inadequate numbers of untrained staff who lacked the resources to provide proper care for them. Lack of sterile medical supplies and the traditional practice of injecting newborn babies with extra blood meant that the AIDS virus soon gained a foothold, and by December 1989, when the Ceausescu regime was brought down, half the babies in Europe with AIDS were Romanian.

CENTRAL AVENUE (BELOW), *built in central Bucharest by Nicolae Ceausescu. Ordinary citizens, some of whose homes had been razed to clear the land, were denied access to this part of the city.*

The empire crumbles

While the people of the communist satellites struggled to assert their independence, the heart of the Soviet system was faltering. Mikhail Gorbachev's radical reforms had alarmed traditional Party members, while most people found themselves faced with even longer food queues, more acute shortages, rising prices and a surge in crime. In 1989 a wave of strikes swept across the Soviet Union, from the Ukraine to the Arctic. In August more than a million people in the Baltic states – Estonia, Latvia and Lithuania – joined hands, forming a human chain to protest against Soviet domination.

Many Russians who had initially supported Gorbachev felt disillusioned. 'The reforms were so great that life had changed and the people had changed,' says Yevgeny Mahaev. 'Now it was money that was important, rather than friends.' Andrei Ozerskii, a physicist working in Zelenograd, the Soviet electronics centre, at first believed that Gorbachev would strengthen the nation; then he too began to have doubts: 'By 1988 and 1989 I knew that the changes in the leadership and party were not good for the country. 'Gorbachev's words were empty....But my final disillusionment came in 1990 when he met the leaders of the seven capitalist countries. I realized that it would not bring any benefit to our country.'

Gorbachev, struggling to appease both the Communist Party hardliners and the restless radicals, satisfied neither faction. On May Day 1990 the people of Moscow gathered in Red Square, where every year they turned out to cheer military parades and political leaders. But on this occasion jeers and chants rang round the square. Gorbachev and the Politburo were shouted down, and had to retreat.

Boris Yeltsin, a prominent member of the group demanding faster reform, began to overtake Gorbachev in popularity, and in February 1991 he publicly challenged the president, declaring that he should either increase the pace of reform or resign. In

MINERS ON STRIKE
(BELOW) *in the Ukraine in 1989 demanding political change. The Ukraine was the second most populous republic in the Soviet Union, and also one of the most conservative. But once the forces of change were unleashed, resentment of Soviet domination grew into widespread public protest.*

STANDING IN LINE
(OPPOSITE) *Despite the economic changes introduced by Mikhail Gorbachev, most Soviet citizens still had to endure hours of queueing to purchase even the most basic foodstuffs in 1989. Family members often took it in turns to wait. In the worst-hit regions people waited throughout the night.*

GESTURE OF DEFIANCE
(ABOVE) *Lithuanian protesters impaled their passports on the barricades to symbolize their rejection of Soviet citizenship.*

June Yeltsin became the first democratically elected president of the Russian Federation.

As the situation continued to deteriorate, Communist Party conservatives decided to take matters into their own hands. People watching television on 20 August 1991 knew that something was wrong when the usual programmes were replaced by the ballet *Swan Lake*, interspersed with announcements that Gorbachev was 'undergoing treatment' at his holiday home in the Crimea. In fact there had been a coup: a self-appointed emergency committee announced that it was in control, and tanks moved into the centre of Moscow. 'We were horrified,' remembers Dasha Khubova, who listened to a foreign radio station to find out what was happening. 'At first we didn't speak, we just listened. Then my mother said, "I

CIVILIANS SURROUND
a Soviet tank (ABOVE) in Moscow during the coup in August 1991. Boris Yeltsin, the Russian president, defied the coup, challenging its leaders – the Emergency Committee – and calling for a general strike. The planned attack on the White House, the parliament building, did not take place.

had hoped that your life would be better, but it's the end".'

Boris Yeltsin was in his dacha outside Moscow when the coup took place. He heard the news on his return, and made his way to the square in front of the White House, the parliament building. Joined by thousands of supporters, he climbed onto a tank and urged people to resist. Within hours, crowds of civilians had surrounded the White House to protect the rebels. Natasha Kusnetsova was among them. 'I wasn't afraid,' she says. 'I couldn't just stand by. I knew that if I had to live behind the Iron Curtain again I would do something extreme....I would rather die.'

Sergei Evdikimov was one of the officers in the tank regiment that had been ordered to the White House. 'Moscow was flooded with troops,' he recalls. 'Civilians gathered all around them and talked to the soldiers. The people built barricades right in front of my tank.' Uncertain of his orders, and having lost all radio contact with his commanding officer, Sergei Evdikimov found out about what was happening by reading the resistance leaflets distributed by the White House. 'One young guy climbed on my tank and we started discussing the situation...."Why don't you come over to our side?" he asked.' After an appeal from the White House, and despite his fear of reprisals, Sergei Evdikimov decided he would join them. 'I could tell that the public supported Yeltsin,' he says. 'I was joining the people.'

Without the support of the public, the army or the police, the coup failed. It proved to be a beginning, not an end. Mikhail Gorbachev returned to Moscow still defending the Party, but it was Boris Yeltsin who took charge during the final months of the communist empire, transforming Soviet institutions into Russian ones. Other republics declared their independence from the Soviet Union. On 25 December 1991 Gorbachev resigned, and the red flag of the Soviet Union was lowered from the roof of the Kremlin. It was an extraordinary moment. 'I had such mixed feelings,' says Dasha Khubova. 'All my generation had been born under this flag ....It was the symbol of our life, and now it was coming down. It was frightening because it seemed like the end of everything, but it was also exciting. We knew that things were changing.'

STANDING TOGETHER *Civilians in Moscow befriended those sent to threaten them. They gave the soldiers gifts of food and cigarettes, and persuaded them to support the people rather than fight them.*

COMMUNISM BROUGHT DOWN (RIGHT) *The people of Moscow celebrated the collapse of the coup and Boris Yeltsin's challenge to the power of the KGB in Russia by toppling the huge statue of Felix Dzerzhinsky, founder of the Soviet secret police. The numerous statues of Vladimir Ilyich Lenin all over the country were later also removed as the Communist Party he had led was banned, and the Soviet Union he had founded more than seventy years earlier was dismantled.*

1 9 8 0 – 1 9 9 5

Back to the Future

TOWARDS THE MILLENNIUM

WHEN THE ARMIES OF Iraq crossed over the border into Kuwait in August 1990, the world held its breath. After issuing threats over many weeks, Saddam Hussein, the Iraqi president, had decided to invade Kuwait and take over its immense oil wealth for himself.

Less than a year after the Soviet empire had begun to crumble, the Gulf war was a reminder that although the Cold War might be over, the world was far from peaceful. The Iraqi invasion was condemned in the United Nations, and by January 1991 forces had assembled in Saudi Arabia to challenge it. Tens of thousands of people – most of them Iraqis – died as the international army, three-quarters of a million strong, forced the invaders back to Iraq.

The Gulf war reflected many of the issues facing the world as the century ended. It had been fought over a key energy source – oil. The pall of black smoke that hung over the burning oil wells, visible for hundreds of kilometres, was a reminder of the damage being inflicted on the environment not just in the war, but by human activities across the globe. The war was fought using sophisticated military technology, by forces often so far removed from the fighting that they never saw the suffering it inflicted. It was closely followed on television all over the world. Edwin Nerger, who watched in Fort Wayne, Indiana, says: 'Just about everybody in the country and a lot of the rest of the world actually lived that war....I'll never forget it.'

In the century's last decades there were many local conflicts that had international implications. Growing ethnic tensions mirrored the nationalism that had proved to be one of the principal causes of the First World War. Many people's lives were affected by economic upheavals far beyond their control in the world's repeated cycles of expansion and recession. The technological optimism of the age of electricity reappeared in the age of the computer. In some ways, people's hopes, fears and expectations at the end of the twentieth century seemed remarkably similar to those of their great-grandparents at its beginning.

DESERTED LANDSCAPE *Kuwaiti oil wells burn on the horizon following the Gulf war.*

New nationalisms

In 1900 many peoples, subjects of the European empires, were beginning the long struggle for independence for their nations and a voice in the political process for themselves. As the century ended, this was still true. From 1945 the Cold War that had divided much of the world into two ideological camps made national identities seem less important than whether to be communist or anti-communist. But by the mid-1980s the rigid polarization of the Cold War years began to ease, and from 1989 in Eastern Europe and the Soviet Union political independence was gained by many people, citizens of the new states established when the Soviet empire collapsed.

The voice of minority peoples was increasingly being heard: Basques and Catalans in Spain, Belgian Flemings, Bretons, German-speakers in northern Italy, Scots and Welshmen all demanded more self-government or autonomy. Sometimes this led to bloodshed and civil war. In 1991 the people of Chechnya, an autonomous province in the Russian Federation, declared their independence. At first the Russians responded by imposing economic sanctions; those did not subdue the Chechens, and in December 1994 a military invasion was launched. It was fiercely resisted, even when Chechen villages were shelled and Grozny, the capital, reduced almost to rubble.

There were many other ethnic groups still hoping for greater recognition, among them the people of Kashmir, mostly Muslims, who were forced to remain part of predominantly Hindu India by an army of more than 600 000 Indian soldiers; the plebiscite that should have been held after the 1949 intervention by the United Nations had never taken place. One of the largest stateless nations remained that of the Kurds, who made up nearly a quarter of the population of Iraq and Turkey, and about a tenth that of Iran and Syria; their homeland straddled the borders of these countries. The revolt in Iraqi Kurdistan, which had begun in the 1960s, was brutally put down in the late 1980s.

The most poignant reminder of the century's early years came on 5 February 1994, when a mortar bomb exploded in the

KASHMIRIS STAND *in front of the ruins of their home. Possession of Kashmir, situated on the mountainous northern border between India and Pakistan, remained a source of conflict between those two countries, as it had been ever since Indian partition in 1947.*

WAVING THE FLAG
Chechen soldiers in Grozny celebrate outside the presidential palace after successfully beating off an attack by Russian forces in January 1995. Hundreds of ethnic and local groups within the Russian Federation demanded more autonomy after the Soviet Union collapsed in 1991.

old market square in the Bosnian city of Sarajevo, killing sixty-nine people. The bomb had fallen within a few metres of where a Serbian nationalist, Gavrilo Princip, had assassinated Archduke Franz Ferdinand of Austria eighty years before. In the spring of 1991, realizing that the federal state of Yugoslavia was doomed, Serbs and Croats had tried to forge independent states, seizing as much territory as they could from their neighbouring Yugoslav republics. Among the first outsiders to realize how dangerous this process might be was a group of Italian tourists, who found themselves in the middle of a gun battle between Croatian police and Serbian nationalists. A Croatian policeman and a Serbian butcher were killed, the first of some 200 000 people to die in the bitter ethnic conflicts between the peoples of Yugoslavia, whose rivalries had been submerged under communism. The fighting took the heaviest toll in Bosnia, where the Serb forces intimidated and murdered Muslim inhabitants whom they tried to expel from areas they controlled, a process known as 'ethnic cleansing'.

MUSLIM REFUGEES *at the Tuzla camp near the Bosnian town of Srebrenica. Bosnia was an ethnic patchwork of Croats, Muslims and Serbs. As the conflict continued, hundreds of thousands of refugees fled or were forced to leave their homes; as evidence of mass graves, concentration camps and other atrocities emerged, it became increasingly clear that a new generation would inherit the old legacies of fear and hate.*

The atrocities committed in the breakup of Yugoslavia were dwarfed by events in Rwanda. One of the most densely populated countries in the world, this small African state was inhabited by two principal ethnic groups, who had lived together peacefully before it became first a German, then a Belgian colony. Since Rwanda had gained its independence in 1962 the minority Tutsi dominated both Rwandan society and the majority Hutu people. Attempts to resolve the conflict between them in the early 1990s seemed to be making progress, but on 6 April 1994 the presidents of Rwanda and neighbouring Burundi, returning from negotiations in Tanzania, were killed when their aircraft was shot down by a surface-to-air missile. The old enmity erupted afresh – the result was genocide. In the bloodbath more than half a million Tutsis and any Hutus who were suspected of supporting them were killed – men, women and children were hacked or bludgeoned to death by axes, machetes and any other weapons that could be found. Fearing reprisals, millions of Hutus fled Rwanda hoping to find safety in neighbouring Tanzania and Zaire; those who managed to survive the difficult journey and reached the border had to endure terrible conditions in the refugee camps.

People across the world watched and listened in horror as news of events in Bosnia, Rwanda and the world's other trouble spots was brought to them. It was television – the medium that more than any other tended to make the world a smaller, more homogenized place by allowing everyone to watch the same films, be seduced by the same advertisements, and desire the same lifestyle – that also ensured that everyone knew of the tragedies taking place. They were a grim reminder of the high price being paid by those who identified themselves with ethnic struggles and the new nationalism, which often denied them both the political stability and the economic opportunities that many people elsewhere in the world were able to take for granted.

HILLSIDE OF HUNGER
Food supplies from the International Red Cross are handed out to Rwandan refugees in the Goma camp in Zaire. Diseases such as cholera quickly spread in the unhygienic conditions of the camps, despite the help of aid workers from many international charities.

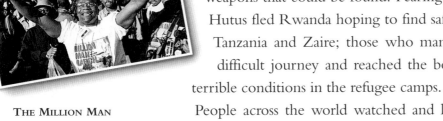

THE MILLION MAN MARCH *in Washington DC on 23 October 1995 was the largest black rally to be held since the civil rights march led by Martin Luther King in 1963. Issues of race and inequality had still not been resolved. Many black Americans found their identity in their race rather than in their citizenship of a country that they felt still denied them an equal place.*

PEACEKEEPING FORCE
American soldiers under the auspices of the United Nations in Somalia in 1993. The UN's role as international peacekeeper was becoming more difficult – and more expensive: in 1988 the peacekeeping budget was $230 million; by 1995 it was more than $3 billion. In the decade from 1985 the UN was involved in twenty-five peacekeeping operations.

Capitalism takes over

In Western Europe, where during the first half of the century many millions of people had lost their lives and livelihoods in war, a new spirit of cooperation had been established. Through the close economic ties established among members of the European Community, it was hoped that the political hostilities that so often in the past had led to war could be ended for ever. The six states that had founded the European Community in 1957 – Belgium, France, Germany, Italy, Luxembourg and the Netherlands – were joined in 1973 by Britain, Denmark and Ireland, and during the 1980s first by Greece and later by Spain and Portugal. In 1995 Austria, Finland and Sweden also joined; by this time Cyprus, Malta and Turkey had also applied for membership. So had Hungary, Poland, Romania and Slovakia, which looked westwards once the Iron Curtain had fallen.

The end of communism in Eastern Europe in the late 1980s brought economic and political change, and new hardships as well as new opportunities for the people living there. Three hundred million people were affected; many of them had skills comparable to those of people in the West, but continued to earn far less. The contrast in prosperity was most startling in Germany, a divided nation from 1945 until 1989. It was estimated that the economy of the eastern part of the country would not catch up with that of the west for at least ten years, though 150 billion Deutschmarks were being invested in its economy each year.

Since the Second World War, both the socialist states under communism and the Western democratic nations had been more closely involved in their citizens' lives than ever before. In the communist bloc, state control still limited individual rights and freedom of speech, but it ensured full employment, free education and health care for all. A social welfare programme had also been introduced in the capitalist democracies, funded by the prosperity of the boomtime years of the 1950s and 1960s. But in the late 1970s and 1980s politicians and voters began to question whether the state was the best owner of industries and services such as coal, electricity and railways. In the United States President Ronald Reagan declared: 'Government is not the solution to our problem – government *is* the problem'. Margaret Thatcher, the British

prime minister, said, 'There is no such thing as society'. Public services and welfare were cut back. The 'enterprise culture' was supposed to replace the promise that the state would take responsibility for its citizens' well-being 'from the cradle to the grave'.

In the former Soviet Union the political revolution that ended communist rule was followed by equally dramatic economic change. As well as democracy, people were to have capitalism. As subsidies were removed from factories, and the safety net that had protected the people was suddenly removed, pensioners were impoverished, miners and soldiers were not paid for months, and increasing numbers of people experienced the bitterness of unemployment – unknown under communism. Others found that their enterprise could make them millionaires.

In China, where almost a quarter of the human race still lived under a communist regime, the economy was also changing with the times. China's leaders embraced the market, and instead of insisting on equality said that the Chinese should try to make themselves rich; individual enterprise and increased spending on consumer products was the only way China would be able to fulfil its 'Four Modernizations' policy and become a major economic power by the end of the century. While the Chinese came to resemble Western capitalists in the ways they acquired and spent money, with production soaring by some 10 per cent a year, their elderly leaders remained in unchanged political control, determined to stamp out any sign of dissent or desire for democracy.

China's economic growth depended on the manufacture of consumer goods for export to the rest of the world. By 1995 some

MALL OF AMERICA (LEFT) *in Bloomington, Indiana. The largest shopping mall in the United States, it could offer 7 km (4.3 miles) of shop fronts, a wedding chapel, Legoland, amusement arcades and restaurants – the ultimate shopping experience.*

CAPITALISM COMES TO MOSCOW (RIGHT) *Fast food outlets such as Pizza Hut and McDonald's catered for a vast new market in the former communist world. In 1992 a Big Mac hamburger bought in Pushkin Square cost the average customer a day's wages.*

SIGNS OF THE TIMES *Hong Kong* (ABOVE), *one of the most successful economies of East Asia, was due to be returned to China by Britain in 1997. The small, crowded islands represented a triumph of capitalism on the communist coast. China gave assurances that Hong Kong's autonomy would be respected; its promise of economic partnership is shown on the poster at the border* (BELOW).

60 per cent of toys for the international market were made in southern China, where 3000 factories were staffed by more than a million workers, most of them young women. Their wages were lower than those that would have been paid to workers in most other countries, but they were for the first time earning money that enabled them to make consumer choices of their own.

Some of the companies whose products were being made in Asia were household names in the West. They were part of a new approach to manufacturing that no longer heeded national or even continental boundaries. The rapid developments in international communications systems and the removal of trade barriers meant that multinational companies could choose where to process raw materials, where to make the components, and where to assemble goods of all kinds – from toys to cars. These companies grew ever larger and ever richer; by 1992 the 500 largest companies between them accounted for nearly a third of the world's total gross domestic product, and nearly three-quarters of world trade; more than half of the 'greenhouse emissions' produced by global industry

were the result of their activities. In 1993 up to 90 per cent of trade in a wide range of commodities – cocoa, coffee, copper, cotton, iron ore, pineapples, tea, tobacco – was controlled by no more than six giant corporations, whose activities affected numerous small farmers, craftsmen and shopkeepers in the developing world. As the wealth of the multinationals grew, so did their economic power. Accountable only to their shareholders, these companies began to replace governments as shapers of the world economy. At a time of rising unemployment, people in industrialized countries were also affected: as the multinationals sought cheaper labour for their factories, unemployment in developed nations increased.

Eager to play their part in the world economy, and to improve trade as a way of acquiring foreign currency and reducing their debts, many developing countries set up special Export Processing Zones (EPZs) to attract multinational corporations. While there were benefits for the host nations, conditions for the workers were often poor, and the countries themselves became more vulnerable to fluctuations in world markets. This was true in predominantly agricultural countries as well, where farmers were encouraged to abandon subsistence crops such as maize or sweet potatoes in favour of cash crops such as coffee or exotic vegetables to stock the shelves of Western supermarkets. Their customers had an ever greater range of goods to choose from, and once-seasonal fresh foods could now be obtained all year round.

TOYS FOR EXPORT
Barbie dolls being packed in a toy factory in Indonesia. By the end of the 1980s no Barbie dolls were made in the United States: they were all manufactured in South America and East Asia.

These efforts ensured that during the 1980s and 1990s more countries – in Central and South America and particularly in parts of Asia – began to share in the new prosperity, though much of Africa was being left behind. The poorest developing countries came under pressure from the international lending organizations such as the World Bank to carry out what was called 'structural adjustment': cutting public expenditure to reduce state budgets, deficits and inflation. Investment in education and welfare was reduced; the one area where cuts were not made was in defence budgets – they absorbed ever higher proportions of national wealth in many countries, including those that could least afford it.

The result of all these economic and political changes was that across the world in almost every country, developing and developed, the gap between rich and poor widened.

CHILDREN OF THE STREET

THE PLACARD LEFT BY THE BODY of a boy killed on a beach in Rio de Janeiro read: 'I killed you because you had no future'. In the 1980s and 1990s in the cities of Brazil, where many street children died violent deaths at the hands of the authorities, it was the police, rather than poverty or loneliness, that those whose home was on the street most feared.

As the populations of the world's cities grew during the century, so the numbers of young people living in them rose. Both in industrialized and in developing countries, the numbers of children working and even living on the streets also grew. By the mid-1990s there were millions of them; it was impossible to calculate exactly how many. The highest number, about two million children, were estimated to be in Brazil; there were large numbers elsewhere in some countries in Central and South America, particularly in Colombia, Guatemala and Mexico. There were street children in India, many of them belonging to families known as 'pavement dwellers'; and others in Ethiopia and Sudan, in Sri Lanka and Vietnam.

Most of the children were forced onto the streets by poverty, having to help support their families by selling roasted peanuts, cleaning car windscreens or 'guarding' cars, shining shoes

or begging. These children went home at night. A small minority had abandoned or been abandoned by their families, and had to find what care and companionship they could among other street children. In industrial countries they were most often runaways escaping family discord. An estimated 80 per cent of North American homeless children had left because they had been physically or sexually abused; this was said to be true of only 20 per cent of street children in Central and South America. In the developed world there were about the same number of street girls as street boys, whereas in cities of the developing world the vast majority were boys.

Concern for the children's fate led to a number of projects to help them, and they also took initiatives of their own. In 1985 the National Movement of Street Boys and Girls was founded in Brazil. The second national meeting, in 1989, exposed the authorized killing of children; the resulting publicity forced the government to recognize what was taking place. In Guatemala the staff of Covenant House (Casa Alianza), an organization set up in the mid-1980s to offer shelter to street children, decided to document the violence after a child was kicked to death by four policemen. When they publicized the violence and attempted to prosecute the perpetrators, the workers themselves received death threats.

Many children encountered hostility not only from the authorities but also from the general public, who saw them as drug-abusing, violent delinquents. But the street children – like all the other children whose childhoods were being disrupted by famine or exploitation, or the traumas of war – did not create the world in which they were growing up. Living on its margins, they merely reflected it.

HANGING ON *Street children in Rio de Janeiro, Brazil. All street children were at risk of violence, abuse and exploitation by adults and older children. Many of those with no other prospects drifted into crime as they grew up.*

THE INTERNATIONAL AIRPORT *at Orly, near Paris. In the early 1990s it was Europe's third busiest airport – after London Heathrow and Frankfurt am Main in Germany – with more than twenty-three million passengers a year. As air traffic increased, airports became increasingly congested not only in the terminals but in the air above, and computer-controlled air traffic control systems became more sophisticated and complex.*

The shrinking world

The changing patterns of world trade would not have taken place without the technological revolution that accompanied them. At the beginning of the century it had been the discovery and the many applications of electricity that had the greatest potential and brought about the most dramatic technological change. In the 1990s technological innovation continued, and at an increasingly rapid pace. The exploration of space, developed during the Cold War years, had led to a greater understanding of the outer world; this was being matched by an unparalleled exploration of our inner world: the workings of the human body.

The most dramatic impact on people's lives was to come through the electronics and computer revolution. The computer developed from advances in mathematics, miniaturization, silicon chemistry, engineering and many other fields. In the 1980s the manufacture and widespread use of personal computers made it possible for individuals as well as companies to link up around the world faster and more cheaply than ever before. The giant dustfree

SURFING THE NET at the Cyberia Internet Café in London. It was impossible to establish how many people were using the Internet by the mid 1990s; estimates varied from sixteen million to forty million, and the number was said to be doubling every year. Users could gain almost instant access to an extraordinary range of information and activities.

mainframe computers of the 1960s had centralized power in large institutions, and had to be operated by white-coated specialists; the personal computer dispersed power to individuals. Anyone able to afford the hardware (which became cheaper every year) could word-process, calculate, operate spreadsheets, and access databases of every kind. Huge amounts of information could be processed and transmitted in seconds. By the early 1990s people in almost every field – from shopkeepers to doctors and tyre-fitters to financiers – were using computers in their work. Children were taught how to use them in school, and enjoyed the games that could be played on them at home.

By the early 1990s the personal computer was being transformed from a self-contained desktop tool to a gateway to every other computer in the world via the Internet. People around the world could now communicate directly and instantaneously with each other for little more than the cost of a local telephone call. The Internet began as a United States military project to develop a communications system that would not be destroyed in the event of a nuclear attack. In the late 1970s the system was opened up to other government departments, and to research organizations and universities. In 1992 permission was granted to private companies to offer subscriptions giving individuals access to information on the Internet. Access to the Internet began to grow most rapidly in the prosperous West, and also became available elsewhere in the world: India and South Korea opened up a full service; and it was spreading in Indonesia and the Philippines.

It was too early to predict the full impact of this technology. Among its probable consequences were the increasing dominance worldwide of 'American' English in business, and the dispersal of 'office work' from city centres to people living and working in small towns and villages. It was already possible to ignore national boundaries and employ people for clerical work in countries where labour costs were lower: American airlines used computer operators in the Caribbean to prepare their tickets, and British banks sent figures to be processed overnight in India.

By the mid-1990s it was clear that the computer revolution was still only beginning. In addition to numerical data (military and intelligence information,

GREEN FUEL *While the roads became ever busier, attempts were made to reduce the noxious effects of vehicle exhaust emissions. One of these was unleaded petrol.*

The silver disc

COMPACT DISCS *were first launched in 1980; by the end of the decade the sale of discs was already overtaking that of vinyl records. They offered improved sound quality, and because they were read by a laser beam rather than having a needle running in a groove, did not wear out. They could store vast amounts of information, and were soon used not just for music recordings but as an alternative to books and videos, combining text, graphics, sound and animation.*

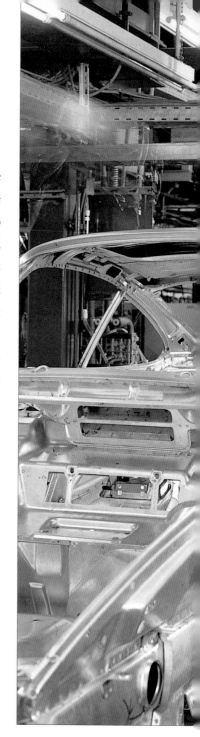

ROBOTS ON THE LINE (ABOVE) *The heavy, hot, repetitive work of making cars, such as this Porsche in Germany, was undertaken faster and more accurately by robots than by humans.*

SCANNING THE BRAIN (RIGHT) *A medical technician examines the brain of a patient at a New York hospital. Non-invasive diagnostic techniques were a valuable medical tool.*

MAPPING OUR GENES

FOR MUCH OF THE TWENTIETH CENTURY, the exploration of space was one of the most exciting scientific adventures. By the late 1980s another kind of exploration was taking place that was likely to have a huge impact on the future of the human race.

The instruction manual of the human body is written in a chemical code found in the nucleus of cells. These coded messages determine our biological inheritance: our appearance, our inherent abilities, our predisposition for different diseases, and much more. This chemical instruction manual is known as DNA – deoxyribonucleic acid. The structure of DNA was discovered in the 1950s; within its structure, which is like a spiral ladder, are the units – called genes – that carry the coded instructions for the individual characteristics of every organism. During the 1980s a research project was initiated whose aim was to map the genetic code of human beings. Such a huge and costly venture needed international cooperation, and in 1988 the Human Genome Organization (HUGO) was established; by 1990 it already had 250 members – all research scientists – from twenty-three countries.

A complete genome map would cover the whole of the DNA sequence, but this would be prohibitively expensive. As only 2 per cent of the entire sequence of DNA consists of active genes, about 100 000 in all, it was decided to concentrate on these. The messages of the genetic code are 'written' in pairs of chemical bases; a short message would consist of a few hundred bases, while long ones require many thousands. By the end of 1995 more than five million bases had been identified – still only a fraction of the total.

From the outset the most compelling reason for the research was to help eradicate inherited disease. There are thousands of these diseases, including asthma, certain cancers, cystic fibrosis, haemophilia and sickle-cell anaemia. It is 'mistakes' in the message of a particular gene that can trigger the disease in an individual.

While some scientists undertook the painstaking work of mapping the genes, others developed techniques to change them. Genetic engineering speeds up the process that naturally takes place in any sort of selective breeding – long used to produce more fragrant or colourful flowers, crops with greater yields or improved animal breeds. Selective breeding works only within a species; genetic engineering can transfer characteristics between very different species – a process was developed to produce insulin, the hormone humans need to regulate sugar in the blood, within genetically engineered bacteria. By the mid-1990s the possibilities of gene therapy were offering new hope to many thousands of people. There was some concern about the ethical implications of genetic engineering, yet it might also prove enormously beneficial, perhaps improving the health of entire populations by correcting the faults in genes that carry disease from generation to generation.

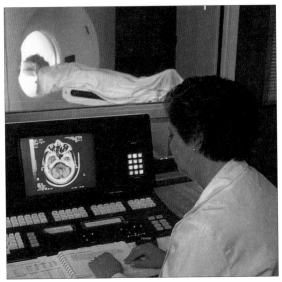

FROZEN CONTINENT (ABOVE) *A biologist undertakes research in the harsh conditions of Ross Island on the coast of Antarctica. Activities other than scientific research were banned for fifty years in 1991. The continent is of particular interest to environmental scientists, as its thick covering of ice – an average of 2000 metres (6500 feet) deep – holds the history of the Earth's atmosphere.*

VIRTUAL REALITY (LEFT) *first became available in March 1993. This uniquely interactive form of computer entertainment was hailed as an exciting new experience – and as an addictive hi-tech hallucinogen.*

SPACE LAUNCH (OPPOSITE) *A satellite is released from a space shuttle cargo bay. The first manned space flight took place in 1966; in 1981 the space shuttle, the first manned spacecraft designed to be reused, was launched. Space programmes were developed for both military and scientific purposes.*

telephone banking, scientific calculations, commercial transactions) voice communication, music, maps, still and moving images could be translated into digital information, stored, retrieved and reproduced at amazing speed.

The computer was not the only important technology of the late twentieth century. During the previous hundred years, people's lives had been changed as much by the achievements of medical scientists as by those of engineers and physicists, and now biotechnology promised further possibilities for curing disease. Some people embraced the new possibilities; others urged caution, and called for more stringent ethical and environmental controls.

By the 1990s concerns about the environment had become a constant reminder that the development of new technologies could be dangerous as well as beneficial, and that their effects were often not understood at the time; like so much else, it had become a global issue. Scientists and environmentalists increasingly agreed that uncontrolled human activity was damaging the Earth, and that the carbon dioxide emissions resulting from industrial activity were likely to bring about dramatic, potentially disastrous climatic change. It was feared that over-consumption of water would threaten whole regions, and water shortages provoke conflicts as dangerous as earlier wars over land and oil.

On the brink of the new millennium, humans could for the first time truly be said to be living in the global village, where the actions of people in one country directly impinged on those in other countries. Technological advances challenged the power of institutions; governments could no longer so easily restrict their citizens' access to information, or pursue policies in isolation. Fast, cheap communication enhanced people's opportunities to take part in the global economy, and education and skills became increasingly important: in time, the world would be divided between the information haves and have-nots. Many people faced an ambiguous future, and lived poised between fear and hope in a world of rapid change. As Donald Hodge, who had grown up in the early years of the century, reflects, 'It is an entirely new world ….Everything has changed – the outlook of people, aspects of communication. The world has shrunk down to a tiny ball now, where once it used to extend so far.'

Acknowledgements

Television

Executive Producers
Peter Pagnamenta (BBC)
Zvi Dor-Ner (WGBH)

Archive Producer
Christine Whittaker

Programme Producers
Archie Baron, John Bridcut, Daniel Brittain-Catlin, Peter Ceresole, Graham Chedd, Jenny Clayton, Mark J. Davis, James DeVinney, Sally Doganis, Charles Furneaux, Angela Holdsworth, Bill Treharne Jones, Jonathan Lewis, Ben Loeterman, Angus Macqueen, Marian Marzynski, Anne Moir, Max Whitby

Assistant Producers
Rosalind Bain, Robi Dutta, Nancy Fraser, Harry Gural, Nathan Z. Hendrie, Isobel Hinshelwood, Kevin Huffman, Lisa Jones, Marcus Kiggell, Kathleen Kouril, Gabrielle Osrin, Dominic Ozanne, Liana Pomeranzev, Sun Shuyun, Jonathan Smith, Tony Stiker, Amy Tarr, Eddie Tulasiewicz, Sarah Wallis, Armorer Wason

Film Researchers
James Barker, Michaela Barnes, Maggi Cook, Alex Cowan, Alexandra Crapanzano, Carol Davis-Foster, Deborah Ford, Hilary Goldhammer, Susan Levene, Jill McLoughlin, Lynn Mason, Masha Oleneva, Alf Penn, Alison Smith, David Thaxton, Jeanette Woods

Film Editors
David Berenson, Guy Crossman, Graham Dean, Sally Hilton, Margaret Kelly, Alison Lewis, Roderick Longhurst, Jon Neuburger, James Rutenbeck, Charles Scott, David Simpson, Beth Solomon, Guy Tetzner

Supervising Film Editor
Steve Sampson

Series Managers (London)
Carol Harding
Candida Pryce-Jones

Production Managers (Boston)
Kathy Shugrue
Kathleen Shugrue

Core Team
Laura Azevedo, Sheoko Badman-Walker, Sally Ball, Alexandra Branson, James Dobel, Jill Flippance, Alison Lewis, Sue MacGregor, Fiona Mellon-Grant, Rachel Solman, Alison Whitlock

Publishing

People's Century was produced for BBC Worldwide Publishing by

B·C·S Publishing Limited, Chesterton, Oxfordshire

Editorial Director
Candida Hunt

Art Director
Steve McCurdy

Editors
Deena Daher, Jo Newson, Clare Ramos, Jenny Roberts

Assistant Editors
Tabitha Jackson, Helen McCurdy, Rebecca Simor

Design
Jerry Goldie

Picture Research
Alexander Goldberg and James Clift of Image Select (London), David Pratt

Illustrations
Julian Baker

Index
Sarah Ereira

Picture credits

10 Topham Picture Source, 12 Popperfoto, 12/13 Hulton Getty, 13 *(top)* ET Archive, 13 *(bottom)* Roger Viollet, 14 *(top)* ET Archive, 14 *(bottom)* Ann Ronan at Image Select, 15 Corbis/Bettmann, 16 *(top)* Corbis/Bettmann, 16 *(bottom)* Corbis/Bettmann, 17 *(left)* Ellis Island, 17 *(middle)* Yetta Sperling, 17 *(right)* Ellis Island, 18 *(top)* Amy Sears, 18 *(bottom)* Mary Evans Picture Library, 18/19 Ann Ronan at Image Select, 19 Hulton Getty, 20 *(top)* Elmie Steever, 20 *(middle)* Elmie Steever, 20 *(bottom)* Corbis/Bettmann, 21 *(top)* Arthur Whitlock, 21 *(middle)* Army & Navy, 21 *(bottom)* Ulster Museum, 22 *(bottom)* Cadbury Ltd, 22/23 Corbis/Bettmann, 23 Hulton Getty, 24 *(left)* Hulton Getty, 24 *(right)* Hulton Getty, 25 Ann Ronan at Image Select, 26 Australian War Memorial, 28 Hulton Getty, 28/29 ET Archive, 29 Image Select, 30 *(left)* Bayerisches Armee-museum, Ingolstadt, 30 *(right)* AKG Berlin, 30/31 Robert Harding Picture Library, 31 Australian War Memorial, 32 *(top)* Albert Powis, 32 *(middle)* Albert Powis, 32 *(bottom)* Robert Harding Picture Library, 33 ET Archive, 34 *(top)* Image Select, 34 *(left)* Peter Newark's Military Pictures, 34 *(bottom)* AKG Berlin, 36 *(top)* Ernst Weckerling/Julian Baldwin, 36 *(bottom)* Ernst Weckerling, 36/37 Image Select, 37 *(top)* Image Select, 37 *(middle)* Walter Hare, 37 *(bottom)* Norman Tennant, 37 *(inset)* Norman Tennant/Julian Baldwin, 38 *(top)* Tela Burt/Tony Mayne, 38 *(middle)* Tela Burt, 38 *(bottom)* Image Select, 40 Peter Newark's Military Pictures, 40/41 The Bridgeman Art Library/Imperial War Museum, 42 *(left)* Andrew N. Gagg ARPS, 42/43 *(top)* Mary Evans Picture Library, 42/43 *(bottom)* ET Archive, 43 *(top)* Walter Hare/Julian Baldwin, 43 *(middle)* Walter Hare, 44 *(top)* Peter Newark's Military Pictures, 44/45 Topham Picture Source, 45 The Trustees of the Imperial War Museum, 46 *(top)* Imperial War Museum, 46 *(bottom)* Bettmann Archive, 46/47 Popperfoto, 48 AKG Berlin, 49 AKG Berlin, 50 Archiv Gerstenberg, 52 *(top)* David King Collection, 52 *(bottom)* Novosti (London), 53 David King Collection, 54 The Bridgeman Art Library, 54/55 Alexander Briansky, 55 Alexander Briansky, 55 David King Collection, 56 *(top)* Archiv Gerstenberg, 56 *(bottom)* Novosti (London), 57 Department of Politics, Glasgow University, 58 Archiv Gerstenberg, 58/59 David King Collection, 59 Archiv Gerstenberg, 60 *(top)* Novosti (London), 60 *(bottom)* David King Collection, 61 *(top)* David King Collection, 61 *(bottom)* Novosti (London), 62 *(left)* Ella Shistyer, 62 *(right)* Ella Shistyer, 63 *(top)* Novosti (London), 63 *(bottom)* Novosti (London), 64 Novosti (London), 65 Archiv Gerstenberg, 66 *(bottom)* Novosti (London), 66/67 Roger Viollet, 67 Roger Viollet, 68 David King Collection, 69 David King Collection, 70

(bottom) Boris Yefimov, 70/71 David King Collection, 71 David King Collection, 72 David King Collection, 72/73 David King Collection, 74 ET Archive, 76 *(left)* US National Archives, 76 *(bottom)* Imperial War Museum, 77 Hulton Getty, 78 *(top)* Topham Picture Source, 78 *(bottom)* Culver Pictures, 79 AKG Berlin, 80 Mary Evans Picture Library, 80/81 Topham Picture Source, 82 Topham Picture Source, 83 *(right)* US National Archives, 83 *(bottom)* *The Tacoma Daily News*, 84 Hulton Getty, 86 Edimedia, 87 *(top)* Kobal Collection, 87 *(bottom)* Topham Picture Source, 88 Ann Ronan at Image Select, 88/89 Hulton Getty, 89 Peter Newark's Military Pictures, 90 *(top)* Peace Pledge Union, London, 90 *(middle)* Donald Soper, 90 *(bottom)* Hulton Getty, 90/91 Topham Picture Source, 91 Robert Harding Library, 92 *(top)* Karl Nagerl, 92 *(bottom)* Karl Nagerl, 93 Hulton Getty, 94 Karl Nagerl, 95 *(top)* Geffrye Museum, 95 *(bottom)* AKG Berlin, 96 *(left)* ET Archive, 96 *(right)* Peter Newark's Military Pictures, 97 Hulton Getty, 98 Ford Motor Company, 100 *(top)* AKG Berlin, 100 *(bottom)* AKG Berlin, 100/101 Corbis/Bettmann, 102 *(top)* Ford Motor Company, 102 *(bottom)* Corbis/Bettmann, 103 *(top)* Ford Motor Company, 103 *(middle)* Archie Acciacca, 103 *(bottom)* Corbis/Bettmann, 104 Fiat, 105 Mary Evans Picture Library, 106 Fiat, 106/107 Popperfoto, 107 Les Gurl, 108 Ford Motor Company, 108/109 Ford Motor Company, 109 Corbis/Bettmann, 110 AKG London, 111 *(left)* Corbis/Bettmann, 111 *(top)* Espedito Valli, 111 *(bottom)* Espedito Valli, 112 AKG London, 112/113 Corbis/Bettmann, 113 *(right)* Paul Boatin, 114 Steven Richvalsky, 115 Corbis/Bettmann, 116 Fiat, 117 Corbis/Bettmann, 118 *(top)* Zenaide Provins, 118 *(bottom)* Zenaide Provins/Archie Baron, 119 *(top)* Corbis/Bettmann, 119 *(bottom)* Corbis/Bettmann, 120 Corbis/Bettmann, 121 Corbis/Bettmann, 122 Caruso, 124 Mary Evans Picture Library, 125 *(left)* Hulton Getty, 125 *(right)* Hulton Getty, 126 *(top)* Joe Liguori, 126 *(middle)* Joe Liguori, 126/127 Corbis/Bettmann, 127 *(top)* JL Charmet, 127 *(bottom)* Corbis/Bettmann, 128 Hulton Getty, 128/129 Hulton Getty, 129 *(top)* NBC, 129 *(bottom)* Sidney Garner, 130 Hulton Getty, 130/131 Hulton Getty, 131 *(top)* Diego Lucero, 131 *(middle)* Diego Lucero, 131 *(bottom)* Allsport, 132 *(left)* Caruso, 132 *(right)* Caruso, 132 *(bottom)* Hulton Getty, 133 *(top)* Baseball Hall of Fame, 133 *(bottom)* Corbis/Bettmann, 134 *(top)* Anna Freund, 134 *(middle)* Anna Freund, 134 *(bottom)* Corbis/Bettmann, 135 NBC, 136 Hulton Getty, 136/137 Mirror/Telegraph Newspapers, 137 Mary Evans Picture Library, 138 Hulton Getty, 138/139 Corbis/Bettmann, 139 Corbis/Bettmann, 140 Corbis/Bettmann, 141 NBC,

142/143 Edimedia, 143 *(top)* Helen Stephens, 143 *(middle)* Corbis/Bettmann, 143 *(lower middle)* Allsport, 143 *(bottom)* Baltimore Afro-American, 144 NBC, 145 Corbis/Bettmann, 146 AKG Berlin, 148 Popperfoto, 149 Corbis/Bettmann, 150 *(top)* Edimedia, 150 *(bottom)* Waddingtons, 150/151 Edimedia, 151 Edimedia, 152 Edimedia, 152/153 Edimedia, 154 Hulton Getty, 155 *(top)* Hulton Getty, 155 *(right)* Corbis/Bettmann, 157 *(left)* Corbis/Bettmann, 157 *(top)* Chilean Biblioteca Naçional, 157 *(bottom)* Chilean Biblioteca Naçional, 158 Humphrey Spender, 159 *(top)* Con Shiels/Archie Baron, 159 *(middle)* Con Shiels, 159 *(bottom)* Hulton Getty, 160 Hulton Getty, 161 Edimedia, 162 *(left)* Tore Alespong/Archie Baron, 162/163 *(top)* Swedish Labour Movement Archives, 162/163 *(bottom)* Tore Alespong, 163 *(top)* Göta Rosén/Archie Baron, 163 *(bottom)* Göta Rosén, 164 *(left)* Edimedia, 164 *(top right)* Bill Bailey/Archie Baron, 164 *(right middle)* Bill Bailey, 164/165 Corbis/Bettmann, 166 Corbis/Bettmann, 166/167 AKG Berlin, 167 DC Comics, 168 *(top)* Mancil Milligan/Archie Baron, 168 *(bottom)* Mancil Milligan, 169 Corbis/Bettmann, 170 Photofest, 172 BFI, 172/173 Image Select, 173 Corbis/Bettmann, 174 *(top)* Corbis/Bettmann, 174 *(middle)* Image Select, 174 *(bottom)* Danny Patt, 175 *(left)* AKG London, 175 *(right)* AKG London, 176 AKG London, 177 Peter Aprahamian, 178 *(top)* Image Select, 178 *(bottom)* The Bridgeman Art Library, 179 Corbis/Bettmann, 180 Corbis/Bettmann, 180/181 Corbis/Bettmann, 181 AKG London, 182 *(bottom)* Corbis/Bettmann, 182 *(top)* Image Select, 183 Corbis/Bettmann, 184 *(left)* BFI, 184 *(right)* Rajam Ramanathan, 184 *(bottom)* AKG London, 185 Image Select, 186 *(left)* Cy Locke, 186 *(bottom)* Corbis/Bettmann, 186/187 Popperfoto, 187 *(top)* Image Select, 187 *(bottom)* Corbis/Bettmann, 188 *(top)* Robert Opie, 188 *(bottom)* Popperfoto, 189 *(top)* Walt Disney/Mirror Syndication International, 189 *(bottom)* Popperfoto, 190 O. Winston Link, 191 Image Select, 192 Hulton Getty, 194 Hulton Getty, 196 *(top)* AKG Berlin, 196 *(bottom)* AKG Berlin, 197 *(left)* AKG Berlin, 197 *(right)* AKG Berlin, 198 Hulton Getty, 198/199 Hulton Getty, 199 AKG Berlin, 200 *(top)* Imperial War Museum, 200 *(middle)* Reinhard Spitzy/Jonathan Lewis, 200 *(bottom)* Reinhard Spitzy, 201 AKG Berlin, 202 *(top)* Bundesarchiv, 202 *(bottom)* Pressens Bild, 203 AKG Berlin, 204 *(top)* Gerda Bodenheimer/Jonathan Lewis, 204 *(middle)* Gerda Bodenheimer, 204 *(bottom)* Hulton Getty, 204/205 YIVO Institute for Jewish Research, New York, 206 Hulton Getty, 207 *(left)* Anna-Maria Ernst, 207 *(right)* Ann-Marie Ernst/Jonathan Lewis, 207 *(bottom)* Bundesarchiv, 208 Wiener Library, 208/209 Niedersächsische Tageszeitung Hannover, 210 *(top)* Hulton Getty,

210 *(bottom)* AKG Berlin, 212 Edimedia, 213 *(top)* AKG Berlin, 213 *(middle)* Hans Margules, 213 *(bottom)* Hans Margules, 214 *(top)* Edimedia, 214 *(bottom)* The Jewish Museum, Prague, 215 Edimedia, 216 Hulton Getty, 217 AKG Berlin, 218 Hulton Getty, 220 *(top)* Hulton Getty, 220 *(bottom)* Hulton Getty, 220/221 *(top)* Corbis/Bettmann, 221 *(middle)* Hulton Getty, 221 Imperial War Museum, 222 *(top)* Hulton Getty, 222 *(bottom)* AKG Berlin, 224 Hulton Getty, 225 AKG London, 226 Hulton Getty, 227 *(top)* Mary Evans Picture Library, 227 *(bottom)* Hulton Getty, 228 *(top)* Sid Newham/Lisa Jones, 228 *(middle)* Sid Newham, 228 *(bottom)* Hulton Getty, 229 *(top right)* Margarete Zettel/Lisa Jones, 229 *(bottom right)* Margarete Zettel, 229 *(left)* Hulton Getty, 230 Hulton Getty, 230/231 Victor Cole, 231 *(left)* Victor Cole, 231 *(middle)* Victor Cole, 231 *(bottom)* Edimedia, 232 *(top)* AKG London, 232 *(bottom)* Hulton Getty, 233 *(top)* Edimedia, 233 *(bottom)* Kieko Saotome, 234 *(top)* Leonid Galperin, 234 *(bottom)* Leonid Galperin, 235 *(top)* Edimedia, 235 *(bottom)* Novosti London, 236 Edimedia, 236/237 Novosti London, 237 Edimedia, 238 *(top)* Hulton Getty, 238 *(bottom)* Hulton Getty, 239 Hulton Getty, 240 Hulton Getty, 240/241 Hulton Getty, 242 US National Archives, 244 Bettmann, 244/245 AKG Berlin, 245 *(left)* Anatoly Semiriaga, 245 *(right)* Anatoly Semiriaga, 246 *(top)* Corbis/Bettmann, 246 *(middle)* Topham Picture Source, 247 *(left)* Bettmann, 247 *(right)* Bettmann, 248 Hulton Getty, 249 University of Canterbury, 250 School of Slavonic Studies, 251 Edimedia, 252 *(top)* Gail Halverson, 252 *(middle)* Gail Halverson, 252 *(bottom)* Bettmann, 253 AKG Berlin, 254 *(top)* Tamara Banketik, 254 *(bottom)* Tamara Banketik, 255 Novosti London, 256 *(left)* Alexei Kozlov, 256 *(right)* Alexei Kozlov, 257 Hulton Getty, 258 *(top)* Manny Fried, 258 *(middle)* Manny Fried, 258 *(bottom)* Manny Fried, 258/259 US National Archives, 259 *(left)* Kobal Collection, 259 Bettmann, 260 AKG Berlin, 261 Bettmann, 262 AKG Berlin, 262/263 AKG Berlin, 263 *(left)* Hulton Getty, 263 *(right)* AKG Berlin, 264 *(top)* Anita Möller, 264 *(middle)* Anita Möller, 264 *(bottom)* AKG Berlin, 265 Hulton Getty, 266 Advertising Archive, 268 Popperfoto, 269 *(top)* Topham Picture Source, 269 *(bottom)* Topham Picture Source, 270/271 Topham Picture Source, 271 Edimedia, 272 *(top)* Raymond Jolivet, 272 *(bottom)* Raymond Jolivet, 273 *(top)* SAIS Bologna School, 273 *(bottom)* Popperfoto, 274 Popperfoto, 275 *(top)* Advertising Archive, 275 *(bottom)* Corbis/Bettmann, 276 *(left)* Advertising Archive, 276/277 Popperfoto, 277 *(bottom)* Topham Picture Source, 277 *(right)* Bettmann, 278 *(top)* Advertising Archive, 278 *(bottom)* Gamma, 279 Bettmann, 280 *(top)* Bill Braga, 280 *(bottom)* Corbis/Bettmann, 281 AKG Berlin, 282 *(top)* Ludwiggsen Associates Ltd, 282 *(bottom)* Popperfoto, 283 Popperfoto, 284 Edimedia, 285

(top) Edimedia, 285 *(bottom)* Farabolafoto, 286 *(top)* SAIS Bologna School, 286 *(middle)* Gerardo Ciola, 286 *(bottom)* Gerardo Ciola, 288 Popperfoto, 289 Camera Press, 290 Hulton Getty, 292 *(top)* Mary Evans Picture Library, 292 *(bottom)* Popperfoto, 294 Hulton Getty, 294/295 Popperfoto, 295 Indian Press & Information Bureau, 296 *(top)* Anim Assiful, 296 *(bottom)* Popperfoto, 297 Hulton Getty, 298 Hulton Getty, 299 Popperfoto, 300 Magnum, 301 Popperfoto, 302 Popperfoto, 303 Popperfoto, 304 Popperfoto, 305 *(top)* Hulton Getty, 305 *(bottom)* Edimedia, 306/307 Popperfoto, 307 *(left)* Komla Gbedema, 307 *(right)* Popperfoto, 308 Hulton Getty, 309 *(top)* Popperfoto, 310 *(left)* Popperfoto, 310/311 Popperfoto, 311 John Hill Agency Ltd, 312 Popperfoto, 313 Popperfoto 314 Gamma, 316 *(top)* Corbis /Bettmann, 316 *(bottom)* Corbis/Bettmann, 317 *(top)* Gamma, 317 *(bottom)* Hulton Getty, 319 *(left)* Aleksei Kondratiev, 319 *(right)* Popperfoto, 320 *(top)* Thomas Saffer, 320 *(bottom)* Thomas Saffer, 320/321 US National Marine Archive, 321 Popperfoto, 322/323 Advertising Archives, 323 Popperfoto, 324 *(top)* Sheldon Johnson, 324 *(middle)* Sheldon Johnson, 324 *(bottom)* US National Archives, 325 *(top)* Periodicals Art Library, 325 *(middle)* Periodicals Art Library, 325 *(bottom)* Popperfoto, 326 *(top)* Corbis/Bettmann, 326 *(bottom)* Hulton Getty, 326/327 Popperfoto, 328 *(top)* CND, 328 *(bottom)* Hulton Getty, 328/329 Kobal Collection, 330/331 Gamma, 331 Gamma, 332 *(top)* Valery Staradumov, 332 *(bottom)* Valery Staradumov, 333 Novosti/Gamma, 334 Gamma, 335 *(left)* Leonid Teliatnikov, 335 *(right)* Leonid Teliatnikov, 336 Gamma, 337 Gamma, 338 Hulton Getty, 340 *(top)* Corbis/Bettmann, 340 *(bottom)* Hulton Getty, 341 *(top)* Hulton Getty, 341 *(bottom)* Hulton Getty, 342/343 Magnum, 343 *(left)* Hulton Getty, 343 *(right)* Werner Bischof/Magnum, 344 Werner Bischolf/Magnum, 345 Magnum, 346 Image Select/Sony, 346/347 Corbis/Bettmann, 347 Spectrum, 348 Spectrum, 348/349 Magnum, 349 *(left)* Magnum, 349 *(centre)* Nobuko and Taisuke Sato/Tim Humphries, 349 *(right)* Japanese Embassy, London, 350 Hulton Getty, 350/351 Hulton Getty, 351 *(top)* Hulton Getty, 351 *(bottom left)* Takunori Nagaoka, 351 *(bottom right)* Takunori Nagaoka, 352 Hulton Getty, 352/353 Images, 354 Hulton Getty, 355 *(top)* René Burri/Magnum, 355 *(bottom)* Philip Jones Griffiths/Magnum, 356 Marilyn Silverstone/Magnum, 356/357 Gamma, 357 *(top)* Yi Chong Kak/Tim Humphries, 357 *(bottom)* Yi Chong Kak/Tim Humphries, 358 René Burri/Magnum, 358/359 James Nachtwey /Magnum, 359 *(left)* Kang Sung Ro, 359 *(right)* Kang Sung Ro, 360 Hutchison, 361 Gamma, 362 Ian Berry/Magnum, 364 *(top)* Publisher's Photo Source, 364 *(bottom)* Popperfoto, 365 Corbis/Bettmann, 366/367 Popperfoto, 367 *(left)* Popperfoto, 367 *(right)* Popperfoto, 368/369

Corbis/Bettmann, 369 *(top)* Corbis/Bettmann, 369 *(bottom)* Bernard Lafayette, 370/371 Corbis/Bettmann, 371 *(top)* Ernest Green, 371 *(bottom)* Corbis/Bettmann, 372 Popperfoto, 373 *(top)* Floyd Mann, 373 *(middle)* Floyd Mann, 373 *(bottom)* Magnum, 374 Hulton Getty, 375 Corbis /Bettmann, 376 Popperfoto, 376/377 Camera Press, 377 *(top)* Popperfoto, 377 *(middle)* David Bruce, 377 *(bottom)* David Bruce, 378/379 Magnum, 379 Popperfoto, 380 *(top)* Hulton Getty, 380 *(bottom)* Gamma, 381 Gamma, 382 Hulton Getty, 383 *(top)* Gamma, 383 *(bottom)* Gamma, 384 *(top)* Popperfoto, 384 *(bottom)* Nomathamsanqua Koha, 385 Gamma, 386 Image Select, 388 Magnum, 389 *(top)* Toshio Hamada, 389 *(middle)* Hidenori Yamashita, 389 *(bottom)* Hidenori Yamashita/Max Whitby, 390 Hulton Getty, 390/391 BBC, 391 *(top)* Hulton Getty, 391 *(bottom)* Olga Penrose, 392 Lloyd Kiff, 392/393 Hulton Getty, 393 Corbis/Bettmann, 394 Rex Features, 395 *(top)* Magnum, 395 *(bottom)* Magnum, 396/397 Environmental Picture Library, 397 Panos Pictures, 398 Press Association, 398/399 Environmental Picture Library, 400 Environmental Picture Library, 400/401 Liaison, 401 *(top)* Lois Gibbs/Max Whitby, 401 *(bottom)* Liaison, 402 *(top)* Gamma, 402 *(bottom)* Gamma, 403 Gamma, 401 *(top)* Gamma, 404 *(bottom)* Alain Mingam/Gamma, 405 Gamma, 406 *(top)* F. Sherwood Roland, 406 *(middle)* F. Sherwood Roland/Max Whitby, 406 *(bottom)* Gamma, 407 Gamma, 408 Gamma, 409 Patrick Piel/Gamma, 410 Popperfoto, 412 Hulton Getty, 412/413 Archive Photos, 413 Hulton Getty, 414 *(top)* Corbis/Bettmann, 414 *(middle)* Peter Robinson, 414 *(bottom)* Corbis/Bettmann, 415 AKG London, 416/417 Hulton Getty, 417 Archive Photos, 418 *(top)* Lenore's TV Guide, 418 *(middle)* Hulton Getty, 418 *(bottom)* Popperfoto, 419 *(top)* Magnum, 419 *(middle)* Kamila Mouchkova, 419 *(bottom)* Associated Press, 420 *(top)* Alex Azar, 420 *(middle)* Corbis/Bettmann, 420 *(bottom)* Corbis/Bettmann, 421 *(top)* Hulton Getty, 421 *(bottom)* Hulton Getty, 422 *(top)* Hulton Getty, 422 *(bottom)* Advertising Archives, 423 *(top)* Dorothy and Benjamin Berger, *(middle)* Corbis/Bettmann, *(bottom)* Corbis/Bettmann, 424 *(top)* Popperfoto, 424 *(bottom)* Australian National Film & TV Archives, 424/425 Allsport, 426 *(top)* The Vintage Magazine Company, 426 *(middle)* Steliana Stefonoiu, 426 *(bottom)* Corbis Bettmann, 428 Suman Film Company, 428/429 Mark Edwards/Still Pictures, 429 Children's Television Workshop, 430 Associated Press, 431 Camera Press, 432 *(top)* Gamma, 432 *(bottom)* BBC, 433 Network, 434 Hulton Getty, 435 *(top)* Hulton Getty, 436 *(bottom)* Hulton Getty, 437 National Labour Party, 438 Hulton Getty, 438/439 Hulton Getty, 439 *(top)* Marjorie Cave, 439 *(bottom)* Marjorie Cave, 440 *(top)* Corbis/Bettmann, 440 *(bottom)* Corbis/Bettmann, 440/441 Corbis/

Bettmann, **441** *(above)* Deborah Runkle, **441** *(bottom)* Deborah Runkle, **442** *(top)* World Health Organization, **442** *(bottom)* Hulton Getty, **443** Hulton Getty, **444** Gamma, **445** *(top)* World Health Organization, **446** *(bottom)* UNICEF, **446** Gamma, **447** Santosh Basak/ Gamma, **448** *(top)* Santosh Basak/Gamma, **448** *(bottom)* World Health Organization, **450/451** Environmental Picture Library, **452** Jean Michel Turpin/Gamma, **452/453** Hector Mata/ Gamma, **453** Hulton Getty, **454** Gamma, **454/455** SIPA Press, **455** *(top)* Christian Vioujard/Gamma, **455** *(bottom)* Peter Staley, **456** Gamma, **456/457** Art Directors, **458** Peter Newark, **460** Popperfoto, **461** Popperfoto, **462** Cartier Bresson/Magnum, **462/463** Hulton Getty, **464** Popperfoto, **465** Peter Newark, **466/467** Sun Shuyun, **467** *(top left)* Shao Ai Ling, **467** *(bottom left)* Shao Ai Ling/Jenny Clayton, **467** *(right)* Camera Press, **468/469** Cartier Bresson/Magnum, **469** *(top)* Peter Newark, **469** *(bottom)* Camera Press, **470** *(top)* Camera Press, **470** *(bottom)* Camera Press, **471** *(top)* Sun Shuyun, **471** *(bottom)* He Jin Lua and Lian Tianyun/Jenny Clayton, **472** Camera Press, **472/473** Popperfoto, **473** Popperfoto, **474** Hulton Getty, **475** *(top)* Gamma, **475** *(bottom)* Gamma, **476** *(top)* Topham, **476** *(bottom)* David King, **477** *(top)* Tong Xiang Ling, **477** *(middle)* Tong Xiang Ling/Jenny Clayton, **477** *(bottom)* Hulton Getty, **478** Gamma, **478/479** *(top)* Popperfoto, **478/479** *(bottom)* Popperfoto, **480** Corbis/Bettmann, **481** Gamma, **482** Corbis/ Bettmann, **484** Christie's Images, **484/485** Corbis/Bettmann, **485** *(top)* Hulton Getty, **485** *(bottom)* Corbis/Bettmann, **486** *(top)* Marc Ribould/Magnum, **486** *(bottom)* Kobal Collection, **487** *(top)* Hulton Getty, **487** *(middle)* Rogan Taylor, **487** *(bottom)* Hulton Getty, **488** Apple Corporation, **488/489** Hulton Getty, **489** *(top)* Camera Press, **489** *(bottom)* Rex Features, **490** *(top)* Gamma, **490** *(bottom)* Vivian Rothstein, **491** Andromeda (Oxford) Ltd, **492** Gamma, **492/493** Popperfoto, **494** *(top)* Rex Features, **494** *(bottom)* Martine Algier, **495** Camera Press, **496** Leonard Freed/Magnum, **496/497** Redferns, **497** Hulton Getty, **498** *(top)*

Ron Thelin, **498** *(middle)* Ron Thelin, **498** *(bottom)* Corbis/Bettmann, **498/499** Rex Features, **500** *(top)* Rusty Sachs, **500** *(middle)* Rusty Sachs, **500** *(bottom)* Marc Ribould/ Magnum, **500/501** Leonard Freed/Magnum, **501** *(top left)* Gamma, **502** *(top right)* Romain Goupil, **502** *(bottom)* Popperfoto, **502/503** Rex Features, **503** Jeff Jones, **504** Press Association, **505** ZEFA, **506** Corbis/Bettman, **508** Corbis/ Bettmann, **509** Norman Rockwell/Advertising Archives, **510** Advertising Archives, **510/511** Advertising Archives, **511** Magnum, **512** *(left)* Schering Health Care, **512** *(right top)* Anilu Elias, **512** *(right middle)* Anilu Elias, **512/513** Corbis/ Bettmann, Advertising Archives, **514** Claude Sauvageot, **515** *(top left)* Advertising Archives, **515** *(top right)* Advertising Archives, **515** *(middle)* Dusty Roads, **515** *(bottom)* Advertising Archives, **516** *(left)* Amy Coen, **516** *(right)* Amy Coen, **516/517** Magnum, **518** Corbis/ Bettmann, **519** *(top)* Popperfoto, **519** *(bottom)* Gamma, **520** *(left)* Jaqui Ceballos, **520** *(right)* Corbis/Bettmann, **521** Popperfoto, **522** *(top)* Ginnie Whitehill, **522** *(bottom)* Corbis/ Bettmann, **522/523** Gamma, **523** Telegraph Colour Library, **524** Gamma, **524/525** Camera Press, **525** Corbis/Bettmann, **526** Vibhuti Patel, **526/527** Raissa Page/Format, **527** Grameen Bank, **528** *(top)* Popperfoto, **528** *(bottom)* Corbis/Bettmann, **529** Corbis/Bettmann, **530** Claude Francolon/Gamma, **532** *(left top)* Arsenio Garcia/Peter Sainsbury, **532** *(left middle)* Arsenio Garcia, **532** *(left bottom)* Arsenio Garcia, **532** *(right)* Acme Photo, **533** Popperfoto, **534** Corbis/Bettmann, **535** *(top)* AKG London, **535** *(bottom)* Gamma, **536/537** AKG London, **538** *(top)* Corbis/Bettmann, **538** *(bottom)* Camera Press, **538/539** Popperfoto, **539** *(top)* Earl Young, **539** *(bottom)* Earl Young, **540** Popperfoto, **540/541** *(top)* Duong Thanh Phong, **540/541** *(bottom)* Popperfoto, **542** *(top)* Tran Thi Gung, **542** *(middle)* Duong Thanh Phong, **542** *(bottom)* Duong Thanh Phong, **543** Popperfoto, **545** *(top)* Corbis/Bettmann, **545** *(bottom)* Gamma, **546/547** Gamma, **547** Gamma, **548** *(top)* Courtesy of the Ministry of Defence Pattern Room, **548** *(middle)* Hulton

Getty, **548** *(bottom)* Gamma, **549** Gamma, **550** *(top)* Gamma, **550** *(bottom)* Gamma, **551** Gamma, **552** Gamma, **553** Gamma, **554** Rex Features, **556** *(left)* Popperfoto, **556** *(right)* Popperfoto, **556/557** Gamma, **557** Popperfoto, **558/559** Mohamed Lounes/Gamma, **559** Mohamed Lounes/Gamma, **560** Popperfoto, **561** *(top)* Rex Features, **561** *(bottom)* Rex Features, **562** Popperfoto, **563** *(top left)* Popperfoto, **563** *(top right)* Hadi Gaffari, **563** *(bottom)* Rex Features, **564** G. Uzan/Gamma, **565** Gamma, **566/567** Gamma, **567** *(top)* Gamma, **567** *(bottom)* Michel Artault/Gamma, **568** Rex Features, **570** Gamma, **570/571** BBC, **572** Popperfoto, **572/573** Rex Features, **573** Rex Features, **574** *(top)* Yasser Tawfiq, **574** *(bottom)* Rex Features, **574/575** Gamma, **576** Gamma, **577** Gamma, **578** Gamma, **580/581** Magnum, **581** *(top)* Nina Motova, **581** *(bottom)* Nina Motova, **582** *(left)* Hulton Getty, **582** *(right top)* Dietmar Passenheim, **582** *(right bottom)* Dietmar Passenheim, **583** *(top)* Magnum, **583** *(bottom)* Dietmar Passenheim, **584/585** Gamma, **585** Gamma, **586/587** Magnum, **587** *(top)* J. Czarnecki/Gamma, **587** *(bottom)* Zbigniew Lelental, **588** *(top)* Gamma, **588** *(bottom)* Yevgeny Mahaev, **588/589** Gamma, **590** Gamma, **591** Gamma, **592** *(bottom)* Bärbel Reinke, **592/592** Gamma, **593** Gamma, **594** *(left)* Andrej Krob, **594** *(right)* Andrej Krob, **595/596** Camera Press, **596** *(left)* Associated Press, **596** *(right)* Magnum, **596/597** Camera Press, **598** *(top)* Gamma, **598** *(bottom)* Gamma, **598/599** Magnum, **599** Magnum, **600** Camera Press, **601** Magnum, **602** Camera Press, **604** Camera Press, **604/605** Paul Lowe/Magnum, **605** Magnum, **606** Camera Press, **607** *(left)* Gamma, **607** *(right)* Gamma, **608/609** Martin Parr/Magnum, **609** C. Steele-Perkins/Magnum, **610** Ian Berry/Magnum, **610/611** Camera Press, **611** Gamma, **612** Gamma, **612/613** Gamma, **613** Paul Lowe/Magnum, **614** *(top)* Spectrum, **614** *(bottom)* Images, **614/615** Images, **615** Spectrum, **616** *(top)* Images, **616** *(bottom)* Gamma, **617** Images

The publishers would like to thank all the people who took part in the making of the programmes and kindly lent their own photographs for use in this book.

While every effort has been made to trace the copyright holders of illustrations reproduced in this book, this has not always been possible in every case. The publishers will be pleased to rectify any omissions or inaccuracies in the next printing.

Index

Page numbers in italic type refer to picture captions.

D

G

X

Y

Z